Catholicism,

Popular Culture,

and the Arts in Germany,

1880 – 1933

MARGARET STIEG DALTON

Catholicism,
Popular Culture,
and the Arts in Germany,

1880 – 1933

UNIVERSITY OF NOTRE DAME PRESS
NOTRE DAME, INDIANA

Manufactured in the United States of America

Library of Congress Cataloging-in-Publication Data
Dalton, Margaret Stieg, 1942–
    Catholicism, popular culture, and the arts in Germany, 1880–1933 /
Margaret Stieg Dalton.
        p.   cm.
    Includes bibliographical references (p.   ) and index.
    ISBN 0-268-02566-5 (cloth : alk. paper)—ISBN 0-268-02567-3 (pbk. : alk. paper)
    1. Catholic Church—Germany—History—19th century.   2. Christianity
    and culture—Germany—History—19th century.   3. Popular culture—
    Germany—History—19th century.   4. Catholic Church—Germany—
    History—20th century.   5. Christianity and culture—Germany—History—
    20th century.   6. Popular culture—Germany—History—20th century.
    7. Popular culture—Religious aspects—Catholic Church.   I. Title.
    BX1536.D32   2004
    305.6'8243'09034—dc22

                                                            2004026368

∞ *This book is printed on acid-free paper.*

To the memory of Jack

and

For Robbie and Nicky

contents

acknowledgments

The pleasantest part of writing a book has to be preparing the acknowledgments because it gives the author an opportunity to reflect on the entire process and to remember the many kindnesses along the way. In this case, there were many.

I began my research in the Stadtbibliothek in Mönchengladbach, to which I returned again and again. When the Volksverein was closed during the National Socialist period, its magnificent collection of books, pamphlets, and periodicals was transferred to the Stadtbibliothek. The staff of the special collections division of the Stadtbibliothek could not have been more helpful in my quest for relevant publications.

After orienting myself in Mönchengladbach, I began visiting the diocesan archives that reported holdings that might relate to my interests. Every historian owes a large debt to the generations of archivists who collected and organized the records that are the raw material of historical research. I was the beneficiary of well-developed record practices in the episcopal ordinaries. The archives of the Catholic Church that were especially important for this book were those in Regensburg, Passau, Rottenburg, Wrocław, Mainz, Speyer, and Fulda. The archives of the Archdiocese of Cologne are in a class by themselves. Because of their richness, I spent more time there than in any other single place. I was truly impressed with how exceptionally well the needs of scholars are met. At the Borromäus Verein, although it is not an archive but a working library service, I was permitted to view the records of its early years.

I am grateful for the efforts of the archivists who considered my somewhat imprecise description of what I was trying to do and then drew on their experience and knowledge of their collections to suggest useful material that I would not have known enough about to request. This happened virtually everywhere. Archival staff continued to be helpful as I wrote to inquire about something that needed clarification or asked for a missing fact.

There was also more personal help. I remember with particular appreciation the archivists in Fulda. Knowing that I had no reason to be in Fulda except to use the archives, they found space on a table in the workroom for me, so that during the long midday closing of the reading room I would be able to continue to work.

During the summers I spent doing research in Germany, friends provided welcome breaks and good conversation. Without Helga and Alf Lüdtke, Hanna Bieger, and Elisabeth and Jürgen Schriewer, those summers would have been a lot less enjoyable. I owe a special debt of gratitude to Andrej and Ewa Biłyk of Wrocław. They saw to it that I had a place to stay in Wrocław and was able to get my work done, and they also introduced me to Poland.

On the home front, I received much help from the staff of the University of Alabama libraries. I will never forget a conversation with former Dean of Libraries Charles Osburn. When I apologized for the obscurity of my topic, he cut me off and proceeded to explain to me just why the German Catholic Church's reaction to modern culture was interesting and important. Carole Burke and Angela Wright, heads of the interlibrary loan division, went far beyond the call of duty in filling my requests for materials. With Dean Osburn's support, the library participated in the AAU/ARL German Resources Project to facilitate my requests. The director of the School of Library and Information Studies, Joan Atkinson, saw to it that I had the staff support and assistance I needed. Jewell Sandoval and Nannette Spivey, the school's administrative specialist and secretary, each made important contributions. The graduate assistants who worked on this project, Jason Bolton, Laurie Charnigo, and Leigh Thompson, provided exemplary service.

The University of Notre Dame Press has been everything a publisher ought to be and more. Its director, Barbara Hanrahan, understands her business thoroughly. She manages to combine highly competent professionalism with human warmth and common sense. I have enjoyed working with her and getting to know her. The anonymous reviewer of the manuscript did one of the best jobs of refereeing I have experienced in my career. He read the manuscript, decided that what I was attempting to do was reasonable, and made numerous suggestions that made it a much stronger book. The staff of the press helped turn this book into the kind of publication I hoped it would be.

In the last stages, two people provided special help. Jeffrey Zalar kindly sent me a copy of his outstanding dissertation on the Borromäus Verein and Catholic reading before 1918. Although I had asked to see it because I knew he had information about the participation of women in the Borromäus Verein, it offered stimulating ideas and new interpretations as well. Last, but far from least, has been my former colleague, R. Kathleen Molz. She used her outstanding editorial skills to help me improve my prose. More than that, however, I had someone to talk to who was knowledgeable about European art, literature, and music, and who could set me straight where necessary on points of Catholic practice. She spotted ideas in the manuscript that needed to be emphasized. I shall miss our conversations around the kitchen table. She gave me the kind of help I have not had since my father died.

Finally, I would like to express my thanks for the financial support that I received for this project. A research grant from the School of Library and Information Studies helped with expenses of a trip to Germany in the summer of 1992. The Deutscher Akademischer Austauschdienst awarded me a grant that covered my expenses for research in Germany in the summer of 1993. And the University of Alabama gave me a sabbatical for the 1998/1999 academic year that made it a lot easier to get the first draft of the manuscript completed.

1

Introduction

The Catholic Cultural Movement

In 1892 a German literary critic gave vent to his frustration over the enthusiastic response of German readers to Edward Bellamy's *Looking Backward:* "Bellamy! Indeed, two or three years ago one could hear nothing else but Bellamy. In every railway compartment you could see somebody reading Reclam's Number 2661/2; the student read it during lectures instead of listening to an exegesis, interpretation or conjecture; and even the peasants studied this kind of national economy."[1] *Looking Backward* was but one of the time-travel books that German readers enjoyed. English-language Tauchnitz editions of H. G. Wells's *The Time Machine* (1895) and Mark Twain's *A Connecticut Yankee in King Arthur's Court* (1890) were available in Germany almost as soon as they were published in England and the United States, and German translations were made of both early in the twentieth century.[2]

These well-known English and American books were popular in Germany because they captured a fundamental experience of the age: the sense of shuttling between different eras. Late nineteenth-century Germans lived in a time when both past and future coexisted. Political unification and economic development had turned Germany from a picturesque, somewhat backward collection of principalities into a major world power, but development had not been uniform across regions, economic sectors, or social groups, nor was every town, economic sector, or individual affected in the same way.

Although the impact of these economic and political changes was uneven, no one was unaffected by them, and their impact on most people was enormous. Within the space of a generation the lives of individuals were transformed in fundamental ways. Workers lost autonomy when they moved into factories and were subjected to increased discipline. The mechanization of every aspect of production and communication created a new tempo that extended to daily life. Radical social, geographic, economic, and behavioral changes destabilized institutions and accepted norms, bringing psychological stress in their wake. The community in which the older generation had lived and the traditions that had sustained that community no longer commanded the ability to direct individual behavior. Nor did change cease with the industrialization of the economy and the establishment of the nation. The new was always in the process of becoming. "The world," as the French writer Charles Péguy remarked in 1913, "has changed less since the time of Jesus Christ than it has in the last thirty years."[3]

Intellectual change matched the political and economic transformation: revolutionary ideas of all kinds permeated the *Zeitgeist;* advances in the natural sciences were redefining the physical world; Darwinism was reconstructing the world of biology; the new criticism of the Bible, Marxism, and the discovery of the unconscious brought changes that were just as dramatic in their own areas. Such ideas threatened the existing truths that underlay and supported political and social institutions.[4]

Inevitably, the period also brought major changes to culture. As the nineteenth century progressed, culture began to emerge as a separate sphere of activity and meaning. In the agricultural villages and market towns of preindustrial Germany, work and leisure had been intertwined, church and world had been closely connected. By the 1890s industrialization had disrupted these traditional patterns, and the economy, society, church, and state were beginning to be viewed as distinct components. Culture had become not only a separate subsystem but also a subsystem that was professionalized. Men and women ceased to be both audience and creators and became consumers. Whole new industries arose to feed the growing hunger for certain kinds of culture.[5]

In sum, the era was one of contradiction and contrast, and, above all, change. There was self-doubt—and self-confidence. There was the condemnation of progress—and the embracing of it. There was the retreat from the old absolutes of a supposedly unified worldview to uncertainty and plurality, the questioning of all received wisdom—and the search for new absolutes. There was enthusiasm for the new opportunities technological and economic development brought—and grief for what was being lost. Not surprisingly, nervousness was the pathology of the age.[6]

For German Catholics, whose faith was firmly rooted in the Middle Ages, the sense of living in conflicting worlds was particularly acute, as well as particularly painful. Put at a political disadvantage by the solution to German unification that made Germany a predominantly Protestant state, left behind economically, and belonging to a religious confession that science and scholarship appeared to make increasingly outmoded, Catholics had every reason to dislike the new world that was emerging. They lived in the dichotomous world strikingly described by Henry Adams in "The Dynamo and the Virgin," but they venerated the Virgin, and alienation was their principal reaction to the dynamo and all it represented.[7]

Rejection of the world was not, however, an option for a Church that had, early in its history, chosen to participate in the world. Instead, the fundamental question Catholics faced was one of degree: To what extent should Catholics integrate into the emerging world? The differentiation of life into substructures that accompanies modernization facilitated response. A way of life was no longer a totality but a menu of choices. At the highest level, even in states with established churches, church and state were separate entities. Work and family were now distinct spheres, and leisure was an identifiable activity. This differentiation permitted the Church to fight for its interests on one front but not another. It permitted the individual to accept a job in a factory while maintaining traditional Catholic values within the family, to enjoy a movie while at the same time participating in a society dedicated to piety. Differentiation was not, however, necessarily appreciated. Friedrich Muckermann, S.J., a leading cultural thinker,[8] argued that "through the confusion of the structures of life, through the unnatural separation of state and church, of religion and culture, of the holy and the profane, out of the free and happily developing Catholic soul are created difficulties that are nearly insuperable."[9]

Culture was one important arena in which Catholics tried to resolve this fundamental question of the extent to which they could accept the modern world yet still remain good Catholics. At one extreme were the Catholics who wanted nothing to do with modern culture; for them cultural conflict was an unambiguous duel between good and evil. At the other extreme were those who had so completely embraced the new world that they had left the Church, leaving their views unrepresented in Catholic discussions. And in the middle were the Catholics who, whether, at worst, reluctantly or, at best, enthusiastically, recognized that they must be involved with their own period. For them there was no alternative to participating in German culture.[10]

Educated Germans of all religious persuasions found culture an increasingly appropriate focus for consideration of these often dichotomous issues. They recognized that culture could influence how people thought and that it was not neutral but ideologically based. In the land of poets and philosophers, culture had long been an object of concern and national pride. Culture was, moreover, an important element in the Catholic tradition. In the early nineteenth century, Johann Michael Sailer, S.J., bishop of Regensburg,[11] had described the mutuality of religion and the arts in the following terms: "There is a bond of the Church with the fine arts that is not arranged but is nonetheless essential. A religion that gives up this bond with the fine arts is quite dead. It is dead if no inner revelation moves it, and it is in contradiction with itself if it wants to reveal itself but lacks the essential means to put this revelation in motion."[12]

THE BOOK AND ITS THEMES

This book is a study of the German Catholic cultural movement that flourished from the late nineteenth century until 1933, a loosely organized movement made possible by rapidly advancing industrialization, the beginnings of mass communication, and a singularly self-conscious Catholic minority. German Catholic culture was more than just culture produced by an individual who happened to be Catholic: it was intellectual and artistic activity with a specifically Catholic stamp, a unique blend that offered distinctive variants of art, literature, and music. It was produced for Catholic consumption but competed on the national stage, and, like another major and more studied variant, socialist culture, was intended to reflect and promote a specific worldview and to create a particular structure of meaning. Both Catholic and socialist cultures were alternatives to the majority culture and were based on a partial rejection of it.[13] The majority culture, Protestant and nationalist, came in either liberal or conservative flavors, but, by virtue of its position as majority culture, its worldview was far less deliberately purposive.

Culture is not, however, only about creation; it is also dissemination. The acts of reading, viewing, listening, and responding are what give cultural artifacts their larger meaning. This book, therefore, pays as much attention to efforts to diffuse culture as it does to creation. Dissemination was an activity that was as much a part of the Catholic cultural movement as creation, and the activities of

dissemination and advocacy of culture had considerable influence on the definition of what was acceptable Catholic culture.

This book is primarily an intellectual history that examines the ideas of
Catholic intellectuals, both lay and clerical, about culture and its various forms.
The principal questions of the Catholic intellectuals provide the book's central
themes: What should be the Catholic response to cultural modernism? What
should be the Catholic response to popular culture, whether the traditional culture of the *Volk* or the emerging mass culture? What is the relationship of Catholic culture to the Protestant-dominated national culture? Most of these issues,
minus the word Catholic, were also subjects of debate in the wider culture, and
the divisions within Catholic culture are the divisions of that wider culture. Other
questions are the questions of those of us who look back, rather than those who
lived through the events: Who were the individuals who attempted to develop
and direct this movement? What efforts were made to transform ideals into programs? How did larger economic and social factors influence it? And what was
the role of the Church universal?

In this study, emphasis will be upon Catholic culture as a national movement. The historian can look at larger phenomena broadly or smaller phenomena
in great detail. Knowing a particular parish so well that one recognizes that Hans
Schmidt and Georg Müller married sisters, or that the statue of the Virgin Mary
is a source of considerable local pride, is appealing, and local history and the history of particular social units like university students is much in vogue. This book
takes the broader approach in the interests of a more comprehensive if less precise picture. It covers the late nineteenth and early twentieth centuries. Although
the Weimar Republic is usually treated as a sharp break with the past rather than
an extension of Wilhelmine Germany, in the case of Catholic culture, the 1920s
built on prewar foundations. The Nazi seizure of power in 1933, on the other hand,
quickly brought a clear termination to Catholic cultural efforts.

The history of Catholicism has been described as touching more aspects
of the world than the history of almost any other subject.[14] Adding culture to Catholicism only widens the possibilities and makes it advisable to state the boundaries of this book, as well as its ambitions. One road not taken is the political.
Much research on nineteenth- and twentieth-century German history has focused on politics, but the Catholic cultural movement had only an indirect connection to that arena. Similarly, cultural artifacts as such do not receive much
attention: this is not a study of German Catholic literature, art, music, drama, or
cinema but a study of the debates, conditions, and context surrounding their
creation. Catholic theology and Rome appear only peripherally. The large themes
of secularization and modernization are present, but the stress lies on what
secularization and modernization theories reveal about the Catholic cultural

movement rather than on contributing to the scholarly debates on secularization and modernization.

One regrettable absence is that of the audience of Catholic culture. Audience is an essential element in culture, but it appears in this book almost exclusively through the perceptions of cultural leaders rather than in the words of the individuals who enjoyed a book from the libraries of the Borromäus Verein (Association of St. Charles Borromeo) or appreciated a painting at an exhibit of Christian art. The intended (and actual) beneficiaries of the Catholic cultural movement left little trace of their reactions. Predominantly rural, tending to lack education beyond the elementary level, and belonging to a Church that emphasized the group rather than the individual, the majority of Catholics were neither cultural enthusiasts nor autobiographers. The fine arts did not bulk large in their lives.[15]

THE OBJECTIVES OF CATHOLIC CULTURE

The English Catholic historian James Froude once compared the writing of history to making a selection from a child's box of letters. Just as one can spell any word by making the appropriate choice of letters from the box, he argued that it is possible to defend any historical interpretation by a judicious selection of facts. The historian has only to take the facts that support his position and to say nothing about those that do not suit his purpose.[16] The rich array of possibilities for selection presented by the Catholic cultural movement could have been designed to illustrate his metaphor.

The goals of the leading figures concerned with Catholic culture were sometimes contradictory and almost always vague, circumstances that invite multiple interpretations. Most commonly expressed was a strong will to fight. Later historians have commented on the friend/enemy dichotomy that dominated Catholic thinking of the period, and a general aura of combativeness definitely pervaded the cultural movement.[17] The enemy could be concrete and personal; it might be Protestants and Protestantism, socialists and socialism. The fault line—the phrase is David Blackbourn's—separating Catholic and Protestant went back to the Reformation, and the Catholic revival of piety in the earlier nineteenth century had reinforced it.[18] In the late nineteenth century, a Catholic milieu in the process of consolidation and densification sought to match every activity and organization with a Catholic counterpart. Just as Catholics were anti-Protestant, Protestants were anti-Catholic. In 1886 what would become the most important Protestant organization, the Evangelischer Bund zur Wahrung der deutsch-protestantischen Interessen (Protestant League for the Protection of German-Protestant Interests), was founded because Protestants felt that they were losing power to the Catholics. An acid remark by an unidentified Catholic convert that a group for the promotion of bee-keeping sponsored by a Protestant pastor would include the struggle against Rome in its articles illustrated a profound truth.[19]

Both confessions feared socialism, a fear Hans-Ulrich Wehler traces to the events of 1848, although the common enemy did not lead to cooperation. Socialist electoral victories in the 1890s only exacerbated fears. Socialism's philosophical materialism, class basis, urban orientation, and antagonism to religion and to the church made it antithetical to any form of Christianity and particularly to late nineteenth-century Catholicism. Socialism's success also made it dangerous. Some of its organizational features might be worthy of imitation, but Catholic writing on culture is full of diatribes against its godless and materialistic culture.[20]

Catholic intellectuals recognized that the enemy could be abstract, impersonal forces, as well as identifiable individuals and groups. They could see that religion was losing its power to shape men's minds. They understood that moral consciousness was no longer based primarily in religiously defined guilt and anxiety but determined by self-confidence and autonomy. Fate and coincidence were being challenged by new scientific findings; and action, often on the national level, rather than resignation, was the order of the day. Rhetorically, Catholic writers juxtaposed modern culture to secularism, individualism, and materialism, treating these isms both as processes and as conditions and comparing all unfavorably to Catholic teachings. They used terms interchangeably: modern for secular, materialistic for modern, and also individualist or some equivalent for secular. They talked about asserting eternal values, but they acted as if Catholicism was in the process of becoming one more competing ism. A statement by the Australian Aboriginal writer, Mudrooroo Narogin, could, with appropriate substitution of terms, be an expression of the Catholic position: "The Aboriginal writer is a Janus-type figure with one face turned to the past and the other to the future while existing in a postmodern, multicultural Australia in which he or she must fight for cultural space."[21]

The concept of secularization as it is used today in research is only distantly related to the secularism that these Catholic intellectuals perceived as so aggressive and so iniquitous. A major phenomenon of the nineteenth and twentieth centuries, in the hands of scholars secularization has become a major tool for understanding the history of the modern era. It encompasses a host of changes, from the transfer to secular control of activities and functions that had formerly belonged to religion and the decline in resources commanded by religious institutions to a major shift in norms and thought patterns from religiously based to rational and temporal systems. One frequently encountered definition describes it as the loss of social significance by religion. Hugh McLeod, who has studied religious change in nineteenth-century Germany, prefers to see secularization in terms of levels of the beliefs and practices of individuals, an approach shared by Thomas Mergel, who uses the term "inner secularization" to describe the attitudes of the bourgeoisie he has studied. In the cultural context of this book, McLeod's approach is particularly useful, since confession was the major feature of social identity in imperial Germany, a fact that testifies to its social and historical significance.[22]

Both secularization and modernization pervade the study of Catholic culture; in a sense, this entire book can be read as a commentary on the secularization and modernization of German Catholics. By any scholarly measure, imperial Germany was a society in the process of becoming more secular and more modern, and secularization and modernization are latent in specifically cultural questions. Was the Catholic cultural movement offensive or defensive in its purpose? Indictments of modern culture, statements of the necessity to protect Catholics from the threat of the contemporary world, and pleas for a morally based culture can be interpreted as either offensive or defensive moves, but in either case "secular" and "modern" are essential elements.

Did the Catholic cultural movement attempt to integrate Catholics into the wider German culture and society or isolate them from it? The answer to this question is as ambiguous as the answer to whether the movement was offensive or defensive in character. Arguments that Catholics needed to familiarize themselves with contemporary ideas, a position in which modernization is viewed as necessary if not positive, can be matched by exhortations that Catholics be protected from exposure to dangerous ideas, a viewpoint in which the only variation was what kind of evil came with modern changes. Defensiveness among Catholics tended to correspond with a desire to isolate themselves from modern culture, while the desire to integrate corresponded with greater openness to secular ideas. It was, however, possible for an individual to be defensive yet an advocate of greater openness.

Underlying these questions was the all-important question of the relationship of German Catholics to the larger nation. Those Catholic intellectuals who advocated cultural integration rather than separation and who accepted contemporary culture rather than rejected it were considered to be nationalists. The dilemma was plain: to oppose the Protestant-dominated culture placed the German Catholic at odds with his new-minted German nationality; to accept it too wholeheartedly could compromise his Catholic faith. The further 1871 receded into the past, the less exigent and absolute the alternatives became, but the problem remained. Whether it was the Second Reich or the Weimar Republic, Germany remained Prussian dominated, which meant that, to the extent religion was a factor, the nation remained Protestant dominated. The Roman Catholic Church remained the Church universal, seated in Rome.

No Catholic participant in cultural discussions advocated either secularization or modernization as such, although some came close. Without being consciously aware, however, all who promoted a Catholic culture were contributing to the inexorable advance of those complementary phenomena. By working to create a specific cultural option that would shore up or compensate for a receding religion that no longer pervaded all of life, they were furthering the privatization of religion. Privatization is that condition in which religion primarily manifests itself as an individual experience, and its growth has little to do with action in the public domain; it was a noticeable feature of the period covered in this study.[23]

One of the few points on which there was general agreement was the importance of reinforcing Catholic identity. Catholic leaders wanted Catholics to respond to the basic question, "Who am I?" with a resounding, "A Catholic!" A movement that could induce them to substitute cultural experiences that reinforced their Catholic values for those that eroded them was a valuable supplement to other sources of Catholic ideas.[24]

Identity is a postmedieval concept. As modernization created increased mobility, diversity, and opportunity, social identity became a matter of choice, not birth. The right to marry without official permission, the elimination of feudal services, religious toleration, advancing industrialization with its urbanization, and an increasingly self-conscious working class all meant greater freedom for the individual. These changes also meant that an individual's concept of his identity was continuously challenged. The erosion of the old certainties that determined life left people uneasy and seeking orientation and guidance. For the governing and intellectual classes, the formation of the "right" identity was a matter of urgency.[25]

Catholic intellectuals saw the Catholic cultural movement as a means of providing needed orientation. Literature and other cultural modes were a way of influencing, reinforcing, or changing norms.[26] This combination of a purpose that sought to guide the most fundamental beliefs and behaviors of individuals, and the use of the media of mass communication to do so, meant that the Catholic cultural movement was, in fact, a form of propaganda.

Debate over the form in which persuasion should come usually took place in terms of education versus entertainment. Linked together by the common goal of persuasion to a Catholic point of view, the two were not necessarily mutually exclusive, although their respective supporters often argued as if they were. Because it was the more worthy, not to mention more compatible with the prevailing gospel of hard work and self-improvement, education was the more frequently mentioned. But entertainment had its defenders. At the very least, appropriate Catholic entertainment would protect Catholics from unwholesome influences by keeping them suitably, as opposed to unsuitably, occupied. What everyone did agree upon was that the products of a rapidly developing popular culture industry could only undermine the Catholic point of view.[27]

The choice between education and entertainment involved questions of major significance: Who was the intended audience? Was the culture of the Catholic cultural movement part of the effort to keep educated Catholics within the Church or was it intended to be culture for the masses? Should its emphasis be on contributing to the Protestant- and Prussian-dominated national culture or on competing with the emerging commercial popular culture? The overwhelmingly bourgeois orientation of the Catholic culture movement heavily influenced the answers to these questions.

PERSPECTIVES ON CATHOLIC CULTURE

History is more than the recounting of facts; it is facts presented in support of a particular interpretation. As Froude recognized, possibilities of interpretation are abundant, and it is a favorite sport of every generation of historians to attempt to overthrow previously received wisdom. In modern German history, the *Sonderweg* debate, a disagreement over whether German economic and social development was unique, is probably the most far-reaching and significant example, but opinions vary widely on many other topics. Among historians of German Catholicism, the role of the Center Party, the function of Catholic organizations, and the nature of Catholicism itself, to name only a few of the more notable debates, are also subjects of considerable disagreement. Which position a historian holds on one or another often has implications for how he or she views the Catholic cultural movement.[28]

The study of Catholic culture offers numerous dichotomous possibilities of exposition. Is the Catholic cultural movement forward-looking or backward-looking? Some Catholic intellectuals evinced a sincere interest to adapt their faith, lives, and culture to the changing world in which they live. Others argued with equal sincerity for a renaissance of the Catholic cultural greatness of the Middle Ages. Novels and plays with modern settings and modern challenges can be matched by novels and plays that deal with traditional themes in historical settings and give traditional answers. Their relative significance is at the discretion of the historian.

Another matched pair of questions is whether the Catholic cultural movement is the consequence of Catholic revival or Catholic decline. Jonathan Sperber makes a convincing case for the revival of Catholic piety and the reinvigoration of the Catholic milieu in the *Vormärz* period; Michael Gross's work on Catholic missionary crusades reinforces Sperber's conclusions. Both the Borromäus Verein, the most important Catholic library and literary group, and the Cäcilien Verein (Association of St. Cecilia), the organization founded to restore Gregorian chant and purify the liturgy, can be seen as part of the Catholic revival. On the other hand, particularly in some of the later organizations, a defensive posture aimed to prevent further attrition is the stated motivation.[29] Revival and decline are also related to but not identical with cohesion and erosion within the Catholic milieu. Was the Catholic cultural movement an expression of the milieu's solidarity or was it an attempt by leaders to strengthen ties that were losing their strength? Evidence can be found to support either position.

A question that does not involve a choice between two alternatives is who the Catholic intellectuals concerned with culture were. Inadequate biographical information prevents firm conclusions, but it does hint at a direction. The writers who discussed the issues and proposed policies and programs were usually undistinguished people, both socially and professionally. The few who achieved enough prominence for their biography to interest their contemporaries and therefore be recorded for posterity were predominantly from the petty bourgeoisie. Those who founded organizations tended to be more socially prominent; it was not unusual to have a substantial merchant or even a member of the nobility listed among founders. Clergy were involved in both intellectual and organizational aspects and were likely to be higher clergy or men singled out for some other form of advancement rather than ordinary parish priests. Cause and effect differ; advancement could have been for their work with culture, or their interest in culture could have been made possible by their position. The presence of Jesuits in key positions is noticeable, especially as writers and thinkers, although they were not numerous.

Other issues relate to factors outside the Catholic milieu. To what extent was this culture German, the product of a society consolidating its newly achieved nationality? How did social and religious purpose adapt to economic realities? Culture was in the process of becoming a commodity in late nineteenth-century Germany, a process antithetical to expressed Catholic cultural values; but creators and producers had to receive an adequate return on their offerings if they were to continue production.

Evolution

The Catholic cultural movement has been discussed as if it were an entity, but it was neither unified nor unchanging. It was a miscellaneous assortment of local, regional, and national organizations with widely varying interests. Coordination of cultural organizations across diocesan boundaries or areas of interest was rare until the 1920s. The Church certainly possessed the capacity for organization, but its leaders preferred to use that capacity for its more traditional activities, such as helping the poor, rather than developing an alternative culture.

Cultural organizations, although separate and unorganized, shared some commonalities, and different periods can be distinguished within them.[30] In the early years, up to about 1895, features that would be characteristic of the movement emerged in embryonic form: organization on the national level; the employment of new means of communication; and a division of interest between culture that related directly to the Church and culture for the members of the Church. The dominant organizations were the Borromäus Verein, the Cäcilien Verein, and the Christlicher Kunstverein (Christian Art Association), all founded well before the beginning of the *Kulturkampf.*

The period between 1895 and 1914 was in many ways the most exciting for the Catholic cultural movement. Organizations grew rapidly, both in terms of the number of organizations and the size of their membership. Efforts were made to put cultural activity on a firmer and more professional organizational basis and to secure stable financial support. The Borromäus Verein exemplifies both these trends, but other groups show some of the same intentions, if not success.

These years, the years of the debate on theological modernism within the Catholic Church, were of particular significance in creating the Catholic cultural movement's intellectual foundations. The theological issues had only a limited connection to culture, but the fundamental question of how the Catholic Church should respond to the new ideas and the new world that was coming into being was very directly related. Artists had to grapple with these questions, existing organizations could not ignore them, and new groups were organized in response to one or another aspect. Debate was often intense, and the expansion of the Catholic press made possible thorough discussion and wide dissemination. The suppression of theological modernism that took place after the turn of the century was accompanied by efforts to rein in other potentially dangerous tendencies that were seriously affecting Catholic cultural activity.

This period of intellectual ferment, organizational development, and high interest was followed by the four years of the Great War.[31] The war's impact was enormous, but little was particular to Catholic culture. As it did to other German institutions, the war brought a consciousness of new tasks and reduced the resources available to undertake any task. In the cultural arena one of the most significant features was the outpouring of trashy literature (*Schmutz-* and *Schundliteratur*) and pornography, an early manifestation of the trivialization and brutalization described by George Mosse in his discussion of the impact of the war. Pornography and trash had long been themes of Catholic cultural discussion, but the war years turned them into obsessions.[32]

The last period of the Catholic cultural movement covered the years of the Weimar Republic, a time of cultural vibrancy and political instability that retains an enduring fascination. Catholic intellectuals and artists may have deplored most of what its wide-ranging experimentation produced, but they were not uninfluenced by new ideas. Artistic works began to reflect contemporary stylistic trends. In the Catholic cultural organizations, there was an increased emphasis on coordination of cultural efforts, significant losses of membership, and greater participation of women as consumers and producers of culture. A heightened sense of the dangers of commercial, secular cultural offerings encouraged expanded activity in all areas and involvement in the new media of film and radio.[33]

One purpose of an introduction is to give the reader a framework for what follows, and that has been the primary objective of this introduction. It cannot, however, provide a single, sense-making thread, and in this case a single explanation would be impossible. The ambivalence of the age does not encourage a neat presentation. The collection of ideas, individuals, organizations, and events that constitute the Catholic cultural movement yields no overarching explanation, only a series of explanations. For too many questions, the evidence suggests that it is not a choice between either/or, but more a case of both/and, or yes, but. The totality is a miscellany.

If the reader still finds a hypothesis indispensable to use as a touchstone in the chapters that follow, it would have to be that the Catholic cultural movement was ultimately defensive in its outlook. There were advocates of accommodation and adaptation to modern culture, but the dominant theme of the movement was defensiveness. Its most frequently stated purpose was to immunize Catholics from the dread disease of modernism and to isolate them from the surrounding culture. That purpose required its products to have wide appeal, but content consistently reflected bourgeois cultural values. This fundamental contradiction predestined the movement to disappoint its participants and supporters.

The Catholic cultural movement was one element in the attempt of the Church to adapt to new conditions, while maintaining its doctrine and preserving its position of intellectual and political power. The nature of the sources on which this book is based dictates that it is primarily a study of policy and intention and secondarily of implementation. In sum, it deals with the official rather than the unofficial, the formal rather than the informal. It is a study of the mentality and activities of the cultural elite, of what contemporaries thought of when they thought of Catholic culture.

2

The Catholic Milieu and Its Organizations

THE CONCEPT OF THE MILIEU

Catholic culture is unthinkable without the Catholic milieu. In 1941 Friedrich Muckermann, S.J., used the term "milieu" in his memoirs, but milieu in a scholarly sense appears to have been first applied to German Catholicism by Carl Amery in his 1963 book *Die Kapitulation oder Deutscher Katholizismus heute*. M. Rainer Lepsius, however, can take credit for the term's present wide currency. In his classic essay "Parteiensystem und Sozialstruktur: Zum Problem der Demokratisierung der deutschen Gesellschaft," Lepsius attributed the stability of German political parties in the late nineteenth and early twentieth centuries to their firm foundation in stable milieux. A milieu denoted the presence of socially unifying characteristics, among which he included the structural dimensions of religion, regional tradition, economic situation, and cultural orientation. Used in this way, milieu added a fruitful social and moral dimension that supplemented the narrowness of analysis based on economic and class interests. He identified four milieux in pre–World War I Germany: Catholics; the conservative feudal aristocracy and government officials; the Protestant bourgeoisie; and the socialist working class. Since Lepsius, it has been impossible to write the political history of nineteenth- and twentieth-century Germany without considering the social context more comprehensively.[1]

Subsequent scholarship has refined the concept of milieu considerably, and the Catholic milieu has become an object of study in its own right, fed by the growth of interest in social history. Much attention has focused on its role in modernization. Differences within the Catholic milieu have been studied, as well as the milieu as a whole. How a scholar sees the Catholic milieu depends on which characteristics are emphasized; some scholars interpret it as a transitional phase of modernization, others as an attempt to resist modernization. Even the most fundamental fact, religion itself, is a variable, since not every Catholic was equally faithful to the Church. Many Catholics existed on the fringe of their local milieu or had no connection with it at all. Some were connected to the Catholic milieu for one purpose but with a different milieu for another.[2]

Milieux, like individuals, had multiple identities. No individual, or milieu, was just Catholic, even if Catholicism was the foundation and raison d'être of the milieu. Social composition, economic activity, and political views mattered. Studies of Catholic workers and the Catholic bourgeoisie demonstrate that the milieu of a Catholic urban merchant had little in common with the milieu of a Catholic peasant. In a land of regions, geographic distinctions were also significant. Olaf Blaschke and Frank-Michael Kuhlemann argue that we should think in terms of separate milieux at each level—local, regional, and national. The essence of a local milieu was determined by the particular mix of economic, social, geographical, and historical conditions; at the macromilieu level the unifying bond of a common faith overshadowed differences.[3]

Although our understanding is now more nuanced, appreciation of these refinements has not significantly altered our perception of the Catholic (macro)-milieu. Most scholars would agree that it was a community bound together by the Catholic faith, in which life was lived within a framework of norms and rituals defined by the Church, reinforced by the organization of social and economic life, and supported by a strong Catholic press and numerous associations. It consisted of real villages and real neighborhoods, but it was also a virtual community. Its boundaries, geographic, social, economic, and cultural, were permeable; the term "osmotic" has been used. Agreement even extends to some of its characteristics. Catholic society was indeed, as contemporaries held, separate and backward. It was backward economically and backward culturally. Ultramontane clergy, reactionary in terms of nineteenth-century ideas, dominated, and modernization was slow to make headway against a ghetto mentality.

Late nineteenth-century Catholics would have recognized this description. They knew that their values and their way of life both unified them and separated them from other elements of society, and by the end of the century they were applying the term "ghetto" to themselves. This ghetto was to a considerable extent self-imposed. Although a fully developed ghetto Catholicism existed only in Germany, in the nineteenth century it was not uncommon for political and religious communities to form a subculture. Such subcultures were a transitional phase in modernization, a response that offered stability in the face of change. They provided conditions in which groups could preserve traditional ways and begin the process of adaptation to the new without being fully exposed to all its dangers.[4]

Whether German Protestants also had a milieu remains an open question. Much depends upon the specifics of definition. Historians write of Protestant milieux,[5] but the term milieu appears to be less applicable to Protestants than to Catholics. Protestants spoke with a far less unified voice; their theology emphasized individual responsibility; and it was less clear where authority lay in their organizational structure. As members of the majority, Protestants lacked the self-consciousness that accompanies minority status. Counterparts to the forms that upheld the Catholic milieu—the Catholic press and the numerous associations—were present, but they were weaker and less important to a group whose identity was essentially subsumed in the larger national identification. If one wishes to compare the Catholic milieu with another milieu, the socialist/working-class milieu exhibits some similar features, although its unifying factor, of course, was not a shared religion.[6]

RISE AND DECLINE OF THE CATHOLIC MILIEU

Although the physical separation between Catholic and Protestant created by the Treaty of Westphalia (1648) was diminishing in the wake of the territorial adjustments that followed the Napoleonic Wars and the internal population shifts brought by industrialization, other kinds of separation were increasing. The greater mixing of the confessions brought more conflict and a sharper definition of social and cultural—cultural in the broadest sense—differences. Each confession created institutions to resist the perceived opponent and to support the like-minded.[7]

The dominant intellectual trends of the eighteenth century had had the effect of decreasing confessional tensions, but greater emphasis on religion and renascent popular piety in the nineteenth century contributed to the sense of difference. The nineteenth century may have been, as Thomas Nipperdey argues, the century in which Germans ceased to see themselves as Christian, but declining church attendance was not the only trend. Blaschke writes of the reconfessionalization of life, Wolfgang Schieder of "religious mobilization." Gangolf Hübinger describes Protestant intellectual and organizational renewal, and Sperber convincingly portrays a Catholic revival, although not everyone agrees with his post-1848 timing.[8]

In German Catholicism, administrative reform reinforced increasing piety. The mid–nineteenth century was a period when the Church was attempting to tighten its control. The Church's bureaucracy was growing, and operations were being centralized as Rome more and more asserted authority. Diocesan administration improved. Organizations addressing every need and interest proliferated on both diocesan and parochial levels to create the thick net that is associated with the Catholic ghetto.[9]

Events outside of Catholicism played a major role in the establishment of the milieu, the single most important of which was the Prussian *Kulturkampf*.[10] Variously interpreted as a political maneuver on Bismarck's part, an attempt to assert a unified national culture, and a defensive reaction of local elites to groups that challenged their local dominance, the *Kulturkampf* was a struggle between the new national state and the universal Church for power that helped define the role of Catholics within the empire. It permanently shaped their thinking, affected their actions, and colored their emotions.

Its principal features are straightforward. After some preliminary skirmishing, the Prussian government passed the notorious May Laws of 1873. These laws regulated the training and employment of the clergy, clerical discipline, the use of clerical punishment, and provided for an easy withdrawal of priests from the Church. In 1875 a law followed that attempted to regulate the administration of parishes. The Church responded with a papal encyclical that condemned all the Prussian ecclesiastical legislation and threatened excommunication for those who complied with it, a move that the Prussian government then answered with a law that stopped all financial support to the Church from state sources. This law was soon extended to the monastic orders as well. What had begun as an attack on the Catholic Center Party had quickly become an attack on the Church.

Enforcement of these laws wreaked havoc with the life of the Church and the faithful. They affected the most fundamental relationships: those of the hierarchy with its priests and the Church with its parishioners. They often worked, moreover, to impede or injure Catholics in their secular relationships and activities, as well as in their religious relationships and activities. The following figures of arrests reported by the *Frankfurter Zeitung* in 1875 convey some idea of the extent of the devastation: 241 priests; 136 editors; 210 members of the Center Party, beyond those included in the numbers for priests and editors; and 55 other persons. In addition, house searches, expulsions, and the dissolution of meetings took place. By 1878 only three of the eleven Prussian bishops remained in office;

the other sees were vacant, either by the bishop's removal or death, or because the bishop had fled into exile. Several bishops administered their sees from adjacent foreign territory. By 1881, 1,125 of the 4,627 Prussian parishes, or 24 percent, were vacant, a catastrophe for millions of the faithful.[11]

At the beginning of 1878 Pope Pius IX died, and Leo XIII was chosen as his successor.[12] This event set the stage for the abandonment of the *Kulturkampf,* and over the next nine years negotiations between the Prussian government and the Vatican gradually dismantled it. Who won the "battle" is not entirely clear; Bismarck argued in his memoirs that the *Kulturkampf* had given the state control over the schools. But the Center Party survived and emerged from the fires strengthened, while the punitive measures had little long-term effect. At the same time, the legal basis of the Catholic Church in Germany remained somewhat insecure; the relevant laws were suspended, not repealed.[13]

For our purposes, the most important result of the *Kulturkampf* was psychological. Whether one is talking about a collective Catholic psyche or the perceptions and self-awareness of millions of individual Catholics, the *Kulturkampf* put Catholics on notice that they lived in a new era. The accelerating pace and new conditions of a semi-democratic political life sharpened issues and compressed the time available to work out solutions. German Catholicism had experienced state-led oppression before, but the way the *Kulturkampf* had come about and its intensity were different. And, because it touched the life of virtually every German Catholic, its shock effect was felt well beyond the political arena. In the *Kulturkampf* the powerful political, economic, and social forces of the late nineteenth century were interconnected, and Catholics could no longer preserve the illusion that they could remain untouched by these forces.

The *Kulturkampf* forced Catholics to recognize the uncomfortable fact that the Protestant majority in Germany was fundamentally and widely anti-Catholic.[14] In a society where religion was the primary identifying social feature and the confessional difference the most important of all,[15] this anti-Catholic feeling was both distressing and dangerous. In a country intoxicated with the success of its recent national unification, the perception that Catholics were unpatriotic only increased the menace. Already convinced that their position was being eroded,[16] Catholics emerged from the fires of the *Kulturkampf* with a defensive mentality and a determination to protect themselves, their faith, and their way of life, although they did not necessarily agree on the best way to accomplish that object.

The *Kulturkampf* was a pivotal event in the consolidation of the milieu, but it alone did not create it. Dating the beginning of the Catholic milieu, like dating its decline, varies among scholars because so many other factors are relevant. If, for example, a historian chooses to emphasize the revival of *Volk* piety already mentioned, the milieu's formation would have to be placed early in the nineteenth century. The Münster-based Arbeitskreis für kirchliche Zeitgeschichte assigns the formation period from 1830 to 1914, its fully fledged operation to 1914–1955, and places its deterioration after 1955. Wilhelm Damberg argues that the Catholic milieu was systematically dismantled after 1933. Oded Heilbronner sees World War I as instrumental in tearing down its walls, while Thomas Mergel places the beginning of its erosion at the end of the *Kulturkampf*.[17]

That the milieu flourished in the late nineteenth and early twentieth centuries was an essential factor in the development of the Catholic cultural movement. By the end of the *Kulturkampf* a strong sense of community based on the shared bond of religion and Catholic values existed among the Catholic population. Catholics often lived in communities that were ghettos in fact if not law and where social and economic ties strengthened the bonds of a common faith. In its broad outline, the milieu survived until the Nazis gained control of the state. It provided a base for Catholic cultural activity, it offered a market for cultural products, and it socialized the creators and organizers of Catholic culture. And, because the milieu was so closely identified with Catholicism itself, its ethos reinforced the imperative for Catholic culture: that it was necessary to keep the *Volk* faithful, not just to the Church, but to a particular way of life.

At the same time, a second important fact should not be ignored. The milieu and its way of life were changing; the word "eroding" has been used by both contemporaries and historians. Formal religious observance among Catholics was slower in its decline than among Protestants, but it did decline. Males, members of the working class, and residents of large cities were increasingly less likely to attend Church services. External measures are not the only measures of faith, and indications exist that many individuals found a deeper, firmer faith after examination in the light of challenges. The general opinion of Catholic commentators throughout the period was, however, that religion was in decline. That was a fact to be deplored and fought. It was a fact that could either reinforce defensiveness and attachment to the old ways or encourage new ideas and hasten adaptation to changed conditions.[18]

Emphasizing the separateness of German Catholics can go too far.[19] Although they were unquestionably a distinct and identifiable group, they shared with all other Germans a world in which everything seemed to be in a state of flux.[20] Rapid industralization was perceptible, and the traditional agricultural village was plainly losing vitality. The basis of society and social relations was shifting. The intellectual certainties of the past faced challenges from every direction. In themselves, economic, social, and intellectual changes were impersonal and devoid of values. But, although impersonal and undiscriminating, they had enormous impact on the lives of individuals who lived them, whether the individual was Catholic or Protestant, male or female, a resident of Munich or a farm in Schleswig, a butcher, a baker, or a candlestickmaker.

CATHOLIC VIEWS AND ATTITUDES

Probably the most obvious of the ideas that dominated the Catholic milieu, the ideas that established the framework of permissible thinking, was reverence for tradition and a parallel suspicion of all that was modern. This mind-set conferred great influence on the clergy, who were usually the ones who defined the "tradition" to be applied in a given set of circumstances. Issues to which it was applied ranged from the relevance of the Middle Ages to the present to employer/employee relations.

Tradition venerated the rural and agricultural world and conveniently ignored the fact that it was changing. The new industrial society was viewed with distaste; reluctance to admit that it was a new world that called for new measures greatly complicated the Church's relationship with the working class. The big city was condemned as a source of evil. On a personal level, sexuality was, in theory, limited to marital relations, and homosexuality was considered anathema. Sexual roles were more strictly differentiated in Roman Catholic circles than elsewhere.

Reverence for tradition meant that Catholics reacted to some of the most powerful currents in their society with disinterest or disdain. They viewed with qualified enthusiasm the triumphant establishment of the Reich in 1871 that put them in a minority; Sedan Day was a Protestant celebration. The fundamental faith in progress, achieved through the use of reason, that was so characteristic of the age was acceptable only if reason was given a specifically Catholic interpretation. The individual and his importance were minimized, and among the consequences was a relative indifference to education. Catholics were consequently viewed as enemies of the Reich, who resided culturally in the Middle Ages and saw themselves as minors in need of guidance from the pope and the Jesuits.[21]

Can the term "*mentalité*" be used to describe this outlook? Although, as with so many theoretical constructs, consensus has yet to emerge on exactly what *mentalité* means, *mentalités* can be defined broadly as the glue that hold milieux together. Three general features characterize use of the term: it is applied to collectivities, not individuals; it includes unconscious as well as conscious assumptions; and it refers to ideas that are part of an interrelated structure, not those in isolation. Simply defined, *mentalités* are a group's values and modes of thought, grounded within a particular cultural environment.[22] The problem in describing a particular set of attitudes and ideas such as the Catholic *mentalité* lies in the definite article "the." Although the above statements about reverence for tradition and attitudes toward progress are true, they are not universally true of all Catholics or all Catholic groups. Gender, class, and regional differences introduce variations. In looking at collectivities, one loses sight of the individual, and no individual was just Catholic, any more than any milieu was just Catholic.

Catholics, like other religious groups, were divided into conservatives and modernists. The ultramontanes, who saw every aspect of life through the lens of Catholicism, have to be considered the conservatives. By the end of the *Kulturkampf,* theological and political events had thwarted their only possible rival claimants to that title—those whom Mergel describes as the traditional Catholics, who tended to regard the world and religion as two separate categories. Ultramontane derives from the Latin words *ultra* for beyond and *mons* for mountain, and the name captures the fundamental principle of ultramontanism, that is, the supremacy of the Roman pope. Ultramontanism is usually viewed as a reaction to the growing separation of church and state in the early nineteenth century; Mooser sees it as a conflict between the pope and bourgeois society. Originally a jurisdictional battle, it evolved into a sweeping Catholic fundamentalism with particular emphasis upon the role of the clergy. McLeod summarizes the essence of ultramontanism as a combination of a dogmatic and antirationalist theology with a warmly emotional piety and a preference for life within a Catholic ghetto, where the faithful could be protected from infection by Protestant or rationalist views. The ultramontanes' encouragement of pilgrimages and the cult of the Virgin Mary enabled them to present themselves as protectors of the religion of the *Volk.*[23]

The high point of ultramontanism can be assigned to the 1850s and 1860s or to 1870, the year of the declaration of the doctrine of papal infallibility. Most historians consider ultramontanism in Germany to have been moderate in comparison to, for example, that in France. As an ideology,[24] however, it continued to dominate the outlook of the parish clergy until well into the twentieth century and was, therefore, a potent force in shaping the views of those who were part of the milieu. Its development was, in fact, a precondition for the development of the milieu.[25] One list of the principal features of ultramontanism includes a tradition-based conservatism, authoritarianism, religious fanaticism, a historical dualism that categorizes everything as either good or bad, economic romanticism, antifeminism and antisexuality, an antidemocratic political philosophy, the rejection of modern scholarship and science, ritualism, mysticism, glorification of Gothic and Nazarene art, and a view of history that drove the ultramontanists to seek renewal in the past. Not coincidentally, these themes appear again and again in cultural commentary.[26]

In contrast to ultramontane fundamentalism stood the modernists. Hardly a system, barely a movement, modernism was little more than a collective name for diverse, often unrelated ideas and could be found wherever the Church was found. Modernists advocated recasting the Church's conception of religious and social order in the light of the important ideas of the nineteenth century, bringing ecclesiastical institutions up-to-date, and adapting the lifestyle of Christians to the modern world; they resisted the restoration of traditional Thomistic theology. Pius X[27] needed fifty-eight paragraphs, many running to hundreds of words, to condemn modernism to his satisfaction in his 1907 encyclical *Pascendi Domenici gregig*.[28]

Modernism remained relatively moderate in Germany, largely a movement of academics and intellectuals. It attracted theologians who opposed neoscholasticism; scholars who wished to incorporate the methods and ideas of the natural sciences into Catholic thinking; historians who wanted to discuss history as an evolutionary process; laymen who wished for more independence and a larger role in their church; supporters of the Reich who hoped for greater prominence for German culture and thought; advocates of a miscellany of reforms ranging from the use of German in the liturgy to an end to clerical celibacy; and some deeply religious men who wanted to replace the legalistic Church, mired in worldly interests, with a Church of love and the spirit. What the modernists had in common was a deep loyalty to the Church and the conviction that it was important to open the Church to new ideas and approaches.[29]

The leading German modernists included Franz Xaver Kraus, professor at the University of Freiburg; Hermann Schell, professor at the University of Würzburg from 1884; and Albert Ehrhard, successively professor of church history at the Universities of Würzburg, Vienna, Strasbourg, and Bonn.[30] Schell is probably the single most important figure. In his widely read and widely disputed pamphlet *Der Katholicismus als Princip des Fortschritts* (1897), Schell articulated the fundamental premise of modernism: that the Catholic Church needed to "ally itself with progress in whatever form." He condemned isolation and argued for freedom of thought. In his scholarly work *Der Katholizismus und das zwanzigste Jahrhundert im Lichte der kirchlichen Entwicklung der Neuzeit* (1901), Ehrhard argued that the Middle Ages was not the high point of the Catholic Church and that the Church of the twentieth century needed to be involved with its own period. Schell's book was placed on the Index; Ehrhard's book probably cost him a prelate's cap.[31]

The spectrum of beliefs among Catholics had many similarities to the spectrum of beliefs in the nation. Emphasis on family, emphasis on tradition, and a romanticized view of the country and rural way of life were typical of German conservatives of all kinds. Openness to the new was the definition of any modernist. What set Catholic conservatives apart from other conservatives and Catholic modernists apart from other modernists was their Catholicism. This is not quite the obvious statement it appears to be. There had to be an acceptance of the fundamental teachings of the Church. If that acceptance was not there, the viewpoint ceased to be a Catholic viewpoint. Catholic modernists recognized that when their ideas were judged incompatible with those fundamental teachings, it was a choice between the idea and Catholicism. When the Church condemned their writings and positions, they generally allowed themselves to be silenced because the alternative was to cease to be a Catholic.

CATHOLIC INFERIORITY

The attraction for Catholics of fundamentally defensive ultramontane ideas was closely related to what was referred to by contemporaries as Catholic inferiority. In 1871 Catholics comprised 36.2 percent of the population of Germany, a slight increase over their previous position, thanks to the annexation of Alsace-Lorraine. A generation later, in 1907, that statistic was virtually unchanged at 36.5 percent.[32] After the territorial changes following the end of World War I, which detached the predominantly Catholic areas of Alsace-Lorraine and the Polish part of Upper Silesia, their numbers declined slightly to 32.4 percent.[33]

The general figures do not reflect the wide regional variation nor do they reflect the fact that in some states Catholics were dispersed in small clusters among the population, while in others they were concentrated in a particular area. Another point to consider is that Catholics were a minority overall, but they were not a minority in all states. In the states of Bavaria and Baden the majority of the population was Catholic and in both Württemberg and Hesse, where they constituted over 30 percent of the population, Catholics were a substantial presence. In Prussia itself they were the majority in the provinces of Westphalia and the Rhineland. They were also a majority in Prussia's eastern provinces of West Prussia, Posen, and Silesia, but significant numbers of Catholics in those provinces were Polish Catholics rather than German Catholics. In many of these areas Catholics had the numerical potential to dominate state and local politics and society, because both the empire and its successor, the Weimar Republic, were federal rather than unitary states.[34]

But Catholics were not only a minority in Germany, they were also a disadvantaged minority, and they knew it. In 1896 Georg, Freiherr von Hertling,[35] future chancellor of Germany, addressed the Görres Gesellschaft (Görres Society)—a society founded by Hertling to encourage scholarly research among Catholics—on "The Causes of the Backwardness of German Catholics in the Areas of Scholarship." Hertling demonstrated Catholic educational deficiencies. Hans Rost[36] supported Hertling's argument and added to it with a 1908 book, *Die Katholiken in Kultur- und Wirtschaftsleben der Gegenwart.* Rost's book was one of those provocative discussions of a significant issue that catches public interest and stimulates lively commentary, and three years later he followed it with a second, more comprehensive book on the same themes.[37] He substantiated his argument that Catholics were economically and socially disadvantaged with statistic after statistic, documenting what had been vague common knowledge. He showed that Catholics, who were 36.5 percent of the population, constituted 44.2 percent of the agricultural work force, 36.2 percent of industrial workers, but only 29.9 percent of the military officers, civil servants, and members of the independent professions. The conclusion was clear: Catholics were less likely to be engaged in the most progressive and rewarding areas of the economy. They were, therefore, less wealthy and had less social and political power.[38] Other statistical evidence of relative backwardness included the fact that infant mortality was higher among Catholics.[39]

Two closely related facts were particularly important for cultural activity. First, the bourgeoisie, a group that has a central role in the transmission of culture, was a relatively small proportion of the Catholic population.[40] Second, the level of educational attainment was lower among Catholics, creating a smaller number of potential consumers of Catholic culture. Rost demonstrated that the higher the level of education, the lower the percentage of Catholics. He showed that there was a connection between a father's social and professional standing and his son's educational attainments. Moreover, because Protestants were more likely than Catholics to be engaged in learned professions, they were more likely to send their sons on for further education; the percentage of educated Protestants would therefore only increase. In the case of the clergy, a group that placed an especially high value on education, a celibate Catholic clergy had no sons to educate.[41]

A third of Rost's social and economic factors that had significant implications for culture was that Catholics were less likely to live in big cities than were Protestants. Their world remained the largely preindustrial world of the countryside and small town. The numbers of Catholics living in cities did increase dramatically by the end of the nineteenth century, but a principal effect of that increase on Catholic thinking was to exacerbate hostility.[42] Catholic writers, along with many other intellectuals, concentrated on what was unpleasant about the city. Deploring its amorality and immorality was virtually universal.

Large cities posed a challenge to the Church that it was not particularly successful in meeting. The parochial system did not expand rapidly enough to accommodate the rapid growth in their populations, although some cities, like Cologne, were less disadvantaged than others. In Frankfurt am Main, for example, in the mid-1920s only sixty priests cared for the approximately 162,000 Catholic souls, or one priest for every 2,700 people. The wonder is not that only 35–40 percent of the Catholic men and 65–70 percent of the women continued to observe their traditional religious duties, but that so many did so. To say that a large city required an heroic pastor, as did Johannes Chrysostom Schulte, O.F.M.,[43] was a major understatement.[44]

What critics rarely saw, or perhaps merely failed to value, were the cultural opportunities of cities. The late nineteenth century saw the rise of the first mass media—newspapers of mass circulation and illustrated magazines—which had a decisive role in cities. The city made the products of popular culture—products noted for their marketability rather than religious acceptability—physically accessible. The early twentieth century saw the rise of the cinema. Theater had always been a predominantly urban art form. Usually, Catholic writers dismissed these amenities as "temptations." Joseph Mausbach's[45] attitude was typical: "Because our big cities of today are centers of worldly culture, they do not maintain a friendly or saintly face for Christian eyes." At most, a reluctant appreciation was visible. The ambivalence was caught in a review of Franz Herwig's[46] novel *Die Eingeengten,* where Berlin was described as "our much hated, much loved, much admired Berlin."[47]

The causes of Catholic disadvantage were vociferously debated. Rost himself attributed them to such factors as less fertile land, poorer educational opportunities, inequality, the dissolution of the old Holy Roman Empire, secularization, poor pay for the educated, clerical celibacy, and a lack of appreciation of scholarship and wealth.[48] A Protestant critic added a racial motif: Protestants were of predominantly German stock, Catholics from Roman stock.[49] There was, however, no arguing the fact of Catholic disadvantage; in the Protestant state Catholics were not only unable to participate fully politically but were also excluded from important areas of social and economic activity. The disadvantage, moreover, persists today.[50]

Generally speaking, historians accept Rost's facts and his conclusion of relative Catholic inferiority. What has been modified is the emphasis. Nipperdey, for example, stresses the greater openness of Protestantism to new ideas. Heilbronner urges a more particularized view, using as examples the considerable Catholic bourgeois presence and domination of politics in cities like Cologne and the power of the Center Party. The causes of "inferiority" continue to stimulate lively debate.[51]

Social Groups of the Milieu

The broad contours of German Catholicism's social demography are apparent from Rost's statistical data. The class structure of Catholics mirrored the class structure of the nation, but with some important differences. Many of those differences had particular implications for cultural activity. Thomas Mergel opened his landmark book on the Catholic bourgeoisie of the Rhineland with the comment that Catholics have been almost totally absent from research on the bourgeoisie and the bourgeoisie almost completely absent from research on Catholics. Fortunately, research interests have begun to change. The Catholic bourgeoisie may have been small, both numerically and in proportion to the entire Catholic population, but they had the same central position in cultural activity as the bourgeoisie of other religious persuasions. The bourgeoisie determined both high culture and the culture of daily life. It was tremendously influential, transforming noble, peasant, and worker in its own image in the course of the nineteenth century.[52]

Defining the bourgeoisie is a basic research problem that many historians avoid by using the word as if their readers understand what it means.[53] A definition of bourgeois that can be applied requires an unambiguous and knowable standard, such as income level or education, but definitions that do not accommodate ambiguity and variation take into account neither two generations of intensive research on the subject nor the uncertainties inherent in the nature of class. The bourgeoisie of the nineteenth century were themselves uncertain about exactly what constituted that status and were riven by a host of "subtle distinctions and sweltering conflicts."[54] The meaning of the term has changed over time. Historians in the nineteenth century tended to define the class in terms of its members' economic role as accumulators of capital and entrepreneurs. Now it is more common to emphasize a shared value system and common way of life. Lepsius defined the bourgeoisie as that which remains after nobility, clergy, peasants, and workers—groups bound together by social function or working and living conditions—are removed. This solution has much in common with how the bourgeoisie defined itself, since the typical bourgeois thought of himself as neither a nobleman nor a peasant.[55]

The Catholic bourgeoisie had the same general economic and cultural functions as other German bourgeois groups, but Catholicism and *Bürgertum* (the condition of being a member of the bourgeoisie) were not always comfortable companions. The problem lay principally in the area of values. Financial prudence, a passion for order, hard work, a strong sense of duty, and punctuality, all characteristics universally associated with the bourgeois mentality, are hardly incompatible with Catholicism. Contradictions emerge, however, when one adds to that list other bourgeois values, like admiration for success, a rational way of life, inner direction, a skeptical view of authority, and emphasis on the individual and individual responsibility. That the educated were leaving the Church is a persistent theme in German Catholic writings of the period covered in this book, although historians like Mergel have qualified that perception to some extent.

Some members of the bourgeoisie were able to reconcile their Catholicism with their bourgeois status, but there were many who found the two incompatible and chose the latter, thereby ceasing to be either consumers or contributors to Catholic culture.[56]

Like the bourgeoisie as a whole, the Catholic bourgeoisie was divided between the *Bildungsbürgertum* (educated bourgeoisie) and *Besitzbürgertum* (propertied bourgeoisie), or as it is more commonly called now, *Wirtschaftsbürgertum* (economic bourgeoisie), that is, between those whose claims to bourgeois status were based on education and profession and those whose claims were rooted in wealth. The German *Bildungsbürgertum* enjoyed and enjoys great prestige. In Wehler's words, "Bildung geht vor Besitz" (education takes precedence over property). Normally, the *Bildungsbürgertum* takes a particularly active cultural role, but the Catholic *Bildungsbürgertum* was handicapped by its smallness and by the nature of its education. At the secondary-school level, attendance at the *Gymnasium,* the hallmark of *Bildung,* was far less common among Catholics than among Protestants. If Catholics did continue their education beyond the elementary level, it was more likely to be at the highly traditional classical *Gymnasium* than at the *Realgymnasium* or *Oberrealschule* where modern subjects were taught.[57]

Another important distinction was the distinction between the *Kleinbürgertum* (petty bourgeoisie) and the members of the bourgeoisie with a more certain claim to the status. The *Kleinbürger* were the shopkeepers and the clerks, whose income might be indistinguishable from a worker's wages, but whose pretensions were definitely different. In a small town, the *Kleinbürgertum* often provided local leadership in the absence of men of a higher social rank. This group dominated the Catholic milieu and remained faithful to the Church as the upper bourgeoisie was being lost. For Catholic culture, their dominance had unfortunate consequences, because the *Kleinbürgertum* has never been noted for good taste. Some historians urge that this perception is unjust. Their taste is not necessarily bad, just different, and the Latin proverb *De gustibus non est disputandum* should apply. But the conventional wisdom expressed in a thousand novels and cartoons—that the culture of the petty bourgeoisie was imitative, not to say deplorable—is not easy to dispel or deny.[58]

One group not prominent in the Catholic milieu was the industrial working class. Historians usually suggest that religion had lost its hold on the working class in the course of the nineteenth century, although Catholic workers were less likely to abandon their Church than Protestant workers. In the Roman Catholic Church, individual priests were not indifferent to the plight of industrial workers, but the response of the institutional Church left much to be desired. Efforts to develop Catholic unions were made, and the Volksverein (People's Association) came into existence to address the social question, but success was qualified. A strong socialist milieu competed for the loyalty of workers, and by the Weimar period Catholic workers were increasingly likely to vote for socialist candidates rather than those of the Center Party. The working class appears in Catholic writing on culture predominantly as a group to be attracted, not as a group already engaged in Catholic cultural life.[59]

The *Kleinbürgertum* is a group of particular consequence for the milieu, not just because it dominated the milieu, but because it provided the majority of the clergy. Irmtrand Götz von Olenhusen's study of the priests of the Diocese of Freiburg demonstrates that at the end of the nineteenth century priests were less likely to be of bourgeois origin than earlier, they were unlikely to come from the new industrial working class, and they were unlikely to come from a big city. Instead, they tended to come from the traditional preindustrial commercial classes and to have been born in small towns that were not quite villages. German Catholic history is not as rich in research on the clergy as French, but, to the extent that it is available, the same social trends as in France are apparent.[60]

By the late nineteenth century two competing ideals of the cleric existed: the enlightened priest, who was oriented to the modern, bourgeois, dominant culture, and the ultramontane priest, a man who held strictly to the system in which all meaning was religious and was represented by the official Church. It was not, however, a contest. Everything in the education for the priesthood was designed to produce a cleric of the ultramontane type.

A major element in the Tridentine reforms of the sixteenth century had been improving the standards of the priesthood. Priorities were piety, obedience, and morality, and seminary training inculcated these qualities. The education of the typical late nineteenth-century German priest was sketchy and, although an improvement over the education of his earlier counterparts, rarely intellectually rigorous. A long list of things was forbidden. Avoiding sexual relations, of course, and avoiding even the appearance of impropriety were of the utmost importance, but proscription extended much further. Certain kinds of dress, active or passive participation in the theater, dances, ballets, and masquerades, gambling, frequent or regular visits to taverns without justification, excessive alcohol consumption, bearing arms or hunting, and practicing improper occupations were also forbidden. Residence was enjoined. In contrast to their Protestant brethren, Catholic parish priests were not perceived as belonging to the world of the educated and rarely did they emerge from their training with any openness to modern culture.[61]

The community expected the priest to fulfill his clerical duties, to hold services regularly, catechize the children, advise parishioners, visit his flock, and generally to be a good person. Many were good men. The cleric of literature and memoir is usually a good and faithful shepherd. The autobiography of Ludwig Ganghofer,[62] a novelist reared in a small town in the Black Forest, contains an affectionate portrayal of Father von Hegnenbach. Ganghofer describes him as the most pious and faithful man he ever knew and from whom, even when he was silent, "good cheer and contentment with life emanated like scent from a blooming bough."[63] In the course of the nineteenth century, the Catholic clergy became steadily more important in the face of historical and intellectual challenges, and they exercised considerable power over the lay world. Poorly educated as they were, they provided intellectual, social, and political leadership. They defined norms and to the best of their ability saw that those norms were followed. They were prominent in discussions about culture. They may have been the lowest level in the church hierarchy, but they were the intermediaries between God and man.[64]

Not all scholars agree, however, with this picture of the priest's influence and control. An underlying theme of Margaret Lavinia Anderson's discussion of Catholic politics in the late nineteenth century is that "the Catholic population were not mere creatures of any clerical 'milieu.'" Obviously, such factors as intelligence, level of education and interest, energy level, personality, and individual opinions, not to mention the magnitude of his responsibilities, would have greatly influenced how effectively a priest could guide his flock in any area. One can also expect that the range of cooperation and obedience visible in every other human group was present in German Catholics.[65]

The clergy were not the only Catholic intellectuals, if intellectuals are defined as those "who employ in their communication and expression, with relatively higher frequency than most other members of their society, symbols of general scope and abstract reference, concerning man, society, nature, and the cosmos." There were also Catholics whose professions had strong intellectual components—judges, civil servants, doctors, engineers, editors, and educators—even if they were less numerous, relatively and absolutely, than their Protestant counterparts. They were less numerous for reasons similar to the reasons that premodern societies are not rich in intellectuals: their relative poverty; their limited access to higher education; and the discrimination that restricted their participation in government. At the same time, the Roman Catholic Church tended to deplore rather than encourage the use of intellectual training to transcend and transform traditions, which is one of the principal functions of intellectuals. From this group, editors, journalists, and educators, and those engaged in the practice of specific art forms were most likely to contribute to debates about culture.[66]

Women represent a further group for consideration. In the model of the bourgeois family, the woman was responsible for culture, as she was for religion. As the nineteenth century progressed and religion became less public and more privatized, the home became a religious center where mothers laid the ground-work for future piety and interpreted the world for the children; statements like "the mother is appointed priestess" and "the mother is the soul of the family" were not uncommon. If culture was to have a firm Catholic foundation, accomplishing it was up to her; but her cultural role was not a public one. Memoirs attest to women's considerable success, but women were also blamed for failure. Rost attributed the decline of "our culture" to the lack of culture among women, their superficiality, lightness, and scorn for the moral principles of Christianity, a disparaging viewpoint that many of his contemporaries shared.[67]

CATHOLIC ORGANIZATIONS

Organizations were the signature of the Catholic milieu. With an organization for every political, economic, social, and cultural purpose of life, the system had a crucial role both in consolidating and maintaining the Catholic milieu and in providing a base for action, although their relationship to the Church was never formally clarified. *Vereinsprotestantismus* (associational Protestantism) could not compete with *Vereinskatholizismus* (associational Catholicism) in size, scope, or effectiveness. During this period—the nineteenth century is known as the century of the association and the twentieth carried on the good work—Catholic organizations in Germany reached such heights that the country was considered "the classical land of the Catholic organizational movement."[68]

Catholic organizations may not have been "without number," as one contemporary wrote, but at times they seemed so. As the laws regulating association were liberalized, they mushroomed. They matched the structure of the Church: there were national organizations, diocesan organizations, and organizations for individual parishes. In some cases an organization would be hierarchical, in other cases it might exist at only one level. August Pieper,[69] an official of the Volksverein, the influential Catholic organization formed in 1890 to encourage social reform on a Christian basis, created a six-part taxonomy to categorize their breadth of interest. His schema included organizations of piety that either attempted to encourage Christian virtues or supported specific Church needs; organizations devoted to charity; organizations based on class or profession; organizations devoted to the ideals of scholarship, art, and literature; political groups; and social groups. The fourth category—organizations dedicated to the ideals of scholarship, art, and literature—is his cultural category, even if he does not use the word culture, and it is the smallest. Specific, conscious, cultural activity formed only a small part, numerically, of Catholic organizational activity, but the fact that it was reified in institutions capable of action made a cultural movement possible.[70]

The 1923 edition of the *Kirchliches Handbuch*, a compilation of statistics relating to German Catholicism, had a similar cultural category. Its title, "Societies for the Care of Culture and Adult Education," announces an important development in the generation after Pieper wrote his article: the linking of culture and adult education. The many associations founded after 1900 (seventeen out of twenty-five of the cultural organizations listed in the handbook, or 68 percent) testify to the increasing interest in "feinere Kultur" (high culture) and to the energy expended in its cause. The 1923 handbook as a whole lends support to the description of the Catholic Church as an "organization-forming" organization.[71]

The primary purpose common to all Catholic associations was to be "truly Catholic."[72] All were dedicated to the preservation of the Catholic outlook and to religious and moral "toughening." The Diocesan Synod of Freiburg declared early in the 1920s: "The Catholic associations are important statements of the life of the Church and witness to its unbroken strength and fullness of life. The Church makes use of the associations in order to maintain the faithful of all classes in the life of the Church and to strengthen them in faith and morals, to awaken them to apostolic labor and to prepare them for it, and with their help to solve the tasks of the present and secure important Church interests in all areas of public life." Other statements include more specific goals, like the care and support of the Catholic press, but the fundamental purpose of Catholic associations was to strengthen Catholic identity.[73]

Contemporaries recognized that declared purposes were not necessarily the only purposes of an association in the eyes of its members or even, perhaps, the most important ones. Entertainment was a particularly thorny issue. By the turn of the century scathing comments on the subject of pleasure seeking had become common. One priest saw the origins of Catholic associations in the replacement of a presumed former contentment and satisfaction with a search for pleasure. The only redeeming feature was that such activity took place in an environment in which Catholic values were preserved and practiced. The bishop of Passau, Baron Sigismond-Felix Ow-Felldorf,[74] found it necessary to declare firmly in 1924 that entertainment and pleasure could never be the chief objective of Catholic associations. His words indicate a certain resignation to the fact that entertainment was going to be an objective, if not the chief objective.[75]

In the absence of personal testimony we can only surmise what these organizations meant to their members. The fact of membership says something, although, as anyone who has ever belonged to an organization knows, it may not say much. Basic data are scattered and accidental; unfortunately, neither the Church nor anyone else kept reliable statistics.[76] At best, there are occasional figures for an individual organization. The Volksverein, for example, arguably the single most important Catholic organization, had 805,000 members before World War I.

It lost members during the war, but by 1921 it had recovered to almost 696,000. That was its postwar high point, and membership then declined. The pattern of membership in the Borromäus Verein, the premier Catholic library organization, shows some similarities, although the Borromäus Verein numbers rose steadily after the setbacks of World War I and postwar inflation. It is possible that these two sets of statistics represented a shift in interest from the general organization to the more specialized.[77]

Two exceptions to the general lack of information are the parish of St. Josef Gelsenkirchen-Schalke in the Ruhr and the Diocese of Paderborn. Schalke, a town with some 19,000 Catholics, had thirty-three church-related organizations, which counted 10,476 members in 1913. A study of the Diocese of Paderborn estimates that for its Westphalian portion, 17 percent of members of some Catholic association at the turn of the century were members of the educational societies, principally of the Borromäus Verein. The organizations of religious piety, the brotherhoods, congregations, prayer societies, and mission societies, had the most appeal with 60 percent of all Catholics being members of some association. Statistics varied considerably. In the Deanery of Büren (province of Paderborn), 80 percent of all Catholics who belonged to some association belonged to an organization of religious piety; in the working-class town of Gelsenkirchen, the corresponding figure was 55 percent. The religious brotherhoods and congregations would have been the most effective organizations for providing a focus of Catholic identity. Nonetheless, the high membership statistics may more reflect the clerical pressure brought to bear on parishioners to join these particular associations than testify to widespread piety.[78]

To the clergy organizations meant work. The priest was expected to be the leader, to provide the impetus that would get an organization started, as well as the labor to keep it going. An anonymous set of instructions that dates from the period declared that "[t]he success of association activity depends primarily on the priest's direction." How impossible his task was is made clear by what we know about the associations active in the parish of St. Clemens, Hannover, in 1912. St. Clemens, the original parish church in Hannover from which new parishes were being carved during this period, offered its parishioners a comprehensive assortment of organizations from which to choose. There was the Casino "Constantia," a club for "independent" Catholics (that is, upper bourgeois and professional Catholics); four organizations for craftsmen and apprentices; a branch of the Volksverein; the St. Vinzenz-Verein (St. Vincent [de Paul] Society) that aided the poor; the St. Elisabeth-Verein (St. Elizabeth Society) that aided individual poor women and women workers; two groups for working women; a society for girls who had left school; a branch of the Borromäus Verein; the Casimir-Verein (Casimir Society) for Polish-speaking workers; the Paramenten-Verein (Decoration

Society) that worked to outfit poor churches; a Cäcelien Verein; and the Katholisches Kreuzbündnis, a society for Catholic teetotalers. A list of societies sponsored by the parish of St. Josef in the working-class district of Gelsenkirchen-Schalke, active between 1872 and 1927, identifies a total of forty-four organizations. With two exceptions, a sports group and the Verband der katholischen Vereine Schalke (a society of societies founded in 1898 by the local priest to coordinate and publicize the activities of all the other associations), they were either branches of the same organizations to which those of St. Clemens organizations belonged or the same kinds of societies. Associations are fundamentally an urban form, but rural parishes had them too, if not in such superabundance as St. Clemens, Hannover, and St. Josef, Gelsenkirchen-Schalke.[79]

Work with associations was work for which the priest was not particularly well prepared. Ideally, he would have acquired at seminary the foundation of "a social knowledge and understanding of economic and class problems" and then extended it by practical experience and participation in short-term courses and conferences. He would have sufficient subject knowledge for cultural associations like the Borromäus Verein. The reality, however, was that preparation for work with associations was to all practical purposes nonexistent. Laypersons were viewed as a necessary, but not especially welcome, source of relief for the priest.[80]

By the 1920s the voluntary associations of the Church had ceased to be the source of pride they had once been. A keynote speaker at the 1928 Katholikentag (Congress of Catholics),[81] the largest annual gathering of German Catholics, might still praise organizations as "a pillar of the life and work of our Church," but their costs were being counted. Criticism had begun to appear by the turn of the century, but it became common after 1918. More than one cleric made the important point that the demands of working with associations interfered with his primary duty, the care of souls. *Vereinsmüdigkeit* (fatigue with associations) replaced *Vereinsfreudigkeit* (joy in associations); *Vereinsmeierei* (associational obsessiveness) disappeared. Tellingly, with rare exceptions, memberships declined.[82]

In a sense, associations had been too convenient. Eugen Weiss was one voice among many when he grumbled, "Without doubt we suffer from a superfluity of associations. And they never become fewer, only more." Every perceived problem spawned a new organization. The fundamental complaint was that Catholic organizational activity was overextended and that it was not of the right kind, whatever the right kind might be. In 1928 the archbishop of Bamberg, Johannes Jacobus Hauck,[83] wrote in his Lenten letter: "Willingly it is to be acknowledged that our Catholic organizational life carries traces of the weakness and insufficiency that adhere to all human institutions. It is likewise to be acknowledged that our Catholic organizational life is sometimes overstrained and that it developed too diversely. It is also to be acknowledged that in many cases it corresponds too little with the high purposes of the apostolic spirit." Wilhelm Marx,[84] leader of the Center Party and a former official of the Volksverein, agreed. "Catholic organizational life has become too diverse and too motley," he wrote. A set of guidelines for clergy referred to "mindless multiplication." There was also some sense that their very existence placed too much reliance on man's ability to deal with social ills and not enough on supernatural means of grace.[85]

A major grievance was a perceived emphasis on pleasure. Because associations, with the exception of the music groups, regularly met at their local tavern, they were too often synonymous with beer and noise. They made Sundays less holy and damaged Christian morals. Nearly everyone who wrote on the subject considered Catholic organizational activity to have been infected by this "Vereins-bazillus" (associational bacterium).[86]

Some went so far as to question their very reason for existence. The unidentified author of the following statement was clearly unimpressed with what associations accomplished. His account has an immediate quality to it that suggests a disgusted man, coming home after one too many irritating, pointless meetings, probably of an organization dedicated to art, and venting his frustration.

> I am a declared enemy of associations that collect dues, write annual reports, and create the largest executive boards possible. The members of the executive board are usually the founders, who bring nomination documents with them in their pockets. There are people who cannot belong to enough organization boards, who look on this membership as a thing of honor, not, however, the work, the practical work, and without that associations are born dead. We have a sufficiency of Christian art societies; they all grew out of the best of intentions. After some years of existence, however, the scepter for the most part goes over into the hands of—cliques.[87]

The universal solution to these manifold problems was simplification. A common suggestion was that all the Catholic organizations of a parish should hold one common festival, rather than separate ones, a proposal that is an unintended comment on what organizations meant to the men and women of the 1920s. Consolidation was, however, easier to suggest than to accomplish. On the local level, economic interests were at stake; taverns made good money from association meetings. In terms of the Church, other interests were involved, but the real problem was administrative; who had jurisdiction was not always clear. Catholic associations spanned such a wide range of type and organizational pattern that no single authority could command, "Let there be consolidation." And, had it succeeded, consolidation would have eliminated many sources of strength and done away with the virtues of specialization, as the occasional naysayer pointed out.[88]

Church officials did make periodic attempts to assert the authority of the Church. In 1921, for example, the Freiburg Synod reminded priests that while "association activity in all its branches is the cure of souls," the regular pastoral cure of souls—preaching, catechizing, hearing confessions, taking services, and caring for the sick—must not suffer. The Diocese of Rottenburg issued particularly detailed guidelines in 1931 that dealt with virtually all of the complaints of the previous decade. The Catholic Action movement, which began as a papal initiative in the 1920s, can be seen as an attempt of the Church to channel and direct lay participation in a more readily managed form. In Germany, however, the devastating economic conditions of the Depression and the Nazi takeover of the state in the end imposed "reform" by necessity and by force.[89]

Discussions about organizations within the Catholic community were in concrete rather than abstract terms. Only occasionally were their latent functions dimly perceived.[90] One critic, with anything but approval, described them as *Nebenkirchen,* or secondary churches. Like the home, the association was becoming an alternative site of religious activity. The greater its success, the greater the potential threat to the Church.[91] Whether recognized or not, however, the organizations did collectively fulfill the many functions of voluntary associations. From the point of view of the individual, they gave the opportunity for sociability, service, and social action and served as an arena in which to develop organizational and political skills. They offered educational opportunities. They replaced spontaneous neighborliness with more formal arrangements. As Hürten puts it, "The voluntary associations simply replaced what custom and tradition had created in the village. . . ."[92]

From society's point of view the contribution of Catholic organizations is more debatable. The founding ideals of the associations seem too often to have been lost, and activity became activity for its own sake. Where one scholar sees them as a modernizing force, another sees them as using modern means for achieving conservative ends. There is more agreement that they hardened the lines within German society and contributed to fragmentation. They strengthened inner homogeneity, but they cut Catholics off from the wider national culture.[93]

Without its organizations, the Catholic milieu would not have been the Catholic milieu. In a period when identity was defined by the organizations to which a person belonged, they added to an individual's Catholicity and strengthened the group's Catholicity. Without Catholic cultural organizations, there would have been no Catholic cultural movement. Those organizations with cultural interests helped define a specifically Catholic culture, stimulated its creation and production, disseminated it, and preserved it.

3

Culture in Theory and Practice

THE DISTURBING NEW WORLD OF CULTURE

As the end of the nineteenth century approached, a sense of cultural crisis developed in Germany; after World War I it would become a sense of calamity. This perception was visible in all Western countries but was particularly acute in Germany, where the need to define the new nation was urgent, and economic and social change had been experienced so recently and so rapidly. This sense of crisis was even more acute among Catholics, who recognized that they stood "in the middle of a decisive change in intellectual life (*Geistesleben*)," understood that the trends of the day did not favor them, and feared what the outcome might be.[1]

The emergence of cultural modernism, a collection of ideas, attitudes, and artistic events in which technological, political, and economic developments played an essential role, was the principal source of these feelings of anxiety. Cultural modernism was not an integrated movement but, as Georg Bollenbeck puts it, an "ensemble" of assorted arts. It had no formal intellectual relationship with the theological modernism opposed by the Church except a fundamental openness to the new. Cultural modernism was not the same thing as modern culture, although the two shared many characteristics, and critics would often attack one as a surrogate for the other. Cultural modernism was primarily process, although it could at times be product. Modern culture, on the other hand, was primarily product, the assortment of all the cultural artifacts, attitudes, ideas, and ways of life that were available, its heterogeneity reflecting the diversity of cultural modernism. Cultural modernism played a major role in making culture a political issue.[2]

Because cultural modernism often defined itself in terms of what it was not, capturing its essence is difficult. One point on which there is general agreement is that its dominant feature was rejection: rejection of the past, rejection of whatever was the prevalent style, rejection of whatever was established. Modern art, modern literature, modern music, and modern theater were by definition experimental. Other characteristics frequently associated with cultural modernism and its products are internationalism, an identification with the bourgeoisie, and a high degree of subjectivity. The mixture had something to aggravate almost everyone. It offended national sensibilities, left indifferent those who did not share the dominant bourgeois values, and displeased those who did not consider the individual the most important element in society.

From the last decade of the nineteenth century on, artistic experimentation, personal anger and bitterness, and rejection of conventional political and social values are consistently visible in all forms of modern culture. One needs only to mention the writings of the philosopher Friedrich Nietzsche, the plays of Gerhart Hauptmann, the paintings of Lovis Corinth, or the music of Richard Strauss to appreciate how great must have been the impression of rebellion, disillusion, and alienation on the casual observer—as was intended. Such works helped focus and advance the discussion of theories of culture. They reflected attitudes and at the same time made statements that contributed to the shaping of attitudes. Continuity with the past, whether the point of reference was a landscape of Caspar David Friedrich or a symphony of Beethoven, seemed to have disappeared.

Many Germans found such manifestations of cultural modernism an affront, un-German, and destructive of all they cherished. The new works certainly had little affinity with such traditional German characteristics as thoroughness, love of order, rationality, or conformity.[3] They might receive critical acclaim, they might seem to be the wave of the future, but they held little appeal for ordinary individuals. Works like Kurt Weill's *Die Dreigroschenoper,* a genuine hit, and Thomas Mann's *Der Zauberberg,* with its initial printing of 50,000 copies, were exceptions. Popularity was generally reserved for less challenging and more accessible works, like the operettas of Franz Léhar and the novels of Ina Seidel.[4]

With its international outlook, cultural modernism ran counter to nationalist feelings, so powerful in a nation that had only recently achieved nationhood. In commenting on German opera houses and orchestras after the founding of the empire, the music scholar Christoph Wolff writes that "[t]hese years were also marked by often exaggerated cultural bombast, from which there gradually, yet unmistakably, evolved feelings of nationalistic superiority whereby German music was considered to be pre-eminent and foreign works were scarcely allowed to have their say."[5] His remarks could be applied to other cultural forms with equal validity.

Exaggerated admiration for all arts German easily became chauvinism, and a connection between opposition to cultural modernism and anti-Semitism is often apparent. It was true that the assimilation of Jews had proceeded further in the arts than in any other area of German life, but only occasionally were leading artists in the various expressions of cultural modernism Jews. This fact did not prevent them from being perceived as dominating the cultural world and using their position to undermine true German culture.[6]

The early twentieth century added variations to what the late nineteenth century had begun. World War I intensified both the compulsion of modernists to innovate as well as the debate about culture. Rejection of the past became an attack on the past.[7] Theories of decline, moral and otherwise, were widely discussed. Emphasis was on irrationality, spontaneity, and despair. The United States became a cultural factor, its influence either to be deplored or welcomed, depending on the point of view. The psychological novels of Hermann Hesse, the "decadent" paintings of Max Beckmann, Leopold Jessner's innovative staging, the politically radical theater of Erwin Piscator, and the twelve-tonal music of Arnold Schönberg surpassed their predecessors in discontinuity.

During the 1920s modern culture had the additional misfortune of becoming associated with leftist politics in popular perception. Although a shared desire to break with the past justifies the association, only a few prominent figures were, in fact, Marxists. When artists were politically radical, their political radicalism tended to be vague and undisciplined. Peter Gay describes the proponents of expressionism, the dominant movement of the early twentieth century in all the German arts, in the following terms: "[T]hey were in general revolutionary without being political or, at least, without being programmatic . . . rebels with a cause but without clear definitions or concrete aims."[8] What was truly revolutionary was "their unremitting search for reality behind appearance."[9] Facts, however, were almost irrelevant, and a vague perception of revolutionary sympathies was enough to give rise to cries of decadence, insufficient Germanness, and, after 1918, so-called *Kulturbolschewismus* (cultural bolshevism).

THE SOCIAL BASES OF CULTURE

The concurrent shift in the social bases of culture and the emergence of popular culture that was taking place heightened cultural anxieties. By 1900 three distinct cultures could be identified: high culture, *Volk* culture, and popular culture. Even if innovation was an increasingly important element in high culture, socially and economically high culture was what it had been for centuries: culture primarily for the upper classes, created by self-conscious artists and writers who argued fiercely over theories and practiced distinctive styles. *Volk* culture, too, remained much what it had always been: a largely unwritten culture of the lower orders with a traditional content. The only new feature of *Volk* culture was its discovery by the intelligentsia, who in the course of the nineteenth century had turned it into an object of study and veneration. Because the *Volk*[10] supposedly remained true to ancient German ideals,[11] *Volk* culture was now seen as a repository of semi-mystical Germanness. Finally, there was popular culture, which was a genuinely new phenomenon. Technological development, a newly literate population, increased disposable income and leisure time in the working class, and urbanization had combined to generate a mass culture. Unlike other forms of culture, popular culture was a principally commercial product, its main purpose to make money for its producers and purveyors. Its content, moreover, like the content of modern high culture, had few antecedents recognizable by bourgeois cultural critics.[12]

Not that popular culture was an exclusively lower-class phenomenon. In fact, it often served to bridge the wide gap between the entertainments of high society and the coarser amusements of the lower classes. Contemporaries recognized that older patterns were being modified. Writing in 1926, Siegfried Kracauer,[13] a founder of film theory, offered a sophisticated analysis of the audience's reception of modern culture. The new commercialized art, literature, and theater, he wrote, acted as homogenizing forces to eliminate class divisions. *A-Kunst* (*allgemeine Kunst,* or general art) joined *E-Kunst* (*elitäre Kunst,* or elite art) and *U-Kunst* (*Unterhaltungskunst,* or entertainment), and the public made stars of the representatives of this new type.[14]

During this period, high culture ceased to be the exclusive property of the upper classes, even if they remained its primary market. Annual art exhibitions in major German cities like Berlin received much attention in the press and attracted large numbers of visitors. Other areas of culture, especially the performing arts, provide additional examples of occasional wide popular interest in the products of cultural modernism. Such interest guaranteed that the debate on cultural modernism would extend well beyond the elites for which it was created and contributed to its politicization. The occasional particularly outrageous novel, play, or painting easily became a cause célèbre.[15]

The products of cultural modernism were not, however, the only culture that was available, if, indeed, its writers, artists, and composers shared enough in common to group their works under one umbrella. In the early twentieth century what is now called modern culture was only one of several possibilities. Literature had serious authors who glorified the comradeship of war in traditional genres, poets who continued to write lyrical poetry, and *Heimat* writers who celebrated the people and places of their particular locale. In music and theater Franz Léhar carried on the operetta tradition, and Richard Wagner produced immense musical glorifications of the Germanic past. Some painters continued to paint portraits, landscapes, and still lifes in representational and/or Romantic and/or other traditional styles. Such works reflected different values, made different statements, and supported a different position in the cultural debate. That they would be the ones largely ignored by the future was not yet determined.

Catholic Positions on Modern Culture: The Negative and the Less Negative

Catholic responses to modern culture were overwhelmingly negative. The seminal document was the *Syllabus of Errors* issued in 1864 by Pius IX, a document that established the Church's policy for decades to come. Most of the eighty errors in the Syllabus addressed political issues, but the last error, number 80, defined the Church's position on culture: "The Roman Pontiff can, and ought to, reconcile himself, and come to terms with progress, liberalism and modern civilization."[16] In an explication that appeared very soon after, the French bishop Felix Dupanloup[17] put the papal quotations in their original context: in error 80 the pope had been specifically attacking the spoliation of convents in Piedmont and harassment of nuns and clergy. Four decades later the German historian Albert Ehrhard was still trying to explain away the words of error 80. But such explanations failed to make much impression. The syllabus was viewed as an exhortation to reject the modern world without equivocation, and, considering the pope's view of Catholic modernism, this view is not unreasonable. Pius IX had declared, "Catholic liberalism has one foot in the truth and one foot in error, one foot on my side and one foot on the side of my enemies."[18] Albert Lotz[19] might rejoice in 1924 that the mentality of the syllabus no longer prevailed, but his statement was more hope than reality; Catholic thinking on modern culture generally followed Pio Nono's lead.

The central premise in Catholic thinking about culture was that it should be, by nature, Christian. By the late nineteenth century, however, Christianity, which for so long had been the foundation of Western thought, was being replaced by other, nonreligious intellectual structures. Catholics commonly attributed the cultural crisis to this displacement. Friedrich Muckermann's comparison of culture to the apartment houses of Berlin, "where one discovers that the foundations are no longer reliable," captured the essence of this view. Modern culture was no longer based on Christian truths but on its own questionable strengths. A crucial separation had taken place, and modern culture and religion belonged to two separate worlds.[20]

Each Catholic critic of culture had his own list of grievances, which ranged from the tastelessness of mass-produced missals to philosophical profundities like the absence of spirit. High on the list of complaints was materialism, a word that covered a wide range of sins. Most often it was used broadly to summarize the spiritual costs of economic development; the reader was expected to respond to it with instinctive condemnation. Materialism signaled hedonism and a meaningless search for pleasure, conspicuous consumption, an emphasis on the good things in life that money can buy. Sometimes other characteristics associated with late nineteenth-century capitalism and industrialization were subsumed under it, like urbanization and bureaucratization. Few writers distinguished between its original philosophical meaning and its contemporary popular meaning.[21]

Again and again, Catholic commentators asserted the incompatibility of materialism and culture, or at least the brand of culture they endorsed. Materialism was portrayed almost as a force that displaced ideals in the individual's consciousness. Richard von Kralik,[22] a leader of the *Gral* movement (an Austrian literary movement that sought to revive an idealized medieval Catholicism) presented one definitive statement on the subject: A great culture was incompatible with materialism; to be culture, a culture had to be idealistic; and to be the highest culture, a culture had to be religious. The economic problems of the 1920s gave a sharper edge to discussions about the evils of materialism, but the fundamental objections did not change.[23]

Denunciations of materialism were frequently accompanied by charges of moral decline. Moral decline might be equated with the decrease in church attendance that had been observed in Protestants before and in Catholics after 1870, or it might be used more generally. If the latter, moral decline might mean spiritual emptiness, negativism, an excessive emphasis on reason, an excessive emphasis on man and not enough on God, and an excessive emphasis on success. Alternatively, it might be left to the reader to infer moral decline from descriptions of the characteristics of the modern world and contemporary human behavior. Language sometimes got colorful. Franz Zach's[24] claim that "[m]odern life has become a dance around the golden calf and an orgy of Venus" packs powerful images that enhance the initial charge.[25] By the mid-1920s "moral decline" had become a cliché, although that fact did not stop its use. In a public letter to the Ministry of the Interior about the pernicious influence of films, Cardinal Adolf Bertram,[26] presiding bishop of the Fulda Conference of Bishops, prefaced his remarks with a reference to moral decline.[27] A sermon prepared by the Borromäus Verein for use on the day designated St. Charles Borromeo Sunday by the Fulda Conference of Bishops raised the level of hyperbole with the words "moral emergency."[28] This perception of moral decline was widely shared.

Another focus of Catholic cultural criticism was unity (*Einheit*), usually in the guise of a treasure that had been lost. Unity implied wholeness and harmony; often it seemed to have almost metaphysical properties. Different writers used unity in different senses. The theologian Arnold Rademacher's[29] unity was psychological; he asserted that culture had lost all unity, but his explanation of this assertion suggests that he really meant that the individual personality had lost its unity and that therefore life had lost its unity. Victor Cathrein, S.J.,[30] saw unity in a philosophical sense; for him, the great strength of Catholics was their unified worldview. Hans Grundei's[31] unity was political; the creation of a "formal" democracy in 1919 had split the formerly unified Catholics.[32]

Most often, however, Catholic writers meant social unity when they used the word unity. Essentially, they used the distinction between community (*Gemeinschaft*) and society (*Gesellschaft*) developed by the sociologist Ferdinand Tönnies,[33] an agnostic of Lutheran background. *Gemeinschaft* was a type of social relationship that "is intimate, enduring and based on a clear understanding of each individual's position in society. Culturally, societies characterized by *Gemeinschaft* are relatively homogeneous, since their culture is enforced quite rigidly by well-recognized moral custodians—the church and the family." Such societies usually enjoy "greater emotional cohesion, sentiment, continuity and authenticity." *Gesellschaft*, in contrast, referred to "impersonal, contractual and calculative" social relationships, the kind of relationship that was increasing in an industrializing, urbanizing society.[34] Some Catholic writers, like Rademacher, used the words *Gemeinschaft* and *Gesellschaft;* others spoke less precisely but clearly all yearned for *Gemeinschaft*. Many contrasted *Gemeinschaft* unfavorably with individualism, a characteristic of modern life that was blamed for many of society's problems.

Richard von Kralik joined the idea of unity to culture. "In unity," he wrote, "lies the greatness of all high cultures." Greatness of culture could not be achieved through individual efforts but required a wholeness in which the entire society—the whole *Volk*, all classes—would be comprehended. Kralik claimed that societies that prized unity did respect individuals; the exaltation of individualism, however, when accompanied by the destruction of unity, paradoxically led to a devaluing of the individual.[35]

Laments for lost unity were often interwoven with laments for the lost Middle Ages. From a twentieth-century perspective, medieval society appeared to have had an underlying intellectual, social, and political unity that had since disappeared, taking with it much of man's sense of well-being. Franz Zach can again represent many voices. Zach extolled the "wonderful unity" of the medieval worldview. He applauded the Christian character of its culture and deplored the destruction of this worldview by the subjectivism of modern times.[36] A rare exception to the general glorification of this apparent age of cultural unity was Albert Ehrhard, who pointed out a widespread failure to see the dark side of the Middle Ages, but even Ehrhard acknowledged that the period was a shining hour of Catholicism (*Glanzepoche*).

The persistent evocation of the Middle Ages is the clearest example of the nostalgia that was such a large part of Catholic attitudes toward culture. A yearning for something better than what was currently attainable was virtually universal, and writers looked to the undeniably rich Catholic past rather than to some uncertain future utopia. The conditions for nostalgia were present in abundance:[37] a linear, as opposed to cyclical, view of time; a sense that the past was "better" than the present; and the presence of tangible reminders of that past. Regrettably, this idealization of the Middle Ages stamped Catholic responses with a retrogressive air that, in turn, imparted an air of futility, a major disadvantage in an era that valued progress and conviction.

Nostalgia is as much an emotional response as it is an intellectual one, and emotions were as important as ideas in Catholic responses to modern culture. In the impersonal words on the pages, fear is palpable—fear of the power of the emerging mass media, fear of the power of culture to usurp the place of religion.[38] Defensiveness is conspicuous. There are numerous declarations that the Protestant version of something was not as good as the Catholic version. Rost, the same Rost who demonstrated Catholic economic inferiority beyond a doubt, argued that the collections held in all Protestant museums could not equal in value and beauty the art treasures preserved in the museums of Italy and Spain. Others tried to claim that cultural giants of the past like Goethe, Shakespeare, and Leibniz were crypto- or half-Catholics. Such comparisons suggest a collective cultural inferiority complex,[39] a not uncommon reaction of disadvantaged minorities.

Catholics who were more positive about modern culture did exist, but no comparable list of points in praise of modern culture, not its censure, can summarize their views. Such men were far more likely to criticize Catholic culture, which they considered inferior, than to linger over the attractions of modern culture. Their acceptance of modern culture, and to some extent cultural modernism, was more a matter of general attitude than of particular features. The quintessential example of this quasi acceptance is the journalist Karl Muth's[40] electrifying 1898 pamphlet *Steht die katholische Literatur auf der Höhe der Zeit?* (Does Catholic Literature Stand at the Pinnacle of the Times?), although examples of his arguments can be found as early as the eighteenth century. Muth answered the rhetorical question of his title with a resounding no. He and others like him feared the consequences of cultural isolation far more than they feared modern culture. By the 1920s the ideas of these advocates of involvement and adaptation were being described as a powerful current and, such as it was, constituted the Catholic avant-garde.[41]

Differences between those Catholics who opposed modernism and its cultural creations and those who argued for some accommodation with modernism should not be exaggerated. All Catholic intellectuals shared the conviction that culture could only be a true culture if it was a religious culture. They also agreed that, although culture has been linked with religious practice from mankind's earliest days, culture had a separate identity, and, even more importantly, so did religion. No one challenged the view that the Church existed for religious purposes. It might have a major role as a bearer of culture (*Kulturträger*), but that was not its raison d'être. The theologian Joseph Mausbach, considered a modernist in theological terms, stated the case: While there was a close tie between religion and culture, culture was neither the purpose nor measure of religion. Religion, on the other hand, was perhaps a precondition of culture, creating art and enriching research, but it was itself more than all culture. The explication of the aesthetic philosophy of Pius X in Kralik's journal *Der Gral* offers a more ornate version of the shared view of art and culture's subservience to religion: "Religion gives art the breath of life, inspiration, strength, fruitfulness, fullness, fire, light, and warmth. Art gives religion beauty, brilliance, honor, appearance, splendor, ornament."[42]

THE MAJOR ISSUES

Culture was not a discovery of the late nineteenth century. In the years after the *Kulturkampf* Catholic intellectuals could build on the work of men like Friedrich Schleiermacher, Friedrich von Schlegel, Bishop Johann Michael Sailer, Joseph von Görres, and Martin Deutinger,[43] who had addressed fundamental concerns about the condition of Catholicism, often in the context of literature. Most of these men were Romantics, and their literary ideals, their discussions of aesthetics, and their thinking on the relation of art and religion provided essential structure for their successors.[44]

The central issue for Catholic intellectuals of the late nineteenth and early twentieth centuries was the same as it had been in the early nineteenth century: What is the proper relationship between religion and culture? This question underlay discussion of virtually every aspect of cultural criticism in the long-running debate. Too close a relationship was as objectionable as too distant a relationship. Opinion was not divided along factional lines. The modernist Schell considered a split between the two as un-Catholic. Rademacher attempted conciliation, arguing that religion and culture were related powers. Muckermann compared the relationship to that of church and state. Andreas Jerger-Schwennebach[45] crisply asserted that religion should be measured by religious values and culture by cultural values. On the whole, culture was subsumed under religion, although occasionally one finds statements that it was culture that encompassed religion.[46]

The definition of culture was likewise contentious. Most writers on culture felt obliged to attempt to make clear their use of the term. When they did not, it might be done for them, as when the editors of the *Allgemeine Rundschau* attached the following note to an exchange between Albert Lotz and Ludwig Hänsel[47] on the subject of culture and Christianity: "The solution of the contrast between Lotz and Hänsel lies, in our opinion, in the fact that they understand culture differently. Lotz includes in it applied morality and politics, Hänsel probably only the free human creativity that in each culture has a different style."[48] As a general rule, Catholic writers were no more agreed on what culture was than non-Catholics, and they reproduce the same fundamental variations of definition as writers without a confessional focus.[49] Mausbach was one of the few writers to acknowledge diversity of usage:

> The word culture is used in different senses. H. St. Chamberlain[50] places it in sharp contrast to civilization; to him culture is the creative activity of men in religion and morality, philosophy and art; civilization is an existence improved through industry, acquired learning and richness. Others understand by culture education and the development of men's strengths, of religious and moral as well as intellectual and worldly strengths. Thus culture would include the religious life apart from the actions of God in religion, His manifestations, and grace. Most frequently, however, one thinks of the word culture as it has been adopted in German: as that circle of human deeds and arrangements that have the creative as object, body and soul, nature and world; God and the otherworldly side of life, religion and morality in their absolute, transcendental aspects, therefore stand outside and above culture.[51]

Richard von Kralik's eight-page discussion of the concept in his tendentious and more than slightly self-indulgent *Ein Jahr katholischer Literaturbewegung* is worthy of the philosopher he considered himself to be. Kralik began with the Latin origins of culture as agricultural cultivation and concluded with a summary of the views of those who disagreed with him. The positions that he imputed to them were that culture is the worldly accomplishments of the century, that the Catholic Church has no cultural mission, and that an equilibrium between Catholicism and modern culture can and must be achieved, notions that he considered seriously misguided. His own idea was that true culture is "a shaping, well-bred organizing of a man's life." Kralik saw the Catholic Church as having a broad cultural task and dreamed of a unified idea, a Christian culture in the Catholic sense.[52]

A further group of definitions treated culture in humanistic terms. One proponent of the broadest definition of this type was Josef Kreitmaier,[53] a Jesuit who wrote extensively on art and music. Kreitmaier described culture as "nothing other than the development of the spiritual strengths and abilities of mankind that have been lent to it by the Creator." He was concerned with the goal of refinement, with man achieving and realizing his humanity. For some Catholic intellectuals, this humanistic element was culture. Others treated it as part of a broader definition, while still others viewed it as one type of culture.[54]

The variety of definitions of culture, as well as the diversity of opinion on the proper relationship between culture and religion, reflect different conceptions of the role of culture. Just as an assortment of definitions of culture by Catholic intellectuals can be compiled, so can an assortment of statements on the role of culture. For Albert Ehrhard the role of culture included improving the worldly relations of mankind, helping in the identification of truth, realizing morality, ensuring the rule of law, satisfying aesthetic needs, and caring for religion. Joseph Mausbach saw culture as in itself a condition of religion; Franz Xaver Walter[55] and Otto Müller[56] saw it as education, a means to raise the moral and spiritual level of the broad masses. To Romano Guardini,[57] an influential Catholic thinker in the 1920s, culture's task was to be a repository of truths; it was the means God had given mankind to carry on spiritual and intellectual activity. No one of these interpretations, it should be noted, was dominant, any more than any one definition of culture or any one view of the proper relation of culture and religion was dominant.[58]

Attempts to define culture frequently involved comparison with other concepts. The most common contrast was with civilization, but *Bildung,* translated variously as education, foundation, or culture, is also encountered, and, on occasion, even art or the arts. Michael Pflaum's exhaustive examination of this confusion concludes that in the late nineteenth century culture usually included

Bildung, Wissenschaft (scholarship or knowledge), *Kunst* (art), and *Sprache* (language); that culture and civilization were used synonymously between 1850 and 1880; and that after 1880 culture was associated only with positive values of art, literature, and religion, and civilization with things of lesser value.[59]

These generalizations, however, are at best only partially true of Catholic usage. Writing in 1925 Franz Zach described the linguistic anarchy: "What is civilization? Many use the words civilization and culture as meaning the same thing. Others assert that culture and civilization stand in the same relation as economic well-being and intellectual education. Many today use culture for what earlier was exclusively termed civilization, education of the intellect, and refinement of morals."[60] A year later Friedrich Muckermann made much the same point about *Bildung:* "The recurrent word *Bildung* is the most problematic there is. It plays in a thousand colors and must be reduced to thin abstractions if *Geist* [spirit, intellect] and heart, religion and culture, holy and profane, old and new are to be accommodated." Each individual writer used culture, civilization, and *Bildung* as if they had distinct meanings, but, for Catholic writers as a group, the terms were virtually interchangeable. Ehrhard noted that others often used civilization and culture in ways precisely opposite to his own, and Walter declared that at times, "*Bildung* is almost the German word for culture."[61]

These semantic squabbles were not unique to Catholicism, to Germany, or to the late nineteenth and early twentieth centuries. Wilhelm von Humboldt[62] had offered a formulation that became a classic: "*Civilisation* is the humanising of peoples in their external institutions and the related inner attitudes. To this refinement of the social, *culture* adds scholarship and art. When, however, in our language we say *Bildung,* we mean at the same time something more elevated and more spiritual, namely the disposition which harmoniously affects perception and character out of understanding and feeling for overall intellectual and moral striving."[63] Johann Herder had written extensively on the topic — his description of *Bildung* is quite different from Humboldt's — and Giambattista Vico, Marquis de Condorcet, Auguste Comte, Karl Marx, and Matthew Arnold were among the many who made important contributions. No one, however, succeeded either in conceptually distinguishing the various terms in a way that achieved general acceptance or in establishing the dominance of one interpretation of culture and its content. There is meaning, but logical precision is not present. Catholic writing is no exception to the resulting confusion.[64]

The primary function of words in Catholic discussions of culture was to organize thought, but some became slogans that signaled appropriate responses. Positive, for example, meant the creation of healthy alternatives to the "excrescences" of modern culture, or even better, the creation of substitutes for the popular novels and films and undesirable social activities, alternatives that were not just healthy but that would actively promote Catholic values. Negative was the inseparable *Doppelgänger* of the positive, never forgotten if not always mentioned. Negative meant doing everything possible to protect good Catholics from excrescences, protection that would have the added benefit of contributing to a more wholesome society. Healthy and unhealthy were another matched pair, while to label something organic conferred an aura of desirability.

The Intellectual and Economic Context

Tortured and seemingly endless discussions of the meanings of *Kultur, Zivilisation,* and *Bildung* are only one way in which German Catholic writing on culture reproduced non-Catholic writing on culture. Catholic writing exhibits the same mixture of rejection, adjustment, and affirmation as non-Catholic writing, if not in the same proportions. Catholic writing also shares the generally heightened rhetoric that followed World War I and shows the same gradual accommodation and eventual acceptance of modern high culture, the same reluctant tolerance of popular culture, even if Catholics were slower to reach the new consensus than others and never really endorsed cultural modernism.[65]

Cultural conservatism had been a well-established intellectual tradition in Germany since the Wars of Liberation, and the Catholic variant is virtually indistinguishable from the non-Catholic.[66] Whether a critic was Catholic or non-Catholic, the basic message was one of pessimism. Cultural conservatives of all kinds denounced and rejected capitalist society, materialism, and the bourgeois mentality, along with the literature, art, and music that were their products. These conservatives held the life of an industrialized, urbanized society to be spiritually empty and devoid of moral virtue.

Degeneration was a popular catchword of the period that summarized the perception of moral decline. In 1892 and 1893 a medical doctor, Max Nordau,[67] published an exhaustive consideration of degeneration (*Entartung*) that both described modern culture and gave the condemnation of modernism a scientific basis. The book displayed an exceptionally broad and accurate knowledge of modern thought; its application of science to art was innovative. The term "degenerate" expressed perfectly the revulsion so many Germans felt for the products of cultural modernism, and its use spread rapidly, quickly becoming a convenient expression in political debates. It became a particular favorite of the Nazis, who in 1937 mounted one of the most distinguished exhibits of modern art, *Entartete Kunst,* as a prelude to destroying the paintings.[68]

Non-Catholics were as likely as Catholics to lament that industrialization and modern politics had destroyed social unity. One of the few differences is that while both groups saw themselves as guardians of the national soul, non-Catholics tended to emphasize the national soul's political elements more than its religious elements. Georg Steinhausen, a professor at Heidelberg,[69] in his magisterial history of culture offered a litany of ills that summarized the situation from any conservative's point of view: loss of spirituality (*Entgeistigung*), loss of idealism (*Entidealisierung*), loss of soul (*Entseelung*), and loss of individuality (*Entindividualisierung*).[70]

Julius Langbehn's[71] best-selling magnum opus *Rembrandt als Erzieher* presented the basic argument of all cultural conservatives: "It has gradually become an open secret that the contemporary spiritual life of the German people is in a state of slow decay, according to some, even of rapid decay."[72] The book offered an inchoate series of motifs out of which could be fashioned a worldview, although it was not itself, as one reviewer claimed, "a coherent *Weltanschauung.*" Although at the time Langbehn was not a Catholic, his themes were the staples of conservative Catholics. He rejected contemporary culture, which, in his view, was being destroyed by science and excessive intellectualism. He railed against materialism and ranted against the Americanization of German culture. Berlin epitomized the evil of the big city. Anti-Semitism was a prominent theme, more prominent than in any writings by Catholics. Contemporaries recognized that his views were "at once typical of a *Weltanschauung* of hundreds, even thousands of Germans," and the book sold well, running to multiple editions.[73] Langbehn was not a Catholic when he wrote *Rembrandt als Erzieher,* but later editions of the work show an increasing sympathy toward Catholicism that eventually led to his conversion.

More specifically Protestant writing on culture shared with its Catholic counterpart a sense that it was important that culture have a religious base.[74] Pious Protestants were no more pleased than devout Catholics that German culture had been largely secularized by 1890. Like Catholics, Protestants were divided into conservatives and what passed for modernists. The fundamental arguments were the same in both confessions; cultural pessimists agreed on the sickness of modern culture, the cultural realists agreed on the need for accommodation. To a degree, these positions have characterized Christianity's response to culture from the beginnings of Christianity.[75]

The single greatest difference between the views on culture of the two confessions stemmed from the different relationship of the two groups to the national culture. Protestants had a strong sense of identity with the new German Empire and took for granted that, just as the German Empire was ruled by the Protestant Hohenzollern family and the German state was dominated by Protestant Prussia, German culture was and should be based on the Protestant worldview. They feared the erosion of their cultural hegemony. That their Protestant culture was being supplanted by a secularized modernism rather than Catholicism did not make its loss any more acceptable. Catholics, on the other hand, could not feel that this contemporary national culture was *their* culture; they retained a vision of an earlier Reich in which Catholicism and Catholic culture had been not only an essential element but a dominant one.[76]

At this point it becomes pertinent to raise the question: Which national culture? Most theories of culture offered by intellectuals were developed in the context of high culture, whether it was culture that achieved that status or culture that merely had ambitions. In reality, however, the vast majority of cultural artifacts by the end of the nineteenth century were representatives of popular culture, not high culture. The new popular culture was aimed at a population that was now literate, enjoyed more disposable income, and was conveniently concentrated in urban units. It was culture with no pretensions, created solely to make money. The literature of popular culture was a detective story or a romance, its art brightly colored reproductions, its films visually titillating. The possibilities for music would only become apparent with the development of the recording industry.[77]

Catholic intellectuals, like many other intellectuals, recognized that a decisive break with the past had occurred. Culture had become a commodity like any other commodity, subject to the same laws of supply and demand. The industry's only consideration was the salability of the cultural artifact, not its content. The wise entrepreneur understood his market and offered it what it wanted. He used new techniques of production and dissemination to achieve considerable efficiency and therefore profit. Complaints, as will be seen in subsequent chapters about individual cultural forms, were legion. Tastelessness was the least of them. Cheap novels and their counterparts in other cultural forms were accused of corrupting the innocent and of inculcating false values. Even religion itself was subject to what was perceived by intellectuals as the same debasement; the nineteenth century saw much growth in religious kitsch.[78]

Interestingly, the cultural theories of the Frankfurt school[79] resonate strikingly with the insights of Catholic intellectuals on the subject. The Frankfurt school had the distinction of naming the culture industry, but many Catholic intellectuals, too, recognized that there was such thing as a culture industry, the complex result of technological, economic, and social development. Both groups, moreover, agreed that the impact of the culture industry on its consumers was neither enlightening nor uplifting, however different their view of enlightenment might be. In an address to the 1926 Katholikentag in Breslau, Johannes Hönig,[80] an educator in Leipzig, warned, in a statement worthy of Theodor Adorno, of the intellectual enslavement that the new media of radio and film could easily produce.[81]

What the two groups did not share was the Marxist view that popular culture was an aspect of a capitalist plan to reinforce economic and political control, although a few of the more perceptive Catholic writers appreciated that culture and class were interconnected. Such individuals saw that the culture they discussed endlessly was the culture of an elite minority, created by and for an educated bourgeoisie. Karl Muth presented the following picture in a 1923 essay: "In the pyramid of the social structure of Catholic Germany, 90 percent are not at all concerned with the poetic literature that the times produce. The Catholic book trade sells its literary novelties to a group of at most 8 percent, and at the very most 2 percent are literarily highly educated and creators."[82] The frequent assertion that the Catholic *Volk* deserved something better than the available popular culture acknowledged that popular culture was the culture of those of a lower social status.

THE ORGANIZATION OF CULTURE

Catholics and socialists shared many of the same perceptions of the culture industry, they had similar assets with which to work, and both stood somewhat apart from the dominant national culture. In these circumstances, it is not surprising that the response of the two groups was essentially the same: to make available and encourage the consumption of culture based upon (different) true principles. Although the socialists would have liked a proletarian literature, art, and music, just as the Catholics would have liked a Catholic literature, art, and music, both groups emphasized adult education more than the creation of culture.[83]

The relationship between culture and adult education, *Kultur* and *Bildung*, was close; intellectuals often used the terms interchangeably. In German Catholicism the years between 1900 and 1920 saw the forging of a link between cultural activity and *Bildung* based on common assumptions and the identification of education with culture. At the turn of the century, adult education was largely directed to bringing to the underprivileged, that is, the lower classes, the benefits their lack of higher education denied them. Since higher education was predominantly humanistic, adult education focused on the humanities. And, as long as the humanities remained the foundation of higher education, they would remain at the heart of any efforts to improve the condition of the working classes and thus within the scope of an organization like the Volksverein. Cultural consciousness was held to fulfill the educational ideal of Catholicism.[84]

This approach to adult education evolved out of practice rather than theory, and it is significant that both then and now Catholic adult education has been more distinguished for its practical accomplishments than its theoretical foundations.[85] Theoretical discussions tended to get mired in cloudy concepts like "organic."[86] Emil Ritter,[87] a leader of the Volksverein who was personally active in adult education, expressed the one principle on which all agreed: Catholic adult education was to protect against fallacy, that is, it should provide a proper theological framework for practical experiences and prevent the misapprehension of the values of life. Beyond this basic provision, those interested in adult education held varying, often discordant opinions. Ritter argued that adult education should not be "narrow-hearted"; culture mirrors the eternal, and narrowness is neither organic nor Catholic.[88] Yet Ritter's view is not entirely compatible with Father Robert Grosche's[89] emphasis on the necessary Catholicness of adult education.[90] And at least one major publication emphasized adult education's practical side—goals like improving one's professional knowledge and critical thinking—even though it, too, placed religion at the heart of adult education.[91]

What would become the principal coordinating agency of Catholic adult education and cultural efforts, the Zentralbildungsausschuß (Central Committee for Education), was founded in 1919. The initiative came from Johannes Braun,[92] director of the Borromäus Verein, the oldest of the Catholic cultural organizations. He invited representatives of twelve of the largest organizations concerned with education to meet in Bonn in July. The group agreed to found a working committee to which was given the task of renewing and expanding the work of adult education in the Catholic population.[93]

The political and social circumstances of the postwar world had created a cultural crisis "in which the radical upheaval of educational stratification of society dissolved the old unity of culture into a chaos of trends." These Catholic leaders saw an interdependence of education and culture. The initial explanation of purpose of the Zentralbildungsausschuß emphasized that cultural policy was not an attempt to claim power or to kindle a social movement, but only an effort to awaken the instinctive desire for education of the individual.[94] Its statutes declared that it was to advance and deepen independent adult education on a Catholic foundation and to coordinate central Catholic educational organizations. It would accomplish these objectives by founding local educational coordinating committees of Catholic organizations, establishing a business office, preparing annual reports to be sent to the cooperating organizations, and holding public conferences at least annually.[95]

Many of the most severe problems of Catholic organizations were practical problems, although this aspect was not emphasized. Organizations transformed ideas and attitudes into a cultural movement; they were the cultural infrastructure that made possible Catholic culture. As Friedrich Muckermann later described them, they were fighting battalions on the cultural front. But Catholic cultural organizations, like other Catholic organizations in the difficult postwar environment, were experiencing financial adversity and loss of membership that sharply curtailed their ability to fulfill their objectives.[96] The Zentralbildungsausschuß was intended to be a national organization, but it, like the Borromäus Verein, was located in the Archdiocese of Cologne and its director reported to the archbishop of Cologne. To judge from its reports and the lists of organizations that participated in it, the Zentralbildungsausschuß never truly became a national body, confining its activities largely to the areas outside of Bavaria. As in many other things, Bavaria went its own way.[97]

The first managing director of the Zentralbildungsausschuß was Emil Ritter, a prominent figure in the activities of the Volksverein. Bernhard Marschall,[98] a religion teacher active in the Borromäus Verein, ran the office and did most of the work.[99] Marschall later replaced Ritter as director and was released from his teaching responsibilities so that he could give his full time to the Zentralbildungsausschuß.[100] Friedrich Muckermann regarded Marschall with some mistrust but described him as "a sympathetic man, an organizer, and a far-seeing leader in his area." Marschall was not popular in Volksverein circles, where his narrowly confessional approach was deplored and the Zentralbildungsausschuß considered incompetent. He was derogatorily labeled "Bildungsmarsch[all]" (the marshal of education), and described by Franz Hitze, a leading figure in the Volksverein, in the following terms: "He impedes thoroughly through noise and dilettantism."[101]

Despite these leadership issues, the Zentralbildungsausschuß sponsored activities that focused on the common interests of participating groups, it endeavored to coordinate the efforts of the individual groups, and it worked in areas of adult education for which no Catholic organization existed, most notably in radio and film. Conferences figured prominently, both in the activities of the Zentralbildungsausschuß and in its newsletter; after the organization was well established, semiannual conferences were considered necessary. The agenda of the second conference in July 1924 gives some idea of their character. It included a report by the managing director, a lecture on the role of music in Catholic organizations, discussions of the Zentralbildungsausschuß at the Katholikentag and the meeting of academics, and the prospective meeting of the Zentralbildungsausschuß on the subject of the Church and adult education. The fall 1930 conference tackled two questions: the task of the organization in the changed world of the theater and the organization's attitude toward the Hohenrodter Bund and the Deutsche Schule für Volksforschung und Erwachsenbildung (two related, non-Catholic enterprises involved in, and at the time perceived as monopolizing, the movement for adult education). For the Zentralbildungsausschuß, the fundamental issue in Catholic adult education was to find a balance between helping Catholics learn what they needed to know to participate fully in German society and maintaining the cohesiveness that helped preserve their religious faith.[102]

The newer media, radio and film, were a major area of endeavor for the Zentralbildungsausschuß. It represented German Catholic interests in these media to governments and to other organizations concerned with these media, and it furthered the development of Catholic radio and film efforts whenever possible. As the use of both radio and film exploded in the 1920s, and as their potential became apparent, activity related to these media came to dominate the work of the Zentralbildungsausschuß, although it did not coordinate very well with the organization's other responsibilities.

By the end of the decade, the Zentralbildungsausschuß was attracting considerable criticism, and complaints were expressed openly at the winter conference of 1928. Although there was talk of incorporating the Zentralbildungsausschuß within the Volksverein, the organization survived as an independent body, and its central responsibility of coordination was reaffirmed.[103]

The Media of the Milieu

No consideration of Catholic culture would be complete without at least some attention to the media in which discussion and debate about it took place. Some discussion, of course, was in the form of lectures, but permanent records exist of only the most important addresses at the most important conferences, like the Katholikentag. There were the Catholic newspapers, estimated to number 608 in 1933,[104] where the noisiest and most conspicuous encounters took place or at least were reported. In terms of culture, the most influential newspapers over the long term were *Germania,* the newspaper of the Center Party published in Berlin, and the *Kölnische Volkszeitung,* published in the heart of the Rhineland. The principal editors of the *Kölnische Volkszeitung* during the period of this book, Hermann Cardauns and Karl Hoeber,[105] also made significant contributions to the debate in their own right.

The case of *Germania* demonstrates how considerable a contribution a newspaper could make. In 1898 it was hard to find any article on any aspect of culture in it. By the mid-1920s *Germania* was offering special sections devoted to light fiction and poetry, to serious essays on cultural topics (*Aus Zeit und Loben,* or "From Time and Praise"), to culture per se (*Das neue Ufer,* or "The New Shore"), and to Catholic concerns, which, of course, included culture (*Werk und Wert,* or "Work and Worth"). In addition, *Germania* offered regular film and book reviews, a daily story on some cultural aspect, be it an archaeological dig, liberal Judaism, a new opera, or peasant pottery in the Odenwald, serialized novels, and both lists of contents and occasional summaries of important articles from other cultural publications.

Journals, especially the reviews aimed at the educated middle classes, were the arena for the most serious and significant discussions about culture, although the general-purpose, family-oriented journals that had multiplied in the later nineteenth century would occasionally publish brief essays on cultural topics. The most prominent reviews emphasized literature, the dominant cultural format. They included *Hochland,* probably the single best-known Catholic periodical outside the Catholic milieu, the Austrian *Der Gral* (later *Schönere Zukunft*), the ultramontane *Literarischer Handweiser,* and *Bücherwelt,* the journal of the Borromäus Verein. The *Allgemeine Rundschau,* published in Munich, had a broader cultural focus, asserting an "emphatic concern" for all cultural interests. In its view, politics and culture were inseparable, supporting and enriching one another. *Stimmen aus Maria-Laach* (later *Stimmen der Zeit*) and the *Historisch-politische Blätter für das katholische Deutschland* also had a broader scope. Individually, these journals had different orientations, which could change over time. *Stimmen der Zeit* was a Jesuit publication, *Historisch-politische Blätter* expressed reactionary views, and *Hochland* represented the Catholic avant-garde that played a large role in overcoming the ghetto mentality. *Der Gral* began as *Hochland*'s adversary, but *Der Gral* under Friedrich Muckermann's editorship in the 1920s was a notably different *Der Gral* from what it had been earlier.[106]

By the end of the 1920s, the Volksverein was making an important contribution to cultural journalism. Its own journals included *Volkstum und Volksbildung* (1913–1933, renamed *Volkskunst* in 1928), which was aimed at the parish priest and adult-education worker. *Volkstum und Volksbildung* was strong in ideas for cultural programming. Its *Bild und Film* (1912–1914/15) was the first Catholic journal devoted to film, and its *Musik im Leben* (1925–1930) presented music for everyman. The Volksverein also published some journals of other organizations, including the Cäcilien Verein's *Musica Sacra,* an activity that enhanced its centralizing role in Catholic culture.[107]

Another publication of some importance was *Keiters katholischer Literatur-kalender,* a Catholic counterpart to the biographical directory *Kürschners deutscher Literatur-Kalender* that had begun publication in 1879. Although both used the term literature in the title, both included a range of authors that went well beyond what is usually thought of as literature. The first edition of *Keiters* was 1891, the last 1926. *Kürschners'* practice of designating Catholic authors with a *K* had earned some resentment, since it was felt that the *K* was a sign of lesser value. Ironically, by creating a separate directory for Catholic authors and readers in an attempt to demonstrate the quality of Catholic literature, *Keiters* widened the gulf between Catholics and the larger national literature even further.[108]

Voluminous Catholic writing on the subject of culture failed to produce a clear theoretical base for a Catholic cultural movement. It did produce insights. By 1933 Catholic intellectuals seemed to share an understanding that the dominant contemporary culture was no longer based on a religious foundation. They also recognized that a culture industry now existed to provide the masses with entertainment. They appreciated that the very functions of culture had changed. But no individual or group of intellectuals succeeded in developing an intellectual foundation for Catholics in their approach and response to culture that achieved wide acceptance. Such coherence as the Catholic cultural movement enjoyed derived from agreement that its specific goals should be to uplift, to (re)educate, and to reinforce the identity of Catholics. Interpretation of those goals depended on whether the Catholic intellectual addressing the subject rejected modern culture unequivocally or advocated a degree of accommodation.

In his history of German society, Hans-Ulrich Wehler portrays Wilhelmine Germany as a society in transition to a communication society. Culture was an integral part of that transition. In the years covered by this study, both the meaning and substance of culture changed significantly. The Catholic cultural movement was an attempt to temper and direct that change.

4

Literature

THE FUNCTION OF LITERATURE

Catholics, like non-Catholics saw literature from different perspectives. For Friedrich Muckermann, literature was a battlefield of ideas. Another critic offered the less belligerent image of literature as a playground of ideas, a place where religion and moral viewpoints met and tested one another. Or literature could be seen as the intellectual development of peoples, manifested in "lively" words.[1]

What Catholics did agree on was literature's importance. Literature was perceived as having the power to change norms. On the political side, this provoked fear that reading could lead to revolution. In terms of religion, the reading of bad books was condemned for trapping good Catholics in negative, relativistic modern thought.[2]

Catholic intellectuals considered fiction an especially important genre because of its intellectual accessibility. "The representatives of belles lettres have the greatest influence among all powers that influence a time," pronounced Heinrich Keiter,[3] author of *Konfessionelle Brunnenvergiftung: Die wahre Schmach des Jahrhunderts*, a book that essentially tried to show that anti-Catholic novels had done even greater damage than anti-Semitic novels. "They form public opinion, the trend of the times, and culture, and they determine the relationship of a time to religion." Keiter expressed the apprehension that so many Catholics felt: "The most dangerous books are not by Strauss or Renan, Nietzsche or Haeckel,[4] but are the novels that awaken in all men a lingering fever and those 'art works' that invade the depths of the soul, the low, and the hostile." Karl Muth felt that no one would argue with the statement that bad novels had brought more harm to the world than good deeds had brought good.[5]

At the same time, the influence of literature, including fiction, could be turned to Catholic advantage. A 1929 article reported the affecting tale of how a story in one of the Sunday journals that portrayed the dangers of a mixed marriage saved a woman in America from the perils of marriage to a Protestant. Many Catholics saw literature as something close to propaganda, one more way of "taking up the fight" with those who were the enemies of the Church, its institutions, and true culture. It was a particularly important way since many people no longer attended church regularly.[6]

But whether its positive or negative potential was emphasized, literature mattered, and by 1880 it mattered considerably more than it had earlier. In the late eighteenth century approximately 15 percent of the population was literate. By 1870 the figure had risen to 70 percent, and by 1900 it was 90 percent. The potential audience for literature had greatly expanded, and books had become more important in life. They offered information; they enabled readers to experience vicariously alternative visions of the world; they reinforced values; they entertained and comforted. In short, reading complemented the gospel of self-improvement and seriousness of purpose that was characteristic of the period.[7]

Artistic developments within literature, however, were a source of concern for Catholics, as they were for many other Germans. With the dominance of the artistic credo of art for the sake of art, the new literature accentuated the individual. Heightened subjectivity, the interior life, and the all-important *I* replaced larger themes. Nietzsche became the hero of a generation of writers. To state the obvious, these were not the values of a community-minded, idealist Catholicism. A new prominence of sex in general in literature, and the portrayal in particular of sexuality without love, not to mention a fascination with decadence, gave still more reason for Catholic concern.[8]

Most Catholic writing on literature addresses one or both of these aspects: who was reading, and what was being read. The two were, in fact, connected: what was being read gained importance because of who was reading it. By the turn of the century, intellectuals were beginning to contrast literature, which just happened to be read by the educated, with what we now call genre fiction, which was read by the lower classes. On the one hand, debate about literature, which was largely a debate about the literature of high culture, thrived. On the other, there was not just discussion but reaction relating to the enormous growth in the less than "true literature" category that was so popular. This chapter discusses, not works of literature as such, but the debate about literature, whereas chapter 5 is primarily about the social response to (pseudo)literature.

Literature was primus inter pares among cultural activities, and it was often used as a metaphor for culture. Its nature presented possibilities for sophisticated discussion, the numbers of books and readers gave it magnitude, and it had an established communication system that facilitated debate. Because it was the first modern mass-communication medium, most of the themes discussed in this book were first framed by contemporaries in terms of literature, and it was therefore in relation to literature that most of the responses to cultural innovations of the period emerged.[9]

CATHOLIC LITERATURE

Jakob Kneip,[10] a Catholic author of *Heimat* novels, wrote in 1931, "What we call Catholic literature is scarcely twenty years old. Before this time there was scarcely any feeling in the Catholic part of the population for an artistic or generally intellectual task within the whole *Volk*. The revolution came with Karl Muth."[11] Not everyone agreed with his perception. To Muth's opponents, it seemed to give the man too much credit, but there was much truth in it, if one defines Catholic literature as Kneip did, as belles lettres written with a Catholic outlook but that met artistic standards.

The foundations of German literature lay in the sixteenth and seventeenth centuries and were firmly based in Protestantism. Luther's translation of the Bible by itself had created a language for modern literature. A culture developed outside of Church control, and Protestant emphasis on education produced an educated laity. German Protestants contributed major thinkers to the Enlightenment, but Catholics remained relatively untouched by it.[12]

At the beginning of the nineteenth century, the literati considered Catholics uneducated; literature simply had not had the same function for Catholics that it had had for Protestants, who were encouraged to consider for themselves the terms of their salvation. As the century progressed, however, Catholic intellectuals began to pay more attention to literature. The desire to realize the early Romantic vision of a Catholic utopia was a significant stimulus, and literature became an ongoing topic of discussion among Catholic intellectuals. Unity, variety, and universality were to be proclaimed poetically and guaranteed religiously. Dissatisfaction with contemporary trends was a frequent theme, and the recatholicization of society a common solution. Much of the subsequent discussion on literature followed the lines laid out in the early nineteenth century by Friedrich von Schlegel, Schleiermacher, and Görres.[13]

By the 1890s a body of writing that could be considered Catholic literature existed, if one defines it as literature written by Catholics and supportive of, or at least not in opposition to, what were generally considered Catholic values. Ida, Gräfin Hahn-Hahn,[14] for example, had, after a scandalous early life and subsequent conversion to Catholicism, produced numerous novels of doubtful literary merit but ostentatious Catholicism. Other lesser known Catholic figures had achieved some popularity. Novels and stories were most likely to be read, but there was also some Catholic poetry. Annette von Droste-Hülshoff[15] is an outstanding example of a Catholic poet of the early nineteenth century, who with her aristocratic background and elegant verse could hardly be a greater contrast to her contemporary, the somewhat dubious Countess Hahn-Hahn.

KARL MUTH

Against this background, Karl Muth published in 1898 his pamphlet *Steht die katholische Belletristik auf der Höhe der Zeit?* under the pseudonym Veremundus. Muth was no newcomer to the literary scene. As a journalist, he had written extensively on literary topics, primarily for the *Mainzer Journal* and *Der Elsässer*. He had presented several of his ideas in embryonic form in an 1893 pamphlet, *Wem gehört die Zukunft? Ein Literaturbild der Gegenwart,* but it was *Steht die katholische Belletristik . . .* that made him a leading figure in Catholic literary circles.[16]

Steht die katholische Belletristik . . . inaugurated the first of three significant literary controversies in which questions were posed that forced the discussion of basic issues. This first controversy took place between 1898 and 1900. The controversies of 1909–10 and the mid-1920s earned the names of the first and second *Literaturstreit* (literary dispute), respectively. The ideas presented in *Steht die katholische Belletristik . . .* were not new—Wilhelm Kreiten[17] had anticipated Muth's assertions of the low quality of Catholic literature and its excessive prudery in an article in *Stimmen aus Maria Laach* earlier in the year—but Muth presented them in a way that caught the public imagination and sparked a lively response.[18] His basic argument was that Catholic literature could not be at the peak of excellence because of the current state of the Catholic Church in Germany. He offered a multicausal explanation of inadequacy: Catholics lacked interest in literature; Catholic novels were confessionally biased and inaccessible to others; Catholic novels were characterized by a schoolmasterly tone; Catholic literature was dominated by prudery; Catholic literature did not enjoy competent literary criticism; Catholics had no belletristic journal that sought its readers only among educated adults; and Catholic publishers were generally unwilling to take risks. Muth did not mince his words. Catholic novels displayed an outmoded quality. Artistically, their excessive moralizing killed off humor, and their prudery promoted ignorance, not innocence, which invited possibly disastrous consequences. Muth was asserting a fundamental opposition to the literary ideas that had prevailed in the Catholic milieu.[19]

Its assertion of Catholic literary inferiority made *Steht die katholische Belletristik . . .* part of the more general ongoing discussion about Catholic inferiority, and its attitudes and spirit placed its author firmly alongside Hermann Schell in the important modernist controversy in Roman Catholic theology. One rival went so far as to compare its impact to that of Schell's *Der Katholizismus als Princip des Fortschritts,* a work that achieved international and lasting notoriety.[20] The analysis of inferiority was what attracted the most attention, but *Steht die katholische Belletristik . . .* was more than an indictment. Muth's clear distinction between literature and works of lesser quality paralleled his concern that educated Catholics had no Catholic literature to read. He emphasized the importance of artistic and aesthetic criteria. His detractors dismissed this as amoral "art for art's sake," but it was a useful corrective to the heavy emphasis on morality. Another major idea, one that became increasingly influential in later years, was his view that a novel ought to address the concerns of the present, the time in which its readers had to live, rather than those of an overvalued past. This opinion was frequently abridged to the idea that a novel had to be of its own time.

Hard upon *Steht die katholische Belletristik . . . ,* Muth (again writing as Veremundus) published in 1899 *Die literarischen Aufgaben der deutschen Katholiken,* in which he outlined steps that might be taken to improve the condition of Catholic literature. Muth summarized *Steht die katholische Belletristik . . . :* "The Catholic novel is primarily a tendentious novel [*Tendenzroman*], therefore it is not at the height of art." This theme was a kind of preparation for his argument in *Die literarischen Aufgaben . . . ,* that art is central. Whether Catholic novels should be tendentious was a matter much debated, and Muth's opponents could cite no less a personage than Bishop Ketteler of Mainz, who had pronounced, "Every novel should and must have a position [Tendenz]; and a Catholic novel should and must have a Catholic position." On the other hand, by the canons of German bourgeois aesthetics, depoliticized and, by extension, disinterested writing was considered more valuable than writing that argued a particular point of view.[21]

Muth took the position that either Catholics had a literary ideal or they did not; but if they did, rationally speaking, it could only be an artistic one.[22] He was careful to make clear that by art he meant true art, art for all time, not just for the present. To be artistic a work had to be a picture of purified reality. He amplified these familiar platitudes with an attempt at hypothesis: the nature of art (objectively) consists of both thought and beauty and requires that the internally perceived ideal be rendered to satisfy a fundamental spirituality, that is, the ideal should be transcendental.[23]

Muth's consideration of art included consideration of its relationship to its time, another idea that had been introduced in *Steht die katholische Belletristik . . . .* In order to lead into a discussion of the novel's place in contemporary life, he used the statement of one of its reviewers, who had modified Muth's conclusion that the Catholic novel did not stand at the height of art to "the Catholic novel did not stand at the height of the times." This discussion evolved into a serious engagement with the ideas of modernism in the context of literature.

Muth was not an unreconstructed reactionary, but neither did he blindly embrace the new for the sake of its newness. He was scathing on the word modern itself: "There is no dumber word in art criticism!" Modern derived from "Mode" (fashion), and fashion, in essence the eternally changing surface, should have nothing to do with true art. Modern was nothing but a superfluous word for new. "Modern art—new art, modern technique—new technique! It's all the same."[24]

He shared the dislike of less progressive Catholics (and Protestants) for what he labeled "dirty naturalism and similar artistic nonsense." The modernism he found desirable lay in technique, in a strongly developed sense of realism, in careful observation and characterization, and to some extent in choice of topic. Not only did Muth find this kind of modernity acceptable, he welcomed it; he saw nothing in it inherently incompatible with religion. To him form was a matter of indifference and only the spirit mattered. Forms and languages might change, but the spirit of Christianity, of Catholicism, remained the same. It was always capable not only of adaptation to different cultural forms but also of accommodating the spirit and spiritual needs of different ages and peoples. He viewed such flexibility neither as sin nor betrayal. Change was normal, inevitable, even tolerable.[25]

Steht die katholische Belletristik . . . provoked an immediate and abundant reaction. Muth had the gift of provocation; he inspired, aroused, aggravated, and incited. Many praised the pseudonymous author for the accuracy of his insights. Others, who were often of the ultramontane persuasion, criticized Muth for exaggeration, for superficiality, for disloyalty, for failing to appreciate "the golden fruits on the green bough of Catholic literature," and for not properly understanding the importance of morality in literature. His self-appointed role as the conscience of Catholic literature was held to be a sign of hubris. *Die literarischen*

Aufgaben . . . aroused less opposition, not only because it was more positive and less censorious, but because it gave more attention to morality as such.[26]

The immediate reaction to the two Veremundus pamphlets was not, however, a measure of their true significance. Muth would go on for another four decades as a major Catholic cultural leader, but these two pamphlets focused attention on Catholic cultural weakness and mark the beginning of the Catholic literary movement. References to ideas first brought to the public in them were frequent in subsequent literary criticism. The charge of inferiority rankled but had enough justification to stimulate a generation of young Catholics to do better. Even those not in the Muth camp, like Friedrich Muckermann, had come to appreciate him by the end of the 1920s.[27]

LITERARY JOURNALS

Some ten years elapsed between the publication of *Die literarischen Aufgaben . . .* and Muth's next work, *Die Wiedergeburt der deutschen Dichtung*. Literary debate continued, if not at quite the same pitch. Several new journals that would have great importance for Catholic literature were begun. In 1903 Muth himself founded *Hochland* to fill a perceived gap in Catholic cultural life: "Up to now we have had no review in the grand style on a Catholic-Christian basis that would enable an efficient and comprehensive organization of its inner activity and be in the position of being part of today's cultural life, of influencing it, and of surveying all the judgments of it." Under different auspices and with a different philosophy, Richard von Kralik and a group of collaborators founded *Der Gral* in 1906. The style of its opening statement was as informative as the words themselves: "*Gral* [grail] journey—journey to the heights! Should we develop a program? Is not the name that stands at the top of this journal the deepest, the most beautiful ever to describe the planned program of a Catholic literary journal? To become a guide on the trip to the heights to this old, holy symbol of ideal life and spiritual direction, that shall be our effort and our principal task that encompasses and specifies our work." *Der Gral*'s underlying philosophy, its somewhat ostentatious religiosity and distinctive antimodernism, are plain on the first page: "Art in our day has wandered far from the ways that lead to the heights of this true symbol of the Christian outlook. . . . The tempestuous, fermenting movement that characterizes our image of the age, a movement that overturns everything fixed and permanent, is to be explained by the transition from the harmonious peace that guarantees full possession of truth to the restlessness of a vain search for truth. . . . In God, truth, goodness, and beauty unite to form a simple, inseparable light."[28] These two journals, along with *Stimmen aus Maria-Laach*, now renamed *Stimmen der Zeit,* and a few of the more general publications with an interest in culture, like the *Allgemeine Rundschau,* would play an important role in shaping Catholic literature.

THE FIRST *LITERATURSTREIT*

The introductory statements of *Hochland* and *Der Gral* foreshadow the second notable Catholic literary controversy, the *Literaturstreit* of 1909–1910, and contain the principal themes that would later be developed in detail.[29] Richard von Kralik, one of the chief protagonists, summarized these themes as the diminished role of the clergy (*Entklerikalisierung*), the loosening of ties to the papacy (*Entultramontanismus*), and the deemphasis of Catholicism's exclusivity (*Interconfessionalismus*). He omitted the theme that encompassed, or at least touched on, all others, the modernity of Catholic literature, but his formulation does show the cast of mind of the *Gral* group.[30] The debate also addressed the role of the laity, Catholic literature's relation to German literature, the extent to which Catholics should read non-Catholic literature, and Catholic literature's relation to its own time.

When the first *Literaturstreit* began is somewhat unclear, although twenty years after the fact Johannes Mumbauer[31] claimed that his own 1907 article on the literary ghetto was the opening volley. Kralik's *Die katholische Literaturbewegung der Gegenwart* (1910) has also been credited with that honor. In fact, the reality was more gradual. Brief disputes of increasing sharpness went back to the days of Muth's *Steht die katholische Belletristik . . .* Kralik, for example, had given a lecture to the Leo Gesellschaft (Leo Society) on March 21, 1900, that was essentially a rebuttal of Muth. In the next few years there was a slow coalescing of forces. Mix in some personal hostility, and, with the two rival journals in place to publicize the quarrel, the conditions were set for a full-blown literary war between two groups that had radically different views of what Catholic ought to mean in literature.[32]

The first of these groups was a loose alliance identified with *Hochland,* which stood for relative liberalism in the sense that it welcomed new ideas, or at least some of them. Karl Muth did not exactly lead the group, but as the editor of *Hochland* and the individual who had formulated the fundamental questions and written extensively on Catholic literature, he loomed largest. In contrast to 1898, when his *Steht die katholische Belletristik . . .* had sparked instant polemics, Muth did not stand alone. The maturing Catholic literary movement had not only encouraged the involvement of new men but also greatly increased communication among the like-minded, as Muth's voluminous correspondence files testify. Johannes Mumbauer and Martin Spahn[33] were other prominent names associated with the *Hochland* group and its contribution to the *Literaturstreit* in this period.

A second alliance centered around the journal *Der Gral,* which upheld the conservative position. The alliance began when a group of authors met through the Leo Gesellschaft, an organization founded in 1892 in Vienna, and found that they shared a common outlook. The principals of this persuasion, who often referred to themselves as members of the Gralbund, were Kralik, Eduard Hlatky, Adam Trabert, Karl Domanig, and Franz Eichert.[34] According to Kralik, *Der Gral* stood for the positive elements in Catholic cultural life while the criticism of Schell, Muth, and Ehrhard was negative, disruptive and threatening. *Der Gral's* opponents saw the Gralbund as arrogant, reactionary, and immersed in a medieval past that never was. Its members were criticized as antiquated and tendentious, pro-clerical, pro-Jesuit, and pro-Rome. The Gralbund, on the other hand, argued that it did not isolate itself, but participated directly in the exciting development of a national literature.[35]

Finally, there were those who chose to stay aloof from the acrimony, both then and subsequently. Efforts were made to involve the Borromäus Verein in the quarrels, but the official position of the society was noncommittal: "For us there is no *Literaturstreit.* We rejoice in every good book." In fact, the association was probably less neutral than that statement implies, because to its director "good book" meant a book that would give the Catholic *Volk* what it needed for its spiritual foundation and would not "submit to the modern spirit of the times, but conquer it."[36]

What the above-mentioned national literature was, aside from the Catholic relation to it, was cloudy. The term usually implied Protestant involvement and was closely connected to the development of a national identity, an identity from which Catholics did not want to be excluded. Catholic discussions on the subject were complicated by the fact that many of the figures associated with the Gralbund were Austrians, most notably Kralik himself, an association that tied the literary debate to the political controversy concerning whether a united Germany should be a *Großdeutschland* that included Austria or a *Kleindeutschland* that exclued it. That the Catholic Church was in the process of resolving the relationship of the national churches to the papacy added further complexity.[37]

Kralik's assertion of direct Catholic participation in the national literature, however, ran counter to fact and to perception. Instead, there were two separate literary cultures. Whether one is talking about a "reichsdeutsch" (imperial German) literature or a broad German literature shared by all of the German tongue, Catholic writers simply were not mainstream authors, as far as German Protestants, educated German Catholics, German literary critics, or statistics of reading preferences were concerned. Whether Catholics should endeavor to participate in German literature or not was more debatable, and much depended upon the nature of national literature and the terms on which they participated.[38]

The preface to *Der Gral* advocated a "true" national literature, which in this case usually meant restoring art to the *Volk*. That art of the *Volk* was perceived as having been appropriated by a small exclusive group and having lost its connection with the masses.[39] *Der Gral*'s explanation of this tragedy contained the usual elements of the Catholic indictment of the modern world: the relationship was lost when the social principles of Christianity were replaced by the self-seeking individualism of the modern world outlook. It was not enough that the unity and commonality of the highest interests in life were torn apart by religious anarchy, but the unity of artistic practice and artistic feeling was also destroyed. Because the goals of life and life's relationships were now focused on the individual personality, the artist no longer created his works from the eternally fresh well of the soul of the *Volk* but from the strangest, concealed depths of the *I*.

The Germanness of German Catholic literature was another topic of discussion in this controversy. One writer asserted that what was modern corresponded with what was read. German literature was modern and therefore was read; German Catholic literature was neither read widely nor was it modern. Like it or not, to be read, Catholic literature had to become modern—or become German, which was the same thing. This writer strongly urged that Catholic literature should become modern, only adding the qualification that it should become modern the Catholic way.[40]

Germanness and modernity were inextricable, and what connection Catholic literature should have to German literature was one facet of the larger and more important question of what relation should Catholic literature have to the intellectual and cultural trends of the day. That question was usually subsumed under the code word "modern," and writers on both sides of the debate used the word freely, albeit loosely. Ironically, they did agree that they were against "modern," even if they did not agree on what "modern" was.

Modern could mean the specific school of thought within Roman Catholic theology known as modernism, represented in Germany by Hermann Schell, whose most important works were eventually placed on the Index. In the context of literary debate, however, it tended, in the sense it is frequently used today, to establish an association with the present time; in *Die literarischen Aufgaben* . . . Karl Muth had, in contemputous tone, equated modern with new. On the other hand, Eichert (a member of the Gralbund) would have nothing to do with modern when it meant a break with all inherited traditions, but he liked modern when he could identify it with "everything lively, whether born today or one hundred years or more ago." Kralik saw philosophical modernism as related to the old—and discredited—sophistry. He described cultural modernism as not only "modern-ist" in the sense of the papal encyclical "Pascendi," but also a tendency to rela-tivism, a denial or weakening of strong, lasting, eternal truths in theory, history, morals, and aesthetics. He equated it with the view that everything changes and develops, that everything progresses to something essentially different, that every-thing needs reform, and that everything is subject to criticism, assumptions that were in conflict with his idea of eternal truths.[41]

When the discussion shifts from "modern" as a set of abstractions to "mod-ern" as a complex of attitudes, the gulf between the sides in the controversy be-comes more comprehensible and still wider. Muth and his *Hochland* colleagues were frequently and justly, in the attitudinal sense, accused of being modernists. They had taken the crucial step of recognizing and acknowledging that they lived in a distinctly different time from previous generations. Muth had pushed this recognition to its logical conclusion: just as their forefathers had lived in their own time, so must they live in theirs.[42] Muth urged novelists to write for their own times. He practiced a kind of modernism when he published in *Hochland* controversial novels like Antonio Fogazzaro's[43] *Il Santo* and the historical novels of Baroness Enrica von Handel-Mazzetti.[44]

This approach and these actions were a far cry from those of the Gral-bund. In their circle, the past and tradition, referred to in hushed tones and with a slight obeisance, loomed large. Tradition was the criterion against which the present was measured. In the plural, traditions were the glories of the Catholic past. Kralik might declare that he did not overvalue the era of post coaches, but the heart of the Gralbund was in the past.[45] Its members praised the past, usually with-out differentiating between its more and less desirable attributes. They proclaimed their loyalty to the ideals of the Middle Ages, and they wrote old-fashioned poetry and drama.[46]

In addition to the philosophical divisions, personal animosities embittered the discussions. A near duel between two Austrians over a literary question testi-fies to how deeply interested parties cared about the issues, which many per-ceived to be issues of faith and not merely of literature.[47] Muth and Kralik had at one point had a relationship of sorts—Kralik had been named a collaborator of *Hochland* when it had begun—but the relationship had soured.[48] *Der Gral* pub-lished open letters to Muth pointing out his errors, and Muth riposted in kind. Kralik's *Ein Jahr katholischer Literaturbewegung* is an exhaustive chronology of each thrust and parry, a kind of he said, she said, then he said, and then she said to what seems ad infinitum.

An article by Alexander Baumgartner,[49] a literary historian and critic who had made important contributions to the study of Goethe and to the revival of in-terest in Calderón, represents the general opinion of the *Gral* group. Baumgartner, a Jesuit, was one of the leaders of the *Gral* movement.[50] He described as a "punch in the face" Muth's assessment of the Catholic population as a stronghold of illiterates. He accused Muth of being too interested in French literature, which made him un-German, and criticized Muth for his praise of Henry Sienkiewicz,[51] author of *Quo Vadis?*, because Sienkiwicz had failed to understand the pedagogical and social meaning of the martyrdom of St. Agnes. Baumgartner viewed with distaste Muth's exhortations to more realism, darker shadows, and sharper contrasts. He felt that Muth had been corrupted by the tinsel shine of French novels and by the rational and materialist point of view, and that he had lost that moral sensitivity that draws one away from the darker side of life. When Muth complained of narrowness, self-consciousness, philistinism, and prudery, Baumgartner heard disloyalty and decadence. In Baumgartner's opinion, Muth's call for more freedom for novelists stretched that freedom so far that it passed all bounds of moral consideration.[52]

Baumgartner's bill of indictment is comprehensive and conveys a very real anger. Although the relationship between art and morality was fundamental to all of the polemicists' interpretations of Catholicism, the *Hochland* group would not have accepted the judgment that it was unconcerned with morality any more than the Gralbund saw itself as uninterested in art. Each faction would have argued that its adherents represented both "true" art and "true" morality. Only when the purpose of literature is what is in question are the differences unambiguous. The *Hochland* allies saw literature as rooted in religion but serving literary ideals. Mumbauer spoke for all when he wrote that the true artist "does not teach religion and truth in his writings; like reason in nature, they lie within them." Hermann Herz,[53] secretary of the Borromäus Verein and not identified with either *Hochland* or *Der Gral*, had come to this same point of view for quite another reason. The reviewer of many novels, he considered sickly sweet piety and devotion, like their antithesis of complete neutrality, "sure signs of a minimal artistic talent." The *Gral* view was expressed by Baumgartner: like all the arts, literature was a helper in the fight against the animal nature of man. Like all activity, its purpose was to honor God.[54]

Additional points of consequence separated the two factions; for example, what should be the role of the clergy? In general, *Hochland* was considered pro-laity, which the Gralbund interpreted as anti-clergy, and the Gralbund was held to be pro-clergy, which the *Hochland* group perceived as anti-laity. While partisans in each group were careful to state their position in positive terms, the combination of implication, logical conclusions to be drawn from what was said, and behavior indicates that there was some justice in the respective opponents' view.

The proper roles of clergy and laity was another topic that went back to *Steht die katholische Belletristik . . . .* Muth had urged that the laity become more involved in the writing of literary history and criticism because they had a "more varied emotional life and greater impartiality in the questions raised by the passions of life."[55] The obvious implication, of course, is that the clergy had less understanding of human nature, but his real concern was the dominance of cultural life by the clergy.

The Gralbund was not only strongly pro-clergy, it was also notably pro-papacy. Kralik's identification of great culture with religion presumed a strong clerical presence. Any suggestions of greater lay involvement were answered sharply. Kreiten acknowledged that the more restricted emotional experience of priests might make them less than desirable as novelists, but that did not affect their ability to evaluate. Because the Gralbund equated the Church with its clergy and hierarchy, it interpreted any questioning of the clergy as criticism of the Church.[56] In practice, however, laymen were prominent within the group, and the Gralbund would probably have subscribed to Samuel Taylor Coleridge's concept of a "clerisy" in which the educated constituted a class with special responsibilities, particularly in the area of culture.

The appropriate role of the clergy was closely related to the question of what was the appropriate role of religion and of confession. Whether or not this was one question or two was a significant part of the issue; there were those Catholics, especially on the side of *Der Gral,* who equated religion with Catholicism. During this period of the first *Literaturstreit,* what the role of religion should be was debated primarily in terms of openness to non-Catholic cultural influences. The *Gral* adherents rejected anything modern that was non-Catholic, although Greco-Roman classical civilization was an acceptable influence. Baumgartner went so far as to argue that participation in German culture was a defection to the Protestant side.[57]

The *Hochland* adherents just as clearly stood for greater cultural and literary accessibility, a condition they saw as mutually interactive. Catholic literature would benefit from non-Catholic literature, and non-Catholic literature would be enriched by Catholic influences. Mumbauer's article on the literary ghetto painted the dangers of the ghetto mentality in dark colors; by isolating themselves from national life and general (worldly) culture, Catholics would become intellectually, economically, socially, and politically stunted and degenerate. He disagreed strongly with Kralik's assertion that a great literature was only possible on a Catholic basis, listing numerous examples of famous writers who were not Catholic. Heinrich Falkenberg[58] argued that Catholic literature was too Catholic for many of the faithful and urged Catholics to "hear the other side"; he excepted only authoritative Church teachings from this tolerance. Muth, too, advocated openness, as much by example as by assertion. One of the things the *Gralbund* held against him was his praise of authors and dramatists like Zola, the Goncourt brothers, Nietzsche, Ibsen, Tolstoy, Dostoevsky, and, among German authors, Hermann Sudermann, Gerhart Hauptmann, and Gottfried Keller. Baumgartner had dismissed these authors as "the whole swarm of naturalists, impressionists, and symbolists" and what they created as "a literature of decadents to which the dechristianization of France had contributed the greatest part."[59]

Yet another point where the *Gral* and *Hochland* groups differed was in their view of educated Catholics, although the point was not debated as such. Both sides recognized the loss of the educated from the Church, but Muth used that fact as the foundation of his concern that Catholic literature needed to be improved. Literature was one means that could reclaim them. Educated Catholics did not read Catholic literature. Instead, there was "a great hunger in broad Catholic circles for non-Catholic writings." Certainly, those allied with *Hochland* read widely in Western European literature. During a 1904 convalescence Muth enjoyed a lift from his reading, which included Thomas Mann's *Buddenbrooks*, and books by Selma Lagerlöf, Ricarda Huch, Peter Rosegger, Leo Tolstoy, Maxim Gorky, Maurice Maeterlinck, and John Ruskin.[60] "Unfortunately," he reported, "nothing particularly impressive has been available from Catholic pens." The *Gral* group, on the other hand, was more concerned with the *Volk*, a word it used in the usual late nineteenth- and early twentieth-century way to mean a (German) peasant close to the reality of the earth or his industrial counterpart.[61]

How the two factions applied their theories can be seen to some extent in the journals they produced. Both printed original poetry, stories, and novels, but a comparison of the second volume of *Hochland* (1905) with the second volume of *Der Gral* (1907) shows the broader reach of the former. *Hochland* gave itself a more general cultural role; its articles and reviews included attention to art, music, and theater, as well as some to politics and economics, and even some to science and technology. *Der Gral* was almost exclusively limited to literature. The real differences, however, are in the substance rather than form of what was printed. In *Hochland* one can find contemporary authors, both as authors of literature printed and as subjects of reviews and essays, authors from a variety of countries, and non-Catholics as well as Catholics; this was far less true of *Der Gral*. Another distinction lies in what was published: the contrast in these respective second volumes between the subject matter of Hermann Schell's "Worte Christi: Das Charakterbild Jesu nach Houston Stewart Chamberlain" (The Words of Christ: The Character of Jesus according to Houston Stewart Chamberlain) and Engelbert Karlinger's, "Eichendorff als Gralsritter" (Eichendorff as a Knight of the Holy Grail), is both enormous and indicative. In the *Hochland* article a leading Catholic modernist theologian comments on the ideas of a racial theorist; in the article in *Der Gral* Joseph von Eichendorff,[62] the German Romantic lyricist of the previous generation, is presented as a precursor of the *Gral* group.

All of these differences added up to a wide gulf between the two sides of the debate, differences that were irreconcilable. To the *Hochland* group, the Gralbund represented everything that kept Catholics intellectually, economically, and politically "inferior." To the Gralbund, the *Hochland* group and other Catholic modernists hardly deserved to be considered Catholic at all. The adherents of *Der Gral* prided themselves on their ownership of virtue: "We can boast about being in possession of the right principles, which we . . . explain untiringly." With their criticism, Muth and his allies threatened both the Church and true religion.[63]

The future might favor Muth and the *Hochland* group, but in 1910 the Gralbund awarded itself the decision in the contest. They had the support of a substantial number of German Catholic authors who had published a manifesto in the *Augsburger Postzeitung* in August 1909 that accused Muth and Falkenberg of wanting to suppress the expression of religion in the realm of culture for the sake of artistry.[64] And they could point to the support of the most powerful figure in the Roman Catholic Church, the Holy Father himself. In a 1910 public letter to Kaspar Descurtins,[65] a Swiss author, Pius X took issue with modernism in general, and with modern literature in particular: "This new assistance in the spread of error, that proceeds openly from day to day under the concealing mantle of the pursuit of literature and of literary criticism, has troubled us painfully, because by this means the error is the more veiled, and consequently more readily disseminates its poisonous seeds." Descurtins had conspired—there is no other word—with the *Gral* group to damage the reputation of *Hochland* with the papal authorities. Less than a year later, the pope wrote to his "beloved son Franz Eichert and the other associates of the literary society 'Gralbund,' " praising them for having avoided yielding too easily to the trend of the times and for having displayed themselves in their writing as "open and unconcealed Catholics." These words stand in stark contrast to papal efforts to place *Hochland* on the Index. The self-admiration of the *Gralbund,* however, needs to be taken with a large grain of salt. As the Franciscan Expeditus Schmidt[66] commented in 1907, the *Gral* group had proposed its distinctively Catholic literary program "without finding general applause."[67]

Like most literary wars, the *Literaturstreit* did not so much end as decline into sporadic sniping. In the years that followed it, important topics were discussed—the war years brought attempts to define a "good" novel—but not until the mid-1920s did literary debates again become so heated. Toward that decade's end, a debate emerged of sufficient density and acidity to be called the *Literaturstreit* of 1928 to 1929.

The Second *Literaturstreit*

The "new" quarrels were a mixture of old and new. The tone of high seriousness was unchanged, as was the conviction that it was important to create true literature. Catholic literature was still considered inferior, and Catholic readers were still viewed primarily as consumers of trash. The concern with the Catholic relationship to the national literature remained. Even some of the players of the prewar decades were present. *Hochland* and *Der Gral* were still leading Catholic literary journals, although *Der Gral* became *Schönere Zukunft* in 1927, and Karl Muth continued to contribute to the ongoing discussion. The description of the discussions of the 1920s as "out of the same bed as earlier literary feuds," had considerable aptness; most of the topics could be subsumed under the basic theme of the first *Literaturstreit:* the conflict between art, understood as literary art, and religion.[68]

The opening act in the *Literaturstreit* of the postwar period was an address made by Jakob Kneip to a conference of writers that was held in Koblenz in 1927. Born in 1881, Kneip came from the peasantry of the Hunsrück. He was heavily influenced by Muth and the excitement of the literary "revolution" of the late 1890s, although he was not a member of the generation of the first *Literaturstreit;* his own reputation was largely achieved after World War I. One admiring critic went so far as to equate him with the major figures of Goethe and Annette von Droste-Hülshoff: "Kneip is to today's lyric poetry what Goethe was to the time of the Anacreontic and Droste was to the Romanticism that was splitting up and coming to an end."[69]

Kneip's fundamental point in his Koblenz talk was that the clergy exercised too much influence over culture. In the early Christian period and in the Middle Ages the poet was "the interpreter of the eternal, the keeper under seal of the divine." Since Luther, however, and especially since the *Kulturkampf,* "the representatives of the Church in Germany had been seized by a great touchiness, even an estrangement with respect to art." To make his point, Kneip used a picture of the Last Judgment by Stephan Lochner,[70] a fifteenth-century artist of the school of Cologne, which portrayed a bishop, an abbot, a pope, and a king among the damned in hell. He asked whether any painter in Cologne would today be able to paint such a picture and which Catholic newspaper would dare to introduce the work of old masters to its readers? His next question, whether today there would be letters to the editor complaining of the presentation of clergy as frivolous and blasphemous, implied a pessimistic answer.[71]

Clerical oversight could only stifle imagination and prevent artists and writers from doing their jobs, which was, according to Kneip, to "give a picture of life and the confession, of the times and of the future." When a writer attempted to do this, external considerations and pressures inhibited him and distorted his achievements. Self-censorship was pervasive and damaging. An unwritten requirement that the writer had to declare himself as either for or against the times was a further constraint. These opinions are far distant from Martin Deutinger's mid-nineteenth-century definition of artistic freedom as voluntary submission to the teachings of the Catholic Church. For Deutinger, artistic freedom is liberation from non-religious artistic concerns, a condition achieved by giving sovereignty to religion.[72]

This second *Literaturstreit* was more limited in its scope than the first; the fundamental question was still the relationship of art and religion, but debate was less wide-ranging. Discussion focused on the issue raised by Kneip, the role of the Catholic Church in monitoring artists and writers, and did not move beyond it. The position of those who disagreed with him is self-evident: no, the Church did not stifle art, and if it did, it was necessary in the cause of religion. Variations within this argument were minor.

But if the scope of the second *Literaturstreit* was limited, the interest and intensity it aroused were not. Kneip's speech was printed in *Germania* and later in *Schönere Zukunft*, where its editor, Joseph Eberle,[73] took the opportunity to respond. Much editorializing followed in other publications, and Kneip's talk was described as having been "much noticed and discussed" in Catholic Germany. Some of the more substantial reaction included an article by Joseph August Lux[74] that used Kneip's talk as the starting point of his own questioning of the reality of German Catholic literary life. Otto Kunze[75] addressed the same question as Kneip and came to much the same conclusion. Gustav Keckeis[76] attempted to reconcile the different views theoretically, and a Bavarian cleric presented the parish priest's view. An article in the *Fränkisches Volksblatt* inquired plaintively, "Shall we disagree further?" *Schönere Zukunft*, the journal in which the most important articles opposing Kneip had appeared, sought to close the debate with a statement acknowledging the respects in which Kneip had been right. In the following year, the Jesuit Wilhelm Wiesebach[77] summarized discussions, concluding with the ambiguous principle with which all "agreed": What is morally contestable is substantially valueless or outright ugly. Kneip had clearly voiced a widespread concern.[78]

A comparison of the second *Literaturstreit* with the prewar controversies shows important changes that had taken place in the intervening years. Intra-Catholic communication had increased considerably with the multiplication of literary journals and specialized conferences and meetings. The general public was now more involved with cultural questions, thanks to such differences as *Germania*'s added attention to culture. The anticipated public reaction to a Lochner-type picture referred to by Kneip was something new.

Looking at content rather than form shows other variations. The narrower scope of the second *Literaturstreit* fitted a new pattern; not every dispute within the confession became a debate over theological fundamentals. Criticism was not necessarily a challenge to the faith or to the power of the Church. Another change was that some interest in the questions on the part of non-Catholics was assumed. These contrasts suggest that the modernist challenge was no longer an active, open issue in the Church and that Catholics were feeling more secure within German society than they had a generation before.

A DEFINITION OF CATHOLIC LITERATURE

The discussion about Catholic literary inferiority and the two *Literaturstreite* were the high points of Catholic literary life between the end of the *Kulturkampf* and 1933. They dramatized critical discussions and addressed fundamental issues. They rarely produced consensus. Even within camps, there was diversity of opinion on what Catholic literature was and what it ought to be, the themes around which most discussion revolved.

In fact, Catholic intellectuals inherited a usable definition of Catholic literature from the great Romantic lyricist, Joseph, Baron von Eichendorff. Eichendorff designated Catholic literature as a literature that is produced by a Catholic author; a literature that is intended for Catholic readers; and a literature that bears the Catholic outlook and expresses Catholic ideas. His views of the distinguishing features of Catholic literature were widely shared. The English Catholic priest and writer Ronald Knox defined the Catholic novel in very similar terms as a novel written by a Catholic, a novel with a Catholic background, and a novel with Catholic morality.[79] But perhaps in the same way that every generation needs to rewrite history, every generation needs to redefine its basic terms.

It was a task made more difficult by the variety of meanings of the term "literature." By the end of the nineteenth century, literature was used in three principal ways: literature as the totality of literary production, that is, everything in print; literature as the great books, that is, the books that have had an historical impact; and literature as imaginative writing.[80] One of the more common definitions of Catholic literature, as the sum of the contributions of individual Catholic authors, is a Catholic version of the first.

Another approach, one used by the novelist Joseph Lux, was to define Catholic literature by explaining what it was not. Catholic literature was no more solely concerned with artistic and aesthetic questions than it was solely concerned with religion, the supernatural, and the Catholic viewpoint. It was not limited to religious writing. Nor was it holy kitsch or moral preaching, although it did have a moral basis and it did have religious roots. Karl Muth preferred to avoid the term Catholic literature altogether, holding that Catholic fiction and poetry (*Belletristik*) did not deserve the title because they lacked the element of artistry. Instead, he used the less ambitious term *Belletristik* or more specific words, like novel, prose, or *Tendenzroman* (tendentious novel).[81]

Much discussion was in the form of questions. How Catholic did something have to be to qualify as Catholic? In what way should it manifest Catholicism? For some, being written by a practicing Catholic was enough to make a novel Catholic. Others wanted a Catholic setting or a Catholic tone. Maria von Ebner-Eschenbach[82] was Catholic, but not Catholic enough to be counted as "one of us." In 1922 Franz Herwig, a novelist much influenced by *Hochland,* wrote,

> Catholic ought to mean a particular intellectual and spiritual frame of mind, unintentional but more than a little strong and convincing, that penetrates the work. It means the possession of an inner harmony, which discreetly illuminates every word, every sentence, which explains or eradicates shame, and which enlightens all human events, emotions, and deeds. It does not require a judgment be expressed: the way of presentation, the way of putting deeds and opinions in an eternal light is judgment enough. The wonderful art of arranging all things in harmony, the art that the old mystery play possesses, should be what Catholic writing of the present and future has.

In another article comparing the novels Sigrid Undset[83] wrote before and after her conversion to Catholicism, the critic Georg Schäfer provided the less intricate criterion that a Catholic author was distinguished by his or her sense of sin.[84]

The need to protect themselves from undue limitations on freedom of expression gave writers a powerful incentive to avoid a strict interpretation of the Catholic of "Catholic" literature. Too often, precision meant narrowness and led to restriction and prescription, especially since sensitive matters of faith could be perceived as being at stake. But there was no agreement on how much freedom there should be. Where one critic argues that artistic freedom meant "the right of the author to serve God by his means," another could say, alluding metaphorically to inquisitorial methods of torture, "We can't put our writers in Spanish boots but must let them romp about in the life of our times." The second *Literaturstreit* was a broad discussion of the issue of artistic freedom.[85]

For all their verbiage, the various stages of *Literaturstreit* did not exhaust all relevant topics relating to Catholic literature. One important issue that received little attention was the role of the critic. In Germany at the turn of the century, the function and activity of criticism was becoming pedagogic. The critic both instructed in correctness and informed his audience about new works. At the same time, critical judgment no longer adhered to traditional canons of aesthetics. Instead, subjective reaction became the norm.[86] Among Catholics, Muth gave the topic one of its more thorough treatments in his 1909 *Die Wiedergeburt der Dichtung,* in which he asserted the creativity of criticism. The critic could influence both writer and audience. The critic could also address the moral considerations raised in a work. Muth's critic was, in short, very much in the new pedagogical tradition of literary criticism.[87]

Most Catholic writing about criticism, however, tended to address very specific points. An exchange of views between Friedrich Muckermann and Arthur Friedrich Binz[88] in the mid-1920s produced a series of essays, commentaries, summaries, and articles, but it did not rise above the level of questions such as whether Catholic critics should recommend non-Catholic authors.

THE ECONOMICS OF LITERATURE

Another topic of concern that cut across the literary spectrum was economics. Catholic men of letters were aware of the importance of economics in a capitalist society, and their awareness is woven through their discussions. One of the most common indications was the view that Catholic critics should neither recommend non-Catholic writers nor criticize Catholic authors harshly. This judgment is one expression of a ghetto mentality that has a significant economic as well as intellectual dimension. Stated crassly, the economic version was, "Buy Catholic." Buying Catholic, however, was never sufficiently widespread to support anything beyond a Catholic literature of modest dimensions.

In the period 1880–1933, German book production increased, although not steadily. In 1870, 14,179 titles were published; in 1910, 30,317; in 1914, 34,871. Numbers dropped precipitously during World War I, but in 1920, 32,245 titles were published. In the following years of inflation and depression production was unstable, responding to each new crisis. Although fiction's share of the market was growing, the largest single category was children's and school books at around 15 percent, followed by the natural sciences and the applied sciences.[89]

The period was one of profound change in the economics of publishing. That kitsch and trash were economic rather than intellectual phenomena had long been understood, but that literature was a business as well as an art was not widely recognized until the 1920s. The role of publishers was growing in importance; authors were now dependent upon them instead of on patrons. Publishers spoke with increasing frequency on literary occasions. In an article discussing the economic meaning of the book, Georg Schäfer[90] recognized the phenomenon of writing for the market, of targeting a specific audience segment, and using a formula to appeal to readers. Schäfer perceptively observed that the more writing is a commercial endeavor, the more the spiritual sensitivity of the author decreases.[91]

The economics of literature have four basic elements, authors, publishers, booksellers, and readers, who may or may not be the same as book buyers. They form an interconnected chain and each element is necessary to the others. In the Catholic case, each element exhibited features that contributed to the limited economic viability of Catholic literature.

One inescapable underlying problem was simple lack of interest in Catholic literature. Non-Catholic booksellers did not stock the publications of Catholic presses. Why? Because non-Catholics did not read them. Even worse, neither did most Catholics. The fact was stated in different ways: Muth referred to lack of interest; Falkenberg declared that "a reading public is lacking," terminology frequently adopted by others; Joseph August Lux used the familiar Latin formulation, "Catholica non leguntur."[92] That Catholics did not offer much of a market for books was undoubtedly the result of their generally lower educational level; their disinclination can only have been intensified by the availability of the new, less intellectually demanding, entertainment media of the 1920s, radio and films. And even if Catholics were interested, they would find books difficult to afford. The price of books put them beyond the reach of most working-class families. In the late 1920s the entire book-publishing industry was experiencing an economic crisis, and Catholics were not the only non-buyers.[93]

How large a share of the industry Catholic publishers represented is questionable.[94] There were substantial Catholic publishing houses: Herder in Freiburg im Breisgau, Schöningh in Paderborn, Kösel in Kempten and Munich, and Bachem in Cologne. There were also other smaller and less stable firms, as well as the occasional specialist firm like Pustet in Regensburg, which had a major role in music publishing. Contemporaries were not unaware of the importance of market share. In 1917 Albert Rumpf[95] of the Borromäus Verein raised the question of whether Catholics, who constituted 36 percent of the population, accounted for 36 percent of German books and pamphlets produced each year. It is not clear whether he was thinking of Catholics as publishers or readers, but however he meant the question, the unstated answer was that they did not.[96]

Not surprisingly, Catholic authors found it difficult to make a living, and making a living had become increasingly important as the percentage of lay Catholic authors, in contrast to Catholic clerical authors, grew. From time to time the authors' plight was acknowledged. A brief article in 1901 raised the question of whether Catholic literary inferiority was not really a matter of the inadequate pay received by those who wrote for Catholic journals. Enrica von Handel-Mazzetti, perhaps the most important and successful of the Catholic novelists, expressed the author's dilemma in personal terms. After thanking Karl Muth in a letter for publishing in *Hochland* several of her novels, especially the controversial *Jesse und Maria* (1905), she commented that she could earn more if she wrote for non-Catholic journals: "If I were selfish and my Catholic art not more important to me than gold and possessions, I would have long since taken one of the hands that were held out. But my profession as a German Catholic artist was and is more to me than anything else." By writing for the secular journal *Rundschau,* she might be able to demonstrate to non-Catholic Germans that Catholics could compete, but she would have had to be noncontroversial and adjust her writing for a non-Catholic readership.[97]

More than one Catholic man of letters deplored the commercialization of cultural life and the dominance of the profit mentality, but what they were usually deploring was the development of a mass culture. Art and literature had always been economic enterprises; the difference was in how they were financed, not that they were financed. Those who lamented the new patterns tended to congratulate themselves that Catholic literature was not completely dominated by money, but Catholic publishers and booksellers were subject to the same economic constraints as others. The true difference was one of scale, not one of kind. Publishers were criticized for being unwilling to take risks—Kösel was singled out as an exception—but the cold fact was that to stay in business, Catholic journals, publishers, and booksellers had to succeed economically. They were essential to the production of Catholic literature; the substitution of organizations for publishing houses and subsidies for profits could be no more than an occasional alternative.[98]

Economic viability is determined by what sells. In the case of literature it is a matter of what people will read and buy, and, to the extent that most Catholics did read, they did not read serious literature. As Lux put it, the "higher" the literature, the less likely it was to be read, a curse that was particularly applicable to religious literature, since at its most desirable it was mystical and symbolic.[99] Distressing though it might be, few Catholic readers had any appetite for the classics or serious literature. Instead, they, like other Germans, read the light, popular, entertaining writing that was known as *Unterhaltungsliteratur* (light fiction). This writing was decried as shallow. Sometimes it was equated with immoral literature. It had no literary pretensions. But no critical disapproval could nullify its seductiveness, and no critical acclaim could enhance the charms of more serious literature.

Catholic authors and publishers did respond to the fundamental imperative of demand.[100] There were hundreds of magazines that served Catholic consumers of *Unterhaltungsliteratur.* Newspapers published novels in installments, even newspapers as serious as *Germania.* The reviews in *Bücherwelt,* the journal of the Borromäus Verein, and the catalogs it periodically published are full of light novels, many written by Catholics and with a Catholic slant and setting. A novel like Jassy Torrund's *Hannas Lehrjahr* (1919)[101] is typical. Hanna is a good Catholic girl who looks after her sick mother, wins a prize at a garden show, and marries her former teacher. Catholic values are affirmed and advocated by example. *Hannas Lehrjahr* is a Catholic version of the stereotypical light novel that lacks the dimension that would have made it literature to the critics, but for most German Catholics this kind of writing passed for Catholic literature.

The authors who wrote entertaining novels and stories were not, by and large, the authors to whom critics like Muth, Kralik, and Kneip referred when they spoke of Catholic authors. There was the same gulf between serious authors and other authors among German Catholic writers that there was in mainstream German literature. To enhance the presence of Catholic literature, a few writers were probably taken more seriously than they would have been had the pool of Catholic authors been larger. Karl Muth, for example, considered Maria Herbert[102] a writer of *Unterhaltungsliteratur* rather than literature, but the Gralbund sharply disagreed with him.[103]

For the most part, authors, unless they were also critics, like Kralik and Kneip, wanted only to stand aside from the quarrels and get on with their writing. Enrica von Handel-Mazzetti doubtless expressed the views of many when she wrote, "I will be quiet about all the sad things that burden us in literary life and say only that my joy in work blooms above all." She acknowledged all she owed Muth and stated that she would not publish in any journal that attacked him, but she also made it clear that she did not consider herself a member of any party, on either side of the *Literaturstreit*.

THE ACHIEVEMENTS OF THE CATHOLIC LITERARY MOVEMENT

By the beginning of the 1930s, the Catholic literary movement had been in existence for more than thirty years, and a sense that it had burnt out as a movement begins to be detectable. Disillusionment was not universal, but some hard questions were beginning to be asked.

Probably the most important of those questions was put in the title of one article, "Gibt es ein deutsches katholisches Literaturleben?!" (Is There a German Catholic Literature?!). Certainly there were novels and poetry written by Catholics, but had it achieved the status of literature? Not every critic would have been able to give an unqualified, enthusiastic "yes." Instead, many literati wrote of a pervasive dreariness. Not that Catholics were incapable of writing literature. Georges Bernanos in France, Sigrid Undset in Norway, and G. K. Chesterton in

England had managed to be true both to Catholicism and to art. But German Catholic literature could not point to a comparable figure and lacked, moreover, examples of "the good, outstanding novel that corresponds to modern sensitivity, that is presented in a gripping fashion, and that depends on and is based through and through on the Catholic worldview."[104]

Explanations for the pallid condition of German Catholic literature were advanced. One assertion that implies deficiency was that Catholic literature was too "feminine." Coupled with the prevailing identification of women with forms of religion and piety that were unappreciated, a subtle but unmistakable depreciation of women as authors, denigration of novels written for women, and disparagement of women as readers, this judgment was devastating. These views were particularly apparent in Muth and those sympathetic to his ideas. An occasional outstanding woman writer, like Enrica von Handel-Mazzetti, did not change the general perception.[105]

A 1927 canvas of a number of well-known Catholic authors elicited other explanations. Three questions were asked. Can we Catholics in Germany be satisfied with our accomplishments in the overall literary picture of the times? Have we truly left "exile" and won our own place? Is the future promising, or is a retreat already taking place after the efforts of recent years? Opinions were naturally mixed, but overall the tone was one of discouragement. At one extreme was Martin Rockenbach,[106] who considered the circumstances of the times propitious. At the other was Karl Borromäus Heinrich,[107] who dismissed the questions with the assertion that "the accomplishments of contemporary, so-called Catholic authors and writers in German are—with isolated exceptions—so bad that they can claim to have no significance for national and world literature!" Most of the authors recapitulated the long-familiar laments, but without the commitment to change and optimism that had characterized earlier discussions. Two explanations were common, the first economic, the second intellectual. Peter Dörfler,[108] one of the most successful Catholic authors, summarized the first with his complaint about the lack of a Catholic Maecenas. The intellectual alternative was that the Catholic worldview was incompatible with modern literary trends.[109]

One suggestive new theory surfaced: over-organization. Twenty years before, the standard response to a problem had been to create an organization, as when the Wolframbund (an association named for Wolfram von Eschenbach) had been founded to raise literary taste.[110] Now, the solutions had become the problem. Authors complained of sterility and oppressiveness. Karl Gabriel Pfeill[111] wrote of the "superfluity of tinny, bustling, deadening 'organizations.'" Josef Georg Oberkofler[112] described how "true Catholic works of art" were attacked because what had begun as an individual's bright idea had been institutionalized and then degenerated into academicism and sterility. Pfeill used the term "dead to life" to characterize organizations.[113]

Comparison of Germany, with its undistinguished German Catholic novels, and France, where the works of Catholic writers like Georges Bernanos, François Mauriac, and Paul Claudel achieved international renown, suggests the possibility of additional contributing factors. Certainly, the intellectual climates in the two countries were considerably different. In Germany, the principal opponent of Catholicism was Protestantism; in France the principal opponent was secularism. The French Revolution had enshrined in France the forces that most aggravated and stimulated Catholic novelists: faith in progress, a secular society, capitalism, and egalitarianism. These forces of modernization were less firmly established in Germany. The concentration of German Catholics on internal national concerns rather than international Catholic issues cannot have enhanced their artistic perspective, and their relative lack of access to higher education would only have further limited their potential.[114]

Inevitably, any movement that begins with the high hopes of the German Catholic literary movement is bound to disappoint, and late in the 1920s Lux went so far as to say that he did not believe in the possibility of a Catholic literary life. His contemporary Johannes Mumbauer was more positive. In the same year that Lux made his pronouncement, Mumbauer pointed out that the literary picture might be depressingly cheerless, but years ago it had been worse. Criticism was improving. Richard von Kralik had envisioned a grand purpose for the Catholic literary movement of giving a unified confessional meaning to art in the Romantic sense and replacing a multifaceted Christian culture and worldview with a Catholic one. This it had not done, but it could take credit for the serious debate of important topics, the encouragement of young authors, and facilitating the adjustment to a new era of authors, readers, and critics.[115]

Its accomplishments, however, were limited by its elitist character. Whether conservative or progressive, whether of the *Hochland* or the *Gral* party, Catholic intellectuals were primarily concerned with the reading of the Catholic intelligentsia and the opinions of their non-Catholic counterparts. Less educated and less socially and economically elevated Catholics figured only as raw material to be improved. Popular literature was noticed only to be vilified. The disapproval of the critics did not stop the expansion of popular literature any more than it stopped the ordinary Catholic reader from reading it. In fact, the Catholic literary movement had the worst of both worlds: novels written to conform to the persistent and prevailing precepts of Catholic literary critics achieved neither artistic greatness nor popularity. Like all writers, Catholic writers found themselves caught between irreconcilable desiderata: pleasing critics precluded wide sales, but writing for a mass market discouraged critical acclaim. Even if an author succeeded in producing a work of literary merit with sales potential, if it had been written to be a Catholic work, that sales potential could not be expected to extend beyond the Catholic population.

A few attitudes display some flexibility and change. A slight but perceptible increase in tolerance of non-Catholic literary contributions sets the 1920s apart from the prewar period. Unyielding resistance to change disappeared. The Jesuit Wiesebach urged greater openness. *Der Gral* under Friedrich Muckermann was no longer the *Der Gral* of Kralik and Eichert. Speaking at the Katholikentag of 1928, Muckermann encouraged Catholics to view literature as a treasure from the past, but also to participate in the literature of the present.[116] Nostalgia for past glories, veneration for a simple, straightforward Catholic way of life that never was were still present in the unappreciated Catholic *Unterhaltungsliteratur,* but they were part of the more elevated literary discourse only as emotional undertones, not as the intellectual system they had constituted in Kralik's heyday.

The fundamental questions of concern to the Catholic literary movement remained the same: How far could a Catholic writer go in adapting to an increasingly secular world? What was the proper relationship of literature and morality? What was the role of the clergy in determining literary canons? The underlying assumption of all who wrote on Catholic literature was implicit in the name: it had to belong to both the world of Catholicism and to the world of literature, or, as Friedrich Muckermann put it, to two kingdoms. Working out the appropriate relationships had only become more difficult as the twentieth century progressed, and what passed as German Catholic literature in 1933 remained, despite a number of good Catholic novels, disheartening to those of good taste.[117]

5

Books, Reading, and Catholic Libraries

If debates about serious literature have a remote and somewhat inconsequential air about them, debates about the real reading of real people suggest an intellectual brawl. They are full of sound and fury, and never far from action. An intellectual component is present, but the imperative to do something is always close behind. With the decline of regular church attendance, Catholics were hearing fewer sermons, and other forms of communication were becoming increasingly important. Reading offered a means to strengthen a sense of Catholic identity. The improvement in the literacy of Catholics that had taken place in the years before the *Kulturkampf* made it essential to influence reading. This chapter describes the Catholic effort to encourage Catholics of all classes to read, particularly through its library organizations.[1]

But what should Catholics be reading? An answer to that question was a precondition to effective library service, and librarians took the lead in Catholic efforts to distinguish good reading from merely acceptable reading and to identify what was not acceptable reading under any circumstances. The same fundamental contradiction plagued the efforts of Catholic librarians that plagued the efforts of non-Catholic librarians. Catholic libraries, like public libraries, were considered institutions of adult education. They were expected to educate readers in both a broad humanistic sense and a narrower practical sense, to spread culture, and to strengthen Catholic identity. At the same time, however, they had to offer readers what they wanted, or there would be no readers, and what readers wanted was amusement. The conflict between the ideals of librarians and what was practical forced them to ask: Was the act of reading so valuable in and of itself that it was better for a library user to read something of "lesser" value than not to read at all? For Catholics, there was an additional question: How Catholic did something have to be to be acceptable? Was it enough if a book merely refrained from undermining Catholic principles, or did it need to do something more positive? Catholic librarianship was a delicate balancing act.

LITERATURE AND ITS POOR RELATIONS

An expanding and developing publishing industry offered German readers of the late nineteenth century a diverse assortment of publications from which to choose. There was the literature of high culture, but there was also entertaining literature, colportage literature, trashy literature, pornography, and nonfiction.[2] Catholic librarians had to develop principles that would help them decide how each category related to their work. Even literature of the highest quality had to be treated with caution, since it could easily have elements that rendered it inappropriate from a Catholic perspective.

To accomplish the Borromäus Verein's goal of stimulating Christian thought and activity, the 1900 statutes of the organization prescribed "the promotion, encouragement, and dissemination of good writings." A selection of writings was to be assembled that was in equal part, "edifying, instructive, and entertaining." This statement affirmed a commitment to quality and at the same time tried to clarify what "good" meant. It combined aesthetic, religious, and practical considerations with the good bourgeois values of edification, earnestness, and propriety.[3] In its conciseness it is an exception; most efforts to define good reading tended toward verbosity and vagueness.

More typical of attempts to describe good reading was that of Alois Wurm.[4] In a book published by the Volksverein in 1913, he equated literature with the representation of life's (proper) values. If these values were not at least minimally present, their absence said something important about the book, even if it bore the other marks of a refined, aesthetic culture. Wurm denied that his standard was a moral one, but instead considered it a "general spiritual standard." A work of literature ought not to destroy spiritual life, but promote it. Wurm was interpreting in terms of adult education one of the few points of agreement that had emerged out of the critical debate on literature: to be literature, a work had to have a moral dimension.[5] Five years later Albert Rumpf, then-secretary of the Borromäus Verein, described a good book as a teacher and guide, a friend and comfort to people. A good book should announce the greatness, power, grandeur, and wisdom of God, praise the good men who serve and honor God, and celebrate the wonders of nature that are the manifestation of God's power, indeed, celebrate all goodness and beauty. Like the Gospels, a good book should inspire men to honor God and the Church and to preach to the young.[6]

To a considerable extent, good books were defined by what they were not. A speech at the 1926 Katholikentag entitled "The Good Book" was, in fact, largely devoted to bad books; the closest the speaker came to defining good books was to assert that they should redirect the faithful from the restless bustle of life to the stillness of a healthy, Christian-based family life. Joseph Froberger's[7] lecture at the fourteenth Borromäus Verein course for librarians presented an exhaustive and detailed list of contrasts. Bad books, such as sentimental love stories divorced from reality, exhibited a sloppy, enervating frame of mind, while good books, like the Tyrolean novels of one Schrott-Fiechtl,[8] took a vigorous path, enlivened by a "healthy breeze" blowing through them. Bad books had no clear worldview, especially in the area of religion, but would shake the foundations of the spiritual personality; good books portrayed a clear and true view of the world. Modern books that contained confused social ideas were dangerous, whether they were written from a reactionary or revolutionary point of view; what was needed were novels that portrayed social ideals of justice and love. All books that cast doubt on the moral principles of family were to be strongly opposed, and such proscriptions included not only novels dealing with divorce but all books that led to disdain for the family. To be applauded were those Catholic novels that could lead to deeper family feeling, novels exemplifying maternal and filial love, and novels depicting scenes of home life. All works that loosened moral principles were to be avoided; those that were full of moral strength were to be welcomed. Books that stimulated the passions or portrayed immoral behavior were to be fought with books that represented the ideal of Christian purity. At times, Catholic librarians came very close to saying that a good book was any book that did not endanger morals, corrupt the young, or plant dangerous doubts; aesthetic considerations did not enter the equation.[9]

A more germane consideration of a good book was that of Hermann Herz, the de facto director of the Borromäus Verein from 1903 to 1912,[10] who defined "good" in terms of library service. Less peremptory and more practical than other analysts, Herz put the reader at the center. Whether a book was worthwhile for a reader depended not only on the book but also on the reader. From this premise Herz concluded that "the greatest part of our classical writing (belles lettres), like that of the present, so far as it achieves high artistry, demands immersion, quiet consideration and reflection, even an intellectual effort, and is only possible with intellectual and at least average physical freshness." Such reading made too great a demand on the man who worked eight to twelve hours at physical labor, or even at less physical and more intellectual work. For such a man, a book of less literary merit but that was easier to read served his needs better than a more aesthetically demanding one. Herz concurred with the view of Walter Hofmann,[11] the librarian of the public library of Leipzig and a leader in the library profession, that a book had to fall within the circle of a reader's experience to reach him. The most valuable literature needed to be in a library for readers with literary understanding and taste, because for such people only the truly valuable book was appropriate, but for the average reader from the "better" bourgeoisie and the lower classes, a less exalted type of literature offered more. The librarian should have no regret in obtaining such books and making them available.[12]

Herz was fundamentally idealistic; he wrote of the good that grew from the seed good books planted, of instruction from instructive books, of edification from religious books, of artistic pleasure from poetry, and of the joy and improvement from all three types. Johannes Mumbauer, too, believed that the true, substantial book was full of life and life-giving, and thus leading to the education of humanity. Although Mumbauer was an author rather than a librarian, he agreed that when the right book was in the hand of the right guide and true adult educator, it could be effective. Along with most of the individuals who were responsible for the local libraries, Herz and Mumbauer recognized that "good" books did not necessarily have much appeal. They might seek to promote the reading of good books, but the task was almost hopeless because the average reader was "without question" overtired and because there were too many more alluring alternatives. Inexpensive reading material designed to be commercially successful, rather than "good," was readily available at newsstands and lower-end booksellers; even working-class individuals could afford a single installment of a serial novel. Lending libraries maintained as a sideline by newsdealers or stationers were another option. Filled with numerous popular novels of doubtful character that could be borrowed for a small fee, they offered serious competition to Catholic libraries and to secular public libraries.[13]

Librarians frowned upon popular novels that were classified as entertaining literature (*Unterhaltungsliteratur*) or as *Trivialliteratur* (trivial literature), the latter being the *Unterhaltungsliteratur* of the bourgeoisie. They considered novels in these categories worthless but basically harmless. Totally unacceptable were the novels in the category a step lower down, a category labeled "Schundliteratur." *Schund* is the German term for trash. The *Schund* novel was pure entertainment, with no literary pretensions and less literary merit. It came with assorted settings, the more exotic the better, and its heroes bore no resemblance to anyone, living or dead. It was a genre novel and might be an adventure novel, a western, a detective story, or a romance.[14]

Catholic concern about this pseudo-literature increased as its volume increased. At the 1885 Katholikentag Paul Haffner,[15] who was named bishop of Mainz in the following year, spoke on the dangers of questionable novels, a category in which he included the novels of Zola. Haffner concluded that whoever read bad novels would of necessity lose their principles of faith and morality. Significantly, he was less concerned about the effect on the "lady" who read such books than about the effect on women of the lower classes.[16] The problem of bad literature was discussed at virtually every Katholikentag of the 1890s. Catholic attitudes were not significantly different from those of other conservatives, but the uncompromising stance was unusual.

In 1910 a long article in *Die Bücherwelt* defined the basic Catholic, and Borromäus Verein, position on *Schund*. After lengthy definitions and descriptions of *Schund* literature and *Schmutz* (dirt) literature, and a presentation of their evils, its author, Johannes Braun (Herz's successor as general secretary of the Borromäus Verein) outlined a plan of action. First, youth who enjoyed reading were to be taught to ask themselves such questions as: What should I read and what should I not read? Second, parents were to be informed and warned. Third, good, cheap reading material was to be offered. Braun saw a major role for the Borromäus Verein in this third line of attack: "Each leader should remain conscious of the organization's high task that these libraries have to fulfill. They must endeavor with all means to hold their libraries to the heights. These 3,700 Borromäus Verein libraries are a powerful phalanx that will do their part in protecting our *Volk* from the plague of *Schund* and *Schmutz* literature."[17]

Church officials encouraged the Borromäus Verein, and it became the most important positive force in the fight against *Schund*, fighting bad literature by offering a healthy Catholic alternative. In 1927 the Fulda Conference of Bishops praised and recommended the Borromäus Verein for its efforts in the fight against *Schund*. The sermons for Borromäus Sunday, an annual fixture after 1919, were prepared by the the central office of the Borromäus Verein but distributed to the parishes by episcopal ordinaries. Almost invariably these sermons combined condemnation of *Schund* with the recommendation that parishioners become members of the Borromäus Verein.[18] Nor was the Borromäus Verein the only Catholic library organization for which *Schund* literature was a focus of activity. Throughout the period, virtually every Catholic library organization or society founded to disseminate literature mentioned the need to fight the plague of *Schund* in its organizational plans.

By the 1920s *Schund* was the obsession and the perpetually, monotonously repeated theme of the leaders of the Borromäus Verein. The organization cooperated with other groups, both Catholic and non-Catholic, to fight this evil, and in 1928 the Borromäus Verein sponsored a conference devoted to the theme. Local branches of the Borromäus Verein understood their role in the fight against *Schund*. An article in the newsletter of the parish of Essen-Borbeck proclaimed, "A mass of newspapers, books, and writings is daily distributed in our area, but it includes not only good but unfortunately also many bad and pernicious writings, writings that undermine faith, speak of authority with scorn, and appeal to the lowest instincts. . . . If you, Catholic father, want to be sure that only good books come into your house, you must join the Borromäus Verein."[19]

In the writing of intellectuals, colportage literature was usually equated with *Schund* literature, although the historian Rudolf Schenda argues that this merely illustrates how completely intellectuals failed to understand colportage literature. Colportage literature was the reading of people for whom books were an unaffordable luxury. For them, reading had to be, above all else, cheap. Using price alone as a criterion, the 1926 edition of Enrica von Handel-Mazzetti's *Meinrad Helmpergers denkwürdiges Jahr* (a novel about the conversion of a Lutheran youth to Catholicism) at 5 M did not appear attractive in comparison with *Der verlorene Ring* (1928) by the prolific but little esteemed author of romances, Hedwig Courths-Mahler, for 2.75 M; nor could Franz Herwig's *Die Eingeengten* (1928) at 8 M compete with *Der Rote Kreis* by the popular American writer of mysteries, Edgar Wallace, at 3 M. Even more attractive was an installment of a *Schund* novel that could be had for a mere 0.20 M, when a single issue of *Hochland* cost 1.75 M in 1928. Only a newspaper like *Germania* at 0.10 M for a daily issue in 1927 was really cheap and offered good reading.

Unsophisticated readers wanted the written word to offer a sense of familiarity; literary novelty was a secondary consideration. In fiction they preferred escapism, sensational stories, and well-worn plots. They looked for brisk, economical, and direct prose. Colportage literature delivered these things in an inexpensive format. The colporteurs brought entertaining reading, works by popular authors like Eugenie Marlitt, Ottilie Wildemuth, and Johanna Spyri[20] and formulaic genre fiction, but they also brought nonfiction and devotional works to the rural village. Schenda estimates that a mere 6 percent of the colportage trade was in dirty and trashy novels and emphasizes that the colporteurs delivered ideas to large classes of the population that were otherwise without print.[21]

Equating colportage literature with *Schund* concentrated attention on the moral aspects of colportage literature. Subsequent scholarship has broadened that perspective, and the sociological implications of the opinions of intellectuals are now apparent. Rudolf Schenda makes a compelling connection of popular reading with the old oral traditions of the lower classes; early colportage novels were frequently print versions of familiar tales but were demonstrably more violent and bloodthirsty versions of these stories, packaged for bourgeois readers. Print gave new visibility to what had previously remained largely underground. Since it sold so well, colportage fiction was viewed as reflecting the outlook, tastes, and opinions of the lower classes, and what it reflected had to be frightening in a society of deep class divisions, although colportage literature also preached the doctrine of obedience to established authority.[22]

In addition to its violence, the commercial character of colportage literature disturbed intellectuals. Like *Schund,* and like *Unterhaltungsliteratur,* it was produced for a market. It was created not by, but for, the *Volk* by aggressive entrepreneurs. The fundamental issue was influence: because what made money rarely met the standards of good reading, readers ran the danger of having their moral values corrupted. Publishers of colportage literature and *Schund,* who might—horrors!—not even be Christian, were subverting the faith of Catholic readers in the interest of filthy lucre. In this situation, it was convenient for intellectuals to invoke the biblical warning that money is the root of all evil.[23]

READERS AND READING

A report in the local newspaper on the 1914 diocesan conference in Eichstätt of the Preßverein, the Catholic library organization for the dioceses of Bavaria, manifests appreciation of both the potential of reading and its possible dangers:

> There are gates in our souls that are broader and more accessible than any other, and through these gates walks Death, as well as life. In multiple forms, in captivating colors and shapes, as beauty and glistening gold, Death pushes through these gates. But in no form is it so fruitful as when it enters in showy words and intoxicating sentences, when it strides over printed paper. It is a whole army, legion is its name. Every small black printed letter is a soldier in its service. But these small soldiers can also be put to the service of grace. How often grace speaks in the soul, while eyes are skimming over lines of print! What soul-winning and soul-bewitching, soul-cultivating and soul-destroying strength reading possesses![24]

Reading presents new worlds, whether it is an exotic locale or a society where lives, thinking, and behavior are very different from the reader's. When it portrays the reader's world from a somewhat different perspective, it can bring new insights. It is particularly effective in communicating complex ideas; the act of reading encourages reflection. Reading is a powerful source.

As discussed in chapter 4, literacy increased significantly in Germany in the course of the nineteenth century. Starting from somewhere around 30 percent in 1830, by 1890 only a small percentage of the German-speaking population of the Second Reich was unable to read. Literacy varied by gender, region, class, and religious confession. In the Kingdom of Prussia, for example, in 1871 the rate of illiteracy among men in Saxony and in Hessen-Nassau was 2 percent, in Hanover 4 percent, in Silesia 11 percent, and in Posnan 32 percent. Among women in the same provinces the statistics were 5 percent, 8 percent, 17 percent, and 41 percent respectively. Catholics were generally less literate than Protestants, although that too varied by region. Schenda gives the figure of 85 percent literacy for male Catholics and 78 percent literacy for female Catholics, but those 1871 figures were the average for the entire Kingdom of Prussia and included the many Polish Catholics of the provinces of Posnan and Prussia, as well as the Catholics of the Rhineland and Westphalia, where illiteracy was much lower.[25]

The nature of reading also changed during the course of the century. Where previously a few books of great importance, particularly religious texts, had been read, reread, and read yet again, now the pattern was to read many books, but to read them only once. Extensive reading, in which the goal is to get an overall understanding of a work, replaced intensive reading, in which the purpose is complete and detailed understanding of one work.[26]

What was read is less certain. Helmut Walser Smith describes the reading of those in the rural areas, towns, and small cities of Germany in the late nineteenth century, whether readers were Catholic or Protestant, as predominantly confessional material. Confessional material ranged from devotional works to moralistic tales and was more often read for its entertainment value than for the sake of piety. If readers were Catholic, they might read local Catholic newspapers and journals. If they owned a calendar, then a far more interesting and substantial thing than the calendar of today, it was a Catholic one. Catholic popular literature was decidedly anti-Protestant.[27] Jeffrey Zalar presents a somewhat different picture, arguing that while the lower classes in the Rhineland and Westphalia read devotional and other religious works in the mid–nineteenth century, they read a great deal more besides.[28]

Reading was influenced by the same factors that affected literacy. Those who lived in urban centers had wider reading opportunities than rural people, but accessibility did not necessarily translate into more or better reading. The author of an article from the Weimar period complained that little true reading was done in large cities, a fact he attributed to the lack of poetry in big city life.

Young men were more interested in sport than literature, and young women consumed only *Hintertreppenromane* ("below-the-stairs" novels).[29]

Patterns of reading and book ownership among the bourgeoisie were different from those of the lower classes. As a matter of course, the bourgeoisie read books, owned books, and belonged to reading societies. By the beginning of the nineteenth century, the Catholic bourgeoisie was very similar in this respect to other members of the bourgeoisie. Rudolf Schlögl has demonstrated that by 1830 in the Catholic towns of Aachen, Cologne, and Münster, not only was a private collection of books common, the single largest category of books in private libraries was that relating to history, politics, and social issues. By the end of the nineteenth century, diocesan offices were "flooded" with requests to be allowed to read contemporary works that had been placed on the Index, books like the novels of Zola and Tolstoy, the philosophy of Nietzsche and Schopenhauer, and the pseudo-science of Houston Stewart Chamberlain; others asked for a more general dispensation. Many young professionals, members of both *Bürgertum* and *Kleinbürgertum*, sought permission to read contemporary books from church officials, convinced that they needed to read both the scholarly and literary books of the day in order to succeed and to gain the respect of their compatriots.[30]

The central premise of Johann Chrysostom Schulte's book on the Church and the educated[31] was that although the Church served all classes equally, the same treatment was not appropriate for all classes. In his chapter on reading, Schulte observed that the educated of the day (1912) did not welcome efforts to influence what they read, and he therefore advised the clergy to proceed with caution. For a priest to set himself up as a literary mentor, he needed to be widely knowledgeable in literature and familiar with the literary taste of the educated, or his recommendation would disappoint and irritate. On the other hand, while Schulte acknowledged that much Catholic religious writing was seriously out of date, all Catholics nonetheless had a religious duty to read religious literature corresponding to their educational level and position in life.[32]

Two surveys offer firm evidence about reading in the post–World War I years. The first asked female workers what they read. Data were probably collected in Coesfeld, a small town in the Münsterland, in 1920. These women favored romance above other types of reading; their favorite authors were Hedwig Courths-Mahler, Friedrich Lehne, and Anny Wothe.[33] Second came mystery novels. All had read Ferdinande von Brackel's *Die Tochter des Kunstreiters*,[34] but Enrica von Handel-Mazzetti was considered too difficult because of the dialect in which her characters spoke. They had been introduced to the classics of German and European literature in school but did not otherwise read them. Of the group, 30 percent were members of the Borromäus Verein, but book buying was common, and the women lent one another books.[35] A second survey in 1928 studied what travelers read, based on information collected from railway newsstands. Daily newspapers were most common. Scholarly journals were rarely bought, and the sales of general cultural journals like the *Allgemeine Rundschau* and *Hochland* had dropped precipitously since the introduction of magazines that featured scantily clad stars of stage and film. Romance magazines that printed advertisements of those seeking partners were available; women's magazines sold briskly. Nudist magazines and outright pornography sold well enough for dealers to keep them in stock. Sale of books depended upon price; according to the survey, those at 1 RM did best. The novel and detective-novel series of the publisher Ullstein were also popular.[36]

The results of these surveys of reading can only have confirmed what the individuals who conducted them already knew: "good" books were not popular. In fact, the Church had lost control of what its members read by the late nineteenth century. By that time reading material of all kinds was multiplying rapidly and disseminated widely; in such an environment priests simply could not control what parishioners read. Constantly reiterated throughout the period was the responsibility of priests to fight bad reading, but they were markedly unsuccessful at it, as Zalar documents. Newspapers that contained new, often unwelcome, ideas, were widely read. Subliterature of a doubtful and frequently suggestive character was readily available. Catholics read what came to hand, particularly distressing for the clergy when it was Protestant material, and even more distressing when the readers were children. Zalar's evidence comes from the Rhineland and Westphalia, an area more confessionally mixed than most Catholic regions, but there is no reason to believe that priests in other regions were any more successful, then or later. Priestly discussions of intellectual discipline, writes Zalar, "recognize the powerful currents of individual choice that had penetrated the Catholic milieu, even as its boundaries were being defined." Choices only became wider as the nineteenth century gave way to the twentieth and priestly influence over reading declined even further. In cultural matters, Catholics all too often chose the popular, secular, and non-Catholic option, undermining the efforts of Catholic intellectuals to develop acceptably Catholic cultural possibilities.[37]

The reluctance of many priests to act as literary police was one reason their efforts to fight "bad" literature were so ineffective. Their education had not equipped them for the task, and the numerous other demands for their services left little time for it. Disagreement within the clergy over what was suitable reading for parishioners diminished effectiveness still further. Reading the Bible, for example, was strongly discouraged, but the clergy in predominantly rural Württemberg considered it acceptable for their parishioners to read the Old Testament with supervision. Zalar gives several examples of young men who, wanting to read a book that was on the Index, would be encouraged to do so by one cleric but denied permission by another.[38]

To make good reading as widely available as possible and to offer informed guidance to readers in its pursuit, as well as to create an alternative to the many undesirable sources of reading, an expanding network of Catholic libraries, supplemented by book clubs and reading circles, was developed and strengthened. The premier library organization was the Borromäus Verein, founded in 1845 by August Reichensperger[39] with headquarters in Bonn, but a Bavarian counterpart and an assortment of smaller groups and independent efforts were also part of the picture. Still active today, the Borromäus Verein provided good books, training for librarians, and leadership to German Catholic librarianship.[40]

The Borromäus Verein had the distinction of being the first German Catholic organization devoted to cultural activity. Its initial bylaws stated that its purpose was "the stimulation of Catholic thought and inclination to corresponding action." It was to encourage and spread good literature that would work against the corrupting influence of bad literature on all classes of bourgeois society. One or more free publications would be sent to all who participated, in accord with their contribution and the means of the association. The association would also be responsible for publishing a list of writings that served its purpose and making them available to participants for purchase at the lowest possible cost. Only two years after the association's founding did the managing committee[41] decide to add a third approach, the establishment of libraries.[42]

After early experiments with a variety of literature-related activities that included publishing, libraries became the dominant enterprise. Statistics of the 1870s and 1880s show the impact of the *Kulturkampf.* From 1,526 local groups in 1874, the Borromäus Verein declined to 1,493 in 1875, 1,358 in 1876, and 1,266 in 1881. Not until 1890 did the number of local societies recover to its 1874 level. Fluctuations in membership followed the same pattern.[43]

The need to rebuild after the *Kulturkampf* was intensified by the growing interest of Catholics in reading. Again and again, descriptions from the early 1890s cite a desire and need of Catholics to read (*Lesebedürfnis*). Improved education had produced a generation that not only could read but did read, and because the Borromäus Verein did not offer the books Catholic readers wanted, they stayed away from its libraries and obtained what they wanted elsewhere. Priests complained that Catholics were exposed to unsuitable reading of all kinds. Clearly, a more controlled environment was called for.[44]

Johannes Braun, the society's director for much of the first half of the twentieth century, described the subsequent revitalization of the Borromäus Verein as an upturn after a long period of sleep, a second spring. When reformers gained control of the managing committee in the late 1890s, the objectives of the organization were redefined. Emphasis was placed on adult education. Efforts were made to reach more Catholic readers. To symbolize the new outlook, the name used for local libraries was changed from *Vereinsbibliothek* (association library) to *Volksbibliothek* (people's library). But the new name not only implied a wider audience, it was also the contemporary term for an institution of adult education. The *Volksbibliothek* might provide some entertaining reading on the side, but its raison d'être was educational. The statutes of the Borromäus Verein were amended in 1900 to give local groups the right to admit nonmembers to their libraries, either free of charge or with a small deposit, should the local group wish to do so. In 1920 they were amended again to permit women to be members. Zalar interprets this reorganization and rebuilding effort as an attempt by the leaders of the Borromäus Verein to meet the demand in the Catholic population for modern literature and learning. It can also be interpreted, however, as an attempt to make certain that Catholic readers stayed within acceptable boundaries.[45]

The emphasis on adult education brought the Borromäus Verein closer to the growing public library movement. The decade of the 1890s was a period of great significance for German public libraries. In 1895 Constantin Nörrenberg[46] presented the lecture that is the manifesto of German public librarianship, arguing that the public library had an essential educational role, and holding up the achievements of public libraries in England and the United States as a model. Previously, the bourgeoisie had maintained libraries that were usually called *Stadtbibliotheken* (city libraries), but these libraries served their needs and interests rather than those of the general population. After 1890 cities, especially large cities, began opening popular libraries intended for all classes.[47] A library profession began to emerge. The new model libraries held much promise and appealed to leaders of widely differing outlook.

Catholics were aware of these developments. The 1898 Katholikentag passed a resolution encouraging the founding of libraries. A year later Philipp Huppert[48] urged the Borromäus Verein to shed its character as an organization of membership libraries and become an organization of popular libraries. In the years preceding World War I the Borromäus Verein saw itself as very much a part of the public library movement, although this image became less common after the war, when public libraries were identified with state support and the representation of diverse viewpoints.[49]

By the turn of the century, change was well underway. The statutes adopted in 1900 replaced a self-perpetuating committee with a committee elected by the society's membership conference. The roles of the managing committee and the membership meeting were clarified, and the goal of the society was officially re-defined to the "promotion, advance, and spread of good writings of edifying, in-structive, and entertaining content."[50] A new journal, the *Borromäus-Blätter,* was founded to replace the existing newsletter, and Augustin Esser[51] was appointed its first editor. Esser filled it with practical advice for the operation of the local orga-nizations and discussions of contemporary topics, like colportage literature and public libraries. During his leadership a literary commission was founded with the intention of making the Borromäus Verein the literary counterpart to the Volks-verein. These years were "a time of soul-searching and reflection, indeed, a time of crisis, but also one of finding a new way."[52]

Esser resigned as editor in May 1903 and, after a brief interlude, was suc-ceeded by Hermann Herz. A Swabian priest, Herz came recommended by Ansgar Pöllmann,[53] a member of the Benedictine congregation at Beuron and editor of a new journal of religious poetry, *Gottesminne.* Herz, the only professional at the Bonn office, had two responsibilities: to edit the *Borromäus-Blätter;* and to do "agitation" work for the Borromäus Verein in the dioceses. Endowed with ability, self-confidence, and boldness, he carried out both tasks with great success.[54]

The introduction to the first issue of the *Borromäus-Blätter* edited by Herz outlined the fundamentals of his program: to spread knowledge of good books among Catholics and to encourage Catholic libraries as a counterforce to god-less public libraries. Herz aimed the journal at his own generation, the genera-tion that had been influenced by Hertling's ideas on the need of Catholics for scientific knowledge, by Muth's writings on culture, and by Albert Ehrhard's *Der Katholizismus und das zwanzigste Jahrhundert.* Herz was, however, committed to a balanced approach, and leading Catholic writers of different generations and varying opinions contributed essays to the *Borromäus-Blätter,* renamed *Die Bücherwelt* in 1906. Herz's own sympathies lay with Muth, but he felt that the *Borromäus-Blätter,* as the publication of the Borromäus Verein, needed to in-clude both progressive and conservative cultural views, because the organization was committed to promoting the writings of both groups. A steadily growing cir-culation testifies to how well the journal met the needs of its audience.[55]

Herz proved equally capable at organizing branches of the Borromäus Verein. A general secretariat for literature and library affairs in Bonn was created in 1908, formalizing a supervision that already existed. How necessary it was is demonstrated by the fact that in 1905 a mere 20 percent of the local societies submitted the reports that they were required to file on their membership and activity and sent a percentage of their income to finance the central administra-tion.[56] The new secretariat was to provide unified direction, to verify that local groups were living up to the Borromäus Verein ideal, and to provide services to local groups. It quickly expanded its existing activities of preparing recommendations for acquisition and acting as a fulfillment agency and soon added training for local librarians.[57]

Herz's success generated a need for additional staff, and in 1909 Johannes Braun, a young priest in the Diocese of Trier who had completed his *Abitur* and had pursued additional study in the seminar for priests, was named the second professional on the staff. When Herz returned to parish work in his native Württemberg in 1912, Braun succeeded him as general secretary and did not retire until after World War II. Braun was a man who enjoyed good wine and a fine cigar and who was well suited to the work of organization and encouragement needed by the society, even if there were those who thought a more intellectual outlook would have been appropriate.[58]

Although the personalities and intellectual interests of the two men were very different, administratively speaking the Herz era and the Braun era had many similarities. Both men possessed abundant energy and worked hard to inspire existing local societies to better performance, to improve the professional knowledge of library staff, and to encourage the foundation of new Borromäus societies. A sampling of statistics from significant years[59] demonstrates their success and the appeal of the reorientation of the society to adult education, although Herz's remark in 1918 that Catholic educational efforts were "a slave to the tyranny of numbers" is a warning to take these figures with a grain of salt.[60]

	Societies	Membership	Average Membership per Society
1895	1712	61,538	35.9
1903	2519	106,170	42.1
1912	4466	237,245	53.1
1929	5387	263,681	48.9
1933	5198	187,865	36.1

The statistical picture was not one of unbroken progress. In the war years of 1915 and 1916 there was a decline in the number of societies, and in 1915 there was a decline in membership. The period 1920–1933 brought greater losses; five of those years saw a decline in the number of societies, seven in membership. Equally important, the growth in average membership per individual society that marked the pre–World War I period was reversed.[61]

Statistics make clear that the Borromäus Verein was overwhelmingly an organization of the Rhineland and Westphalia with the distinctive brand of German Catholicism found in those regions; Breslau and Freiburg were the only dioceses outside of the Archdiocese of Cologne that participated to any considerable extent. The six dioceses with the most Borromäus societies in 1933 were, as they had been in 1903, Cologne, Breslau, Freiburg, Münster, Paderborn, and Trier. The percentages of Catholics who were members of the Borromäus Verein confirm the regional character of the society. Only in the dioceses of Trier, Münster, and Hildesheim were more than 1.5 percent of Catholics Borromäus Verein members in 1933.[62]

Braun built on the administrative foundation laid during the Herz years. In the early 1920s he worked to create diocesan organizations to support the local Borromäus Verein libraries in the different dioceses. Later he tried to create yet another layer, district organizations. The worth of this elaborate administrative structure was debatable, even if it did parallel the hierarchical organization of the Church; there were those who argued that the societies in direct contact with the central administration were stronger than those that had to work through intermediate organizations.[63]

Informal connections and independent endeavors sometimes supplemented formal organizational structure and the efforts of the Bonn central administration in areas where there was a sufficient density of Borromäus Verein groups. In a series on activities of local groups, a librarian in Gelsenkirchen reported a considerable degree of cooperation among the fifteen Borromäus Verein libraries and fifty Borromäus Verein workers in the city. Regular monthly meetings were held and the group organized a shared exibition.[64]

Because the libraries of the local Borromäus Verein societies were poor, small in size, and open only limited hours, staffing was problematic. Although efforts began at the turn of the century to increase lay participation, partly to offer relief to overworked priests and partly to reduce clerical domination, the local priest was frequently the librarian. If he was not, he was nonetheless expected to exercise supervision over the library. The librarian was usually assisted by volunteers and occasionally by a part-time worker. Although women could not be members of the Borromäus Verein until 1920, some served as librarians of the society's libraries before that date, and they were often found as assistants. Some spoke at meetings.[65]

To remedy the complete lack of preparation of these individuals for the task of running the libraries, in 1911 the central administration in Bonn began to offer continuing-education courses to librarians and other staff on a regular basis; a library school was opened in 1921. The sixteenth course, offered in 1928, can stand as an example of these educational efforts. It lasted five days, during which those who attended listened to lectures on the pedagogical and psychological basis of librarianship, the preparation of the librarian, technical matters, especially cataloging, literature and the *Volk,* the Catholic book trade, the modern novel, and various types of readers. There were practical exercises after the presentation on cataloging, a visit to the press in Cologne, and an evening for socializing.[66] The attendees took home preprinted notes and guidelines to assist them in their subsequent work.

Another kind of expansion was the creation of the Buchgemeinde (Book Community) in 1925, a kind of book club cum publishing program that recalled the early purpose of the Borromäus Verein. It attempted to do for Catholics what, as Braun put it, a liberal Berlin organization was doing for liberals.[67] Its goal was to bring well-qualified literature into the Catholic home, and religious, instructional, and entertaining reading were included in its offerings. Braun presented the Buchgemeinde as a counter to the economic need, religious indifference, and spiritual superficiality that ruled the modern world. Fewer people could afford to buy books after the war and, even worse, fewer seemed to want to buy them. Within five years the Buchgemeinde claimed 400,000 satisfied members. That was the positive side. On the other side, Friedrich Muckermann felt that the Buchgemeinde interfered with the established book trade.[68]

Figures conceal the weak financial base upon which Borromäus Verein activity rested. Zalar describes Prussia's contribution to Borromäus libraries in the prewar period as "niggardly."[69] That had not changed by 1933. In 1933 expenditures of all Borromäus Verein societies totaled 1,543,511 M. Money from the Church covered 14 percent and money from collections 6 percent. The state provided 3,528.78 M, the districts 4949.71 M, and the localities 23,059.64 RM, bringing subsidies by all governments to a grand 2 percent. An additional 64.7 percent was categorized as "other library income," most of which came from membership fees.[70] Because the society was so dependent on these membership fees, any decline in membership had serious consequences, and during the postwar period membership volatility hampered sustained development. Between 1929 and 1933 the Borromäus Verein dropped from 263,165 members to 187,865, a loss of 28 percent.[71] It experienced similar vicissitudes in the unstable economic conditions of the early 1920s.[72]

Small as it was, financial assistance from local governments could create problems. In some small communities, especially in predominantly Catholic areas, the Borromäus Verein library was expected to serve as the de facto public library in exchange for such a subsidy. Because their Catholic character could not be guaranteed under such circumstances, the central administration in Bonn discouraged these arrangements, but their advice can have been heeded only rarely. In the early 1930s large numbers of communities that had only a Borromäus library claimed to have public libraries.[73]

Borromäus Verein growth and achievements were not accomplished without controversy. Herz's changes were not universally welcomed by conservative

Catholics, and Heinrich Falkenberg, an early ally and fellow progressive, criticized him so sharply for lack of accomplishment that, at the suggestion of the managing committee, Eduard Müller,[74] a lawyer from Koblenz, had to speak at the 1909 membership meeting of the Borromäus Verein in support of Herz.[75]

Braun, who was energetic and capable but also abrasive, stimulated a different kind of opposition. Friedrich Muckermann considered him a disappointed man. There was a brief row over efforts to organize books for soldiers at the front in 1915 that involved the Borromäus Verein in the person of Braun, a Reich committee, the Volksverein, and the Catholic publishers, and the early 1930s saw serious internal discord. The first trace of this discord is a letter from Prelate Albert Lauscher,[76] the chair of the managing committee, to another committee member, Johannes Henry,[77] in which Lauscher expresses concern about the audits of the Borromäus Verein. Two years later discord had become full-scale war. Braun was under attack, and not only the committee, but the staff of the central administration, the archbishop of Cologne,[78] and the diocesan leaders of the Borromäus Verein were drawn in. The issues were varied, although how Braun was interpreting the mission of the organization was not one of them. Primarily concerned with the financial difficulties brought on by the Depression, the managing committee wanted to scale down the enterprise. Its members proposed cuts in salaries and staff. They wanted to consider which areas of activity—library school, Buchgemeinde, or distance lending—could be dispensed with. In addition, the committee objected to Braun's lack of cooperation, his attendance at conferences, and his general independence.[79]

Braun countered the charges against him by citing the success of the Borromäus Verein under his direction. He quoted remarks made by the society's patron, the archbishop of Cologne, when the archbishop had been bishop of Paderborn: "The priest who today does not see that he has a good Borromäus Verein and associated library sins against his duties for the care of souls." Braun certainly had the support of the diocesan leaders of the society, who saw him as indispensable. In the end, proposals for reorganization never proceeded beyond the proposal stage, as the Nazi takeover in 1933 forced the society to refocus its attention on the external enemy to its activities.[80]

THE COLLECTIONS OF THE BORROMÄUS VEREIN LIBRARIES

What a library contains and what is absent from it demonstrate how it interprets its mission. In his recollections, Johannes Mumbauer, who was born in 1867, paints a dreary picture of the Borromäus Verein library of his youth. Dominated by books such as the novels for young adults by Wilhelm Herchenbach,[81] it was a place in which few good things were to be found. Catholic family magazines that published Karl May[82] and other authors of similar ilk were available, but those who wanted something "higher" had a choice only between the "good" Ferdinande von Brackel and Flammersfeld.[83] Heinrich Falkenberg described the Borromäus Verein libraries of twenty years later as "lost posts."[84]

The abysmal condition of the collections of Borromäus Verein libraries was a major stimulus to the changes of the mid-1890s. Motives were mixed. Fear of the competition from other organizations offering reading opportunities, a desire to encourage Catholic literature, the need to educate Catholics for economic success in the modern world, and the hope of preparing them intellectually for the challenges the times presented to their faith were all prominent. The changes of the late 1890s can be interpreted either as a move toward the modern world or as an effort to restrain the intellectual involvement of Catholics in that world. In fact, it was both—a compromise that made some opportunities available to ordinary Catholics to acquaint themselves with contemporary thought, but to do so within distinct limits. The collections reflect that same compromise.[85]

To provide guidance to local Borromäus societies in selecting books, as well as to help individuals make informed purchases for their home libraries, still an aspect of Borromäus activity, different publications were developed. Under Herz the *Borromäus-Blätter* published essays that offered general guidance and lists of recommended books. A model catalog was published in 1907 and by 1918 was in its fourth edition under the name *Literarischer Ratgeber der Bücherwelt.* These various lists give much information about the Verein's idea of the ideal Catholic library. Despite the fact that readers' tastes ran strongly to fiction—by its own admission, at most 7 percent of the circulation of Borromäus Verein libraries was nonfiction—nonfiction dominated them, as it did all library lists of the period. An educational purpose for libraries seemed to preclude serving a need for recreation; justifications of lighter fare for those uninterested in education have a defensive air about them.[86]

Catalogs and lists had a strongly Catholic tinge, although books did not have to be Catholic to qualify as "good." This had been Borromäus Verein policy from its beginning. Herz made it clear that while it was relevant to ask whether a book contradicted the faith or moral teachings of Catholicism and whether it was suitable for "true" entertainment and "genuine" adult education, it was not relevant to consider the author's confession as such. Braun reaffirmed this policy.[87] At the same time, tolerance of non-Catholics was grudging. Johanna Spyri, author of the classic children's book *Heidi,* was slighted with the words, "Johanna Spyri is a believing Protestant; her books, however, contain nothing to damage a Catholic mind." Yet, limited as it was, tolerance in the form of inclusion of non-Catholic authors in Borromäus Verein collections provoked criticism from other Catholics.[88]

All lists included substantial sections on various church-related topics, history, Jesus and the Virgin Mary, piety, and apologetic literature. And the Catholic viewpoint appeared in other ways. The history section of Philipp Huppert's basic collection published in 1899 omitted the great German historians of the nineteenth century Leopold von Ranke, Friedrich Christoph Dahlmann, and Heinrich von Sybel[89] but included the assertively Catholic Johannes Janssen,[90] a historian of lesser importance; the 1918 *Literarischer Ratgeber* did not add them.[91] Few Borromäus-sponsored lists gave much attention to the professional, work-related knowledge that Josef Zimmermann, a member of the staff at the Borromäus Verein's central administration in Bonn considered essential, recommending instead nonfiction that was more general and less immediately practical.[92]

In the area of belles lettres, the confessional orientation is less obvious, particularly as the twentieth century progressed. The 1918 *Literarischer Ratgeber* listed modern authors like Thomas Mann and Rainer Maria Rilke. It included the plays of Karl Schönherr, which were excoriated by Catholic reviewers when performed, even if the description given of his works emphasizes their pitfalls. Classics of European and American literature, past and present, were numerous, but not those of non-Western culture. English and American authors were particularly well represented. The English writers included not only John Milton, John Keats, Alfred, Lord Tennyson, Charles Dickens, and George Eliot, but also writers of lesser stature like R. D. Blackmore, Dinah Maria Mulock Craik, Wilkie Collins, H. G. Wells, and Jerome K. Jerome. The American writers included a similar range of major and minor figures.[93]

The emphasis on adult education dictated that the advising of readers was a central function of librarians. They were there to advise, and to advise in a particular way. Wurm captured the stern, somewhat elitist essence of that view: "The basic principle was that the public library is an institution of adult education, therefore its director, the librarian, must be an adult educator. The library staff, therefore, in no way has as its first obligation the task of giving the public the book it wants, but instead of taking care that the right book goes to the right person." Librarians were educators, whose duty was to try to raise the taste of the reader who wanted only the lightest fiction. The librarian was described as "a field marshal who commands powerful forces" and reminded that "he must also know his battalion."[94]

Emphasis on education tended to limit the librarian's interest in reading to what was educational. Johannes Hönig, something of an expert on books and reading, expressed the adult educator's view of what a man should read. He argued that reading should include a newspaper for breadth, books and well-rounded journals for depth. There should also be literature in all its forms, including novels, epics, and drama. Hönig, like most adult educators, Catholic and otherwise, believed that the goal of education was to produce a harmoniously unified personality, an individual who would find the reading of books not only work but also a pleasure. He acknowledged the right of men and women who had spent their entire day in toil to relax, but his ideas about relaxation showed little understanding of the effect of hard manual work. Relaxation should not be in the cinema, tavern, or dance hall, nor should it come from listening to a radio. What these harassed individuals needed was to repair their damaged nerves, and in his view that could only come through reading. Only reading could establish unbroken intellectual relationships.[95]

A major influence on the thinking of Catholic librarians was the librarian Walter Hofmann. Considerably more authoritarian in his attitudes than the opposing school of public librarians, Hofmann was uncompromising in his insistence that only books of educational value belonged in a library. For those who felt that the true library was distinguished by its educational goals, this was attractive, but there were those who found the emphasis on education overdone. In a speech to a group of Catholics in Hannover that was later printed in *Die Bücherwelt,* Georg Schäfer described Hofmann's approach as "exaggerated educational darkness," and an article in *Germania* in 1926 poked fun at some of the excesses of adult education's adherents.[96]

The reality was that Borromäus Verein libraries might hold educational ideals, but they also provided some entertaining reading, because that was what readers wanted. Fiction was important, whether librarians liked it or not, because from its beginnings a major purpose of the Borromäus Verein had been to combat the abundant material of doubtful character. This material only became more abundant and more accessible as the nineteenth century gave way to the twentieth. If Borromäus Verein libraries did not offer the light reading people wanted, they would get it at a lending library (as opposed to a subscription library like the Borromäus Verein) or newsstand.[97]

Selecting fiction for the libraries was particularly vexatious. In his description of the 1926 edition of the Borromäus Verein's *Literarischer Ratgeber,* Josef Zimmermann described the basic dilemma from the Catholic librarian's point of view. Literature was shaped by the writer's worldview. Authors not only described life, but interpreted it, and, if they had a negative attitude to Catholic moral and religious values, a destructive tendency would inevitably be present in their works. Fiction did not have to be explicitly anti-Catholic to be dangerous to the Catholic reader. The problem was compounded by the fact that few Catholic writers wrote fiction.[98]

Almost all librarians of the period, Catholic and non-Catholic alike, viewed novels as, ipso facto, objects of suspicion; Herz considered 90 percent of them worthless. A 1902 list of books for good Catholic daughters on the subject of novel reading declared: "Not so early! Not so much! Not for such a long time!" Even if the necessity of including fiction was reluctantly accepted, the problem of find-ing appropriate novels still remained. Herz endorsed the publications of Catho-lic presses tepidly, declaring that while they might be worthless, at least they were morally and religiously above reproach.[99]

The 1933 annual report boasted that the Borromäus Verein, taken as a whole, had collections of 4.8 million books, a circulation of 10.4 million, and 490,156 readers. How much they had grown is apparent from a comparison with 1912 when there were only 107,453 volumes, a circulation of 1.8 million, and 237,245 readers. The annual report of 1928 had compared the Borromäus Verein statistics with those of public libraries. In that year the Borromäus Verein fig-ures claimed 3.9 million books, a circulation of 8.4 million, and 415,553 readers. The corresponding statistics of public libraries in 1928 were only slightly larger: 4.3 million books, 11.3 million circulation, and 501,258 readers.[100]

By 1933 the typical Borromäus Verein library was larger and more diverse, vastly different from that used by Johannes Mumbauer in his youth. Broader in scope and outlook, it included recent books on a wide variety of subjects in addi-tion to religious books and books written from the Catholic point of view. In 1924 Georg Schäfer enthused, "Our libraries are not only inexpensive places of pleasure from which one obtains entertainment for a boring Sunday afternoon, but places of serious recuperation and at the same time missions, because books hide forces that can make men better or damage them."[101] His accolades, however, need to be treated with some caution and may well have been true only for larger towns. Im-portant changes had undoubtedly taken place, but the lists of the collections that the Nazis required every village Borromäus Verein library to submit after the 1933 takeover do not present an image of up-to-date, appealing reading.[102]

LOCAL BORROMÄUS VEREIN LIBRARIES

When one switches the focus of attention from the central administration of the Borromäus Verein to the local groups, one enters a different world. Probably the most notable feature is the smallness of most local societies. Naturally, this was not something that the secretariat chose to emphasize, but when a Father Hille-brand reports in 1924 from Grossenlüder in Fulda that he has twenty-four read-ers and lends twenty-five to thirty books each Sunday, or the Deanery of Laup-heim in the Diocese of Rottenburg can claim only five Borromäus Verein groups with a combined total of thirty-one members and fifty-six readers in 1920, the conclusion is inescapable.[103] The vast majority of Borromäus Verein libraries were village libraries, and potential readership was limited in an environment where only the priest and schoolmaster passed for educated. The wonder is not that Grossenlüder had only twenty-four readers, but that it had so many.

Urban areas steadily increased their share of the population in the twentieth century, and big cities became more prominent in Catholic thinking and in Catholic librarianship. At the 1932 Katholikentag in Essen a program on the big city as a cultural entity included a presentation by Braun on the book. He spoke not about reading in general, but about the reading of books and, even more specifically, about the reading of "good" books. By 1933 the annual report of the Borromäus Verein was at least providing statistics on Borromäus Verein service in individual big cities, although its chief boast was its service to villages and small towns. In communities with under 5,000 inhabitants, the average number of volumes held, volumes circulated, and circulation per reader in Borromäus Verein libraries exceeded the averages of the secular public libraries. The report does not make a similar comparison for communities over 5,000, and the statistics are not clear enough for readers to make their own assessment, although a veiled reference to the confessionally mixed nature of big cities suggests that Borromäus Verein usage did not outpace national averages in that category. Whatever the statistics, however, large cities never replaced the village and small town as the dominant milieu of Catholic librarianship, even if the fact that cities were the battleground where the fight against *Schund* and *Schmutz* was being waged did increase their importance.[104]

At the local level, social distinctions were omnipresent. Like public libraries, Borromäus Verein libraries were intended for, and appear to have primarily been used by, the less well-to-do. In the parish of Grossenbaum membership in 1919 was divided as follows: 69 wage employees, such as factory workers, railway employees, and servants; 43 apprentices and assistants in industry and commerce and their wives and children; 31 independent craftsmen, sales people, and handworkers, plus their dependents; 10 civil servants, teachers, lawyers, doctors, and others of similar professions; 4 rural workers; 5 students; and 4 individuals without profession, such as retirees. Equally telling are the figures for membership: 46 percent of the 78 members were "Class III" members, which cost 4.20 M; only 15 percent were 10 M "Class I" members. Anecdotal evidence confirms the scattered statistical data. As a 1929 article in *Die Bücherwelt* began, "It is generally observed and deplored that the registered users of our Borromäus Verein libraries are limited almost exclusively to the lower and middle classes. Only isolated examples of members from the so-called better classes are to be found in our ranks." More than three decades had gone into trying to increase the use of the society's libraries by just such Catholics.[105]

These social demographics were a source of both pride and frustration for the Borromäus Verein. As Herz reminded the readers of *Die Bücherwelt*, the Catholic library rejected the training of a small group of leaders as the purpose of the library. At the same time, the failure of educated Catholics to use the Borromäus Verein was a frequently repeated lament and a matter of deep concern. The reluctance of educated Catholics to use Borromäus Verein libraries touched the fundamental question of the purpose of the society. Educated Catholics might read Catholic literature—although there are some suggestions that Catholic literature roused little interest in anyone—but they also wanted to read other things. They wanted, in short, the books that the Borromäus Verein had decided to forego. Some compromises were made. One example was that certain books, like Sienkiewicz's *Quo Vadis* and Twain's *The Adventures of Tom Sawyer,* were made available to the educated, but only to them.[106]

Librarians took seriously their responsibility to provide readers with the "right" book. Their advice was not something readers could avoid, since they did not have access to the bookshelves. A spirit of tutelage and hierarchy pervaded librarians' advice, which was dispensed on the basis of the reader's profile. Rural readers were treated differently from readers who worked in industry. Women were advised differently from men. The priorities of the librarian were education and the improvement of taste; the readers' preferences were there to be changed.[107]

The upper classes also received special consideration in reading circles. A local society could not offer books that conflicted with the Borromäus Verein's fundamental principles of selection, but it could offer other attractions. If membership in a circle allowed members prompt access to the newest books, it would obviate such complaints from the "educated" as the lengthy wait in lines, the soiled, shabby condition of books that had been used by "other people," and the lack of the newest publications. How widespread this solution was is unknown, but there are reports from some parishes that mention reading circles, and the central administration in Bonn published a handbook that gave practical information on how to organize and manage one.[108]

The Borromäus Verein expected its readers, whatever their social class, to be pious, righteous and, perhaps above all else, earnest. Rules for readers published in 1904 indicate its view of its readers and, in passing, reveal some of the social values it was trying to promote: never read if by doing so you neglect work, because duty takes precedence; never read a book that opposes faith or Christian morals; it is better to read serious and instructive books than purely entertaining books; families cannot be urged too strongly to read aloud together.[109]

Although women did not become members until 1920, they had long been readers, but either as less than full members or as part of a family in which the male head was the Borromäus Verein member. Collections did not reflect their interests and needs, however, unless a special effort was made, as it was in Trier, where a group of Catholic women created and maintained a special collection on women's interests. Recommended lists had nothing for women comparable to the special sections on youth reading.[110]

Probably the most important distinction in the Borromäus Verein was the distinction between clergy and laity. After the *Kulturkampf,* clergy became more and more prominent in the Borromäus Verein, as they did in the activities of the growing network of Catholic associations. The parish priest usually provided much of the initial impetus to establish a Borromäus Verein library, and, as has been mentioned, he then often became the librarian. The role of the higher clergy was exhortation and encouragement. The bishop of Limburg commended the Borromäus Verein, the bishop of Mainz recommended it. The Fulda Conference of Bishops urged Catholics to become members. Pope Pius XI, after much effort by Braun and the papal nuncio Cardinal Eugenio Pacelli (later Pope Pius XII),[111] was eventually persuaded to applaud it.[112]

How large a role clergy should have was a matter of occasional discussion. As librarian, a priest could provide continuity, some assurance of administrative control, and dependable guidance to readers; a layman, however, would be more likely to raise the level of lay participation. In 1912 dissatisfaction with the content of the Borromäus Verein library in Bingen led to charges of declining clerical involvement; in 1931 the clergy of the Diocese of Rottenburg pleaded for more support personnel from the laity. These could be examples either of the swing of the pendulum or the human tendency to pine for what is not.[113]

Ultimately, the test of any library is its success with its users. Statements by Borromäus Verein leaders paint the rosiest of pictures, but evidence that the society libraries themselves provided has to raise questions. Statistics show very low levels of membership, although it must be remembered that secular public library use was also very low. The starkness of the figures is only slightly mitigated by the facts that not all readers were necessarily paying members of the Borromäus Verein.[114]

At the same time, statistics cannot be the only guage of the libraries' influence on individual readers. Readers enumerated in Georg Schäfer's article, the uneducated reader, the naive reader, the romantic, the rationalist, and the aesthetic reader, represent stereotypically the real Borromäus Verein readers, who without the society might not have had access to the same range of reading materials. Deacon Joseph Gerads used even more concrete examples to convey the nature of the Aachen library's work: the mother who came weekly to the library to fetch books for herself and her children, the unemployed youth, the *Gymnasium* student.[115] Borromäus Verein officials would certainly have rejoiced if a library had saved even one soul from the corruption of *Schund* or the dangers of the godless secular public libraries, where librarians practiced so-called neutrality and collections represented a variety of opinions on controversial issues. The very high per capita circulation figures of Borromäus Verein libraries in confessionally mixed urban areas like Berlin suggest that individual readers did find the holdings of these specifically Catholic libraries relevant to their lives.[116]

OTHER CATHOLIC LIBRARIES

Although the Borromäus Verein was the largest Catholic library organization, it was not the only one. A separate society, the Preßverein, was organized for the Bavarian dioceses in 1901, where the Borromäus Verein had not taken root.[117] The Preßverein had many similarities to the Borromäus Verein, but it was not a mere imitation. According to its flier, its goal was "to advance the Catholic press as broadly as possible and to protect the Catholic *Volk* against the dangers presented by an immoral press that was the enemy of faith." Its activities were to include the dissemination of Catholic daily newspapers, dissemination of Catholic periodicals and magazines to reading circles, organization of a Catholic book trade, creation of Catholic libraries, and establishment of public reading halls, a comprehensive plan that reflects the level of social and economic development in these areas in Bavaria. In the Rhineland, commercial channels for dissemination of newspapers and books were more abundant and their producers and publishers better organized.[118]

   If the ambitions of the Bavarian-based Preßverein were large, its accomplishments were modest. Its fastest growth occurred before World War I. Between 1908/1909 and 1913 the number of local Preßverein societies increased from 117 to 326, the number of members from 12,331 to 21,978, the number of volumes from 106,240 to 261,693, and the number of loans from 363,773 to 648,645. As of the end of 1927 there were 804 societies, 34,929 members, 731,178 volumes, and 1,199,536 loans; as of 1931 there were 887 societies, 30,493 members, 854,341 volumes, and 1,387,066 loans. In contrast, the statistics for the Borromäus Verein (which had no geographic limits to its area of influence, despite its focus in the Rhineland) in 1908 indicate that there were 3,418 local societies and 167,030 members; 4,466 societies, 237,245 members, and 1,770,141 loans in 1912; 4,294 societies, 216,266 members, and 5,583,361 loans in 1925; and 5,525 societies and 260,650 members in 1930. The Borromäus Verein was therefore six times as large as the Preßverein in 1925 and 8.5 times as large in the early 1930s. A comparison of the loans in the mid-1920s, however, shows that those six times as many Borromäus Verein members borrowed only 4.6 times as many books, probably because the areas served by the Borromäus Verein, especially the Rhineland where it had its greatest strength, were more urbanized and offered more access to other forms of popular culture than did the areas served by the Preßverein.[119]

Comparing figures emphasizes similarities, but the two organizations had significant differences that numbers do not reveal. Generally speaking, the Preß-verein was perceived as working with Catholic publishers and booksellers instead of competing with them, as the Borromäus Verein was. Reading circles loomed larger in the Preßverein; from the beginning, reading circles were viewed as a useful way to make Catholic journals known, to spread these journals, and to introduce the journals into families that had known only non-Catholic pub-lishing.[120]

Another subtle difference lay in the Preßverein's relation to the clergy. Where the Borromäus Verein was managed by a largely lay committee, although with clerical involvement, the Preßverein was managed primarily by clergy. The Preßverein was founded by the general vicar of the Diocese of Eichstätt, Georg Triller;[121] the Borromäus Verein had been founded by laymen. At a very early stage, Triller was in close contact with the Vatican about his society. In 1902 Cardinal Mariano Rampolla,[122] on behalf of Pope Leo XIII, praised the managing commit-tee of the Preßverein for having responded to the danger posed to the faith by founding the Preßverein. The 1911 annual report of the Preßverein included praise from Leo's papal successor, Pius X.[123] As in the Borromäus Verein, Preßverein ac-tivities were often on a very small scale. A local society could be founded with only twenty people and the membership fee was only 2 M a year. And, as in the Bor-romäus Verein, women could be readers but not members. Among the reading circles, the largest was in 1913 Regensburg with 117 members and 63 journal sub-scriptions; Obereichstätt had four members and sixteen journals.[124]

To some extent these two library organizations, the Preßverein and Bor-romäus Verein, were in competition, but the competition was mainly in dioceses like Speyer and Rottenburg. Rottenburg, a diocese coterminous with the King-dom of Württemberg, is adjacent to Bavaria, but its history and culture were quite different from the history and culture of Bavaria, nor was Rottenburg under the jurisdiction of the archbishop of Munich and Freising. Speyer was one of the Bavarian dioceses, since its territory was part of the Kingdom of Bavaria, but physically and culturally it belonged to the Rhineland. The Borromäus Verein seems to have made particular efforts in Rottenburg, and its records show steady growth there. In 1908 Herz visited Rottenburg to recruit and promote Borro-mäus Verein libraries; in 1915 Rumpf made another such trip; and in 1928 Braun made a third.[125] Lists of libraries show, however, that neither organization achieved complete dominance in either diocese. Local societies of both organizations existed in both dioceses, but the libraries of the two together were far outnumbered by parish libraries with *no* affiliation. The formally constituted library organizations may have been the leaders of Catholic librarianship, but they did not constitute its sum total. It is clear, moreover, that even in dioceses that were central to their activities, as, for example, Mainz was to the Borromäus Verein, diocesan officials expected that general-purpose non–Borromäus Verein Catholic libraries would exist.[126]

The two lists that resulted from surveys by the diocesan authorities of Speyer and Rottenburg (the Rottenburg survey probably dates from 1908, the Speyer survey from 1921) communicate the reality of library service in rural parishes. The "libraries" were very small; collections of less than one hundred volumes were not uncommon. Efforts, even Catholic efforts, were dispersed. Ravensburg, for example, a town of some 50,420 in 1925, had six Catholic libraries. The largest was that of the Familienkreuz (Family Society), which contained 994 volumes. The Catholic associations of bricklayers, workers, apprentices, journeymen, and female workers also had libraries. The comments on the Speyer survey hardly display the burning *Leselust* (desire to read) trumpeted by Preßverein and Borromäus Verein advertising. Instead, phrases like, "There is no interest to be awakened," "little used," "little read," "poorly used," "disbanded," and "no base for a library" are to be found, balanced only by an occasional "great need for reading," "in good order and enthusiastically used," or "steadily increasing borrowing." Großsteinhausen, with a collection of twelve volumes, was described as having a worn out priest. Differences in region and in how urbanized a community was account for some of the differences, but not all.[127]

Despite an occasional rivalry within the fold,[128] the real competition to the Catholic libraries during the period was not internal. It came from the many alternative attractions offered by the modern world, that is, the modern secular commercial world, just as it had in 1845 when the Borromäus Verein was founded. Like all librarians of the period, Catholic librarians felt that the attractive new media of radio and film and the growth of organized sports had cut into their sphere. They felt particularly threatened by the efforts of the socialists to do precisely what the Catholics were trying to do: to create a culture based on a particular worldview.[129]

The most direct competition was from the public libraries. Borromäus Verein leaders and priests alike reiterated again and again that secular public libraries and secular reading groups posed a threat. Typical were the words of the 1929 annual report of the Borromäus Verein director for the Diocese of Cologne: "The intention of opponents' efforts to establish in every district libraries that include all viewpoints in their collections, which will work against the efforts of the libraries with a worldview, becomes ever more obvious. Our libraries must exist to put up competition and to make the founding of such libraries superfluous." In 1930 Braun wanted the bishops to recommend the Borromäus Verein rather than other reading societies to their flocks because "thousands of Catholics, who should belong to us, are members of independent book groups."[130] More vitriol could be found in less formal documents. Father Weyer of Post Lutzerath, Kreis Cochem, prepared a mimeographed letter that he sent to all the dioceses to complain about the reading collections put together for non-Catholic reading circles. Although he wrote at length about the obscenity and shamelessness of the reading groups, he felt that he nonetheless lacked the words to express adequately his outrage at the damage they did in city and country.[131]

When one looks at the German library scene of the 1920s, what Catholic libraries and secular public libraries shared is more striking than their differences. Both tended to be small and both were heavily dependent on membership and user fees for funds, although local government could subsidize either and did occasionally give small supplements. Both had the same mission: the librarian was a relatively educated individual, whose role it was to advise the reader, a relatively uneducated individual. Neither kind of library encouraged anything except serious reading.[132]

The one point that did truly distinguish a Catholic library—whether Borromäus Verein, Preßverein, or independent parish effort—from a secular public library was the philosophical basis, or, as their custodians would have put it, worldview. Catholic libraries were designed to limit the reading of Catholics to books and magazines that were acceptable to the Church, or even better, to books and magazines that would strengthen the Catholic views of Catholics. "Modern" books and entertaining literature were tolerated because readers were going to read them even if the library did not provide them, and it was better to have them make their choice from a collection that excluded the most obnoxious examples. Public libraries were nowhere near as permissive as Catholic opponents painted them, but, from the Catholic point of view, they were too tolerant. The formal resolution of the general meeting of the Preßverein in Bamberg in October 1927 that rejected the guidelines developed by Walter Hofmann, a major figure in public librarianship, because they included books of all views, stands as a defining moment in the history of German Catholic libraries. When it came to the point, the priorities of Catholic libraries had to place the protection of faith and the preservation of their confessional identity above all or else lose their rationale as Catholic libraries.[133]

6

Catholic Art and Its Organizations

An Outline of the Debates

By the late nineteenth century it was no longer possible for Europeans to ignore the metamorphosis in the visual arts that had been underway for some time. One classic history of modern art summarizes this metamorphosis that began in France as a constellation of separate developments: "shifts in patterns of patronage, in the role of the French Academy, in the system of art instruction, in the artist's position in society, and, especially, in the artist's attitude toward artistic means and issues—toward subject matter, expression, and literary content, toward color, drawing, and the problem of the nature and purpose of a work of art."[1] The full impact of the sweeping changes was felt somewhat later in Germany, with expressionism rather than impressionism, but the revolution affected all Western art.[2]

For contemporaries, this revolution in the visual arts was at once bewildering, beguiling, shocking, and sensational. The late nineteenth century was seminal in the visual arts, as it was in so many other areas of human enterprise, and works that have since become clichés were then new, fresh, and exciting.

When the transformation occurred was not quite clear—the dean of German Catholic art historians, Albert Kuhn,[3] ascribes it to the 1870s and especially the 1880s—but by 1900 the perception that there was such a thing as modern art was widespread. The visual arts might have their roots in the traditions of the past, but they were qualitatively different from what they had been before, and artistic creativity had outstripped understanding.[4]

In recent years Hans Belting has argued that the visual arts had greater impact in Germany than in other western European countries. Certainly, Germans took great interest in the visual arts. They saw art as a means, as one more tool to be used in the vital and urgent tasks of inventing their national identity and integrating the German nation. Artistic achievements, like the completion of Cologne Cathedral in 1880 according to the original medieval plan, were national achievements. Art was, in short, a measure of identity. This association of art and identity was nothing new in Germany. Martin Luther had banished Catholic painting from his reformed religion and encouraged his friend Lucas Cranach the Elder[5] to develop a new, Protestant form of religious painting. Artistic styles expressed ideologies.[6]

Because the visual arts communicated meaning beyond their aesthetic purposes, they were a major battleground in the culture wars of the 1890s and continued to be a focus of heated discussion until the Nazi takeover suppressed free speech and artistic expression. The decade of the 1890s was a defining period culturally. Artists and intellectuals had to make judgments about modernism in art, and the resulting divisions were superimposed upon existing divisions.

Although the transformation of the visual arts polarized Catholics along the same lines as it did non-Catholics, setting those who resisted anything new against those who felt change necessary, the terms of discussion in the two groups had important differences. Similar arguments might be used, but they were used to different ends. In the non-Catholic world, cultural modernism was seen as "a threat to the very heart and soul of what it meant to be German." Controversy over museum purchases, the emperor's imposition of his own traditional taste upon the choices of paintings for the St. Louis Exhibition of 1904, and the less well-known argument over an exhibit in 1909 were as much political disputes as they were artistic disagreements. Resistance to cultural modernism had many facets, but the central issue among conservative Germans was the definition and defense of German identity.[7]

This national element was largely absent from Catholic writing on the subject, where the central issue was the relation of art and religion. The question was not whether the Church had a relationship to art, but what that relationship was. A century earlier Bishop Sailer had declared that a religion that gave up its bond with the fine arts was dead; his words may have overstated the case, but Catholic thinkers and clergy clearly believed that art was not something that could be neglected. Conservative Catholics perceived cultural modernism's threat as a threat to the heart and soul of what it meant to be Catholic; those more open to the new insisted that adaptation was necessary for survival.[8]

To some extent Catholic response in the visual arts paralleled Catholic response in literature. It displayed the general pattern of hostility to modern ways, offset by a few scattered voices urging accommodation. It displayed the slow and partial modification of attitudes. There was the same insistence on a narrow morality. There were the complaints about Catholic inferiority and an urgent sense that appropriate Catholic art had to be developed for the new times.

At the same time, the different natures and divergent functions of art and literature in Catholic life produced significant variations in the responses. Art, which for the purposes of this chapter is primarily painting and to a lesser extent the less contentious areas of sculpture, architecture, and decoration, communicates differently from literature and affects its audience differently. Visual where literature is verbal, art easily transcends national boundaries. Its messages tend to be either more subtle or more explicit than those of literature, and it offers different—some would say fewer—opportunities for the expression of values. One contemporary writer expressed these fundamental contrasts in the following words: "Visual art, as such, is an aesthetic shaping for the eye, not for the understanding; poetry is for the ear and for fantasy."[9]

The visual arts were intertwined with the Catholic past in a way that literature was not. The great cathedrals of the Middle Ages, built to worship a Catholic God, were a physical presence in many cities and a daily reminder to passersby of the connection between the Church and art. The paintings of the Middle Ages and the Renaissance had been painted at a time when religion in western Europe was synonymous with the Catholic Church. Rost may have been defensive when he argued that all the art treasures held in Protestant museums could not equal in value and beauty those preserved in the museums of Italy and Spain, but his statement contained more than a little truth.[10]

The absence of the popular-culture dimension was another factor that distinguished debates about cultural modernism in the arts from those in literature. The lower classes were simply less interested in art than they were in novels. Efforts like the journal *Kunst für alle* (Art for All)[11] notwithstanding, art was, as one article in *Hochland* put it, "not generally as important in the life of a *Volk* as artists and those who concern themselves with it would like it to be." This lack of interest in art was to some extent dictated by economics. The working classes were obviously less able to afford art than the bourgeoisie, although Emil Ritter of the Volksverein confused his categories when he wrote, "Without money, there is no enjoyment of art." Art was largely the preserve of the educated and was associated with, indeed, was an indicator of, middle-class identity, and Catholic discussions only occasionally express concern with the impact of art upon the lower classes.[12]

In consequence, relatively few artistic products were produced for lower-class consumption. Nothing in art could compare, either in quantity or content, with the flood of entertaining literature. And such decorative items that were produced for the lower-end market, items like glass paintings and chromolithographs, did not challenge the bourgeois norms of intellectuals in the same way that a trashy novel did. These objects frequently had religious themes; when they did not, the picture was likely to be an unexceptional representation of nature or an historical event. These objects differed from their counterparts in bourgeois homes in quality, not content.[13]

Art's relative lack of resonance in the *Volk* and the absence of threatening commercial artistic products diminished the motivation of Catholic intellectuals to interest themselves broadly in the visual arts. The direct impact church buildings and their decoration could have on religious faith, on the other hand, gave them a strong motivation to concentrate their attention on religious art, which is what they did. In literature Catholic intellectuals had hoped to influence the national literature, but in art their interests were much narrower. Catholic art became largely a matter for the clerics who purchased art, the artists who produced art, and the critics who dominated discussions of artistic issues in cultural journals.

DEFINITIONS OF ART

As in all areas of culture, Catholic critics fiercely debated fundamentals. Definitions tended to be broad statements about art in general, not clear and precise delineations. They included the notions, drawn from various philosophical, theological, cultural, and aesthetic theories, that art consists of the thoughtful, beautiful, and true rendering of an ideal, with internally perceived spiritual satisfaction, that is transcendental; that art is the creation of being; that art springs from the insufficiency of men; that art always reveals something typical and characteristic of the essence of the appearing thing; that art is the most beautiful and finest bloom of all *Volkskultur,* and that it is a powerful spiritual force, a disseminator of ideas, an awakener of the spirit, and a conqueror of the heart; that art is a piece of truth and reality, seen through the medium of individuality; that art is the embodied ideal of beauty, the most beautiful and finest bloom of all culture; that art is complete being, the highest consciousness of the world relationship, and the secret spiritual clarity that gives the true impulses to truth; that art is the transfiguration of nature to truth; that art is not one of the things on which the well-being of man depends, but a trimming and decoration; that art is the expression of human thought; and that art is a heightened ability, a command of the means of expression in the realm of language, tone, or colors, of physical means, which aspires not to be of practical utility, but to give pleasure by means of a quieting of the soul.[14]

Some Catholic writers went a step farther and attempted to define an art that was better and greater in some ways than mere "art," but their efforts produced only a similar collection of inchoate and indeterminate assertions. One writer defined true art as having the power to speak *to* the soul, while for a second it was where the artist spoke *from* the soul. Another saw true art as that which was in accord with nature, by which he meant representational art. Great art, according to another critic, could only be created by great men using the artistic materials of their times, and truly great art was described as that which came, not from ideas (a view derided as the false wisdom of professors), but from spiritual needs that demanded satisfaction. The most perfect form of art was that in which there was complete mastery of form, technique, and material; the highest art was that which served the supreme, religious, and divine idea.[15]

What was meant by Christian art was considered self-evident, but self-evidence did not stop efforts to describe it. Christian art was at once the highest song of art, a bloom on the cross of the Savior, a beam of the transfiguring glance of the resurrecting and triumphant Christ, a way to interpret the Catholic faith, not to mention an economic enterprise. It carried the mark of Christian being. It should come out of the religious experience but not be confessional. It should be a progressive scale to help the faithful to reach God. On the one hand, Catholic art should accord with the spirit of the Church, with Church teaching, and with Church prescriptions. On the other, some critics refused to acknowledge that there was such a thing as a specifically Christian art. A content-oriented approach described it as the art concerned with the person of Christ, with what he had brought into the world, and with the artistic enhancements to the places of worship of the various Christian cults. Nor was the cause of clarity advanced by the fact that critics used Christian, Catholic, confessional, and Church as interchangeable adjectives. In the end, the modern reader is forced to do what contemporary readers must have done: to assume that Catholic writers on art identified Christian with Catholic and Catholic with Christian, unless they made specific distinctions, and to include within Christian art all works created by and for Catholics.[16]

THE PURPOSE OF ART

Like literary theorists, art theorists argued within their own terms rather than addressing essential points of conflict. Their debates, however, lacked the drama of the antagonism between *Hochland* and *Der Gral* in contemporary Catholic literary debates. Consensus existed on the major point: that art had a purpose, one that most Catholic intellectuals agreed was to serve God and the Catholic Church. Secondary objectives like the satisfaction of aesthetic needs, the provision of a bridge between social classes, and the expansion of the printed word were occasionally mentioned, but the dominant view was that art did not exist for its own sake. More than one writer explicitly rejected the popular slogan *l'art pour l'art,* which, according to Conrad Gröber,[17] the archbishop of Freiburg, equated art with God and removed moral constraints. Even a progressive thinker like Johannes Mumbauer expressed art's task in fundamentally religious terms: "to allow the eternal ideas to be reflected in thoughtful creations, to seek to grasp with longing hands divine things and to give them earthly form."[18]

To serve religion had been one of art's earliest functions, and the Second Council of Nicaea (787) had given its role in the Catholic Church precise definition. The Council of Trent (1545–1563) reaffirmed and elaborated the principles articulated at Nicaea. Archbishop Gröber gave them modern phrasing: "Art had soul-caring tasks." The goal of art was not individual expression, or beauty, or education, or any one of a dozen alternative ideals then current in artistic circles, nor was it a substitute for religion. Beauty had value, since man responded to beauty, but beauty was not an end in itself, only a means to some end, such as raising man to a higher world of thought and feeling.[19]

To hold that art is purposeful is to view it as a means, a position most directly stated by Archbishop Gröber: "Art is a way, not a goal." Art, specifically Christian art, was one more way of conveying the Catholic message and carrying on the business of the Church. Pius XI[20] credited art with the ability "to charm the spectator, like prayers rising from the depths of the heart, like hymns of faith, like triumphs of God's heavenly glory." The well-known author of *Heimat* literature Peter Rosegger described it as "an important, unfortunately underappreciated educational factor in modern life; it lifts the heart, it seeks, even nobly, the way to the soul's nobility, it is a Samaritan in time of need, it is an impressive preacher of faith and morals." Catholics agreed with socialists that disagreements about new art were really disagreements about worldviews, not the harmless amusements of artists. Art was yet another field on which Catholics battled, another way of "countering the dangerous effects of modern views." Although Catholics conceded that Protestants had the advantage in music, in art they believed that the advantage was theirs. Rosegger wrote in 1899, with what was considered only slight exaggeration, "One can find many Germans who would like to transfer to the Protestant confession, if the art of the Catholic Church did not have such a strong hold on them."[21]

The development of psychology had given discussions of artistic purpose new significance. An article appeared as early as 1911 on the psychological effect of art on religious feeling. It asserted a relationship between aesthetics and religious life, argued that art strengthened feeling, and attempted to explain the process. In passing, it proclaimed the superiority of Catholic visual arts, of the paintings and carvings of holy images that so effectively awakened the imagination of simple men. These insights may not have been very sophisticated, but they were an important beginning and found, moreover, wide acceptance. At the 1921 Tagung für christliche Kunst (Conference for Christian Art) one Father Remigius Boving[22] declared, as if it were common knowledge, "that [i]t is a psychological law that a work of art affects, not only through what it is, but also through the association of ideas and feelings that it awakens." Art's influence could be used to good or ill effect, as an adjunct to preaching, or to corrupt. Art could strengthen the soul and raise the spirits. At its most fundamental, art was religious.[23]

The Relation of Art and Religion

Religious, yes, but not religion. By the end of the nineteenth century, art had developed a quasi-religious function in western Europe. Some historians go so far as to see art emerging as a replacement for religion, but this blurring of the distinction between the two was not apparent in Catholic discussions: "Art cannot compensate for religion or replace it, as many hastily assert; it can prepare a spiritual atmosphere, in the best case, be a John of a future religion."[24] This 1910 statement did not appear in a Catholic journal, but it expressed perfectly the view of Catholic intellectuals.

Because art's right and proper purpose was to glorify God and strengthen the Catholic Church, artistic issues mattered greatly. The welfare of the Roman Catholic Church was not a goal to question or to compromise. The corollary to the principle that the purpose of art was to serve religion was that artistic interests were subordinated to religious imperatives; the end dominated the means. Content was paramount, good art secondary. Josef Kreitmaier, the Jesuit art expert who wrote extensively on art for *Stimmen der Zeit*, provided a theological basis for this view, although he also argued that the highest artistic standards were essential. The religious function of art also prevented Catholics interested in Christian art from dissociating themselves completely from popular art. They had to accept that what was politely called conventional art, and less politely religious kitsch, was "more suitable for devotional purposes than art sharply stamped by the personal." Given art's primary purpose, they might work to improve popular devotional art, but they could ignore neither it nor those housewives who had the responsibility for the home.[25]

The primacy of religion was stated in various ways, as in the view that to qualify as art, art needed to be rooted in Christian principles. Thorn Prikker,[26] an artist who worked in stained glass, was quoted as having said, "Tell him that art is not the highest thing, that it is much better to be a good man, that art is not more beautiful than a pure soul." Konrad Weiss[27] asserted the same principle, but in more polished terms, when he wrote that art and religion have equal standing, but that religion is what does the conditioning, while art is that which conditioned. Primacy was not, however, a topic that really needed to be explored, since it was unquestioned, and statements on it tended to be more comments made in passing than assertions to be proved.[28]

One unfortunate result of assigning artistic priority to religion rather than to aesthetic considerations was that art acceptable to Catholics was often of exceedingly low quality. If Christian art was underappreciated, as Rosegger had said, it was for good reason. Catholic art had become identified with the Beuron group of painters, and once that identification was established, it was difficult to change. At its best, the work of the Beuron school, following its founding in the 1860s, and that of its predecessors, the Nazarenes, has the charm of good Pre-Raphaelite painting, with which it has much in common.[29] Regrettably, their many imitators did not produce work of the same quality, a fact that was widely recognized. Kreitmaier described religious art à la Beuron as artistic "sweets." The architect Georg Lill[30] was less metaphorical but equally blunt, ascribing the "tragedy" of Christian art to the lack of artistic quality, to cheapness, banality, and hastily done work.[31]

Mass-produced kitsch in the Beuron style was a particularly unfortunate manifestation of Catholic art, and during the period the quality of devotional objects deteriorated markedly. Lill asked the pointed question of what Christian house art can be and answered it with a description of an eighteenth-century wooden crucifix that had been passed down in his mother's family. In his opinion, devotional objects had lost their connection with art and been reduced to objects to entertain and instruct. Kreitmaier tended to emphasize the loss of connection with the *Volk* but shared Lill's perception of the consequences.[32]

ART AND MORALITY

The relationship between art and morality was the most important facet of the relationship of art and religion. Art was not identical with morality any more than it was with religion, but non-Catholics as well as Catholics expected art to provide moral guidance to society. Art was deemed subordinate to morality, as it was to religion, "the bloom on the branch of a moral life and not its root." The two "stood close to each other in friendly fashion." Attempts to be precise about morality were not particularly successful, however, since there was no single, authoritative definition of artistic morality, nor were any statements of moral principles extant that could be readily applied to the visual arts.[33]

Few difficulties were created by general statements like the following from Ehrhard: "For art, that freest of the children of God, these limits [to freedom] are marked by its harmonious link with the remaining factors of the highest cultural life, with truth, which enlightens the spirit, with morality, which arouses and strengthens the will, and with religion, which binds all mankind with God, the prime source of truth and all holiness." More specific guidance about morally positive art was rare, and the usual refuge was to equate morality with the artist's morality. Art was moral or immoral, depending on the intention of the artist.[34]

But intention was interpreted by the critic, and the immoral tended to be defined as whatever offended the critic's sensibilities. Nudity in religious and secular art was a critical issue, as pictures, like literature, became steadily more explicit; the nudity, not only of sexually mature adults, but also of the Christ child was condemned.[35] Gerhard Gietmann[36] described as shameless any portrayal and celebration of nudity. He argued that God had created man good, and the representation of nudity was objectionable since it aroused sensuality. The increase of nudity in the arts was evidence of decadence. Canon Zimmern of Speyer Cathedral disagreed. In Zimmern's opinion, Praxiteles' sculpture of Aphrodite of Knidos demonstrated why nudity had a place in art; she removes her clothes, not to pass the time or to make a public exhibition of herself, but to serve what he saw as a reasonable purpose. After World War I, Kreitmaier, generally conservative though his views were, approvingly quoted Albert Kuhn, the Nestor of Catholic art history, who had written:

> In general, our time is, on the one hand one of reckless freedom in the presentation of the nude, and on the other one of horrifying prudery. . . . This prudery is to be deplored, because it is not a mark of pure, healthful, and strong sexuality, but of an hysterical, effeminate time that demands forbearance and consideration like a disease.

Kreitmaier defended the naked human form; he reminded his readers that the famous papal art collections contained numerous nude works of art, although he qualified his defense by acknowledging that young people must still be protected from exposure to such images.[37]

ANTIMODERNISM

Omnipresent immorality was the principal Catholic objection to modernism. The basic argument was that the present times could not produce great art, and particularly not great Christian art, because they were godless. This position made hostility to all that was contemporary almost inevitable. Antimodernism was a theme in virtually all Catholic writing on any area of culture or culture in general, but it comes through particularly strongly in the visual arts. As Mumbauer put it, "Ecclesiastical interests have generally been very reserved and suspicious toward modern art and not seldom rejected it strongly."[38]

Modern art was condemned for embodying all the iniquities of the present. Not only did it impart a general unhealthiness, its more specific sins included materialism, arrogance, licentiousness, decadence, destruction of public feeling and the sense of shame, and pessimism. It was criticized for its suspicion of everything that had come before it, for its rejection of the laws of nature and all spiritual, religious, and moral laws, and because it was producing too much bad art. Its emphasis on the individual contributed to the erosion of the sense of community. Worst of all was the aid and comfort it gave to revolution.[39]

Although the unacceptable content of modern art loomed larger than its objectionable form, both form and content were subjected to severe criticism. One of the most devastating and comprehensive indictments came from Kreitmaier. In one of his early articles, a review that appeared in 1912, he began by describing modern art as sick in content. His reasons covered a broad range. Kreitmaier considered modern art to be without intelligence, a quality he felt it could not display, since the perpetrators of modern art believed themselves to be descended from apes. Modern art expressed unwelcome viewpoints: it was revolutionary, antistate, and inimical to the Church. It served only the devil, not God. In addition, it was sick in form. Color dominated; mood, color and tonal values, daring contrasts, and soft harmonies were goods that the modernists sought to achieve. The graphic was subordinated, and, if it could not be completely eliminated, modern artists tried to make it as ugly as possible with eccentric movements, bodies with crooked limbs, and false proportions. He concluded bitingly that modern art was displeasing in structure, difficult in outline, hard to understand, and harder still to enjoy. It turned pleasure into torture.[40]

Kreitmaier used *Simplicissimus,* the satirical journal famous for its cartoons, as a symbol of what was wrong with modern art. But *Simplicissimus* was more than a symbol; it brought the antipathy to cultural modernism to a head, outraging Catholics by its mockery of religion, the Church, and the clergy and by its violation of artistic values. Kreitmaier described it as "Satan's work" and charged it with rejecting true art and harming both state and church. Expressing fears for the future, he commented, "The satirical press and mocking art offensively seek not true art—that can be found even in the darkest part of the world or the depths of big cities—but only "*Schlager*," the shock effects that, through their audacity and insolence, astonish and arouse the negative, the *Schadenfreude* that is part of man, ill will, jealousy, and quiet hate.[41] In its depths, the drive to destruction dominates."

Kreitmaier was not the only Catholic to single out *Simplicissimus* as a particularly heinous example of cultural modernism. The *Allgemeine Rundschau* reprinted an editorial from the *Augsburger Abendzeitung* that criticized *Simplicissimus* for its attitude to the fatherland. When the Katholischer Preßverein passed a resolution at its 1913 conference urging Catholics to support the Catholic press through subscriptions and advertisements and to avoid making purchases at businesses that displayed immoral pictures or literature harmful to Christianity, it emphasized that this resolution applied to *Simplicissimus* with particular force. Perhaps *Simplicissimus*'s greatest sin, however, was that it was read by many Catholics.[42]

Catholics were not the only Germans to revile *Simplicissimus,* nor were they the only Germans hostile to cultural modernism in the visual arts. Antimodernism in Germany has been the subject of recent scholarly research, and its strength and pervasiveness from the late nineteenth century onward are now much better understood. Modernism roused the same feelings of threat and abomination in non-Catholics as in Catholics; non-Catholics shared the "diffuse discomfort with modernism" that is clear in Catholic writing. Many of the objections were the same in both major Christian confessions, but, as in literature, a perceived endangerment to German national identity is a much stronger element in the Protestant criticism. With regard to modern art, Catholics (according to Kreitmaier) became uncharacteristically iconoclastic, seeing themselves as more Calvinist than Calvin, but even liberal Protestants had many of the same problems with the ethics and aesthetics of modern art as they had.[43]

Catholic antimodernism in the visual arts contained a strong Luddite element. The organizational meeting of the first society for Christian art in Germany passed a resolution in 1857 excluding mass-produced works from its purview. Again and again writers inveighed against the tasteless outpourings of factories. All the Catholic art organizations included opposition to factory products in their statements of purpose and one, the Tagung für christliche Kunst, in summarizing its accomplishments between 1920 and 1933, proudly declared, "The Tagung für christliche Kunst has fought almost all arrangements that sought to bring kitsch and factory ware, in whatever form, into the Church and the Christian home." This hostility had two sources, one aesthetic, one economic: machine production was equated with kitsch, and machine production threatened the livelihood of the independent artist and craftsman. Both judgments were probably accurate, but opposition to machine-produced art irretrievably stamped Catholic art activity with an elitist character, since that was the only art the working class could afford. A pronouncement in guidelines issued to the clergy was especially arrogant in its phrasing and claimed that everything produced for commercial reasons was trash, an unconscious adoption of the decidedly non-Catholic idea of art for art's sake. In addition this view displayed an overwhelming ignorance of the economic history of art.[44]

Veneration of the art of the past, especially the art of the Middle Ages, paralleled hostility to the art of the present. Catholic preferences, like those of the majority of Germans, were unquestionably traditional.[45] The most positive employment of this nostalgia was to use old art as something from which to learn, and many intellectuals, non-Catholic as well as Catholic, sought to find a distinctively German style in the Middle Ages. What was old, however, had a particularly strong hold on Catholics, because they saw the art of the past as embodying the Catholic values of a Catholic past. To urge Catholics to stand by their principles was to urge them to cling to traditional art, and vice versa. A taste for modern art could be interpreted as disloyalty to the great traditions of Catholicism. The folios distributed annually to their members by the art societies, especially before the war, contained predominantly representations of traditional art.[46]

THE EVOLUTION OF TASTE AND THEORY

As the twentieth century progressed, however, changing tastes began to influence artistic canons. Artists had been creating art that ignored aesthetic "rules," some intellectuals had found the results pleasing, and critical judgments slowly began to accommodate the new realities. In a 1916 article in the Catholic journal *Allgemeine Rundschau,* Oscar Doering[47] denied that there was any absolute concept of beauty. Kuhn himself offered the opinion that all styles are of their time and have no universal but only relative justification. In 1932 Archbishop Gröber rejected the idea that the Church put some specific ideal of beauty before the artist; neither the form of Christian antiquity nor that of the Gothic Middle Ages could be an absolute canon. To do so would be inappropriate, "because the Church is catholic, comprehending West and East, past, present, and future, and knows well that the picture that is beautiful to a *Volk* or race or time corresponds to the character of the time, the *Volk,* and the race." The definitive judgment, however, was that of the Church. Papal guidelines issued in 1925 recalled the principle that beauty is the sister of simplicity, truth, and purity and decreed that therefore nothing that was ostentatious or untrue should be accepted in what was placed in churches, but that everything should be maintained in accord with conscience and purity.[48]

By the end of the period, uncompromising repudiation of contemporary art and a fixation on the past had ceased to be the all-but-universal Catholic point of view. Attachment to the past had begun to be criticized as an attachment to a cold, empty classicism. Few would have agreed that modernism had won, but writers increasingly advocated accommodation. That a compromise was necessary was widely accepted, because, as an article in *Hochland* put it, "The Church must engage the world of today." At a very early point in the discussions, Karl Muth's words, made with specific reference to art, had stated the obvious: "Only if the Christian world places itself in the service of the times . . . will it become lord of the new 'barbarians.' "[49]

Comparison of *Germania*'s treatment of art in the 1920s with the debates of the cultural literati suggests that the majority of educated lay Catholics shared neither the hostility to modern art nor the suspicions of the ecclesiastical interests. In *Germania* modern art was a commonplace, not a matter that needed to be treated with particular sensitivity. Catholic art was well reported, but exhibits of modern artists were also regularly reviewed. *Germania* displayed appreciation of the Bauhaus group[50] and of the modern art of Saxony. Important contemporary German artists like Paula Modersohn-Becker, Franz Marc, and Lovis Corinth were discussed; one article on Corinth raved about his work, its author describing himself as overwhelmed by it. Major foreign figures like Picasso were considered to be of interest. *Germania* covered thematic exhibitions and clearly recognized that each new phase in the development of art would be succeeded by yet another.[51]

Eventually "ecclesiastical interests" and more conservative (*strenggläubiger*) Catholics would bring themselves to tolerate modern art on the basis of the truth that no one time period could claim for itself the totality of the divine artistic ideal. One early advocate of accommodation was August Rumpf, a Munich lawyer and honorary papal official, who argued at the 1909 Katholikentag that Christian art must be modern and speak in the language of the times. What was needed from the artist was service to the faith and honor of God, rather than service or honor in any specific style. His view was repeated with increasing frequency, especially in the 1920s, and often in virtually the same words, that art should speak in the voice of the times. By 1930 Cardinal Faulhaber,[52] archbishop of Munich, was proclaiming that the second law of Christian art was that it should speak *to* its own time. In 1932 the Fulda Conference of Bishops announced: "The Church understands, too, that religious art speaks in the forms of the current times; the Church is no fundamental opponent of a 'modern' art form, provided the latter adhere to the fundamental laws of true art and correspond to the Church's requirements." That same year Pope Pius XI declared that modern art was not automatically to be rejected: "to every good and progressive development of true traditions shall all doors stand open and a hearty welcome be given."[53]

Modern art even began to receive a little praise as Catholic intellectuals showed that they were not immune to the accomplishments of modern artists. In 1926 Kreitmaier admitted that he enjoyed some modern art and credited expressionism with having brought a new way of seeing. Van Gogh's ecstatic curves and his efforts to reach a higher reality, Cézanne's ability to surpass the bounds of nature, and Rodin's pathos were commended. Picasso himself received some kind words. Another writer admired Ferdinand Hodler,[54] a properly Catholic Swiss artist, but also appreciated the work of Käthe Kollwitz.[55] It probably helped that a case could be made for a fundamental similarity between Gothic art and expressionism—the distortions, the starkness of figures, the simplicity of paintings.[56]

This adaptation grew out of new interpretations of what art was. Catholic aesthetics had been classical aesthetics, in which the good and the beautiful were one and the same. Praxiteles and Raphael had been the standards against which all art was measured. But arguments like Doering's—that because there was no absolute beauty, there were no greater or lesser epochs in art—prepared the way for change. Gradually, questions began to be asked like: Why should art not be considered to achieve the highest even when it did not copy the external world? One of the most influential works of the period, Johannes van Acken's[57] *Die christozentrische Kunst,* urged that the healthy principles of modern art should be adopted: its concern for the whole, its simplicity, its closeness to the *Volk,* and its national orientation. Expressionist Christian art became less objectionable, and Kreitmaier's elaborately argued dismissal of it implies that many Catholics were strongly in favor of putting expressionist art in their churches.[58]

The fact was that public taste was changing. As one critic put it, "[T]he old churches with their Romanesque arches, Gothic pinnacles, and baroque pilasters no longer affect the man of today as they worked on those who witnessed their construction." Another pointed out that pastoral needs were now different from what they had been in the twelfth and thirteenth centuries. Not that change was always for the better. Some critics trusted the healthy reactions of the *Volk,* but often popular taste ran to kitsch rather than what the cognoscenti considered art. The commercially successful devotional pictures with their heavenly blues, pretty pinks, and beams of light, the ugly monuments that littered cemeteries, and the coarse plaster-of-Paris figurines invited the epithet of *Schund* (trash) and provided frequent, visible reminders that the *Volk* was not necessarily the best judge of beauty.[59]

As in all cultural discussion, *Volk* was a concept frequently invoked in writing about art, not that it achieved any more clarity in this arena than in any other.

The assumption that the *Volk* was the repository of true virtue conflicted with the undeniable bad taste of many of its members. The *Volk* was described as interested in art and also as uninterested in art. Its purported interest derived from the fact that art was not a luxury but a natural need, its lack of interest from the excessive refinement of art and art's loss of the view of the whole. Some writers argued that art could serve as a bridge between the classes, even to elevate the lower classes; others treated it strictly in terms of its impact on the individual. One of the few uncontested points was that the Church had to interest itself in art for all classes, not just in high art for the educated. With Christian art, the necessity was still more obvious, since Christian art was for the entire Christian community.[60]

ARTISTS AND CRITICS

Most important, of course, in the modernizing of Catholic art were the artists themselves. Like their audience, they too were of their times. As the new century wore on, Catholic artists in all areas of the visual arts began working in the styles seen in non-Catholic art, such as expressionism. Descriptions of the windows of Thorn Prikker, reports of exhibits of modern Christian art in all forms, like that in Munich in 1922, and the portfolios of the 1920s distributed by the art organizations, which include pictures of distinctly modern paintings, sculpture, and graphics, all indicate that by the 1920s Catholic artists were producing recognizably modern art, and modern religious art at that. In 1931 a priest, obviously with some experience in dealing with artists, pointed out that most artists who pursued Church contracts were not interested in making what had always been made, but in doing something different and new. "How," he asked, "can we as shepherds in the Church hold back the 'new' in Church art? Should we admit these works to holiness or should we exclude them from it?" He concluded that artists should be given artistic freedom and buttressed his argument with the tale of two altars by the same individual, one commended, the other, for which the priest had issued instructions that it correspond to the views of the Catholic *Volk,* ignored.[61]

By the 1920s artistic freedom was a frequent topic of Catholic commentators. Earlier discussions of art had approached the issue indirectly, by asserting a particular ideal of beauty or rejecting certain forms, styles, and content. Similar judgments continued to be expressed, but the idea of artistic independence had gradually become more acceptable, with the obvious limitations imposed by the Church's teachings on faith and morality. One cynic argued that artistic freedom meant that the artist was dependent upon the buyer, but by and large writers recognized that artists had to find their own way. The definitions of art that required it to be individual reinforced this view.[62]

Allowing artists independence required faith that they would produce satisfactory works. Above all it required faith in their abilities and character, since art work was held to be good depending on the intention of the artist. There were many attempts to identify appropriate personal characteristics. Rumpf demanded of the artist depth of religious faith, consciousness that the artist creates for the honor of God and the edification of man, and mastery of artistic techniques. Kreitmaier called for firmness, steadfastness, and high spiritual love, and believed that the experience of suffering was a prerequisite for the true artist. Clemens Holzmeister, a practicing architect, felt that a good Catholic upbringing gave the artist a sure sense of what the people and the times needed. Like good Christian art, the Christian artist was to unite Christianity and art; he was to be both the good religious man and the talented artist. He had to experience faith and be able to express it.[63]

Critics, too, had their own identifiable role in Catholic art activities: imparting meaning to the artistic creation. For more than a quarter of a century Josef Kreitmaier wrote numerous articles for *Stimmen der Zeit* that ranged over art in its entirety. Remarkable for his intellectual depth and breadth, no other Catholic cultural journal had any writer on art who compared with Kreitmaier. *Germania* offered regularly intelligent description and commentary from Otto Gehrig, but while his range was as broad as Kreitmaier's, his aims were less ambitious. Georg Lill edited and published frequently in *Die christliche Kunst*, and Fritz Witte and Sebastian Staudhamer[64] in the *Zeitschrift für christliche Kunst,* but their interest was limited to Christian art. Art received some attention from Karl Muth and Emil Ritter, but for Muth it was as an aspect of his broader interest in culture, for Ritter of his interest in adult education. The occasional parish clergyman would write an article to express his outrage at one or another artistic "excrescence," but such individuals usually chose to write angry letters to their ordinary or local newspaper rather than articles for journals with a national circulation.

THE ECONOMICS OF ART

Art was a commercial enterprise as well as a religious and aesthetic endeavor, and because Catholic art usually meant religious art or church art, priests were the most frequent purchasers. Ideally, priest and artist would agree on the form and the way in which the art in question would be executed, but that was the ideal. The reality was that the two had fundamentally different roles in the process, and considerable mistrust was often present. Professional and sometimes personal value systems that had little in common with each other exacerbated the situation. The erudite way to put it was that the clergy were objectively oriented, artists subjectively oriented and individualistic; but in truth, priests were no different from any other buyers. They might not know art, but they were paying, and they knew what they wanted and what they did not want. An elderly artist, looking back in the late 1920s on his own career that had begun with an association with the Beuron group, expressed envy of the younger generation of artists: "They have it easier today; at least they don't have to imitate any one style. I would have been a different fellow if my Church contractors hadn't always prescribed in which style I was to paint."[65]

Priestly taste was no more reliable than that of anyone else. A few, not particularly successful, efforts were made to include art in the instruction of priests, but with the acknowledgment that many men "do not possess an organ for the visual arts." One priest complained to the bishop of Regensburg that parish priests were replacing old church equipment with galvanoplastic ware in an attempt to modernize. A particularly pious priest was reported to permit in his church only what would not offend mothers and children. Proposed solutions included an artistic advisor for the priest. Priests had the additional problem of maintaining parochial harmony; one can sympathize with the parish priest to whom a wealthy parishioner presented a new "ornament" for the church, the obvious cost of which did not redeem its essential ugliness.[66]

The economic features of Catholic art activity had much in common with those of non-Catholic art, although there were differences, primarily deriving from the fact, as Kreitmaier wrote, that "one gets at the values of a religious work of art not exclusively from the artistic side." The market for Christian art was limited, and artists had difficulty finding buyers. No longer were the Church and the princes of the Church the generous patrons they had been before the secularization of much of the Church's property early in the nineteenth century. And with art regarded as of relatively low priority, priests were reluctant to spend what money there was on it. Why, asked a Darmstadt architect plaintively, should an artist be expected to work for nothing, when no one expects a lawyer, doctor, or civil servant to?[67]

Even when they were paid for their work, artists were rarely economically secure. The most fundamental problem was the basic economic law of supply and demand. Whether one is talking about the art world in general or the Catholic art world in particular, by the 1920s an oversupply of artists was a fact of artistic life. In 1934 Bishop Johannes Baptista Sproll[68] stated flatly that there were simply too many artists in the Diocese of Rottenburg. The onset of the Depression had exacerbated difficulties, but signs of trouble had been apparent earlier. As Kreitmaier put it in an essay from 1923: "Many artists live under conditions like those of the simplest unskilled laborers. With remarkable idealism and willingness to sacrifice they fight for their existence and would rather go hungry than leave their beloved art." There were also efforts to restrict what market there was within the Catholic community to Catholic artists.[69]

CATHOLIC ART ORGANIZATIONS

As in the non-Catholic art world, Catholic art societies assumed important functions in the distribution of art. During the period covered by this book, four Catholic art organizations had a national presence: the Deutsche Gesellschaft für christliche Kunst (German Society for Christian Art), founded in 1893; the Gesellschaft für christliche Kunst (Society for Christian Art), founded in 1900; the Tagung für christliche Kunst, founded in 1920; and the Christlicher Kunstverein. In addition, the Mainz Katholikentag of 1851 had created a national Catholic art organization that had held a few general meetings. The central organization did not survive the *Kulturkampf,* but a number of its diocesan offspring reorganized themselves afterward and carried on. Enjoying both a strategic location in the heart of the Rhineland, where so much surviving medieval art was located, and committed leadership, the Christlicher Kunstverein für die Erzdiözese Köln (Christian Art Society for the Archdiocese of Cologne) functioned in many ways as if it were a national organization. The Rottenburg branch of the organization took advantage of its early start to dominate art activity within its diocese. Other organizations existed. A discussion of art organizations that participated in exhibits in 1931 included an Arbeitsgemeinschaft für christliche Kunst (Working Group for Christian Art); branches of a Vereinigung christlicher Künstler (Union of Christian Artists) in Berlin, the Dioceses of Münster, Trier, and Meißen, and the Archdiocese of Freiburg; an Institut für religiöse Kunst (Institute for Religious Art) in Cologne and a Marienthaler Künstler Kreis (Artists' Circle of Marienthal) in Wesel. But to judge from the absence of records and the failure of writers on Catholic art to mention them, they did not have the presence of the Christlicher Kunstverein, Deutsche Gesellschaft für christliche Kunst, and Tagung für christliche Kunst.[70]

With the possible exception of the Tagung für christliche Kunst, the principal associations had strong roots in resistance to modern art and proclaimed similar interests. The Christlicher Kunstverein described its purpose as, "to awaken a taste for Christian art in all forms, to stimulate and direct it in the right paths, both by the research, preservation, and restoration of the old and the care of the new." Like many other mid-nineteenth-century cultural organizations, its scope was broad; its definition of Christian art included Christian architecture, Christian sculpture, Christian poetry, and Christian music. The Deutsche Gesellschaft für christliche Kunst's purpose was to pursue scholarly activity in the area of art on the model of the Görres Gesellschaft and to effect, as soon as possible, a unification of efforts for true Christian art, although a history written thirty years later claimed that it had been founded with the idea of "weaning Christian art from the condition of torpidity and shallowness into which the epigones of the Nazarenes had brought it." The Deutsche Gesellschaft für christliche Kunst's rival, the Gesellschaft für christliche Kunst, asserted that it would both produce and reproduce the Christian art of past and present so that the public would have the opportunity to buy, and it would attempt to create ties between the public and artists, particularly by mediating contracts. The post–World War I Tagung für christliche Kunst had five areas of concern: the future of art in the wake of the recent separation of church and state; the building and furnishing of the new churches and church buildings that needed to be erected; the increase of so-called church art workshops that were not directed by artists; the preparation of future clerics and artists and the education of those already practicing; and support for the efforts to bring good Christian art nearer to the *Volk*. An effort to establish yet another Catholic art organization, the Allgemeine Vereinigung für christliche Kunst (General Union for Christian Art), by joining the Deutsche Gesellschaft für christliche Kunst and the Gesellschaft für christliche Kunst was abortive, but had it been successful, its goals would have been the most ambitious of all. The chosen tasks of the Allgemeine Vereinigung für christliche Kunst included the development of an advisory body for church construction, a professional library, permanent and travelling exhibits of Christian art, diocesan museums, a school of Christian art for both artists and clerics, and workshops for clerical artists.[71]

Although diocesan branches usually duplicated the objectives of the national societies, local statements of purpose are sometimes illuminating. The goal of the Rottenburg diocesan branch of the Christlicher Kunstverein was the care of Christian art in the Diocese of Rottenburg and the advancement of architecture, sculpture, painting and crafts for church purposes. The organization saw itself as having multiple tasks: to provide theoretical instruction in the aesthetic and liturgical principles of Christian art; to describe and study existing art works and their care and repair; to advise on the renovation, construction, and acquisition of art works; and to discourage the production and purchase of unchurchly, unreliable, and unartistic works. The statutes of the Speyer branch of the Deutsche Gesellschaft für christliche Kunst provide a different kind of insight. After affirming its intention of advancing the goals of the Deutsche Gesellschaft für christliche Kunst, it added sharply that "local, personal, and party interests are excluded, and the tasks assigned to the jury of the Deutsche Gesellschaft für christliche Kunst, like all professional business with artists, will not be touched by the diocesan group."[72]

Differences among these organizations lay primarily in practice. The Deutsche Gesellschaft für christliche Kunst set out to be a meeting point for all those artists and friends of artists who cared about art in the Christian sense. Its inaugural statement declared, "Direct communication between the public and the artists will be sought." Its reports on the exhibits it sponsored and its annual portfolios emphasize their economic functions, although both also served educational purposes. The Deutsche Gesellschaft für christliche Kunst's success was contested by one of its founders, the Munich sculptor and professor Georg Busch,[73] who claimed that the society was not fulfilling this responsibility adequately. Seven years later it was Busch who organized the rival Gesellschaft für christliche Kunst, which sponsored exhibits and maintained a gallery in Munich of Christian art.[74]

Exhibits of Christian art, both medieval and modern, were numerous. Most were organized by the Catholic art societies, a few by other groups, like museums or craft associations. Large meetings like the annual Katholikentag might have Christian art exhibits of general character associated with them. There were independent exhibits, special exhibits (often within larger exhibits), smaller local exhibits (often by the diocesan branches of the national art organizations), and "more representative" exhibits for both Germany and foreign countries.[75]

These exhibits were marked by considerable variety. For example, Kreitmaier considered three 1922 exhibitions held in Düsseldorf, Cologne, and Munich to exemplify, respectively, progressive, conservative, and radical trends in modern religious art. Visitors were not universally pleased. The strong emphasis on medieval religious art, whether original or contemporary imitations, undoubtedly left those interested in modern art unsatisfied, but the lack of surviving complaints from promodernists indicates something about their expectations. Objections did come from conservatives. Ernst Lennartz,[76] chair of the Männerverein zur Bekämpfung der öffentlichen Unsittlichkeit (Men's Organization to Fight Public Immorality), protested that at the famous Deutscher Werkbund exhibit in Cologne in 1914, paintings of *saints* were presented in the modern style, that is, in complete *nudity.* (The emphasis is his.) Dissatisfaction with the exhibit at the Essen Katholikentag of 1932 produced the suggestion from the Tagung für christliche Kunst that a series of local exhibits be organized from which a selection could be made for the national event. And the visit of a priest from Iggensbach to the Deutsche Gesellschaft für christliche Kunst's exhibit room, where he was mightily offended by a Madonna he described as a cripple and a freak, prompted a five-page letter in which he gave his views on what Christian art was and was not.[77]

The exhibit at the Essen Katholikentag in fact stimulated a debate, much of which took place in the popular press, that was an abridged version of the larger, long-running debate on art within Catholic circles. The theme of the exhibit, "The Big City and Religious Art," had made controversy almost inevitable, and in the discussions deep divisions were apparent. How experimental should religious art be? How experimental could art be and still be Catholic? And what did "Catholic" mean, in any case, when one was talking about art? The traditionalists attacked the exhibit, the more progressive defended it. Even the antagonisms between North and South were expressed, because the exhibit, which emphasized the experimental, was dominated by the artists of the Rhineland and Westphalia.[78]

Education, particularly of the clergy, was a major goal of all the Catholic art organizations, although they emphasized different aspects and fulfilled it in different ways. Their mere existence, by directing attention to Christian art, made an important contribution. The Verein für christliche Kunst published the *Zeitschrift für christliche Kunst*,[79] and the Deutsche Gesellschaft für christliche Kunst published *Die christliche Kunst*, both of which were scholarly in character. The Verein für christliche Kunst opened and maintained a museum of Christian art. The lectures at the meetings of the Tagung für christliche Kunst were intended to be educational.

The art organizations also provided advice to clergy who were building, restoring, and making purchases of art works. This responsibility was largely left to the diocesan branches where it could be actively pursued, as the report on travel costs of the chairman of the Rottenburg Verein für christliche Kunst shows. In the first six months of 1929, Father Pfeffer[80] visited seventeen towns and villages, all of which were engaged in either adding to or restoring churches, and advised two other paishes on their cemetery monuments.[81]

Educational activities were addressed to other audiences as well. From its earliest days, the first art organization, the Christlicher Kunstverein, hoped to influence artists. The museum it established in Cologne was intended "to stimulate a pure style in art." Its journal, the *Zeitschrift für christliche Kunst*, stated in its foreword that its primary objective was to be a guide and advisor to the practicing artist and that it would provide patterns and plans for art work.

Museums were an especially effective way of reaching the third major audience of the art organizations, ordinary Catholic laypersons, individuals who as consumers of art were viewed with considerable ambivalence, and whose taste was alternately praised and execrated. They were disdained for spending their hard-earned wages on the much-maligned tasteless outpourings of factories. At the same time, a lingering romanticism idealized the uneducated Catholic *Volk* whose rejection of arrogant modern art was considered an attitude to be applauded. Artists, critics, and art societies had to curb their feelings of superiority. However execrable their taste, ordinary laypeople constituted a marketing opportunity, and none of these art organizations wanted Christian art to be just for the upper classes. From an early stage in their activity, public taste had been one of their concerns. In the announcement of its establishment, the Deutsche Gesellschaft für christliche Kunst illuminatingly combined aesthetic and economic elements: "It is of the utmost importance to cultivate and educate the taste of the public, with the intention of awakening an understanding of and need for original works. From this it is hoped that the supremacy of industrialism, the worst enemy of art, will be broken." Museums could be an antidote to poor taste, as well as a means to reach people who would not otherwise be exposed to what they considered good Christian art.[82]

The art societies helped support artists. By bringing their work to the attention of potential buyers in exhibits and portfolios, they performed an indispensable service. In addition, they provided some subsidies to artists. A different kind of support was the attempt to offer spiritual and emotional support. The Notgemeinschaft katholischer Künstler (Emergency Organization for Catholic Artists) was founded in 1932 for that specific purpose. Robert Svoboda, its organizer, dismissed the economic difficulties of the times with the exhortation that churches employ artists rather than craftsmen. The help that seemed most necessary to him was spiritual sustenance. Father Svoboda felt strongly that the artistic personality was the source of many problems, a personality he saw as a schizophrenic type, in which the professional-artistic *I* was separated from the humane-personal *I*. To address the presumed psychological plight of artists, he had earlier organized a committee for "religious deepening" within the confines of the Tagung für christliche Kunst, and this became the primary goal of the independent Notgemeinschaft.[83]

Not that all initiative came from outside the community of artists. A group of Rottenburg artists in the 1920s urged that a retreat for artists be organized at a suitable place, as did the Catholic artists in the Notgemeinschaft. They wanted lectures and participation in the liturgies of the Church that would offer them something they were missing that was important for useful participation in the creation of religious art. The plans materialized; in 1929 Father Pfeffer informed his bishop that the good experience of the previous year's retreat for artists was leading them to repeat it; another retreat was announced in 1932.[84]

Although the Catholic art organizations had many activities in common, each also had its own identity. The annual reports from both before and after World War I of the Christlicher Kunstverein für die Erzdiözese Köln communicate a picture of a group that emphasized preservation of the past. They report in detail each year's acquisitions for the museum, the museum's visitors, and, of course, the number of members. The 2,298 who purchased tickets of admission to the museum in 1909/1910 represented a particularly successful year. October 1910 saw the ceremonial opening of the annex to the museum, an annex built to house the large collection Alexander Schnütgen[85] had transferred to the city four years previously. Those 2,298 patrons, however, represent only slightly more than 6 visitors per day, and the number of visitors fluctuated; three years later only 919 purchased admission tickets, and during the war the numbers dropped even further. Articles in the society's journal demonstrate an emphasis on medieval Christian art. The Christlicher Kunstverein took pride in, and was very much an organization of, the Rhineland, the center of German medieval art.[86]

The Deutsche Gesellschaft für christliche Kunst, on the other hand, was located in Munich, the city of the Munich Secession and a center of modern German art. An organization of the present, its activities focused on bringing artists and the friends of art together, and its decision to hold a meeting in Berlin reflects the assertion of a desire to move beyond Munich and to be a national organization. Like the Christlicher Kunstverein in Cologne, the Deutsche Gesellschaft für christliche Kunst made purchases, but their collection remained a permanent exhibition rather than a museum, and they regularly sponsored competitions and exhibits. Their annual portfolio was sufficiently important to be reviewed periodically. Over time, the reproductions in these portfolios show the increasing influence of contemporary movements like expressionism, a development that ignored the organization's original goal to resist modern art.[87]

The Tagung für christliche Kunst was primarily an annual meeting. Lectures delivered at these meetings covered a wide range of interests, with perhaps an orientation to the practical. A summary of the decisions taken at its meetings by its executive committee shows that they primarily related to practical matters, such as the standards for Christian art, the desirability of professional advice in construction, and the interests of artists. Because a different provincial committee took charge of the upcoming meeting each year, its only geographic stamp was peripatetic.[88]

Inevitably, the associations frequently stepped on one another's toes. Their fundamental similarity of interest was reinforced by organizational similarity. Each followed the same pattern: first a national organization was established, then the national organization tried to establish diocesan organizations. In the end, the small number of Catholics with an interest in art effectively limited each diocese to one art organization. In Cologne it was the Christlicher Kunstverein, in Speyer the Deutsche Gesellschaft für christliche Kunst. The bishop of Rottenburg, at the behest of the Rottenburg Christlicher Kunstverein, wrote to the Deutsche Gesellschaft für christliche Kunst to inform them that he could not endorse the diocesan branch they were trying to organize. He was patron of the Rottenburg Christlicher Kunstverein, which had operated successfully for seventy years; the Rottenburg group, not without reason, feared that the diocese could not support two organizations with such similar aims. The episcopal rebuke did not, however, prevent the Deutsche Gesellschaft für christliche Kunst from recruiting individual members in Rottenburg, and they had already enrolled 260.[89]

The chairman of the Christlicher Kunstverein in Rottenburg had identified a basic truth: the art associations were addressing the same individuals, and many of those individuals were able to afford membership in only one art organization, if that. The membership profiles of the Catholic art societies display marked similarities. In the diocesan organizations the bishop was invariably the patron. In all of them, clergy were a substantial presence and were prominent in carrying out the business of the organization. Artists were, if not rare, in a decided minority, and architects were more likely to be members than painters. Typical members were dedicated individuals, like Alexander Schnütgen in Cologne, a collector and journal editor, Robert Witte,[90] the Dresden architect who was executive secretary of the Tagung für christliche Kunst, and Canon Staudhamer of the Deutsche Gesellschaft für christliche Kunst. How large these groups were is difficult to state with authority, since consistent reports are lacking. The 13,000 members of the Munich-based Deutsche Gesellschaft für christliche Kunst in 1926 and the 1,011 members of the Christlicher Kunstverein für die Erzdiozese Köln of 1909 do, however, make crystal clear that organized efforts to develop Catholic art reached relatively few people, certainly far fewer than were touched by the literary activities of the Borromäus Verein. Ultimately, art was not a form of culture that could easily be popularized.[91]

For all their notable contributions to Christian art, the Catholic art organizations had a carefully circumscribed role. They encouraged, they supported, they promoted, and they advised. They sponsored conferences at which art was explained in learned fashion. But authority over art remained with the Church hierarchy, and it was the role of the Fulda Conference of Bishops to endorse and recommend the activities of the societies. The visual arts were simply too intimately related to religious practice to be left to chance or to the laity.[92]

EMERGING TOLERATION

On the official level, acceptance of cultural modernism in religious art was on the increase as the twentieth century progressed. The contrast between the edict regulating church architecture issued by Archbishop Antonius Fischer[93] of Cologne just before World War I and the statements of Bishop Sproll of Rottenburg in the late 1920s epitomize the transition and the qualified nature of what became acceptance. Archbishop Fischer decreed that only buildings of Romanesque or Gothic style were to be built in the Archdiocese of Cologne; nothing of a later style was acceptable. In contrast, Bishop Sproll of Rottenburg welcomed new styles. He answered his rhetorical question, "Why shouldn't we follow new ways?" with, "The new ways of architecture are certainly not to be rejected if they serve the needs of God's service." In painting Sproll was somewhat more cautious: "the new must be created, taking into acount the sensitivities of our people"; but there, too, he accepted the new.[94]

By 1933 a series of declarations by high Church officials had established acceptance of modern art as the norm. In his 1930 New Year's Eve sermon, Cardinal Michael Faulhaber, archbishop of Munich, summarized the consensus that was developing: the traditions of the Church should be maintained; artists should speak in the voice of their own time; the religious character of art should be preserved; and art should serve God. The 1932 meeting of the Fulda Conference of Bishops affirmed the sacred character of art, but also acknowledged that art had to be of its own time. A 1932 statement from the pope offered a similar qualified, conditional acceptance of modern art. Church officials had come to recognize that modernist styles could serve any ideological interest and that modernist religious art did not threaten religious faith.[95]

Official permission did not mean, however, that the priest who was making an artistic decision about his church would necessarily choose an abstract painting or an expressionist sculpture. To tolerate is not the same thing as to require. Georg Lill credited Cardinal Fischer's decree that all new churches in his archdiocese be built in Romanesque or Gothic style with producing results exactly the opposite from what the cardinal had intended; the temperamental clergy of the Rhineland chose to prefer the opposite of "retrospective" art, namely, expressionism. Lill's comments would seem to indicate that the individual cleric enjoyed considerable latitude, whether or not Catholic officialdom berated modern art.[96]

For enthusiasm about modern art one has to look outside the hierarchy of the Church and to some extent outside religious art. Enthusiasm did exist and it was probably more widespread than conservative Catholics liked to recognize. The articles in *Germania* on important contemporary artists, the abundance of exhibitions featuring modern religious art, the illustrations in Catholic magazines, and even the changes in typography in Catholic newspapers and journals all attest to the interest and growing appreciation of modern art among Catholic critics, artists, and audiences, as well as cultural gatekeepers like editors.

On the individual level, Josef Kreitmaier, the distinguished conservative Jesuit critic, reflects in a personal way the pattern of Catholic activity in art: his writings exhibit slow, often reluctant accommodation, which in the end is followed by acceptance. In 1912 Kreitmaier had condemned modern art as sick; by 1926 he was acknowledging in print that art should be different from what it had been eighty years before; by 1928 he had found some good things to say about modern art; and by 1932 he was beginning to show some signs of appreciating even Emil Nolde, whom he had earlier detested.

Compromise with new times and new ways had been accepted as necessity. By the end of the 1920s even the most conservative of the organizations, the Christlicher Kunstverein für die Erzdiözese Köln, was including modern art in its programs. Nor was this accommodation solely prompted by realism. Irrational though it may have been, despite all the diatribes that deplored Christian art's current condition, throughout the period a small but persistent current of optimism can be perceived. In 1853 Christian art was described as experiencing "a strong and fresh upturn," in 1909 it was judged to show signs of healing, and in 1930 a recent upswing was detected. Christianity might not create art, but individual Catholics, the Catholic art organizations, and the Church worked hard to foster art within the framework of the Church's teachings and traditions, while coming to terms with the challenges posed by developments in secular modern art.[97]

7

Music, Church Music,
and the Cäcilien Verein

Music in Its Varieties

"Music remains the only art, the last sanctuary, wherein originality may reveal itself in the face of fools and not pierce their mental opacity." These words of James Huneker[1] unintentionally describe the effect of a fundamental property of the music of high culture: impenetrability. Incomprehensible to all but an informed few, music does not tend to generate the hostilities that other art forms do.[2]

Unless, of course, we are talking about music in Germany in the late nineteenth and early twentieth centuries. Germans felt a particular sense of proprietorship in music; their musical accomplishments persuaded them that music was *their* national art, in the way that sculpture had been particularly Greek and painting particularly Italian. During the nineteenth century music was "sacralized." A perception that music could be dangerous added to its significance, because it was regarded as having an essential role in shaping German identity. Despite its abstract nature and claims to the contrary, music was also confessionalized and just

137

as politicized as literature or the visual arts. Polemical articles on music appeared in newspapers and journals of general circulation.[3]

Catholics shared this perception that music was important, and their appreciation was not limited to religious music. The discussions about music exhibit much the same configuration as Catholic discussions about literature or the visual arts. The arguments are the same arguments, applied in a different context; the fundamental division is the same division between antimodernists and modernists.

If the transformation of the visual arts introduced an abundance of images that did not conform to people's ideas of art, the revolution in music gave birth to sounds nineteenth-century Western ears found alien. The candidates for a date to mark the beginning of modern music convey the cumulative changes: in 1889 Richard Strauss's tone poem "Don Juan" and Gustav Mahler's First Symphony were performed for the first time; 1907 was the year of Arnold Schönberg's transition to atonality; and by 1920 the new aesthetics of music were well established. An early study of twentieth-century music summarized the change in the following way: "The uninitiated listener seeks in vain for familiar landmarks in this new tonal country which, so far, has been explored principally by those imbued with the pioneer spirit. Melody, harmony, rhythm, form, have changed. There is nothing to guide him; nothing shows him whether he is on the right path." The common denominator in all responses to the arts of the early twentieth century was bewilderment. Laws believed to be immutable had been shown to be not so immutable after all.[4]

Like the other arts, music was divided, between a music of high culture and an emerging and quite separate popular music; during the 1920s the latter steadily increased its prominence in relation to serious music. The two differed both in how they were disseminated and in the social classes with which they were identified. The milieu of the music of high culture was the concert hall and opera house, its most devoted admirers the upper classes. Popular music was less confined, its performances taking place wherever people might gather, whether it was the parish hall or the public park, and was associated by contemporaries with the petty bourgeoisie and lower classes. Both kinds of music were affected by industrialization, as new technology like the invention of sound recording enormously expanded the potential audience for music, but popular music was able to benefit far more from the new opportunities. Entrepreneurs produced music to take advantage of the expanded potential audience. Their music observed very different conventions from the music of high culture.[5]

Commercial music was not, however, the only form of popular music, if popular is used in the sense of widespread. Music was, in the nineteenth century and early part of the twentieth, a part of a way of life "in which education and conviviality each served as the goal of the other." Unlike other art forms—theater is the one exception—music was often a participatory art form as well as a spectator art form. Amateur music making was widespread, both as a social activity in choruses and instrumental groups and within the family. If nothing else, as the music educator Walter Berten[6] pointed out, every human being has a voice. Music was an important part of bourgeois family life. To play the piano was de rigueur for every bourgeois daughter. A painting by Adolf Menzel[7] of the Menzel family around the piano illustrates well this commonplace activity.[8]

Music presented German Catholics with the same conditions that literature or art presented: an experimental music of high culture and a commercialized popular music, in both of which Catholic values were irrelevant. Their fundamental dilemma was the same as in other art forms: Which music was acceptable to Catholics? Which was not? How far could they accommodate change without losing their Catholic identity? To what extent could they use new conditions as opportunities? But an important difference set music apart from other areas of cultural activities. Unlike any other form of culture, music had specifically religious functions; music was not just a decoration but an integral part of the liturgy. Church music was of vital importance, and its importance enhanced the importance of music in general. Speaking to a liturgical meeting in 1928 at Klosterneuburg, one choir director summed up what he believed to be at stake: "A *Volk* that doesn't sing any more is a dying *Volk*, and a religion that doesn't sing any more is a dying religion."[9]

DEFINITIONS OF MUSIC

As in other areas of culture, the nature of the art form was a primary question. What was music? The unstated but taken for granted definition was that music was sounds that had rhythm, melody, or harmony, compositions with both unity and clarity. Stated definitions were both more prolix and more opaque. Catholic writers did not define music much differently from non-Catholics; both usually offered some variant on the Greek conception of music as "an earthly reflection of a higher cosmic order," linked to morality through the theory of ethos.[10] Catholic intellectuals also used metaphors to describe music, metaphors such as speech raised to a higher power, or the true voice of unfalsified and untrammeled nature, or the direct speech of the soul. It was the child of pain, a gift of the deity that had the power to reconcile such contradictions of religion as freedom with dependence and the feeling of being one human among other humans with the feeling of owing obedience to God. It was the expression of life, the mirror of life, a jewel of life, and a true companion; it was the mirror of the times, the mouthpiece of the times. At its most profound it could express a particular world-view. When music was particularly spiritual, as in church music, it was considered to be an aspect of religion and singing a form of prayer. Although articulated by Catholics, these descriptions on the whole complement rather than contradict society's own working definition of music and its role in culture.[11]

In statements of purpose, the religious tinge perceptible in many Catholic definitions of music became more pronounced. One mixed classical elements with Christian: "The purpose of good music is to bring the spirits of men together and in accord with God, which can only happen if the spirit of each individual is in harmony for and within itself." Another commentator presented music as a means to bring warmth to the soul, true joy to life. As far as most Catholic intellectuals were concerned, the principal purpose of music, and not just church music, was as an aid to the care of souls, a way "to bring the loftiness and loveliness of supernatural truths to the *Volk* in sensually appealing forms." Music, as all the arts must, would lead man to God. It had a role in helping man to achieve his ultimate purpose, which was defined as glorifying and serving God and achieving holiness.[12]

MUSIK IM LEBEN

Much Catholic writing about music other than church music came in the form of reviews of performances of the music of high culture or articles in cultural reviews like *Stimmen der Zeit.* Quite different were the articles in *Musik im Leben,* a journal published by the Volksverein that began circulation in 1925. In its relative indifference to both the music of high culture and to church music and its focus on music for everyman, *Musik im Leben* often seems akin to a counterculture publication. No other cultural area had anything like it. Its inclusion of articles by non-Catholics, like the distinguished musicologist Alfred Baresel[13] and the novelist Franz Werfel,[14] only enhances this impression. *Musik im Leben* sought to bring music and life closer together and was interested both in the role of music in the life of the individual and in the social function of music. The journal was the Catholic contribution to the post–World War I challenge to autonomous music[15] that was known as *Gebrauchsmusik* (music for use) or *Gemeinschaftsmusik* (when amateur or community music was emphasized.)[16]

The editor of *Musik im Leben* described music as a "good thing in life, a source of life, a power in life" and saw music as a way to develop the inner life, a way to serve joy. He compared it to the lost paradise of Vineta, the Baltic Atlantis, which occasionally sent sounds from under the sea to particularly needy persons. Another *Musik im Leben* article described music as a guide to religion and philosophy, a means for the individual to achieve a better and more balanced life. Although it subscribed to the premise that "[t]he need for music and the longing for music are fundamentally a religious need and longing," *Musik im Leben* could also publish an article saying that entertaining music was needed. Looking beyond the individual, a fundamental premise of the journal was that music had the potential to strengthen the sense of *Gemeinschaft* (community). This general idea—that music had the power to cure social ills—was a belief shared by many Germans.[17]

Musik im Leben did not merely celebrate music; its editor and contributors interpreted its orientation to the common man as an educational mission. Not just any music could be a means of inner development and a source of joy. *Musik im Leben* wanted to see a discriminating musical public developed and advocated such programs as the development of a second orchestra in big cities that would provide adult musical education and be a source of pleasure for the *Volk*. The music the journal considered appropriate for such an orchestra ranged from works by Haydn and Mozart to Strauss waltzes.

At times concern for the musical life of the *Volk* comes across as condescending, but the sincerity of *Musik im Leben* is patent. Its editor, Josef Müller, set the tone in his 1925 introduction when he declared that music was for all the *Volk*. It was a theme he returned to frequently; three years later he argued that in a *Volk* that considered itself a *Kulturvolk*, all men were worthy of culture, not just those in a narrow social group. The possessing classes had turned culture into something capitalist, cruel, and a means of power, just as they had done with material necessities like housing, clothing, and food. The consequence was a great cultural crisis, especially in music, which had been deprived of its foundations (*Mutterboden*) in the *Volk*. The music of the petty bourgeoisie was disgraceful, a music of overflowing sentimentality alternating with military music of coarse rhythms. Not that Müller's thinking was always consistent. At times the *Volk* was the source of true music, at times it needed to be won for music.[18]

While *Musik im Leben* was the most determined advocate of what one might call "music for the *Volk*," its contributors were not alone in their ideas. Most German intellectuals believed that music should be for a purpose; Catholic church music, after all, was nothing if not *Gebrauchsmusik*, music intended for use. A low opinion of the taste of the lower classes prevailed among those who wrote on cultural topics. The sense of the importance of the *Volk*, *Musik im Leben*'s emphasis on the *Volkslied* as a source of true music, and its belief that the participation of the *Volk* in music needed to be increased were widely shared opinions. What was unique about *Musik im Leben* were its consistent attention to the music in which the *Volk* was actually interested and its efforts to work within that context. The *Volk* was more than just a catchword.[19]

MUSIC, RELIGION, AND MORALITY

Both the power of music and its potential moral menace, underlying themes of much Catholic writing on music, have been appreciated since ancient times. In his 1910 book on the aesthetics of Catholic church music, Anton Möhler[20] described music as both the most democratic and the most dangerous of the arts and marshaled an impressive array of Catholic and non-Catholic philosophers in support. Hegel had written of the great power (*Allgewalt*) of music, Schopenhauer of its unconscious effect, Deutinger of the "inconceivable power of sounds" on the unconscious elements in the soul, and Wilhelm Wundt had described how music directly awakened thoughts.[21] The power of music and its dangers were premises underlying much Catholic writing on music.[22]

Appreciation of the moral potential of music did not, however, produce the same kind of discussion of the relationships between religion and music as emerged in other art forms. The slogan "art for art's sake" was far less frequently heard in music than it had been, for example, in the visual arts. Writers on music firmly asserted purposes for music, but they took for granted that "art" was not one. The abstract nature of music helped mute dissension. An article in the *Monatshefte für Kirchenmusik* did complain that chords without thirds were American, but it was one of a kind.[23] Equally important, the priority of church music in Catholic interest eliminated a large area of debate. No one had to argue that church music should embody moral and religious principles.

Debate about musical morality, therefore, was largely confined to the category of popular music. "Good" music was deemed capable of exercising an improving influence upon the *Volk* and bad music of corrupting. Operettas, for example, were regarded as morally harmful, and modern hit songs decried.[24] A song with piquant lyrics or a tune that used "primitive" rhythms was frequently interpreted by cultural arbiters as a challenge to social propriety, a particularly grievous sin if the song or tune compounded its error by becoming wildly popular. As in the battles over rock music in the second half of the twentieth century, class distinctions and generational conflict were factors, as well as distaste for the commercial character of much popular music.

Usually, the problem of assuring morality was resolved in music as it was in art and in literature by insisting that the creator be a moral person. Desiderata for composers were the same as those for artists and writers: sound faith and good moral character. Whether artistic or literary ability was to be taken for granted or whether it was less important than religious principles was not addressed. One writer offered the following comprehensive analysis: the musician who lived his life without firm moral principles and was unconcerned with heavenly, supernatural ideals, with God and his commandments, could not compose "noble, classical, good music." No matter how much he studied or how refined his musical taste, no matter how accurate his imitations of the great masters, he could not do it. Another writer suggested that the composer imitate the artist of the Middle Ages in his anonymity as well as his music; in this way he would moderate the individualism that modern times fostered. An intimate relationship to the Eucharist would purify and prepare his heart and mind for service of the Most High. An article published in *Hochland* was only slightly more subtle, concluding that, even if musicians were good Catholics, no true work of art could originate without an inner compulsion rooted in religious feeling.[25]

ANTIMODERNISM

Most expressions of Catholic antimodernism concerning music that was not church music are concentrated in the period that followed World War I. Although what Catholic critics found offensive in music had been present before the war—Möhler labeled the big city a musical cesspool (*Musikseuche*)—hostility only became widespread and shrill in the 1920s, when a general pattern of cultural ruin seemed to prevail. The inner confusion of music symbolized the chaos of the times, and music was described as "a sure sign that our social life is sick."[26]

A new element in cultural criticism was the use of psychology. Critics had long talked about the effect of music on men's souls, but now the word "psychology" itself and the insights of the new science appeared frequently. Möhler, the aesthetician of church music, described these insights as psychological facts: "None [of the arts] is so sensual [as music], none works so much on the lower sensing organs of the body and spirit, none exercises so easily an enervating and softening influence on the character, none leads so readily to the creation of an imaginary world and the abandonment of the existing world . . . none leads [people] astray so frequently to disorder, one-sidedness, forgetfulness of duty, imagination, fantasy, enthusiasm. None makes [people] so irritable, obstinate, conceited, capricious, domineering, quarrelsome."

Others used similar language. Walter Berten, who frequently contributed articles to *Musik im Leben*, quoted Schopenhauer approvingly: "No art works so directly upon men as music, because no other lets us recognize the true nature of the world so deeply and directly (direct through feeling) as this." Another critic saw music's role as bringing natural strength out of the duel between unconsciousness and consciousness. The tie between music and the erotic was acknowledged to be "natural."[27]

Antimodernists often singled out individual composers for criticism. Richard Wagner, a man who had dreamed of the regeneration of music, was denounced for having brought only anarchy and decadence. He was blamed for the evolution of music into the opiate of the nihilists and into the fulfillment for the sick desires of soulless big-city dwellers. Mahler had wrestled with the lost spirituality of music but had created only "cabalistic" music. Bruckner's[28] offerings were dismissed as "empty." Max Reger's[29] efforts to fill the forms of old church music with the wasted feelings of modern music were condemned as wicked. Richard Strauss was trashed.[30]

In the 1920s antimodern critics, Catholic and non-Catholic alike, frequently linked modern music with undesirable foreign influences. *Musikbolschewismus* (musical bolshevism) was a conglomeration of referents that associated Schönberg, expressionism, and atonal music—in short, anything that was musically innovative—with political radicalism and chaos, impotent intellectuality, pathology, and the unnatural. According to antimodernist discourse, a bolshevist plot was subverting German music and, by implication, Germany. The angel of darkness came clothed in the light; crowds heedlessly pursued the new fashion in music because fashion was everything. Equally unwelcome, and sometimes equated with *Musikbolschewismus,* was the American influence, which was seen to promote the overthrow of traditional forms and was accused of attempting to kill the spirit of German music. Jazz thus became a paradigm of *Musikbolschewismus.*[31]

MUSIC AND THE *VOLK*

All the heat and hyperbole of the discussions about the music of high culture, however, do not disguise their limited significance. Modern music—intellectualized, atonal, and, above all, strange—had little audience appeal. What did appeal was light, entertaining, and readily available music. Music was fashionable, played everywhere people gathered, in parks, cafés, and beer gardens. Gramophones, records, and, by the end of the period, radio spread it still further. As in literature and art, a capitalist economy was supplying a product to meet a demand.[32]

But acknowledging in the abstract that sentimental music was important in the lives of people was one thing, accepting what was played, sung, and sold was quite another. Criticism of popular music encompassed a variety of complaints; that it was kitsch, that it polluted true music, that it threatened the *Volk*. The situation was described as a "spiritual epidemic" and light music was often described as *Schundmusik* (trashy music). After the sexual explicitness and violence of late twentieth-century popular music, it is difficult to get excited about songs with titles like "Isn't There a Chair for My Hulda?" or "Doll, You Are the

Star of My Eyes," but contemporaries found them, at best, silly and, at worst, offensive and dangerous.[33]

Carnival music was a particular object of censure. Damned for appealing to man's lowest instincts, carnival music was reviled for lacking "the inner values that are a condition of true joy." Josef Müller compared it to alcohol in its failure to nourish, a comparison that reminded the reader of the licentiousness and dissipation for which the German carnival was famous. The German carnival was also associated with the suspension of class, a condition that was almost worse than the spectacle of the riotous lower orders.[34]

Müller's condemnation is one example of the strong correlation that exists between the critics' disapproval of music associated with the lower classes and their disapproval of popular music in general. A regular complaint was the stubborn refusal of the Catholic *Volk* to enjoy what the cultural intelligentsia thought they should enjoy. Paul Marsop,[35] a writer who had some influence on Catholic writers, wanted "better" music offered to people. Karl Schaezler commented sadly in *Hochland,* "It is a particular tragedy that the art of our time, although it stands so close in time and space to the public, through the new technical possibilities of dissemination closer than earlier art to its contemporaries, finds so little resonance in broad circles." Schaezler was something of an elitist, but he was far from alone in this. The raison d'être of *Musik im Leben* was the improvement of the taste of the lower classes.[36]

Much of the hostility to popular music was rooted in its commercial character. Commercialism was a symbol of and surrogate for changing values, social relations, and economic patterns, indeed, for change itself. One writer was acute enough to recognize that it was the low price of popular albums that made them so dangerous. As with pornographic literature, as long as the undesirable was so expensive that only the wealthy could afford it, it was acceptable. When every apprentice and workman—and, where music was concerned, every schoolgirl and seamstress—could enjoy it, the threat to good taste became a threat to society. Democracy in music was not necessarily desirable.[37]

Intellectuals offered two possible solutions. The first was education. Although the suggestion that "secular songs receive Christian baptism" was made, no serious effort was made to produce acceptably Catholic popular songs.[38] Instead, Catholic intellectuals called for the improvement of taste. To win the lower classes for culture, the lower classes needed to be musically educated. For music to strengthen their Catholic cultural identity, they needed to be musically educated. Exactly how this education was to be accomplished was left vague, although Catholics were clearly to take advantage of whatever means civilization had at hand. Concerts, lectures, congregational singing, Catholic clubs and associations, and the good Catholic home were all mentioned. Even popular music, because it helped interest people in music, might, of itself, be used as a path to something better. An article on *Volksmusik* opened with a lengthy quote from Hedwig Courths-Mahler, the queen of trashy fiction, in which she argued that people did not read Jakob Wassermann[39] or Thomas Mann, they read her; it was she who gave them a taste for books. Readers would not have missed the implied analogy.[40]

The second favored way to improve musical taste was through *Volksmusik* and especially the *Volkslied* (*Volk* song), which offered, so it was believed, the particularly attractive feature of a close relationship to nature. The fundamental contradiction was recognized; the *Volkslied* revolution of the early nineteenth century had been largely the work of the bourgeoisie. The *Volk,* a basically rural social unit, was disappearing, and the village was being musically invaded by the big city, facts that did not stop Catholic intellectuals from romanticizing the *Volk* or its music. One article on village musical life rhapsodized about the bells in the morning, the organ in the church, community singing, and the young farmer singing "like a bird's song" as he guided his plow. Only the smallest village would do; larger villages had houses with pianos and phonographs that played foxtrots and popular songs. Articles in *Musik im Leben* were hortatory, and articles in *Volkskunst* gave practical advice, but even in the Catholic associations, *Volksmusik* enjoyed only limited popularity.[41]

DANCE

Catholic responses to dance, a subcategory of culture closely related to music, follow the same general outlines as those in other areas of culture. Like music, dance can be divided into the dance of high culture and popular dance. Apart from an occasional review of a ballet, dance received little attention until after World War I. In the postwar period, new foreign imports like the Charleston and the tango replaced the old prewar social dances. At the same time, the modern-dance movement with its sensuous movements and figure-revealing costumes began to attract interest.

The modern-dance movement stimulated controversy. The most acerbic exchange of views, one might call it a small-scale "*Tanzstreit,*" began when Friedrich Muckermann, editor of *Der Gral,* spoke at a conference on dance in Munich in 1930. Muckermann gave a brief history of the relation of dance to Christianity, including mention of a conciliar prohibition in 622 and two papal interdictions in 731 and 741. He then argued, however, that the modern dancer Rudolf von Laban[42] was doing nothing against Christianity, but rather was building community spirit (*Gemeinschaft*) organically through his dance. Muckermann spoke briefly, and

positively, of another Jesuit, Father Schröteler of the Katholische Schulorganisation (Catholic School Organization), who encouraged the participation of children in rhythmic dancing, and applauded the enrichment that the work of such
dancers as Rudolf Bode, Emile Jaques-Dalcroze, and Isadora Duncan[43] brought
to old forms of dance. He concluded by citing the classical ideal of *mens sana in
corpore sano.* For Muckermann, dance united in a model way activity and pas-
sivity, the individual with the social community, and the soul with the body.[44]

The principal figure on the negative side was the political economist and
aristocrat Paul Westerholt.[45] He criticized Muckermann's remarks but reserved
his main ire for Father Schröteler, who was endangering Catholic education by
exposing the young to the rhythmic-dance movement. Westerholt's condemnation of modern dance was total and vitriolic: modern dance emphasized
the body, in particular the minimally clad female body. He saw it as part of a
American-Freemason-Jewish plot, one element in a larger plan to corrupt the
Volk and undermine the Catholic way of life.[46]

In the criticism voiced by Catholic cultural critics of social dancing, the
language was slightly different, but sexual danger remained the basic theme. According to these critics, the combination of music and dance acted as a narcotic
on the body and soul, and on the fringes of the dance lurked the demimondaine,
ready to seize her opportunity. On a lower social level, the danger was that a young
man might take a girl home after a dance. The more liberal-minded did not find
these possibilities so threatening, but instead argued that German Catholics
needed to learn to enjoy themselves and that dance could help in this by afford-
ing a heightened sense of life.[47]

Catholic discussions of dance produced a fascinating instance of insight
and self-awareness with regard to modern culture as a whole. Contemporaries
recognized that the rhythm of the new dances, "restless, the everlasting, the ham-
mering noise," was, like the rhythm of the race driver, characteristic of the times.
Some understood that the dances symbolized an even more profound change:
the rhythm of life itself had a new rhythm. One critic suggested that the young
were not overwhelmed by this new rhythm because they had been born into it.
Such a statement communicates volumes about the feelings of alienation of the
older generation.[48]

CHURCH MUSIC AND REFORM

Although the underlying issue, the extent to which Catholics should adapt to
modern trends, was fundamentally the same as in other categories of music, we
are in a different world in many respects with church music. For Catholics, it

had to be the category of highest priority. Because music was interwoven with the liturgy itself, church music had the potential to do far more damage than popular music, however obnoxious that popular music might be. Consequently, church music received the preponderance of attention from intellectuals and Church officials. On the other hand, because it was an internal matter, the Church could control it in a way that it could not control other forms of music, and church music could in turn be used to exemplify Catholic values. Church music was, by definition, Catholic music.

Catholic interest in music was so heavily concentrated in religious music that the two often seemed to be synonymous in Catholic thinking. Many Catholics would have found the statement of purpose for religious music given in *Tra le solleci tudini*, Pope Pius X's 1903 *motu proprio* on the topic, an acceptable statement of purpose for music in general: "Sacred music, being an integral part of the liturgy, is directed to the general object of this liturgy, namely the glory of God and the sanctification and edification of the faithful. . . . [i]ts object is to make that text [of the liturgy] more efficacious. . . ." A more poetic description pictured liturgical music as the garment of the Word of God.[49]

Throughout this period, various attempts were made to describe the desired characteristics of church music. The program of the Fifth General Assembly of the Cäcilien Verein in 1874 listed the uplifting of the faithful, religious pathos, and value to the service of God as necessary characteristics of church music, but, because church music was the art school of the common man, popular appeal was also essential. Popular appeal required simplicity, conciseness, and comprehensibility, which might or might not be compatible with more lofty goals. A parish music director used a more down-to-earth list: church music had to be cheerful, spiritual, interesting, and "true." Nearly sixty years later at the Twenty-fifth General Meeting of the Cäcilien Verein in 1932, Bishop Buchberger of Regensburg[50] declared that, like the Church itself, church music had to be built on the firm ground of faith; it must acknowledge authority, historical tradition, and catholicity and generality. These assertions, while illuminating the concerns of those interested in church music during the period, do not exactly provide standards for evaluation.[51]

Because music was central to the Mass, church music was regulated by the Church in a way that no other of the arts was. Among the more significant decrees was that from the Council of Trent in the sixteenth century that nothing "lascivious or impure" be used as church music. A 1749 encyclical of Benedict XIV[52] elaborated on that stricture, specifying that "theatrical music" was not permitted and that instruments like drums, flutes, horns, and lutes were to be excluded from the church. Individual dioceses added additional guidelines; the Archdiocese of Cologne, for example, announced in 1854 that only organ music would be permitted at Advent and during times of fast and that during the last days of Holy Week even the organ was prohibited.[53]

These regulations are a symptom of a discontent with church music that had its roots in the character and innovations of the baroque. As the sixteenth century gave way to the seventeenth, the chant and polyphony of the Middle Ages were replaced by ever more elaborate music. Just as painting, instead of endeavoring to "fortify dogma and elevate the spirit," chose to "gratify the desire of the eye and delight in the display of technical skill," so too did postmedieval music emphasize whatever were the contemporary aesthetic imperatives. An early twentieth-century description of the resulting settings of the Mass uses adjectives like dramatic, sensuous, even flippant. Like opera, church music now had arias and solo performers; composers expressed their emotions. The liturgical consequences were, as the *New Catholic Encyclopedia* puts it, "disastrous." Liturgical considerations were subordinated to aesthetic, and "there were festive occasions that might best be described as 'church concerts with liturgical accompaniment.'" The performance orientation of baroque music also introduced an aristocratic element. Just as the church was supposed to be for all, church music was supposed to be for all, but elaborate productions were expensive. There was good reason for the widespread concern for church music in the mid–nineteenth century.[54]

Despite efforts to reform church music, the problems persisted, and in 1903 Pius X issued his *motu proprio,* a directive that carried the weight of papal authority. It was the work of a pope with a life-long interest in church music, who had introduced reforms as parish priest, as bishop of Mantua, and as cardinal and patriarch of Venice. Building on a century of efforts to reform church music, the *motu proprio* asserted broad principles, covered a wide range of problems, systematized an approach, and gave strong direction to Catholic church music. It went well beyond previous attempts to reform and it dominated church music during the period of this book.

As its introduction makes clear, the pope hoped to eliminate "abuses in the matter of the singing of sacred music." These abuses were of long standing, but earlier efforts by other popes, bishops, and the Congregation of Sacred Rites had failed to eliminate them. Pius X declared, "We think it Our duty to lift up Our voice without delay in order to reprove and condemn everything in the music of divine worship that does not agree with the right principles so often laid down." His fundamental concern was very general, the contrast between the gravity and piety of the celebration of the Mass and the current condition of church music. The passage of time had brought changes in taste to the detriment of sacred music, whether from the unhappy influence of secular and theatrical music or from the pleasure excited by the music itself.[55]

Among the points on which he ruled that concerned ordinary parishioners were those relating to the use of Latin, organ music, and women's voices. The document stated that "[t]he language of the Roman Church is Latin" and affirmed the prohibition of the vernacular during solemn liturgical functions. It effectively limited the role of German church songs in Catholic services and can be interpreted either as an affirmation of the Church's universality or a lack of concern with communication. Because organ music was only reluctantly allowed, and other instruments permitted only with special leave from the bishop of the diocese, much important church music was relegated to church concerts and secondary status. The *motu proprio* defined singers as having a real liturgical office, and because women were incapable of holding such liturgical office, they were therefore not to be admitted to the choir. This issue of women's participation had been a running controversy for several decades between individual parish priests, who needed alto and soprano singers, and their diocesan authorities.[56]

Principles that were of wider significance, but less obvious to those without a particular interest in church music, were the assertion of the primacy of vocal music, the enthronement of Gregorian chant, and the carefully circumscribed acceptance of new music. The *motu proprio* declared that, because of its function, church music had to "eminently possess the qualities which belong to liturgical rites, especially holiness and beauty," qualities found "most perfectly" in Gregorian chant. The more a musical composition was like Gregorian chant in its movement, inspiration, and feeling, the more worthy it was of use in the liturgy. Polyphony of the classical school was cited as a model and pronounced to have reached its greatest perfection with Giovanni Pierluigi da Palestrina in the sixteenth century.[57] Modern music was admissible in churches, "since it has produced compositions good and serious and dignified enough to be worthy of liturgical use," although caution had to be used because modern music was chiefly a secular art. This last statement was prefaced by the acknowledgment that the Church had always recognized and encouraged progress in the arts and used what was good and beautiful in different centuries. The sanctification of Gregorian chant, however, had greater effect than the cautious acceptance of contemporary music.[58]

At the same time, a parallel movement was taking place within the Protestant Church, whose members regarded church music as having been in decline since Bach. Protestants objected to the music of the later eighteenth century because its roots were in Enlightenment rationalism, Catholics to its performance characteristics. But the solution was the same: restoration of past music, although the idealized past of the Protestants was the Reformation Church rather than the medieval Church.[59]

THE CÄCILIEN VEREIN

Pius X's *motu proprio* unequivocally endorsed efforts to reform church music that dated back to the beginning of the nineteenth century. Initially, scholars had sought to restore the original texts of Gregorian chant and polyphonic chorale, and subsequently an organization was founded in Germany that worked to develop choirs to perform the texts. This organization was the Cäcilien Verein, officially the Allgemeiner Cäcilien-Verband (General Association of St. Cecilia), which began in Germany in the 1860s. The Cäcilien Verein was the focus of official German Catholic interest in music throughout our period, and, because more laymen participated in its choirs than in any other cultural activity with the exception of the Borromäus Verein, the laity was significantly involved as well. The scholarly effort to restore liturgical texts and the creation of a society to educate the performers of these texts were intertwined, as evidenced in the Cäcilien Verein's encouragement of musical scholarship; but the two enterprises also remained to some extent independent.

At the center of the reform movement was the desire to assert liturgical correctness as the first rule of church music. The reformers wanted to restore "true" church music, by which they meant choral music. Revolting against what was perceived as the belittling effect of the church music of the eighteenth and nineteenth centuries upon the liturgy, they defined progress as a return to the past. Choral music was the highest form of church music, and Gregorian chant was the highest of the high. Gregorian chant symbolized the Church; its "quiet, measured melodies, because they don't use attention-getting effects, are festive and soulful and advance the piety of the *Volk*." In the words of Pius X's *motu proprio*, Gregorian chant embodied most perfectly holiness, art, and universality, the qualities required in sacred music. The genuine excitement shared by those who cared about church music emerges even from the formal phrasing of the papal document: "Gregorian chant, . . . [is] the only chant which she [the Church] has inherited from the ancient Fathers, which she has jealously kept for so many centuries in her liturgical books, which she offers to the faithful as her own music, which she insists on being used exclusively in some parts of her liturgy, and which, lastly, has been so happily restored to its original perfection and purity by recent study." One priest invoked the words of St. Teresa of Avila to describe it as "a still, steady stream of peace, its own sure blessedness." Gregorian chant was the hallmark of the Cäcilien Verein. The *Volk* might not understand it, but it was good for them. The pope wrote about restoring it to the people, others saw it as a way of improving musical taste, and optimists worked hard to convince themselves that it was becoming popular.[60]

The Cäcilien Verein was founded by Franz Witt,[61] one of those individuals whose interests and abilities seem perfectly matched to their times. Witt was born in 1834 in the village of Walderbach in the Oberpfalz. The son of a teacher, he attended the *Gymnasium* in Regensburg and was then a pupil, and later cathedral prebendary, at the Regensburg Royal Study Seminar. He completed his theological studies in 1855, and a year later, with papal dispensation, the twenty-two-year-old Witt was ordained priest. He was such an exceptional student that his professors encouraged him to pursue further study at the University of Munich with the idea of becoming a professor of theology, but Witt chose instead to serve as a parish priest. [62]

Witt's interest in music began in childhood; the village church of Walderbach was unusually well provided with music. By the time he was fourteen he knew some three hundred masses by heart, in addition to assorted motets, vespers, and litanies. His ability in music was recognized and encouraged during his years as a student in Regensburg. Valentin Riedel,[63] bishop of Regensburg from 1841 to 1857, had committed himself to improving the condition of "degenerate" church music, and the cathedral Kapellmeister, Joseph Schrems,[64] was working to introduce a cappella singing, or song with only organ accompaniment. Witt worked closely with him, and Schrems had hoped he would succeed him.

Witt left Regensburg convinced that only the old masters were "churchly" and that to be churchly, a composer had to compose like them. By 1859 he had written his first compositions, ten verses of a Stabat Mater for three voices and the *Missa septimi toni* for a male choir, both in the style of Palestrina. Performed at the consecration of a church, Witt's work so impressed the new bishop of Regensburg, Ignatius Senestrey,[65] that Witt was recalled to Regensburg where he served as priest and as instructor for chorale, homiletics, and catechism at the seminary for priests. Music had to be relegated to his early morning and late evening hours. During this period Witt became acquainted with Karl Proske,[66] the canon of the Alte Kapelle in Regensburg, a leading scholar of church music with a fine library that Witt was invited to use. Witt described these years as his "musical novitiate."

His years as a parish priest had broadened Witt's understanding of the musical problems of the Church, and in 1865 he published a pamphlet on the state of Catholic church music, *Der Zustand der katholischen Kirchenmusik zunächst in Altbayern—Allen Geistlichen, Chorregenten und Freunden der Musik zu Erwägung vorgelegt. Der Zustand* . . . was simultaneously an indictment of current practices and a call to action. Witt began with the Tridentine decrees that prohibited all that was lascivious and impure in music and demonstrated how what he described as trashy church music (*kirchenmusikalischer Schund*) violated these decrees. He asserted the primacy of choral singing. He then outlined his proposals for reform:

a society for Catholic church music; a popular journal of church music, especially for rural choir directors and instructors; an intensive schooling in church music at the various seminaries for clergy, young men, and teachers; and a school for church music to be founded by the society.[67]

Witt began the popularly oriented journal *Fliegende Blätter für katholische Kirchen-Musik* in 1866 and used it to help create the conditions that would make it possible to establish the society. At the 1867 Katholikentag in Innsbruck he delivered his famous speech about the necessity of reforming church music, a speech that was both a call to arms and a statement of fundamental principles. He published the speech, which contained the proposed statutes for a society, along with detailed criticism of the music offered at the meeting. A year later, the Allgemeiner Cäcilien Verband was founded at the Katholikentag in Bamberg. The school would come later. It was not the first organization formed to reform church music and promote Gregorian chant during this period in Germany, but it would soon become the largest and most influential. In 1886 the Cäcilien Verein was described, with some exaggeration, as "a small world power."[68]

The statutes of the Cäcilien Verein declared its purpose to be the introduction or advancement of "true" (*ächte*) church music everywhere. True music included chorale or Gregorian chant, figured polyphonic music of both past and present, German church songs, and serious music worthy of being played on the organ. The Verein would concern itself with instrumental music only to the extent that it was considered liturgical music and only as it was urgently needed to advance reform.[69]

The statutes explain how the society was to accomplish its reforms. First, conferences for choir directors of four to eight members would be organized. These choir-director groups would hold meetings at least once a year to advise and support choir directors in their task of putting on musical festivals, the second means by which the society would achieve reform. Each year, or perhaps every two or three years, the society of a province or diocese would hold a grand music festival, *not* a concert or a competition, but a church festival with meetings. Third would come the encouragement of composers, choir directors, and organists, for whom an academy within the society would be organized. There would be competitions and grants, medals, honorary gifts, and decrees for them. The most important concern of all, the establishment and education of permanent, continuing choirs, was understood but not stated in these initial statutes.

The initial statutes were vague on the subject of organization, making provision only for a president and executive committee. The bishops were named as potential protectors. From the description of how the organization would reach its goals, it is clear that some sort of diocesan organization was assumed, although it was not described. At the first general meeting, however, it was decided that the society would be organized by diocese, district, and parish. The society's general president would be elected at the general meeting by the membership, then approved by the cardinal protector.[70]

Witt, the obvious choice, became the first president, an office he held until his death in 1888, and began to organize diocesan branches of the Cäcilien Verein. One of the first was established in Cologne, where he sought the archbishop's approval of the statutes in 1868 with assurances that it would not infringe upon his authority. Rottenburg was also quick to organize a diocesan group. The Cäcilien Verein grew rapidly and soon spread to other countries; the ills to which it was a response were not particular to Germany. By 1901 the society could boast that thirty-two (most but not all) of the dioceses in Germany, Austria, and Switzerland had created diocesan organizations.[71]

THE PARISH CHOIRS

The parish societies that carried out the organization's most fundamental task of singing at regular church services were the primary unit of the Cäcilien Verein. As with the other units, their administration gradually became more formal. In 1871 Witt wrote that statutes for these parish groups were urgently needed. He proposed that the parish priest would be the honorary chair, attend choir practices when possible, and look after the Christian behavior of the members. There would be a professional choir director. Anyone willing to practice regularly could be a member, an "anyone" that included unmarried girls, although Witt was uncertain whether married women should also be allowed.[72]

Examples of parish statutes are very similar, and by the beginning of World War I they had become so standardized that forms were being printed in diocesan registers. Parish statutes usually cite, as the foundation of the organization, the papal letter of 1870 that endorsed the Cäcilien Verein, the *motu proprio,* and relevant diocesan legislation. These statutes assert the local organization's care for Gregorian chant, polyphonic chorale both ancient and modern, and German church songs, and emphasize the strict adherence to Church regulations relating to the organ and other instruments. They establish a local administrative committee and specify its functions. They mandate specific activities, such as the preparation of an annual report, special celebrations of the Mass for the Cäcilien Verein, and the acquisition of music, and they prohibit certain other activities. Purely secular entertainment, dances, and Shrove Tuesday celebrations were not acceptable for a group that had a liturgical office to perform. Adherence was expected and enforced, as the example of the parish of Muffendorf in the Diocese of

Cologne shows. An attempt to persuade diocesan officials that the Church could not possibly object to plans for a proposed dance was slapped down sharply with the instruction to conduct the Cäcilien Verein in accord with the statutes.[73]

From the point of view of a parish choir, these Cäcilien Verein statutes, national, diocesan, and parochial, were rigorous, and not every church choir chose to turn itself into a parish Cäcilien Verein; in 1914 the president of the church choir in Gummersbach wrote to Archbishop von Hartmann of Cologne, who was putting pressure on choirs to join the Cäcilien Verein, that the church choir had existed for twenty-three years and had sung to the best of its ability and the satisfaction of its priest without being associated with the Cäcilien Verein. Witt estimated that there were some 2,000 branches of the Cäcilien Verein in all of Germany in 1886. In the Diocese of Speyer around 155 parish branches of the Cäcilien Verein had been organized by 1895, but the diocese had over two hundred parishes. Generally speaking, the Cäcilien Verein was strongest in the Bavarian dioceses, especially Regensburg, and the Archdiocese of Cologne, although inconsistencies existed even in these areas of strength. The president of the Regensburg diocesan society complained that the number of parish branches of the Cäcilien Verein was small for such a large diocese, yet the city of Regensburg had an abundance. That the bishops were periodically persuaded to urge their foundation is a sure indication of the Cäcilien Verein's lack of complete success.[74]

The use of Latin is a good example of the way in which a Cäcilien Verein choir was more demanding than the ordinary parish choir it often replaced. In the late nineteenth century many places used the Latin text of Mass settings only on festive occasions. It was none too popular among the Catholic *Volk,* and there are references to the preference of the people of the Palatinate for German songs and to the attachment of the people of Franconia to the German offices. Latin was sung on feast days, but it was of poor quality in many places. But Cäcilien Verein groups had to use Latin because the music that was its primary concern, Gregorian chant and polyphonic choral music, was in Latin. Discontent persisted, finally resolved by the liturgical reforms of Vatican II in which the vernacular replaced Latin.[75]

Participation in a parish choir that followed the statutes of the Cäcilien Verein made demands upon the individual, although there were many members who served for twenty-five years or more; the Cäcilien Verein of Zweibrücken in the Diocese of Speyer could point to Karl Henn who had joined the choir in 1868 at the age of eighteen and was still singing and attending choir practices regularly in 1930. The initial statutes of the Cäcilien Verein specified only that anyone, including the musical laity, who accepted the principles and purposes of the Cäcilien Verein and paid the dues could be a member, but requirements in regard to personal character were soon imposed. While a good voice was obviously desirable, it was not essential, and in addition to singers, groups also had large numbers of a second class of membership, called "passive" members. These were individuals without musical ability who did not sing. One wonders how the parish of Erbsendorf in the Diocese of Regensburg, which in 1894 had only passive members, managed.[76]

The social class of choir members reflected the social composition of its area. A controversy in two urban parishes in the Cologne area shows significant numbers of members who were teachers, but most choir members in the Cäcilien Verein choirs in Speyer were farmers or workers. One question in a survey in Speyer in 1930 requested information about the social background of members, but no other records suggest any real interest in the social status of choir members; it was assumed that church music was for all. There was also a sense that parents, regardless of social status, had an obligation to encourage boys with good voices to participate.[77]

The truly indispensable qualification was a good moral character, because when singers exercised their holy office, "they represented the angels." Pius X's *motu proprio* declared, "[O]nly men of known piety and integrity who, by their modest and reverent demeanor during the service, show themselves worthy of the sacred duty they perform, may be allowed to sing in the choir." At least some societies took this monition seriously. A testimonial for Karl Johann and Karl Kirsch of Mittelbexbach describes their lives as thus far blameless and their families as "also good." Writing to the Cäcilien Verein of Mittelbexbach, the parish priest of Jägersburg, for example, obviously had some doubts about one of his parishioners: this man was the father of thirteen children, eight of them living; he normally fulfilled his religious duties, but the education of the children left something to be desired, and his daughter Marie's moral character was questionable; he had not been a continuous member of the Cäcilien Verein.[78]

Once in the choir, members were expected to observe the rules of discipline. Good intentions and goodwill were most important, but "each singer had to be imbued with the idea that the demand of the best possible performance can only be fulfilled *through practices,* which are attended diligently, in their entirety, promptly, and with a willingness to sacrifice." In the winter of 1907/1908 in Fürfeld in the Diocese of Mainz, all members of the choir agreed to pay 10 Pfennig for each unexcused absence. The use of young boys in choirs inevitably brought additional disciplinary problems, and after the war there were complaints that these difficulties had increased. Witt's own position seems to have been generally accepted: "I judge the performance ability, the goodness, the educational level of a choir almost completely by its discipline. If it is quiet, very attentive, intent and serious, pious and worthy, it will with its weak abilities achieve excellence, while carelessness, lack of attention, and frivolity will sink even the highest abilities deep into mediocrity."[79]

This level of discipline was one aspect of the first principle of the Cäcilien Verein, obedience to the Church, a quality that made it popular with the church hierarchy, although Witt had denied any ambition of the society to be "more Catholic than the pope." Another attractive feature was that it offered an alternative to non-Catholic choruses, which were viewed as repositories of the revolutionary spirit, a view shared by conservative Protestants. Within two years of its founding, the pope officially sanctioned and recommended the society and appointed a protector for it. The archbishops and bishops willingly issued calls from time to time to their priests to found local chapters. Not surprisingly, despite the obvious necessity for lay participation, the Cäcilien Verein was perceived as being dominated by the clergy, a perception that was strengthened by the customary appointment of clergymen as diocesan presidents.[80]

Not that all parish clergy were uniformly enthusiastic, although in a liturgical matter like this, they had to provide the leadership because they were responsible for the parish's compliance with the musical regulations of the Church. The Cäcilien Verein statutes made the priest the honorary chair of each parish group's executive committee but also expected him to participate actively, selecting music, and maintaining discipline. The outcome was not always happy. Uninterested, incompetent, or abrasive priests could do considerable damage in a parish. Ideally, a musically knowledgeable priest engaged himself to advance church music, which could be a valuable ally in his fundamental task of caring for souls. Ideally, the priest had a good voice and was skilled in chant. Ideals were not, however, always the reality, and the clergy were often the biggest obstacle to improvement. Throughout the period there were repeated calls for more education in music for the clergy.[81]

Of equal if not greater importance in musical affairs was the choir director. Generally, directing the choir was a duty added to the other duties of the local schoolmaster, but the position was a secondary one, and the individual's qualifications for it can only have been a secondary consideration when he was hired as a teacher. Choir directors received little if any training, and the Church was periodically called upon to take over responsibility for their preparation. Musical incompetence was not rare, and there must have been more than one schoolmaster like Herr Geiger, the schoolmaster of Ranfels in the Diocese of Passau, who, in the opinion of the curate, preferred the pleasures of the hunt to the interests of music.[82]

Priest and choir director had no option but to work together. At its best, the relationship was exemplary, such as that of Eichendorf in the Diocese of Passau, where priest and teacher united to found a Cäcilien Verein. But the reality could be quite different, and complaints from one about the other litter diocesan files. Both parties in a quarrel that revolved around the lack of discipline in Marienheide in the Archdiocese of Cologne are represented by letters in the general vicariate. No fewer than twenty-five teachers complained about the parish priest of Waldsassen in the Diocese of Regensburg who, contrary to pastoral instructions, ordered fanfares and marches and prohibited singing at the appropriate points in the service.[83]

That the choir director frequently served without any, or with only token, remuneration cannot have helped the situation. As the Cäcilien Verein report in the Diocese of Rottenburg in 1877 put it, teachers paid more attention when part of their income was related to music. Although parishioners recognized that directing a choir was demanding, they also felt that the schoolmaster, who was often the only educated man in the village besides the priest, was to some extent a Church official. To pay or not to pay was a choice between a traditional idea of obligation and a newer view that contemporaries would have labeled materialistic, although the factor that settled the question was usually the poverty of the parish.[84]

The first annual report of the diocesan Cäcilien Verein of Passau offers a picture of a model choir. After enthusing about the willingness of the members of the parish Cäcilien Verein of Innstadt to sacrifice for the honor of God, the author described the joy of the choir in the beauty of the Catholic service. He praised the "first-class" choir director, the musically educated clergy, and the true cooperation among citizens that permitted the awakening of feeling for all branches of art among the parishoners. He delighted in the rapid growth of the choir in numbers and extolled its performances.[85]

For the most part the activities of the Cäcilien Verein are fairly obvious. Like all church choirs, the choirs of the Cäcilien Verein practiced regularly and performed at church services. What set them apart from other choirs was the emphasis on musical festivals, which took place at the district, diocesan, and international level. These festivals displayed the accomplishments of the Cäcilien Verein and helped maintain morale and attract new members. The international festivals were impressive occasions, biennial events with great pomp and ceremony, involving hundreds of choirs and large numbers of people. A report on the sixteenth festival, held in 1901 in Regensburg, recounts in loving detail the ceremonial Masses, the lectures, the visit to Karl Proske's grave, and the music performed. The report communicates the exaltation of the author; his words convey some of the flavor of the occasion: "the 'Ave verum Corpus' for four voices by Aug[ust] Wiltberger reveals itself as a pearl of nonliturgical music and was excellently sung."[86]

Although the primary emphasis of the Cäcilien Verein was the liturgical role of music and its spiritual contribution, its activities added a dimension that was quite different: a social dimension. The Cäcilien Verein involved the laity in significant numbers and significant roles; without choir members and choir directors, Gregorian chant would have remained unperformed, festivals nonexistent. Participation in a Cäcilien Verein or, for that matter, any church choir, realized in a special way the idea that church music was for everyone.[87]

Members developed a strong sense of Catholic identity and of the behavior appropriate for those who had an important role in the liturgy. A priest in the Palatinate described the effect of the society on youth: "Young Cecilians are now and then attracted away from the blunting search for pleasure to more noble deeds. They regularly attend church services, they remain in contact with their priest and teacher, they join well-run societies where they find an atmosphere of holy art, peaceful activity, and the harmonies of music." Members of the Cäcilien Verein were, in a sense, model Catholics, who were held to a high standard of personal behavior and who publicly affirmed their commitment to the Church and the Cäcilien Verein at special celebrations of the Mass.[88]

Despite the prevailing tone of high seriousness, the parish Cäcilien Verein also offered choir members entertainment. For many, especially in rural parishes, there were few alternatives, although the parish priest of Homburg argued that the social role of the Cäcilien Verein was equally important in industrial areas. But this lighter side was officially acknowledged only by exclusion; Cäcilien Verein statutes prohibited "as such, dances, balls, secular concerts, and theatrical productions of secular content." Interpreting these words was, of course, fraught with difficulties, and every diocesan archive yields examples of disciplinary action over dances or secular concerts. The number of such disciplinary actions increased in the 1920s, one symptom of a major problem the Cäcilien Verein faced after the war: competition from secular culture. Catholics had not been the only busy organizers of societies for this or that purpose, and music groups were particularly popular. The Cäcilien Verein competed with secular choirs for members, and "secular song had more attraction." To survive, church choirs began to perform more secular music, and consequently they ceased to be, in one writer's opinion, true church choirs. Certainly, the fact that many adopted names like "Men's Singing Group and Cecilian Church Choir" reinforces the impression that the focus of the Cäcilien Verein had shifted.[89]

The 1920s were, on the whole, a difficult time for the Cäcilien Verein. One commentator asked, "Has the Cäcilien Verein had its day?" Josef Müller wrote of its fatigue (*Müdigkeit*), of the sameness of the organizations, and of the efforts of performances and festivals to pretend to a liveliness that was not there. Some said the Cäcilien Verein was dying, while others proclaimed its revival. There were calls for renewal. Some groups disbanded, other parishes formed new groups, but the overall trend was downward. Reports of financial difficulties can be found in several dioceses. The diocesan president of Passau wrote to the episcopal ordinary that after the "fizzling out [*Einschlafen*]" of parish branches of the Cäcilien Verein during and after the war, they were now limiting their activity.[90]

And tastes were changing. Church concerts were in favor, at least with singers and listeners, and the "modern" composers disdained by the Cäcilien Verein leadership, Haydn, Mozart, and Beethoven, were now prominently featured in them. These concerts were dangerously close to the secular entertainments prohibited in the Cäcilien Verein statutes, but, for the most part, Church officials seem to have permitted them. The episcopal ordinary in Mainz created an elaborate set of guidelines for such occasions. Josef Kreitmaier addressed the fundamental conflict between pleasure and the original religious purpose of the music that was at the root of objections to the concerts. After considering in detail the difference between secular concerts and concerts of church music, he concluded that religious duty did not preclude enjoyment and that the aesthetic pleasure to be found in church music was different from the aesthetic pleasures of secular music. The pope was less accommodating. In *Divini Cultus,* the 1928 apostolic constitution on divine worship, Pius XI wrote, "It is greatly to be deplored that in certain places these wisest of laws have not been fully observed"; he then proceeded to specify and admonish some of the pretexts used.[91]

Controversy was a feature of the Cäcilien Verein, as it is of any organization with a theoretical foundation, but, perhaps because the Cäcilien Verein was the embodiment of an ideal, controversy was particularly prominent.[92] Many issues were never truly resolved or were obscured by personal animosities. The single most important question was the extent to which modern church music should be permitted.[93] The original statutes permitted their music, and it was frequently performed in church concerts by Cäcilien Verein groups, but the Cäcilien Verein as a whole was never truly comfortable with it. What was promoted, and promoted in a way to exclude all else, was Gregorian chant and polyphonic chorale of a determinedly archaic kind. Palestrina was glorified, his style enshrined as a model and a protection against the dangers of the modern world. The pope was even convinced that Palestrina, had he lived at the end of the nineteenth century, would still have been composing as he did in the sixteenth: "Nor let it be said that if Palestrina were alive today he would write a completely different kind of music. Were Pierluigi da Palestrina among us today he could not, as one understanding thoroughly the rules of the liturgy and art, give us any but music in harmony with the sanctity of the place, and derived from that perennial spring of all sacred music, Gregorian chant."[94]

CÄCILIEN VEREIN MUSIC

An abundance of near-formulaic pseudo-Palestrina liturgical music was composed and served as the staple of Catholic church choirs. All the usual names found in surviving programs and reports were included in a list of music performed in the parish church of Zwiesel in the Diocese of Passau in 1915. Masses by Peter Griesbacher, Vinzenz Goller, Max Filke, Ignaz Martin Mitterer, Michael Haller, and Franz Witt, were sung, and other music by Raphael Molitor, Joseph Gregor Zangl, Josef Ett, and Josef Renner, among others[95] was used.[96]

Palestrina may have been the greatest Catholic composer of all time, he may have been more Catholic than Beethoven, but to freeze everything in his style was to anchor the Cäcilien Verein firmly in the past. Not everyone found that desirable. Wilhelm Kurthen[97] pointed to the Byzantine Church as a cautionary example of what could happen to a church that refused to adapt to new times. The fundamental fact was that "our secular twentieth-century voice . . . sings out in different forms than that of the sixteenth. . . . In our times even the common man of the *Volk* is well acquainted with a much richer world of sound and a much more gripping rhythm." Even an early member of the Cäcilien Verein acknowledged that not everything old is good and not everything new is bad. Kreitmaier praised the modern chorale: "The chorale in its present reconquering form is a high work of art, full of brilliance and splendor. In its simpler forms, like psalmody, hymns, and vesper antiphonies, it is full of quiet greatness. That all songs do not stand at the same heights does not change the general character." The conflict between a sixteenth-century ideal and a twentieth-century audience placed the composer in a quandary. If he followed the path of Palestrina, he was criticized for copying and told that creative church music was needed; if he tried to do anything modern, he was criticized as unliturgical. At the very least, his artistic personality was obscured.[98]

The comment has been made that no composer of distinction wrote Catholic church music during the period in which the Cäcilien Verein thrived. This assertion was largely true, but it is true of Protestant church music as well as Catholic. In the nineteenth century, composers preferred to write religious music suitable for concert performance rather than liturgical music. Where Catholics are concerned, the explanation is not hard to find. Artistic freedom was not an issue. The nature of music produced only the most general guidelines, such as, "What all art, and above all Catholic church music, needs is optimism, joy in faith, hope of salvation, and that splendor, that radiance with which the Catholic liturgy is stamped." It was the pressure to compose à la Palestrina, the austere modernism of atonal music, the then-current fashion, and the minuscule market that added up to a powerful disincentive to compose for the Church.[99]

This question of style, the *Stilfrage* that was at the root of most Cäcilien Verein quarrels, along with the association's musical arrogance and inflexibility, detracts from its many accomplishments. But the problems should not be allowed to overshadow its enormous contribution. To have accomplished its initial objective of replacing the commonly used church music with Gregorian chant and chorale, to the great benefit of the liturgy, was no small feat. It imposed high standards of all kinds on its choirs, and it insisted on compliance with Church regulations. The example set by the Cäcilien Verein influenced other church choirs and encouraged diocesan officials to demand more of everyone. Sober contemporary evaluation applauded its effectiveness.[100]

Unfortunately, the organizational skill of the Cäcilien Verein leaders was not matched by their artistic understanding and accomplishments. The emphasis on excluding bad music rather than encouraging good new music had a paralyzing effect on creativity. The Cäcilien Verein did not nurture creative forces. Instead, it valued new works for their similarity to old and made the basic mistake of believing that art could be created by formula.[101]

Cecilianism had much in common with the Nazarenes, the German version of the attempt to resuscitate medieval art, a similarity that was noticed as early as 1886. Both were rooted in an uncritical admiration for the Middle Ages, both masqueraded as replications of medieval art forms. Yet the Cäcilien Verein and its quasi-medieval music survived where Nazarene art did not, a tribute to the strength of its organization and to the success with which it fulfilled an essential liturgical function.[102]

OTHER ISSUES IN CHURCH MUSIC

At this point, it is well to note that the Cäcilien Verein was not, in the words of Johannes Hatzfeld,[103] the Church, nor was it even church music, and there were many issues relating to church music that extended beyond its confines. One of these was the question of women in choirs. The traditional exclusion of the female voice from the Catholic Church was based on the conventional view that there was "something sensuous and passionate in the female voice—something at variance with the austerity of the ideal that should prevail in the music of worship." The suggestion was also made that the association of men and women "in the sympathy of so emotional an office as that of song" was prejudicial to the complete absorption demanded by the sacred function; certainly, fears that morality could survive such an association are explicit as well as implicit in the records relating to music in this period. The 1903 *motu proprio* unequivocally declared that singers in a church were substitutes for an ecclesiastical choir of clerics and that women, being incapable of liturgical office, could not be admitted to the choir, but this declaration did not resolve the matter.[104]

Women were the exception in church choirs, but they did participate to a limited extent in some parishes, and there was pressure throughout the period to admit them, especially in the 1890s and after World War I. Church music was predominantly choral music, and much choral music required a range of voices. Because the supply of boys able and willing to sing alto and soprano parts was insufficient, many choirs wanted to admit women. The priests and choir directors of these parishes presented a variety of arguments to buttress the obvious; without women's voices they would be limited to a narrow range of compositions. The priest of Bieber bei Offenbach in the Diocese of Mainz tried to convince the episcopal ordinary that since the boys' choir was no longer viable, a mixed choir should be permitted. It would serve to good purpose and "spare our enemies gloating over our misfortune." An entire choir in the Archdiocese of Cologne signed the following, perhaps slightly exaggerated, statement: "The singing in the Mass was so uplifting when women joined in that the church was filled; otherwise, when boys alone sang, it always was emptier. The singing in the minster church especially was so much more appreciated through the addition of women that people from all over the city, people who otherwise did not go to church, attended Mass. Indeed, for that reason alone, many Catholics have not left the Church. Many have even been so moved by women's singing that they remained true to the Church."[105]

Official Church opinion showed signs of uncertainty and transition, but the weight of tradition and pronouncements was definitely on the side of keeping women out of choirs. An 1891 report by the cathedral Kapellmeister in Cologne to the archbishop on the subject began with the Council of Laodicea (ca. 360 A.D.) and the opinion of St. Cyril,[106] who permitted women to sing in a choir but only if they sang softly; men's voices had to dominate in the choir in order to avoid a feminine sound. He also reminded the archbishop that the provincial synod had decided in 1860 to exclude women's voices.[107] An exhaustive article written in 1916 on the liturgical basis for the participation of women harked back to St. Paul's injunction that a woman should not make herself conspicuous by singing and preaching.[108]

In this area, however, practice did not always follow the rules. In the same report that he referred to the provincial synod's decision to exclude women, Kapellmeister Karl Cohen[109] listed the choirs in the Cologne area that included women. Of the subsequent statements from the concerned parishes, that from St. Martin's is the most detailed. Its history of women's participation begins with a graphic account of the difficulties the choir encountered in finding the right voices to sing the high parts. By the time they were ten, the boys from good families were completely withdrawn; bourgeois youth were putting their energy into school. Payments for substitutes were unattainable, and so women were the only hope. Mixed choirs might need discipline, but so did boys' choirs, as any choir director faced with fifty boys taking a break from a practice session knew. The women, on the other hand, were for the most part pious teachers; the implication was that they could be depended upon to keep out of mischief during such breaks. The priest of St. Martin's, Father Linden, concluded with an appeal to authority; Cardinal Bartolini had said that if there was an advantage to using women's voices, then they should be used. He clearly felt he had made that case.[110]

The choir director and organist of Altenessen (Rhineland), A. A. Knüppel,[111] leader of one of the Cäcilien Verein factions in the 1920s, made many of the same points in a 1912 article, "Werden in Zukunft in unseren Kirchenchören Knaben oder Mädchen singen?" (In the Future, Will It Be Boys or Girls Singing in Our Church Choirs?).[112] Exclamation points convey his exasperation at the difficulties of working with boys. He also raised the question of whether it was better to have women singing in a choir than spending time in a dance hall or at the theater.

Nor was the Rhineland the only place that women's voices were used in Germany. In the period before the 1903 *motu proprio*, Oberndorf in the Diocese of Rottenburg reported that it was experiencing difficulties in expanding its Cäcilien Verein repertoire because of the frequent change among female members of the choir. Lists of long-time members from parishes in the Diocese of Speyer show that a number of parish choirs had female members both immediately before and after 1903. Even after the *motu proprio*, it was apparently customary for women to sing in church choirs in southern Germany.[113]

Women's voices again became a prominent issue after World War I. Cries that boys were in short supply were heard. The explanations of the shortage are similar if not identical to earlier ones: secular societies competed with the church choirs for the boys; the boys were needed at home or had jobs; the boys had parents who were socialists and therefore prohibited their involvement. What is different is that the choir members themselves, including the women, were writing to diocesan authorities and not leaving it to the parish priest or choir director. These letters demonstrate an assumption of religious equality and the reality that women as well as men were part of the congregation. They also convey a sense that the times were changing; the minster choir in Essen wrote: "In this time of democracy, when the world of women is seen as equal, the opinion of the archiepiscopal officials is bound to incite [opposition]. This is most regrettable given everything that has to be done. All of goodwill must work together so that the Church remains the victor in the fight against her enemies."[114]

Another choir in Essen produced two extraordinary documents that movingly communicate both the feelings of the women who were being denied the privilege of participation and the men who were their colleagues. In 1919 the choir of St. Maria Empfängnis did not have enough boys' voices. The male singers of the choir were not satisfied with what could be done in these conditions, and so women were asked to join it. They did so, to the edification and satisfaction of the faithful. Now the women were being told by diocesan authorities that they would not be permitted to continue:

> In all other organizations in which we participate, only work and sacrifice are asked of us women. Here we have found a field where we can give expression to our deepest feelings. We experience personal satisfaction in singing in a choir of God. If we are good enough in these times to work in a profession that is not easy, to be active in the Parament and Elizabeth Societies, if we're good enough to do the major work in the Young Women's Organization in caring for the young who have just left school, if we're good enough to cope with the great work of the Borromäus Library, if we're good enough to prepare the First Communion classes, if we're good enough to further the cause of children within and outside of the Jesus and Boniface Societies, if we're good enough to take over the instruction of converts, then ought we not to be allowed to participate in a society where we find not only work but also some personal joy?

These words, from the women themselves, express with unparalleled directness their anger and disappointment, as well as make clear the extent to which the Church relied on women to keep its social organizations going. The women, for the most part teachers, were, moreover, supported by the male singers, who were also primarily teachers. The men wrote that once women's voices were added, song became uplifting and worthy. If women were excluded, it would be detrimental and be interpreted by interested parties as a backward step.[115]

Although no statistics exist, the evidence suggests that by the mid-1920s the presence of women in a choir was no longer the rare exception it had been earlier. The decision was up to the individual diocese, whether it chose to interpret Church decrees strictly or not. The 1914 church-music regulations of the Archdiocese of Cologne announced that in rural areas schoolgirls might be permitted to sing with the choir with the permission of diocesan officials. Archbishop Schulte explained the compromise to the diocesan convocation of the Cäcilien Verein in 1926. A reply from the general vicariate of the archdiocese to a 1930 query makes the details clear. After quoting the 1903 *motu proprio* to the effect that singers had a liturgical office to which women could not be admitted, the official admitted that because boys were lacking in many places, women had been allowed to sing in choirs in the last decade. But this leniency came with the understanding that women's voices should only strengthen the boys' voices. Many parishes overlooked this limitation and used only women for alto and soprano parts, but their practice corresponded in no way to the opinion of the Church, still less had it compelled the archbishop to license women to be full members of choirs.[116]

Officials in Mainz were less flexible, at least in tone. A 1927 document sent to all deans informed them that Mainz would adhere strictly to the Church's regulations, although, at roughly the same time, the choir of St. Paul in Offenbach announced in its semicentennial history that women had been singing with the choir for three years. Pope Pius XII finally resolved the conflict between rules and practice some years later with his pronouncement that women were allowed to sing in choirs, providing they remained outside the sanctuary and behaved appropriately.[117]

Another aspect of church music that was broader than the Cäcilien Verein was the German hymn, much beloved by the *Volk*. Although the Cäcilien Verein statutes included the advancement of these hymns among their goals, the association's dedication to Gregorian chant did not leave much room for anything else, and the furtherance of hymns was left to others. Kreitmaier compared choral music and hymns: "Church music has much trouble with, and concern for, her favorite children. While the firstborn, the chorale, has achieved a thoughtful, poetic nature that is always close to the ideal, it puts up with practical life with difficulty. The *Volk* hymn possesses a sanguine tendency that brings the good side of a character to dominance only with the most farsighted and intelligent instructional methods."[118]

To a considerable extent the hymn was a *Volkslied,* beyond official control or the influence of the intellectual elite. Musically, it flouted aesthetic principles. The long-time president of the Cäcilien Verein of the Diocese of Cologne, Friedrich Koenen,[119] wrote to Witt, "If we demand that the church *Volkslied* agree in tonality with Gregorian chant, few of our present church songs will remain." The familiar Christmas carol "Silent Night," attacked in 1897 by the cathedral Kapellmeister of Mainz for its lack of judgment, false sentimentality, worldliness, and tastelessness, survived unscathed in the affections of the *Volk*. Church officials were forced to recognize that the *Volk* had its own taste and to make some musical concessions.[120]

Most dioceses had their own hymnals and saw them as important elements in their local identity. Passau, for example, sharply rejected a collection of church songs put together to promote loyalty to the Kingdom of Bavaria: "This book may be appropriate for Bamberg and Würzburg, but for the Diocese of Passau it is *not*." During World War I a national songbook became a priority; the many variations and different versions of hymns meant that German soldiers had few in common. In 1916 a collection of twenty-three hymns was published. Protestants, too, developed a common hymnal during the war.[121]

Hymns were as popular with the clergy as they were with parishioners, but for different reasons. A document from the early 1920s in the Cologne archives states the archdiocese's position: "Of the greatest pastoral importance is the most frequent possible participation of the faithful in church singing. It fills their hearts with true joy in faith and lets them properly experience the beauty of the Catholic liturgy and recognize the Church year in its wonderful celestial significance. It fills hearts completely with love and thankfulness toward the Church, influences in a beneficial way the complete religious life of the faithful, in particular family life, and offers strong protection against the dangers that threaten the religious life of Catholic Christians." Priests were advised to devote their best efforts to encouraging parishioners to participate in singing and then given some practical suggestions: they should not turn over the selection of hymns completely to the organist or choir director; they should avoid introducing too many new songs; they should not allow the choir to sing too fast or permit inappropriate organ playing, which, because of its tempo and poorly chosen harmonies, would make singing difficult instead of enhancing it.[122]

Ultimately, church music of all kinds was significant because of its effect on the listener. The skeptic may find claims of the efficacy of hymns or other music in saving Catholics from lapsing from the practice of their faith less than convincing, but personal testimony suggests differently. A Dr. H. offered the following ecstatic impression:

> Chorale! You wonderflower of music. . . . A blessing of wishing to be a child again sweeps through my breast as I quietly hum to myself the Gloria as it resounds to heaven. And I sing it again. And so it compels me from the Sanctus to the Dona nobis pacem. Yes, you, O sweet Virgin, brought peace with your birth, the peace of heaven, how wonderful, how blissful it sounds in those soft F-major sounds. And in the hymn of the Communio my soul rejoices in the *Beata viscera* (beautiful being) of the Bride of the Holy Ghost. And how many of these cadenzas sound jubilantly through all this wide-ranging song. Whole lines without a word. Which spoken word would be adequate to praise the Queen of Heaven with her due?
>
> Outside blows the cold autumn wind. The heavens, cloudless for weeks, are darkly covered, deep down. What do I do? I don't see it. In my soul there is a heaven full of brightening colors. You wonderflower chorale! How I give thanks to my good God, that He has given the gift of you, the wonder of all music wonders, a whole world of delight, full of beauty and joy, as it has been in my heart for days. Today it became for me a flower

garden, where I could pick roses, asters, and bright feathery blooms to praise the one, the heavenly Woman.

Not every statement was so florid, but even a sober description of the role of a choir in a rural area conveys some idea of the centrality of church music to German Catholic life, as Maria Müller-Gögler's[123] memoirs of her childhood attest. In the parish church, all Catholics who attended a Mass with music were being exposed to what was unquestionably high culture, even if their reason for being there was not cultural. In the area of music, the Church was truly functioning as a school of the arts for the common man, although its instruction was limited to traditional forms of music.[124]

Concern for the musical taste of the *Volk* was one element in how the didactic role of the Church was understood. Critics argued that, because music was an intimate part of the edification to which the *Volk* had a right and a way of winning the proletariat for Catholic culture, the clergy had an obligation to study the difficulties latent in the "soul of the *Volk*"—the strength of prejudices, the power of the familiar, and the weaknesses of human ability. Then, slowly, the *Volk* needed to be led to an appreciation of greatness and beauty. It could be done and had been done before. When Gregorian chant was revived, the *Volk* had initially found it alien, cold, and inimical, but the admirers of Gregorian chant believed that they had nonetheless come to appreciate it.[125]

With all the regulation to which church music was subject, the personal taste of parishioners was allowed practically no latitude; taste became an issue only when secular music was involved. For the many social groups that were an integral part of parish life, music was an essential part of almost every gathering. The following description is no exaggeration: "At presentations of a play, one likes to hear music in the interval. For the evening of song by a choral group and choral division, one wants breadth in selections and additional instrumental music. A lecture evening will be more appreciated with music, and a true family evening is unthinkable without music." In addition, there were Catholic music groups other than choirs, such as the Catholic trumpeters of Oberflörsheim in the Diocese of Mainz. The Church appreciated that music had important socializing functions and demonstrated that awareness by encouraging the musical activities of societies.[126]

Establishing musical standards for these groups was relatively easy. They could be advised in earnest articles in *Volkskunst* and in other Catholic journals. Reviews were available, and the journals suggested sample programs. More direct influence came from the parish priest, who exercised at least nominal supervision to ensure that the activities of these groups remained within the boundaries of accepted Catholic patterns.[127]

Technological developments during the period created important new means of bringing music to people. One such innovation was musical recording. Initially, Catholic intellectuals greeted records with distrust. They were criticized for being commercial, for appealing to a popular audience, and for being technological. As the opportunities the new medium offered became clearer, opposition began to abate. Catholic musicians had to approve of the availability of no fewer than thirty examples of Gregorian chant on records in 1932, although they felt that much more needed to be done before Catholic interests could be considered well served. Acceptability increased as records proved themselves in choral practices and in music instruction in adult-education programs. One writer described them as a powerful weapon in the fight against "spiritual proletarianization." He urged that they be in the hands of the individual Christian family, an indication of the changing perception of the role of the family. By 1933 even recording technology and Christianity no longer seemed quite so irreconcilable, although the use of records in church services inspired suspicion and, as in response to many cultural developments during the period, charges of "bolshevism."[128]

The development and successful commercialization of records was one significant change among a host of changes that music experienced during the period between the end of the *Kulturkampf* and 1933. Willi Schmid[129] described the regrouping of musical undertakings that had followed "the spiritual catastrophe" of the Great War: concerts no longer dominated, and the home had become a cultural center in its own right. Private choirs, and informal circles of young musicians had replaced more formal efforts; a strong demand for commercial music had arisen. According to Schmid, the different elements in the contemporary musical environment, elements such as the music of Schönberg, the subjectivists, or the young men of a choir that sang old German choral music, had so little in common with each other that no understanding between them was possible.[130]

Schmid concluded that change must come and that it had come. Even the Catholic world, a world that was trying to maintain some distance from the larger, secular world, experienced change in its music. Some changes could easily be perceived as positive, like the rise and activity of the Cäcilien Verein. Others, like records, a means to an end rather than an end in themselves, were accepted without too much strain or, indeed, too much discussion. Still others were ignored, which made them easier to live with. It remained rare for Catholics to consider the cost of their isolation from the most stimulating currents of contemporary music or to acknowledge their failure to encourage genuinely new music.

For Catholics the issues in popular music and in religious music throughout the period were variations on the same theme: change. In popular music, the question was the extent of accommodation; in church music, the extent to which the past should be perpetuated. The results, however, were quite different. Because it was beyond the power of the Church to influence popular music in an acceptably Catholic direction, the Church had to live with what was available. Popular music could never be expected to reinforce Catholic identity. Nor could the Church restrict effectively the access of individual Catholics to popular music. Religious music was a completely different story. There the Church not only regulated what was and was not permissible, it could also use the institution of the choir both to strengthen an individual sense of being Catholic and to mold specific behavior.

8

Theater, Cinema, and Radio

THEATER

The Threat of the Theater

"The theatre is irresistible: organise the theatre!" These words of Matthew Arnold might well have served as the motto of the self-appointed Catholic cultural intelligentsia.[1] By the end of the nineteenth century, the German theater, in its broadest sense, was a considerable enterprise. No longer a limited and occasional event, the court theaters, traveling companies, and carnival shows of eighteenth-century Germany had become a rich mix of professional and amateur offerings, extending from the highest of high culture to simple, often crudely humorous entertainment, designed for the uneducated. Almost every city of any size had its professional theater, music halls, vaudeville, and cabaret, and amateur productions abounded. New plays reflected the intellectual and artistic influences that were dramatically changing other forms of literature. This potent combination made the theater an object of social and political concern. Anxious about what Catholics were being exposed to, many Catholic cultural leaders condemned what they

found unacceptable and tried to encourage the creation of theater that would satisfy *their* ideals. The spectacular rise of the film industry, with its even greater accessibility and fewer constraints, would multiply that anxiety and expand both
opposition to the undesirable and efforts to improve quality.

Drama has been recognized since antiquity as a particularly compelling
idiom in which to convey ideas. In 1918 Jakob Overmans, S.J.,[2] the theater expert
of *Stimmen der Zeit,* wrote, "The uniqueness of theatrical art consists in its pre-
senting an artistic experience to a festively gathered crowd and disseminating it
in the most effective form." The theater was neither inherently good nor inherently bad but could be "a powerful force either for the salvation or for the destruction of our future." Overmans emphasized its negative effects; he credited
lascivious plays with undermining religion, destroying morally necessary feelings
of shame, and upsetting the nervous system. Other Catholic leaders were equally
extravagant in their optimism; the Catholic amateur theater, for example, was
touted as an antidote to bolshevism. Archbishop Faulhaber of Munich and Freising waxed poetically, if unspecifically, on the subject in 1918: "What a healthy theater art as a great power in today's cultural life could do for good, if it would show
the *Volk* the bright side of moral greatness, feminine worthiness, and fidelity to a
calling, instead of the dark side of life . . . if it raised a star for our youth instead of
drawing them to the dust, if it tried to educate the taste of the *Volk* instead of bow-
ing to the confusion of the taste of the times!" How this was to be accomplished
the good archbishop did not explain.[3]

The theater as danger is a theme that recurs frequently in Overmans's writing, and many traditionalists, Catholic and non-Catholic alike, shared this perception. Before the success of Gerhart Hauptmann, the plays of the nineteenth
century had been largely historical dramas; the few exceptions, like the plays
of Georg Büchner,[4] had remained unperformed. Dominated by mediocrity, the
stages of Germany had been a means of "sustaining decadent social institutions."
The founding of the Freie Bühne (Free Stage) as a private club in Berlin in 1889
began a revolution. Exempt from official censorship, the Freie Bühne brought to
the stage plays of a kind that had never before been presented. Its first production,
Ibsen's *Ghosts,* was followed by Gerhart Hauptmann's naturalist drama *Vor Son-
nenaufgang.* The Freie Bühne was committed to newness and to influencing German drama, and it went from the plays of one ism to those of another with a
success that encouraged others to follow its lead. The political and social ideals advanced in these plays varied, as did the artistic presentation, but almost universally they showed human beings "caught up in a world that gave no indication of
ultimate, immutable truths," a worldview that undercuts the foundations of Catholicism, not to mention Christianity.[5]

By 1920 German dramatists were offering the public a steady flow of plays that rejected tradition in all its forms, each more offensive to traditionalists than the last. Articles in Catholic journals criticized the theater for satisfying every kind of sensational hunger. Frequently labeled a "cesspool," the theater was accused of spreading its poisons not only in big cities—where one presumably expected nothing better—but also on the "healthy ground" of the provincial towns. Critics also complained about the artistic merits of contemporary theater: one writer described the professional theater as 90 percent kitsch, another as the playground of the worst kind of individualism.[6]

Plays that in retrospect are viewed as theatrically exciting, innovative, and significant, at the time many Catholics found malevolent. Yet the replacement of mediocrity with plays about such controversial themes as suicide, female emancipation, generational conflict, and class tensions was hardly an improvement from a Catholic point of view. The content of these modern plays was correctly perceived as often violating Catholic teachings and, more questionably, as threatening morality. Divorce was a particular sore point, although virtually any idea that took issue with established forms, opinions, and social conventions was undesirable. The 1913 offerings of the Bavarian State Theater were so outrageous that Catholics and Social Democrats joined together in high-mindedness to dismiss them.[7]

Expressionist playwrights, including Frank Wedekind, most famous for *Frühlings Erwachen* (1891), a drama of adolescent sexuality, and Carl Sternheim, whose comedies satirized the "arrogance, hypocrisy, impotence, and aggression" of middle-class Wilhelmine Germany, earned particularly strong Catholic disapproval.[8] The *Allgemeine Rundschau* labeled them both "poisonous." Equally unpopular was the Austrian Karl Schönherr.[9] His play *Der Weibsteufel* (1914) provoked Archbishop Faulhaber's wrath, probably as much in retribution for his earlier play *Glaube und Heimat* (1910), which had portrayed the Catholic Church in an unfavorable light, as in its own right. The Austrian Arthur Schnitzler[10] was another playwright whose work provoked attack from Catholic critics. Dramatists who did not write in German were mentioned less often, but Oscar Wilde[11] and Ibsen were sufficiently well-known to be regarded as dangerous.[12]

Serious, artistic modern drama was disliked because it was considered depressing and stylistically problematic. Innovative dramatic resolutions like the defeat depicted in Hauptmann's *Die Weber* (1892), the suicide in Wedekind's *Frühlings Erwachen*, the murder in Schönherr's *Der Weibsteufel*, or the lack of any resolution at all as in Hauptmann's *Der Biberpelz* (1893) consistently contradicted traditional Christian values and social ideals. Hope through salvation, the optimistic message that is the foundation of Christianity, is conspicuously absent from these dramas, and a finale like the repentance and subsequent redemption in Hugo von Hofmannsthal's[13] 1911 reworking of the medieval morality play *Jedermann* is unthinkable.[14] The style of serious, modern drama added to the problem with its efforts to reflect characteristics of modern life disliked by many Catholics. Michael Patterson relates the telegram style of playwrights like Wedekind and Sternheim to the pervasive speeding up of modern life. Rapid speech was, moreover, associated with the city; country folk typically spoke slowly.[15]

Catholic distrust of the theater was nothing new. An 1860 Church edict had forbidden the clergy to attend theatrical productions. The republication of this ban in 1914 suggests that the decree was not being observed as faithfully as the hierarchy wished. Its basic premise was certainly questioned. A 1904 *Allgemeine Rundschau* article argued that priests were educated men and should not be excluded from an important area of culture, even if operetta and cabaret had nothing to offer them and their presence there would make a bad impression. The author concluded that priests should "[t]ry everything, hold[ing] fast to what is good." Another objection was raised along somewhat different lines: How could priests, the educators and advisors of the *Volk,* judge for others what they had not been allowed to see for themselves?[16]

Complaints about the decline of the theater manifest the pervasive Catholic nostalgia for the past, although in this case it is for a past that was more recent than the more usually invoked medieval or pre-Reformation eras. The periods that produced the medieval *Jedermann* and the plays of Shakespeare were held up for admiration as the periods of the greatest dramatic accomplishment; but the past for which the Catholic writers of the 1920s longed was in this case no further back than 1914: "We were never blind to the excrescences [of the theater] and certainly fought them bitterly, but the intellectual forms of 1914 stood so much higher than those of this pitiless time that began with the bleak November Revolution, that there is no comparison."[17]

Many blamed commercialism for the theater's ills. Ignoring the fact that theater had a long history as an economic enterprise, they complained that the theater had become a business like any other and that the cashier's report was now the most important reality. The traditional assignment of theatrical oversight to the commercial police (*Gewerbepolizei*) rather than the ministry of culture demonstrates that the government, too, saw the theater as commerce, not culture.[18] Economic considerations were perceived to have preempted cultural interests: "If only the business character of our theater were annihilated and the theater director independent of the treasurer's report, then our theater could again be an expression of the national cultural will," lamented Heinrich Heimanns,[19] an author of inspirational books. But a capitalist economy did not permit this vain hope to be fulfilled. Theater owners, directors, and producers had to "make concessions to the unculture (*Unkultur*) of the masses." They had to offer what the public would pay to see and the public, regrettably, did not share the artistic views of Catholic cultural leaders. Its deplorable taste was a constant grievance. Audiences had, supposedly, no taste for serious drama and opera, and the most attended plays were the worst plays. Bad plays, sniffed the *Allgemeine Rundschau* in 1913, make more money than good plays.[20]

Coexisting with condemnation of the theater public was the complaint that the theater was out of step with the feeling of the *Volk*, which was believed to be in closer touch with the ethical forces of life than were dramatists and producers. When commenting on the sickness of theatrical life in 1916, Expeditus Schmidt asked rhetorically, "How can it be otherwise?" Berlin, he declared, set the tone of theatrical life, but Berlin had only a "public," not a *Volk* rooted in its land as culture required. The distinction between *Volk* and public reflects an important aspect of Catholic cultural thought during the period. *Volk* was used in writing about the theater as it was typically used: as a term reserved for the idealized German peasant/worker/citizen, who existed only in the minds of the theorists; the public, however, was composed of real people. In contrast to both, the owners, directors, and producers were described as freethinkers, whose views of art and its purpose did not correspond to Christian views. Commentators remarked on the Jewishness of many, and one writer declared, betraying a latent anti-Semitism, that an Eastern Jewish culture was being imposed on the warmhearted (*gemütig*) Germans.[21]

The Purpose of the Theater

Catholic intellectuals were dissatisfied with the theater as it was, but what did they think it ought to be? To the extent that they held a theory of the theater, it derived from that of Friedrich Schiller, a man who was not himself a Catholic. Although Schiller praised the theater as an especially effective means of entertainment, the basic premise of his essay "Die Schaubühne als eine moralische Anstalt betrachtet" ("The Stage as a Moral Institution") was that the stage is a moral force and its task the reinforcement of laws and religion. Citing the terrible infanticide of Euripides' Medea and the conscience-induced sleepwalking of Shakespeare's Lady Macbeth, Schiller asserted that because such scenes are dramatically staged, the theater acts more powerfully in the interests of morality and religion than either can in their own interest. The theater can not only condemn vices, but, unlike the law, it can also honor virtues. Theater can portray folly and prepare us for human weakness. It can teach us to be more considerate of the unfortunate and to judge gently: "The thoughtful and the worthier section of the people diffuse the light of wisdom over the masses through the stage." Such statements must have been particularly attractive to proponents of the Catholic cultural movement, even if they found less welcome Schiller's typically Enlightenment conclusion: "Purer and better principles and motives issue from the stage and circulate through society: the night of barbarism and superstition vanishes."[22]

Disagreement came over what to emphasize. To what extent should the theater be an educational institution? Was entertainment a legitimate function, or merely to be tolerated as an economic necessity? Overmans was unequivocal; the most important task of the theater was education. Friedrich Muckermann declared that modern man expected the theater to provide him with a metaphysics, an effective ordering of the world that provided a balance between individual freedom and common bonds, a religion that sanctified fulfilled existence, and, of course, poetry. An essay in *Germania* argued that theatrical art had the obligation to shake men out of the hollowness of daily life, to awaken them and keep them awake to the idea and to the ideal, and, most importantly, to make laughable and kill the stupid seriousness of daily life. Other purposes assigned to the theater included the transmission of culture, of intellectual life, and of experience.[23]

An understanding that pleasure was a function of the theater did exist. In 1920 Overmans described how, after the sufferings of the war, people wanted relaxation and an escape into a happier world. Slightly later, an author in *Hochland* discussed the need for relief of those who worked nine hours a day at demanding work that required concentration. A respite was not only not offensive, it was also socially desirable: "Let us be happy that the nerves, thoughts, and souls of agitated men can be calmed, that for a few hours they can forget their cares, that the irritation they have accumulated or the despondency that oppresses them perishes in quiet pleasures, and that then refreshed fighters can face inexorable life again, somewhat more confidently and more patiently." Pleasure was not, however, high on any Catholic priority list.[24]

Schiller provided the intellectual foundation, but by 1930 Catholic thinking on the theater was showing some influence from theatrical events of the previous three decades. The shift in emphasis from historical dramas to plays about contemporary characters confronting contemporary problems had been accepted, even endorsed. In 1930 the theater critic of *Der Gral* noted that it had taken ten years for dramatists to begin writing about World War I, the implication being that it was overdue. A year earlier Overmans had made a related point in *Stimmen der Zeit* in more critical terms. In his opinion, what most concerned individuals was *not* dealt with in dramas, the most compelling example being the war.[25]

Catholic Drama

Some attention was given to what Catholic drama ought to be. The perennial cultural questions were put in terms of the theater: Was a Catholic dramatist one who treated Catholic material? Was personal piety the sine qua non that defined a Catholic dramatist? The obvious was stated: Catholic drama must be not only religious and moral but also artistic. An ideal was proclaimed: "[D]rama that is born out of the Catholic or Christian spirit is the high point of dramatic creation." But generalizations can be interpreted in different ways, and sometimes specifics accompanied vague exhortations. Overmans might say that theatrical art "wants always to show the nature of things," but he also explained that the playwright must avoid exploration of "strange areas." Georg Raederscheidt, director of the pedagogical academy in Bonn,[26] urged dramatists not merely to represent subjective spiritual experiences but also to show that behind the citizen stood the state, behind the individual was the *Volk,* behind freedom was responsibility, behind the world eternity, behind guilt sin, and behind authority the heavenly world order.[27]

Raederscheidt argued that the Catholic viewpoint was especially appropriate to the theater because it demanded fullness, completeness, and variety; but he was virtually alone in this opinion. Most discussions of the Catholic element in drama and theater convey a recognition that in the twentieth century Catholic moral teachings were not a foundation for successful theatrical production. Catholic playwrights did not write about contemporary life or address the questions that troubled people; instead, they produced historical dramas that were pale imitations of Schiller or plays on religious themes. To some extent, exciting dramatic innovations just did not mesh well with the virtually immovable traditionalism of the Church. Reinhard Johannes Sorge,[28] a Catholic convert who wrote a limited number of plays that were a "unique fusion of religious fervor and expressionist style" before his death on the Western Front, was the exception. By and large, Catholic dramatists chose to address the Catholic world and to do it in terms of its own canons rather than those of the larger German society. In 1913 Overmans wrote, "No one denies that the number of performable Catholic plays, thanks to the [small number of playwrights], is very small. A reliable means of increasing this number or increasing it quickly, is not known, because the writers have yet to be born." Later he would dismiss available Catholic drama along with other forms of Catholic literature as basically boring.[29]

Leo Weismantel[30] was a "typical" Catholic dramatist whose dramatic career clarifies some of the difficulties of Catholic drama. A teacher and politician who served as a member of the Bavarian Landtag in the 1920s, Weismantel was one to whom journalists turned when they wanted the opinion of a Catholic literary figure. Born in 1888, he exemplified the Catholic intellectual. On one occasion he wrote that "to each Catholic is given the sacramental focus of the Church's life of community, before whose strength all disruption is like chaff." Weismantel wrote a number of plays in the years immediately after the war before concentrating his literary efforts in other forms. The plays were primarily experiments with form or vehicles for disseminating his views on cultural policy. As he himself described it, he used the stage as a pulpit between 1918 and 1924. His plays were on the usual historical or religious themes. *Der Kurfürst* (1925), for example, treated Elector Balduin of Trier[31] at the time of the Avignon papacy and the fight between pope and emperor. An article in the journal of the Borromäus Verein unintentionally sheds light on the dramatic failure of such plays: the author enthuses over Sorge's vision and achievement in the innovative *Der Bettler* (1912); but he is carefully polite about Weismantel's work. Gustave Stezenbach[32] may well have had Weismantel in mind when he wrote in 1923: "Catholic writers can write for libraries. Their works remain book dramas, and we Catholics don't care whether they're performed."[33]

Stezenbach's comment is an expression of the unyielding fact that lay beneath the surface of Catholic discussions of theater: the ordinary German Catholic had no interest in serious modern drama. Again and again the point was made that Catholics did not attend the theater and, except for the occasional protest, were indifferent to it. In 1928 the *Kölnische Volkszeitung* reported a particularly telling example. Special performances of two of Max Mell's[34] irreproachably Catholic religious plays, *Das Apostelspiel* (first performed in 1924) and *Die fröhlichen drei Könige*, had been commissioned in Cologne. The deaneries were informed, memos were sent to two hundred Catholic clubs in the city of Cologne, and the performances were announced in the *Kölnische Lokal-Anzeiger*'s calendar of events and in the diocesan newsletter. Yet only seven tickets sold. Catholics not only rejected the theater, they rejected Catholic theater.[35]

Catholic indifference, however, was almost certainly limited to serious drama. There are no statistics on Catholics as theatergoers, but the fact that the Platzl, a music hall in Munich, a city with an overwhelmingly Catholic population, was invariably sold out suggests that Catholics consumed popular theatrical entertainment as eagerly as Protestants or Jews. The Platzl offered faux Bavarian entertainment, singers of *Volk* music, comedians, short skits, and the like.[36]

Theater Groups

The failure of Catholics to buy tickets to serious theater productions had its inevitable consequence: theater directors made no attempt to attract them. In turn, the lack of suitable plays reinforced Catholic reluctance to buy tickets. Overmans recognized the connection; it did not help to call for Christian and Catholic literature, theater, and films if those who called for them did not concern themselves with identifying prospective readers and viewers for them.[37]

Organizing a theater group was one way to influence the theater. In September 1916 an article in the *Allgemeine Rundschau* by Maximilian Pfeiffer,[38] a member of the Reichstag, announced that a group of politicians, literary figures, and representatives of economic and artistic groups had founded the Verband zur Förderung deutscher Theaterkultur (Organization for the Advancement of German Theatrical Culture) in Hildesheim during the previous month. The organization united Catholics and Protestants in a program that condemned the morally poisonous influence of libertine and pseudo-literary imported plays, vowed to improve the quality of German theater in the spirit of German literature and civilization, and viewed the theater's task as one of education and moral improvement.[39]

A year later the Verband zur Förderung deutscher Theaterkultur claimed 100,000 members from all classes and political parties, as well as branches in over one hundred cities. Its success attracted criticism. Artists were concerned about artistic freedom, and liberals worried that the group was too Catholic. Catholics wanted an organization, but not this organization with its multiple groups and different priorities and values. In addition, some fundamental inconsistencies had become clear. Catholic members too often were non-theatergoers. They wanted to fight the theater rather than participate in it.[40]

The work of the Verband zur Förderung deutscher Theaterkultur occupied one phase in what was beginning to be called the Catholic theater movement by the mid-1920s. The movement's antecedents went back to prewar days, a 1910 lecture series on the topic by Expeditus Schmidt; a Calderón association in Munich; a traveling theater company in Upper Silesia; a speech by Jakob Overmans addressed to a Catholic woman's group in Hannover; and a proposal in 1914 by Carl Sonnenschein, a Berlin priest and leader in the Catholic social-welfare movement, for a central organization to interest Catholics in the theater.[41]

Rather than the Verband zur Förderung deutscher Theaterkultur, however, a new organization became the central Catholic theater organization. At a meeting in Frankfurt am Main in April 1919 a group of "Christian-thinking men," many with practical experience from the Verband zur Förderung deutscher Theaterkultur, founded the Bühnenvolksbund (People's Association for the Stage) because they wanted an organization better designed to work with local and regional groups than the Verband zur Förderung deutscher Theaterkultur. Jakob Overmans was given credit for inspiring the foundation of the Bühnenvolksbund; his remark about the pointlessness of calling for Christian and Catholic literature if no attention was paid to their audience was quoted in a memorandum detailing the enterprise's early years. The Bühnenvolksbund proclaimed two objectives: to make theater accessible to the masses and to raise the artistic condition of theater. The one was related to the other: the power of group ticket buying could be used to influence the schedules of theaters.[42]

Officially, the Bühnenvolksbund was independent. An undated leaflet attributed the big difference between the Volksbühne (People's Stage), a similar theater organization, and the Bühnenvolksbund to the fact that "the Volksbühne is bound to the spirit of socialism while the Bühnenvolksbund has no political orientation and no political party's program to apply." The original goal of the Bühnenvolksbund was to advance the art of the theater and dramatic literature, both in the sense of national German culture and in Christian outlook. The phrasing of the organization's statement of purpose emphasized inclusiveness and was, according to the anonymous author of the report on the conference that founded it, deliberate. He believed that while the founders of the Bühnenvolksbund applauded confessional goals and activities, they wanted the Western, Christian cultural idea to be central because it helped to bind society together.[43]

From the beginning, Catholics were prominent in the Bühnenvolksbund, even if it was not a specifically Catholic organization. It had close ties with the Volksverein, which provided leadership and assistance, such as offering free issues of *Volkskunst* to its members. Its first executive committee included prominent Catholic cultural leaders like Cardinal Faulhaber, Professor Adolf Dyroff of Bonn University and the Borromäus Verein, Wilhelm Marx and Emil Ritter of the Volksverein, the author Johannes Mumbauer, the editor Karl Muth, Hans Rost, Expeditus Schmidt, and the playwrights Leo Weismantel and Ilse von Stach.[44] As the decade of the 1920s wore on, the Bühnenvolksbund acquired more and more the appearance of a Catholic organization. It sought episcopal approval and worked closely with the Zentralbildungsausschuß (Central Committee for Education [see p. 182]), although it never became quite Catholic enough to satisfy the demands of many theologians, academics, and members. The uncomfortable reality of Ritter's comment that an exclusively Catholic theater organization would be too weak to influence the theater life of the public forced Catholic leaders to tolerate the interconfessional Bühnenvolksbund, but they were not happy with it.[45]

The first task of the new group was to get organized, and a 1921 newsletter communicates that first flush of energy and enthusiasm. The movement was spreading in southern and western Germany, and there were now local groups in Württemberg, Freiburg im Breisgau, Mannheim, Saarbrücken, and Trier. The industrial areas of the Lower Rhine were interested; the Dresden group was in difficulties; the Bühnenvolksbund leaders were particularly pleased that the Berlin group was already developing its own performances; Breslau was about to have its first performance; and the Upper Silesia group was sponsoring its first

conference. Four years later an open letter soliciting new members radiated satisfaction: a membership of some 400,000 and "the happy certainty that we, in the
last few years, have created a Christian national theater movement and that from
these new forms the atmosphere can develop in which the *Volk* can again become
healthy."[46]

The mature Bühnenvolksbund of the mid-1920s was involved in a number
of activities. Its interest was broad, encompassing professional theater, traveling
theater, *Heimat* plays, puppet theater, amateur and youth productions, and film.
At the center was the purchasing of tickets for its members to "valuable theater
productions that are above reproach." It published Christian playwrights, sponsored continuing education courses for amateur and youth actors, and maintained an advisory center for amateur theater. In 1928 there were no fewer than
300 local groups, 17 provincial groups, 180 full time employees, 3,000 part-time
workers, and 100 artistes in the traveling-theater groups.[47]

As a group, the Bühnenvolksbund was notably prone to controversy. Much
of the dissension stemmed from the fact that it had to accommodate a wider
range of viewpoints than an exclusively Catholic organization would have found
necessary. In 1923 it was attacked on the one hand by the Rhein-Mainsiche Verband für Volksbildung as "a danger to a free German culture" and on the other
hand in the *Allgemeine Rundschau* for halfheartedness in its efforts at moral purification. In 1926 Robert Grosche, a leading Catholic advocate of ecumenism and
the then–university chaplain in Cologne, and Wilhelm Gerst,[48] director of the
Bühnenvolksbund, exchanged accusations. Grosche objected strongly to the
balance of Catholics and Protestants in the Bühnenvolksbund, and he and Emil
Ritter eventually left its board of directors. Publication of Otto Brüe's novel *Jupp
Brand*[49] in 1927 by the organization attracted another kind of criticism; the world
knew enough of the dark side of life. Nor were all performances sponsored by
the Bühnenvolksbund equally acceptable. A priest in the Diocese of Fulda, who
had been asked to attend one of its meetings in October 1932, reported that at the
meeting's end, Shakespeare's *King John* was performed. He commented that with
two divorces of high nobles, a peace-disturbing intrigue of the papal delegate, and
the murder of a monk by poison, it could hardly be acceptable from a Catholic
point of view.[50]

Amateur Theater and the Catholic Associations

Probably the most serious issue in the faultfinding was the relationship of the
Bühnenvolksbund to Catholic amateur theater. From the beginning, the Bühnenvolksbund had included amateur drama in its scope; one of its goals was "the
exercise of influence on the dilletantish performances of societies and the like."

Amateur theater was thought of as a form of adult education, and this facet was strengthened by its connection with the Zentralbildungsausschuß, which had gone so far as to draw up guidelines for such performances. To support amateur theater better, at the end of the 1920s the Bühnenvolksbund proposed a comprehensive program to the Catholic bishops that would combine conferences and courses, advisory material, especially the publication and circulation of its own journal, an advisory group for each diocese, and the publication of how-to manuals, like the series *Buch von Fest und Feier* (The Book of Holidays and Celebration). Such activity seems unexceptionable, not to say worthy, and Emil Ritter, the individual who probably had the most comprehensive grasp of what was going on in Catholic amateur theater, endorsed it cautiously. It was, after all, very similar to what the Volksverein, of which he was the general secretary, was already doing. Others, however, accused the Bühnenvolksbund of suppressing amateur drama in the Catholic groups and clubs.[51]

Amateur theater performances were a staple of Catholic voluntary associations. When, as evidence of the ceaseless search for pleasure that dominated the times, the bishop of Fulda[52] used the fact that every Catholic organization offered a play between Christmas and Lent, he may have been exaggerating, but dramatic performances were clearly a major activity in Catholic associational life. The professional theater attracted only a small minority of Catholics, many more attended amateur performances. Every city and village had its theatrical society that presented at least one play a year. In addition, many groups whose primary interest was not theater would offer plays or skits at their social evenings. A suggested program for the Kaiser's birthday, which included a prologue, an anthem, a recitation, scenes from a play by Ernst von Wildenbruch, a choral thanksgiving, a speech with a toast, and concluded with another anthem, gives an idea of their character.[53]

Catholic amateur theater was the repository of many illusions: that this motley collection of efforts would be an antidote to the ills of the modern stage; that it would be a school for the professional theater; that it would offer educated Catholics a substitute for the professional theater; that it would be a true expression of the *Volk;* and that it would revive the Christian art of the seventeenth-century Spanish dramatist and poet Calderón. The reality was another world. Amateur theater aped professional theater, which meant that its offerings were just as frequently kitsch as those of the professional theater. Amateur groups did perform religious plays, but a description of how plays were chosen makes it clear that piety was not the most important feature. External features were primary. Were there bright costumes? Was there a fight scene? Father Humpert, who analyzed no fewer than 269 reports on Catholic amateur theatrical performances, had reason to raise the question of whether a play could be educationally effective if the most important consideration was that something eye-catching had to occur. The abysmal quality was generally conceded, and when Ritter wrote in 1923 that amateur theater used to be a joke, one only wonders at his use of the past tense.[54]

For all its ubiquity, however, amateur theater was never the cultural issue for Catholics that professional theater was. The leaders of the Catholic organizations that performed the amateur plays retained control and direction, guaranteeing that nothing would be presented that was offensive to Catholic sensitivities. Quality might be appalling, taste execrable, but content, the primary object of Catholic concern with the theater, was acceptably circumscribed.

By 1930, amateur theater was all that it would ever be, and professional theater was no longer the cultural issue that it had been. Neither provided the ideal educational experience or moral force, but among Catholic intellectuals, they were both generally accepted for what they were. The shift is particularly significant in the theater of high culture, where traditions of all kinds were increasingly ignored. Catholic intellectuals had, in the end, proved no more immune to the excitement of modern German theater than other intellectuals were. As early as 1914 an article in *Hochland* praised the work of the innovative director Max Reinhardt. Leopold Jessner's production of *Die Weber* was favorably reviewed in *Germania*. A 1930 article in *Der Gral* noted approvingly that dramatists had begun to write about the war. An article in *Germania* summarized and made explicit what was tacitly recognized: he who wants to live in his own time and be fulfilled must recognize its particular sense. The nature of theatrical art was to personalize abstract ideas and to make forces seem alive, to use characterization to illuminate and contrast, and in the process to unleash the power of ideas. In doing this, theater had begun, as it had had to begin, a new direction.[55]

Film

The Beginning of Catholic Interest in Film

Theater is older than Christianity, and the Church had had long experience dealing with it. Not so the cinema. In the late nineteenth century a new entertainment phenomenon, the moving picture, appeared and rapidly became the world's fourth largest industry. One perceptive cleric commented, "Through the discovery of printing in the fifteenth century mankind was given the greatest technical means for the mass dissemination of ideas. For the technical progress of our time has been reserved the placement of two additional, new means at the side of the Gutenberg art: film and radio." Catholics were faced with the necessity of developing a response to these new media that offered such great cultural potential.[56]

Catholic responses to film displayed somewhat different characteristics from the responses to literature, art, and music, or even theater. Discussions of fundamental issues like cinema's proper purpose and its appropriate relationship with religion were far less common. An emphasis on action takes the place of endless, mind-numbing debate. The rise of the film industry was so rapid, its technology and techniques so constantly changing, that there was little room for leisurely discussion of what seemed an overwhelming phenomenon. By the time an issue had been thoroughly considered, it was likely to be irrelevant.

The reactions of Catholic intellectuals to film were similar to those of other German intellectuals. Initially, they were almost total indifference. The early cinema was closely identified with the industrial lower classes and labeled "a child of the big city." It therefore lay outside the interests of the Catholic intelligentsia and seemed irrelevant to the predominantly rural Catholic experience. Nor was it perceived to have any redeeming social or cultural value. Film production in its first decade emphasized novelty and sensationalism. The prevailing means of dissemination was the *Wanderkino,* a traveling enterprise that would put on performances at carnivals or in a rented tavern room. Film was seen as entertainment and diversion, a curiosity rather than something to be taken seriously.[57]

By the end of the first decade of the new century, interest was displacing indifference. Occasional articles about film began to appear in Catholic journals, and calls for control of pornographic films began to be heard. Concern about physical conditions in movie theaters was expressed and, even more importantly, about the effect of film on a viewer. Reaction in the prewar period tended to be a blanket dismissal. As one commentator crisply remarked, "It is clear that . . . the cinema, as it is today, is a mischief, a nuisance, and a scandal." A standard litany of complaints developed.[58]

In response, Catholics created organizations. The most important Catholic film organization of the prewar period was the Lichtbilderei of the Volksverein that was founded in 1909 to loan suitable films to Catholic groups. Its 1912 catalog boasted no fewer than 700 titles, to which it was adding new titles at the rate of about thirty a week. Its director estimated that the Lichtbilderei was supplying forty weekly theaters and between fifty and sixty Sunday theaters. It published a journal, *Bild und Film,* as well as a series that treated technical problems of the use of moving pictures. A Bavarian film organization, the Zentrale der süddeutschen katholischen Arbeitervereine (Headquarters of the Southern German Catholic Workers' Associations), usually called the Leo Gesellschaft (Society of St. Leo) or Leohaus (House of St. Leo), was established in 1912. Its most significant accomplishment before 1914 was the creation of a *Wanderkino* to provide film showings for communities without their own cinemas; later it would become the single largest German producer of Catholic films.[59]

By the time World War I broke out, Catholic responses to film ranged from rejection to approbation. The Church hierarchy tended to be strongly negative, despite such anomalies as Pius IX's appearance on film in 1901. A pastoral letter from the bishops of the Fulda Bishops' Conference in 1908, "Über den Kampf gegen die Unzucht und Unsittlichkeit" (On the Fight against Lewdness and Immorality), did not mention the cinema by name but was widely recognized as a warning against it. Some Catholic intellectuals held more optimistic views. At the 1912 Aachen Katholikentag Joseph Mausbach asked if literature, painting, and music had been "conquered" with great success and theater somewhat less so, why could the same not be done for film? A year later, the Metz Katholikentag defined a program for Catholic activity: to demand governmental oversight of production; to influence the programming of movie theaters; and to demand the establishment of a Catholic film-producing organization. This program is remarkably similar to that of German Protestants in the same years.[60]

Both positive and negative reactions strengthened during World War I and the immediate postwar period, and by the middle of the 1920s the scope and magnitude of Catholic involvement with film bore little resemblance to prewar efforts. When Father Karl Walterbach,[61] president of Leohaus, remarked in 1926 that Catholic indifference to film was beginning to disappear, he was sadly out of date. By then Catholic parishes and organizations regularly showed films. There were Catholic organizations to pressure the film industry, to distribute films to Catholics, to produce films suitable for Catholics, to educate the Catholic viewing public, and even an organization to coordinate the work of other Catholic organizations. The first Catholic International Film Congress would be held in 1928 in Paris, and the second a year later in Munich.[62]

The Church hierarchy recognized early the need to influence cinema viewing habits. The veiled warnings of the Fulda Bishops' Conference of 1908 were supplemented with strict guidelines in 1913: school-age children were to be excluded from public cinema showings; special showings for school children of suitable films were to be arranged and overseen by religious instructors; children not yet of school age must be excluded from all film showings; parish priests had the responsibility for oversight of public cinema offerings; the dangers of the cinema were to be held up to adults and children in church and school. Their 1926 decree on morals treated film much more briefly. Linking film and theater with *Schundliteratur,* the bishops warned Catholics that they should never expose themselves to such undesirable influences. The brevity of the injunction can probably be attributed more to a pragmatic recognition that such decrees were often futile rather than to the success any previous guidelines had had. There was no way to enforce these warnings, and there is every reason to think that they had little effect.[63]

The Popularity of the Cinema

The maturing of film as an art form, its tremendous popularity, and its obvious potential for influence[64] transformed initial lack of interest into intense concern. Catholics awakened to the fact that they did not need to create a stage theater for the masses; it already existed in the cinema. Richard Muckermann,[65] a leading Catholic expert on cinema, described the appeal: "Dressed in working clothes, one goes in from the streets, usually without needing to make one's way far. The prices are low, it is dark, one can come when one will, the film rolls steadily on." His description of a typical program at a suburban cinema, two big dramas, a two or three act comedy, and then a trick film,[66] makes clear that there was something for everyone. Alois Funk,[67] a priest in the Diocese of Trier who wrote several articles on film and radio, saw the cinema as offering "pleasant, light, and cheap entertainment." It does not take much imagination to understand why someone who had spent the working hours typing or on an assembly line would find such an experience pleasurable.[68]

The numbers spoke for themselves. In 1900 there were two movie houses in Germany. By 1910 that number had grown to 480, and by 1913 to more than 2,500. By 1927 estimates were running 3,800 movie houses with 47 million visitors a year, or one-third of the entire population. When he spoke at the Katholikentag in Essen in 1932, Richard Muckermann interpreted the figures in terms of that city. In 1931 some 6 million people visited the 60 cinemas of Essen. With a population of around 640,000, that meant that almost ten times as many people had visited the cinema as the city had residents. What Muckermann did not say, but what he must have known, was that, while many of those visitors were not residents of Essen but of the surrounding area, the city also had to have had a great many resident film addicts. And Essen was hardly alone. Statistics for Cologne, Düsseldorf, Dortmund and Bochum were very similar. Friedrich Muckermann, Richard's brother, gave the same facts a slightly different slant with the comment that even faithful Catholics were spending more time in the cinema than in church. The cinema was clearly as popular with German Catholics as with everyone else.[69]

These numbers testify to the magnitude of the cinematic phenomenon, and by the 1920s Catholic cultural leaders, whether they fought it or tried to work with it, knew that it was a force to be reckoned with. Friedrich Wolf, a communist intellectual, described this phenomenon in the following terms: "Film is a great power today in the West, economically and intellectually." Catholic intellectuals used only slightly different words to express identical views in phrases such as "Film rules the masses" and "within thirty years film has become a power." A negative version of the same perception of power was the statement of Josef Ettl, a parish priest: "In recent times hardly anything has been more pernicious for faith and morality than the cinema."[70]

It became a cliché to speak of the cinema as "the theater of the little man." Its low prices gave it a significant economic advantage over the theater, an advantage that was quickly apparent. Willy Rath traced the changing balance between theater and cinema in Elberfeld, an industrial city of 180,000 that is now part of Wuppertal:

	The City Theater	Cinema	
1906		2 cinema houses	126,093 visitors
	118,601 visitors		
1907		3 cinema houses	259,514 visitors
1908		4 cinema houses	332,365 visitors
	109,843 visitors		
1909		6 cinema houses	449,616 visitors
1910		8 cinema houses	555,580 visitors
1911		9 cinema houses	880,647 visitors
	99,055 visitors		
1912			

Film was truly, as Richard Muckermann stated, an enemy of the theater, and, in economic terms, it was winning the battle.[71]

The low price created a sociological difference between the theater public and the movie public. Theater was largely for the educated and refined, while movies had something for everyone, although they were particularly associated with the working class. Most intellectuals made their disdain for the cinema clear, but one writer made a point of thanking film for the immense intellectual stimulation it had given him. Many intellectuals, he believed, were ashamed to acknowledge their interest publicly. This class distinction was the source of much of the concern about films, Catholic as well as non-Catholic, because, for all the idealization of the *Volk,* few intellectuals had much confidence in its powers of discrimination and judgment. Individuals who had never attended a play or concert, but had found their entertainment in taverns and at carnivals, now enjoyed a medium of a different cultural level that would influence them and that they would in turn influence.[72]

Intellectual accessibility paralleled economic accessibility. Films tended to be simple and direct, suitable to the modest abilities of their viewers, whose expectations were considered to be equally modest, although the most successful film companies appealed to all classes. Cultural elitists might complain that when a work of world literature was filmed, its true value was lost, but enthusiasts praised the ability of films to reduce the content of a bulky work to a single hour and reach thousands of spectators who spoke a variety of languages. Films might be lacking in artistry, psychologically superficial, and overly dependent upon deus ex machina–type solutions, but they were also undemanding. Viewers wanted characters to be depicted in the same black and white terms as the film itself.[73]

The methods of filmmakers were undeniably effective. The editor of the special cinema issue of the *Augustinus-Blatt* summarized the result: "No new invention in the sphere of the intellect ... stimulates the fantasy in so lively a fashion, for the content is transmitted without great effort of reading or hearing." Funk considered this visual medium particularly successful in portraying otherwise abstract ideas.[74]

Catholic intellectuals recognized that they needed not only to praise or criticize but also to understand. By the end of the 1920s the psychological impact of film had begun to receive attention. When speaking to the 1929 Catholic Film Congress, Luitpold Nusser, director of the Leo Gesellschaft, offered this rather pretentious assessment:

> But how powerful the inner, soulful effect that emanates from a film that is artistically and aesthetically above reproach and that presents opinions honestly can be on viewers! Surely everyone who has ever been in a movie theater has experienced that. The enormously suggestive effect of the film is conditioned by the magical darkness of the room, which concentrates the vision on the square piece of linen and excludes—apart from the impressions of a reinforcing music—all other possibilities of impression. It is truly no wonder that the naive viewer takes the pictures that appear there for absolute reality, because his consciousness of the simulated action is completely erased by the apparent life on the white wall.[75]

This blurring of the distinction between reality and unreality was considered a major problem, but by the 1920s films, their audiences, and their critics, had reached a considerable level of sophistication. When Victor Schamoni considered the question of film as art in *Hochland,* he concluded, "Not only does the film show what is, perceived through the observant eyes of conscious men, but the artist, the thinking, creating, forming, intuitively shaping man, has in film the possibility of a representation, an expression of his point of view. Film brings something completely new: as from words poetry and from sounds music, so from pictures a picture-poem, a picture-play for the eyes." An even more perceptive commentator wrote, after discussing new technologies of communication, "The newness is not only in how but also in what it is, in material that now for the first time can be directly, intelligently presented." He gave examples from two recent films, one showing a wild animal in the freedom of the primeval forest, the other life on a sinking ship.[76]

Sophistication is also apparent in the beginnings of a multifaceted understanding of the relation of films to their context; the dislike of the speed and tempo so apparent in films is an interesting expression of this understanding. The very act of projecting a series of images onto the screen to produce the illusion of movement led to the association of films with speed. Speed was inherent in the contrast between the minutes required to view a story reduced to a film and the hours required to read the print version. Speed became a plot element when a film portrayed modern urban life, so much faster than the life of the traditional agricultural village. More than one Catholic intellectual considered the effects of the speed of films to be highly detrimental, whatever the form; their speed was blamed for "untrue and unnatural" effects, for overstimulation of the nerves, for inviting superficiality, and, ultimately, for causing the *Volk* to forget all its moral principles. These negative judgments were not only judgments of the tempo of films per se, they were also judgments of the accelerated, technologically driven times in which the critics lived.[77]

Film and Morality

Like any other artistic medium, the cinema could be "an angel of light or a path to destruction," but many Catholics saw the cinema only in the darkest of terms. It acquired a bad reputation, and in its early years newspaper stories like one reporting a young girl's theft to obtain the price of a ticket were not unusual. Little boys expressed feelings of shame that they had attended a film showing; students wrote that the cinema had harmed them. Some intellectuals went so far as to see it as a threat to the Church itself. One 1932 article quoted, of all authorities, Trotsky: "The cinema is the greatest competition, not only of the tavern, but of the Church. It liberates [people] from the need to cross the threshold of a church." That same article credited the cinema with destroying millions of souls on a daily basis.[78]

Intellectuals argued that the easy confusion of fantasy for reality was an important element in the moral threat posed by film. Overmans urged that films show "real life from all over the globe"; but the world of commercial feature films bore little resemblance to any real world. In his classic 1927 essay, "Die Kleinen Ladenmädchen gehen ins Kino" (The Little Shopgirls go to the Movies), Siegfried

Kracauer wrote, "Stupid and unreal film fantasies are the daydreams of society, in which its actual reality comes to the fore and its otherwise repressed wishes take on form." It was a point that Catholics interested in film understood. Writing in *Germania,* Otto Behrens criticized the de rigueur happy ending for lacking reality and censured the frequent connection between happiness and money in films. Another Catholic critic wrote of viewers seeing things they would like to have: a life without work but with elegant clothing and romantic intrigue. His words lacked the bite and disdain of Kracauer's, but they said much the same thing.[79]

When Catholic intellectuals expressed concern about the compatibility of Church and cinema, however, it was more likely to be because films presented a world that affronted Catholic values than because they presented an unreal world. Friedrich Muckermann's keynote address at the 1929 Catholic Film Congress opened with the words, "If you put the world of Catholicism and the world of film next to each other like two independent greatnesses, there are so many gaping contrasts that they appear to be irreconcilable." Among the contrasts: Catholic heroes were saints, but the heroes of the movies were impostors; Catholicism prized virginity and the Christian family, but the movies proclaimed the rule of the demimonde and licentiousness; Catholicism fostered a just appreciation of the classes for each other, but the movies showed respect only for money and property; Catholicism's roots lay in the reality of nature and grace, but the movies displaced reality in fantasy.[80]

Muckermann's points were all related to morality in a broad sense, but, as in other cultural areas, Catholic concerns with film were primarily moral in a narrow, sexual sense, rather than philosophical or aesthetic. Morality was fixed and defined. Again and again, from *Der Gral* to *Hochland,* in newspaper columns and diocesan journals, readers were told that the cinema represented a serious moral danger. The fundamental argument was that "[o]n a daily basis the cinema endangers, destroys, and damages in millions of souls the treasures of knowledge and faith, those highest guidance-giving natural and supernatural values." Films were "a good school for sin and crime." The argument was made with mind-numbing specificity. Writing to the Ministry of the Interior in the name of the Fulda Bishops' Conference in 1923, Cardinal Bertram declared that the cinema was a major contributor to moral decline. The cardinal reveled in the details: "the greedily demanding glances, the flirting, kisses, and hugging, the undressing with almost complete removal of clothing, the disappearance of lovers after an intense love scene through doors or something similar in a heightened atmosphere and with nerve-stimulating lighting are bound only to prod sexual instincts, especially if the viewer, as today is often the case, participates with heightened nerves. . . ." In his opinion the depiction of such behavior wounded viewers in body and soul and caused people to lose their self-respect and esteem, to become hard and common.[81]

Seen from a Catholic point of view, or from a Protestant, or even, perhaps, from a socialist point of view, the movies did indeed present a world inimical to morality. The *Allgemeine Rundschau* reported in 1913 that an article in the *Deutsche Tageszeitung* had substantiated its own previously reported findings of 51 movie divorces and 19 movie seductions and identified a further 97 murders, 45 suicides, and 22 abductions in 250 additional movies. In those movies the public was in the company of 176 thieves, 25 prostitutes, and 33 drunkards. Nor did the situation improve with the passage of time. The end of censorship that followed the fall of the Hohenzollern Empire brought a flood of *Aufklärungsfilme*, or "enlightenment" films, a term used for sex films with only the thinnest veneer of education. Although new censorship laws dealt with the immediate problem, in the years that followed eroticism in films seemed to increase and to be the point of many films rather than a mere suggestion. In the world of films, the Catholic Church itself was tainted with sex; Cardinal Bertram found the frequency with which the plots of movies turned girls who had violated prevailing standards of sexual morality into nuns particularly offensive.[82]

A column in *Bild und Film* proclaimed, "The *Schundroman* is dead, long live the cinema!" The same evil effects that had been attributed to *Schund* literature were now attributed to the cinema; *Schund* cinema offered in livelier form what *Schund* literature offered in printed form. A survey of seventy-eight girls, asking them to describe their experiences in the cinema as a warning to others, was published in *Pastor Bonus*. Eight girls reported "bodily injury," by which they meant sore eyes and nervous excitement. Thirteen reported that they lost interest in work and in prayer as a consequence of the cinema. Their statements supported the general impression that the cinema had an "unfavorable effect" by, for example, giving them a preference for movies over school. Inability to forget pictured scenes, unwelcome approaches in the movie theater, and disobeying parents to visit the cinema were other results. The most serious consequence, of course, was that thirty-seven girls stated, "in the most bitter terms, that it had led them into sin." Sin included inappropriate dancing and immodest clothing. Many could identify scenes from specific movies, like *Das Land des Lächelns* (Land of Smiles [1930]), the American *Das Großstadtmädel* (City Girl [1930]), and the French *Unter den Dächern von Paris* (*Sous les toits de Paris* [1930]), that had prompted the "sinful" behavior.[83]

Good Films, Bad Films

The accepted explanation for the disgraceful condition of the movies was their commercialism. It was recognized that without the businessman there would be no film industry. But recognition did not make the fact less inflammatory or more palatable: "Reckless, egotistical commercial spirit and commercial dominance embody themselves infernally in modern films." Catholics, like other conservatives, agreed that there was a disturbing lack of responsibility on the part of people to whom destiny had given an unmistakable influence on the broadest ranges of the *Volk*. In 1931 the papal nuncio in Munich, Cardinal Pacelli, used his message to the Reichsverband deutscher Lichtspieltheaterbesitzer (Organization of German Movie Theater Owners) to declare: "The cinema today conveys a view of the world and principles of life and becomes thereby the school of those who visit it, whose numbers grow daily. In this fact, however, lies the duty for those who convey these principles and impressions. These are the theater owners."[84]

As usual, however, the problem was less commercialism per se than it was public taste. To remain profitable the film industry had to make concessions to public taste, and public taste in films was, in the perception of Catholic intellectuals, at least as deplorable as it was in art, literature, music, or theater. It may well have been even worse. Any expression of confidence in the good sense and good taste of the *Volk* with respect to films is rare, although an occasional echo of this theme can be found among the many diatribes. One film expert equated the taste of the international public with that of children and the uneducated, who demanded strong passions and sharp contrasts. He quoted an article from *Hochwacht*, the journal of a group in which Catholics were prominent that was dedicated to rooting out immorality: "The sentimental and horrible, the impudent and burlesque, wild eroticism and fascinating crime thrill primitive men everywhere more strongly than the complicated problems in the intellectual lives of more highly cultivated individuals." Novels lost their artistic value when translated into film, and the famous director Fritz Lang was accused of having reduced the Siegfried myth to kitsch in his film *Die Nibelungen: Siegfried* (1924). That not much could be expected from films was the prevailing wisdom.[85]

Cause and effect of this unfortunate circumstance were not always clear. Did the public get the films it wanted and would pay for, or was the film industry engaged in a diabolical plot to degrade the public? Otto Behrens suggested that the decline of the feature film "has almost the appearance of a systematic striving to ban the more fastidious and intellectual public from the cinema."[86]

Americans were frequently blamed for the ills of the cinema. From the beginning the film industry was international, and from a very early stage American films dominated German screens. German Catholics found a variety of things to resent about this fact. There were the usual conservative objections to the Americanization of Europe and to the invasion by American capital. There was the assertion that American films were inferior to German films and declining in quality. Some objections had an anti-Semitic cast. It did not escape the notice of German Catholic writers that the American film industry was dominated by immigrant Jews. An alleged loosening of bonds between the individual and the group and a weakening of mankind's recognition of its responsibilities on earth counteracted Catholic emphasis on the group over the individual. The religious diversity of American films, which reflected the religious diversity of that country, and the prominence given in them to the Bible conflicted with Catholic positions.[87]

At the same time, some appreciation of the American contribution can be found in Catholic commentary; a review of the Russian *Battleship Potemkin* (1925), for example, commented that not everything good had to come from America. The compliment was indirect, but it was nonetheless real. Individual films, actors, and directors often received a favorable reception from the German Catholic media. Charlie Chaplin was a particular favorite. *Germania*'s reviewer described *Circus* (1928) as "imposing," and a story on Chaplin's work lauded him for having raised film to artistic stature. On a more general level, knowledgeable critics clearly respected the understanding of the medium that produced the enormous success of American films, even if they might deplore particular examples.[88]

What made films good was far less clear than what made them bad, and Catholic discussions of the aesthetics of film in the 1920s range from the murky to the meaningless. Words like artistic, educational, good, and cultural were bandied about without clear definition. That artistry was desirable was taken for granted, but whether it could be achieved was less certain. By 1925 films had proven to most people's satisfaction that they could be art, but that did not stop Hans Steckner, writing on Lang's *Nibelungen* film, from posing the question yet again of whether film could be an art. Steckner was troubled by the fact that film's artistry depended on mechanical means, a problem that concerned others as well. Steckner concluded that "[t]he cinema is a sin against the spirit of art." Bernhard Marschall flatly disagreed that mechanical implementation negated art. The cinema had its own art, gesture (in this era of silent movies), where the theater had the art of the spoken word, but it was, undeniably, art.[89]

More theoretical and less polemical was the position of Otto Steinbrinck[90] in his contribution to a 1925 volume that was intended to summarize the Catholic experience of film. Although Steinbrinck took the artistry of film as axiomatic, he also attempted to define it. In the context of film, art meant not only films that were externally refined and "artfully" manufactured but also included films that mirrored the times *and* the godly and sublime human life in the *Volk*. Steinbrinck even found grounds for optimism in the dominance of kitsch over art and in the decadence of the literary and artistic elements in such films: "After the expressionist addiction to intoxication and the fashionable idolization of 'mystical visions,' the constraint of a stronger, more ascetic, and livelier abundance of pictures and of more modest and more natural vividness that film relentlessly imposes can signify nothing less than a healing bath to the sick writers of our time—often indeed a good cold bath."[91]

Alois Funk was writing for clerics or lay committees who would supervise the local cinema, and his consideration of good and bad therefore emphasized the concrete and practical. According to Funk, Catholics approved of films that enriched knowledge and rejected films that glorified evil. Evil was only acceptable in the context of action. To be welcomed were nature films, historical films like *Ben-Hur* (1925), Lang's *Die Nibelungen,* films that showed the love of parents and children, and those that portrayed worthy heroes. To be rejected were films that glorified criminals, films that were socially and religiously inflammatory— predictably, controversies had followed the release of highly publicized films about Martin Luther and Joan of Arc—and films dominated by eroticism and sex. Funk connected film with Schiller's prescription of the theater as a moral institution.[92]

By the time Funk wrote in 1930, Catholic newspapers regularly reviewed films, a measure of their acceptance as a cultural medium. A contributor to *Bild und Film* had called for reviews in 1913, arguing that they were essential if the cinema was to be improved. Such reviews are an interesting contrast to the more general, and usually condemnatory, articles that had appeared in the cultural journals. Critics in *Germania,* for example, understood and appreciated the remarkable achievements of German filmmakers of the 1920s. The photographic techniques of *Berlin—Eine Symphonie der Großstadt* (1927) were described as brilliant. *Höhere Töchter* (1927) was praised for naturalness and lack of sentimentality. The films of Fritz Lang, the famous *Dr. Mabuse, Der Spieler* (1922) and *Der müde Tod* (1921), as well as Karl Grune's *Die Straße* (1923), were judged especially worthy, in contrast to the historical *Fridericus Rex* (1921–1922), which was labeled superficial and banal. A glowing review of *Der Blaue Engel* (1930) in the *Allgemeine Rundschau,* the same journal that had published the 1913 article tabulating the murders, suicides, thieves, and prostitutes of film, shows how much Catholic attitudes toward film had changed in twenty years. Emil Jannings as Professor Unrat was "inconceivably good," Gerron as the magician "excellent," and Marlene Dietrich as Chansonette, "the best." Even the film's subject matter, libertinism, was lauded as relevant.[93]

The review of the film *Battleship Potemkin* is particularly significant. Catholics had every reason to be negative about this famous film. Banned in the United States and Britain, it celebrated revolution; no Catholic was unaware that socialist revolutions invariably attacked the clergy and confiscated Church property. Its cinematographic techniques, the use of characters as symbols rather than individuals, and its emphasis on rhythm rather than story were far from what usually received applause. Yet the reviewer in *Germania* not only praised it, he called it a masterpiece.[94] The reception of *Battleship Potemkin,* particularly when it is seen not as an exception but an example of a growing enthusiasm for innovative films in which it was not unusual for Catholic values to be ignored if not contradicted, suggests an increasingly tolerant Catholic intelligentsia.

The Catholic Film Movement

In 1928 Arthur Klein-Ehrenwalt insisted, "Twenty-five million Roman Catholic Germans have a right to see in the cinema what corresponds to their sensitivity, to be able to show their children what is necessary for their development." Although he was alone in asserting that this was a right, it was certainly the objective of every Catholic cultural leader. The optimistically labeled Catholic film movement sought to offer a positive alternative to what was commercially available. "Positive," that favorite slogan of Catholic cultural activity, was used with particular insistence in the area of film.[95]

Richard Muckermann, the brother of Friedrich Muckermann, was at the center of the Catholic film movement. Friedrich described their division of labor; he, as editor of *Der Gral* and a frequent lecturer, worked on the aesthetic and educational aspects of film, his brother on many other aspects, especially economic and propagandist. (This was an era before "propaganda" acquired its present connotations.) In fact, this description does not seem to have been quite fair to Richard. Richard Muckermann published numerous articles on film that addressed philosophical issues in Catholic newspapers like the *Kölnische Volkszeitung;* he was to be found at most conferences on the subject. His papers reveal a man both visionary and practical. Richard Muckermann had a well-defined sense of purpose of the Catholic film and throughout the 1920s worked with groups to create an effective production organization.[96]

Another key individual was Bernhard Marschall of the Zentralbildungsausschuß. By 1927 the Zentralbildungsausschuß had founded a film committee that concentrated in its first years on facilitating film reviews in the Catholic press, creating a Catholic film journal—the Lichtbilderei's *Bild und Film* had died some years before—and fostering cooperation among existing Catholic film organizations. Later it occupied itself with preparing film lists. Perhaps Marschall's most conspicuous accomplishment was the International Catholic Film Congress that was held in Munich in 1929, followed immediately by the International Catholic Radio Congress. The resolutions of the film congress show how Catholic acceptance of the medium had grown. The importance of film was asserted and its influence emphasized. Catholics in all countries were urged to form film committees, to work extensively with the film industry, and to demand censorship laws. The congress also wanted the luxury tax for film to be at the same level as for theater, and for Catholic politicians to concern themselves with the film question.[97]

The Catholic film movement is primarily identified with an array of new organizations created specifically to produce and distribute films, although existing organizations like the Caritasverband (Organization for Charity) and the Katholischer deutscher Frauenbund (Association of German Catholic Women) participated in Catholic film work in the vague sense of promoting good films. Some individuals, primarily adult educators, made important intellectual contributions. The new film organizations tended to have a short life span. The vicissitudes of the prewar Lichtbilderei were typical. It failed to survive the difficult years of the war and postwar period in its original form. Its work was absorbed by its parent organization, the Volksverein, which in 1921 founded Neuland-Kinematographie (New World Films) to carry that work on. Neuland in turn went bankrupt, to be briefly rescued with support from the Leo Gesellschaft, but then disappeared. Other prominent groups of the Weimar period were Richard Muckermann's Stella Maris in Düsseldorf, the Spera-Gesellschaft (Spera Society) in Berlin, and the Bild- und Film-Zentrale (Central Office for Pictures and Film) in Cologne.[98]

A film list of the Bild- und Film-Zentrale in Cologne gives some insight into its operations. The Bild- und Film-Zentrale distributed standard, popular American films, like *The Mark of Zorro* (1920), movies about the famous fighting dog RinTinTin, and westerns. Film versions of prominent literary classics were abundant, as well as more recent works like *Soll und Haben* (1924) by Gustav Freytag, *Die Weber* (1927) by Hauptmann, and a novel by Selma Lagerlöf. The film list did not reinforce the star system; only rarely were performers listed. On the whole, its work showed no distinctively Catholic orientation, but—an important but— the management was Catholic.[99]

Popular hunger for movies was virtually without limit, and a Catholic distribution network was essential; to control the supply was to control what was viewed. A 1921 position paper advocating the establishment of a Catholic film organization identified seven different viewing clubs in the Rhineland, ranging from a Düsseldorf group of 1,400 members with fourteen show days per month to a Duisburg group with 300 members and six show days per month. In addition, many Catholic societies showed films. There was some talk of a network of Catholic theaters, preferably managed by the Volksverein, but it never materialized, and a drive to establish parish cinemas (*Pfarrkinos*) later in the decade was probably a substitute.[100]

For Catholics who wished to be protected from undesirable influences, the parish cinema provided an alternative to the offerings of the local cinema. By the 1920s they were widespread; a national organization was founded for them in 1929. As in other parochial organizations, the priest was likely to have a prominent role, and much depended upon his level of interest. Josef Ettl, the priest and moving spirit of a parish cinema in Guntersdorf, took his self-imposed task very seriously indeed. He described his pain when he felt that a film "injures the tender feeling of simple, modest people." When he showed *Ben-Hur,* he wished that the worst scenes had been omitted.[101]

Production of Catholic films was the capstone of Catholic film work. To replace bad films with good Catholic films was the ultimate positive answer to the film industry. A Catholic film would "make a positive presentation of the Catholic, of the Christian ethos." Richard Muckermann described the purpose of the Catholic film as "to give a small insight into the greatness and sublimity of the Catholic Church [with its ability] to stop the hearts of the peoples of the world." It was not important for it to deal with Catholic material, but it did have to convey the Catholic spirit. And what was the Catholic spirit? One writer defined it as awakening the conscience, lifting the heart, and showing the path to peace.[102]

The Catholic film movement forced Catholic intellectuals to think about the relationship of culture and film in a way they had not done before. Disparaging dismissals of film as belonging merely to civilization rather than culture were common enough, as were paeans to the art form: "Film is more than a great invention. It is a great cultural achievement." But the production of films could lead to more sophisticated thinking. Friedrich Muckermann spoke for virtually all Catholics interested in film when he argued that progress in film could only be made in connection with a living culture, which should, obviously, be defined by Catholicism. For Muckermann, form and content were inseparable, a striking insight that anticipates later cultural theory. Admittedly, for most Catholic intellectuals, who continued to focus on content, the medium was *not* the message, but Friedrich Muckermann was not alone in his comprehension of new possibilities.[103]

The appropriate artistic level for the Catholic film was debated at length. Most who pronounced on the subject entertained artistic ambitions, but high culture had to be balanced with popular appeal, or there would be no point in the effort. One critic cautioned that Catholics should not forget the role of film in entertainment: "The tired, overworked, angry man needs, now and then, to forget what oppresses him and makes him angry during the day, day after day." For such individuals, it was acceptable, even necessary, for there to be light Catholic films and Catholic kitsch.[104]

The first German Catholic film, *The Life of St. Elizabeth,* was produced in 1917 by the Leo Gesellschaft of Munich. Criticized for being too strongly affected by the spirit and form of the average modern film, the Leo Gesellschaft would be the dominant Catholic film organization of the Weimar period. Of the 186 films of Catholic origin made between 1917 and the end of 1932, the Leo Gesellschaft produced 72. A miscellaneous assortment of film organizations, Catholic non–film organizations, clerical orders, commercial firms, and one-time endeavors accounted for the remaining two-thirds.[105]

The Leo Gesellschaft liked to think of itself as the only Catholic producer of Catholic film, although it was not. It did bulk large in its own perception and in the perception of others among its associates because of the kinds of films it made. Three-quarters of those Catholic films that were most like the feature films shown in the cinema, that is, films that were Catholic but without specific religious reference, were made by the Leo Gesellschaft, and three-quarters of its production was in this category. This group comprised the largest group of Catholic films, 72 of 186. Most of the remaining films fell into the following categories: Church missionary activity (25); life and activities of Church youth groups (18); Church social work (15); and popular religious life, such as honoring the saints, pilgrimages, and processions (12).[106]

How much of an impact did the Catholic film movement have? In quantity, its impact was small, or there would not have been the constant complaints of a lack of suitable films for Catholic groups. In quality, its impact was probably even less. Catholic films undoubtedly were hits on the parish film circuit, but they lacked wider appeal and failed to cut into the insatiable appetite of the public, including the Catholic public, for the usual commercial fare.

By 1932 some leaders of the Catholic film movement were beginning to face the painfully obvious ineffectiveness of their efforts. Richard Muckermann told the Essen Katholikentag that the idea that Catholics could collectively influence the film industry to produce better films was an illusion. Two directions were possible: Catholics could produce films, or people could be taught to prefer good films. Muckermann was blunt: the second option, education, was the only realistic approach. Catholic capital was simply not sufficient to expand beyond the modest efforts of the Leohaus group and a new Berlin effort, Eidophon, that was backed by money from Holland. The onset of the Great Depression had exacerbated the difficulties of a perennially underfunded enterprise. At least as critical was the lack of enough Catholic writers, actors, and directors.[107]

Secure in his conviction that there was a demand for the Catholic film, Bernhard Marschall would continue his organizational busyness until the Zentralbildungsausschuß was disbanded under the Nazis, but the Catholic film movement as a whole was a failure. Even Marschall had to acknowledge that only private film companies existed; there was no Catholic film work planned by the administrative hierarchy. The German Catholic film movement was ephemeral; its realities were the viewers' societies, the clubs that put on film programs, and the unorganized collectivity of parish movie nights, not formal systems of pro-

duction or distribution that could compete with the industry. Friedrich Muckermann summed it up: a great Catholic international film movement existed only
on paper.[108]

The Catholic film movement may have failed, but it bears witness to considerable Catholic acceptance of the medium. That acceptance is the more remarkable because it was so indisputably new. Not only did film reflect the times,
far more significantly, it incarnated the times and was recognized as doing so. In
Funk's words, film is "a true child of our fast-moving times." Its very newness may,
indeed, have facilitated acceptance. With no past history to be overcome, more
imaginative responses to the medium were possible.[109]

RADIO

Regular radio broadcasting began in Germany in October 1923, and by the end
of 1924 there were fifteen German transmitters and 99,000 receivers. The number of receivers increased rapidly: 1.2 million in 1926, 2 million in 1928, 3.5 million in 1931, and 6.1 million in 1935. Nine regional radio organizations were established in 1924 and a national umbrella organization in 1925. Regulations designed
to preserve "the multifaceted cultural life of Germany" were issued in 1926. They
guaranteed that the new medium would offer a diversity of opinion, although it
was left to the individual states to regulate content.[110]

Because it was strictly controlled by the government from the beginning,
radio presented Catholic cultural leaders with fewer problems than any other medium. How radio would be used and what messages it would communicate were
determined, not in the marketplace and by the public's willingness to pay, but
bureaucratically. Policy was largely a matter of political debate, and opportunities to influence policy were limited but real.

Partly because of this tight governmental control, radio attracted less attention from Catholic intellectuals than film or theater. In addition, because it seemed
to have less impact, radio was less interesting. Moreover, radio broadcasting was
not as "new" as film had been. By the mid-1920s people were becoming, if not
jaded, at least accustomed to technological changes in their daily lives. Radio,
the newest comer, presented few major cultural issues that had not already been
thoroughly considered in terms of film.

As in society at large, Catholic understanding of the power and importance
of radio was virtually immediate. Experience with film seems to have made it
easier to accept that "[r]adio has become a phenomenon important to life world-
wide, a power that affects all areas of political, economic, and cultural life." Although there was some anti-radio sentiment in the Catholic Church—the bishops

of the Milan Province, for example, forbade the use of radio—no serious consideration was ever given to the question of whether or not to participate in radio broadcasting. There was, on the other hand, great concern that radio not be allowed to develop without Catholic involvement, as many felt film had been allowed to develop.[111]

Radio was recognized as an extraordinarily effective medium of mass communication. Many Catholic writers pointed to its success in reaching broad masses. Others went a step beyond to the understanding that it was both inherently democratic and democratizing: "It removes the exclusivity of pleasure in art, entertainment, knowledge and, in favorable cases, even education." Skeptics found this something of an overstatement, since they assumed that radio's educational and cultural effects were more likely to be limited to those who were already educated and already cultured, but art, knowledge, and education were available, even if listeners selected only the entertainment options. Some intellectuals expressed fear. In the wrong hands radio could bring much harm. What, they asked, would have happened if the founder of German socialism, August Bebel, had been able to broadcast against Bismarck in 1891? Or Bismarck against the leader of the Catholic Center Party, Ludwig Windthorst, in 1874?[112]

Radio's great allure for proponents of the Catholic cultural movement was its perceived educational potential. The first formal conversations about radio among Catholics in 1926 produced a declaration that radio should be treated as an "educational establishment" (*Bildungsstätte*), and soon articles with titles like "Rundfunk und Volksbildung" (Radio and Adult Education) began to appear. The new medium fitted well with the Catholic concept of adult education that was being forged in the 1920s. Whereas before World War I humanistic learning had been emphasized, a kind of "the classics for the common man" approach, after the war the objective of adult education was to provide the individual with what he needed to understand about the reality of his life. The format of radio programs and the very nature of radio communication would not have served that earlier ideal well, but, in terms of format, radio suited the new approach, as did its emphasis on current events and information.[113]

The cultural potential of radio also seemed promising. Like film, radio was declared to be a carrier of culture. Radio added a new, aural dimension at a time when films were still silent, but radio was not itself seen as a creator of culture. The recommendation of the first Catholic meeting on radio in 1926 that the number of radio organizations be limited to increase the possibility of making radio a cultural force in fact increased the chances that a culture acceptable to Catholics would prevail. With points of creation few and content subject to political review, the anarchy that prevailed in film production was eliminated.[114]

Opinions on the broadcast of music illustrate some of the ambivalence about culture, about what culture was, what it ought to be, and for whom it ought to be. Each radio establishment boasted a concert hall along with its theater and lecture hall, and music was an important part of radio programming; music was a staple in Catholic offerings on the radio. Listeners doubtless thought of music in terms of pleasure, but Catholic cultural leaders saw it in more serious terms. The broadcast of *Volkslieder* could be used to educate taste by demonstrating the difference between true *Volk* music and commercial kitsch. Good music would fight popular music. Catholics were exhorted to participate in radio in order to ensure musical presentations that reflected Catholic life. Catholic intellectuals did not debate whether music and radio were mismatched. The ideal remained "self-performance of a work of art in complete harmony with intellectual, spiritual, and rational forces and the possibility of experience," but when that was not possible, mechanical means were better than nothing. Technology had earned respect as a good helper.[115]

The first Catholic participation in radio programming was in lecture series. Some Protestant sects had participated eagerly, but in the beginning neither the Roman Catholic Church nor the traditional Protestant groups had been especially interested in radio. The bishops displayed their usual reluctance. The Fulda Conference of Bishops' protocol of August 12, 1926, recommended a certain distance in the interest of the *disciplina sacra*. Within a few years, however, religious offerings had become standard radio fare. Although reluctant, Catholics felt that they had to match the Protestants.[116]

The regular religious programs took different forms; an address alone or a reading by itself; an address plus music; a reading from the Bible or other texts plus music; or music alone. The planned program for the Catholic religious offerings of the Westdeutscher Rundfunk (West German Radio), first based in Münster and later in Cologne, for the first five months of 1928 included talks with the following titles: "The Pilgrimage to the Manger"; "The World of the Supernatural (Angel and Devil)"; "Man, the Crown of Creation"; "Resurrection in Christ"; "Peace in Christ"; and "Mother Mary." Frequently a theme was chosen to give some unity. In 1931 Cologne was in the first year of a three-year topic: the sacrifice of the Mass; Stuttgart's theme was God's grace; and Frankfurt had chosen Church history, presented through the saints. As time passed, the Church became more comfortable with the medium, and new applications were added to the basic weekly religious program. A part of the 1932 Essen Katholikentag was broadcast. The 1932 Christmas Eve message of the pope was broadcast, as well as a Midnight Mass from Weingarten. In addition, Catholic programs included cultural content. The Catholic committee for the Frankfurt regional station was quite proud that 1930 had seen a "stately" row of Catholic programs, with such jewels as a broadcast from the abbey of Maria-Laach on Benedictine monasticism, Erich Przywara[117] on "Technology and Religion," and Anton Neipperg[118] on "The Cultural Crisis of the Present and Catholicism."[119]

Deep Catholic concern for maintaining the sacred character of the Mass imposed restrictions on the religious programs. The clergy remained adamant that the radio broadcast of a religious service was *not* a substitute for the Mass. The conversations at the 1926 meeting on radio produced the following statement about the two-hour period allotted to a Catholic religious program: "This hour shall, however, be no 'religious celebration,' still less a 'religious devotional hour' in which the liturgical service is broadcast. Rather, in Breslau, and soon in Berlin, the cultural works of Catholics shall be treated and broadcast. It shall be more an 'educational hour.'" More detailed guidelines issued later in the same year added a directive, endorsed by the Fulda Bishops' Conference, that church music performances should only be broadcast if they were *not* part of a Church service. The fact of technological transmission added to reservations. The question of how the presence of a transmitter and a receiver in the nave affected the character of the cure of souls was posed but not answered.[120]

The Catholic response to the new medium was facilitated by the existence of the Zentralbildungsausschuß. Its energetic director, Bernhard Marschall, eagerly appropriated radio as its responsibility, an acquisition aided by the general lack of interest elsewhere. Marschall was a man for all media and would go on to add film, press, and records to his empire, which eventually included both groups interested in adult education and groups interested in communication in its many forms. The Zentralbildungsausschuß held its first discussions on radio in February 1926 and in the following year organized a radio division. A local committee was organized for each broadcasting region. The Bavarian dioceses cooperated with the Zentralbildungsausschuß to a limited extent, but the Bavarian bishops issued separate declarations on the subject.[121]

The Zentralbildungsausschuß represented Catholic interests in radio nationally and internationally. It organized the 1929 International Catholic Radio Congress, the first of its kind, to demonstrate Catholic readiness to work positively. Most real work, however, took place at the local level. Particularly full records from the Diocese of Rottenburg, a diocese that had both a diocesan radio group as well as radio groups for the individual deaneries, enable us to appreciate some of the day-to-day problems of the Church in working with radio authorities. Guaranteeing Catholic independence and control over its assigned radio time and speakers required constant vigilance. At the same time, the individuals representing Catholic interests worked constantly to influence radio authorities as much as possible. And they had to develop appropriate and attractive programs. As a group, they must have been exceptionally effective, because the regional organization of the Rottenburg Diocese was noted for its Catholic programming.[122]

A different kind of organized activity was the listening group (*Hörgemeinde*). Most such groups were doubtless very informal, a few members of a Cäcilien Verein who listened to a particular set of musical programs together, or several people who met at the parish house to do their listening, but one optimist went so far as to suggest that they be directed by a clergyman or teacher. These listening groups disappeared as ownership of the apparatus needed for radio reception became more common. By 1931 the family was being described as the true listening group.[123]

Catholic involvement with radio was one of its happiest cultural endeavors. Thanks to strict governmental control, radio was almost totally devoid of what Catholics found morally offensive. Because of the guidelines under which radio operated, the Catholic viewpoint was well represented and, in addition, radio officials were sensitive to Catholic opinions. In what was surely a unique event, the director of the Westdeutscher Rundfunk sent a letter to Marschall, apologizing because a crude program had been broadcast. Finally, the very nature of radio seemed to reinforce what Catholics wanted reinforced: the group, the family. For so much positive benefit, the fact that other viewpoints were equally well represented and that radio's cultural offerings were a potpourri that included much popular culture could be tolerated.[124]

In the performing arts, modernity appeared at its most direct and unmitigated. Each medium, theater, film, and radio, was described as a metaphor for the times, and all were considered to be especially effective in reflecting their times. Catholic success in taming them would have established an important precedent.

With the exception of radio, however, success is not the word that immediately springs to mind to describe German Catholic engagement with the performing arts. Instead, the pattern is the same one that characterized Catholic engagement with other art forms: opposition and acceptance, the channeling of responses into organizational entities, relatively uncoordinated activity in pursuit of different and sometimes conflicting purposes, and, in the end, accommodation. The themes are long-standing, played with variations appropriate to the form, and with differing degrees of intensity.

Catholic rhetoric concerning the performing arts invoked the familiar abominations. Morality was the first and foremost consideration, the denunciation adapted to fit the examples in each medium. The same distaste for technology that appears in discussions of other cultural activities was expressed, although a fresh element was added to this particular aversion. Johannes Hönig warned—sapiently—that the new methods of dissemination could easily lead to intellectual enslavement (*Geistesknechtung*).[125]

The familiar illusions that kept the Catholic cultural movement alive were present. Those engaged with theater, cinema, and radio regarded popularity as an aberration. They were convinced that crass capitalists dictated what was available, and, all evidence to the contrary, that what the people *really* wanted was the good Catholic play, the good Catholic film, or the good Catholic radio broadcast. Good plays would conquer the stage—if only there were good plays; good films would replace bad—if only good films were made available; and on radio the good music of great composers would convert listeners from light-weight, popular fare.

Likewise, the familiar problems manifested themselves. The division between laity and clergy that was the product of different priorities created or exacerbated difficulties in working together; with a few notable exceptions, Catholic laymen were much more positive about the new theatrical offerings and the new media of film and radio than were clerics. The lack of money, no more abundant in these than in any other cultural area, was keenly felt. Film was especially expensive, but theater was not cheap.

Proposed solutions were equally familiar. The two-pronged approach, positive and negative, was the foundation of work in the performing arts as it was in all other cultural areas. Positive efforts addressed both production and dissemination, but there was also great reliance on censorship. Thanks to the role of the performing arts in mass communication, the concept of the *Volk* was prominent, but less trust was placed in the wisdom of the *Volk* than in censorship as a force for improvement.

At the same time, Catholic engagement with the performing arts was not a tale already completely told. The performing arts were distinguished by a newness that was present in such quantity, in such strength, and with such suddenness that it forced Catholics, whether reluctantly or enthusiastically, to face the fact of profound cultural change in a way that they had not before. In a particularly insightful passage, the novelist Arnold Ulitz[126] wrote: "The cinema first makes us lie, and we become liars and actors. . . . Everything is theater, love, politics, and sport. . . . The girls make eyes as they have seen it done in the movies, the men offer one another their hands, and light cigarettes as the counterfeit gentlemen do on film. But so it is: first, man made the film, now film makes men."[127]

The new media had enormous potential as creators of culture, but what they were depended on how they were used; their effectiveness could serve either good or bad ends. Monsignor Eugène Julien[128] urged the First International Catholic Film Congress to "meet the new art with trust and accept it as the Church earlier accepted poetry, painting, sculpture, and music, if placed in the service of religious feeling"; but complete trust was never achieved. Although its "strong realism" led German Catholicism to be actively involved with the new media, and there were certainly many Catholic intellectuals who were extremely positive about them, film and radio continued to meet resistance from conservative Catholics. Despite the many fine films of the 1920s, despite all the rhetoric about educational value, in 1931 the episcopal ordinary of Mainz could sharply inform one of its deans that it was not appropriate to recommend a film from the pulpit, even if it contributed to religious edification: "The pulpit is not the place to make the faithful aware of a film performance, which primarily serves pleasure, and to urge them to visit it." For the majority of Catholic intellectuals, films, although carriers of culture, were never themselves quite culture but instead belonged to the world of civilization. They were thus associated with the material world, not the spiritual, with technology, not aesthetics. Only its antiquity saved the theater from a similar fate.[129]

9

Struggling with the Objectionable

Opposition and Censorship

PERILOUS TIMES

Censorship acknowledges that ideas can have behavioral consequences; its fundamental premise is that dangerous ideas need to be prevented from threatening or influencing the public. Employed to protect the state or another entity from ideas that pose a threat to political stability or to the morals that underlie political, social, and religious stability, censorship is exercised by an institution that is deemed to be legitimate and that has the power to enforce whatever restrictions are imposed on the medium of communication. Whether or not censorship is perceived to be necessary, the form it takes and its successes and failures are embedded in the particular context of political, social, economic, and technological conditions.

Although examples of censorship can be found in almost any organized society, the invention of printing introduced qualitative changes to its theory and practice. When the printing press replaced the scriptorium as the means of reproduction, the number of copies of any particular work, and therefore the potential audience, multiplied greatly. As a 1928 article in *Pastor Bonus,* the journal for parish priests, pointed out, the heretics of the fifteenth and sixteenth century "productively misused" this opportunity to spread their pernicious ideas. The decline of unit production costs that resulted from the mechanization of printing and the spread of wood-pulp paper in the nineteenth century expanded the accessibility of ideas further, and in the twentieth century the new technology of film multiplied them yet again.[1]

The convergence of the development of mass media, great economic and social change, improved education of the lower classes, and the beginnings of democracy presented late nineteenth- and early twentieth-century Germans with a set of circumstances that virtually guaranteed that censorship would be a major subject of debate. People who had previously had only the most limited access to revolutionary political ideas, titillating pictures, and smutty literature could now readily obtain such items at their local tobacco shop or newsstand. Suggestive films were screened at local cinemas. The government and propertied classes became steadily more concerned about what the lower orders were reading, hearing, and viewing; recent history made social and political instability all too imaginable. Justifications for censorship needed to be reasserted, new procedures needed to be developed.

In the context of Catholic culture, censorship has been related primarily to moral concerns, because culture is perceived as the crucial link between corrupting values and immoral behavior. At the 1912 Katholikentag, Joseph Mausbach expressed the widely held view that literature and art determined the spiritual atmosphere. The obvious corollary was that if one cared about the spiritual atmosphere, one had to care about what was read, what was viewed, and, by extension, what was heard. Some saw literature and art more as a product than a cause of the spiritual climate. The 1908 declaration of the Fulda Bishops' Conference proclaimed both views at the same time: that immorality led art astray and infected literature and that a spiritual (*geistig*) syphilis was the product of pornographic books and pictures.[2]

By the beginning of the twentieth century the perception of pervasive moral decay, widespread throughout western Europe, was prevalent in Germany. In 1903 Hermann Roeren,[3] a Cologne lawyer, morality warrior, and Center Party deputy in the Reichstag, expressed a widely shared view: "A few years ago those who asserted that even here in Germany morality was declining in the name of 'culture' and 'free art' were dismissed as benighted and called moral zealots, . . . but no one now argues that there is no moral decline." The Fulda Conference of Bishops complained that society was plagued by an epidemic of immorality. Moralists used terms like moral emergency and cited a mind-numbing catalog of noxious social ills, ranging from prostitution to embracing on the stage. The lists were endless. Immorality was inherent in modern life.[4]

Count Albert von Oberndorff's[5] brief moral history of the Germans presented at the 1931 Katholikentag in Nuremberg illuminates the Catholic frame of reference. Oberndorff began with Tacitus, who had praised the virtue of German women, then moved on to the Middle Ages. The count admitted that the medieval period was not free from moral errors but argued that moral errors were then recognized as such and labeled: "Good was good, and bad bad." The Renaissance had taken the unfortunate step of reviving lax heathen viewpoints, and the eighteenth century had imposed a "Versailles-mistress" economy on the German peoples. The count's assessment of the present was that many Germans were ripe for the ills of "geistiger Bolschewismus" (spiritual bolshevism). Militantly he asserted that "we Catholics" were in the front line and needed to stand shoulder to shoulder with other respectable men in the fight against the unacceptable in dress and in social life, against smut in word, in picture, in the theater, and in the cinema, against abortion, and against the "shameless pushiness of perverts." The laws of Christian tradition needed to be defended.[6]

Particularly painful to the many who shared this dark view, Catholic and non-Catholic alike, was the sense that moral deterioration was taking place before their eyes. They were living through a time in which "basic value orientations . . . primarily rooted in tradition and in institutional religion" were giving way to values "increasingly based on individual autonomy, self-interest and personal preferences," and they knew it. The old German virtues of thrift, modesty, and godliness were growing scarcer. Germans had entered World War I with the hope that war would bring moral renewal, but instead moral conditions had only worsened. By the mid-1920s the following broad trends were regular objects of complaint: the destruction of ideals; the diminution of authority and abolition of old ties and limits; the stress on "naturalness," especially in sexual relationships; the spread of American influence; the growth of socialism and a materialistic worldview; the increase of Jewish influence; and the change in the role and activities of women, which was often equated with a decline in the family. Intellectually, anti-Christian isms like aestheticism, atheism, individualism, materialism, and pantheism were on the rise; worship of the body was rampant. The declining birthrate, ever-rising number of divorces, large numbers of prostitutes, increasing homosexuality, alcoholism, lack of suitable housing, and mass psychoses were symptomatic social ills.[7]

There was broad-based public distaste for the cultural products that reflected these trends. Art, literature, music, and later films challenged the dominant late nineteenth-century bourgeois conventions, and the tone, form, and style in which they did it brought great discomfort. The decisive break of the artistic avant-garde with the traditions of centuries created a high culture that empha-sized innovation, disdained rules whether artistic or otherwise, was international in its orientation, and was socially engaged in a new way. New cultural offerings were often judged both un-German and un-Christian, as German and Christian were generally understood. An article in the *Allgemeine Rundschau* described everything that was ugly, decadent, or dirty, three adjectives frequently applied to new cultural offerings, as alien to the Germans and only permitted by their "stu-pid" good nature.[8]

Commercially produced popular culture was equally loathed. Indecent pic-tures, trashy novels, cartoons that pilloried clerics, generals, and politicians, music that appealed to primal instincts, and sexually suggestive films exemplified de-teriorating public morals. There was a strong feeling that the *Volk* was being ex-ploited. Cultural decline was both cause and effect of moral decline; moral decline was cause and effect of religious decline.

Articles and letters offer specific examples of what Catholics found unwel-come in modern culture. In art they objected, for example, to the morality (or lack of it) in artists' circles, to the large naked statues in the Feldherrnhalle in Munich, to a reproduction of a Hieronymous Bosch work in the *Kölnische Volkszeitung*. In literature, the books in lending libraries brought offense, and merely holding a bad book in the hand was held to destroy purity. Music had its trashy songs and tunes. The theater, with its embracing on the stage, crudities of language, and portrayal of what Catholics opposed, such as divorce, was rife with condemnable scenes and themes. The cinema was perceived as the school of the criminal.[9]

Censorship was the solution of choice. Most Catholics saw it as requisite to the success of their cultural program. The creation of healthy alternatives to the products of modern culture was the positive part of their cultural efforts. Cen-sorship was the indispensable negative *Doppelgänger,* necessary to protect good Catholics from the cultural temptations and evils of the world.

THE SYSTEM OF STATE CENSORSHIP BEFORE 1914

Despite the existence of laws intended to restrict the availability of what was un-desirable, "excresences" of modern culture were present in German cultural life before 1914. The system of censorship within which Germans lived under the em-pire was a mixture of local and national law and regulation, all of which depended heavily on enforcement by local police. As far as the morality of art and litera-ture was concerned, the crucial law was Paragraph 184 of the 1872 Criminal Code, which defined pornography. Before 1924 only Braunschweig and Württemberg had laws that specifically regulated films.[10]

Paragraph 184 was not intentionally applied in a manner to hinder art or scholarship, since both the police and the courts of imperial Germany accepted that human sexuality was a legitimate and necessary object of study and art. They limited their efforts to what endangered public morality, recognizing that if they began confiscating and prosecuting works of great art and scholarship, they would merely make themselves ridiculous. Through judicial decisions, however, Paragraph 184 did acquire a dangerous subtext, the doctrine of relative obscenity, which could and often did harm art and scholarship. Relative obscenity made external circumstances, like place of presentation, intended use, and, most significant of all, intended audience, factors in the determination of the obscenity of a cultural artifact. It permitted the Dresden Royal Gallery to display publicly Vecchio's *Reclining Venus* and Giorgione's *Sleeping Venus,* but required the confiscation of inexpensive postcard-sized reproductions of the paintings.[11]

Beginning about 1890 there was much popular agitation, agitation in which Catholics like Hermann Roeren were prominent, to extend what was illegal to include what was morally undesirable. The many marches, petitions, and public meetings of this effort, however, had little impact. A representative of Chancellor Theobald von Bethmann-Hollweg[12] did propose a law to protect youth from salacious advertising to the Reichstag in February 1914, and the Prussian Landtag petitioned the state government to fight the "increasing immorality, especially in the big cities" in March 1914, but the outbreak of the war prevented further action. The principal legacy of the prewar movement was to convince many politicians and a significant section of the population that something had to be done about the cultural artifacts that did not meet accepted moral standards.[13]

An exception, if a very partial exception, to this campaign's general lack of results was the Lex Heinze. Originally intended to expand the definitions of pornography already existing in the 1872 Civil Code, during the eight years it was debated it helped make culture a major political issue and contributed to the polarization of right and left. Vigorous opposition outside the Reichstag involved leading intellectuals, artists, and writers in defense of intellectual freedom. The final political compromise permitted only an attenuated version to be passed in 1900, but enough substance remained to save the face of the right. Among Catholics, it revealed in the political arena "the growing division" between the doctrinaire and those willing to compromise to some extent with modern society.[14]

THE BATTLEGROUND

The primary cultural setting in which Catholic views on censorship evolved was print, especially in that category of publications called *Schundliteratur* (see pp. 86–89). Usually published in the form of weekly installments costing only a few Pfennig, it was the first widely available commercial cultural product aimed at the lower classes. Produced purely, or not so purely, to entertain, *Schundliteratur* fell somewhere between true literature, which was defined by its merits and ambitions, and pornography, which was defined by its obscenity. The question, of course, was where it fell. This in-between position of *Schundliteratur* made it the area where those who believed greater moral restraints needed to be imposed contended with those who wanted to expand the limits of acceptability.

Schund meant trash, but how dangerous really was this form of cultural trash? Opponents of *Schundliteratur* presented it as a major factor in the degeneration of society, and from the 1880s on it was regularly included on any list of modern ills, usually right next to prostitution. *Schundliteratur,* even if it was not openly pornographic, subtly led the reader to the wrong side of the boundary between good and evil. By concealing its true face, *Schundliteratur* was all the more dangerous. *Schund* was held responsible for poisoning the soul, destroying faith, and stirring up dissatisfaction and radicalism. It worked against everything that made for a healthy life.[15]

Schund was accused of damaging taste and hindering education. Individuals who read nothing but *Schundliteratur* would not only be morally corrupted, they would also be so habituated to sensational and tasteless tales that they would never seek out literature that was more challenging to read but more intellectually and spiritually rewarding. If *Schund* were censored, vulnerable youths would be more likely to fulfill their spiritual, intellectual, and, presumably, economic potential, a line of reasoning that endowed censorship with a positive character.[16]

Nonetheless, *Schund* had many attractions, and Catholics were not immune. Slickly marketed, it had the charm of the forbidden. It appealed to readers who wanted something undemanding to read on the train or at the hairdresser. Readers of "sluggish mentality," a group one opponent equated with *Schund* readers, did not understand that reading was supposed to be intellectual work and could cultivate thought. If a work created a sufficient stir, those who wanted to be in the know had to read it, moral impurity or no moral impurity. Too many people preferred to be thought morally inadequate rather than not conversant with the latest trend.[17]

One aspect of the campaign to tighten the law relating to pornography was an effort to expand the legal definition of censorship to include *Schundliteratur*. At virtually every Katholikentag of the 1890s the evils of *Schundliteratur* were a topic of discussion, Catholics were active in groups that advocated censorship, and Catholic groups like the Borromäus Verein worked to bring more censorship about. By 1914 the anti-*Schund* reformers had succeeded in getting a bill introduced into the Reichstag that added *Schundliteratur* to the jurisdiction of the *Reichsgewerbeordnung* (National Commercial Regulations), evidence that *Schundliteratur* was viewed as a commercial product rather than a cultural artifact. The outbreak of World War I put the anti-*Schund* campaign on hold; the proposed legislation was not even debated. The flood of *Schund* publications brought by the war were handled under the regulations of the strict military censorship the government imposed.[18]

The issue, however, had not died. The influence of the prewar reformers can be seen in the Weimar Constitution. This attempt to create the foundation for a democratic Germany renounced censorship in principle: "Every German has the right within the limits of the general laws to express his opinion freely in word, writing, print, picture, or other means. . . . No censorship will take place. . . ." At the same time, it made two important exceptions: "No censorship will take place, but laws that deviate from this principle may be made for films. Also in the fight against *Schund-* and *Schmutzliteratur,* as for the protection of youth from public advertisements and displays, legal rules are permissible."[19]

The Reichstag used the exception to pass immediately a film censorship law, but it took seven years for a law regulating *Schundliteratur* to materialize. Opponents of *Schundliteratur* across the political spectrum mounted a sustained, vigorous campaign for such a law. Finally, in August 1925 Martin Schiele,[20] the leader of the DNVP (Deutschnationale Volkspartei, or German National People's Party) and minister of the interior, sent a draft of a law to supplement the existing law on pornography to the Reichstag. This legislative proposal stimulated intense debate, as opponents of censorship organized to counter its advocates, but a law against *Schund* and *Schmutz* was finally enacted in December 1926.[21]

The *Schund* and *Schmutz* law provided for the creation of a list of dirty and trashy publications that were not to be sold, given, or traded to anyone under eighteen. Following the model of film censorship, a review board (*Prüfstelle*), established by the minister of the interior in cooperation with provincial governments, was to decide whether or not a publication should be placed on the list. Decisions of a review board applied throughout the Reich. A national review board had the responsibility of informing the minister of the decisions of all review boards and heard appeals to remove items. The review boards consisted of a chairperson from the civil service and eight members, two from art and literature, two from the book trade and the art trade, two from youth organizations, and two from teaching and adult education.[22]

Passage of the law did not solve the problem. No sooner was the long-sought law providing for restrictions on *Schundliteratur* in place, than a chorus of complaints began. The 1926 law was not a true censorship law. It neither examined works before publication nor affected production but only limited dis-

semination under certain conditions. Another objection was that implementation of the law was slow, and when enforcement did begin, it was inadequate. A
full year elapsed between the law's passage and placement of the first item on the
list. After *Schund* was finally defined, the police failed to forward complaints. The
resulting list was therefore "thin" and disturbingly full of material about which
no one cared any more, like the Buffalo Bill stories. Opponents of *Schundliteratur*
realized that they had won an empty victory. They might gain psychological satisfaction from having a law and from placing a few items they had long condemned
on a restricted list, but they knew that the law had not made a significant impact
on the reading of *Schundliteratur*.[23]

Film was the other major cultural setting in which Catholic views on censorship developed. Film, like print, was a mass medium, but there were significant
differences in some of the issues and even larger differences in the solutions.
Discussions about censorship of film exhibit a more limited range of opinion
and less subtlety than those of print culture. They were also more compressed,
both because film did not become a cultural force until the first decade of the
twentieth century and because the first film censorship law was passed in 1920.

Catholic intellectuals divided film into the same categories they used in literature: films with artistic ambitions and merits; *Schund* films; and clearly pornographic films. *Schund* films were merely *Schundliteratur* in another guise. Unlike
literature, however, the assumption was that the vast majority of films were trash.
How could it be otherwise? Because film was an industry, the artist was not in the
forefront; instead the principal creator of the art work was the capitalistically oriented, industrial, mostly anonymous "entrepreneur." A Cologne group of moral
crusaders that viewed more than 150 films found only *Der Wunder des Schnee-
schuhs* (The Wonder of Snowshoes [1920]) completely acceptable. They dismissed
the vast majority of films as "completely without value, their principal object to
satisfy the crowd's desire for sensation." Most intellectuals would probably have
been slightly more generous, but they would have agreed with the crusaders that
film was far from providing either entertainment that was above reproach or education that was free of aesthetic and moral objections.[24]

A vague dislike of the medium as such is apparent in many discussions relating to film. Not even a possible contribution to religious piety made it acceptable
to recommend a film from the pulpit. Because film was a business, dominated by
its need to always offer something new, conservative intellectuals argued that it
could not serve the purposes either of culture or education, let alone religion.[25]

Other arguments against films were grounded in particular objectionable
features that offended Catholic sensibilities. In 1927 Arthur Klein-Ehrenwalt insisted, "Twenty-five million Roman Catholic Germans have a right to see in the
cinema what corresponds to their sensitivity, to be able to show their children

what is necessary for their development." Too many films featured prostitutes and criminals, too many portrayed an unreal world of consumption and luxury, too many took absolutely no interest in morals for that to be possible.[26]

Until after World War I Catholic efforts to impose controls on films were primarily directed toward protecting children. The circumstances of 1919 forced advocates of censorship to broaden their focus. As one writer on the film scene of 1919 put it, it was as if the demons of the world had been unloosed. The combination of the "moral enervation of broad classes" brought by the war and the end of effective censorship by local police permitted a flood of "Aufklärungs-filme." Masquerading as sex education, most of these "enlightenment" films were outright pornography.[27] Klaus Petersen emphasizes the conflict of interests in the development of censorship in the Weimar period, but this effusion of pornographic films created a consensus that something had to be done to regulate what was available at the local cinema.[28]

The new Reichstag, under considerable pressure to move quickly, took almost immediate advantage of the constitutional exception to pass a law to censor films. As with the later 1926 law regulating *Schundliteratur*, the May 1920 law provided for review boards to be created as needed in the centers of the film industry, with a national review board at the head. Members of review boards included representatives from the film industry, art, literature, social work, youth work, and adult education. Grounds for censorship included the endangerment of public order (a concept that took political, social, religious and ethical considerations into account), the wounding of religious sensitivities, harming the perception of Germany abroad, and satisfying the baser instincts without any redeeming value. In addition, films to which youth under eighteen were admitted had to be free of damaging effects on their physical, moral, and intellectual development and should not overstimulate their imaginations. Children under six were not admitted to any film showings.[29]

In its final form the film law of 1920 was a compromise that failed to satisfy all the factions, and by 1922 revision was being seriously discussed. Most Catholic intellectuals urged more rigorous censorship of films. In 1923 the Catholic bishops sent a petition to the minister of the interior placing responsibility for the moral decline of Germany on the shoulders of the cinema. The bishops were particularly concerned about the portrayal of crime, which they believed would lead to imitation in real life, and the representation of religion and religious figures. They wanted a more thoroughgoing rejection of films that were dirty or trashy and the age of restriction raised from eighteen to twenty. They urged that the representation of the film industry on the review boards be reduced in favor of other interested parties and that individual state governments take a more prominent role. Although the patchwork of local jurisdictions that had licensed films in imperial Germany had been an uneven and minimally effective system, from a Catholic point of view the national character of the new arrangement was a problem. What could be shown in Wedding, Giesing, or Hernals, could not, as one writer put it, be shown in the shadow of the Gedächtniskirche, the Frauenkirche, or the Stephanskirche.[30]

CATHOLIC ADVOCACY OF CENSORSHIP

Generally speaking, Catholics, whether as individual Catholics or as the official Church, endorsed censorship; the idea that freedom has limits is fundamental to Christianity. Catholic interests were not, however, identical to those of the state. Catholics might fear political instability, but they feared it for what such instability could mean for the Church. Both Catholics and the government were alarmed by immorality, but the government's alarm was rooted in fear of possible social consequences, the alarm of Catholics in concern for the impact of immorality on religion. Such differences, however, had little effect in practice. Catholics wanted censorship to accomplish what most other Germans wanted censorship to accomplish: protection from culture that damaged religious feelings, that endangered public order, that debased morality, and that satisfied (or was it really stimulated?) the lower instincts of mankind. Some wanted aesthetic censorship as well, by which they meant restrictions on what damaged the artistic and aesthetic values of the *Volk,* a concept that broke new theoretical ground.[31]

The family, both the family as symbol and the family as reality, was a particularly strong theme in the advocacy of censorship by Catholics. Throughout the Western world fundamental attitudes toward family life had changed in the course of the nineteenth century. The home had become a refuge for men from the rough and tumble of the world. Women were idealized, and the wife and mother was expected to be pure and virtuous. Childhood was now an identifiable stage in life; and the child by definition was innocent. Catholic moralists wanted censorship applied to the cultural manifestations of what they equated with damage to the family, the declining birthrate, divorce, and prostitution. Books about prostitutes and plays that featured divorce were potential sources of corruption. Pornography might lead to the sales of contraceptives. Stories that demeaned women were deplored. The relationship of parent and child required protection; parental control was necessary for a proper "German" family.[32]

Youth was idealized. Even big-city youth had a "holy" right to a happy, innocent time; they should *not,* wrote one commentator, be better informed than medical students had been twenty-five years before. For them, it was particularly important that the moral level not be allowed to degenerate, but for it to reach the highest possible height. Limiting their access to films and their visits to art galleries where nude pictures were on display was important.[33]

Anticapitalist sentiments appear frequently in the arguments of Catholic intellectuals who favored stricter censorship. The unstated assumption that art should not be part of the cash nexus created fundamental hostility to the products of modern culture. A 1926 article in *Hochland* attributed most of art's problems to its materialism. After art's separation from the Church, it had to serve the rich, a task that made it necessary always to come up with something new, striking, and extravagant. Too often, to be new, striking, and commercially successful, the producer of a cultural artifact had to ignore moral standards. Capitalism was sweepingly condemned for seeking "to draw its profit from the ruin of the morality of our *Volk*."[34]

Discussions of commercialism included consideration of the role of the merchant. Both advertising that attracted people to undesirable films and the commercial techniques that helped booksellers sell *Schund* and *Schmutz* were resented. The rejection of a Catholic clergyman's request to the owner of a "pleasure business" to refrain for the general good from producing an offensive "offering" was reported with some indignation in an article with the title "Cynicism." (The owner told the clergyman that he would cancel the offensive "offering" only if the clergyman would guarantee the wages of his employees.) Distinctively Catholic was the idea that the merchant had responsibilities to the community. He was not solely a distributor of goods, in business only to make money. He was there to serve "real needs," unlike the slave traders of North America or the traders in trashy books and pictures. His business should rest on foundations of truth and justice. Moral law demanded that he take only a "fair profit." If merchants adhered to these principles, there would be no need for censorship. Such ideas hark back to the Middle Ages and were as anachronistic as the term merchant itself in the industrialized, urbanized German economy of the early twentieth century.[35]

The most common justifications of censorship were the most convincing: an assertion, often richly embroidered with detail, that some evil consequence results from reading the wrong book or seeing the wrong film. Catholic intellectuals buttressed these statements with more abstract arguments, all of which ultimately rested on the thesis that faith could be weakened by contact with the ungodly. Mausbach emphasized the Church's responsibility to see that man did not come into conflict with what interfered with the adoration of God that was enjoined upon him. The Church was the custodian of divine revelation, and its duty was to interpret the teachings of Christ. Morality was an eternal truth.[36]

Censorship was a practice with which Catholics were familiar and comfortable, as Georg Schreiber,[37] a professor of moral theology, pointed out in the debates on the proposed film censorship law of 1920 in the Reichstag. Church-approved censorship can be said to have begun with the burning of the books that followed Paul's mission to Ephesus (Acts 19:19). From a Catholic point of view, censorship had positive features, protecting individuals from being slaves to their baser instinct and preventing them from choosing reading that would not help develop literary maturity.[38]

But was it for *all* individuals? An underlying condescension is plain in statements on censorship's anticipated benefits. Throughout all discussions of censorship the assumption is that it is the common people who need to be protected, just as it was the young who should have the priest tell them what to read. Gary Stark and Klaus Petersen both comment on this class-based reaction, a commonplace in movements to impose censorship, but contemporaries, too, sensed its presence. An American Catholic criticized Karl Muth sharply for saying that priests might perhaps judge the suitability of a work for the young or common people, but not for educated gentlemen. An anonymous article in the *Historisch-politische Blätter* in 1906 made the point that most people demanded a culture close to the interests of their own profession or group. In fact, the commercial success of *Schundliteratur* and "bad" films demonstrates that the cultural interests of the *Volk* were being satisfied, even if those interests were not what the essentially bourgeois Catholic intellectuals thought they were or ought to be.[39]

CATHOLIC RESERVATIONS ABOUT CENSORSHIP

With the bishops giving such a strong lead on the issue, outright opposition to censorship was rare, although a significant group of Catholic intellectuals was less opposed to what most Catholics wanted banned. These individuals considered the light novels, adventures, romances, and detective stories of *Schundliteratur* to be pseudo-literature, richly deserving of the label trash but nonetheless tolerable. Some equated it with kitsch and saw it as silly, sentimental, even pointless, but basically harmless. More than one Catholic remembered the adventure stories of his youth with fondness. No self-respecting Catholic intellectual could actually be in favor of *Schundliteratur,* though; if his Catholic faith did not prevent it, his intellectual values did.[40]

A questionnaire that *Germania,* the Center Party's newspaper, sent to a number of well-known Catholic writers, literary, and cultural critics while the 1926 *Schund* and *Schmutz* law was being debated in the Reichstag, gives some idea of the extent of the diversity of opinion. The group, which included Friedrich Muckermann, editor of *Gral,* Karl Muth, editor of *Hochland,* Johannes Mumbauer, author and parish priest, Emil Ritter of the Volksverein, the dramatist Leo Weismantel, Helene Weber, a Center Party deputy in the Reichstag, and Eduard

Schöningh,[41] head of a major Catholic publishing house, was unanimous only on the necessity of a law. Their greatest division was over the importance of a definition of *Schund:* Muth, for example, believed that literature would be endangered only if the ideas of *Schund* and *Schmutz* were not made more precise; Helene Weber insisted flatly that it was impossible to define them. Most of the respondents chose not to address the question of whether creativity would be harmed; Leo Weismantel alone responded unequivocally, answering with an emphatic "Absolutely!" (In the Reichstag debate a Communist Party deputy quoted a statement of Weismantel's that the uncomfortable spiritual chaos in the *Volk* revealed in the uproar over his *Totentanz* [1921] had left him reluctant to recommend such a law.) Muckermann's response went beyond immediate issues. He pointed out that placing a book on what he revealingly designated "the Index" advertises bad literature.[42] He saw the law's greatest value in its effect on the area of morality, although he neglected to explain what he meant by that.[43]

Underlying the question of whether or not censorship would harm creativity lurked the dominant issue in censorship in Germany in the late nineteenth and early twentieth centuries: What was the relationship between art and morality? As we have seen, it was an immensely complex question, stimulating continuing debate in every artistic form. It was an issue central to any conception of a Catholic culture, since morality was inseparable from Catholicism. Intellectuals had to concern themselves with definitions. What was art? What was true art? Was immoral art a contradiction in terms? Some Catholics argued that to be art, a work had to be moral. Many more, though, took the position that art could, however regrettably, be immoral. In cultural censorship the problem was one of balance and of how much art one was willing to sacrifice for the sake of the presumably better moral environment that could be achieved by its suppression.[44]

By the end of the Weimar period, fewer Catholic intellectuals were defending censorship vigorously, and reservations were more frequently expressed than had been true previously, although there were still very few who were willing to argue against it. One of the rare Catholics to condemn censorship outright was Johannes Mumbauer. His opposition was twofold: he argued that censorship was basically ineffective and he questioned the right of the Church to impose its cultural values on society as a whole. The Church had the right to judge its own art, such as the decoration of a church or liturgical music, but did it have the same right outside that purview? For Mumbauer the answer was an unequivocal no. Although one of the most outspoken to recommend "accommodation to the times," he was not alone.[45] Morality, at least as it related to culture, was in fact in the process of being recast.

Supplementing Government Censorship

In order to achieve a properly moral cultural environment, several different strategies were advocated by some Catholic intellectuals and adopted by Church officials. The first—first because it was part of the production process—was self-censorship by all concerned. The abundant attention to the character and confession of the artist or writer was one aspect of this approach. A 1928 article in *Bücherwelt* was very direct. It argued that in a state with an average educational level, a law like the 1926 *Schund* and *Schmutz* law would not be necessary. Instead, the intended functions of the law would be silently accomplished by all concerned—authors, publishers, bookdealers, and, not least, readers. Not everyone was convinced of the virtues of self-censorship. The Catholic correspondent of the *Frankfurter Zeitung* argued that only brave publishers like Kösel dared publish "heart-stirring" novels and that the morally safe but low-value works produced by the clergy, a category which in his opinion accounted for a large part of the entertainment of Catholics, were cheap in every sense.[46]

The Church had its own methods to curb immoral culture, some effective, some somewhat less so. One was the *Index librorum prohibitorum* (List of Prohibited Books). Although primarily aimed at what was theologically unacceptable, the Index could also be used to control culture. Karl Muth was forced to cease publication of a German translation of Fogazzaro's *Il Santo* when it was placed on the *Index librorum prohibitorum*. Muth and his circle did wonder how effective the *Index librorum prohibitorum* was, but it succeeded in forcing their compliance. At the least, placement on the *Index librorum prohibitorum* could still be used to make a statement, as it did when the Holy Office put the entire category of *Schundliteratur* on the Index in 1927. The Fulda Conference of Bishops periodically issued rules and guidelines. Priests were exhorted to be vigilant in protecting their parishioners from *Schund*. At one time, a Catholic Zentralstelle that would be similar in function to the review boards created by the 1920 film censorship law and the 1926 *Schund* and *Schmutz* law was discussed, but it was not created.[47]

Education was seen as a vital tool to protect the faithful from cultural evil. The bishops' 1913 declaration on films included the directive that adults and children were to be instructed in their dangers. The 1927 plan to fight *Schund* and *Schmutz* reminded Catholics that in this war it was crucial to educate the young to clear Catholic ideas and to Catholic self-confidence. Teachers were expected to instill moral precepts in their pupils; the organization of Catholic women teachers issued a long list of the values that they considered essential to instill. Education to an appreciation of beauty was a slightly different approach, but optimists hoped that it would have the same effect.[48]

Ultimately, the Church was asserting its right to decide for Catholics which cultural experiences were open to them and which were not. A 1927 bishops' directive to the clergy on the subject of *Schund* and *Schmutz* stated, "The Church must again become *the* [sic] authority in the inner life and activity of every Catholic." Exercising authority is essential in the Church's position on censorship; to live in a society, to be a Catholic, individuals give up some rights that they would otherwise have in a natural state. Both the Church and the state had the right to make rules.[49]

Catholics were regularly reminded of their responsibilities as individuals by official, semi-official, and unofficial Catholic individuals and organizations. Time after time, the family, particularly the mother, was invoked as the most important opponent of trash. A resolution at the seventh general meeting of the Preßverein in 1908 stated, "We regard it as a duty that every Catholic man and every Catholic woman watch over the entertaining reading in the family, spread Catholic literature, and choose primarily Catholic literature when buying books, especially at Christmas." The 1928 regional Katholikentag at Cologne recommended to Catholics this same vigilance within the family in even more specific terms and added films to literature. It expanded personal responsibility into a wider social and economic setting. Catholics were to boycott stores that carried *Schund* and *Schmutz,* they were to work with state and local officials to make existing regulatory laws effective, they were to refrain from supporting *Schund* and *Schmutz* publishers with subscriptions, purchases, advertisements or recommendations, and they were to support and advance the spread of good literature, especially good Catholic literature. The diocesan commissioner of Freiburg saw individual responsibilities in that same wider setting; he urged personal interaction with store owners who placed unsuitable advertisements and "a strong word" with those who sold bad literature.[50]

Whatever their dissatisfaction with existing censorship laws, Church officials emphasized that it was important to stay within the law. Catholics worked within the political structure to change conditions, to obtain new laws, to make existing laws more effective, and to revise laws. They tried to have added to the 1926 law against *Schund* and *Schmutz* a review board for Cologne, the center of Rhineland Catholicism. They recommended Catholics to serve on the national supervisory review board. The Fulda Conference of Bishops devised a plan to supplement the 1926 law by establishing a central organizing committee, together with diocesan and local committees, to fight *Schund.* The main goal of the plan was to create favorable public opinion in the battle against *Schund.* Local groups were charged with the tasks of identifying *Schund* and *Schmutz* in the sense of the 1926 law, observing newspaper stands, railway booksellers, stationery stores, and bookstores, and sending incriminating material to the central committee. They were to establish good relations with police and bring about seizures of material banned under the laws against pornography. At the same time they were to work in a positive direction, establishing Borromäus Verein libraries so that good reading would be available.[51]

Some efforts were made to mobilize the economic power of Catholics to fight the good fight, but they were rarely successful. From time to time Catholics were urged not to patronize anyone who sold *Schundliteratur,* but there is no evidence that any boycott had a significant impact. Catholics were neither united enough nor did they command enough buying power to be effective. When a priest complained to a newspaper about its advertisement for the film *Das Mädchen aus der Ackerstraße* (1919), the editor replied that he could not reject such advertising because the support of Catholics was not sufficient. The priest's case was not strengthened by the fact that Catholic newspapers, too, accepted advertisements for this movie.[52]

MORALITY MILITANT

Particularly aggressive and tenacious in their opposition to *Schundliteratur* and undesirable films were the morality groups. These were organizations, not all of them Catholic, of predominantly middle-class individuals who had come together to fight immorality; schoolteachers and clergy were prominent in their membership. Moral militants shared a vision of the world that featured strong men and pure women, who were faithful to their religion and loyal to their emperor. Each had a well-defined role within the family. Their children were likewise strong, pure, devout, and loyal, and, moreover, obedient to their parents. Sex took place only within marriage. But in contrast to this vision stood reality, a society that seemed anything but virtuous. Morality groups channeled fear and anger into action. Exactly how many existed is unknown, but they were sufficiently numerous to hold a conference in Cologne in 1904 that was immortalized in a satirical poem in *Simplicissimus.* In 1912 Mausbach noted that the last eight years had seen growth in their numbers.[53]

Because so many of these groups were transitory or ad hoc in their activity, they have left few traces. One that did was the Munich Männerverein zur Bekämpfung der Unsittlichkeit (Men's Organization to Fight Immorality). Founded in 1904 by the Catholic journalist Armin Kausen,[54] it claimed 53,510 members in 1908. Its concern was principally with "the spread of immoral pictures and writings" and "the impudence of their shameless display in show windows." Not everyone welcomed its creation. The artist Hans Thoma[55] and Ernst Müller-Meiningen,[56] a Liberal politician who had been a prominent opponent of the Lex Heinze, criticized it sharply. The police showed a marked lack of gratitude for the Männerverein's assistance. This reception did not impair its zeal, and in its first year the group petitioned the police to proceed against prostitution, remonstrated against performances of the play *La Mandragola* by Niccolò Machiavelli, blocked the public appearance of a nude dancer in Richard Strauss's opera *Salome* by organizing successful public protests, objected to the postal authorities that the regulations relating to cards on which nudity was pictured were not being enforced, and closed an exhibition of photographs.[57]

An association of morality associations, the Verband der Männervereine zur Bekämpfung der öffentlichen Unsittlichkeit (Association of Men's Organizations to Fight Public Immorality) was founded in Cologne in 1907 to facilitate cooperation and coordination. Most of the founding organizations were in towns like Aachen, Koblenz, Cologne, Mainz, and Mönchengladbach, although there were a few from large cities, like Essen and Duisburg, and one or two from areas outside the Rhineland and the Ruhr, like Frankfurt am Main and Munich. Officially, the new organization was interconfessional, but it was dominated by Catholics from the beginning. The Cologne Männerverein, a fundamentally Catholic organization, had a particularly important role in the new association, providing it with both leadership and essential support. Hermann Roeren, the chairman of the Cologne group, was instrumental in the formation of the new association, and Ernst Lennartz, the Cologne group's secretary and vice chairman, became its chairman. The editors of the new association's monthly journal *Volkswart* (People's Watch), first Josef Pappers,[58] then Johann (Hans) Fröhlings, were also both Catholics.[59]

Within a year the new association began publication of *Volkswart,* which combined news from the different local groups, hortatory calls to action, reports on legislation, and pseudo-scholarly articles on relevant topics. The magazine was, in a very real sense, the raison d'être of the association. Its articles educated the moral warrior, while its regular column "Aus den Vereinen" (From the Organizations) assured him that he was not alone. But its significance to the association went far beyond the impact of any one issue. In 1925 Lennartz described the journal as both "root and fruit" for the association, root in that it nourished the association, and fruit in that it spread seeds that perpetually renewed the morality movement. The relationship of journal and association was synergistic, and the journal's continuity gave the organization stability. Appropriately, it gave its name to the parent organization in 1927.[60]

Technically, the association was a supraorganization, and its work was far from the unsavory streets where the real fight against immorality took place, although those involved in efforts to fight moral decline did not make such distinctions. To them, the movement to fight immorality was one movement. From

the journal it is clear that the association regarded the activities of the local organizations as its own activities, in fact if not in theory.

In the years before World War I the association and its constituent local
groups worked to keep the issue of *Schundliteratur* alive and before the public.
The January 1909 issue of *Volkswart* printed reports of the activities of several
groups. Aachen's had complained to a judge about a bookseller that sold a series,
"What One Doesn't Say Aloud." The bookseller had been found guilty and fined
50 M, although the fine had been reduced to 10 M plus court costs since it was
a first offense. The Breslau group had sponsored a lecture on how to fight immorality in youth, in which the speaker declared that the most effective ways to
counter *Schundliteratur* were to buy folk tales and to support Catholic libraries.
Mönchengladbach announced the publication of a pamphlet by the Catholic
teachers' organizations intended to educate parents on the dangers of *Schundliteratur*. Cologne had filed complaints about seven immoral writings and petitions
about eleven. The Cologne Männerverein had joined with the Protestant Cologne Männerverein to found an organization devoted solely to fighting *Schundliteratur* and its companion, *Schmutzliteratur*.[61]

Fighting *Schundliteratur* was the association's highest priority in the prewar period, but it was not its only cultural concern. Parents were warned to supervise carefully their children's visits to theaters, where plays that treated sex,
divorce, and the misery of the poor might be encountered. Museums were viewed
with disfavor because they too often displayed paintings that pictured nude subjects.[62] As interest in the cinema increased, the number of articles about films in
Volkswart increased. Such articles, of course, invariably emphasized negative features of the new cultural medium.

The association survived World War I intact, although it was "significantly
behind" in its work when the war ended. The immediate postwar years offered
both scope and stimulus for moral activities. Cinema was now the primary object of attention. Debates on the film law were well reported in *Volkswart,* and the
morality groups supported it strongly. The law of 1920, however, fell short of their
expectations and the association and its groups continued to press for greater
limitation.

In 1927 the Verband der Männervereine zur Bekämpfung der öffentlichen
Unsittlichkeit became an exclusively Catholic organization and was renamed the
Volkswartbund (People's Watch Federation). Pressure for the formal reconstitu-
tion came from Archbishop Schulte of Cologne. One factor in Schulte's thinking
has to have been financial; he had been supplying the organization with much-
needed support. Confessional cooperation had been smoother than in the Bühnenvolksbund but had apparently become more difficult as the years wore on.

At least equally relevant, the climate of the mid-1920s did not favor interconfessional cooperation. The papal encyclical *Mortalium Animos* of January 1928 condemned ecumenical discussions, and its general tenor has to have discouraged interconfessional cooperation. Catholics were warned not be deceived by "the outward appearance of good," no matter how worthy the objective seemed.[63]

The establishment of the Volkswartbund on a Catholic basis came at a time when Catholic concern with immorality was growing. In 1925 the Fulda Conference of Bishops issued guidelines for Catholics "to counter the modern heathen revolution in moral ideas and views to which our *Volk* more and more often falls prey to a tremendous extent." The guidelines explained in theological terms the relation of body and soul and provided specific rules on moral issues that ranged from gymnastics to fashion to socializing to trashy literature. Moral renewal was the theme of the 1928 regional Katholikentag that took place in Cologne.[64]

Reorganization clarified the Volkswartbund's role. Its function was now "to work steadfastly in the Catholic faith for the application of Christian morality to the public."[65] At the same time it became part of the network of Catholic organizations that offered it both a base of support and a means to reach the engaged part of the Catholic *Volk*. Within this network, the Volkswartbund had a clear identity. It was the militant arm of Catholic morality—at one point it referred to itself as a storm troop—and worked closely with other Catholic organizations, particularly the Borromäus Verein, that were concerned with the same problems but had a different function. The terms "positive" and "negative" were frequently used: the Volkswartbund was to eliminate bad reading, the Borromäus Verein was to provide good reading.[66]

The lot of the Volkswartbund improved in practical ways, as well. Schulte became its protector and its finances became less precarious. The intermittent general secretariat was reopened in November 1927, and the energetic Michael Calmes[67] was appointed its director. New local organizations were founded. By 1930 the eight member organizations of 1927 had grown to fifty-three. It began to function more as the directing unit in a hierarchy and less as the agent of its member organizations.[68]

The Volkswartbund used this new strength to intensify its activity with renewed purpose, increased energy, and improved organization. The general secretariat worked to found new local groups, educate other groups with an interest in morality, and mold public opinion through the organization of conferences and the publication of articles in newspapers and journals. The Volkswartbund boasted that it was responsible for sixty-four of the 185 publications on the national *Schmutz* list. Some of the claims are undoubtedly exaggerated, like the one that took credit for the "flight of *Schmutz* publishers, dealers, writers, and painters abroad" and the "purification of German and Austrian magazines of *Schmutz*," but the Volkswartbund was a force in shaping public opinion.[69]

A prime example of the new efficiency and outlook is the document, *Zehn Gebote für Schundkämpfer* (Ten Commandments for the *Schund* Warrior), prepared for distribution to local groups. The commandments simultaneously convey its vigilante outlook and elitist values:

1. to bring immoral writings, prints, and representations to the attention of the public prosecutor immediately (the legal definition of immoral was provided);

2. to present to the nearest police station writings and pictures that offended in a moral or religious sense;

3. to carry a copy of the *Schmutz* list (produced by the review boards under the 1926 law against *Schund* and *Schmutz*) and point out to a storekeeper anything on the list that he was selling;

4. to inform police immediately of erotic writings with nudes on the cover;

5. to keep the local *Schundkampfstelle* (the agency to fight *Schund*) informed of observations of kiosks, lending libraries, and *Schmutz* sellers;

6. to report bad, but not purely local, examples of *Schund* and *Schmutz* to the Volkswartbund in Cologne and never to destroy any advertisements of *Schund;*

7. to speak courageously against dirty literature at kiosks, bookstores, and hairdressers;

8. to participate in the oversight of kiosks and bookstores, a task not regarded as snooping but as corresponding to the democratic principle of the duty of a concerned citizen;

9. to buy and support, above all, Catholic newspapers, magazines, and journals and to demand that they be available in railroad bookstores;

10. to handle oneself courageously and skillfully, but not with prudery.

Such indoctrination was indispensable in an activity where the greatest enemies were perceived as, on the one hand, broadmindedness and, on the other, tunnel vision.[70]

In addition to these voluntary associations, several bishops founded a *consilium a vigilantia* (advisory body for vigilance); Canon 1397 enjoined upon them the responsibility of watching over the books published or sold within their territory. The most active *consilium* appears to have been in the Archdiocese of Munich and Freising, which published a series of memoranda on a broad range of moral issues. Many of these memoranda were thoughtful, informative, and substantial. A report on young adult reading, for example, ran to fifteen large single-spaced pages, presented facts, and considered issues. The Munich *consilium a vigilantia* cooperated with other, more militant Catholic morality groups to pressure police and government officials to greater strictness.[71]

By the end of the 1920s numerous Catholic organizations were involved in the fight against the cultural manifestations of immorality. The general impression is kaleidoscopic. The Volkswartbund was prominent in the Archdiocese of Cologne, where it had its headquarters, Catholic Action in the Archdiocese of Breslau, and Munich-based organizations in Bavaria. The organization might have a particular interest in *Schund*, like the Borromäus Verein or a teachers' association, or it might be a Catholic society of more general character, like a women's organization a workers' group. To bring some order and direction the Fulda Conference of Bishops created a Zentralarbeitsausschuß (Central Working Committee) in 1929, designed to be a central, national committee with diocesan committees and local committees. On each level it would be an umbrella organization to bring together and coordinate the many Catholic groups engaged in the fight against cultural immorality, particularly the fight against *Schundliteratur*. With the Volkswartbund and Borromäus Verein as the core, the Zentralarbeitsausschuß would represent the Catholic point of view both nationally and internationally to non-Catholic opponents of *Schund*. Only one diocesan committee was founded, in Freiburg, and the plan never seems to have progressed beyond an organization on paper, probably because there was a widespread sentiment that the *Schund* fight did not need still another organization.[72]

The thick files of the Volkswartbund in diocesan archives create an impression of activity and accomplishment. Activity there was, but how much it accomplished is more debatable. Recently, Petersen has demonstrated that censorship in the Weimar Republic was fundamentally ineffective. Catholics of the period would have agreed with him. The Volkswartbund might boast of being responsible for sixty-four of the 185 publications on the *Schund* and *Schmutz* list, but they recognized that those sixty-four were a drop from an overflowing bucket. Karl Walterbach, president of the Leo Gesellschaft, captured some of the bitterness of the *Schund* fighter. His report on films argued that thanks to the efforts of *Schund* opponents, well-intentioned and faithful Catholics recognized a bad film and stayed away. But producers had no incentive to produce films that corresponded to the views of these faithful Catholics because there simply were not enough of them to offer the prospect of sufficient profit. Instead, according to Walterbach, they produced films for the "Jews and nonbelievers" who filled the movie theaters. The director of the film review board made the same point: censorship could only hinder the bad, it could not produce good.[73]

The uncomfortable, unavoidable facts were that the *Volk* wanted to read *Schundliteratur*, it wanted pictures that were not necessarily great art, and it wanted films that entertained rather than instructed. In a capitalist economy publishers and producers were going to provide what was marketable. Nor was a democracy going to be willing to pass a law restrictive enough to eliminate *Schundliteratur*. By 1933 even the most stalwart morality fighters were discouraged. Ernst Lennartz himself, chairman of the Volkswartbund for twenty-five years, in reflections written shortly before his death referred to those years as years of much success but of greater disappointment.[74]

The effectiveness of censorship, however, is not only a matter of how many novels have been suppressed or how many films banned. Fights for censorship involve subtle psychological and social motivations, and Catholic participation in the fight against *Schund* had additional consequences. The discussions, articles, campaigns, demonstrations, and other assorted activities offered an unparalleled opportunity to assert and publicize Catholic values. The issue helped tighten the bonds within the Catholic minority, since there was a cause and rules were enjoined upon Catholics. The talk might be of what Catholics were doing for that vague, and interconfessional, entity known as the *Volk*, but the primary focus was on the Catholic part of the *Volk*.

For the individuals involved, there was personal affirmation, of one kind for the member of the militant Volkswartbund who found a storekeeper selling *Schund*, of another for the organizers, publicists, and contributors to the debate. A strong streak of self-righteousness is present in morality movements, and the anti-*Schund* campaigns of the German Catholics were no exception. Those who advocate censorship are convinced that they know best, that they are protecting those not as educated or as virtuous as they. Ambiguities do not trouble them. Elitist values are assumed; only films of "serious character" are acceptable, and reading should be *work*. The elite can even perceive itself as a super-elite; Karl Muth therefore trusted priests to censor only for the young and for the common people.[75]

Occasionally, there is a hint that simple Catholics were not as appreciative of the morality fighters' efforts as they should have been and that public concern about *Schundliteratur* was not as great as it should have been. Little incidents— a complaint that the older generation no longer fights *Schund*, a charge that even Catholics display general indifference to and ignorance about the possibilities of opposition, the Bonn Volkswartbund's difficulty in finding a chair, the constant emphasis on the importance of shaping public opinion—suggest a certain lack of commitment to the cause in the broad ranks of Catholics.[76]

STRUGGLING WITH THE OBJECTIONABLE: A SUMMATION

More than any other, censorship was the cultural issue that forced crystallization of opinion. Catholics had to make choices, not about whether the preservation of morality was more important than anything else (a position with which no Christian could argue), but about the extent to which "excrescences" of modern culture could be accepted without compromising what was truly important. The militant campaigns against *Schundliteratur* and other undesirable cultural forms made the choice a matter of urgency and introduced an element of belligerence that was not present in positive efforts to create acceptably Catholic culture.

Positions on censorship grew out of positions on fundamental questions like the responsibilities of society, the nature of authority, and the scope of individual rights. They were influenced by hopes and by fears, by what a given person prized most highly. In the discussions of Catholic intellectuals on the subject, a stratified society is taken for granted, and all contributors, regardless of their position in the spectrum of opinion or, indeed, place in the social hierarchy, saw themselves as appropriate judges of whether a particular book should be read, a play performed, or a film shown. This attitude reflects consciousness of privilege and presumes superior knowledge, but it also reflects a sense of responsibility for those less fortunate. For those less certain of their social position, participation in a fight for censorship was an affirmation of status.

Both consciousness of authority and respect for institutions of authority are present in the discussions; they are not taken for granted. Initially, the government was perceived as the appropriate party to be responsible for the morality of the cultural environment, and, by including the sale of pornography in the criminal code of 1872, the government accepted a major role in that endeavor. By the end of the nineteenth century Catholic advocates of censorship were working hard to expand censorship to include *Schundliteratur,* unacceptable films, and undesirable drama. Neither the film law of 1920 nor the *Schund* and *Schmutz* law of 1926, however, were rigorous enough for Catholic advocates of censorship or the Church hierarchy. Faith in the government's ability to control all except the grossest forms of cultural immorality was further eroded by the half-hearted enforcement of the laws that had been passed. By the late 1920s the family had become the institution upon which reliance was placed. Organizational efforts had shifted from attempting to influence government policy to convincing the *Volk* of the evils of immoral cultural products.[77]

Some important ideas are strikingly absent from discussions of censorship in the Catholic press and in official statements on the subject. The question of the costs of censorship was rarely treated seriously. The one exception was the *Germania* survey of 1926, and the only reason for its inclusion there was the frequency of the objection to the *Schund* and *Schmutz* bill on the grounds that censorship would dampen creativity. The usual position, if an article addressed the problem at all, was to assert that "true" art would not be affected. The following statement expressed prevailing Catholic opinion on the subject: "It is remarkable that more is said about the fight against the law to control *Schund* and *Schmutz* than about the fight against this epidemic of the *Volk*." In Catholic eyes, the costs of no censorship far outweighed the costs of censorship.[78]

Nor was serious consideration given to the relationship of censorship and democracy. With rare exceptions, no understanding that rights were in conflict, the right of Catholics to be protected versus the right of others to express themselves, was displayed. What the bishops saw as the cause of the ineffectiveness of the *Schund* and *Schmutz* law could also be interpreted as a triumph of democratic procedure. Despite an occasional plea for tolerance, Catholic writings show little broad-mindedness. Dismissing "everything that offends against Catholic faith and moral teachings" as bad literature was fairly typical. Respect for the desire of individuals to make decisions for themselves, even if they were poor or uneducated, was not a concern. Catholics did not, however, have the final word in a secular state, a state, moreover, in which they were a minority. Their ideas about censorship, which was ultimately a matter of law, differed significantly from the institution that did have the final word—the government—and the government's concern was primarily in the area of politics rather than culture.[79]

Much of the response to what was perceived as immoral culture was driven by emotions. Neither detective stories nor pornographic films had been available in the idealized village of recent memory. Anxiety at the quantity and increasingly brazen character of products was palpable. Steadily increasing fear stimulated increasingly sophisticated organization, ever more militancy, and a tone that became more and more shrill. The ineffectiveness of the 1920 film law and the 1926 *Schund* and *Schmutz* law only brought new commitment to opposition to bad films and bad literature.

Censorship makes the existential dilemma of Catholic intellectuals painfully clear. They were caught between their Catholic morality, defined for all time in a very different past, and the cultural world in which they lived, a world that was increasingly international, multicultural, profit-oriented, and antagonistic to tradition.[80] As the nineteenth century gave way to the twentieth and the Wilhelmine Empire to the Weimar Republic, the writing of Catholic intellectuals shows a growing awareness that modern culture was a cohesive package; what was unwelcome about the modern world could not be readily separated from what was desirable. A sense that modernity was inevitable added to their discomfort. Hostility and rejection were the prevailing responses, but, quietly, voices for accommodation were beginning to speak out. Even in Catholic journals, by the end of the 1920s articles regularly presented ideas very different from those that the Volkswartbund so intransigently defended.

10

Conclusion

Looking back on the Catholic film movement after the Second World War, Friedrich Muckermann would comment that its biggest problem was the gap between concept and reality. That insight is just as true of the entire Catholic cultural movement, if not more so. The discontinuity between theory and practice, hope and reality, promise and performance is apparent in each of the arts discussed in this book and in the totality of the movement. Johannes Mumbauer recognized it at the time: "We insist on our great ideas and true principles in order to deceive ourselves about our lack of accomplishments."[1]

Accomplishments were undeniably in short supply, at least if the standard is the stated objectives. The Catholic cultural movement created neither an authentic alternative to the contemporary, increasingly secular, modern high culture nor an effective alternative to the burgeoning commercial popular culture. The movement did make a contribution, but it was a contribution that did more to make its participants feel good about themselves than to improve the cultural environment. Existence can be an end in itself, and the existence of organizations and cultural objectives could and did help to sustain Catholic identity, both individually and collectively. Certainly, the movement was very real to its participants, as a 1926 statement by Hans Rost demonstrates: "Christian culture suffers the test of its eternal values by the destroying influence of the modern spirit. Will the Catholic cultural movement, and Catholic family life in particular, assert its cultural strength in the future and even emerge the victor?"[2]

The foundation of the German Catholic cultural movement was an acknowledgment that the arts were important, that they influenced the outlook of an individual, and that the more accessible the form, the more dangerous the ideas. Interested parties could not agree upon what exactly culture was, but that did not really affect their activities any more than did the absence of a comprehensive theory of culture, because the Catholic faith provided an integrating worldview, functioning in many ways as an ideology. In the different areas of the arts, discussion emphasized issues with more immediate applications. Some generalizations were derived from these more circumscribed considerations, especially from those in literature and art, but they did not constitute a comprehensive theory.

Catholic views on culture in the late nineteenth and early twentieth centuries grew out of contemporary changes in the arts. They were usually phrased negatively, anti-this, or against that. Many terms or expressions were code words, not only describing a situation, but prescribing the appropriate response to it. Among the two most common were materialism and immorality, the first as a synonym for commercialized popular culture, the second for all representations of sexuality outside of marriage. Opposition to "immorality" could be carried so far as to be criticism of the emphasis on love, romance, and relationships between men and women that were the substance of most novels, films, and other forms of artistic expression. Individualism was another negative term. In the context of culture, opposition to it took two forms: opposition to the glorification of the artist and opposition to art's focus on the individual. The Catholic cultural movement also verbalized its rejection of elitism, paradoxically in the light of the generally elitist attitudes of the cultural leaders. All of these separate negations were the consequence of one great negation: a rejection of the increasing secularism of the dominant worldview of modern Germany.

Catholic ideas about culture deserve, however, to be seen in something other than negative terms. Many Catholic intellectuals did indeed oppose new ideas and new ways of doing things, but they did so for what they perceived as positive reasons and in the confidence that they were holding fast to eternal verities. Their antimaterialism emphasized positive spiritual and intellectual values. Antiimmorality was promorality, a defense of chastity and marriage, the traditional family, and the traditional role of women. Antiindividualism was seen as a defense of one of those most sacred of German ideals, the *Volk*.

One area that received relatively little attention from Catholic writers was aesthetics, a surprising omission in view of its central role in culture and the extensive exposure to medieval philosophy that most educated Catholics had experienced. When it was discussed, discussions tended to be one-dimensional. Only the aspect of the moral was considered seriously, and that was limited to the constant invocation that art had to avoid offending morality. Fundamental questions about how art is experienced, how it is judged, and how it is produced attracted little interest, nor was there any serious attempt to articulate a theory of beauty that could have given the movement a foundation for creativity. Neither of the two substantial treatments of aesthetics that did appear, Gietmann in art and Möhler in music, attained much stature, nor was there any attempt to develop aesthetic principles in terms of the new media of film and radio.

What converted Catholic thinking and writing about culture into a Catholic cultural movement was the conviction that eternal norms had to be asserted. Existing culture was insufficient, and a new spirit had to be created. The irony that the "new" being offered was anything but new escaped its advocates. Catholic ideals were what they had always been; that was both their strength and weakness. And it was the Catholic that was the dominant element in the Catholic cultural movement. Assertion of Catholic, in contrast to socialist culture, secular culture, or modern culture, was, after all, why the movement existed.

When compromise was necessary, it was culture that was compromised, not Catholic faith and morals. The offerings of Catholic culture, the books, the paintings, the sculptures, and the motets that could be applauded as being truly Catholic, were in fact frequently close to being truly propaganda, a circumstance that tended to rob them of artistic viability and popular appeal. In the absence of anything better, kitsch with a Catholic gloss passed for culture. For most Catholics, to consider a work Catholic, that work had to promote not only the glory of God but also the glory of the Roman Catholic Church. In the setting of a religious service, where the celebration and advocacy of the faith are central, the fundamental incompatibility of the goals of propaganda and art was less damaging, and pseudo-medieval paintings of the Virgin and imitations of baroque oratorios had a place. Otherwise, the call to arms that is the imperative of propaganda was a serious drawback, interfering with artistic creativity and turning the artist into a preacher. Muth argued that direction, by which he meant a Catholic outlook, was acceptable when it was expressed in the "organism" of a creative work, that is, in the "flesh and blood" of a work, but not when it was expressed in words. Few Catholic artists, however, were capable of such delicate balancing, and, as a result, Catholic culture was too Catholic even for most Catholics. Catholics were, as Falkenberg observed, not just religious individuals, and so a literature that was a mixture of "sky blue and gold," in his opinion, disgusted the average person. Falkenberg's opinion is borne out by the general lack of interest in Catholic culture on the part of those for whom it was intended, the Catholic community.[3]

Although there are common elements that make Catholic thinking on culture Catholic, the most important being the desire that culture remain within the framework of Catholicism, that thinking was hardly monolithic. Intellectually as well as organizationally, the Catholic cultural movement had essentially two phases, divided by the war. The prewar period was a time of enthusiasm, in which organizations were founded and projects launched. After 1918 organizational activity diminished as some of the older groups lost members, but at the same time it expanded as Church-sponsored groups moved into new areas. Pessimism began to replace optimism. There were some conceptual differences between the two periods, but changes of tone and emphasis are more evident than changes of substance. At an early stage Catholics had recognized the fundamental transformations in culture for what they were and rightly considered the "revolutionary" changes of the 1920s an intensification and expansion of prewar trends, rather than a novelty. What alarmed cultural leaders with a national perspective during the 1920s was the widespread diffusion of these revolutionary ideas. Catholic intellectuals continued to deplore the ideas and practices they had deplored before the war, but time and events blunted their reactions. In contrast, the writings of country priests that found their way into print in the 1920s still communicate a sense of outrage. Thanks to the growth of mass media and the mass marketing of other media, the country was catching up with the city, culturally speaking, although not everyone perceived that as a blessing.[4]

World War I increased the attention Catholic writers gave to the spirit of the times in quantity if not quality. The complaints of 1926 were much the same as the complaints of 1910. Cultural critics continued to explore the impact of the erosion of traditional spiritual and moral values on culture, but with a new bewilderment added to prevailing disapproval. They deplored the hedonism and narcissism that were characteristic of the 1920s and bemoaned the loss of acceptance of traditional authority and values. Yet for all the angst, critics did not seem to understand the deep sense of loss of meaning individuals experienced. How could they? Those who were building Catholic culture were committed Catholics, men for whom traditional spiritual and moral values had not lost their meaning and for whom life consequently retained a sense of purpose. For them, generally speaking, the external manifestations of culture did not need to change radically because the fundamental premises underlying culture had not changed. They found their own times abnormal and completely failed to grasp the enormous potential of the new world.[5]

Strong religious faith did not protect the Catholic intellectuals who were trying to create a Catholic cultural alternative from anxiety and pessimism. Although often obscured by the zeal and optimism of the professional enthusiasts like Johannes Braun of the Borromäus Verein and Bernhard Marschall of the Zentralbildungsausschuß, discouragement and dispiritedness come through many accounts. Throughout the 1920s the evidence mounted that the Catholic population was not an eager consumer of what was being offered. In addition, the creators, particularly those engaged in the areas of literature and theater, were finding the creative canons of Catholic culture constraining and were beginning to say so in print.

As was true in so many situations, the prewar and postwar periods approached cultural issues somewhat differently. Although the principal cultural questions remained much the same, for Catholic intellectuals, the question of how to resist contemporary trends was quietly replaced by the question of how to accommodate new trends and participate in the culture of our times, while yet preserving a Catholic outlook. This is a shift of some magnitude and reflects, in the cultural realm, the collective realism of a Church that had survived the centuries; the example of the Byzantine Church, frozen in its own past, had not escaped its Roman counterpart. This change in attitude came about partly because individuals altered their attitudes, partly because new men with different views replaced older thinkers. The extent of the shift, however, should not be overstated. It was a matter of attitude rather than argument, more what was not said than what was made explicit. It was, moreover, limited. Compromise did not extend to fundamental principles, nor did everyone concur. There were still plenty of assertive dinosaurs around, pining in print for the good old days before the war or the even better days before the Reformation.

Among Catholic intellectuals, emphasis varied from critic to critic. When differences dictated by the fact that Muth's area of interest was literature, Kreitmaier's art, and Overmans's theater are removed, distinguishing characteristics remain. Muth's infectious enthusiasm for new ideas, Ehrhard's emphasis on inner holiness, Mausbach's sophisticated understanding of morality, Kreitmaier's genuine effort to grapple with uncomfortable ideas, and Friedrich Muckermann's impressive universality are among the more memorable. Johann Chrysostomus Schulte saw culture through the filter of his desire to retain the educated, more sophisticated Catholic within the Church, while Emil Ritter's orientation was to the interests of the working class. For all these men, however, the fundamental issue was the creation and dissemination of cultural ideas and objects that were informed by the Catholic faith.

The Catholic cultural movement was the collection of many different efforts to accomplish that end. The multitude of organizations that comprised it were typical of this age of associations, a time when every purpose and every problem had its own voluntary association. Catholic culture was too important to be left to the individual Catholic artist or to the individual Catholic theatergoer. The statutes of Catholic cultural organizations, whether the activity of choice was art, literature, music, or the performing arts, had many similarities. Stated goals reified the concerns of critics: materialism, morality, and the basic underlying anxiety to preserve the Catholic outlook. The typical organization asserted that it was going to promote morality, an activity it usually construed in negative terms, by keeping Catholics away from the immoral and replacing the immoral or the less moral with the more moral. More positively, an organization would help to preserve the Catholic outlook by encouraging production and facilitating the dissemination of specifically Catholic cultural artifacts. Few organizations asserted a desire to obstruct or bypass the commercial channels that embodied materialism, but Catholic associations clearly endeavored to offer an alternative means of dissemination.

Differences among organizations are found primarily in their operations. Their statutes might be identical, but there was leeway for interpretation. The degree of independence correlated with how important the group was to the Church; a parish's Cäcilien Verein was more closely supervised than its amateur theatrical club. Geographical location influenced activity; much depended on whether an organization was located in an urban area or a rural one, in Bavaria or the Rhineland. And, as in any human activity, the personalities of the local priest and society members made a difference in the level of activity and in which particular objectives the group chose to emphasize.

Cultural organizations served other purposes besides their stated ones, purposes that their leaders sometimes, but not always, understood. Inherent in the act of association and shared activities was the strengthening of intra-Catholic bonds. Coming together in an organization, while more formal than the customary social interaction of village life, offered a supplement to village neighborliness; it could be a substitute for it. The groups contributed to stability and order. They may have been intended to strengthen Catholics politically, but they also strengthened the existing national political system. These factors, as much as any burning interest in a Catholic culture per se, led Church authorities to support and encourage cultural organizations.

In the Catholic cultural movement, the local Church hierarchy had a limited role. Never well-defined, that role seems to have nonetheless been understood by all concerned parties. Episcopal policy statements tended to address quite specific cultural issues, but only after much discussion had taken place in the Catholic press and elsewhere; the bishops defined consensus more often than they originated ideas. With respect to the organizations, bishops endorsed the worthiness of new ones, sent small subsidies as a token of goodwill, and occasionally arranged special collections to benefit a particular association. Once an organization was functioning within a diocese, whether on the diocesan level or on the parochial level, the bishop had some responsibility for supervision, and normal established reporting practices regularly brought him the required information.

Intellectual leadership in the arts came primarily from an elite, non-parochial clergy with a sprinkling of energetic and engaged laymen. New ideas about culture were disseminated primarily through the medium of Catholic journals aimed at the cultivated citizen. Among the editors and contributors to these journals, Karl Muth, the editor of *Hochland,* Karl Hoeber, the editor of the *Kölnische Volkszeitung,* Jakob Overmans and Josef Kreitmaier of *Stimmen der Zeit,* and Friedrich Muckermann of *Der Gral* were the most important. Significantly, all three of the individuals who were clerics, Overmans, Kreitmaier, and Muckermann, were Jesuits. Novelists and poets and, less frequently, artists and composers themselves made occasional forays into this area of cultural commentary and criticism.

Leadership of cultural organizations also involved both clergy and laity, but only rarely were these the same individuals who provided the intellectual leadership. If one looks at the founders of organizations, examples of both are readily available; the founders of the Borromäus Verein were laymen, the founder of the Cäcilien Verein a parish priest who had taken on additional educational and cathedral duties. The day-to-day operations of the organizations involved both clergy and laity, but the clergy was indispensable. At the national and diocesan level, the chief administrators of cultural organizations tended to be clerics, such as Johannes Braun of the Borromäus Verein. On the parochial level, clergy provided the continuity that made the difference between the survival and demise of organizations; parish priests were responsible for keeping groups like the local Borromaus Verein or Cäcilien Verein going. This functional centrality easily translated into intellectual dominance, and whether the clergy's values should control Catholic culture was a real question throughout the period. Hotly defended in the early years, by the 1920s clerical supremacy was being called into question by advocates of a more independent cultural position. Jakob Kneip, for example, could publicly blame the clergy for the condition of writers and artists in 1927.

And what was that condition? Or, to put the question Kneip was really raising, what was the condition of Catholic culture? By the end of the 1920s it was clear that the Catholic cultural movement had failed. Failure is, of course, in the eye of the beholder, but a movement that did not rouse wide interest in its intended audience, that did not achieve economic viability, that did not produce works that survived their own time, and that did not attract a younger generation to carry it on does not suggest great success. The educated Catholics who denied the existence of Catholic culture may have gone too far, but there can be no doubt that it was indeed "a modest blossom" and its accomplishments distinctly limited. Perceptive observers recognized this fact at the time. In 1927 Friedrich Muckermann wrote, "The complaint that Catholic organizations often fail to reach the summit is not infrequent. . . . The same thing is repeated again and again—that the plays produced lack artistic value, that the forms of pleasure are in all decency common and ordinary. A refined tone, spiritual nobility, and educated culture are rarely detected there."[6]

On one level, the failure was economic. As Rost's analysis of Catholic inferiority had made so plain, Catholics, a minority within the Reich, were less likely to be significant consumers of culture than their Protestant compatriots both because they were less likely to be educated and more likely to be poor. The potential audience for Catholic culture was therefore limited, and a limited audience is synonymous with a limited market. Authors, playwrights, actors, and film directors found it difficult or impossible to make a living if they tried to produce for only a Catholic market. At the very least, subsidies were necessary, whether they came in the form of money from a bishop or depended upon the willingness of a publisher or author to settle for very modest remuneration. The partial exceptions were art and architecture, where the needs of building, outfitting, and decorating churches offered more possibilities, and music, where liturgical practices provided some musicians with steady, if limited, employment.

Intellectual weakness paralleled economic weakness. Catholic culture never succeeded in establishing itself as a viable alternative to the increasingly dominant, increasingly secular, national culture. Catholic ideals did not blend successfully with the canons of the emerging high culture, whichever movement's theories were in the ascendant. Whether it is cultural commentary by an advocate of Catholic culture or a novel that attempts to incarnate its ideals, an aura of unreality always seems to be present. Weakness seemed inherent in Catholicism; Catholics wrote of their "insecurity in spiritual and intellectual things." And the position of Catholics as a minority too often produced a tone of self-consciousness and defensiveness in cultural products that was an additional drawback.[7]

The porous nature of the Catholic milieu was a mixed blessing to Catholic culture. Most Catholics were exposed on a daily basis to the culture of a wider world, which offered new ideas but also competed with Catholic culture. Catholics were free to buy and read any book not on the *Index librorum prohibitorum*. They were free to listen to the music of the Protestant Bach, free to visit art museums, and, unless they were priests, free to attend plays. Many did so. Although separation rather than participation was advocated and clearly preferred, Catholic intellectuals were rooted not just in Catholicism but in German culture. Restriction to the universe of Catholic culture was not a condition of Catholic identity.

In fact, acceptance of cultural diversity among German Catholic intellectuals grew slowly but steadily throughout the period covered by this book. Acceptance was endorsed by Pius XII, who had been the papal nuncio to Germany in the 1920s, in an address to the Tenth International Congress of Historical Sciences in 1955. The pope was direct; the Church's mission was for all time to come and for all men, and in consequence she could not be tied to any specific culture. He repudiated Catholic idolization of the medieval period: "But even the culture of the Middle Ages itself cannot be characterized as Catholic culture; although closely bound to the Church, it drew its elements from different sources also." His statement bestows papal recognition on the cultural cross-fertilization that has been a fact of human life since the Stone Age. Whether he would have made the same statement in 1933 remains open to question.[8]

In its competition with popular culture, Catholic culture enjoyed, at best, limited success. Some Catholic kitsch, such as inexpensive devotional art, did sell. But there was none of the ever-popular *Schundliteratur* with a Catholic outlook—the concepts were a contradiction in terms—and no popular songs. Catholic associations occasionally performed plays with Catholic themes, but Catholic culture was hardly a serious threat to secular, commercial popular culture. The fact was that the Catholic cultural movement, like its perceived rival, socialist culture, could not produce cultural products of a kind and quantity to satisfy the tastes and interests of the intended audience.[9]

The basic dilemma of Catholic culture was recognized by Muth: Which goal had priority, religious or artistic? Every time an artist decided upon a subject, its manner of treatment, and the message to impart, a choice was made, and in a period when economic, intellectual, and social life were increasingly differentiated, one alternative was often more Catholic or more artistic than another alternative. Efforts of Catholic thinkers to reconcile culture and Catholicism by making a religious element a part of a definition of art did not resolve the issue.

Leaders in the German Catholic cultural movement saw themselves as engaged in a heroic struggle with opposing worldviews. They thought of Catholic culture as culture with a Catholic face, but they appreciated that it was just as much Catholicism expressed as culture. Their understanding of the interaction of ideology, culture, and mass-communications media was extraordinary. They recognized that culture was being transformed by new modes of communication, they perceived the fundamental change separating the production of culture and its reception, and they knew that ideology was meaning in the service of power.[10] None of these insights, however, enabled them to prevail; their objectives clashed with too many realities of the times.

Ultimately, the Catholic cultural movement was defeated, not by the Nazi state, which merely delivered the coup de grâce, but by its own inherent weakness. German Catholic culture never became more than an artificial alternative to a vibrant national culture. Unresolved contradictions persisted and sapped its strength. Was its objective to enable Catholics to escape the beleaguered fortress of the ghetto that was late nineteenth-century German Catholicism by educating them and expanding their horizons or was it to strengthen the fortress? Catholic culture was part of the Church's attempt to come to terms with the modern world, but was that coming to terms to be resistance and rejection or adaptation and accommodation? Adherence to its values may have produced worthy creations, but they lacked vitality and appeal. As Erwin Panofsky is reported to have said, "While it is true that commercial art is always in danger of ending up as a prostitute, it is equally true that non-commercial art is always in danger of ending up as an old maid." In a very real sense, the novels, paintings, plays, and films of Catholic culture have ended up on the shelf.[11]

At the same time, the withering and eventual demise of the Catholic cultural movement of the early part of the twentieth century was not an unmitigated loss. For one thing, Catholic culture did not itself disappear. Individual Catholics, like the Nobel prizewinner Heinrich Böll,[12] continued to create artistic works that expressed a robust faith and achieved broad recognition. Organizations like the Borromäus Verein and Cäcilien Verein carried on their activity and thrive today. What ceased to exist was the model, the integrated effort, in short, the mentality. Some perspicacious participants had begun to sense that the movement was a failure by the end of the 1920s. No one had ever disputed that religion was more important than culture, but the suggestion that energies should be concentrated on the essentials of faith and religion rather than a peripheral facet began to be voiced. The Depression of the 1930s, the Nazi persecution of the Church, and World War II deprived participants of a choice, but the end of the movement could be regarded, even by someone like Friedrich Muckermann for whom it brought much sadness, as liberating. Its demise freed Catholics to participate fully in the national culture, and, indeed, it forced them to do so if they wished to be culturally active.

notes

1. Introduction: The Catholic Cultural Movement

1. Arthur von Kirchenheim, "Schlaraffia Politica," in *Geschichte der Dichtungen von besten Staate* [*sic*] (1892), p. 259, quoted in Franz X. Riederer, "The German Acceptance and Reaction," in *Edward Bellamy Abroad: An American Prophet's Influence,* ed. Sylvia E. Bowman (New York: Twayne, 1962), p. 151. *Looking Backward* was translated into German as *Ein Rückblick aus dem Jahre 2000 auf 1887* and then translated three more times before 1933. One translation had gone to a seventh edition by 1891. Also published was an answer to Bellamy, Richard C. Michaelis's *Ein Blick in der Zukunft: Eine Antwort auf Ein Rückblick.* It, too, was available in an inexpensive paperback Reclam edition.

2. See Edgar Hugo Hemminghaus, *Mark Twain in Germany* (New York: Columbia University Press, 1939), p. 11; Roland Innerhofer, *Deutsche Science Fiction 1870–1914: Rekonstruktion und Analyse der Anfänge einer Gattung* (Vienna: Böhlau, 1996), p. 416; and Gertrud Lehnert-Rodiek, *Zeitreisen: Untersuchungen zu einem Motiv der erzählenden Literatur des 19. und 20. Jahrhunderts,* Bonner Untersuchungen zur vergleichenden Literaturwissenschaft, vol. 3 (Rheinbach-Merzbach: CMZ Verlag, 1987), p. 76. Indigenous German examples exist, like a short story that anticipated Wells's idea of a time machine by the *Heimat* author Ludwig Anzengruber. There is even a German translation of Robert Benson's Catholic time-travel novel, *The Dawn of All* (1911).

3. Charles Péguy, quoted in Robert Hughes, *The Shock of the New* (New York: Alfred A. Knopf, 1991), p. 98. For a classic discussion of the change in the nature of time see E. P. Thompson, "Time, Work-Discipline, and Industrial Capitalism," *Past and Present* 38 (1967): 56–97. Thomas Nipperdey, *Deutsche Geschichte, 1866–1918,* vol. 1, *Arbeitswelt und Bürgergeist* (Munich: C. H. Beck, 1998) provides a detailed discussion of many of these issues. An article in the *New York Times* by Steve Lohr, "The Future Came Faster in the Old Days," October 5, 1997, offers an interesting comparison with the experience of the late twentieth century.

4. See H. Stuart Hughes, *Consciousness and Society: The Reorientation of European Social Thought, 1890–1930* (New York: Alfred A. Knopf, 1958).

5. See Wolfgang J. Mommsen, *Imperial Germany, 1867–1918: Politics, Culture, and Society in an Authoritarian State,* trans. Richard Deveson (London: Arnold, 1995), p. 139;

and Urs Altermatt, "Katholizismus: Antimodernismus mit modernen Mitteln," in *Moderne als Problem des Katholizismus,* ed. Urs Altermatt, Heinz Hürten, and Nikolaus Lobkowicz, Eichstätter Beiträge, vol. 28, Abteilung Philosophie und Theologie 6 (Regensburg: Verlag Friedrich Austet, 1995), p. 41.

6. See Nipperdey, *Arbeitswelt und Bürgergeist,* p. 186.

7. Henry Adams, "The Dynamo and the Virgin," in *The Education of Henry Adams* (New York: Modern Library, 1931), pp. 379–90.

8. Friedrich Muckermann, S.J. (1883–1946), editor of *Der Gral* in the 1920s; emigrated from Germany in 1933; leader of Catholic opposition to National Socialism; founder of the magazine *Der deutsche Weg* (1945) in Holland for exiles.

9. Muckermann, "Der Magdeburger Katholikentag: Katholisches Buch, Katholische Presse: Die 2. Öffentliche Versammlung," *Germania,* September 7, 1928, Morgenausgabe.

Karel Dobbelaere summarizes this differentiation of life in the late twentieth century: "Secularization is the product of functional differentiation, with its accompanying processes of rationalization, mechanization, computerization, societalization, bureaucratization, and the segmentation of social relationships—all of which, at the individual level, produce individuation and compartmentalization. These processes are often referred to as 'modernization.'" Karel Dobbelaere, "Church Involvement and Secularization: Making Sense of the European Case," in *Secularization, Rationalism, and Sectarianism: Essays in Honour of Bryan R. Wilson,* ed. Eileen Barker, James A. Beckford, and Karel Dobbelaere (Oxford: Clarendon Press, 1993), p. 28.

There is an immense literature on modernization and its frequent attendant, secularization. Interestingly, while the two usually go together, Islamic countries are the exception. There, economic development has often brought a revival of religion rather than its decline. Although much of the literature relates to non-European countries and the second half of the twentieth century, German modernization in the second half of the nineteenth century displays many of the same features. On the human cultural consequences of modernization, see Ralph L. Beals, "Resistance and Adaptation to Technological Change: Some Anthropological Views," *Human Factors* 10 (1968): 579–88; William R. Freudenburg and Robert Gramling, "Community Impacts of Technological Change: Toward a Longitudinal Perspective," *Social Forces* 70 (June 1992): 937–55; and Robert J. Smith, "Comparative Studies in Anthropology of the Interrelations between Social and Technological Change," *Human Organizations* 16 (Spring 1957): 30–36.

On secularization Bryan Wilson is perhaps the leading scholar. David Lyon's essay, "Rethinking Secularization: Retrospect and Prospect," *Review of Religious Research* 26 (March 1985): 228–43, is a good guide. Peter Ester, Loek Halman, and Ruud de Moor, *The Individualizing Society: Value Change in Europe and North America* (Tilburg, Netherlands: Tilburg University Press, 1994), especially in the introduction and the chapter "Religion, Churches and Moral Values" by Halman and de Moor, address many of the concerns of early twentieth-century German Catholics. The article by Stephan Sharot, Hannah Ayalon, and Eliezer Ben-Rafael, "Secularization and the Diminishing Decline of Religion," *Review of Religious Research* 27 (March 1986): 193–207, analyzes the decline of religion in Israel in the late twentieth century, again a study with many parallels in late nineteenth- and early twentieth-century German Catholicism.

One article in which the concept of modernization is considered specifically in terms of German Catholicism is August Hermann Leugers Scherzberg, "Die Modernisierung des Katholizismus im Kaiserreich: Überlegungen am Beispiel von Felix Porsch," in *Deutscher Katholizismus im Umbruch zur Moderne,* ed. Wilfried Loth, Konfession und Gesellschaft: Beiträge zur Zeitgeschichte, ed. Ansel Doering-Manteuffel, vol. 3 (Stuttgart: W. Kohlhammer, 1991), pp. 219–35.

10. See Albert Ehrhard, *Der Katholizismus und das zwanzigste Jahrhundert im Lichte der kirchlichen Entwicklung der Neuzeit* (Stuttgart: Jos. Roth, 1902), p. 46.

11. Johann Michael Sailer, S.J. (1751–1832), bishop of Regensburg and leading German Catholic philosopher; wrote on aesthetics and Romanticism.

12. Sailer, quoted in Joseph August Lux, "Kirche und Kunst," *Das neue Reich* 37, abridged in "Im Ringen der Zeit," *Germania,* June 26, 1926, Morgenausgabe, Das neue Ufer. See also Eva Kolinsky and Wilfried van der Will, "In Search of German Culture: An Introduction," in *The Cambridge Companion to Modern German Culture,* ed. Eva Kolinsky and Wilfried van der Will (Cambridge: Cambridge University Press, 1998), pp. 2–3.

13. See Wilfried van der Will and Rob Burns, *Arbeiterkulturbewegung in der Weimarer Republik* (Frankfurt am Main: Ullstein, 1982); Vernon L. Lidtke, *The Alternative Culture: Socialist Labor in Imperial Germany* (New York: Oxford University Press, 1985); Lynn Abrams, *Workers' Culture in Imperial Germany: Leisure and Recreation in the Rhineland and Westphalia* (London: Routledge, 1992); and Helmut Walser Smith, *German Nationalism and Religious Conflict: Culture, Ideology Politics, 1970–1914* (Princeton, N.J.: Princeton University Press, 1994), p. 68.

14. See Margaret Lavinia Anderson, "Piety and Politics: Recent Work on German Catholicism," *Journal of Modern History* 63 (December 1991): 715.

15. I have sought autobiographies, queried archives, pursued correspondence, and searched official records to little avail. Such autobiographies as there are include those of the intellectuals who tried to shape culture. Irmtraud Götz von Olenhusen found few clerical autobiographies and ascribes their dearth to the same reasons. See Irmtraud Götz von Olenhusen, *Klerus und abweichendes Verhalten: Zur Sozialgeschichte katholischer Priester im 19. Jahrhundert: Die Erzdiözese Freiburg,* Kritische Studien zur Geschichtswissenschaft, vol. 106 (Göttingen: Vandenhoeck und Ruprecht, 1994), p. 95.

There may be collections that include oral history interviews with ordinary German Catholics of the period, in which they talk about cultural experiences, but they are unlikely to include much comment on culture. Because they are usually written by devoted parishioners, local histories are a good guide to the values of the community, and few of the local histories that were read for this study had anything to say about culture. Typically, they offered a detailed description of the building of the church and a chronology of the clergy but little information on parish organizations. As far as cultural activity is concerned, at most there was a paragraph on the choir or Cäcilien Verein and a brief mention of the Borromäus Verein. Jeffrey Zalar has, however, demonstrated that the cultural interests of Catholic consumers of culture can be studied to some extent, if in a somewhat less direct fashion. In an exceptional dissertation he has put together information from printed sources, requests to ecclesiastical authorities for permission to read books on the index, and parish archives to make a strong case that there were many Catholics who wanted to read modern literature and wanted to keep up with the scientific advances of the century. See Jeffrey T. Zalar, "Knowledge and Nationalism in Imperial Germany: A Cultural History of the Association of Saint Charles Borromeo, 1890–1914" (Ph.D. diss., Georgetown University, 2002); Jeffrey T. Zalar, "The Process of

Confessional Inculturation: Catholic Reading in the 'Long Nineteenth Century,'" in *Protestants, Catholics and Jews in Germany, 1800–1914,* ed. Helmut Walser Smith (Oxford: Berg, 2001), pp. 121–52.

16. James Anthony Froude, "The Science of History," in *Short Studies on Great Subjects,* vol. 1 (New York: Charles Scribner's Sons, 1909), p. 7.

17. See Robert Linhardt, "Kirche und katholische Vereine," *Das neue Reich* 10 (1928): 1085. Irmtraud Götz von Olenhusen sees this mentality extending to within Catholicism in "Klerus und Ultramontanismus in der Erzdiözese Freiburg: Entbürgerlichung und Klerikalisierung des Katholizismus nach der Revolution von 1848/49," in *Religion und Gesellschaft im 19. Jahrhundert,* ed. Wolfgang Schieder, Industrielle Welt, ed. Reinhart Koselleck and M. Rainer Lepsius, vol. 54 (Stuttgart: Klett-Cotta, 1993), p. 133.

18. David Blackbourn, *The Long Nineteenth Century: A History of Germany, 1780–1918* (New York, Oxford: Oxford University Press, 1998), p. 286. Jonathan Sperber, *Popular Catholicism in Nineteenth-Century Germany* (Princeton, N.J.: Princeton University Press, 1984) is a seminal work on the subject of the Catholic revival.

19. See Thomas Nipperdey, *Arbeitswelt und Bürgergeist,* p. 478; the remark about the beekeeper is quoted in Karl Hoeber's *Der Streit um den Zentrumscharakter* (Cologne, 1912) and referred to in Margaret Lavinia Anderson's article, "Interdenominationalism, Clericalism, Pluralism: The Zentrumsstreit and the Dilemma of Catholicism in Wilhelmine Germany," *Central European History* 21 (December 1988): 371. Margaret Lavinia Anderson summarizes and puts in perspective the sharpening of confessional tensions that marked the nineteenth century in "Afterword: Living Apart and Together in Germany," in Smith, *Protestants, Catholics and Jews in Germany, 1800–1914* pp. 319–32.

20. See Hans-Ulrich Wehler, *Deutsche Gesellschaftsgeschichte,* vol. 3, *Von der "Deutschen Doppelrevolution" bis zum Beginn des Ersten Weltkrieges, 1849–1914* (Munich: C. H. Beck, 1995), p. 462. See also Kenneth D. Barkin, "The Crisis of Modernity, 1887–1902," in *Imagining Modern German Culture: 1889–1910,* ed. Françoise Forster-Hahn, Studies in the History of Art 53, (Washington: National Gallery of Art, 1996), p. 19; Hugh McLeod, "Secular Cities? Berlin, London, and New York in the Later Nineteenth and Early Twentieth Centuries," in *Religion and Modernization: Sociologists and Historians Debate the Secularization Thesis,* ed. Steve Bruce (Oxford: Clarendon Press, 1992), pp. 83–84; Leo Weismantel, *Mein Leben* (Berlin: Junker und Dünnhaupt, 1936), pp.40–42; and Nipperdey, *Arbeitswelt und Bürgergeist,* pp. 291–334.

21. Mudrooroo Narogin, *Writings from the Fringe: A Study of Modern Aboriginal Literature* (Melbourne: Hyland House, 1990), p. 24. See also Nipperdey, *Arbeitswelt und Bürgergeist,* p. 186.

22. See Bryan Wilson, *Religion in Sociological Perspective* (Oxford: Oxford University Press, 1982), p. 149; Steve Bruce, introduction to *Religion and Modernization,* pp. 1–7; McLeod, "Secular Cities?" p. 63; Thomas Mergel, *Zwischen Klasse und Konfession: Katholisches Bürgertum im Rheinland 1794–1914,* Bürgertum: Beiträge zur europäischen Gesellschaftsgeschichte, ed. Wolfgang Mager et al., vol. 9 (Göttingen: Vandenhoeck und Ruprecht, 1994), p. 193; and Anderson, "Interdenominationalism, Clericalism, Pluralism," p. 352. Helena Waddy Lepovitz applies the concept in an innovative discussion of the positioning of secular and religious paintings in the home. See Helena Waddy Lepovitz, *Images of Faith: Expressionism, Catholic Folk Art, and the Industrial Revolution* (Athens, Ga.: University of Georgia Press, 1991), pp. 112–13.

23. See Roy Wallis and Steve Bruce, "Secularization, The Orthodox Model," in Bruce, *Religion and Modernization*, p. 13.

24. See Nipperdey, *Arbeitswelt und Bürgergeist*, p. 797; Geoff Dench, *Minorities in the Open Society: Prisoners of Ambivalence* (London: Routledge & Kegan Paul, 1986); and Hans Mol, *Identity and the Sacred: A Sketch for a New Social-Scientific Theory of Religion* (Oxford: Basil Blackwell, 1976).

25. The concept of identity is associated with Erik Erikson, author of such classics as *Identity and the Life Cycle: Selected Papers* (New York: International Universities Press, 1959). It is a major topic in social psychology and sociology, and American historians have found it particularly useful because of the heterogeneous ethnic character of American society. See Arnold Dashefsky, ed., *Ethnic Identity in Society* (Chicago: Rand McNally, 1976); Michael A. Meyer, *Jewish Identity in the Modern World* (Seattle: University of Washington, 1990); and Philip Gleason, "Identifying Identity: A Semantic History," *Journal of American History* 69 (1983): 910–31. A particularly useful article on the subject because it addresses identity in the context of religion is Jeffrey R. Seul, "'Ours is the Way of God': Religion, Identity, and Intergroup Conflict," *Journal of Peace Research* 36 (1999): 553–69.

26. See Nipperdey, *Arbeitswelt und Bürgergeist*, pp. 107, 752.

27. See William J. Brown and Arvind Singhal, "Entertainment-Education Media Strategies for Social Change: Promises and Problems," in *Mass Media, Social Control, and Social Change: A Macrosocial Perspective*, ed. David Demers and K. Viswanath (Ames, Iowa: Iowa State University Press, 1999), pp. 263–81; and Wilhelm Spael, "[Johannes Braun] Lebenswerk im Borromäusverein," in *Bücher in Menschenhand: Festschrift zum goldenen Priesterjubiläum des päpstlichen Hausprälaten und Direktors des Borromäusvereins Johannes Braun*, ed. Leo Koep (Bonn: Verlag des Borromäus-Vereins, 1955), pp. 226–28.

28. Oded Heilbronner, "From Ghetto to Ghetto: The Place of German Catholic Society in Recent Historiography," *Journal of Modern History* 72 (2000): 453–95, examines in detail the major trends in German Catholic social history.

29. See Jonathan Sperber, *Popular Catholicism in Nineteenth-Century Germany*, pp. 3–98; and Michael B. Gross, "The Catholic Missionary Crusade and the Protestant Revival in Nineteenth-Century Germany," in Smith, *Protestants, Catholics and Jews in Germany, 1800–1914*, pp. 245–65.

30. In his foreword Wolfgang J. Mommsen gives a brief synopsis of the periods of German bourgeois culture in the late nineteenth and early twentieth centuries: a far-reaching symbiosis of bourgeois culture and authoritarian order in the national state that followed the establishment of the Empire in 1871; the rise of the artistic avant-garde after 1890 and the consequent challenge to bourgeois culture; and the radical change of cultural paradigms during World War I. Wolfgang J. Mommsen, *Bürgerliche Kultur und politische Ordnung: Künstler, Schriftsteller und Intellektuelle in der deutschen Geschichte, 1830–1933* (Frankfurt am Main: Fischer Taschenbuch Verlag, 2000), pp. 8–9.

31. Modris Eksteins, *Rites of Spring: The Great War and the Birth of the Modern Age* (New York: Doubleday/Anchor Books, 1989).

32. See George L. Mosse, *Fallen Soldiers: Reshaping the Memory of the World Wars* (New York: Oxford University Press, 1991), pp. 126–81.

33. See Heinz Hürten, *Deutsche Katholiken, 1918–1945* (Paderborn: Ferdinand Schöningh, 1992), pp. 145–59, for a discussion of Catholicism in the intellectual climate of the Weimar period.

2. THE CATHOLIC MILIEU AND ITS ORGANIZATIONS

1. See Carl Amery, *Die Kapitulation: oder, Deutscher Katholizismus heute* (Reinbek bei Hamburg: Rowohlt, 1963); Arbeitskreis für kirchliche Zeitgeschichte (AKKZG), Münster, "Katholiken zwischen Tradition und Moderne: Das katholische Milieu als Forschungsaufgabe," *Westfälische Forschungen* 43 (1993): 590; M. Rainer Lepsius, "Parteiensystem und Sozialstruktur: Zum Problem der Demokratisierung der deutschen Gesellschaft," in *Deutsche Parteien vor 1918,* ed. Gerhard Albert Ritter (Cologne: Kiepenheuer und Witsch, 1973), pp. 56–80 (the essay was originally published in 1966); and Frank-Michael Kuhlemann, "Protestantisches Milieu in Baden: Konfessionelle Vergesellschaftung und Mentalität im Umbruch zur Moderne," in *Religion im Kaiserreich: Milieu—Mentalitäten—Krisen,* ed. Olaf Blaschke and Frank-Michael Kuhlemann, Religiöse Kulturen der Moderne, ed. Friedrich Wilhelm Graf and Gangolf Hübinger, vol. 2 (Gütersloh: Chr. Kaiser/Gütersloher Verlagshaus, 1996), p. 316. Other terms used to discuss German Catholics are "Versäulung" (pillarization) and "Subgesellschaft" (subculture). *Versäulung* (fron *Säule,* "column") is applied to a situation in which different groups develop separately, but each supports a common enterprise, such as the nation; see E. H. Kossmann, *The Low Countries, 1780–1940* (Oxford: Clarendon Press, 1978), p. 569. *Subgesellschaft* (*Gesellschaft,* "society") requires two elements: a subculture defined by common values, feelings and behavioral patterns; and a substructure, common bonds, and social relationships (although analysis has tended to be in terms of external features like organizations); see Urs Altermatt, "Katholische Subgesellschaft: Thesen zum Konzept der 'Katholischen Subgesellschaft' am Beispiel des Schweizer Katholizismus," in *Zur Soziologie des Katholizismus,* ed. Karl Gabriel and Franz-Xaver Kaufmann (Mainz: Matthias Grünewald Verlag, 1980), p. 147; and Martin Baumeister, *Parität und katholische Inferiorität* (Paderborn: Ferdinand Schöningh, 1987), pp. 108–9. The concept of *Subgesellschaft* was originally developed by Gabriel Almond. See Gabriel A. Almond and Sidney Verba, *The Civic Culture: Political Attitudes and Democracy in Five Nations* (Newbury Park, Calif.: Sage Publications, 1989), esp. chap. 1, "An Approach to Political Culture," pp. 1–44. Ghetto is a closely related concept.

2. Particularly helpful guides to the literature on the German Catholic milieu include Margaret Lavinia Anderson, "The Limits of Secularization: On the Problem of the Catholic Revival in Germany," *Historical Journal* 38 (1995): 647–70; Heilbronner, "From Ghetto to Ghetto"; Michael Klöcker, "Das katholische Milieu: Grundüberlegungen—in besonderer Hinsicht auf das Deutsche Kaiserreich von 1871," *Zeitschrift für Religions- und Geistesgeschichte* 44 (1992): 241–62; Rudolf Lill, "Der deutsche Katholizismus in der neueren historischen Forschung," in *Der deutsche Katholizismus in der zeitgeschichtlichen Forschung,* ed. Ulrich von Hehl and Konrad Repgen (Mainz: Matthias Grunewald Verlag, 1988), pp. 41–64; Karl-Egon Lönne, "Katholizismus-Forschung," *Geschichte und Gesellschaft* 26 (2000): 128–70; Nipperdey, *Arbeitswelt und Bürgergeist,* pp. 374–95; and Helmut Walser Smith and Chris Clark, "The Fate of Nathan," in Smith, *Protestants, Catholics and Jews in Germany, 1800–1914,* pp. 3–29.

3. See Olaf Blaschke and Frank-Michael Kuhlemann, "Religion in Geschichte und Gesellschaft: Sozialhistorische Perspektiven für die vergleichende Erforschung religiöser Mentalitäten und Milieus," in Blaschke and Kuhlemann, *Religion im Kaiserreich,* pp. 45–51; and Raymond Chien Sun, *Before the Enemy Is within Our Walls: Catholic Workers in Cologne, 1885–1912: A Social, Cultural, and Political History,* Studies in Central European Histories: Studies in German Histories (Boston: Humanities Press, 1999).

4. See Johannes Mumbauer "Ein literarisches Ghetto für die Katholiken?" *Allgemeine Rundschau* 4 (1907): 460–61, 478–79; Oskar Koehler, "The Position of Catholicism in the Culture at the Turn of the Century," in *The Church in the Industrial Age,* ed. Roger Aubert et al., trans. Margit Resch, History of the Church, ed. Hubert Jedin and John Dolan, vol. 9 (New York: Crossroad, 1981), p. 245; Martin E. Marty, "The Catholic Ghetto and All the Other Ghettos," *Catholic Historical Review* 68 (April 1982): 185; and Hugh McLeod, "Building the 'Catholic Ghetto': Catholic Organisations 1870–1914," in *Voluntary Religion,* ed. W. J. Sheils and Diana Wood (Published for the Ecclesiastical History Society by Basil Blackwell, 1986), p. 418.

5. In recent years there have been a number of local and regional studies of Protestants emphasizing social history that use the concept of the milieu. Among the more important are Barbara Becker-Jákli, *"Fürchtet Gott, ehret den König": Evangelisches Leben im linksrheinischen Köln, 1850–1918* (Cologne: Rheinland Verlag, 1988) and Dietmar von Reeken, *Kirchen im Umbruch zur Moderne: Milieubildungsprozesse im nordwestdeutschen Protestantismus, 1849–1914,* Religiöse Kulturen der Moderne, ed. Friedrich Wilhelm Graf and Gangolf Hübinger, vol. 9 (Gütersloh: Chr. Kaiser/Gütersloher Verlagshaus, 1999). Antonius Liedhegener has compared the experiences of Protestants and Catholics in two locales, one urban, the other more rural. Antonius Liedhegener, *Christentum und Urbanisierung: Katholiken und Protestanten in Münster und Bochum, 1830–1933,* Veröffentlichungen der Kommission für Zeitgeschichte, ed. Ulrich von Hehl, series B: Forschung, vol. 77 (Paderborn: Ferdinand Schöningh, 1997).

6. See Blaschke and Kuhlemann, "Religion in Geschichte und Gesellschaft," pp. 34–41; and Jochen-Christoph Kaiser, "Die Formierung des protestantischen Milieus konfessionelle Vergesellschaftung im 19. Jahrhundert," in Blaschke and Kuhlemann, *Religion im Kaiserreich,* pp. 257–89. There are also treatments of several specific regional Protestant milieux in Blaschke and Kuhlemann, *Religion im Kaiserreich.* Gangolf Hübinger in *Kulturprotestantismus und Politik: Zum Verhältnis von Liberalismus und Protestantismus im wilhelminischen Deutschland* (Tübingen: J. C. B. Mohr [Paul Siebeck], 1994) identifies two separate Protestant sociocultural milieux, one of liberal *Kulturprotestantismus* (cultural Protestantism), the other of conservative Protestantism. Other scholars offer different lists. Wolfgang Mommsen identified four: the milieu of the aristocracy and princely courts; the middle-class Protestant milieu; the Catholic cultural milieu; and the working-class milieu. Wolfgang J. Mommsen, *Imperial Germany, 1867–1918,* pp. 120–23. Kenneth Barkin follows Lepsius but emphasizes the cosmopolitan, urban character of the bourgeois subculture, rather than its Protestant element. Kenneth D. Barkin, "The Crisis of Modernity, 1887–1902," p. 22.

7. See Smith, *German Nationalism and Religious Conflict,* pp. 95–98.

8. Nipperdey, *Arbeitswelt und Bürgergeist,* pp. 507–8; Blaschke and Kuhlemann, "Religion in Geschichte und Gesellschaft," p. 8; Olaf Blaschke, "Das 19. Jahrhundert: Ein zweites konfessionelles Zeitalter?" *Geschichte und Gesellschaft* 26 (2000): 38–75; and Wolfgang Schieder, "Sozialgeschichte der Religion im 19. Jahrhundert: Bemerkungen zur Forschungslage," in Schieder, *Religion und Gesellschaft im 19. Jahrhundert,* p. 18.

9. See Heinz Hürten, *Kurze Geschichte des deutschen Katholizismus, 1800–1960* (Mainz: Matthias Grünewald Verlag, 1986); Thomas Nipperdey, *Religion im Umbruch: Deutschland, 1870–1918* (Munich: C. H. Beck, 1988), pp. 25–28; and Josef Mooser, "Das katholische Milieu in der bürgerlichen Gesellschaft: Zum Vereinswesen des Katholizismus im späten Deutschen Kaiserreich," in Blaschke and Kuhlemann, *Religion im Kaiserreich,* p. 89.

10. There are many books and articles on the subject of the *Kulturkampf*. Among the most useful are Erich Schmidt-Volkmar, *Der Kulturkampf in Deutschland, 1871–1890* (Göttingen: Musterschmidt, 1962); Rudolf Morsey, "Der Kulturkampf," in *Der soziale und politische Katholizismus: Entwicklungslinien in Deutschland, 1803–1963*, ed. Anton Rauscher (Munich: Günter Olzog, 1963); Ronald J. Ross, *The Failure of Bismarck's Kulturkampf: Catholicism and State Power in Imperial Germany, 1871–1887* (Washington, D.C.: Catholic University of America Press, 1998); Ellen Lovell Evans, *The German Center Party, 1870–1933* (Carbondale and Edwardsville, Ill.: Southern Illinois University Press, 1981); and Margaret Lavinia Anderson, *Windthorst: A Political Biography* (Oxford: Clarendon Press, 1981), as well as Anderson's article, "The *Kulturkampf* and the Course of German History," *Central European History* 19 (March 1986): 82–115. The following summary of the *Kulturkampf* is primarily based upon their treatment. For an excellent bibliographic essay on the broader topic of historical research on nineteenth- and twentieth-century German Catholicism, see Lill, "Der deutsche Katholizismus in der neueren historischen Forschung," pp. 41–64.

11. See Evans, *The German Center Party, 1870–1933*, p. 76; and Morsey, "Der Kulturkampf," pp. 90–91.

12. Pius IX (1792–1878), born Giovanni Maria Masta-Ferretti; pope from 1846 to 1878; famous for his declaration of the *Syllabus of Errors*. Leo XIII (1810–1903), born Gioacchino Pecci; pope from 1878 to 1903; known for his encyclical *Rerum novarum*, which asserted Christian social norms in contrast to socialist and capitalist values.

13. See Heinhard Steiger, "Karl Muth und das Hochland—eine Art 'Kulturkatholizismus'?" in *Kulturprotestantismus: Beiträge zu einer Gestalt des modernen Christentums*, ed. Hans Martin Müller (Gütersloh: Verlagshaus Gerd Mohn, 1992), p. 266.

14. See Evans, *The German Center Party, 1870–1933*, p. 55.

15. See Thomas Nipperdey, "Religion und Gesellschaft: Deutschland um 1900," *Historische Zeitschrift* 246 (1988): 613. Nipperdey argues that the difference between Catholic and Protestant was more significant than the distinction between Christian and non-Christian because Protestant morality dominated culture. In 1896 Heinrich Keiter described anti-Semitism as a "tiny ball" in comparison with anti-Catholicism. Heinrich Keiter, *Konfessionelle Brunnenvergiftung: Die wahre Schmach des Jahrhunderts* (Regensburg: Verlag von Heinrich Keiter, 1896), p. 4.

16. See Clemens Bauer, *Deutsche Katholizismus: Entwicklungslinien und Profile* (Frankfurt am Main: Josef Knecht, 1965), p. 29.

17. Arbeitskreis für kirchliche Zeitgeschichte (AKKZG), Münster, "Katholiken zwischen Tradition und Moderne," pp. 632–44; Wilhelm Damberg, "An der Jahrhundertwende," in *Im Aufbruch gelähmt? Die deutschen Katholiken an der Jahrhundertwende*, ed. David Seeber (Frankfurt am Main: Josef Knecht, 2000), p. 10; Oded Heilbronner, "The Impact and Consequences of the First World War in a Catholic Rural Area: The Black Forest as a Case Study," *German History* 11 (1993): 21; Thomas Mergel, "Grenzgänger: Das katholische Bürgertum im Rheinland zwischen bürgerlichem und katholischem Milieu 1870–1914," in Blaschke and Kuhlemann, *Religion im Kaiserreich*, p. 185.

18. See Blackbourn, *The Long Nineteenth Century*, pp. 296–302; Albert Ehrhard, *Katholisches Christentum und Kultur*, Kultur und Katholizismus 6 (Mainz: Kirchheim'sche Verlagsbuchhandlung, 1907); Hugh McLeod, "Weibliche Frömmigkeit—männlicher Unglaube?" in *Bürgerinnen und Bürger*, ed. Ute Frevert, Kritische Studien zur Geschichtswissenschaft, ed. Helmut Binding, Jürgen Kocka, and Hans-Ulrich Wehler, 77 (Göttingen: Vandenhoeck and Ruprecht, 1988), pp. 134–56; McLeod, "Secular Cities?" pp. 59–60; and Nipperdey,

Arbeitswelt und Bürgergeist, pp. 437–39. The comparative statistics in Liedhegener, *Christentum und Urbanisierung,* make the similarity of the patterns in secularization of the two confessions and the time lag of the Catholic experience very clear; see especially p. 583.

19. Many of the essays in Smith, *Protestants, Catholics and Jews in Germany, 1800–1914,* represent an attempt to redress the historiographical balance.

20. See Barkin, "The Crisis of Modernity, 1887–1902," p. 19.

21. See Nipperdey, *Arbeitswelt und Bürgergeist,* pp. 420–68; Wehler, *Von der "Deutschen Doppelrevolution" bis zum Beginn des Ersten Weltkrieges, 1849–1914,* pp. 1169–90; and Josef Mooser, "Volk, Arbeiter und Bürger in der Öffentlichkeit des Kaiserreichs," in *Bürger in der Gesellschaft der Neuzeit,* ed. H. J. Puhle (Göttingen: Vandenhoeck und Ruprecht, 1991), p. 260.

22. See Alfred J. Andrea, "Mentalities in History," *The Historian* 53 (Spring 1991): 605–8; G. E. R. Lloyd, introduction to *Demystifying Mentalities* (Cambridge: Cambridge University Press, 1990), pp. 1–13; Blaschke and Kuhlemann, "Religion in Geschichte und Gesellschaft," pp. 12–21; and Peter Burke, "Strengths and Weaknesses of the History of Mentalities," *History of European Ideas* 7 (1986): 439–51.

23. See Mergel, *Zwischen Klasse und Konfession,* pp. 94–97; Christoph Weber, "Ultramontanismus als katholischer Fundamentalismus," in *Deutscher Katholizismus im Umbruch zur Moderne,* ed. Wilfried Loth, Konfession und Gesellschaft: Beiträge zur Zeitgeschichte, ed. Anselm Doering-Manteuffel et al., vol. 3 (Stuttgart: W. Kohlhammer, 1991), pp. 20–45; Mooser, "Volk, Arbeiter und Bürger in der Öffentlichkeit des Kaiserreichs," p. 262; and Hugh McLeod, *Religion and the People of Western Europe, 1789–1989* (Oxford: Oxford University Press, 1997), pp. 47–50.

24. An important way in which an ideology differs from a *mentalité* is that it contains an action element.

25. See Götz von Olenhusen, "Klerus und Ultramontanismus in der Erzdiözese Freiburg," pp. 113–43; Heilbronner, "From Ghetto to Ghetto," pp. 456–63; Hürten, *Kurze Geschichte des deutschen Katholizismus, 1800–1960,* p. 27; and Loth, "Integration und Erosion," pp. 266–81.

26. See Hürten, *Kurze Geschichte des deutschen Katholizismus, 1800–1960,* p. 29.

27. Pius X (1835–1914), born Giuseppe Sarto, pope from 1903 to 1914; known for his reform of Church music; canonized in June 1951 by Pius XII.

28. Aubert, "The Modernist Crisis: Reform Catholicism in Germany," in Aubert et al., *The Church in the Industrial Age,* pp. 422–23; Pope Pius X, *Pascendi Dominici gregig (On the Doctrine of the Modernists),* http://www.vatican.va/holy_father/pius_x/encyclicals.

29. See Aubert, "The Modernist Crisis," pp. 422–30; Nipperdey, *Arbeitswelt und Bürgergeist,* pp. 445–49; Wehler, *Von der "Deutschen Doppelrevolution" bis zum Beginn des Ersten Weltkrieges, 1849–1914,* pp. 1183–34; and Victor Consemius [Conzemius], "The Condemnation of Modernism and the Survival of Catholic Theology," in *The Twentieth Century: A Theological Overview,* ed. Gregory Baum (Maryknoll, N.Y.: Orbis Books, 1999), pp. 14–26. A detailed treatment of the theological issues can be found in Thomas F. O'Meara, *Church and Culture: German Catholic Theology, 1860–1914* (Notre Dame, Ind.: University of Notre Dame Press, 1991).

30. Franz Xaver Kraus (1840–1901), professor at the University of Freiburg; historian who wrote on literature, religious art, and cultural history. Hermann Schell (1850–1906), professor at the University of Würzburg from 1884. Albert Ehrhard (1862–1940), wrote on history, theology, literature, and was papal house prelate.

31. See Aubert, "The Modernist Crisis," pp. 422–30; Hermann Schell, *Der Katholicismus als Princip des Fortschritts* (Würzburg: Andreas Göbel, 1897); and Hans Jürgen Brandt, "Katholische Kirche und Urbanisation im deutschen Reich," *Blätter für deutsche Landesgeschichte* 128 (1992): 222.

32. See Hans Rost, *Die wirtschaftliche und kulturelle Lage der deutschen Katholiken* (Cologne: J. P. Bachem, 1911), p. 125; and *Der Grosse Brockhaus* (Leipzig: F. A. Brockhaus, 1929), s.v. "Deutsches Reich, Statistik, Tabelle 1e: Politische Bezirke: Religionszugehörigkeit der Bevölkerung 1925 (ohne Saargebiet)."

33. Statistics on Catholics and Catholic activities are scarce. Nipperdey attributes this to the episcopacy's lack of interest in statistical information. Nipperdey, *Religion im Umbruch*, p. 22. Erwin Gatz and Lothar Ullrich, "Grundsätzliches zur Minderheitensituation der katholischen Christenheit," in *Katholiken in der Minderheit, Geschichte des kirchlichen Lebens in den deutschsprachigen Ländern seit dem Ende des 18. Jahrhunderts*, ed. Erwin Gatz, vol. 3 (Freiburg: Herder, 1994), pp. 19–36, is a general treatment of Catholic minority status.

34. See Hürten, *Deutsche Katholiken, 1918–1945*, pp. 13–14; and Heilbronner, "From Ghetto to Ghetto," pp. 465–66.

35. Georg, (Graf) Freiherr von Hertling (1843–1919), philosopher and statesman.

36. Hans Rost (1877–1970), editor of the *Augsburg Postzeitung* from 1906 to 1933; Catholic writer on social science, statistics, and cultural history.

37. Hans Rost, *Die Katholiken im Kultur- und Wirtschaftsleben der Gegenwart* (Cologne: J. P. Bachem, 1908), and Rost, *Die wirtschaftliche und kulturelle Lage der deutschen Katholiken*.

38. See Ernst Hanisch, "Der katholische Literaturstreit," in *Der Modernismus: Beiträge zu seiner Erforschung*, ed. Erika Weinzierl (Graz: Verlag Styria, 1974), p. 125; Rost, *Die Katholiken im Kultur- und Wirtschaftsleben der Gegenwart*, pp. 30–37; and Rost, *Die wirtschaftliche und kulturelle Lage der deutschen Katholiken*, p. 14.

39. See Nipperdey, "Religion und Gesellschaft," p. 611.

40. See David Blackbourn, "The German Bourgeoisie: An Introduction," in *The German Bourgeoisie: Essays on the Social History of the German Middle Class from the Late Eighteenth to the Early Twentieth Century*, ed. David Blackbourn and Richard J. Evans (London: Routledge, 1991), p. 10.

41. See Rost, *Die Katholiken im Kultur- und Wirtschaftsleben der Gegenwart*, pp. 39–52.

42. Rost, *Die wirtschaftliche und kulturelle Lage der deutschen Katholiken*, p. 154; Nipperdey, *Religion im Umbruch*, p. 39.

43. Johannes Chrysostomus Schulte, O. F. M. (1880–1943), received his doctorate in theology from the University of Freiburg (1910); church historian, provincial of the Capuchins for Rheinland-Westfalen, and reader in church history from 1912.

44. Alois Eckert, "Grosstadtseelsorge [*sic*]," in *Das katholische Frankfurt: Jahrbuch der Frankfurter Katholiken*, ed. Jacob Herr (Frankfurt am Main: Verlag Carolus-Druckerei, 1928), p. 8; Erwin Gatz, "Katholische Großstadtseelsorge im 19. und 20. Jahrhundert: Grundzüge und Entwicklung," in *Seelsorge und Diakonie in Berlin: Beiträge zum Verhältnis von Kirche und Großstadt im 19. und beginnenden 20. Jahrhundert*, ed. Kaspar Elm and Hans-Dietrich Loock, Historische Kommission zu Berlin, vol. 74 (Berlin: Walter de Gruyter, 1990), pp. 23–38; Johannes Chrysostomus Schulte, O. F. M., *Die Kirche und die Gebildeten* (Freiburg im Breisgau: Herder, 1912), p. 2.

45. Joseph Mausbach (1861–1931), Catholic theologian; professor of moral theology and apologetics at Münster.

46. Franz Herwig (1880–1931), author who combined social and religious themes in novels that portrayed the problems of the proletariat; friend of the Catholic priest Carl Sonnenschein (1876–1929), the Berlin priest and social activist; best known for his novels *St. Sebastian vom Wedding* (1921), *Die Eingeengten* (1926), *Hoffnung auf Licht* (1929), and *Fluchtversuche* (1930).

47. Hanns Heinrich Bormann, "Franz Herwigs Meisterroman," *Germania*, December 17, 1926, Morgenausgabe, Werk und Wert. See also Wehler, *Von der "Deutschen Doppelrevolution" bis zum Beginn des Ersten Weltkrieges, 1849–1914*, pp. 21–36; Andrew Lees, "Debates about the Big City in Germany, 1890–1914," *Societas* 6 (Winter 1975): 31–47; Andrew Lees, "Critics of Urban Society in Germany, 1854–1914," *Journal of the History of Ideas* 40 (January/March 1979): 61–83; and Joseph Mausbach, *Die Kirche und die moderne Kultur* (Munich: Kösel und Pustet, 1921), p. 26.

48. Rost, *Die Katholiken im Kultur- und Wirtschaftsleben der Gegenwart*, pp. 53–62.

49. Johannes Forberger, *Die wirtschafliche und kulturelle Rückständigkeit der Katholiken und ihre Ursachen* (Leipzig: Carl Braun, 1908), p. 73.

50. See Victor Conzemius, "Kirchen und Nationalismen im Europa des 19. und 20. Jahrhunderts," in *Katholizismus, nationaler Gedanke und Europa seit 1800*, ed. Albrecht Langner (Paderborn: Ferdinand Schoningh, 1985), p. 44; and Hans Maier, "Zur historischen Situation des deutschen Katholizismus heute," in *Der deutschen Katholizismus in der zeitgeschichtlichen Forschung*, ed. Ulrich von Hehl und Konrad Repgen (Mainz: Matthias Grunewald Verlag, 1988), pp. 27–28.

51. See Baumeister, *Parität und katholische Inferiorität*, p. 1; David Blackbourn, *Class, Religion, and Local Politics in Wilhelmine Germany: The Centre Party before 1914* (New Haven, Conn.: Yale University Press, 1980), pp. 31–32, 43; Nipperdey, *Arbeitswelt und Bürgergeist*, pp. 450–58; and Heilbronner, "From Ghetto to Ghetto," pp. 458–459, 464.

52. See Mergel, *Zwischen Klasse und Konfession*, p. 1; Nipperdey, *Arbeitswelt und Bürgergeist*, p. 421; and Eric Yonke, "The Problem of the Middle Class in German Catholic History: The Nineteenth-Century Rhineland Revisited," *Catholic Historical Review* 83 (April 2002): 263–80. In "Wohin verschwand das katholische Bürgertum?" *Zeitschrift für Religions- und Geistesgeschichte* 47 (1995): 320–37, Oded Heilbronner argued that the group had not been studied because German social history had been so influenced by the ideas and methods of the social sciences in the 1960s, particularly by the ideas of Max Weber, who virtually identified capitalism with Protestantism. The Catholic bourgeoisie was not seen as an elite or as influential in areas that were important to those disciplines and, as a consequence, was not worthy of scholarly attention. The explanation may be simpler—perhaps there were not enough historians interested in Catholicism to investigate every aspect?—but whatever the cause, the Catholic bourgeoisie has only recently become an object of scholarly interest. In "The European Pattern and the German Case," in *Bourgeois Society in Nineteenth-Century Europe*, ed. Jürgen Kocka and Allen Mitchell (Oxford: Berg, 1993), p. 7, Kocka discusses the limits to this generally accepted notion of *Verbürgerlichung*, or embourgeoisement.

53. Useful discussions on the distinguishing characteristics of the bourgeoisie can be found in Blackbourn, "The German Bourgeoisie," pp. 1–45; Peter Gay, "The Strain of Definition," in *Education of the Senses*, vol. 1, *The Bourgeois Experience* (New York: Oxford

University Press, 1984), pp. 17–44; Kocka, "The European Pattern and the German Case," pp. 3–39; and Mergel, *Zwischen Klasse und Konfession*, pp. 6–14. Gay is particularly good on the problem of multiple contemporary definitions. His explanation that the English "middling orders" were reluctant to separate themselves with distinctive, aggressive class names, and preferred to use middle class or middle classes, clarifies why discussions in English depend so heavily on imported terminology. Awkwardness is unavoidable, and in this section a German term is often used (with an English explanation) because there simply is no adequate English alternative.

54. Gay, *Education of the Senses*, pp. 17–21.

55. See Jürgen Kocka, "Bürgertum und Bürgerlichkeit als Probleme der deutschen Geschichte vom späten 18. zum frühen 20. Jahrhundert," in *Bürger und Bürgerlichkeit im 19. Jahrhundert*, ed. Jürgen Kocka (Göttingen: Vandenhoeck und Ruprecht, 1987), p. 43; and M. Rainer Lepsius, "Zur Soziologie des Bürgertums und der Bürgerlichkeit," in Kocka, *Bürger und Bürgerlichkeit im 19. Jahrhundert*, p. 79. The collection of essays *Bürger und Bürgerlichkeit im 19. Jahrhundert* and the three-volume compilation also edited by Jürgen Kocka, *Bügertum im 19. Jahrhundert* (Göttingen: Vandenhoeck und Ruprecht, 1995) present current scholarship on the subject of the nineteenth-century bourgeoisie in Germany. Wolfgang Mommsen describes the ideal of the bourgeoisie as the increase of profit and wealth, modified by emphasis on honesty, fulfillment of duty, and frugality. The bourgeois lifestyle was one of moderation, avoiding luxury and the superfluous. Mommsen, *Bürgerliche Kultur und politische Ordnung*, p. 25.

56. See Hermann Bausinger, "Bürgerlichkeit und Kultur," in Kocka, *Bürger und Bürgerlichkeit*, p. 122; and Nipperdey, *Arbeitswelt und Bürgergeist*, p. 393. In 1912 the question was raised as to where the needed money would come from if only members of the proletariat were acceptably Christian, and in 1928 Friedrich Muckermann argued that education and leadership went together. See Mooser, "Volk, Arbeiter und Bürger in der Öffentlichkeit des Kaiserreichs," p. 259, and Friedrich Muckermann, "Mitarbeit der Gebildeten: Aus der Praxis des Lebens," *Germania*, November 17, 1928, Morgenausgabe, Kulturelle Beilage. This result would not have surprised Alexander Herzen, who wrote, "Never was Catholicism, never were the ideas of chivalry, pressed on men so deeply, so multifariously, as the *bourgeois* idea." Alexander Herzen, "Post Scriptum" (1921), in *My Past and Thoughts*, trans. Constance Garnett, vol. 3 (London: Chatto and Windus, 1924), pp. 139–49.

57. See Michael Klöcker, "Katholizismus und Bildungsbürgertum: Hinweise zur Erforschung vernachlässigter Bereiche der deutschen Bildungsgeschichte im 19. Jahrhundert," in *Bildungsbürgertum im 19. Jahrhundert*, ed. Reinhart Koselleck, Industrielle Welt, vol. 41 (Stuttgart: Klein-Cotta, 1990), pp. 117–38; Nipperdey, *Arbeitswelt und Bürgergeist*, pp. 556–57; and Wehler, *Von der "Deutschen Doppelrevolution" bis zum Beginn des Ersten Weltkrieges, 1849–1914*, p. 125.

58. See Richard J. Evans, *Rethinking German History: Nineteenth-Century Germany and the Origins of the Third Reich* (London: Harper Collins Academic: 1990), pp. 125–55; Blackbourn, "The German Bourgeoisie," pp. 14–16; Mergel, "Grenzgänger," p. 171; and Geoffrey Crossick and Heinz-Gerhard Haupt, *The Petite Bourgeoisie in Europe 1780–1914* (London: Routledge, 1995), pp. 191–215.

59. See Nipperdey, *Arbeitswelt und Bürgergeist*, pp. 437–38; McLeod, "Secular Cities?" pp. 59–60; Sun, *"Before the Enemy Is within Our Walls,"* p. 280; Thomas M. Bredohl, *Class and Religious Identity: The Rhenish Center Party in Wilhelmine Germany*, Marquette

Studies in Theology 18 (Milwaukee, Wisc.: Marquette University Press, 2000), pp. 151–63; and Wehler, *Von der "Deutschen Doppelrevolution" bis zum Beginn des Ersten Weltkrieges, 1849–1914*, p. 1178; Thomas Schulte-Umberg, *Profession und Charisma: Herkunft und Ausbildung des Klerus im Bistum Münster 1776–1940*, Veröffentlichungen der Kommission für Zeitgeschichte, ed. Ulrich von Hehl, series B: Forschung, vol. 85 (Paderborn: Ferdinand Schöningh, 1999), pp. 385–91.

   60. See Ralph Gibson, *A Social History of French Catholicism, 1789–1914* (London: Routledge, 1989), pp. 68–76; and Götz von Olenhusen, *Klerus und abweichendes Verhalten*, p. 142. Schulte-Umberg does not have statistics on social origins of the Catholic clergy of Münster for the earlier years of the nineteenth century, but in the later nineteenth century the single largest group was of agricultural origin, and its percentage was increasing. Schulte-Umberg, *Profession und Charisma*, pp. 350–52.

   61. See Götz von Olenhusen, *Klerus und abweichendes Verhalten*, pp. 146, 182–83; Schulte-Umberg, *Profession und Charisma*, pp. 367–78; and Nipperdey, *Arbeitswelt und Bürgergeist*, pp. 432, 470.

   62. Ludwig Ganghofer (1855–1920), writer of naive, romantic stories and novels, usually set in the Bavarian and Austrian Alps; noted for his liberally tinged piety and idealistic affirmation of life; his stories were frequently filmed.

   63. Ludwig Ganghofer, *Lebenslauf eines Optimisten*, new ed. (Munich: Drömer-Knaur, 1966), p. 71. See also Gerhard Wurzbacher and Renate Pflaum, *Das Dorf im Spannungsfeld industrieller Entwicklung* (Stuttgart: Ferdinand Enke, 1954), p. 187.

   64. See Olaf Blaschke, "Die Kolonialisierung der Laienwelt: Priester als Milieumanager und die Kanäle klerikaler Kuratel," in Blaschke and Kuhlemann, *Religion im Kaiserreich*, p. 125; Mooser, "Volk, Arbeiter und Bürger in der Öffentlichkeit des Kaiserreichs," p. 264; Sperber, *Popular Catholicism in Nineteenth-Century Germany*, p. 90; and Wurzbacher and Pflaum, *Das Dorf im Spannungsfeld industrieller Entwicklung*, p. 178.

   65. Anderson, "The Kulturkampf and the Course of German History," p. 87. Zalar quotes a statement by Robert Orsi that puts the subject into perspective: "historians have long represented religious leaders and followers like this, setting them within religious context in which everyone does what he or she is supposed to do, in which authority is obeyed and ritual rubrics carefully followed. Yet no one has ever seen anything like this in the real world." Robert Orsi, "Everyday Miracles: The Study of Lived Religion," in *Lived Religion in America: Toward a History of Practice*, ed. David D. Hall (Princeton, N.J.: Princeton University Press, 1997), p. 12, quoted in Zalar, "Knowledge and Nationalism in Imperial Germany," p. 94.

   66. See *International Encyclopedia of the Social Sciences*, ed. David L. Sills (New York: Crowell, Collier, and Macmillan, 1972), s.v. "Intellectuals," by Edward Shils, pp. 399–415; Konrad H. Jarausch, *Students, Society, and Politics in Imperial Germany: The Rise of Academic Illusions* (Princeton, N.J.: Princeton University Press, 1982), p. 231; James Hitchcock, "Postmortem on a Rebirth: The Catholic Intellectual Renaissance," *American Scholar* 49 (1980): 213; Thomas F. O'Dea, "The Role of the Intellectual in the Catholic Tradition," *Daedalus* 101 (1972): 159–60; Hürten, *Deutsche Katholiken, 1918–1945*, pp. 144–59; and Klöcker, "Katholizismus und Bildungsbürgertum," pp. 117–38.

   67. See Irmtraud Götz von Olenhusen, "Die Feminisierung von Religion und Kirche im 19. und 20. Jahrhundert: Forschungsstand und Forschungsperspektiven," in *Frauen unter dem Patriarchat der Kirchen: Katholikinnen und Protestantinnen im 19. und 20. Jahrhundert*, ed. Irmtraud Götz von Olenhusen, Konfession und Gesellschaft, vol. 7

(Stuttgart: W. Kohlhammer, 1995), pp. 9–21; Oded Heilbronner, "In Search of the (Rural) Catholic Bourgeoisie: The Bürgertum of South Germany," *Central European History* 29 (1996): 181; Nipperdey, *Arbeitswelt und Bürgergeist,* p. 52; and Hans Rost, *Katholische Familienkultur,* Politik und Kultur 4 (Augsburg: Literarisches Institut von Haas und Grabherr, 1926), p. 9.

68. Oskar Köhler in *Handbuch der Kirchengeschichte,* vol. 6, pt. 2, ed. Hubert Jedin, (Freiburg, 1973), quoted in Hans-Georg Aschoff, *Um des Menschen Willen: Die Entwicklung der katholischen Kirche in der Region Hannover* (Hildesheim: Bernward, 1983), p. 85. See also Nipperdey, *Arbeitswelt und Bürgergeist,* p. 480; Michael Sobania, "Vereinsleben: Regeln und Formen bürgerlicher Assoziationen im 19. Jahrhundert," in *Bürgerkultur im 19. Jahrhundert: Bildung, Kunst und Lebenswelt,* ed. Dieter Hein and Andreas Schulz (Munich: C. H. Beck, 1996), pp. 170–90; Heinrich Krauss, *Verbandskatholizismus? Verbände, Organisationen und Gruppen im deutschen Katholizismus,* ed. Heinrich Krauss and Heinrich Ostermann (Kevelaer: Butzon und Bercker, 1968), p. 39; and Heinz Hürten, *Deutsche Katholiken, 1918–1945,* p. 119. For studies of Catholic organizations, see Winfrid Halder, *Katholische Vereine in Baden und Württemberg, 1848–1914,* Veröffentlichungen der Kommission für Zeitgeschichte, ed. Ulrich von Hehl, series B: Forschung, vol. 64. (Paderborn: Ferdinand Schöningh, 1995), and Christoph Kösters, *Katholische Verbände und moderne Gesellschaft: Organisationsgeschichte und Vereinskultur im Bistum Münster, 1918 bis 1945,* Veröffentlichungen der Kommission für Zeitgeschichte, ed. Ulrich von Hehl, series B: Forschungen, vol. 68 (Paderborn: Ferdinand Schöningh, 1995).

69. August Pieper (1866–1942), general secretary of the Volksverein from 1892 to 1919, executive director from 1905 to 1922, and head clerk from 1923 to 1930. The Volksverein was the culmination of the Catholic social movement inaugurated by Franz Joseph von Buss (1803–1878) and Bishop Wilhelm Emmanuel von Ketteler of Mainz (1811–1888), both of them delegates to the German National Assembly of 1848 to 1849. Its founders were the industrialist Franz Brandts of Mönchengladbach (1834–1914); Franz Hitze (1851–1921), first director of Arbeiterwohl (an organization of Catholic workers' organizations), a member of the Prussian Landtag and later of the Reichstag, author of many bills of social legislation, and a writer on social theory and politics; and Ludwig Windthorst (1812–1891), the leader of the Center Party.

70. See "Katholisches Vereinswesen und katholische Vereinsaufgabe," *Historisch-politische Blätter für das katholische Deutschland* 165 (1920): 714; and *Wetzer und Welte's Kirchenlexikon,* ed. Heinrich Joseph Wetzer, 2nd ed. (Freiburg im Breisgau: Herder, 1882–1901), s.v., "Vereinswesen," by August Pieper.

71. See Hermann A. Krose, ed., *Kirchliches Handbuch für das katholische Deutschland, 1922–1923,* vol. 11 (Freiburg im Breisgau: Herder, 1923), pp. 224–27; and Burt R. Baldwin, "Formal Volunteer Organization Prevalence among Nations," *Voluntary Action Research* (1973): 89.

72. See Friedrich Schnettler, "Der Seelsorger und die Gefahren und Auswüchse des modernen Vereinswesens," *Der katholische Seelsorger* (1902): 20; F. Norikus, *Katholisches Vereinswesen: Ein Beitrag zum fünfzigjährigen Jubiläum der katholischen Vereine* (Munich: Rudolf Abt, 1898), p. 14; Kalk and Köllen, "Schattenseiten des Vereinslebens," *Pastor bonus* 13 (1901): 496; "Vereinsveranstaltungen auf dem Lande betr.," *Oberhirtliches Verordnungsblatt für die Diözese Passau, 1924* (Passau, 1924), p. 60, Archiv des Bistums, Passau (hereafter PAB); McLeod, "Building the Catholic Ghetto," p. 424; Hans Grundei, "Die Not

der katholische Kulturorganisationen, (Schluß)," *Allgemeine Rundschau* 20 (1923): 54–55; and Heinrich Denzer, "Eine katholische Stadt im protestantischen Preußen," in *Geschichte der Stadt Koblenz: Von der französischen Stadt bis zur Gegenwart,* ed. Ingrid Batorí, Dieter Kerber, and Hans Josef Schmidt, (Stuttgart: Theiss, 1993), p. 263.

73. "Vereinsveranstaltungen auf dem Lande betr.," p. 60, PAB; Anton Retzbach, *Das moderne kath[olische] Vereinswesen* (Munich: Buchhandlung Leohaus, 1925), p. 12. See also Katholischer Burschenverein f[ür] das Königreich Bayer, *Erstes Jahres-Bericht pro 1909/10* (Munich: Franz X. Seitz, [1910?]), pp. 5–6, Bischöfliches Zentralarchiv, Regensburg (hereafter RBZ), OA 1769.

74. Baron Sigismond-Felix Ow-Felldorf (1855–1936), bishop of Passau from 1902.

75. See Schnettler, "Der Seelsorger und die Gefahren und Auswüchse des modernen Vereinswesens, p. 20; Norikus, *Katholisches Vereinswesen,* p. 14; Kalk and Köllen, "Schattenseiten des Vereinslebens," p. 496; and "Vereinsveranstaltungen auf dem Lande betr.," p. 60, PAB.

76. Governments and other institutions dramatically increased the size and scope of their collection of statistics in the nineteenth century, but their activity naturally related to their priorities. Liedhegener, *Christentum und Urbanisierung,* p. 24, comments on the lack of Catholic statistics on urbanization.

77. See Gotthard Klein, *Der Volksverein für das katholische Deutschland, 1890–1933: Geschichte, Bedeutung, Untergang,* Veröffentlichungen der Kommission für Zeitgeschichte, ed. Ulrich von Hehl, series B: Forschungen, vol. 75 (Paderborn: Ferdinand Schöningh, 1996), table 1, p. 420, and table 2, p. 424; Borromäus Verein, "Bericht über die Tätigkeit und den Stand des Borromäusvereins im Jahre 1930," Historisches Archiv des Erzbistums, Cologne (hereafter CHAE), CR 22.5.1; and Michael Ebertz, "Pluralisierung, Verkirchlichung, alte und neue Kristallisationen," in Seeber, *Im Aufbruch gelähmt?* p. 27.

78. See Hans-Jürgen Brandt, "Chronik der Pfarrgemeinde St. Josef Schalke," in *Schalke 91: Eine katholische Arbeitergemeinde im Ruhrgebiet mit Tradition,* ed. Hans-Jürgen Brandt (Paderborn: Bonifatius Druck Buch Verlag, 1991), p. 158; Josef Mooser, "Das katholische Vereinswesen in der Diözese Paderborn um 1900," *Westfälische Zeitschrift* 14 (1991): 447–61; Mol, *Identity and the Sacred,* p. 28; and Gibson, *A Social History of French Catholicism, 1789–1914,* p. 168.

79. See *Jahrbuch der Hannoverschen Volkszeitung 1912* (Hannover-Hildesheim: J. Kornacker, n.d.), pp. 64–75; Aschoff, *Um des Menschen Willen,* pp. 68–79; Hans-Jürgen Brandt, "Kirchliches Vereinswesen und Freizeitgestaltung in einer Arbeitergemeinde 1872–1933: Das Beispiel Schalke," in *Sozialgeschichte der Freizeit: Untersuchungen zum Wandel der Alltagskultur in Deutschland,* ed. Gerhard Huck (Wuppertal: Peter Hammer, 1980), pp. 208–11; Brandt, "Die kirchliche Vereine und Bruderschaften," in Brandt, *Schalke 91,* pp. 353–84; and Klaus Tenfelde, "Die Entfaltung des Vereinswesens während der industriellen Revolution in Deutschland (1850–1873)," in *Vereinswesen und bürgerliche Gesellschaft in Deutschland,* ed. Otto Dann, Historische Zeitschrift, supplement 9 (Munich: R. Oldenbourg, 1984), p. 71.

80. R. Reichenberger, "Referat über das Vereinswesen: Leitsätze und Richtlinien," in *Diözesan-Synode für die Diözese Regensburg, abegehalten 1927 am 11. Oktober (Ir. Teil) und 1928 am 2. Und 3. Juli (II. Teil): Bericht, Beschlüsse und oberhirtliche Verordnungen* (Regensburg: G. J. Manz, 1929), p. 69. See also Wilhelm Niggemann, *Das Selbstverständnis katholischer Erwachsenenbildung bis 1933,* Beiträge zur Erwachsenenbildung, vol. 15 (Osnabrück: A. Fromm, 1967), p.26; and Sun, *Before the Enemy Is within Our Walls,* p. 429.

81. The first Katholikentag was called in 1848 by the canon of Mainz, Adam Lennig, who hoped to found a Catholic movement similar to the Catholic Association in Ireland. Its presidents tended to be from the old aristocracy, although a successful politician like August Reichensperger (1858), Wilhelm Marx (1910), or Konrad Adenauer (1922) was occasionally chosen.

82. See Krauss and Ostermann, *Verbandskatholizismus?* p. 37; "Mehr Organisation, weniger Organisationen," *Der deutsche Weg*, September 1928, Probenummer, Nachlaß Der. Wilhelm Hohn, Stadtarchiv, Mönchengladbach (hereafter MGS), 15/2/128, D.W.; Mooser, "Das katholische Vereinswesen in der Diözese Paderborn um 1900," p. 448; "Die Magdeburger Führertagung: Die katholische Vereine und die Kirche," *Germania*, September 6, 1928, Abendausgabe; Hürten, *Deutsche Katholiken, 1918–1945*, p. 119. Joseph Wittig, "Jesus, Soziale Frage und Christliche Revolution," *Hochland* 19 (1923): 587–96, and G. Kremer, "Das Vereinsproblem," *Theologie und Glaube* 14 (1922): 212–25, are two articles by priests; Kremer's article is especially comprehensive and contains a good bibliography of the negative writings on the subject.

83. Johannes Jacobus Hauck (1861–1943); became archbishop of Bamberg in 1912 after Georg, Freiherr von Hertling, recommended his nomination to Prince Regent Luitpold of Bavaria.

84. Wilhelm Marx (1863–1946), Catholic politician and long-time member of the Reichstag (1910–1918, 1919–1932); delegate to the convention that drew up the Constitution of the Weimar Republic in 1919; chair of the Center party from 1922 to 1928; chancellor of the Republic four times between 1923 and 1928.

85. See Eugen Weiss, "Abbau des Vereinswesen," *Allgemeine Rundschau* 19 (May 27, 1922): 246. The archbishop was quoted in Karl Ulrich, *Die katholischen Gemeinden von Nürnberg und Fürth im 19. und 20. Jahrhundert* (Bamberg: St. Otto Verlag, 1989), p. 193; [Wilhelm] Marx, "Der Volksverein in alter und neuer Zeit," *Germania*, January 1, 1929, Morgenausgabe; *Instruktion für die Beteiligung des Klerus an dem katholischen Vereinsleben der Gegenwart* (n.p., n.d.).

86. See Nipperdey, *Arbeitswelt und Bürgergeist*, p. 168; Kalk and Köllen, "Schattenseiten des Vereinslebens," p. 496; Schnettler, "Der Seelsorger und die Gefahren und Auswüchse des modernen Vereinswesens," pp. 63–65, 115; Retzbach, *Das moderne kath[olische] Vereinswesen*, p. 28; Mooser, "Das katholische Vereinswesen in der Diözese Paderborn um 1900," p. 459; and Father Henseler, "Das Aschenbrodel unter den kath[olischen] Vereinen," *Mitteilungen für die Verein vom hl. Karl Borromäus* 5 (March 1917): 12–13.

87. [Fritz] Witte, "Die Erziehung des Klerus zur Kunst," *Zeitschrift für christliche Kunst* (1920): 20. See also *Instruktion für die Beteiligung des Klerus an dem katholischen Vereinsleben der Gegenwart*.

88. See *Wie überwinden wir die Überorganisation und Anarchie des katholischen Vereinswesens* (Mönchengladbach: Volksvereinsverlag, 1927); Hans Grundei, "Sozialistische und katholische Kulturpolitik und Kulturziele in der Nachkriegszeit," *Literarischer Handweiser* 58 (August 1922): 345; Retzbach, *Das moderne kath[olische] Vereinswesen*, pp. 39–51; Constantin Noppel, "Gärung im katholischen Vereinswesen," *Stimmen der Zeit* 53 (February 1923): 346; Weiss, "Abbau des Vereinswesens, " p. 247; Schnettler, "Der Seelsorger und die Gefahren und Auswüchse des modernen Vereinswesens," p. 120; August Pieper, *Zur Frage: Vereinfachung des Vereinswesen* (reprint from *Führer-Korrespondenz* [1922], vol. 35, pp. 193–201); Sieber, "Ausbau des Vereinswesens," *Allgemeine Rundschau* 19 (1922): 366; Retzbach, *Das moderne kath[olischen] Vereinswesen*, p. 21; and Erwin Gatz, ed.,

Akten der Fuldaer Bischofskonferenz, vol. 3, *1900–1919.* Veröffentlichungen der Kommission für Zeitgeschichte, ed. Konrad Repgen with Dieter Albrecht, Rudolf Lill, and Rudolf Morsey, series A: Quellen, vol. 39 (Mainz: Matthias Grünewald Verlag, 1985), Anlage zu Nr. 203, p. 188.

89. See "Richtlinien für das katholische Vereinswesen," *Kirchliches Amtsblatt für die Diözese Rottenburg* 13 (1931): 262–66; and Dirk H. Müller, "Katholische Aktion versus Vereinskatholizismus: Zur kirchlichen Integration und Emanzipation der katholischen Laien," in Elm and Loock, *Seelsorge und Diakonie in Berlin,* pp. 474–97.

90. Some of these functions were identified early in the century. At the first conference of German sociologists in 1910 Max Weber spoke of the support voluntary associations provided for feelings of individual value, of how membership could facilitate social mobility, and of the contribution they made to democracy in America. Historians have demonstrated that, collectively, Catholic associations fulfill all of these social functions. Max Weber, "Geschäftsbericht," in *Verhandlungen des ersten deutschen Soziologentages vom 19.–22. Oktober 1910 in Frankfurt a. M.,* Schriften der deutschen Gesellschaft für Soziologie, vol. 1 (Tübingen: J. C. B. Mohr [Paul Siebeck], 1911), pp. 53–55.

91. See Wittig, "Jesus, Soziale Frage und Christliche Revolution," pp. 587–96; and Michael Klöcker, *Katholisch—von der Wiege bis zur Bahre* (Munich: Kösel, 1991), p. 126.

92. Hürten, *Deutsche Katholiken, 1918–1945,* p. 21; see also *International Encyclopedia of the Social Sciences,* s.v. "Voluntary Associations: Sociological Aspects," by David L. Sills, pp. 372–76; Wurzbacher and Pflaum, *Das Dorf im Spannungsfeld industrieller Entwicklung,* p. 151; and Klaus Tenfelde, "Vereinskultur im Ruhrgebiet: Aspekte klassenspezifischer Sozialismus," *Duisburger Forschungen* 33 (1985): 22–33.

93. See Ebertz, "Pluralisierung, Verkirchlichung, alte und neue Kristallisationen," p. 27; Nipperdey, *Arbeitswelt und Bürgergeist,* p. 444; and Wehler, *Von der "Deutschen Doppelrevolution" bis zum Beginn des Ersten Weltkrieges, 1849–1914,* p. 1188.

3. CULTURE IN THEORY AND PRACTICE

1. Max Pribilla, "Kulturwende und Katholizismus," *Stimmen der Zeit* 107 (July 1924): 259. See also Heinrich Bachmann, "Das Gesicht des katholischen Heimatromans: Zu einigen wichtigen Neuerscheinungen," *Germania,* November 30, 1928, Morgenausgabe, Werk und Wert. During the period, the question of culture became a subject of intense interest and examination. General treatments of the cultural background of the period can be found in Matei Calinescu, *Five Faces of Modernity* (Durham, N.C.: Duke University Press, 1987), a work that includes a particularly useful bibliography; Raymond Aron, *Progress and Disillusion: The Dialectics of Modern Society* (New York: Praeger, 1968); Monique Chefdo, Ricardo Quinones, and Albert Wachtel, eds., *Modernism: Challenges and Perspectives* (Urbana, Ill.: University of Illinois Press, 1986); *Encyclopaedia Britannica,* 15th rev. ed., s.v. "European History and Culture"; Peter Gay, *Weimar Culture: The Outsider as Insider* (New York: Harper and Row, 1970); Jost Hermand and Frank Trommler, *Die Kultur der Weimarer Republik* (Frankfurt am Main: Fischer Taschenbuch, 1989); Walter Laqueur, *Weimar: A Cultural History, 1918–1933* (New York: Perigee, 1980); and Wolfgang Sauer, "Weimar Culture: Experiments in Modernism," *Social Research* 39 (Summer 1972): 254–84. Among histories of Germany, Nipperdey's two-volume *Deutsche Geschichte, 1866–1918* (Munich: C. H. Beck, 1990–1992) is particularly strong in its coverage of culture.

2. See Georg Bollenbeck, *Tradition, Avantgarde, Reaktion: Deutsche Kontroverse um die kulturelle Moderne, 1880–1945* (Frankfurt am Main: Fischer, 1999), p. 17; and Peter Childs, *Modernism* (London: Routledge, 2000), pp. 2, 12–17. The topic of cultural modernism is attracting increasing interest in its own right. Bollenbeck's *Tradition, Avantgarde, Reaktion* is an excellent examination of the German experience, whereas Childs's book is a basic introduction to and summary of the phenomenon.

3. See Willy Hellpach, *Der deutsche Charakter* (Bonn: Athenäum Verlag, 1954), pp. 171–229; Dean Peabody, *National Characteristics*, European Monographs in Social Psychology (Cambridge: Cambridge University Press; Paris: Éditions de la Maison des Sciences de l'Homme, 1985), pp. 109–23; and Fritz Stern, *The Politics of Cultural Despair: A Study in the Rise of the Germanic Idology* (Berkeley and Los Angeles: University of California Press, 1974), pp. xv–xxx.

4. Ina Seidel (1885–1974), German poet and novelist.

5. *The New Grove Dictionary of Music and Musicians,* ed. by Stanley Sadie (London: Macmillan, 1980), s. v. "Germany, 5. Art music, 1800–1918," by Christoph Wolff, p. 278.

6. See Peter Paret, *German Encounters with Modernism, 1840–1945* (Cambridge: Cambridge University Press, 2000), pp. 1–6, 60–63.

7. See Gay, *Weimar Culture,* p. 17. Richard Mayne (in the section on "European History and Culture" in the *Encyclopaedia Britannica* for which he was responsible) speaks of "cultural parricide," a particularly appropriate term in view of the prominence of parricide in expressionist plays.

8. Gay, *Weimar Culture,* p. 105.

9. Ibid., p. 108.

10. *Volk* was used by intellectuals and politicians as a collective noun to identify the German peasantry and working classes, although the place of the industrial worker within the *Volk* was ambivalent. Virtue was presumed to reside in the *Volk,* which supposedly preserved an understanding of true Germanness that had been lost by the bourgeoisie.

11. For example, the praise of Tacitus for the chastity of German women was periodically mentioned. See [Alfred], Graf von Oberndorff, "Der sittliche Niedergang des deutschen Volkes und die Aufgaben der Katholiken," *Volkswart* 24 (October 1931): 145; "Aus den Vereinen: Aachen," *Volkswart* 3 (March 1910): 43.

12. Those who disliked popular culture conveniently ignored the fact that high culture, too, was an economic phenomenon. I have found Theodor W. Adorno's *The Culture Industry* (London: Routledge, 1991), written by a man who experienced German culture during the period, and Dominic Strinati's *An Introduction to Theories of Popular Culture* (London: Routledge, 1995) particularly useful in my analysis of culture.

13. Siegfried Kracauer (1889–1966), avant-garde film theorist; editor of *Frankfurter Zeitung;* wrote *The Theory of Film: The Redemption of Physical Reality* (1960).

14. See Wilfried van der Will, "The Functions of 'Volkskultur', Mass Culture and Alternative Culture," in *The Cambridge Companion to Modern German Culture,* ed. Eva Kolinsky and Wilfried van der Will (Cambridge: Cambridge University Press, 1998), 153–71; and Hermand and Trommler, *Die Kultur der Weimarer Republik,* pp. 69–71.

15. See Paret, *German Encounters with Modernism, 1840–1945,* pp. 65–67.

16. Pope Pius IX, *Syllabus of Errors,* in *The Encyclical of Pius IX. Dated 8th December, 1864. Proclaiming the Jubilee of 1865, with the Syllabus of LXXX. Errors,* trans. R. Walter (London: George Clark, n.d.), p. 24.

17. Felix Antoine Philibert Dupanloup (1802–1878), bishop of Orléans.

18. Quoted in Roger Aubert, "Internal Catholic Controversies in Connection with Liberalism," in Roger Aubert et al., *The Church in the Age of Liberalism,* trans. by Peter Becker, History of the Church, ed. Hubert Jedin and John Dolan, vol. 8 (New York: Crossroad, 1980), p. 299. See also Ehrhard, *Katholisches Christentum und Kultur,* pp. 40–42.

19. Albert Lotz (1900–?), editor of *Der Rheinische-Merkur.*

20. Friedrich Muckermann, "Die Kulturkrise der Gegenwart und die jüngste Enzykl[i]ka Pius XI," *Germania,* February 11, 1928, Morgenausgabe, Das neue Ufer. See also Friedrich Muckermann, "Der Katholik und das gute Buch," in *Bericht über den Katholikentag zu Magdeburg . . . 1928* (Paderborn: Bonifacius-Druckerei, n.d.), p. 124; Englert, "Kulturpolitik," *Allgemeine Rundschau* 9 (April 13, 1912): 293–94; Hans Rost, *Die Kulturkraft des Katholizismus,* 3rd ed. (Paderborn: Bonifacius-Druckerei, 1923), p. 20; and Rost, *Katholische Familienkultur,* pp. 2, 26–27.

21. See Georg Steinhausen, *Deutsche Geistes- und Kulturgeschichte von 1870 bis zur Gegenwart* (Halle [Saale]: Max Niemeyer, 1931), pp. 143–46.

22. Richard von Kralik (1852–1934), cultural and literary historian, dramatist and poet, and founder of the *Gralbund,* a conservative association of Catholic writers. Kralik was a knight of the Austro-Hungarian Empire, but the *Gral* movement was part of the larger German culture, not just Austrian.

23. See Richard von Kralik, "Kulturideale," *Die Kultur* 3 (1902): 321–29; and D. Blau, "Kulturkrisis der Gegenwart," *Deutsche Blätter in Polen* 6 (April 1929): 173–89.

24. Franz Zach (1876–?), director of the St. Josef Bücherbruderschaft (St. Joseph Fraternity of Books); writer on literary criticism, cultural history; published in feuilletons.

25. Franz Zach, *Modernes oder katholisches Kulturideal?* 3rd ed. (Vienna: Herder, 1925), p. 5. See also Steinhausen, *Deutsche Geistes- und Kulturgeschichte,* pp. 17, 36; and Hans Grundei, "Die Rückkehr des Katholizismus aus dem Exil—durch die Wüste," in *Die Rückkehr aus dem Exil: Dokumente der Beurteilung des deutschen Katholizismus der Gegenwart,* ed. by Karl Hoeber, Verbandes der Vereine Katholischer Akademiker zur Pflege der Katholischen Weltanschauung (Düsseldorf: L. Schwann, 1926), p. 62.

26. Adolf Bertram (1859–1945), bishop of Hildesheim (1906) and archbishop of Breslau (1914); created cardinal in 1916.

27. Cardinal Adolf Bertram to the Ministry of the Interior, "Namens der in den Fuldaer Bischofskonferenzen vereinigten Oberhirten deutscher Diozesen," April 20, 1923, Archiwum Archidecezjalne, Wrocław (hereafter WAA), IA25g49.

28. Borromäus Verein (Zentralstelle), *Der Borromäusverein und die Not der Zeit* (Bonn: Verlag des Borromäus-Vereins, 1927).

29. Arnold Rademacher (1873–1939), professor of theology and religious philosophy at the University of Bonn.

30. Victor Cathrein, S.J. (1845–1931), professor of ethics at Ignatius College, Valkenburg (1882–1910).

31. Hans Grundei (1889–?), tax official and writer on culture.

32. See Arnold Rademacher, *Religion und Leben: Ein Beitrag zur Lösung des christlichen Kulturproblems* (Freiburg im Breisgau: Herder, 1926), pp. 87–89; Victor Cathrein, "Katholische Kirche und Kultur," *Stimmen aus Maria-Laach* 63 (August 1902): 280; and Grundei, "Die Rückkehr des Katholizismus aus dem Exil," p. 66.

33. Ferdinand Tönnies (1855–1931), German sociologist and philosopher.

34. *The Macmillan Student Encyclopedia of Sociology,* ed. Michael Mann (London: Macmillan, 1983), s.v. "Gemeinschaft" and "Gesellschaft."

35. See Kralik, "Kulturideale," pp. 321–23.

36. Zach, *Modernes oder katholisches Kulturideal?* pp. 3, 369–71.

37. See Fred Davis, *Yearning for Yesterday: A Sociology of Nostalgia* (New York: Free Press; London: Collier Macmillan, 1979), pp. 1–30; Malcolm Chase and Christopher Shaw, "The Dimensions of Nostalgia," in *The Imagined Past,* ed. Christopher Shaw and Malcolm Chase (Manchester: Manchester University Press, 1989), pp. 2–4; and Stuart Tannock, "Nostalgia Critique," *Cultural Studies* 9 (1995): 453–64.

38. See Bollenbeck, *Tradition, Avantgarde, Reaktion,* p. 3; Englert, "Kulturpolitik," pp. 293–95; and Joseph Lorenz, "Der Klerus und der moderne Kulturmensch," *Allgemeine Rundschau* 2 (1905): 212–15.

39. See Rost, *Die Kulturkraft des Katholizismus,* p. 72; and Peter Wust, "Die Rückkehr des deutschen Katholizismus aus dem Exil," in Hoeber, *Die Rückkehr aus dem Exil,* p. 22.

40. Karl Muth (1867–1944), journalist; founder (1903) and editor of the Catholic journal *Hochland.*

41. [Karl Muth], *Steht die katholische Belletristik auf der Höhe der Zeit?* (Mainz: Verlag von Franz Kirchheim, 1898). See also Hürten, *Deutsche Katholiken, 1918–1945,* p. 65; and Klöcker, "Das katholische Milieu," p. 260.

42. "Die Aesthetik Pius X. im Brief an den Gralbund," *Der Gral* 5 (July 15, 1911): 656. See also Mausbach, *Die Kirche und die moderne Kultur,* pp. 16–19; "Magdeburger Katholikentag: Der deutsche Katholizismus und die deutsche Kultur," *Germania,* September 9, 1928, Morgenausgabe; and Wilhelm Spael, "Religion, Kultur und christliche Kunst," *Kölnische Volkszeitung,* March 2, 1930, Im Schritt der Zeit (Sonntagsbeilage), p. 1.

43. Friedrich Daniel Ernst Schleiermacher (1768–1834), German Protestant theologian and Romantic theorist. Friederich von Schlegel (1772–1829), German philosopher, critic, writer, prominent originator of German Romanticism, and convert to Catholicism. (Johann) Joseph von Görres (1776–1846), German Catholic apologist, leader in the Romantic movement, and regular contributor to the *Historisch-politische Blatter für das katholische Deutschland,* which he helped to found. Martin Deutinger (1815–1864), German priest and Catholic theologian.

44. See Jutta Osinski, *Katholizismus und deutsche Literatur im 19. Jahrhundert* (Paderborn: Ferdinand Schöningh, 1993), esp. introduction and chaps. 1–4.

45. Andreas Jerger-Schwennebach (1848–1917), priest in Baden; wrote on politics.

46. See Franz Meerpohl, "Zur Kulturphilosophie des Katholizismus," *Literarischer Handweiser* 63 (October 1926): 3–10; Friedrich Fuchs, "Die deutschen Katholiken und die deutsche Kultur im 19. Jahrhundert," in *Wiederbegegnung von Kirche und Kultur in Deutschland: Eine Gabe für Karl Muth,* ed. Max Ettlinger, Philipp Funk, and Friedrich Fuchs (Munich: Kösel und Pustet, 1927), p. 30; Arnold Rademacher, "Katholizismus und modernes Leben," *Vom inneren Frieden des deutschen Volkes* (1916): 90; Friedrich Muckermann, "Kulturfragen der Gegenwart: Zur Sondertagung des Verbandes Katholischer Akademiker in Re[c]klinghausen, *Germania,* January 9, 1926, Morgenausgabe, Das neue Ufer; and Jerger-Schwennebach, "Religion und Kultur," *Historisch-politische Blätter für das katholische Deutschland* 137 (1906): 399.

47. Ludwig Hänsel (1886–1959), *Realschule* professor in Vienna; wrote on literary history and philosophy.

48. Albert Lotz, "Kirche, Kultur und Politik," *Allgemeine Rundschau* 20 (1923): 378.

49. For a discussion of the broader debate, see Arnold Labrie, "*Kultur* und *Zivilisation* in Germany during the Nineteenth Century," in *German Reflections*, ed. Joep Leerssen and Menno Spiering, Yearbook of European Studies/Annuaire d'études européenes, vol. 7 (Amsterdam: Rodopi, 1994), pp. 95–120; *Geschichtliche Grundbegriffe: Historisches Lexikon zur politisch-sozialen Sprache in Deutschland*, ed. O. Brunner, W. Conze, and R. Koselleck (Stuttgart: E. Klett, 1972–1997), s.v. "Zivilisation."

50. Houston Stewart Chamberlain (1855–1927), anti-Semitic racial theorist who preached the superiority of the Aryan race; married to the daughter of Richard Wagner.

51. Joseph Mausbach, "Kultur und Katholizismus," *Theologische Revue* 6 (January 8, 1907): 1.

52. Richard von Kralik, *Ein Jahr katholischer Literaturbewegung* (Regensburg: J. Habbel, 1910), pp. 71–79.

53. Josef Kreitmaier, S.J. (1874–1946), Catholic writer on art and music and regular contributor to *Stimmen der Zeit*.

54. Josef Kreitmaier, "Die Krisis der christlichen Kunst," *Stimmen der Zeit* 104 (1923): 381. See also Dionys Habersbrunner, "Katholizismus und individuelle Kultur," *Der Weg* (1924): 215.

55. Franz Xaver Walter (1870–1950), Catholic theologian.

56. Otto Müller (1870–1944), chief officer of Catholic workers' organization in western Germany; prominent in the Volksverein.

57. Romano Guardini (1885–1968), Catholic theologian.

58. See Ehrhard, *Katholisches Christentum und Kultur*, pp. 363, 420; Mausbach, *Die Kirche und die moderne Kultur*, pp. 16–17; Otto Müller, *Die katholischen Arbeitervereine als kirchliche Bildungsvereine* (Mönchengladbach: Volksverein, 1918), p. 3; Franz Xaver Walter, *Bildungspflicht und Katholizismus: Das Katholische Bildungsideal nach den Grundsätzen der christlichen Ethik*, Schriften des Zentralbildungsausschusses der katholischen Verbände Deutschlands, no. 1 (Mönchengladbach, 1922), p. 170; and Hürten, *Deutsche Katholiken, 1918–1945*, pp. 42–43.

59. See Michael Pflaum, "Die Kultur-Zivilisations-Antithese im Deutschen," in *Europäische Schlüsselwörter*, vol. 3, *Kultur und Zivilisation*, ed. Sprachwissenschaftlichen Colloquium, Bonn (Munich: Max Hueber Verlag, 1967), pp. 288–371.

60. Zach, *Modernes oder katholisches Kulturideal?* p. 19.

61. F. Muckermann, "Kulturfragen der Gegenwart"; Ehrhard, *Der Katholizismus und das zwanzigste Jahrhundert im Lichte der kirchlichen Entwicklung der Neuzeit*, p. 363. See also Walter, *Bildungspflicht und Katholizismus nach den Grundsätzen der christlichen Ethik*, p. 41.

62. Wilhelm von Humboldt (1767–1835), German statesman and philologist; founded Friedrich Wilhelm University (now Humboldt University) in Berlin in 1808.

63. Wilhelm von Humboldt, quoted in Johann Ernst, *German Cultural History from 1860 to the Present Day* (Munich: Nymphenburger Verlagsbuchhandlung, 1983), p. 9.

64. See *Dictionary of the History of Ideas: Studies of Selected Pivotal Ideas*, ed. Philip Wiener (New York: Charles Scribner's Sons, 1973), s.v. "Culture and Civilization in Modern Times," by Frederick M. Barnard. One recent scholar metaphorically threw up his hands, giving his attempt at explaining the definitions the title of "Words, Words, Words." Childs, *Modernism*, p. 2.

65. See Bollenbeck, *Tradition, Avantgarde, Reaktion,* especially the section "Konträre Argumentationsweisen und das ausgleichende Klima des wilhelminischen Obrigkeits-staates," pp. 99–193.

66. Cultural conservatism was often, although not invariably, the companion of political conservatism. That connection has guaranteed voluminous retrospective discussion, because the search for the roots of National Socialism has required intensive examination of all aspects of the conservative environment from which it emerged.

67. Max Nordau (1849–1923), Austrian writer, journalist, and Zionist.

68. See Bollenbeck, *Tradition, Avantgarde, Reaktion,* pp. 21–27; and Hans-Peter Söder, "Disease and Health as Contexts of Modernity: Max Nordau as a Critic of Fin-de-siècle Modernism," *German Studies Review* 14 (1999): 473–87.

69. Georg Steinhausen (1866–1933), also director of the Stadtbibliothek, Cassel, and editor of *Archiv für Kulturgeschichte.*

70. Steinhausen, *Deutsches Geistes- und Kulturgeschichte von 1870 bis zur Gegenwart,* p. 10. See also Stern, *The Politics of Cultural Despair,* pp. xviii–xix.

71. Julius Langbehn (1851–1907), German cultural critic and writer.

72. [Julius Langbehn], *Rembrandt als Erzieher* (Leipzig: C. L. Hirschfeld, 1909), p. 1, quoted in translation in Stern, *The Politics of Cultural Despair,* p. 121.

73. "Vom Zeitalter deutscher Kunst," *Der Kunstwart* 3 (March 18, 1890): 170–79, quoted in Stern, *The Politics of Cultural Despair,* p. 158.

74. For example, see Lempp, "Das Kulturprogramm des deutschen Katholizismus," *Evangelische Freiheit* (1914): 187.

75. See H. Richard Niebuhr, *Christ and Culture* (New York: Harper and Row, 1975).

76. Gangolf Hübinger's *Kulturprotestantismus und Politik* gives the best discussion of Protestant attitudes toward culture, although neither Hübinger nor anyone else has done a detailed examination of their attitudes toward culture in the sense in which it is used in this book.

77. See *New German Critique* 29 (Spring/Summer 1983), which published the essays presented at a symposium at Cornell University in 1983 entitled "The Origins of Mass Culture: The Case of Imperial Germany (1871–1918)."

78. See Hans Rost, *Die katholische Kirche die Führerin der Menschheit: Eine Kultursoziologie* (Westheim bei Augsburg: Gangolf Rost Verlag, 1949), p. 160.

79. Marxist-oriented research center in the social sciences founded in 1923. Theodor Adorno, Georg Lukács, Max Horkheimer, Herbert Marcuse, Erich Fromm, and, more recently, Jürgen Habermas are among the well-known thinkers associated with the Frankfurt school.

80. Johannes Hönig (1889–1954), secondary-school teacher.

81. Theodor Adorno (1903–1969), German, later American, sociologist, philosopher, musical theorist, composer, and leading member of the Frankfurt school. [Johannes] Hönig, "Das gute Buch," in *Die Reden gehalten in den öffentlichen und geschlossenen Versammlungen der 65. General-Versammlung der Katholiken Deutschlands zu Breslau . . . 1926* (Würzburg: Fränkische Gesellschaftsdruckerei, 1926), p. 153. The work of the Frankfurt school has relevance for this study probably because of the shared historical context. Earlier theories of mass culture likewise address more of the same issues than do later theories, perhaps because later cultural theorists have been less hostile to popular culture.

82. Karl Muth, quoted in Johannes Hönig, "Von der Tragik der katholischen Volksbildungsarbeit," *Die Bücherwelt* 26 (May/June 1929): 173.

83. See Frank Trommler, "Working-Class Culture and Modern Mass Culture before World War I," *New German Critique* 29 (Spring/Summer 1983): 64–70; and Gerhard Ritter, "Workers' Culture in Imperial Germany: Problems and Points of Departure for Research," *Journal of Contemporary History* 23 (1978): 165. The shared separation from the national culture was recognized by Theodor Schott in his 1887 bibliography. See Smith, *German Nationalism and Religious Conflict*, p. 68.

84. See "Zur Einführung," *Mitteilungen des Zentralbildungsausschusses der katholischen Verbände Deutschlands* 1 (January 1921): 1. The connection was similar in socialist cultural activity. See Margaret F. Stieg, "The Beginnings of Public Library Service in Vienna, 1887–1914," *Journal of Library History* 21 (Summer 1986): 553–73.

85. See Robert Grosche, "Der Weg aus dem Ghetto," in *Der Weg aus dem Ghetto* (Cologne: J. P. Bachem, 1955); and Niggeman, *Das Selbstverständnis katholischer Erwachsenenbildung bis 1933*, p. 77.

86. See Robert Grosche, "Was fehlt unserer Volksbildungsarbeit?" *Volkskunst* 13 (January 1925): 4–7; Joseph Antz, "Was fehlt unserer Volksbildungsarbeit?" *Volkskunst* 13 (1925): 49–54; and Emil Ritter, "Volksbildung und ihre Organisation," *Volkskunst* 13 (1925): 193.

87. Emil Ritter (1881–1968), official of the Volksverein (1919–1922), writer, and editor.

88. Emil Ritter, "Wo stehen wir?" *Volkskunst* 13 (January 1925): 1–3.

89. Robert Grosche (1888–1967), student chaplain in Cologne from 1920, parish priest from 1930, and leader of ecumenical movement among Catholics.

90. See Robert Grosche, "Volksbildung und Weltanschauung," *Volkstum und Volksbildung* 2 (1930): 193–97.

91. See L. Rieder, "'Grundsätze der Volksbildung,'" *Volkskunst* 2 (1914): 214–18; and Alois Wurm, *Grundsätze der Volksbildung* (Mönchengladbach: Volksvereins Verlag, 1913).

92. Johannes Braun (1879–1958), held different titles but in effect was director of Borromäus Verein from 1909 and was named papal house prelate in 1947.

93. See Bernhard Marschall to Prelate Paschen, office of the archepiscopal ordinary, May 5, 1929, CHAE, Gen. 23.54.1. This thirteen-page letter, a justification for his permanent release from other duties, is a detailed description of the goals, organization, methods, activities, and finances of the Zentralbildungsausschuß. See also Niggeman, *Das Selbstverständnis katholischer Erwachsenenbildung bis 1933*, pp. 133–37; and Bernhard Marschall, "Zehn Jahre Zentralbildungsausschuß," *Volkstum und Volksbildung* 1 (1929): 28–22; "Zur Einführung," *Mitteilungen des Zentralbildungsausschusses der katholischen Verbände Deutschlands* 1 (January 1929): 1–2.

94. "Zur Einführung," p. 1.

95. See Adolf Dyroff and [Johannes] Braun to His Excellency, January 28, 1920, PAB, OA Vereine 44.

96. See Friedrich Muckermann, *Im Kampf zwischen zwei Epochen*, Veröffentlichungen der Kommission für Zeitgeschichte, ed. Konrad Repgen with Dieter Albrecht, Rudolf Lill, and Rudolf Morsey, series A: Quellen, vol. 15 (Mainz: Matthias Grünewald Verlag, 1973), p. 310; cf. Wolfgang Mommsen, "Stadt und Kultur im deutschen Kaiserreich," in *Bürgerliche Kultur und politische Ordnung*, Carl Friedrich von Siemens Stiftung, vol. 4, pp. 11–45.

97. Henrica Stein, "Vom bayrischen Volksbildungswesen," *Volkskunst* 14 (1926): 311–17, is a report on Bavarian activities.

98. Bernhard Marschall (1888–1963), religious instructor (1918); founded Zentralbildungsausschuß (1919).

99. See Emil Ritter to Cardinal Archbishop Karl Josef Schulte, March 24, 1924, CHAE, Borromäus Verein, CR 22.5.1.

100. See Bernhard Marschall, "Aus der Arbeit: Bericht des ZBA," *Volkstum und Volksbildung* 2 (1930): 313.

101. Muckermann, *Im Kampf zwischen zwei Epochen*, p. 310; Horstwalter Heitzer, "Die soziale und staatsbürgerliche Bildungs- und Schulungsarbeit des Volksvereins für das Katholische Deutschland, 1890–1933," in *Katholizismus, Bildung und Wissenschaft im 19. und 20. Jahrhundert*, ed. Anton Rauscher, Beiträge zur Katholizismusforschung, series B: Abhandlungen (Paderborn: Ferdinand Schöningh, 1987), p. 144–45.

102. See "Zweite Tagung des Zentralbildungsausschusses," *Mitteilungen des Zentralbildungsausschusses* 2, in *Volkskunst* 12 (July/September 1924): 5; and Bernhard Marschall, "Der Zentralbildungsausschuß im Jahre 1930," *Volkstum und Volksbildung* 3 (1931): 48. On the Hohenrodter Bund and the Deutsche Schule für Volksforschung und Erwachsenbildung, see Jürgen Henningsen, *Der Hohenrodter Bund zur Erwachsenbildung in der Weimarer Zeit* (Heidelberg: Quelle und Meyer, 1958).

103. See Zentralbildungsausschuß (ZBA) der katholischen Verbände Deutschlands, *Jahresbericht 1927/28* and *Jahresbericht 1930*, PAB, OA Vereine III, 79, and the correspondence of Bernhard Marschall on the matter with Cardinal Adolf Bertram and Cardinal Archbishop Karl Josef Schulte between July and August 1929 held at CHAE, Gen. 23.54.1.

104. See Alfred Wahl, *Cultures et mentalités en Allemagne, 1918–1933* (Paris: Sedes, 1988), p. 183.

105. Hermann Cardauns (1847–1907), editor of the *Kölnische Volkszeitung* from 1876 to 1907, and general secretary of the Görres Gesellschaft from 1876 to 1891. Karl Hoeber (1867–1942), editor of the *Kölnische Volkszeitung* from 1907 to 1923.

106. See H. H. Bormann "Unsere Literaturzeitschriften," *Germania*, June 17, 1926, Abendausgabe, Werk und Wert; H. H. B[ormann], "Drei 'Orplid'-Hefte," *Germania*, July 21, 1926, Abendausgabe; Wehler, *Von der "Deutschen Doppelrevolution" bis zum Beginn des Ersten Weltkrieges, 1849–1914*, pp. 1188, 1246–47; and Hürten, *Deutsche Katholiken, 1918–1945*, pp. 144–55.

107. See Klein, *Der Volksverein für das katholische Deutschland, 1890–1933*, p. 434.

108. See Blaschke, "Die Kolonialisierung der Laienwelt, pp. 118–19; and Osinski, *Katholizismus und deutsche Literatur im 19. Jahrhundert*, p. 305. Margaret Lavinia Anderson notes the pervasiveness and persistence of this kind of confessional identification in Anderson, "Afterword," p. 320.

4. Literature

1. Muckermann, "Der Katholik und das gute Buch," p. 123; Wilhelm Lindemann, *Geschichte von der ältesten Zeiten bis zur Gegenwart*, 3rd ed. (Freiburg im Breisgau: Herder, 1873), p. 1, quoted in Exp[editus] Schmidt, "Das deutsche Literaturleben und die Katholiken," *Allgemeine Rundschau* 1 (December 11, 1904), p. 483.

2. See Nipperdey, *Arbeitswelt und Bürgergeist*, p. 45; Thomas Nipperdey, *Germany from Napoleon to Bismarck, 1800–1866* (Princeton, N.J.: Princeton University Press, 1996), p. 521; and "Im Ringen der Zeit: Für das werthaltige Buch," *Germania*, January 3, 1926, Morgenausgabe, Das neue Ufer.

3. Heinrich Keiter (1853–1898), writer; editor of *Der Deutsche Hausschatz* (1888–98) and *Keiters katholischer Literaturkalender*.

4. David Friedrich Strauss (1808–1874), German Protestant theologian and philosopher; wrote on origins of Christianity. (Joseph) Ernest Renan (1823–1892), French philologist and historian; author of the famous, iconoclastic *Vie de Jesus*. Ernst Haeckel (1834–1919), German zoologist and popularizer of ideas of Darwin in Germany.

5. See Adolf Dyroff, "Das Buch im Kampf um die Weltanschauung," *Die Bücherwelt* 17 (August/September 1920): 219; [Heinrich Keiter], "Konfessionelle Brunnenvergiftung," *Der Gral* 2 (August 15, 1908): 517–18; and Muth, *Steht die katholische Belletristik auf der Höhe der Zeit?* p. 6.

6. See Franz Stärk, "Die Erzählung im Sonntagsblatt," *Die Bücherwelt* 26 (September/October 1929): 344; "Katholischer Press- und Literatur-Verein für die Länder deutscher Zunge," *Katholische Revue* 1 (1900): 2; and E. P. Bundschuh, "Katholische Schriftenmission und Kolportage, eine soziale Aufgabe und ein Zeitbedürfnis," *Soziale Revue* 28 (March 1928): 111.

7. See Ronald A. Fullerton, "Creating a Mass Book Market in Germany: The Story of the 'Colporteur Novel,' 1870–1890," *Journal of Social History* 10 (March 1977): 266; Jochen Schulte-Sasse, "Toward a 'Culture' for the Masses: The Socio-Psychological Function of Popular Literature in Germany and the U.S., 1880–1920," *New German Critique* 29 (Spring/Summer 1983): 86; Rudolf Schenda, *Volk ohne Buch: Studien zur Sozialgeschichte der populären Lesestoffe, 1770–1910* (1970; Munich: Deutsche Taschenbuch Verlag, 1977), pp. 444–45; and Nipperdey, *Arbeitswelt und Bürgergeist*, pp. 752–54.

8. See Nipperdey, *Arbeitswelt und Bürgergeist*, pp. 775–80; and Roy Pascal, *From Naturalism to Expressionism: German Literature and Society, 1880–1918* (London: Weidenfeld and Nicolson, 1973), 229–32.

9. The invention of the penny dreadful and of yellow journalism turned print into the first modern mass medium. When Bernhard Marschall described radio as a mass medium, which he defined as directed at the masses and easily accessible, he included print with his examples of film and records. Bernhard Marschall, "Der Rundfunk," in *71. Generalversammlung der deutschen Katholiken zu Essen an der Ruhr . . . 1932* (Essen [Ruhr]: Fredebeul und Koenen, n.d.), p. 242.

10. Jakob Kneip (1881–1958), Catholic novelist and essayist.

11. Jakob Kneip, "Kirche und Dichtung," *Allgemeine Rundschau* 28 (July 11, 1939): 439.

12. See Osinski, *Katholizismus und deutsche Literatur im 19. Jahrhundert*, esp. introduction and chaps. 1–4.

13. See ibid., pp. 21–25, passim.

14. Ida, Gräfin Hahn-Hahn (1805–1880), German novelist and founder of the Convent of the Sisters of the Good Shepherd in Mainz.

15. Annette von Droste-Hülshoff (1797–1848), German poet; widely regarded as Germany's greatest female writer.

16. [K]arl Muth, *Wem gehört die Zukunft? Ein Literaturbild der Gegenwart* (Frankfurt am Main: A. Foesser Nachfolger, 1893), pp. 166, 180. See also Wilhelm Spael, *Das katholische Deutschland im 20. Jahrhundert: Seine Pionier- und Krisenzeiten, 1890–1945* (Würzburg: Echter-Verlag, 1964), pp. 106–21; Karl Muth, "Bilanz: Eine Umschau aus Anlaß des 25. Jahrgangs," *Hochland* 25 (October 1927): 1–23; and [Karl Muth], *Die literarischen Aufgaben der deutschen Katholiken* (Mainz: Franz Kirchheim, 1899).

17. Wilhelm Kreiten, S.J. (1847–1902), literary historian; associated with *Stimmen aus Maria Laach* from 1874.

18. Hanisch, "Der katholische Literaturstreit," p. 127.

19. Muth, *Steht die katholische Belletristik . . .* , pp. 4, 47–67. See also Osinski, *Katholizismus und deutsche Literatur im 19. Jahrhundert*, p. 342.

20. Alexander Baumgartner, "Die katholische Belletristik und die Moderne." (Zur Beurteilung der drei Veremundus-Schriften), *Stimmen aus Maria-Laach* 77 (August 1909): 121.

21. See Russell A. Berman, "Literary Criticism from Empire to Dictatorship, 1870–1933," in *A History of German Literary Criticism, 1730–1980*, ed. Peter Uwe Hohendahl, trans. Simon Srebrny (Lincoln: University of Nebraska Press, 1988), p. 320. Muth argues this point extensively in *Die literarischen Aufgaben der deutschen Katholiken*. See also "Muth gegen Kralik," *Literatur-Beilage* (September 25, 1909): 177.

22. Muth, *Die literarischen Aufgaben . . .* , p. 17.

23. Ibid., pp. 22, 57.

24. Ibid., p. 72.

25. Ibid., p. 79. See also Osinski, *Katholizismus und deutsche Literatur im 19. Jahrhundert*, pp. 339–41.

26. Muth's personal papers contain several scrapbooks, one of which is filled with clippings of the reaction to *Steht die katholische Belletristik . . .* , held at the Bayerische Staatsbibliothek, Munich (hereafter MBS), Manuscript Division, Karl Muth Nachlaß, Ana 390 I. F.8. The quotation is from the poet Leo van Heemstede's "Steht die katholische Belletristik auf der Höhe der Zeit?" *Dichterstimmen der Gegenwart: Poetisches Organ für das katholische Deutschland* 13 (1899): 22–27.

27. See Friedrich Muckermann, *Im Kampf zwischen zwei Epochen*, p. 210; and Osinski, *Katholizismus und deutsche Literatur im 19. Jahrhundert*, p. 373.

28. [Karl Muth], "Ein Vorwort zu 'Hochland,'" *Hochland* 1 (October 1903): 2; [Armin Kausen], "Unser Programm," *Allgemeine Rundschau* 1 (March 1904): 1; and Franz Eichert, "Gralfahrt—Höhenfahrt!" *Der Gral* 1 (October 15, 1906): 1.

29. It is usually called the first *Literaturstreit*, although the debates begun by *Steht die katholische Belletristik . . .* and carried on with intensity for approximately two years really deserve that title.

30. Kralik, *Ein Jahr katholischer Literaturbewegung*, pp. 101–2.

31. Johannes Mumbauer (1867–1930), priest and writer on literature.

32. Johannes Mumbauer, "Dreißig Jahre katholischer Literaturbewegung und Literaturarbeit," *Literarischer Handweiser* 63 (July 1927): 725. The literary ghetto article to which he referred was "Ein literarisches Ghetto für die Katholiken?" pp. 478–79. See also Hanisch, "Der katholische Literaturstreit," pp. 128, 145.

33. Martin Spahn (1875–1945), German Catholic writer associated with the *Hochland* group; historian and politician.

34. Eduard Hlatky (1834–1913), contributor to the *Der Gral*. Adam Trabert (1822–1914), railroad administrator and literary figure. Karl Domanig (1851–1913), director of the coin division at the Hofmuseum, Vienna; writer. Franz Eichert (1857–1926), Austrian writer, lyricist, and journalist.

35. See Kralik, *Ein Jahr katholischer Literaturbewegung*, pp. 2–3; and Richard von Kralik, *Die katholische Literaturbewegung der Gegenwart* (Regensburg: J. Habbel, 1909), p. 93.

36. Spael, *Das katholische Deutschland im 20. Jahrhundert*, p. 123; Hermann Herz, "Die Bücherwelt und ihr literarischer Ratgeber," *Die Bücherwelt* 17 (August/September 1920): 205–6, quoted in Hermann Herz, "Unser Weg: Referate des 15. Kursus für Leiter und Mitarbeiter von Volksbüchereien des Borromäusvereins," *Die Bücherwelt* 25 (September/October 1928): 362.

37. See Richard von Kralik, *Tage und Werke: Lebenserinnerungen* (Vienna: Vogelsang-Verlag, 1922), pp. 8, 70; and Kralik, *Ein Jahr katholischer Literaturbewegung*, p. 42. Muth took some digs at *Der Gral* for its Austrian associations in *Die Wiedergeburt der Dichtung: Gedanken zur Psychologie des katholischen Literaturschaffens* (Kempten and Munich: Kösel, 1909), p. 30.

38. See Hermann Cardauns, "Das literarische Schaffen," in *Deutschland und der Katholizismus*, ed. Max Meinertz and Hermann Sacher (Freiburg im Breisgau: Herder, 1918), vol. 1, p. 395; and Osinski, *Katholizismus und deutsche Literatur im 19. Jahrhundert*, pp. 303–6.

39. See "Aufgaben und Ziele der kathol[ischen] Literaturbewegung," *Literarische Warte* 2 (1901): 421; and Eichert, "Gralfahrt—Höhenfahrt!" p. 2.

40. See "Aufgaben und Ziele der kathol[ischen] Literaturbewegung," pp. 422–24; and Eichert, "Gralfahrt—Höhenfahrt!" p. 2.

41. F[ranz] [Eichert], "Was ist modern?" *Der Gral* 5 (January 15, 1911): 254–56; Kralik, *Tage und Werke*, p. 173; and Kralik, *Die katholische Literaturbewegung der Gegenwart*, p. 97.

42. See Muth, *Wem gehört die Zukunft?* p. 141; and Muth, *Steht die katholische Belletristik . . .*, pp. 81–82.

43. Antonio Fogazzaro (1842–1911), Italian novelist who advocated lay participation in the Church.

44. Enrica, Freiin von Handel-Mazzetti (1871–1951), Austrian novelist.

45. Kralik, "Kulturideale," p. 325. See also Franz Eichert, "Das katholische Literaturideal," *Der Gral* 4 (November 15, 1909): 98.

46. See Eichert, "Gralfahrt—Höhenfahrt"; Wilhelm Oehl, "Kraliks Kulturprogramm," *Der Gral* 6 (July 1, 1912): 588; Johannes Mumbauer, ["Die Beteiligung der deutschen Katholiken am literarischen Leben und Schaffen,"] in *Bericht über die Verhandlungen der 56. Generalversammlung der Katholiken Deutschlands . . . 1909* (Breslau: Goerlich und Coch [Inh. R. Sprick], 1909).

47. See Kralik, *Tage und Werke*, p. 155.

48. Kralik's letters to Muth are preserved in the Muth collection at the Bayerische Staatsbibliothek. See also Kralik, *Tage und Werk*, pp. 161–62.

49. Alexander Baumgartner, S.J. (1841–1910), literary historian and co-editor of *Stimmen aus Maria-Laach*, to which he contributed for more than thirty years.

50. See Leonhard Wolff, "Spielet Calderons geistliche Festspiele!" *Allgemeine Rundschau* 28 (May 23, 1931): 327; and *New Catholic Encyclopedia* (New York: McGraw-Hill, 1967), s.v. "Baumgartner, Alexander," by R. J. Sealy.

51. Henry Sienkiewicz (1846–1916), Polish novelist, best known for *Quo Vadis?*; awarded the Nobel Prize for Literature in 1905.

52. Baumgartner, "Die katholische Belletristik und die Moderne, p. 125.

53. Hermann Herz (1874–1946), secretary of the Borromäus Verein, later parish priest; wrote on belles lettres, librarianship, and adult education.

54. Johannes Mumbauer, "Die deutschen Katholiken und die Literatur," *Die Bücherwelt* 7 (November 1909): 35; Hermann Herz, "Der Katholizismus in der schönen Literatur

Deutschlands im 19. Jahrhundert und in der Gegenwart," *Die Bücherwelt* 6 (October 1908): 8–12; (November 1908): 33; and Baumgartner, *Die Stellung der Katholiken zur neueren Literatur*, p. 62.

55. Muth, *Steht die katholische Belletristik . . .* , p. 45.

56. See W. Kreiten, "Die katholische Kritik und ihr Kritiker Veremundus," *Stimmen aus Maria-Laach* 55 (November 1898): 510; and Kralik, *Ein Jahr katholischer Literaturbewegung*, pp. 126–27.

57. See Kralik, *Tage und Werke*, passim; and Baumgartner, *Die Stellung der deutschen Katholiken zur neueren Literatur*, p. 19.

58. Heinrich Falkenberg (1869–1928), priest, bibliographer, and bibliophile.

59. See Mumbauer, "Ein literarisches Ghetto für die Katholiken?" p. 460; Heinrich Falkenberg, *Wir Katholiken und die deutsche Literatur* (Bonn: Carl Georgi, 1909), pp. 51, 60; and Baumgartner, "Die katholische Belletristik und die Moderne," p. 124.

60. Selma Lagerlöf (1858–1940), Swedish novelist and poet; first woman to receive the Nobel Prize for Literature (1909) and first female member of the Swedish Academy (1919). Ricarda Huch (1864–1947), German novelist, historian, and poet. Peter Rosegger (1843–1918), Austrian Heimat novelist. Maxim Gorky (1868–1936), Russian writer and leading figure in Soviet literature. Maurice Maeterlinck (1862–1949), Belgian writer, much influenced by symbolists; received Nobel Prize for Literature in 1911. John Ruskin (1819–1900), English critic and social theorist.

61. Baumgartner, *Die Stellung der deutschen Katholiken zur neueren Literatur*, p. 41; Falkenberg, *Wir Katholiken und die deutschen Literatur*, pp. 3, 26; and Karl Muth to Mumbauer, November 23, 1904, MBS, Karl Muth Nachlaß, Ana 390 II. B.

62. Joseph, Baron von Eichendorff (1788–1857), German Romantic writer.

63. "Stand wir Katholiken rückständig?" *Der Gral* 3 (January 15, 1909): 181.

64. "Erklärung," reprinted in Kralik, *Ein Jahr katholischer Literaturbewegung*, pp. 17–19.

65. Kaspar Descurtins (1855–1916), cultural historian; cofounder of the University of Freiburg (Switzerland).

66. Expeditus Schmidt, O. F. M. (1868–1939), theater and literary historian; founder of literary journal *Über den Wassern* (1908).

67. See "Das Literaturprogramm des Papstes," *Der Gral* 5 (November 15, 1910): 72; Pius X, "Dilectis Filiis Francisco Eichert ceterisque sodalibus e Societate litteratorum 'Gralbund,'" *Der Gral* 5 (May 15, 1911): 469; and Expeditus Schmidt, "Die Stellung der Katholiken im deutschen Literaturleben: Ein Vortrag," in Expeditus Schmidt, *Anregungen: Gesammelte Studien und Vortäge* (Munich: Verlag Etzold, 1909), p. 2.

68. See Gustav Keckeis, "Besinnung," *Literarischer Handweiser* 63 (September 1927): 881; and Georg Schäfer, "Der katholische Dichter in unserer Zeit," *Bücherwelt* 25 (March/April 1928): 85.

69. Kneip, "Kirche und Dichtung," p. 439; Martin Rockenbach, "Jakob Kneip," *Die Bücherwelt* 18 (October 1921): 201–7.

70. Stephan Lochner (d. 1451), German religious painter of the school of Cologne, whose brightly colored works incorporate both Gothic elements and naturalism; known for his *Last Judgment*, the panels of which are now in Cologne, Frankfurt, and Munich.

71. Jakob Kneip, "Katholiken und Literatur—Eine Auseinandersetzung: Dichtung und Kirche," *Schönere Zukunft* 2 (August 21, 1927): 999–1000.

72. See Osinski, *Katholizismus und deutsche Literatur im 19. Jahrhundert,* p. 223.

73. Joseph Eberle (1884–1947), writer on culture and publicist; editor of *Schönere Zukunft.*

74. Joseph August Lux (1871–1947), Austrian novelist.

75. Otto Kunze (1885–1929), pseud. Otto Sachse, writer of political and cultural history; editor of *Allgemeine Rundschau* (1921).

76. Gustav Keckeis (1884–1967), novelist, essayist, and editor of *Literarischer Handweiser* 1919–1931.

77. Wilhelm Wiesebach, S.J. (1878–1929), writer.

78. See Joseph Eberle, "Katholiken und Literatur—Eine Auseinandersetzung: Literatur- und Pressefragen der Katholiken. (Antwort an Jakob Kneip)," *Schönere Zukunft* 2 (August 21, 1927): 1000–1003; Otto Sachse, "Des katholischen Dichters Not und Klage," *Allgemeine Rundschau* 24 (August 6, 1927): 488; Joseph August Lux, "Gibt es ein deutsches katholisches Literaturleben?!" *Schönere Zukunft* 2 (September 11, 1927), 1071–73; "Zu der kathol[ischen] Literaturkrisis," *Anzeiger für die katholische Geistlichkeit Deutschlands* 12 (n.d.): 5–6, Borromäus Verein, Bonn (hereafter BBV), file: *Literaturstreit* 1928; "Sollen wir weiter streiten?" *Fränkisches Volksblatt,* September [14], 1927; "Worin Jakob Kneip recht hat," *Schönere Zukunft* 2 (December 8, 1927); and Wilh[elm] Wiesebach, "Zum 'neuen Literaturstreit,'" *Wissen und Glauben* 25 (1928): 162–67.

79. See Ronald Knox, "Der katholische Roman," in *Orplid,* abridged in "Zeitschriftenschau," *Germania,* September 1, 1928, Morgenausgabe, Das neue Ufer.

80. See *Dictionary of the History of Ideas: Studies of Selected Pivotal Ideas,* ed. Philip P. Wiener (New York: Charles Scribner's Sons, 1973), s. v. "Literature and its Cognates," by René Wellek.

81. See Joseph August Lux, "Die Tragik des katholischen Dichters," *Allgemeine Rundschau* 24 (1927): 760–61; and Muth, *Steht die katholische Belletristik . . . ,* pp. 7–12.

82. Maria, Freifrau von Ebner-Eschenbach (1830–1916), Austrian writer.

83. Sigrid Undset (1882–1949), Norwegian novelist; her books were frequently set in the Middle Ages.

84. See Keiter, *Konfessionelle Brunnenvergiftung,* p. 26; Franz Herwig, *Die Zukunft des katholischen Elementes in der deutschen Literatur* (Freiburg im Breisgau: Herder, 1922), p. 13; Franz Herwig, "Rückblick und Ausblick," in Ettlinger, Funk, and Fuchs, *Die Wiederbegegnung von Kirche und Kultur in Deutschland,* pp. 374–82; and Schäfer, "Der katholische Dichter in unserer Zeit," p. 86.

85. Report on a lecture by Gustav Keckeis, editor of the *Literarische Handweiser,* in Herz, "Unser Weg," p. 364; [Philipp] Huppert, "[Katholische Literatur und Presse]," in *Verhandlungen der 43. General-Versammlung der Katholiken Deutschlands . . . 1896* (Dortmund: Gebrüder Lensing, 1896): 364.

86. See Berman, "Literary Criticism from Empire to Dictatorship, 1870–1933," passim.

87. See Muth, *Die Wiedergeburt der Dichtung,* pp. 107–13.

88. Arthur Friedrich Binz (1897–1932), critic and essayist.

89. The statistics given here on overall titles come from Wehler, *Von der "Deutschen Doppelrevolution" bis zum Beginn des Ersten Weltkrieges, 1849–1914,* p. 1233, and Reinhard Wittmann, *Geschichte des deutschen Buchhandels: Ein Überblick* (Munich: C. H. Beck, 1991), pp. 271, 301. The breakdown by category is from Wittmann, *Geschichte des deutschen Buchhandels,* pp. 271–72. For discussions of the publishing industry, see also Russell A. Berman,

"Writing for the Book Industry: The Writer under Organized Capitalism," *New German Critique* 29 (Spring/Summer 1983): 39–56, and Ilse Rarisch, *Industrialisierung und Literatur: Buchproduktion, Verlagswesen und Buchhandel in Deutschland im 19. Jahrhundert in ihren statistischen Zusammenhang*, Historische und Pädagogische Studien, ed. Otto Büsch and Gerd Heinrich, vol. 6 (Berlin: Colloquium Verlag, 1976). Statistics vary slightly.

90. Georg Schäfer (1895–?), teacher, literary critic, and essayist; wrote for *Bücherwelt* in the 1920s.

91. Georg Schäfer, "Lesertypen," *Die Bücherwelt* 21 (September 1924): 118. See also Gary D. Stark, "Publishers and Cultural Patronage in Germany, 1890–1933," *German Studies Review* 1 (1978): 56.

92. Muth, *Steht die katholische Belletristik . . .*, p.50; Lux, "Die Tragik des katholischen Dichters," p. 760. See also Leo Weismantel, "Briefe über katholischen Literatur: An den Toren der Kirche," *Das literarische Echo* 25 (December 15, 1922): 328; Heinrich Falkenberg, *Wir Katholiken und die deutsche Literatur*, p. 38; and Heinrich Falkenberg, *Mehr Literaturpflege* (Bonn: Carl Georgi, 1910), p. 31.

93. See Sachse, "Des katholischen Dichters Not und Klage," p. 488; Schenda, *Volk ohne Buch*, pp. 452–56; and Wittmann, *Geschichte des deutschen Buchhandels*, esp. chap. 10, "Der Buchhandel in der Weimarer Republik."

94. See Michael Schmolke, "Katholisches Verlags-, Bücherei- und Zeitschriftenwesen," in Rauscher, *Katholizismus, Bildung und Wissenschaft im 19. und 20. Jahrhundert*, pp. 102–7.

95. Albert Rumpf (1884–1978), general secretary of the Borromäus Verein; wrote on the topic of librarianship.

96. Albert Rumpf, "Die deutschen Katholiken und der Büchermarkt," *Glaube und Arbeit* 1 (1917): 181.

97. See "Unsere 'Literarische Frage'—eine Honorarfrage?" *Literarische Warte* 2 (1901): 242–45; and Enrica von Handel-Mazzetti to Karl Muth, January 21, [1909], MBS, Karl Muth Nachlaß, Ana 390 II.B.

98. See Karl Wick, "Um die literarische Kritik," *Augsburger Postzeitung*, July 6, 1930, summarized in *Allgemeine Rundschau* 27 (August 23, 1930): 594; Cardauns, "Das literarische Schaffen," pp. 379–83; Falkenberg, *Wir Katholiken und die deutsche Literatur*, pp. 192–200; and Muth, *Steht die katholische Belletristik . . .*, pp. 66–67.

99. Lux, "Die Tragik des katholischen Dichters," pp. 760–61.

100. See ibid., p. 760; and H. A. Berger, "Der katholische Zeitungsroman," *Düsseldorfer Tageblatt*, August 24, 1927.

101. Jassy Torrund, pseud. Josefa Mose, *Hannas Lehrjahr* (Munich: Sonnenland-Bücherei, 1920).

102. Maria Herbert (1859–1925), German popular novelist.

103. Falkenberg, *Mehr Literaturpflege*, pp. 27–28.

104. Adolf Eidens, "Der katholische Zeitungsroman," *Germania*, February 3, 1928, Abendausgabe. In contrast to France, Germany did not produce any great Catholic novels during the period 1880–1933. See also Lux, "Gibt es ein deutsches katholisches Literaturleben?!"; and Heinrich Bachmann, "Um den deutschen Roman: Zur Krisis der Gegenwartsliteratur," *Die Bücherwelt* 27 (May/June 1930): 175. See Theodore P. Fraser, *The Modern Catholic Novel in Europe*, Twayne's World Author Series 841, ed. David O'Connell (New York: Twayne Publishers, 1994).

105. See Hermann Herz, "Zur Beurteilung des Romans," *Bücherwelt* 12 (September 1915): 250.

106. Martin Rockenbach (1898–1948), literary critic and founder of the journal *Orplid*.

107. Karl Borromäus Heinrich (1884–1938), novelist; worked for Volksverein.

108. Peter Dörfler (1878–1955), German novelist.

109. See "Eine Umfrage und ihr Ergebnis: Die heutige Situation der katholischen Literatur" *Germania*, June 23, 1927, Morgenausgabe, Das neue Ufer.

110. BBV, file: Wolframbund.

111. Karl Gabriel Pfeill (1889–1942), German lyricist and art critic.

112. Josef Georg Oberkofler (1889–1962), Austrian writer.

113. Pfeill, quoted in "Eine Umfrage und ihr Ergebnis."

114. See Fraser, *The Modern Catholic Novel in Europe*, pp. 23–66; and Albert Sonnenfeld, "Don Quixote and the Romantic Reactionaries," in *Crossroads: Essays on the Catholic Novelists* (York, S.C.: French Literature Publications Company, 1982), pp. 1–24.

115. See Lux, "Gibt es ein deutsches katholisches Literaturleben?!" p. 3; Mumbauer, "Dreißig Jahre katholischer Literaturbewegung und Literaturarbeit," p. 721; and Kralik, *Tage und Werke*, p. 154.

116. See Muckermann, "Der Katholik und das gute Buch," p. 122.

117. See ibid., p. 126.

5. Books, Reading, and Catholic Libraries

1. See Zalar, "Knowledge and Nationalism in Imperial Germany," pp. 12–55; and Bundschuh, "Katholische Schriftenmission und Kolportage, eine soziale Aufgabe und ein Zeitbedürfnis," p. 111.

2. Except for colportage literature, which meant books delivered by an itinerant peddler, the categories are fairly obvious. Pornography, which prompted multitudinous legal cases and regulations, is an extreme example of how difficult it is to create unambiguous standards for a work of literature.

3. See "Satzung von 1900," in Wilhelm Spael, *Das Buch im Geisteskampf: 100 Jahre Borromäusverein* (Bonn: Verlag des Borromäus-Vereins, 1950), p. 355.

4. Alois Wurm (1874–1968), priest and religious writer.

5. Wurm, *Grundsätze der Volksbildung*, p. 104.

6. Albert Rumpf, "Predigten über gute und schlechte Bücher," *Mitteilungen für die Vereine vom hl. Karl Borromäus* 6 (July 1918): 5.

7. Joseph Froberger (1871–1931), publicist and writer; provincial of the White Fathers from 1905 to 1910.

8. Hans Schrott-Fiechtl (1868–1938), an Austrian who had studied agriculture and written on milk, as well as authored a series of *Heimat* novels set in the Tyrol; a 1916 pamphlet entitled *Der Bruder u[nd] Oesterreich,* published in the series *Flugschriften f[ür] Oesterreich-Ungarns erwachen,* testifies to some political dabbling as well.

9. See Hönig, "Das gute Buch," p. 155; and Jos[eph] Froberger, "Seelische Persönlichkeit und Lektüre," in *Vom Wesen und Wollen katholischer Büchereiarbeit: Vorträge des 14. Kursus für Leiter und Mitarbeiter von Volksbüchereien des Borromäusvereins,* ed. Johannes Braun (Bonn: Verlag des Borromäus-Vereins, 1927), pp. 51–53.

10. Herz did not acquire an administrative title until 1908, when a secretariat was formally established, although he provided such administration as there was from the time he was first appointed.

11. Walter Hofmann (1879–1952), leader in German public librarianship.

12. See Hermann Herz, "Das 'wertvolle' Buch der Volksbücherei," *Die Bücherwelt* 20 (March/April 1923): 49–54.

13. See Johannes Mumbauer, "Buch, Buchkrisis und Buchpflege," *Literarischer Handweiser,* abridged in "Im Ringen der Zeit," *Germania,* August 28, 1926, Morgenausgabe, Das neue Ufer; and Herz, "Das 'wertvolle' Buch der Volksbücherei," p. 49.

14. See Rudolf Schenda, *Die Lesestoffe der kleinen Leute: Studien zur populären Literatur im 19. und 20. Jahrhundert* (Munich: C. H. Beck, 1976), p. 123. For additional information about *Schund* literature, see chap. 9, pp. 210–13.

15. Paul Leopold Haffner (1829–1899), professor of philosophy at the Mainz seminary for priests; named bishop of Mainz in 1886.

16. See [Paul Leopold] Haffner, ["Lektüre"], in *Verhandlungen der XXXII. Generalversammlung der Katholiken Deutschlands zu Münster i. W. . . . 1885* (Münster: Commissions-Verlag der Actien-Gesellschaft "Westfälischer Merkur," 1885), p. 338; and Spael, *Das katholische Deutschland im 20. Jahrhundert,* p. 123.

17. Johannes Braun, "Die Schund- und Schmutzliteratur und ihre Bekämpfung," *Die Bücherwelt* 7 (April 1910): 124–33.

18. See Curate Hoven, "Praktische Bekämpfung der Schund- und Schmutzliteratur," *Mitteilungen für die Vereine rom hl. Karl Borromäus* 8 (February 1919): 7–12; and "Hirtenwort zum Borromäus-Sonntag," *Kirchliches Amtsblatt für die Diözese Fulda* 48 (November 2, 1932): 73.

19. *Kirchenblatt* 1 (1910), quoted in Christof Beckmann, "Katholisches Vereinswesen im Ruhrgebiet: Das Beispiel Essen-Borbeck, 1900–1933" (inaug. diss., Westfälisches Wilhelm-Universität, Münster, 1990), p. 343.

20. Eugenie Marlitt, pseud. Eugenie John (1825–1887), author of serial novels. Ottilie Wildemuth (1817–1877), author of children's tales. Johanna Spyri (1827–1901), Swiss author of children's literature, best known for the *Heidi* novels.

21. See Schenda, *Volk ohne Buch,* pp. 28, 241–70, 473–81.

22. See Fullerton, "Creating a Mass Book Market in Germany," p. 270; Günter Kosch and Manfred Nagl, *Der Kolportageroman: Bibliographie 1850–1960* (Stuttgart: Verlag J. B. Metzler, 1993), p. 40 (Kosch reviews research on the colportage trade in his introduction); and Schenda, *Volk ohne Buch,* pp. 215, 325, 489.

23. See Fullerton, "Creating a Mass Book Market in Germany," p. 270.

24. "Die Diözesankonferenz des Preßvereins," *Eichstätter Volks-Zeitung,* June 9, 1914, RBZ, OA 1773.

25. See Monika Estermann and Georg Jäger, "Voraussetzungen und Entwicklungstendenzen," in *Geschichte des Deutschen Buchhandels im 19. und 20. Jahrhundert,* vol. 1, *Das Kaiserreich 1870–1918,* ed. Georg Jäger with Dieter Langewiesche and Wolfram Siemann (Frankfurt am Main: Buchhändler-Vereinigung, 2001), pp. 21–22; Harvey J. Graff, *The Legacies of Literacy: Continuities and Contradictions in Western Culture and Society* (Bloomington, Ind.: Indiana University Press, 1987); and Rudolf Schenda, "Alphabetisierung und Literarisierungsprozesse in Westeuropa im 18. und 19. Jahrhundert," in *Sozialer und kultureller Wandel in der ländlichen Welt des 18. Jahrhunderts,*

ed. Ernst Hinrichs and Günter Wiegelmann (Wolfenbüttel: Herzog August Bibliothek, 1982), p. 6.

26. See Rarisch, *Industrialisierung und Literatur,* pp. 15–17; Schulte-Sasse, "Toward a 'Culture' for the Masses," p. 86; and Julian Bamford and Richard R. Day, "Extensive Reading: What Is It? Why Bother?" *Language Teacher Online* 21 (1997), http://languehyper.chubu.ac/jb/jalt/pub/tlt/97/may/extensive.html.

27. Helmut Walser Smith describes the evidence for this summary as "strong impressonistic" evidence. Smith, *German Nationalism and Religious Conflict,* pp. 80–85. See also Schenda, *Die Lesestoffe der kleinen Leute,* pp. 38–41. This is the most commonly expressed opinion of historians.

28. See Zalar, "Knowledge and Nationalism in Imperial Germany," pp. 41–54, 58–60. In "The Process of Confessional Inculturation," pp. 121–52, Zalar presents a detailed analysis of the reading of Catholics and comes to conclusions that indicate far greater involvement with the wider national culture than historians usually portray.

29. See Fritz Magon, "Die Freude am Buch in der Großstadt: Einige Beobachtungen und Erfahrungen," *Die Bücherwelt* 25 (March/April 1928): 119–23.

30. See Schenda, *Die Lesestoffe der kleinen Leute,* pp. 38–41; Zalar, "The Process of Confessional Inculturation," pp. 121–22; and Zalar, "Knowledge and Nationalism in Imperial Germany," pp. 280–86.

31. Although he uses the term "educated," he is making a class distinction.

32. See Schulte, *Die Kirche und die Gebildeten,* pp. 161–67.

33. Friedrich Lehne (1771–1836), German novelist. Anny Wothe (1858–1919), German novelist.

34. Ferdinande, Freiin von Brackel (1835–1905), member of the old Catholic Westphalian aristocracy, began writing as critic of Prussian governance but later turned to belles lettres; *Die Tochter des Kunstreiters,* originally published by Bachem in 1875, had reached its seventy-seventh edition in 1924, and was of sufficient popularity to be republished in 1953.

35. See K. Kleebeck, "Was Arbeiterinnen lesen," *Die Bücherwelt* 17 (March 1920): 63–64.

36. See *Consilium a vigilantia* of the Archdiocese of Munich and Freising, Schreiben Nr. 15, October 1, 1928, RBZ, OA 2092. The first survey must have been aimed at finding out what Catholic women read, or the question on the Borromäus Verein would have been irrelevant. Given that the area of the Archdiocese of Munich and Freising is predominantly Catholic, the readers who made purchases at railway newsstands would have been predominantly Catholic, but, in the absence of any knowledge of its methodology, it can hardly be labeled a survey of Catholic reading.

37. See Jose[ph] Froberger, *Weltanschauung und Literatur* (Trier: Paulinus-Druckerei, 1910), p. 52; and Zalar, "Knowledge and Nationalism in Imperial Germany," pp. 89–100 (p. 90).

38. See Schulte, *Die Kirche und die Gebildeten,* pp. 161–67; and Zalar, "Knowledge and Nationalism in Imperial Germany," pp. 28, 53–54, 280.

39. August Reichensperger (1808–1895), politician; member of the Frankfurt National Assembly from 1848 to 1949, worked for a *großdeutsch* solution to the German national problem; opponent of Prussia; member of the Reichstag, where he was a leading member of the Center Party.

40. The most detailed history of the Borromäus Verein is Spael's *Das Buch im Geisteskampf*. For an account in English, see Margaret S. Dalton, "The Borromäus Verein: Catholic Public Librarianship in Germany, 1845–1933," *Libraries and Culture* 31 (Spring 1996): 409–21.

41. The term "managing committee" is used to translate the variety of German terms that over time were applied to the group that made major policy decisions for the Borromäus Verein. Their role was comparable to that of a board of trustees in the public libraries of the United States.

42. See *Die Gründung und Thätigkeit des Vereins vom heil. Karl Borromäus: Festschrift zum fünfzig-jährigen Jubelfeste des Vereins am 30. Mai 1895* (Bonn: J. P. Bachem, 1895), pp. 23–24.

43. See *Die Gründung und Thätigkeit des Vereins vom heil. Karl Borromäus,* pp. 124–25.

44. See Ernst Gystrow, "Der Katholizismus und die neue Dichtung," *Die Gesellschaft* 1 (1899): 422; Alexander Schnütgen, "Der Verein vom hl. Karl Borromäus geschichtlich gewürdigt," *Zentralblatt für Bibliothekswesen* 41 (1924): 330; Gottfried Rohr, "Neue Wege im Borromäusverein: Von der 'literarischen Kommission' 1903–1907," *Die Bücherwelt* 17 (August/September 1920): 193; "Öffentliche Bibliotheken und Lesehallen," in *Verhandlungen der 45. General-Versammlung der Katholiken Deutschlands . . . 1898* (Krefeld: J. B. Klein [M. Buscher], 1898), p. 344; and Zalar, "Knowledge and Nationalism in Imperial Germany," pp. 12–55.

45. See Johannes Braun, "Ansprache bei Eröffnung der Bibliothekarsschule am 16. April 1921," unpublished speech, sent to author by Erich Hodick, director of the Borromäus Verein, in 1995; "Satzung von 1900," in Spael, *Das Buch im Geisteskampf,* pp. 355–56; "Satzung von 1920," in ibid., p. 358, 206; Leo Koep and Alfons Vodermayer, "Die katholischen Volksbüchereien in Deutschland," in *Handbuch des Büchereiwesens,* ed. Johannes Langfeldt (Wiesbaden: Otto Harrassowitz, 1965), vol. 2, p. 394; and Zalar, "Knowledge and Nationalism in Imperial Germany," pp. 158, 165–70, 206.

46. Constantin Nörrenberg (1862–1937), librarian.

47. These popular "libraries" were variously called *Lesehallen* (reading halls), *Bücherhallen* (book halls), and *Büchereien* (usually translated popular libraries). Occasionally, a *Lesehalle* was added on to an existing *Stadtbibliothek* (city library). What unites these new libraries, however, and differentiates them from earlier city libraries, is that they were intended to offer the laboring classes the opportunity to read books, magazines, and newspapers inexpensively. Unlike the public libraries of the United States and Britain, they were neither tax supported nor free to users. They did receive grants from local governments, but they also collected membership fees.

48. Philipp Huppert (1857–1906), writer and editor of the religion and literary sections of the *Kölnische Volkszeitung.*

49. See Koep and Vodermayer, "Die Katholischen Volksbüchereien in Deutschland," pp. 393–94; and Philipp Huppert, *Öffentliche Lesehallen: Ihre Aufgabe, Geschichte und Einrichtung* (Cologne: J. P. Bachem, 1899), p. 1.

50. "Satzung von 1900," in Spael, *Das Buch im Geisteskampf,* p. 355.

51. Augustin Esser (1863–1941), priest and doctor of theology.

52. Spael, *Das Buch im Geisteskampf,* pp. 145–46, 157.

53. Ansgar Pöllmann, O. S. B. (1871–1933), writer.

54. See Spael, Das Buch im Geisteskampf, pp. 162–63.

55. See "Zur Einführung," *Borromäus-Blätter* 1 (October 1903): 1; Spael, *Das Buch im Geisteskampf*, pp. 162–71; Hermann Herz, "Die Bücherwelt und ihr literarischer Ratgeber," pp. 198–99; Borromäus Verein, *Jahresbericht 1929*, pp. 2–3; Koep and Vodermayer, "Die katholischen Volksbüchereien in Deutschland," pp. 393–97; Schnütgen, "Der Verein vom hl. Karl Borromäus geschichtlich gewürdigt," pp. 331–32; and Zalar, "Knowledge and Nationalism in Imperial Germany," pp. 198–99.

56. See Spael, *Das Buch im Geisteskampf*, p. 175.

57. See Borromäus Verein, *Jahresbericht 1929*, pp. 2–3; Koep and Vodermayer, "Die katholischen Volksbüchereien in Deutschland," pp. 393–97; Schnütgen, "Der Verein vom hl. Karl Borromäus geschichtlich gewürdigt," pp. 331–32; *Handbuch für die Geschäftsführer in den Einzelvereinen des Borromäusvereins* (Bonn: Verlag des Borromäus-Vereins, 1921); and Zalar, "Knowledge and Nationalism in Imperial Germany," pp. 204–10.

58. Two articles on Braun give considerable detail about his life and work: Caspar Kranz, "Persönlichkeit und Werk," pp. 23–32; and Wilhelm Spael, "Lebenswerk im Borromäusverein," pp. 33–40. Friedrich Muckermann provided an evaluation of Braun's work in *Im Kampf zwischen zwei Epochen*, pp. 248–49.

59. 1895 was selected to illustrate an approximate beginning of the new adult-education orientation; 1903 as the year Herz arrived at the Borromäus Verein; 1912 because it was the year Braun took over; 1929 as the high point of Borromäus Verein activity in the pre-1933 period; and 1933 as the end of an era. The full range of statistics gives more detail but does not change the overall picture.

60. Hermann Herz, "Das freie Volksbildungswesen," in *Deutschland und der Katholizismus*, ed. Max Meinertz and Hermann Sacher (Freiburg im Breisgau: Herder, 1918), p. 346.

61. See "Die Entwicklung in Zahlen," in Spael, *Das Buch im Geisteskampf*, pp. 372–73.

62. Statistics from "Jahresbericht 1903," *Nachrichten für die Vereine vom hl. Karl Borromäus* 2 (September 1903); "Geschäftsbericht für 1913," *Nachrichten für die Vereine vom hl. Karl Borromäus* 12 (September 1914); and Borromäus Verein, *Jahresbericht 1933* (Bonn: J. F. Carthaus, 1933), pp. 18–19.

63. See episcopal ordinary to general office of the Borromäus Verein, October 12, 1922, Bischöfliches Ordinariat, Archiv, Speyer (hereafter SBOA), 122 Büchereiwesen; Korth to Professor G. Lenhart, June 26, 1912, Dom- und Diözesanarchiv, Mainz (hereafter MDD), Generalakten, Abteilung 44/2; and Andrea Asselmann, "Volksbüchereiarbeit im Spiegel der Zeitschrift 'Borromäusblätter/Die Bücherwelt' (1903–1933)," *Bibliothek: Forschung und Praxis* 19 (1995): 342–44.

64. See Latta, "Von Werk- und Feierstunden unserer Volksbildungsarbeit: Ein Jahr Bezirksarbeit im Borromäusverein," *Die Bücherwelt* 24 (January 1927): 1–14.

65. See Zalar, "Knowledge and Nationalism in Imperial Germany," pp. 211, 219.

66. See *Leitsätze der Vorträge des 16. Kursus für Leiter und Mitarbeiter von Volksbüchereien* (Bonn: Verlag des Borromäus-Vereins, [1928]).

67. In the 1920s at least nine book clubs were operating in Germany as attempts were made to enlarge the market for books. The largest, the People's Association of the Friends of Books, founded in 1919, could claim 300,000 members. The names of the clubs suggest that they, like most cultural organizations, were formed on the basis of a shared worldview. See "Book Clubs of Central Europe," *Publishers' Weekly* 109 (February 27, 1926): 665–66.

68. See Jakob Overmans, *Roman, Theater und Kino im neuen Deutschland*, Flugschriften der "Stimmen der Zeit" 14 (Freiburg im Breisgau: Herder, 1920), p. 19; Hetta Wolff,

"Nochmals: Konzentration oder Zersplitterung? Buchkrise und Buchgemeinschaften," *Germania,* October 9, 1926, Morgenausgabe, Das neue Ufer; Johannes Braun to His Eminence, June 18, 1930, WAA, I A 25b 87; *Kommt zu uns! Wir sind 400 000 zufriedene Mitglieder der Deutschen Buch-Gemeinschaft* (n.p., n.d.); and Muckermann, *Im Kampf zwischen zwei Epochen,* p. 249.

69. Zalar, "Knowledge and Nationalism in Imperial Germany," p. 212. He cites it as an example of the "silent Kulturkampf" of the period. The doctrine that no public support should go to libraries that might exacerbate confessional tensions was applied against Catholic but not Protestant libraries by Prussian officials responsible for distributing library subsidies at various governmental levels.

70. See Borromäus Verein, *Jahresbericht 1933,* pp. 18–19. In 1919 the Fulda Conference of Bishops decreed that the Sunday closest to the feast day of Saint Charles Borromeo (November 4) would be dedicated to the Borromäus Verein. The sermon would be on the subject of books and libraries and the collection of the day given to the society.

71. See Borromäus Verein, "Bericht über die Tätigkeit und den Stand des Borromäusvereins im Jahre 1930," CHAE, CR 22.5.1; and Borromäus Verein, *Jahresbericht 1933,* pp. 18–19.

72. During this period the financial situation was so unstable and figures so meaningless with the hyperinflation of the Mark that the Borromäus Verein did not publish any annual reports. A summary report was published in 1925, Johannes Braun, "Der Borromäusverein von 1922–1924," *Die Bücherwelt* 22 (January 1925): 25–34.

73. See A. Rumpf, "Denkschrift des Borromäusvereins über ein Zusammengehen des kath[olischen] Büchereiverbandes der Pfalz mit dem pfälzischen Verband f[ür] freie Volksbildung," September 23, 1926, BBV; and Margaret F. Stieg, *Public Libraries in Nazi Germany* (Tuscaloosa, Ala.: University of Alabama Press, 1992), p. 199.

74. Eduard Müller (1841–1926), lawyer; president of the Katholikentage held in 1888 and 1895.

75. See Spael, *Das Buch im Geisteskampf,* pp. 188, 194–97.

76. Albert Lauscher (1872–1944), professor of pastoral theology at the University of Bonn from 1917; chair of the Borromäus Verein from 1928 to 1933; named papal house prelate in 1931.

77. Johannes Henry (1876–1958), lawyer; city official in Bonn from 1945 to 1958.

78. Karl Joseph Schulte (1871–1941), bishop of Paderborn from 1910; archbishop of Cologne from 1921; named cardinal in 1921.

79. See F. Muckermann, *Im Kampf zwischen zwei Epochen,* p. 248. Correspondence relating to this was consulted at MGS; the Stadtarchiv, Bonn (hereafter BSA); and CHAE.

80. See Johannes Braun to Cardinal Archbishop Karl Josef Schulte, November 11, 1933; Direske, diocesan chairman, Breslau, to Cardinal Archbishop Adolf Bertram, November 10, 1933; and Sieber, diocesan chairman, Rottenburg, to Cardinal Archbishop Karl Josef Schulte, November 21, 1933, CHAE, Borromäus Verein, CR 22.5.1.

81. Wilhelm Herchenbach (1818–1889), teacher and novelist for young adults.

82. Karl May (1842–1912), writer of enormously popular fiction, often set in the American Wild West, especially for boys.

83. Ferdinande von Brackel's best-known work, *Die Tochter des Kunstreiters,* was translated into English in 1896, as were some of Wilhelm Herchenbach's tales, e.g., *The Armorer of Solingen* (1898), *Angel Hilda* (1886), *Miralda, A Story of Cuba* (1915), and *Wrongfully Accused* (191?). Flammersfeld is of such obscurity as to be unidentifiable.

84. See Mumbauer, "Dreißig Jahre katholischer Literaturbewegung und Literaturarbeit," p. 723; and Falkenberg, *Wir Katholiken und die deutsche Literatur*, p. 118.

85. See Rohr, "Neue Wege im Borromäusverein," p. 193; Zalar, "Knowledge and Nationalism in Imperial Germany," pp. 154–64; and Koep and Vodermayer, "Die katholischen Volksbüchereien in Deutschland," pp. 393–96.

86. See Josef Zimmermann, "Die Führung des Lesers zum belehrenden Schrifttum," *Die Bücherwelt* 26 (March/April 1929): 113; "Die Arbeitsweise des Borromäusvereins im Jahre 1923," BBV; Johannes Braun, "Unsre Volksbüchereiarbeit," *Die Bücherwelt* 17 (August/September 1920): 210; and Herz, "Das 'wertvolle' Buch der Volksbücherei," p. 50.

87. See Spael, *Das Buch im Geisteskampf*, p. 170; Hermann Herz, "Aus dem Vorwort zur dritten Auflage," in *Literarischer Ratgeber der Bücherwelt: Des Musterkataloges für kath[olischen] Volks- und Jugendbüchereien*, 4th ed. (Bonn: Verlag des Borromäus-Vereins, 1918); and Braun, "Unsre Volksbüchereiarbeit," pp. 207–11.

88. Anna Hilden, "Johanna Spyri und ihre Schriften," *Borromäus-Blätter* 1 (October 1903): 13. In 1913 a priest gave a speech at a deanery conference at St. Wendel criticizing the Borromäus Verein for including books by non-Catholic authors on its lists, which gave rise to a minor tempest.

89. Leopold von Ranke (1795–1886), professor of history at Berlin University from 1825 to 1871; considered to be the founder of modern historical scholarship. Friedrich Christoph Dahlmann (1785–1860), taught at various universities; one of the famous seven professors dismissed from the University of Göttingen when the king of Hannover abrogated the constitution in 1837; member of the 1848/1849 Frankfurt National Assembly; founded the *Quellenkunde der deutschen Geschichte*. Heinrich von Sybel (1817–1895), taught at various universities; politically active in support of the nationalist and Protestant cause; founder of the *Historische Zeitschrift* (1859); director of the Prussian state archives.

90. Johannes Janssen (1829–1891), German Catholic historian.

91. See Huppert, *Öffentliche Lesehallen*, pp. 64–65. The distinguished Austrian historian of the "großdeutsch" persuasion, Heinrich, Ritter von Srbik (1878–1951), was likewise absent, but probably because his best work was done later.

92. See ibid., pp. 63–85; and Zimmermann, "Die Führung des Lesers zum belehrenden Schrifttum," p. 113.

93. See *Literarischer Ratgeber der Bücherwelt*, pp. 240–55.

94. Wurm, *Grundsätze der Volksbildung*, pp. 105–6; Schäfer, "Lesertypen," p. 128.

95. See Johannes Hönig, "Vom Bücherlesen," *Die Bücherwelt* 24 (February 1927): 52–57.

96. For a detailed discussion of Walter Hofmann and his ideas, see Margaret F. Stieg, "The Richtungstreit: The Philosophy of Public Librarianship in Germany before 1933," *Journal of Library History* 21 (Spring 1986): 261–76. Both Wurm and Herz were familiar with his ideas, and echoes of Hofmann can be found in many writings of Catholic librarians. The Borromäus Verein staff was familiar with him, as well; it produced a pamphlet entitled *Walter Hofmann und wir Katholiken*, which carefully drew distinctions between his views and the practices of the Borromäus Verein. See BBV, file: Walter Hofmann und wir. See also Schäfer, "Lesertypen," p. 120; and Anton Heinen, "Bildungsrummel?" in *Pflug* 3, abridged in "Im Ringen der Zeit," *Germania*, September 25, 1926, Morgenausgabe, Das neue Ufer.

97. See Osinski, *Katholizismus und deutsche Literatur im 19. Jahrhundert*, pp. 278–79.

98. See Josef Zimmermann, "Zur Neuauflage des 'Literarischen Ratgebers des Borromäusvereins,'" *Die Bücherwelt* 23 (May 1926): 211.

99. G. Rohr, *Empfehlenswerte Bücher und Schriften für katholische Töchter* (Godesberg, 1901), p. 5. See also Herz, "Zur Beurteilung des Romans," p. 250; Josef Karlmann Brechenmacher, "Zeitfragen u[nd] Zeitaufgaben des Jugendbücherwarts," *Die Bücherwelt* 22 (November 1925): 483; Jos[eph] Aug[ust] Lux, "Die Not des katholischen Autors," in *Schönere Zukunft* 50, abridged in "Im Ringen der Zeit," *Germania,* September 25, 1926, Morgenausgabe, Das neue Ufer.

100. See Borromäus Verein, *Jahresbericht 1928* (Bonn: J. F. Carthaus, n.d.), p. 12; and Herz, "Das freie Volksbildungswesen," p. 249.

101. Schäfer, "Lesertypen," p. 117. See also Johannes Braun, "Ansprache bei Eröffnung der Bibliothekarsschule am 16. April 1921," unpublished speech, sent to author by Erich Hodick, director of the Borromäus Verein, in 1995; Spael, *Das Buch im Geisteskampf,* p. 206; and Koep and Vodermayer, "Die katholischen Volksbüchereien in Deutschland," p. 394.

102. See Hürten, *Deutsche Katholiken, 1918–1945,* p. 146; and Stieg, *Public Libraries in Nazi Germany,* p. 196.

103. See Borromäus Verein, *Jahresbericht 1933;* "Borromäus-Verein," 1822–1926, mimeographed survey, Bischöfliches Generalvikariat, Fulda (hereafter FBG), 203–1, Fasz. 1: Büchereiwesen; and Diözesanarchiv, Rottenburg (hereafter RDA), G 1.1, C 16.5d.

104. See [Johannes Braun], "Die Großstadt als Kulturraum: Das Buch," in *71. Generalversammlung der deutschen Katholiken zu Essen an der Ruhr . . . 1932,* pp. 252–27; and Borromäus Verein, *Jahresbericht 1933,* pp. 5–7.

105. See Wurm, *Grundsätze der Volksbildung,* passim; BBV, file: "Berichten der Borromäus Verein Ortsvereine," Grossenbaum, 1920; Matthias Becker, "Von Werk- und Feierstunden: Der Lesezirkel," *Die Bücherwelt* 26 (January/February 1929): 28; and Asselmann, "Volksbüchereiarbeit im Spiegel der Zeitschrift 'Borromäusblätter/Die Bücherwelt' (1903–1933)," pp. 322–61.

106. See Herz, "Das 'wertvolle' Buch der Volksbücherei," p. 50; Becker, "Von Werk- und Feierstunden," pp. 28–29; and "Report on Archbishop Felix von Hartmann's Speech at the Dedication of the New Borromäus Verein Building," *Nachrichten für die Vereine vom hl. Karl Borromäus* 11 (October 1913).

107. See Herz, "Das 'wertvolle' Buch der Volksbücherei," p. 52; *Leitsätze der Vorträge des 16. Kursus für Leiter und Mitarbeiter von Volksbüchereien;* and "Bericht über die Jahre 1920 und 1921," *Mitteilungen für die Vereine vom hl. Karl Borromäus,* 13/14 (August 1922).

108. See Becker, "Von Werk- und Feierstunden," pp. 28–29; and Georg Hauptfleisch, *Praktische Enrichtung von kathol[ischen] Lesezirkeln* (Bonn: Generalsekretariat des Borromäusvereins, 1930).

109. "Leseregeln," *Borromäus-Blätter* 1 (January 1904): 52.

110. See Zalar, "Knowledge and Nationalism in Imperial Germany," chap. 5, passim.

111. Pius XII (1876–1958), born Eugenio Pacelli; papal diplomat; served as nuncio first in Bavaria, then Berlin; elevated to the papacy in 1939.

112. See "Förderung des Borromäus-Vereins," *Kirchlicher Anzeiger für die Erzdiözese Köln* 59 (November 1, 1919): 155; and "Päpstliche Empfehlung des Borromäusvereins," *Kirchlicher Anzeiger für die Erzdiözese Köln* 71 (February 15, 1931): 50. See also letters from the committee of the Borromäus Verein to Cardinal Archbishop Karl Josef Schulte (July 29, 1930), Cardinal Eugenio Pacelli to Cardinal Archbishop Karl Josef Schulte,

December 24, 1930, and Cardinal Archbishop Karl Josef Schulte to Albert Lauscher, president of the Borromäus Verein, January 5, 1931, held at CHAE, Borromäus Verein, CR 22.5.1.

113. See Johannes Braun to Albert Lenhart, April 23, 1912, MDD, Generalakten, Abteilung 44, Borromäus Verein; and Sieber to episcopal ordinary ["Report on First Rottenburg Borromäus Verein Diocesan Conference"], January 28, 1931, RDA, G1.1 C 16.5d.

114. See Borromäus Verein, *Jahresbericht 1933*, pp. 18–19.

115. See Schäfer, "Lesertypen"; and Jos[eph] Gerads, "Von Werk- und Feierstunden unserer Volksbildungsarbeit: Volksbücherei St. Jakob in Aachen," *Die Bücherwelt* 24 (January 1927): 16.

116. See Borromäus Verein, *Jahresbericht 1932* (Bonn: J. F. Carthaus, n.d.).

117. When the Borromäus Verein had earlier tried to expand into the Bavarian dioceses, it had been rebuffed on the grounds that it would compete with an organization sponsored by the king of Bavaria. See F. Auer to the bishop of Munich and Freising, received November 8, 1895, RBZ, OA 622.

118. Katholischer Preßverein für Bayern, announcement, March 30, 1905, RBZ, OA 1773.

119. Statistics taken from Katholischer Preßverein für Bayern, *Jahres-Bericht pro 1908/09* (Landshut: Jos. Thomann'sche Buch- und Kunstdruckerei, 1909); Katholischer Preßverein für Bayern, *Jahres-Bericht pro 1913* (Munich: G. J. Manz, 1914); Katholischer Preßverein für Bayern, *Jahresbericht 1927*; Katholischer Preßverein für Bayern, *Jahresbericht 1931*, (n.p., n.d.); "Jahresbericht des Vereins vom heiligen Karl Borromäus für das Jahr 1908," *Kirchlicher Anzeiger für die Erzdiözese Köln* 49 (November 15, 1909): 131; and "Jahresbericht des Vereins vom heil. Karl Borromäus für das Jahr 1912," "Der Borromäusverein im Jahre 1925," and "Bericht über die Tätigkeit und den Stand des Borromäusvereins im Jahre 1930," CHAE, Borromäus Verein, CR 22.5.1.

120. See Katholischer Preßverein für Bayern, *Jahres-Bericht pro 1908/09*, RBA, OA 1773.

121. Georg Triller (1855–1926), dean of the cathedral of Eichstätt; wrote on theology and asceticism.

122. Cardinal Mariano Rampolla del Tindaro (1843–1913), Vatican secretary of state; close to Pope Leo XIII.

123. See Cardinal Mariano Rampolla to the committee of the Katholischer Preßvereins für Bayern (Alois Frank), March 21, 1902, RBZ, OA 1773; and "Papst Pius X. und der Preßverein," in Katholischer Preßverein, *Jahres-Bericht pro 1911* (Munich: G. J. Manz, 1912): 3.

124. See Katholischer Preßverein für Bayern, *Jahresbericht 1927*; and Katholischer Preßverein für Bayern, *Jahres-Bericht pro 1908/09*.

125. See Herz to episcopal ordinary, October 2, 1908, Albert Rumpf to the bishop, October 30, 1915, Sieber to Reverend Father, February 22, 1928, RDA, G1.1. C 16.5d.

126. Blank questionnaire, MDD, Generalakten, Abteilung 44, Borromäus Verein.

127. See handwritten survey, RDA, G1.1 C 16.5d; and Übersicht über den Stand der kathol[ischen] Büchereiwesen in der Diözese Speyer—September 1921," SBD, Archiv 122, Büchereiwesen.

128. In addition to the assortment of library organizations, there were also groups founded to distribute books, such as the St. Josephs-Bücherbruderschaft. See Spael, *Das Buch im Geisteskampf*, pp. 18–79.

129. See Bernhard Marschall to Cardinal Archbishop Karl Josef Schulte, April 7, 1924; Henseler, "Das Aschenbrodel unter den kath[olischen] Vereinen," pp. 12, CHAE, Borromäus Verein, CR 22.5.1; and Katholischer Preßverein für Bayern, *Jahresbericht 1927*.

130. See Der Borromäus-Verein der Erzdiözese Köln, *Bericht über das Jahr 1919*, CHAE, Borromäus Verein, CR 22.5.1.

131. See Father Weyer to episcopal ordinary, November 11, 1928, FBA, 203–01, Fasz. 1: Büchereiwesen: "Borromäus-Verein," 1822–1926.

132. See Stieg, "The Richtungstreit," pp. 261–76.

133. See Katholischer Preßverein für Bayern, *Jahresbericht 1927*.

6. CATHOLIC ART AND ITS ORGANIZATIONS

1. H. H. Arnason, *History of Modern Art: Painting, Sculpture, Architecture, Photography*, 3rd ed., rev. Daniel Wheeler (New York: Harry N. Abrams, 1986), p. 13.

2. See Nipperdey, *Germany from Napoleon to Bismarck, 1800–1866*, pp. 479–84; and Bollenbeck, *Tradition, Avantgarde, Reaktion*, pp. 39–40, 71.

3. Albert Kuhn, O.S.B. (1839–1929), art historian and professor at the University of Einsiedeln, Switzerland.

4. Albert Kuhn, *Moderne Kunst- und Stilfragen* (Einsiedeln: Benziger, 1909), p. 7. Dating might well depend on what interested the commentator. Kuhn was concerned primarily with questions of style. Another Catholic commentator, whose principal concern was godlessness in art, argued that modern art began in the 1840s. See Mathias Höhler, "Der kirchliche Geist in der kirchlichen Kunst," *Theologisch-praktische Quartalschrift* 44 (1892): 777. A modern critic, looking at the diversity of styles that replaced the single dominant style that had previously been characteristic of Western art, sees its origins "[r]ight from the beginning of the nineteenth century." See Hanns Theodor Flemming, "Painting," in *Late Nineteenth Century Art*, ed. Hans Jürgen Hansen (Newton Abbot, England: David and Charles, 1973), p. 113.

5. Lucas Cranach the Elder (1472–1553), German court painter and engraver; friend of Martin Luther; later referred to as the painter of the Reformation.

6. See Hans Belting, *The Germans and Their Art: A Troublesome Relationship*, trans. Scott Kleager (New Haven, Conn.: Yale University Press, 1998), pp. 1, 7, 31; W. A. Guttsman, *Art for Workers: Ideology and the Visual Arts in Germany* (Manchester: Manchester University Press, 1997); and Jost Hermand, *Avantgarde und Regression: 200 Jahre deutsche Kunst* (Leipzig: Edition Leipzig, 1995).

7. Belting, *The Germans and Their Art*, p. 61 and passim. See also Corona Hepp, *Avantgarde: Moderne Kunst, Kulturkritik und Reformbewegungen nach der Jahrhundertwende* (Munich: DTV, 1987); and Paul Clement, "Contemporary German Art," in *Exhibition of Contemporary German Art*, ed. Metropolitan Museum of Art (New York: Metropolitan Museum of Art, 1909), pp. 5–33.

8. See Steinhausen, *Deutsche Geistes- und Kulturgeschichte von 1870 bis zur Gegenwart*, p. 238; and Johannes Mumbauer, "Katholische Kirche und moderne Kunst," *Der Scheinwerfer* 3 (1930): 10–12.

9. F. X. H., "Bildende Kunst und schöne Literatur," *Historisch-politische Blätter für das katholische Deutschland* 156 (1915): 539.

10. Rost, *Die Kulturkraft des Katholizismus*, p. 72.

11. A journal with this title began publication in 1885, but it was a slogan that was widely and generally used in connection with efforts to educate the taste of the lower classes.

12. See Steinhausen, *Deutsche Geistes- und Kulturgeschichte,* pp. 256–58; Gustav Renner, "Kunst: Über die Freiheit der Kunst," *Hochland* 24 (1926/1927): 547; Emil Ritter, "Über das Verhältnis zwischen Volk und Kunst," *Volkskunst* 2 (February 1914): 184–85; "Um katholische Kultur und Künstlerschaft: Ein Aufruf der Notgemeinschaft katholischer Künstler Deutschlands," received December 9, 1932, RBZ, OA 3344; and Jens Christian Jensen, "Bemerkungen zu Friedrich Overbeck," in *Johann Friedrich Overbeck, 1789–1869,* ed. Andreas Blühm and Gerhard Gerkens (Lübeck: Museum für Kunst und Kulturgeschichte, 1989), p. 13.

13. See Guttsman, *Art for Workers,* p. 5.

14. See Muth, *Die literarischen Aufgaben . . . ,* p. 57; Emil Mauerhof, "Kunst und Religion," *Allgemeine Rundschau* 3 (March 24, 1906): 164; Herman Schell, "Christus und die Kultur," in *Herman Schell: Kleinere Schriften,* ed. Karl Hennemann (Paderborn: Ferdinand Schöningh, 1908), p. 393; "Prof. Thode über Kunst und Sittlichkeit," *Allgemeine Rundschau* 4 (1907): 90; August Rumpf, ["Die deutschen Katholiken und die Pflege der Kunst"], in *Bericht über die Verhandlungen der 56. Generalversammlung der Katholiken Deutschlands . . . 1909* (Breslau: Goerlich und Coch [Inh. R. Sprick], 1909), pp. 343–44; and also Rumpf's view, as interpreted by Oscar Doering, in Doering, "Die deutschen Katholiken und die Pflege der Kunst," *Allgemeine Rundschau* 6 (1909): 776; Christoph, Graf zu Stolberg-Stolberg, "Kunst und Kultur," *Allgemeine Rundschau* 10 (June 28, 1913): 485; Konrad Weiss, "Katholische Kulturwille und die neue Kunst: Offener Brief an P. Desiderius Lenz," *Hochland* 12 (May 1914): 193; J. Schiller, "Kunst und Religion," *Allgemeine Rundschau* 17 (1920): 70; Conrad Gröber, *Kirche und Künstler* (Freiburg im Breisgau: Herder, 1932), p. 12; Mausbach, *Die Kirche und die moderne Kultur,* p. 155; and Gröber, *Kirche und Künstler,* p. 93.

15. See Mauerhof, "Kunst und Religion," p. 164; Oscar Doering, "Von modernster Kunst," *Allgemeine Rundschau* 13 (1916): 548; Benedikt Momme Nissen, "Entwicklung und Entartung christlicher Kunst," *Historisch-politische Blätter für das katholische Deutschland* 171 (1923): 35–40, 68; Romanus Jacobs, "Gedanken über moderne und religiöse Kunst," *Christliche Kunst* 20 (1924): 162; Mauerhof, "Kunst und Religion," p. 164; and H., "Bildende Kunst und schöne Literatur," pp. 543–44.

16. See F. X. H., "Bildende Kunst und schöne Literatur," p. 544; Ildefons Herwegen, "Von dem Wesensgehalt der kirchlichen Kunst," in Herwegen, *Lumen Christi: Gesammelte Aufsätze,* Verband der Vereine katholischer Akademiker zur Pflege der katholischen Weltanschauung, vol. 7 (Munich: Theatiner Verlag, 1924), p. 69; "Das Wesen der kirchlichen Kunst," *Ecclesiastica* 12 (December 3, 1932): 473; Kreitmaier, "Die Krisis der christlichen Kunst," pp. 377–93; Jacques Maritain, "Christliche Kunst," abridged from *Art et Scholastique,* trans. Günther Müller, in "Zeitschriftenschau," *Germania,* November 3, 1928, Morgenausgabe, Das neue Ufer; Konrad Weiss, "Die christliche Kunst der Gegenwart," *Hochland* 6 (September 1909): 676; Nissen, "Entwickelung und Entartung christlicher Kunst," p. 70; and Gustav Langen, "Christliche Kunst," *Der Kunstwart* 23 (May 1910): 160.

17. Conrad Gröber (1873–1948), bishop of Meissen from 1931; archbishop of Freiburg from 1932.

18. See Gröber, *Kirche und Künstler,* p. 91; and Mumbauer, "Katholische Kirche und moderne Kunst," p. 11.

19. Gröber, *Kirche und Künstler,* pp. 4, 45. See also Gerhard Gietmann, *Allgemeine Ästhetik* (Freiburg im Breisgau: Herder, 1899), p. 56; Herwegen, "Von dem Wesensgehalt der kirchlichen Kunst," p. 69; Josef Kreitmaier, "Theologische Grundbegriffe der kirchlichen Kunst," in *Ehrengabe deutscher Wissenschaft dargeboten von katholischen Gelehrten,* ed. Franz Fessler (Freiburg im Breisgau: Herder, 1920), pp. 263–71; Ehrhard, *Der Katholizismus und das zwanzigste Jahrhundert,* p. 422; Walter, *Bildungspflicht und Katholizismus nach den Grundsätzen der christlichen Ethik,* p. 101; Unger, "Brauchen wir illustrierte Zeitungsbeilangen?" *Allgemeine Rundschau* 22 (1925): 635; and P. Hoche, "Hausfrau und Kunst," *Volkskunst* 7 (March/April 1919): 356. Gröber compared the substitution of art for religion to offering the serpent in place of bread.

20. Pius XI (1857–1939), born Ambrogio Damiano Achille Ratti; pope from 1922 to 1939.

21. Gröber, *Kirche und Künstler,* p. 4; "Das Wesen der kirchlichen Kunst," p. 469; Peter Rosegger, quoted in [Fritz] Witte, "Neue Zeiten, neue Ziele," *Zeitschrift für christliche Kunst* 32 (1920): 11, 13. See also Martin Mayr, "Der Kampf um die neue Kunst," *Allgemeine Rundschau* 17 (1920): 399; Richard Müller-Freienfels, "Die psychologische Wirkung der Kunst auf das religiöse Gefühlsleben," *Zeitschrift für Religionspsychologie* 4 (1911): 375; Carl Töwe, "Geschmack und Ungeschmack in der katholischen Kunst," *Theologie und Glaube* (1916?): 308; and Rost, *Die Kulturkraft des Katholizismus,* p. 72.

22. Remigius Boving, O.F.M. (1876–1929), wrote on Gothic architecture, aesthetics, and cultural history.

23. See Müller-Freienfels, "Die psychologische Wirkung der Kunst auf das religiöse Gefühlsleben," pp. 369–75; Remigius Boving, in *Rede auf der Tagung für christliche Kunst 1921,* p. 62, quoted in Gröber, *Kirche und Künstler,* p. 105; "Die Kunst als Gehilfin der Predigt," *Christliches Kunstblatt für Kirche, Schule und Haus* 32 (1890): 177–86; and Schiller "Kunst und Religion," p. 70.

24. Hans Kauders, "Das Religiöse in der Kunst der Gegenwart," *Das Kunstblatt* 29 (1910): 181. See also Nipperdey, *Germany from Napoleon to Bismarck, 1800–1866,* p. 478; Bollenbeck, *Tradition, Avantgarde, Reaktion,* pp. 39–40; and Osinski, *Katholizismus und deutsche Literatur im 19. Jahrhundert,* p. 295.

25. Josef Kreitmaier, "Konfessionelle Kunst," *Stimmen der Zeit* 104 (1922): 61. See also Josef Kreitmaier, "Die Krisis der christlichen Kunst," in *Von Kunst und Künstlern: Gedanken zu alten und neuen künstlerischen Fragen* (Freiburg im Breisgau: Herder, 1926), p. 118; Kreitmaier, "Theologische Grundbegriffe der kirchlichen Kunst," p. 284; and Hoche, "Hausfrau und Kunst," pp. 355–56.

26. Thorn Prikker (1868–1932), Dutch painter who lived in Germany; popular for his stained-glass creations.

27. Konrad Weiss (1880–1940), art expert for the *Münchener Neueste Nachrichten.*

28. See J. Schaefer, "Unsere Ortsgruppen im Kampf gegen Schund und Schmutz im Rahmen des neuen Gesetzes," CHAE, Gen. 23.30.1; and Weiss, "Die christliche Kunst der Gegenwart," p. 669.

29. One has to question, however, the validity of attempting to revive a past style. A style belongs to its own time and when imitated in a later period can be no more than an artificial construct. Herman Beenken acutely observed that the Nazarenes, through reason, wanted to come to the point where the old artists had stood. Herman Beenken, *Das neunzehnte Jahrhundert in der deutschen Kunst* (Munich: Verlag F. Bruckmann, 1944),

p. 89. The Beuron School was founded in the 1860s by Desiderius Lenz, O. S. B., to revive religious art and sculpture.

30. Georg Lill (1883–1951), art historian and principal conservator at the Bavarian National Museum; editor of *Christliche Kunst* (1925).

31. See Kreitmaier, "Konfessionelle Kunst," p. 61; Weiss, "Die christliche Kunst der Gegenwart," pp. 678–80; Josef Kreitmaier, "Stirbt die Kunst?" *Stimmen der Zeit* 116 (1928): 120; and Georg Lill, "Die kirchliche Kunst der Gegenwart und das katholische Volk: Rede gehalten am 6. September 1927 auf der 66. Katholikenversammlung zu Dortmund," *Die christliche Kunst* 24 (December 1927): 76.

32. See Georg Lill, "Christliche Hauskunst," *Die christliche Kunst* 26 (1929): 33–43; E. K. Fischer, "Die neue Kunst und die Kirche," *Kunstwart und Kulturwart* 35 (August 1921): 287; and Josef Kreitmaier, "Zur Kulturaufgabe der christlichen Kunst," *Die christliche Kunst* 23 (June 1927): 284.

33. Josef Kreitmaier, "Expressionistische Kirchenkunst?" *Stimmen der Zeit* 116 (1928): 39; Mausbach, *Die Kirche und die moderne Kultur*, p. 160. See also Belting, *The Germans and Their Art*, p. 62.

34. Ehrhard, *Der Katholizismus und das zwanzigste Jahrhundert*, pp. 420–21. See also Josef Kreitmaier, "Von der Freiheit der Kunst," *Stimmen der Zeit* 102 (1921): 131.

35. The *Kölnische Volkszeitung*'s use of a picture of the Christ child, naked in a manger, as the title picture of its Christmas issue, provoked complaints from a reader that it was advocating immorality. The *Kölnische Volkszeitung* responded by inviting a number of distinguished cultural leaders like Friedrich Muckermann and Arnold Rademacher to comment. One of the resulting essays, M. Laros, "Von christlicher Kunstbetrachtung," was reprinted in *Die christliche Kunst* 23 (May 1927): 251–55. Laros was particularly thorough in his response and included a list of basic writings by Catholics on the topic of nudity. In fact, the nudity of the Christ child had theological implications, as well as being nudity per se. The *Kölnische Volkszeitung* discussion included the assertion that the depiction of the naked infant Jesus was not only an example of artistic freedom, but also a symbol of how the love of the Son of Man has descended even into the helplessness of being naked. See also Georg Lill, "Nacktdarstellung und christliche Kunst," *Die christliche Kunst* 23 (May 1927): 251.

36. Gerhard Gietmann (1845–1912), philologist and art historian.

37. See "Prof. Thode über Kunst und Sittlichkeit," pp. 90–91; G[erhard] Gietmann, "Das Nackte in der Kunst," *Allgemeine Rundschau* 2 (1905): 595–98; and Zimmern, "Zum Nackten in der Kunst," *Allgemeine Rundschau* 2 (1905): 637. Albert Kuhn in *Frankfurter Zeitung*, July 5, 1921, quoted in Kreitmaier, "Von der Freiheit der Kunst," p. 135.

38. Mumbauer, "Katholische Kirche und moderne Kunst," p. 11.

39. Deutsche Gesellschaft für christliche Kunst, [1893] broadsheet, PAB, OA Vereine III 44; Mayr, "Der Kampf um die neue Kunst," p. 399; Nissen, "Entwickelung und Entartung christlicher Kunst," p. 68; Kuhn, *Moderne Kunst und Stilfragen*, p. 10; Herwegen, "Von dem Wesensgehalt der kirchlichen Kunst," p. 80; Fischer, "Die neue Kunst und die Kirche," p. 192; "Bericht über die Ausschuß-Sitzungen der 'Tagung für christliche Kunst' in Paderborn am 8. September 1932," MDD, K XXIII 2: Vereine für christliche Kunst; and Josef Kreitmaier, "Moderne Malerei von gestern und heute," in *Von Kunst und Künstlern*, p. 45.

40. Josef Kreitmaier, "Die kranke deutsche Kunst," *Allgemeine Rundschau* 9 (January 6, 1912): 13–15.

41. *Schlager* is now translated as "hit"; here it means that which startles.

42. See Kreitmaier, "Die kranke deutsche Kunst," p. 14; "Wider den Geist des 'Simplicissimus,'" *Allgemeine Rundschau* 6 (1909): 472; Katholischer Preßverein, *Jahres-Bericht pro
1913*, p. 5, RBZ, OA 1473; and Falkenberg, *Wir Katholiken und die deutsche Literatur*, p. 168.

43. See Bollenbeck, *Tradition, Avantgarde, Reaktion*, pp. 11, 43–43. 165; Jeffrey
Herf, *Reactionary Modernism: Technology, Culture and Politics in Weimar and the Third
Reich* (Cambridge: Cambridge University Press, 1984); and Kreitmaier, "Konfessionelle
Kunst," p. 61.

44. See Kreitmaier, "Die Krisis der christlichen Kunst," p. 383; Kreitmaier, "Stirbt
die Kunst?" pp. 116–27; Carl Christian Bry, "Der Kitsch," *Hochland* 22 (1924/1925): 399–411;
"Bericht über die Generalversammlung in Köln zur Bildung eines christlichen Kunstvereins für Deutschland [1857]," PAB, OA Vereine III 42; Tagung für christliche Kunst, "Sitzungsbericht," Paderborn, 1932, RBZ, OA 3349; and Deutsche Gesellschaft für christliche
Kunst, [1893] broadsheets, PAB, OA Vereine III 43; *Merkblatt für den Clerus und geistliche
Institutionen über die Zusammenarbeit mit Künstler* (Freiburg im Breisgau: Freievereini-
gung für Seelsorgehilfe [1934?], RBZ, OA 3344. Mommsen, "Stadt und Kultur im deutschen
Kaiserreich," pp. 34–35, discusses the growing awareness of the economic role of art and
other areas of culture in the late nineteenth century.

45. In a discussion of art as a political weapon, Willi Guttsmann has contrasted the
artistically radical socialist art with the conservative taste of the worker. Peter Paret, though
critical of William II's tastes in art, has acknowledged that one factor that made them so
significant was that so many Germans agreed with him. Willi Guttsman, "Art as a Weapon:
Social Critique and Political Orientation in Painting and Print in Weimar Germany," in
Arthur Marwick, ed., *The Arts, Literature, and Society* (London: Routledge, 1990), p. 213;
Peter Paret, "Art and the National Image: The Conflict over Germany's Participation in
the St. Louis Exposition," *Central European History* 11 (June 1978): 183.

46. See A. M. Schwindt, "Katholische Kunst: Ein offenes Wort an alle, die es angeht,"
Allgemeine Rundschau 16 (1919): 120; Schäfer, "Die katholische Dichter in unserer Zeit,"
p. 82; "Oberhirtliche Empfehlung des christlichen Kunstvereins, des Vereines zur Verbreitung religiöser Bilder, sowie der Zeitschrift für christliche Kunst," *Kirchliche Anzeiger für die
Erzdiözese Köln* 44 (January 15, 1904): 6; and Langen, "Die christliche Kunst," p. 291.

47. Oscar Doering (1858–?), writer and conservator of monuments for the state of
Saxony.

48. See Doering, "Von mondernster Kunst," p. 548; Albert Kuhn, *Die Kirche: Ihr Bau,
ihre Ausstattung, ihre Restauration* (Einsiedeln: Benziger, 1917), p. 36; Stolberg-Stolberg,
"Kunst und Kultur," pp. 485–86; Mausbach, *Die Kirche und die moderne Kultur*, pp. 155–56;
Gröber, *Kirche und Künstler*, pp. 86, 88; "Päpstliche Anweisungen in Sachen kirchlicher
Kunst, Rom—1925," translated from the pontifical document "Norme e Suggerimenti
pratici per le Commissioni Diocesane, Interdiocesane o Regionali per l'Arte Sacra"; and
Schulte, *Die Kirche und die Gebildeten*, p. 163.

49. See Mumbauer, "Katholische Kirche und moderne Kunst," p. 11; Reinhold Lindemann, "Zur Gegenwartslage der christlichen Kunst," *Bücherwelt* 25 (July/August 1928):
241; and Karl Muth, quoted in Robert Grosche, "Über die Möglichkeiten einer Renaissance der christlichen Kunst," in Ettlinger, Funk, and Fuchs, *Wiederbegegnung von Kirche
und Kultur in Deutschland*, p. 254.

50. Important German school of architecture and design and center of avantgarde art in the 1920s and early 1930s, located first in Weimar, then Dessau. Its first director was the architect Walter Gropius. Other individuals associated with it were Hannes

Meyer, the architect Ludwig Mies van der Rohe, the artists Paul Klee, Wassily Kandinsky, and Josef Albers, and the architect and furniture designer Marcel Breuer.

51. See, for example, Oscar Gehrig, "Die Berliner Corinth-Ausstellung," *Germania*, February 24, 1926, Morgenausgabe.

52. Michael Faulhaber (1869–1952), bishop of Speyer from 1911 to 1917; named cardinal archbishop of Munich and Freising in 1921.

53. See August Rumpf, ["Die deutschen Katholiken und die Pflege der Kunst"], pp. 346–49; Georg Lill, "Die religiöse Kunst der Gegenwart und das katholische Volk," in *66. Generalversammlung der Katholiken Deutschlands zu Dortmund . . . 1927* (Dortmund: Gebrüder Lensing, 1927), pp. 141–43; Michael Faulhaber, "Kirche und kirchliche Kunst," *Die christliche Kunst* 26 (February 1930): 130; Tagung für christliche Kunst, "Sitzungsbericht," Paderborn, 1932, RBZ, OA 3349; and Pius XI, reported in *Osservatore romano*, quoted in *Die christliche Kunst* 29 (November 1932): 53–54.

54. Ferdinand Hodler (1853–1918), Swiss painter and engraver.

55. Käthe Schmidt Kollwitz (1867–1945), German graphic artist and sculptor, known for her illustrations of Hauptmann's *Die Weber* and Zola's *Germinal;* a socialist and pacifist who portrayed the misery of the poor.

56. See Josef Kreitmaier, "Vorwort," in *Von Kunst und Künstlern*, pp. v–vi; Kauders, "Die Religiöse in der Kunst der Gegenwart," pp. 180–89; Josef Kreitmaier, "Von Piloty zu Picasso," *Stimmen der Zeit* 101 (1921): 323–32; Fischer, "Die neue Kunst und die Kirche," p. 192; Witte, "Neue Zeiten, neue Ziele," p. 617; and Kreitmaier, "Stirbt die Kunst?" p. 119.

57. Johannes van Acken (1879–1937), priest; director of the Central Agency in Berlin from 1923; director of the Deutsches Caritasinstitut (German Organization for Charity) from 1931.

58. See Osinski, *Katholizismus und deutsche Literatur im 19. Jahrhundert*, p. 192; Meinrad Bechtiger, "Wir Priester und die kirchliche Kunst von heute," *Theologisch-praktische Quartalschrift* 85 (1932): 106–20; Gietmann, *Allgemeine Ästhetik*, p. 120; Doering, "Moderne Kunst," p. 548; Kreitmaier, *Von Kunst und Künstlern*, p. 38; I. van Acken, *Christozentrische Kirchenkunst: Ein Entwurf zum liturgischen Gesamtkunstwerk* (Gladbeck i. W.: A Theben, 1923), pp. 28–30; and Kreitmaier, "Expressionistische Kirchenkunst?" pp. 116–27.

59. Max Schwarz, "Kirchliche Kunst und Kleriker," *Die christliche Kunst* 28 (1931–1932): 56. See also Nikolaus Irsch, "Aus der modernen Kirchenbaukunst in der Dioezese Trier," *Pastor Bonus* 40 (October 1929): 494; Langen, "Christliche Kunst," p. 159; Hans Eitel, *Altes Eichstätter Grabmäler* (Würzburg: Verlag des Verfassers, [1926]); and Lill, "Christliche Hauskunst," p. 40.

60. See Peter Rosegger, "Das Verhältnis des Volkes zur bildenden Kunst," *Das christliche Kunstblatt für Kirche, Schule und Haus* 60 (1918): 259; Kreitmaier, "Stirbt die Kunst?" p. 118; Walter, *Bildungspflicht und Katholizismus nach den Grundsätzen der christlichen Ethik*, p. 101; and Georg Lill, "Im Streite der Zeit: Rechts oder links in der Kunst? Eine Antikritik," *Die christliche Kunst* 22 (April 1926): 209.

61. Schwarz, "Kirchliche Kunst und Kleriker," pp. 54–57.

62. Renner, "Kunst," pp. 547–49; Walter Koch, "Der Begriff Modern in der Kunst," *Wissen und Glauben* 17 (1932): 649; Gröber, *Kirche und Künstler*, pp. 86–90; Karl Gabriel Pfeill, "Neue religiöse Kunst am Rhein," *Die christliche Kunst* 28 (1931/1932): 225–37.

63. See Rumpf, ["Die deutsche Katholiken und die Pflege der Kunst"], p. 349; Kreitmaier, "Konfessionelle Kunst," p. 64; Kreitmaier, "Expressionistische Kirchenkunst?" p. 45;

Clemens Holzmeister, "Das Katholische in der modernen Kunst," *Das neue Reich* 9 (1926): 261; and Kauders, "Das Religiöse in der Kunst der Gegenwart," p. 181.

64. Sebastian Staudhamer (1857–1945), priest, painter, sculptor, writer on art, Catholic theologian, and papal advisor.

65. "Die Kunst der Kritik," *Germania*, October 20, 1928, Morgenausgabe, quoted in Lill, "Die religiöse Kunst der Gegenwart und das katholische Volk," p. 149.

66. See Dr. Marstaller to the bishop, October 9, 1918, RBZ, OA 3360; Alois Fuchs, lecture, Tagung für Christliche Kunst, 1931, FBG, 850 00, Christliche Kunst, 1857–1937; Bechtiger, "Wir Priester und die kirchliche Kunst," p. 118; H. J., "Tagung für christliche Kunst," *Germania*, October 8, 1926, Abendausgabe; and Höhler, "Der kirchliche Geist in der kirchlichen Kunst," p. 778.

67. Kreitmaier, *Von Kunst und Künstlern*, p. 120. See also Gröber, *Kirche und Künstler*, pp. 81, 12; and Schwindt, "Katholische Kunst," p. 120. Robin Lenman is the established authority on the German art market during the Wilhelmine period. See his *Artists and Society in Germany, 1850–1914* (Manchester: Manchester University Press, 1997), and "From 'Brown Sauce' to 'Plein Air': Taste and the Art Market in Germany, 1889–1910," in Forster-Hahn, *Imagining Modern German Culture: 1889–1910*, pp. 53–69.

68. Johannes Baptista Sproll (1870–1949), bishop of Rottenburg from 1927; noted for his strong opposition to National Socialism.

69. Kreitmaier, *Von Kunst und Künstlern*, p. 117. See also Johannes Baptista to Richard Busching, October 16, 1934, RDA, G 1.1 C16.3b; Tagung für christliche Kunst, "Anträge," Paderborn, September 8, 1932, MDD, Generalakten, K XXIII 3; Kreitmaier, "Von Piloty zu Picasso," p. 331; Robin Lenman, "Painters, Patronage and the Art Market in Germany, 1850–1914," *Past and Present* 123 (May 1989): 109–40; and Robert Svoboda to Ludwig Maria Hugo, December 28, 1932, MDD, Generalakten, K XXIII 3.

70. See supplement to "Organ für christliche Kunst," no. 6, 1852, CHAE, CR 22.10.1; Christlicher Kunstverein, "Einladung zur II. General-Versammlung des christlichen Kunstvereins für Deutschland," August 1, 1857, MDD, Generalakten, K XXIII 1; and Gesellschaft für christliche Kunst, "Bericht über die Ausschuß der 'Tagung für christliche Kunst,'" Würzburg, 1931, SBOA, 804.

71. See supplement to "Organ für christliche Kunst," no. 6, 1852, CHAE, CR 22.10.1; [Deutsche] Gesellschaft für christliche Kunst, "Datum des Poststempels," RBZ, OA 3344; Franz Matt, Deutsche Gesellschaft für christliche Kunst, offprint from nos. 28 and 29, *Allgemeine Rundschau,* July 15 and 22, 1911, RBZ, OA 3344; Jakob Strieder, "Die Deutsche Gesellschaft für Christliche Kunst," *Academia* 40 (1927): 33; Tagung für christliche Kunst, August 1920, RBZ, OA 3349; and Allgemeine Vereinigung für christliche Kunst, [leaflet], January 1909, FBG, 850 00, Christliche Kunst, 1857–1937.

72. "Satzungen des Rottenburger Diözesan-Vereins für christliche Kunst . . . August 1907," RDA, G 1.1 C16.3a; and "Satzungen für die Diözesangruppe," printed, n.d., SBOA, 804, DGCK.

73. Georg Busch (1862–1943), sculptor and academic.

74. See [Deutsche] Gesellschaft für christliche Kunst, "Datum des Poststempels," RBZ, OA 3344; and Franz Matt, Die Deutsche Gesellschaft für christliche Kunst," *Allgemeine Rundschau* (July 1911) special issue.

75. See Gesellschaft für christliche Kunst, "Bericht über die Ausschuß-Sitzungen der 'Tagung für christliche Kunst,'" Würzburg, September, 1–2, 1931, SBOA, 804.

76. Ernst Lennartz (1872–1932), lawyer from Cologne; wrote on law and current events; active in morality organizations.

77. See Kreitmaier, *Von Kunst und Künstlern*, p. 116; Ernst Lennartz to Archbishop Felix von Hartmann, May 11, 1914, CHAE, 22.10.1; Tagung für christliche Kunst, "Sitzungsbericht," Cologne, 1930, RBZ, OA 3349; and Joseph Wimmer to managing committee of the Deutsche Gesellschaft für christliche Kunst, January 25, 1926, PAB, OA Vereine 44.

78. See Georg Lill, "Grenzen und Möglichkeiten: Ein Nachwort zur Essener Ausstellung," *Die christliche Kunst* 29 (October 1932): 23–26; "Beschlüsse der Vertretertagung des 71. Katholikentages zu Essen über 'Gro[ß]stadt und religiöse Kunst,'" *Die christliche Kunst* 29 (1932): 28; and "Das Wesen der kirchliche Kunst," pp. 471–72.

79. In 1926 the editors of *Die christliche Kunst* asked their readers what they thought about the direction of Christian art and what the editorial policies of *Die christliche Kunst* ought to be. The responses came from individuals of all classes, ages, and geographic regions, and "rejection, agreement, and reserve were in balance." In his summary, the author asked readers to remember that the board took its artistic as well as its religious side seriously. He seems to have been trying to convince the readers that a balanced approach, one that "built a bridge" between old and young, was necessary. Lill, "Im Streite der Zeit," pp. 207–10.

80. Albert Pfeffer (1873–?), priest in Lautlingen, Württemberg; wrote on religious art.

81. See Tagung für christliche Kunst, August 1920, RBZ, OA 3349; "Vorträge gehalten auf der Tagungen für christliche Kunst, 1920–1933," RBZ, OA 3349; and Aufstellung der Reisekosten für kirchliche Denkmalpflege und Bauberatung durch den Vorstand des Diözesankunstvereins," Albert Pfeffer, February 2, 1929, RDA, G 1.1, C16.3a.

82. See Kreitmaier, "Konfessionelle Kunst," p. 63; Bechtiger, "Wir Priester und die kirchliche Kunst der heute," p. 115; Fritz Witte, "Wir und die christliche Kunst," *Christliche Kunst* 1 (October 1926): 1; and [Deutsche] Gesellschaft für christliche Kunst, "Datum des Poststempels," RBZ, OA 3344.

83. See Josef Kreitmaier, "Fünfundzwanzig Jahre Deutsche Gesellschaft für christliche Kunst," *Stimmen der Zeit* 95 (May 1918): 206–8; Robert Svoboda to Ludwig Maria Hugo, bishop of Mainz, December 28, 1932, MDD, Generalakten, K XXIII 3; "Rundbrief der Notgemeinschaft kath[olischen] Künstler Deutschlands," received January 21, 1933, CHAE, CR 22.10.3; Tagung für christliche Kunst, "Sitzungsbericht," Würzburg, 1931, RBZ, OA 3349.

84. See Albert Pfeffer to the Diocese of Rottenburg, November 4, 1928, and to Bishop Johannes Baptista Sproll, November 3, 1929; and "Religiöse Einkehr für bildende Künstler," printed announcementt, RDA G 1.1 C16.3a.

85. Alexander Schnütgen (1843–1918), priest and theologian; canon at Cologne from 1887; collector of medieval art and sculpture; founder of the *Zeitschrift für christliche Kunst*.

86. See *Schnütgens Schätze: Ein Sammler und sein Museum*, Kölner Museums-Bulletin, special issue 1 (1993); and various annual reports, CHAE, CR 22.10.1.

87. See Kreitmaier, "Fünfundzwanzig Jahre Deutsche Gesellschaft für christliche Kunst"; and "Deutsche Gesellschaft für christliche Kunst," *Volkskunst* 14 (1926): 108.

88. See Tagung für Christliche Kunst, programs, MDD, Generalakten, K XXIII 3; Tagung für Christliche Kunst, Tagesordnung . . . Sitzung des Ausschusses, 1926, CHAE,

CR. 22.10.1; and Tagung für christliche Kunst, "Vorträge gehalten auf der Tagungen für christliche Kunst, 1920–1933," includes motions and resolutions, RBZ, OA 3349.

89. See Professor J. Rohr, chairman of the diocesan Kunstverein to Bishop Paul Willhelm von Keppler, October 15, 1921; and Bishop Paul to Professor Busch, October 25, 1921.

90. Robert Witte (1881–?), architect.

91. See "Deutsche Gesellschaft für christliche Kunst," p. 108; and "Vereinsangelegenheiten," *Jahresbericht . . . des christlichen Kunstvereins der Erzdiözese Köln für das Jahr 1909*, CHAE, 22.10.

92. See Gröber, *Kirche und Künstler*, p. 41; and Kreitmaier, "Theologische Grundbegriffe der kirchlichen Kunst," p. 267.

93. Antonius Fischer (1840–1912), archbishop of Cologne from 1902; named cardinal in 1903; strong supporter of the work of Catholic associations.

94. See Georg Lill, "Das Problem der christlichen Kunst," *Die christliche Kunst* 21 (1925): 78; Mumbauer, "Katholische Kirche und moderne Kunst," p. 11; A[lbert] Pfeffer, "Bischof Dr. Sproll-Rottenburg über moderne kirchliche Baukunst," *Die christliche Kunst* 23 (1927): 348; and A[lbert] Pfeffer, "Bischof Dr. Sproll über die religiöse Malerei," *Die christliche Kunst* 24 (1928): 343.

95. See "Erlaß der Fuldaer Bischofskonferenz über den sakralen Charakter kirchlicher Kunstwerke," *Die christliche Kunst* 29 (January 1933): 104–5; Tagung für christliche Kunst, "Sitzungsbericht," Paderborn, 1932, RBZ, OA 3349; "Das Wesen der kirchlichen Kunst," pp. 469–71; "Merkblatt für den Clerus und geistliche Institutionen über die Zusammenarbeit mit Künstlern," Handwritten supplement to *Kirchliches Amtsblatt* 10 (1933), FBG, 850 00; and Faulhaber, "Kirche und kirchliche Kunst," pp. 129–35.

96. See Georg Lill, "Das Problem der christlichen Kunst," *Die christliche Kunst* 21 (1925): 78; and Mumbauer, "Katholische Kirche und moderne Kunst," p. 11.

97. See Kreitmaier, "Die kranke deutsche Kunst," pp. 13–15; Josef Kreitmaier, "Der Barometerstand der Kunst," *Stimmen der Zeit* 111 (1926): 453–66; Josef Kreitmaier, "Zum Problem der religiösen Kunst," *Schweizerische Rundschau* 27 (1926): 238; Josef Kreitmaier, "Religiöse Kunst der Gegenwart," *Stimmen der Zeit* 124 (1932): 134–36; Verein für christliche Kunst im Erzbistum Köln, "Einladung zur General-Versammlung . . . 21. Mai 1928," CHAE, CR 22.10.1; supplement to "Organ für christliche Kunst," vol. 3, signed Dr. Baudri, dated the feast of the Holy Apostle Matthew 1853, CHAE, CR 22.10.1; Weiss, "Die christliche Kunst der Gegenwart," p. 668; "Moderne christliche Kunst," *Nürnberg-Fürther Rundschau*, July 19, 1930, n.p., RBZ, OA 3365; and Grosche, "Über die Möglichkeiten einer Renaissance der christlichen Kunst," p. 243.

7. MUSIC, CHURCH MUSIC, AND THE CÄCILIEN VEREIN

1. James Huneker (1860–1921), American musician; music critic for various New York newspapers, including the *New York Times;* author of books on music.

2. James Huneker, *Iconoclasts: A Book of Dramatists* (New York: Greenwood, 1969), p. 142.

3. See H. R. Haweis, *Music and Morals* (New York: Harper and Brothers, 1902), p. 20; Eckhard John, *Musikbolschewismus: Die Politisierung der Musik in Deutschland, 1918–1933* (Stuttgart: Verlag J. B. Metzler, 1994), pp. 20–21; Pamela Potter, *Most German of the Arts: Musicology and Society from the Weimar Republic to the End of Hitler's Reich* (New Haven, Conn.:

Yale University Press, 1998), p. ix; Erik Levi, "Music in Modern German Culture," in Kolinsky and van der Will, *The Cambridge Companion to Modern German Culture,* pp. 233–36; Nipperdey, *Arbeitswelt und Bürgergeist,* pp. 743, 746; and Josef Kreitmaier, "Kirchenmusikalische Fragen der Gegenwart," in *Dominanten* (Freiburg im Breisgau, 1924), pp. 222–23 .

    4. See Carl Dahlhaus, *Nineteenth-Century Music,* trans. J. Bradford Robinson, California Studies in Nineteenth-Century Music, ed. Joseph Kerman, 5 (Berkeley and Los Angeles: University of California Press, 1989), pp. 2, 335; and Marion Bauer, *Twentieth Century Music: How It Developed, How to Listen to It,* new ed. (New York: G. P. Putnam's Sons, 1947), p. 97.

    5. See Dahlhaus, *Nineteenth-Century Music,* p. 36; and "Großstadt und Musik," *Musik im Leben* 1 (June 1925): 81–82.

    6. Walter Berten (1902–1956), German composer and educator; wrote on music.

    7. Adolf Menzel (1815–1905), German painter and illustrator.

    8. Dahlhaus, *Nineteenth-Century Music,* p. 42. See also Anton Möhler, *Ästhetik der katholischen Kirchenmusik* (Ravensburg: Verlag von Friedrich Alber, 1910), p. 2; Walter Berten, "Ziele und Möglichkeiten der Volksmusikpflege," *Musik im Leben* 4 (September/ October 1928): 134–36; and E. Jos. Müller, "Die Frauen und die Musik," *Musik im Leben* 1 (April 1925): 50.

    9. Norbert Stenta, "Der Gesang als Faktor der aktiven Teilnahme des Volkes an der Liturgie," *Bibel und Liturgie* (1928): 6.

    10. See *The New Oxford Companion to Music,* ed. Denis Arnold (Oxford: Oxford University Press, 1983), s.v. "Aesthetics of Music," by Bojan Bujic, p. 22.

    11. See Franz Witt, "Die Kirchenmusik bei der 18. Generalversammlung der katholischen Vereine Deutschlands in Innsbruck," *Fliegende Blätter für katholische Kirchen-Musik* 2 (1867): 67; Möhler, *Ästhetik der katholischen Kirchenmusik,* p. 2; Herbert Schulz, "Psychologie des musikalischen Erlebens," *Musik im Leben* 2 (December 1926): 180; "Vor vierzig Jahren," *Musica Sacra* 41 (1908): 3, quoting Franz Witt; Ludgerus Schulte, "Kirche und Musik," *Pastor Bonus* 20 (1908): 353; Karl Bornhausen, "Musik und Religion," *Schlesisches Jahrbuch für deutsche Kulturarbeit im gesamtschlesischen Raum* 1 (1928): 12; E. Jos. Müller, "Zur Musikpflege in den katholischen Vereinen," *Volkskunst* 12 (July/September 1924): 53, 57; Fidelis Böser, "Christozentrische Kirchenmusik," *Benediktinische Monatschrift zur Pflege religiösen und geistigen Lebens* 6 (1924): 6; Joseph Lechthaler, "Unsere Zeit und die Religiöse Musik," *Musik im Leben* 5 (May 1929): 32; Karl Blessinger, "Die Musik als Kulturfaktor," *Musik im Leben* 5 (1930): 175; Heinrich Lemacher, "'Neue Sachlichkeit' in der katholischen Kirchenmusik," *Allgemeine Musikzeitung* 54 (1927): 813; Josef Lechthaler, "Ist die katholische Kirchenmusik inferior?" *Musica Sacra* 57 (1927): 9; Stenta, "Der Gesang als Faktor der aktiven Teilnahme des Volkes an der Liturgie," p. 6; and *Webster's Ninth New Collegiate Dictionary* (Springfield, Mass.: Merriam-Webster, 1985), s.v. "Music."

    12. Kreitmaier, *Dominanten,* p. 184; Juschka, "Grundsätzliches über Kirchengesang: Richtlinien für Chorsänger," *Gregoriusblatt für katholische Kirchenmusik* 45 (1920): 75, quoting an unnamed Jesuit. See also Karl Norbisrath, "Volksbildung und Volkshebung durch Musik und Gesangespflege," *Wissen und Glauben* 22 (1925): 242; Dominikus Johner, "Kirchenmusik und Seelsorge," *Benediktinische Monatschrift zur Pflege religiösen und geistigen Lebens* 11 (1929): 174; and Gerh[ard] Gietmann, "Steht die Kunst in der Kirche unter ästhetische Gesetzen?" *Musica Sacra* 32 (1899): 87.

    13. Alfred Baresel (1893–?), musicologist; author of *Das Jazz-Buch* (1925).

    14. Franz Werfel (1890–1945), Austrian playwright and novelist.

15. A term current in musicological discussions of the late nineteenth and early twentieth centuries, sometimes used for absolute music. It meant music that was not intended to evoke specific associations, was without extramusical connotations, and was free from programmatic designs and psychological implications. It implied music for its own sake.

16. *Die Musik in Geschichte und Gegenwart,* ed. Friedrich Blume (Kassel: Bärenreiter-Verlag, 1949–1986), s.v. "Absolute Musik," by Wilhelm Seidel.

17. "Musik im Leben. Eine Zeitschrift der Volkserneuerung: Einstellung," *Musik im Leben* 1 (January 1925): 1–7. See also *The New Grove Dictionary of Music and Musicians,* s.v. "Gebrauchsmusik," by Stephen Hinton; E. Jos. Müller, "Musik und Erotik," *Musik im Leben* 2 (February 1926): 17; Schulz, "Psychologie des musikalischen Erlebens," p. 180; E. Jos. Müller, "Religion und Musik," *Musik im Leben* 1 (1925): 107; Alfred Baresel, "Zur Lage der deutschen Unterhaltungsmusik," *Musik im Leben* 4 (April 1928): 53; J[ohannes] Hatzfeld, "Erneuerung des ländlichen Musiklebens," *Musik im Leben* 1 (March 1925): 34–39; F. Molitor, "Dorfmusik," *Musik im Leben* 1 (March 1925): 39–43; and Potter, *Most German of the Arts,* p. xi.

18. See Blessinger, "Die Musik als Kulturfaktor," p. 178; E. Jos. Müller, "Die Arbeiter und die Musik," *Musik im Leben* 4 (September/October 1928): 130; "Musik im Leben," p. 7; and E. Jos. Müller, "Musikpflege als soziale Pflicht," *Musik im Leben* 1 (1925): 162.

19. See Karl Schaezler, "Das Problem der modernen Kirchenmusik," *Hochland* 30 (1933): 543.

20. Anton Möhler (1866–?), Catholic theologian; musical scholar.

21. Georg Wilhelm Friedrich Hegel (1770–1831), German philosopher. Arthur Schopenhauer (1788–1860), German philosopher. Wilhelm Wundt (1832–1920), German physiologist and psychologist.

22. See Möhler, *Ästhetik der katholischen Kirchenmusik,* pp. 3, 54, 58.

23. "Vorträge für die Cäcilienvereinversammlung der deutschen Gemeinden der Diözese Kattowitz . . . 1931," *Monatshefte für katholische Kirchenmusik* 13 (March/April 1931): 73. The speaker did not mean it as a compliment; Americans were responsible for making beer without alcohol. He also complained that the "subversive bolshevist" activity had not been complete with the elimination of thirds.

24. See Fr. Caecilianus, "Musica non sacra," *Musica Sacra* 24 (1889/90): 86–87; and W. Fischer, "Musik, Charakter, Religion," *Der Chorbote* 2 (October 15, 1913): 77.

25. Fischer, "Musik, Charakter, Religion," p. 79; Willi Schmid, "Kirchenmusikalische Fragen der Gegenwart," *Katholisches Kirchenmusik-Jahrbuch* 1 (1928): 133; and Eugen Schmitz, "Zur Frage der modernen Kirchenmusik," *Hochland* (April 1913): 94.

26. See Willi Schmid, "Neue Musik," *Stimmen der Zeit* 118 (1929): 89–96; Blessinger, "Die Musik als Kulturfaktor," p. 178; Müller, "Zur Musikpflege in den katholischen Vereinen," p. 54; Möhler, *Ästhetik der katholischen Kirchenmusik,* p. 10; "Großstadt und Musik," pp. 81–82; and Th. B. Rehmann, "Grundsätzliches in der Stellungnahme des Cäcilienvereins zu dem Stilwandel in der Kirchenmusik," *Musica Sacra* 62 (November 1931): 393.

27. Berten, "Ziele und Möglichkeiten der Volksmusikpflege," p. 134. See also Möhler, *Ästhetik der katholischen Kirchenmusik,* pp. 58–59; and Karl Blessinger, "Musik und Intellekt," *Musik im Leben* 4 (January 1928): 5–8.

28. Anton Bruckner (1824–96), Austrian composer.

29. Max Reger (1873–1916), German composer; best known for his organ music.

30. See Josef Kreitmaier, "Musikpessimisten," *Stimmen der Zeit* 107 (1924): 373; Möhler, *Ästhetik der katholischen Kirchenmusik,* p. 5; and Schmid, "Neue Musik," p. 90.

31. See John, *Musikbolschewismus,* pp. 46–47; "Vorträge für die Cäcilienvereinversammlung der deutschen Gemeinden der Diözese Kattowitz . . . 1931," pp. 66–74; and Schmid, "Kirchenmusikalische Fragen der Gegenwart," p. 130.

32. See Alfred Brasch, "Das Volkskonzert," *Musik im Leben* 4 (September/October 1928): 139; and Irmgard Keldany-Mohr, *"Unterhaltungsmusik" als soziokulturelles Phänomen des 19. Jahrhunderts: Untersuchung über den Einfluß der musikalischen Öffentlichkeit auf die Herausbildung eines neuen Musiktypes* (Regensburg: Gustav Bosse, 1977).

33. See Karl Storck, "Gegen die musikalische Schundliteratur," *Der Türmer* (1911): 418; and Josef Kreitmaier, "Für oder gegen Kirchenkonzerte?" *Stimmen der Zeit* 103 (1922): 233.

34. See Müller, "Musik und Erotik," pp. 17–18.

35. Paul Marsop (1856–1925), wrote on music.

36. Paul Marsop, *Zur "Sozialisierung" der Musik und der Musiker* (Regensburg: Gustav Bosse, 1919), p. 27; and Schaezler, "Das Problem der modernen Kirchenmusik," p. 542.

37. See Joh[ann] Ettl, "Das deutsche Volkslied," *Volkskunst* 13 (1925): 514; Müller-Molitor, "Musikalische Volkserziehung" *Volkskunst* 7 (August 1918): 50; and J. Weisweiler, "Gedanken über musikalische Volkserziehung," *Volkskunst* 2 (August 1914): 397–402.

38. Johannes Hatzfeld, quoted in [Bernhard] M[arschall], "ZBA-Herbsttagung," *Volkstum und Volksbildung* 5 (1933): 26.

39. Jakob Wassermann (1873–1934), German Jewish novelist; internationally translated.

40. See Storck, "Gegen die musikalische Schundliteratur," pp. 411–23; Weisweiler, "Gedanken über musikalische Volkserziehung," p. 398; P[aul] Humpert, "Das Lied im Verein," *Volkskunst* 4 (April/May 1916): 179; "Von der Hebung des Volksmusiklebens einer Großstadt," *Musik im Leben* 1 (June 1925): 82–85; Müller, "Musikpflege als soziale Pflicht," p. 162; Marsop, *Zur "Sozialisierung" der Musik und der Musiker,* pp. 29–31; Müller, "Die Arbeiter und die Musik," p. 131; Blessinger, "Die Musik als Kulturfaktor," p. 172; and Johann Schletter, "Echte und falsche Volksmusik," *Musik im Leben* 1 (February 1925): 23.

41. See "Großstadt und Musik," pp. 81–82; Johannes Hatzfeld, "Ist das Volkslied eine bürgerliche Angelegenheit?" *Musik im Leben* 4 (September/October 1928): 132; Johannes Hatzfeld, "Erneuerung des ländlichen Musiklebens," pp. 34–37; and Molitor, "Dorfmusik," pp. 39–43.

42. Rudolf von Laban (1879–1958), influential European modern dancer.

43. Rudolf Bode (1881–1970), German acoustician and theorist of rhythmic gymnastics. Emile Jaques-Dalcroze (1865–1950), Swiss composer and music educator; created eurythmics. Isadora Duncan (1878–1927), American interpretive dancer and choreographer.

44. Friedrich Muckermann, "Tanz und Gemeinschaft—Der Laientanz in kultureller und pädagogischer Bedeutung," *Der Gral* 24 (August 1930): 961–67.

45. Paul Westerholt (1898–?), political economist.

46. See Paul Westerholt, "Moderne Tanzbewegung und Katholizismus," *Gelbe Hefte* 7 (March 1931): 327–53; Paul Westerholt, "Referat . . . über die Verhandlung in Gruppe IX des Vertretertages bei der Katholikenversammlung in Münster," and Paul Westerholt, "Antwort auf die Denkschrift der Zentralstelle der Katholischen Schulorganisation vom 12. Juni 1931 und die Nachschrift vom 27. Juni 1931," CHAE, 22.30.2.

47. See Georg Straßenberger, "Jazz," *Stimmen der Zeit* 125 (1933): 50–55; Kieffer, "Die heutigen Tanzbelustigungen vor dem Forum der Moral," *Pastor Bonus* 24 (1912): 460–61; E. Jos. Müller, quoted in "Diskussion der Zeit zu Tanz und Jazz," *Musik im Leben* 2 (October 1926): 148; and Beda Prilipp, "Vom Tanz in unsrer Zeit," *Hochland* 28 (May 1931): 166.

48. E. Jos. Müller, "Einiges über die Tanzmusik unserer Zeit," *Musik im Leben* 2 (October 1926): 146. See also Prilipp, "Vom Tanz in unsrer Zeit," p. 167–68; Adolf Lohrer, "Etwas vom Volkstanze," *Volkskunst* 15 (1927): 253.

49. Robert F. Hayburn, *Papal Legislation on Sacred Music, 95 A.D. to 1977 A.D.* (Collegeville, Minn.: Liturgical Press, 1979), pp. 223–24. See also Böser, "Christozentrische Kirchenmusik," p. 3.

50. Michael Buchberger (1874–1961), Catholic theologian; bishop of Regensburg from 1927 to 1950; named titular bishop in 1950.

51. See Johannes Hatzfeld, "Von katholischer Kirchenmusik," *Die Musik* 8 (1908): 217; *Programm für die fünfte General-versammlung des allgemeinen deutschen Cäcilien-Vereines vom 1. bis 7. August 1874 zu Regensburg* (Regensburg: Verlag Friedrich Pustet, n.d.), p. 3, RBZ, OA 2990; G. E. Stehle, "Ueber die Nothwendigkeit der Popularisierung der cäcilianischen Idee," *Fliegende Blätter für katholische kirchen-Musik* 10 (February 15, 1875): 10–11; Richard Zentgraf, "25. Generalversammlung des allgemeinen deutschen Cäcilien-vereins in Regensburg," clipping from *Fränkische Zeitung*, July 12, [1932?], FBG, 215–04.

52. Benedict XIV (1675–1758), born Prospero Lambertini; pope from 1740 to 1758.

53. Edward Dickinson, *Music in the History of the Western Church* (1902; New York: Haskell House, 1969), p. 153; Karl Gustav Fellerer, "Das Konzil von Trient und die Kirchenmusik," in *Geschichte der katholischen Kirchenmusik,* ed. Karl Gustav Fellerer, vol. 2 (Kassel: Barenreiter), p. 7; and Karl Gustav Fellerer, "Die Enzyklika 'Annus qui' des Papstes Benedikt XIV," in Fellerer, *Geschichte der katholischen Kirchenmusik,* vol. 2, pp. 149–50. See Hayburn, *Papal Legislation on Sacred Music,* for lists of relevant statements.

54. Dickinson, *Music in the History of the Western Church,* pp. 190–222. Dickinson analyzes the changes in church music in both social and musical terms. *New Catholic Encyclopedia,* s.v. "Music, Sacred, History of, 5. The Baroque Period," by A. Milner (the quotation about church concerts comes from J. Jungmann whom Milner quotes); Carl Dahlhaus, "Der Streit um die Wahre Kirchenmusik," in *Musik—zur Sprache gebracht: Musikästhetische Texte aus drei Jahrhunderten,* ed. Carl Dahlhaus and Michael Zimmerman (Munich: DTV, 1984), p. 201.

55. Hayburn, *Papal Legislation on Sacred Music,* pp. 222–23.

56. See ibid., pp. 226, 228.

57. Giovanni Pierluigi da Palestrina (ca. 1525–1594), Italian composer.

58. Hayburn, *Papal Legislation on Sacred Music,* pp. 221–25.

59. See Georg Feder, "Decline and Restoration," trans. Reinhard G. Pauly, in *Protestant Church Music: A History,* ed. Friedrich Blume (New York: W. W. Norton, 1974), pp. 319–404.

60. "99 Jahre 'Musica Sacra,'" *Musica Sacra* 100 (1980): 4, quotation from Franz Witt (1868); Hatzfeld, "Von katholischer Kirchenmusik," p. 214; Schulte, "Kirche und Musik," p. 342; Hayburn, *Papal Legislation on Sacred Music,* p. 228; and Wilhelm Kurthen, "Das Problem des religiösen Ausdrucks in der Musik," *Gregoriusblatt für Katholische Kirchenmusik* 45 (1920): 65.

61. Franz Xaver Witt (1834–1888), priest; composer of litanies, motets, and masses; a leader in the reform of church music.

62. The information about Witt comes from August Scharnagl, "Dr. Franz Xaver Witt und die Erneuerung der katholischen Kirchenmusik im 19. Jahrhundert," *Musica Sacra* 104 (September/October 1984): 362–68.

63. Valentin Riedel (1802–1857), bishop of Regensburg from 1841.

64. Joseph Schrems (1815–1872), music scholar and conductor.

65. Ignatius Senestrey (1818–1906), Catholic theologian; bishop of Regensburg from 1858.

66. Karl Proske (1794–1861), choirmaster of Regensburg Cathedral from 1830; active in the reform of church music.

67. Scharnagl, "Dr. Franz Xaver Witt und die Erneuerung der katholischen Kirchenmusik im 19. Jahrhundert," p. 362.

68. See Witt, "Die Kirchenmusik bei der 18. Generalversammlung der katholischen Vereine Deutschlands in Innsbruck," pp. 65–70; P. Utto Kornmüller to the bishop, May 3, 1886, RBZ, OA 2990.

69. See Franz Witt, "Statuten-Entwurf eines Cäcilien-Vereins für katholische Kirchen-Musik in Deutschland (nebst Oesterreich und der Schweiz)," *Fliegende Blätter für katholische Kirchen-Musik* 2 (1867): 81.

70. See "Statuten des 'St. Cäcilien-Vereines für alle Länder deutscher Zunge,'" [1871?], RBZ, OA 2990.

71. See "Die Pflege und Ausbildung des Choralgesanges," Franz Witt to the archbishop, CHAE, CR 20.8.1; and Franz Xaver Haberl, general president of the Allgemeiner Cäcilien-Verband, untitled memorandum, April 15, 1901, RBZ, OA 2990.

72. See Pfarr-Cäcilien Vereine, memorandum from Franz Xaver Witt, [1871?], RBA, OA 2990.

73. See "Statuten des 'St. Cäcilien-Vereines für alle Länder deutscher Zunge,'" [1871?], RBZ, OA 2990; "Normalsatzungen der Pfarrcäcilienverein der Diözese Mainz," undated, MDD, Generalakten, C XII; *Kirchlicher Anzeiger für die Erzdiözese Köln* 54 (November 1, 1914): 152–53, and 69 (January 15, 1929): 6–8; and Joseph Hemann to archiepiscopal vicariate, May 10, 1897, note, CHAE, CR 20.8.1.

74. See C. Köhler to archiepiscopal vicariate, December 8, 1914; Max Sigl, "Organisationsfragen: Musik, Lehrerschaft und Trennungsgedanke," *Musica Sacra* 53 (January 1920): 46; J. Niedhammer, diocesan president, to the bishop, November 5, 1895, SBOA, 815; P. Utto Kornmüller to the bishop, May 3, 1886, RBZ, OA 2990; and "Jahresbericht über den Cäcilienverein der Diözese Regensburg pro 1891," RBZ, OA 2990.

75. See "Bericht über den Stand des Cäcilienvereins der Diözese Rottenburg in den Jahren 1897 und 1898," and "Bericht über den Stand des Cäcilienvereins der Diözese Rottenburg in den Jahren 1892 und 1893, RDA, G 1.1 C16.4; Reither to episcopal ordinary, December 28, 1868, SBOA, 815 C; and Johner, "Kirchenmusik und Seelsorge," p. 190.

76. See Schulte, "Kirche und Musik," p. 340; and "Jahresbericht über den Cäcilienverein der Diözese Regensburg pro 1894," RBZ, OA 2990.

77. See letters from St. Maria Empfängnis, Essen, to Vicar General Vogt, October 11, 1920, CHAE, CR 20.8.1; series of reports, "Fragen über die Tätigkeit der Pfarr-Cäcilienvereine," 1930, SBOA, 815; Schmid, "Kirchenmusikalische Fragen der Gegenwart," p. 135; and Johner, "Kirchenmusik und Seelsorge," p. 186.

78. See Juschka, "Grundsätzliches über Kirchengesang: Richtlinien für Chorsänger," p. 75; Hayburn, *Papal Legislation on Sacred Music*, p. 228; parish priest of Mittelbexbach, June 21, 1931, and parish priest of Jägersburg to Cäcilien Verein of Mittelbexbach, June 29, 1931, SBOA, 815.

79. E. Berger, "Über Kirchenchor-Disziplin," *Czcilienvereins-organ/Musica Sacra* 59 (1929): 286, Witt quoted on p. 282; see also untitled promise to attend practices regularly, November 11, 1907, MDD, Pfarrakten: Fürfeld 524 letter from H. Meiser, conductor

at St. Rochus, Düsseldorf, to Cardinal Archbishop Felix von Hartmann, February 21, 1919, CHAE, CR 20.8.1.

80. See Nipperdey, *Deutsche Geschichte, 1866–1918*, pp. 47–48; Feder, "Decline and Restoration," pp. 322, 383; "Bestrebungen zur Hebung der Kirchenmusik in der katholischen Kirche," *Siona* 27 (1902): 130; F. X. Witt, *Reden an den Cäcilien-Verein*, ed. Christoph Lickleder, Documenta Caeciliana, vol. 1 (Regensburg: Allgemeiner Cäcilien-Verband and Fechtinger & Gleichauf, 1983), p. 18; and Isidor Mayrhofer, "Die katholische Kirchenmusik auf dem Irrwege?" *Kirchenmusikalisches Jahrbuch* 22 (1909): 130.

81. See C. Cohen, "Aufgaben des Klerus bezüglich der Kirchenmusik," *Musica Sacra* 33 (1900): 2; Stockhausen, "Kirchenmusikalische Heranbildung des Klerus," *Cäcilienvereinsorgan* 62 (1931): 117–23; Johner, "Kirchenmusik und Seelsorge," pp. 174–92; and Erhard Drinkwelder, "Der geistliche Kirchenvorstand und die Kirchenmusik," *Cäcilienvereinsorgan* 62 (April 1931), also appeared in *Musica Sacra* 61 (April 1931): 111.

82. See "Cäcilien-Verein Bericht über den Diöcesan-Verein Rottenburg 1885," RDA, G 1.1 C16.4; and "Report on the Condition of Church Music in Tirschenreuth Deanery," Michael Daubenmerkl, Großkornreuth, January 13, 1891, RBZ, OA 2990. This report gives credence to the complaints about poor preparation. A table itemizing by parish shows that of the 27 teacher/choir director grades for each of four different areas, 21, or 19 percent, ranked low. See also Max Sigl, "Der Cäcilienverein als Organisation," *Korrespondenz- und Offertenblatt für die gesamte katholische Geistlichkeit Deutschlands* (1926): 135; and Curate Max Pröbstle, Ranfels, to episcopal ordinary, November 25, 1915, PAB, OA Vereine, III, 23 Cäcilien Verein.

83. See Michael Märtl, president of the Cäcilien Verein of Eichendorf to episcopal ordinary, April 7, 1885; parish priest of Marienheide to the canon, July 22, 1920, CHAE, CR 20.8.1; and Franz Witt to the bishop, October 14, 1871, RBZ, OA 2990.

84. See "Cäcilien-Verein Bericht über den Diöcesan-Verein Rottenburg pro: 1877/78," RDA, G 1.1 C16.4.

85. See "Erster Jahresbericht über den Stand des Diözesan-Cäcilien-Vereins Passau," December 15, 1902, PAB, OA Vereine, III, 23 Cäcilien Verein.

86. Joseph Auer, "Die 16. Generalversammlung des Allgemeinen Cäcilienvereines," *Kirchenmusikalisches Jahrbuch* 16 (1901): 119–28.

87. See Müller, "Musikalische Volkserziehung," p. 50; and Hayburn, *Papal Legislation on Sacred Music*, p. 228.

88. Breitling, parish priest of Homburg, to the bishop, June 22, 1909, SBOA, 815.

89. See "Statuten des 'St. Cäcilien-Vereines für alle Länder deutscher Zunge,'" [1871?], RBZ, OA 2990; and "Die Zersplitterung im ländlichen Chorwesen," *Musica Sacra* 57 (1927): 360.

90. See Max Sigl, "Kirchenmusik und Cäcilienverein," *Musica Sacra* 56 (1926): 38; newspaper clipping, Dr. N., "Ende des Cäzilienvereins," *Augsburger Postzeitung*, February 16, 1921, RBZ, OA 2991; E. Jos. Müller, "Kirchenmusik," *Musik im Leben* 3 (October 1927): 137; Julius Smend, "Neue Organisation zur Hebung der katholischen Kirchenmusik," *Monatsschrift für Gottesdienst und kirchliche Kunst* 35 (1930): 115–17; Max Sigl to episcopal ordinary, March 21, 1929, RBZ, OA 2991; newspaper clipping, "Die Jubeltagung des Allgemeinen Cäcilienvereins," *K[ölnische] V[olkszeitung]*, 1932, FBG, Kirchenmusik: Allgemeiner Cäcilienverband Deutschland, Österreich und Schweiz, 1892–1959, 215–04/1; and Clemens Bachstefel to episcopal ordinary, May 11, 1928, PAB, OA Vereine 23.

91. Hayburn, *Papal Legislation on Sacred Music,* p. 331. See also "Kirchenmusikalische Aufführungen," *Kirchliches Amtsblatt für die Diözese Mainz* 66 (December 11, 1924): 39–41; and Kreitmaier, "Für oder gegen Kirchenkonzerte?" pp. 231–34.

92. Kreitmaier begins his discussion of current questions regarding chuch music with musings on extremes, ideals, the reform introduced by the Cäcilien Verein, and the response of its opponents.

93. Franz Joseph Haydn (1732–1809), Austrian. Wolfgang Amadeus Mozart (1756–1791), Austrian. Ludwig van Beethoven (1770–1827), German.

94. From Pius XI's pastoral letter of May 1, 1895, in Hayburn, *Papal Legislation on Sacred Music,* p. 217. See also Schmitz, "Zur Frage der modernen Kirchenmusik," p. 92; "Vorträge für die Cäcilienversammlung der deutschen Gemeinden der Diözese Kattowitz . . . 1931," p. 118; and *New Catholic Encyclopedia,* s.v. "Caecilian Movement."

95. Peter Griesbacher (1864–1933), German priest and composer. Vinzenz Goller (1873–1953), pseud. Hans von Berthal, Austrian church musician and composer. Max Filke (1855–1911), German composer. Ignaz Martin Mitterer (1850–1924), Austrian composer, best known for sacred works. Michael Haller (1840–1915), German composer and music critic. Raphael Molitor (1873–1948), German musicologist and authority on Gregorian chant. Joseph Gregor Zangl (1821–1897), Austrian Catholic theologian and musician. Josef Ett (1788–1847), German organist and composer active in the revival of church music of the sixteenth and seventeenth centuries. Josef Renner (1832–1895), German choral director at Regensburg from 1858 to 1892.

96. See "Kirchenmusikalische Aufführungen in der Stadtpfarrkirche zu Zwiesel (1915)," PAB, OA Vereine 23.

97. Wilhelm Kurthen (1882–?), priest, composer, and editor of the *Gregoriusblatt.*

98. Wilh[elm] Kurthen, "Moderne Kirchenmusik," *Gregoriusblatt für katholische Kirchenmusik* (1924): 42; Kreitmaier, *Dominanten,* pp. 167–68, 213–15, 227. See also Müller, "Zur Musikpflege in den katholischen Vereinen," p. 59; "Die zweite Generalversammlung des allgemeinen deutschen Cäcilien-Vereines zu Regensburg am 3., 4. und 5. August 1869," *Fliegende Blätter für katholische Kirchen-Musik* 4 (1869): 78; and Schmitz, "Zur Frage der modernen Kirchenmusik," p. 91.

99. "Vorträge für die Cäcilienversammlung der deutschen Gemeinden der Diözese Kattowitz . . . 1931," p. 118. See also M. Sambeth, "Krisis oder Erneuerung der katholischen Kirchenmusik?" *Theologie und Glaube* 20 (1928): 551; A. A. Knüppel, "Christozentrische Kirchenmusik," *Monatshefte für katholische Kirchenmusik* 6 (1924): 3; and *New Catholic Encyclopedia,* s.v. "Music, Sacred, History of, Pt. 8, Post-Romanticism," by F. J. Burkley. Johannes Schwermer, "Der Caecilianismus," in Fellerer, *Geschichte der katholischen Kirchenmusik,* vol. 2, p. 229, gives a more detailed description of stylistic variations. See also Feder, "Decline and Restoration," pp. 402–3.

100. See Heinrich Lemacher, "Die kirchenmusikalische 'Situation' in den Rheinlanden," *Musik im Leben* 3 (October 1927): 139.

101. See Schmitz, "Zur Frage der modernen Kirchenmusik," p. 92; and Lechthaler, "Ist die katholische Kirchenmusik inferior?" p. 13.

102. See Winfried Kirsch, "'Nazarener in der Musik' oder 'Der Caecilianismus in der Bildende Kunst,'" in *Der Caecilianismus: Anfänge—Grundlagen—Wirkungen: Internationales Symposium zur Kirchenmusik des 19. Jahrhunderts,* ed. Hubert Unverricht, Eichstätter Abhandlungen zur Musikwissenschaft, vol. 5 (Tutzing: Hans Schneider, 1988), p. 35; and Lemacher, "Die kirchenmusikalische 'Situation' in den Rheinländen," p. 139.

103. Johannes Hatzfeld (1882–1953), expert on church music and the *Volkslied.*

104. Dickinson, *Music in the History of the Western Church,* p. 30. See also Hatzfeld, "Von katholischer Kirchenmusik," p. 223; and Hayburn, *Papal Legislation on Sacred Music,* p. 228.

105. Boos to episcopal ordinary, May 23, 1929, MDD, Generalakten, C XII; CHAE, CR 20.8.1, Ad 4302/20.

106. St. Cyril of Jerusalem (315?–386), Church father; opponent of Nestorius.

107. Carl Cohen to the archbishop, October 15, 1891, CHAE, CR 20.8.1. See also Georg Laurenz Bauer, *Das Wesen der katholischen Liturgie als Grundlage für die kirchl[ichen] Bestimmungen über die Beteiligung der Frauen am Kirchenchor,* offprint from *Theologie und Glaube* 4 (1916) (Paderborn: Bonifacius-Druckerei, n.d.).

108. This wording is probably a free translation of 1 Corinthians 14:34.

109. Karl Hubert Cohen (1851–1938), cathedral Kapellmeister from 1887 to 1909.

110. Th. Linden to the archbishop, July 22, 1891, CHAE, CR 20.8.1.

111. Anton Alexander Knüppel (1880–?), organist at Essen-Altenessen; editor of *Monatshefte für katholische Kirchenmusik.*

112. *Cäcilienvereinsorgan* 47 (1912): 71–73.

113. See "Bericht über den Stand des Cäcilienvereins der diözese Rottenburg in den Jahren 1892 & 1893," RDA, G 1.1 C16.4; SBOA, 825 Cäcilienverein; and A. A. Knüppel, "Werden in Zukunft in unseren Kirchenchören Knaben oder Mädchen singen?" *Cäcilienvereinsorgan* 47 (1912): 72 .

114. [Choir], Essen, to the archbishop October 18, 1920, CHAE, CR 20.8.1. See also Peter Kleinschmidt, Dietesheim, to episcopal ordinary, August 29, 1929, MDD, Generalakten, C XII; and H. Meiser, Düsseldorf, to His Eminence, February 21, 1919, CHAE, CR 20.8.1; and CHAE, CR 20.8.1, Ad 4302/20.

115. [Women in choir], Essen, to Vicar Genearl Vogt, October 11, 1920, and [men in choir], Essen, to Vicar General Vogt, October 11, 1920, CHAE, CR 20.8.1.

116. See *Kirchlicher Anzeiger für die Erzdiözese Köln* 54 (June 1, 1914): 88; A. Stehle, "Ansprache Sr. Eminenz des H. Kardinals Erzbischof Schulte auf der G.-V. des C.-V. der Erzdiözes Köln in Neuss," *Musica Sacra* 56 (1926): 239–46; and Vicar General to Monsignor Oster, dean at Essen-Steele, [January 1931], CHAE, CR 20.8.1.

117. See episcopal ordinary to the dean of the city and surroundings of Mainz, August 5, 1931, MDD, Generalakten, C XII; *Festschrift und Programm zur Goldenen Jubelfeier des kath[olischn] Kirchenchors Caecilia (St. Paul) Offenbach am Main am 27. Juni 1926* (Offenbach am Main: Druck von Albert Kleinsorge [1926]), p. 53; and *New Catholic Encyclopedia,* s.v. "Music, Sacred, Legislation on," by R. F. Hayburn.

118. Kreitmaier, *Dominanten,* p. 181.

119. Friedrich Koenen (1829–1887), cathedral Kapellmeister at Cologne from 1863 to 1887; academic.

120. Peter Kuhl to archiepiscopal vicariate, December 29, 1898, CHAE, CR 20.8.1. See also Kreitmaier, *Dominanten,* pp. 186–94; and "99 Jahre 'Musica Sacra,'" p. 16.

121. See H. R. Müller to His Eminence, February 7, 1915, CHAE, CR 20.8.1; and episcopal ordinary, Passau, to the royal government of Lower Bavaria, K. d. I., January 21, 1881. The book to which he refers is probably Josef Mohr, *Jubilate Deo! Lieder für den katholischen Gottesdienst . . . ,* 12th ed. (Regensburg: Friedrich Pustet, 1877). See also Vogt (Mainz Kapellmeister) to the bishop, February 12, 1916, CHAE, CR 20.8.1. The common songbook was *Einheitslieder für die deutsche Diözesan-Gesangbücher* (Berlin: Germania, 1916).

122. "Die Teilnahme der Gläubigen am Kirchengesang," undated, CHAE, CR 20.8.3.

123. Maria Müller-Gögler (1900–1987), Austrian teacher and writer.

124. See Dr. H., "Laien-Gedanken über den Choral," *Cäcilienvereinsorgan* 59 (1929): 224; Joseph Hebenstreit, "Kirchenchor auf dem Lande," *Volkskunst* 14 (1926): 449–50; Maria Müller-Gögler, *Erinnerungen: Bevor die Stürme kamen. Hinter blinden Fenstern. Das arme Fräulein* (Sigmaringen: Jan Thorbecke Verlag, 1980), p. 18; and "Die zweite General-versammlung des allgemeinen deutschen Cäcilien-Vereines zu Regensburg am 3., 4. und 5. August 1869," p. 78.

125. See Müller, "Musikpflege als soziale Pflicht," p. 162; and Johner, "Kirchen-musik und Seelsorge," p. 188.

126. Kurthen, "Das Problem des religiösen Ausdrucks der Musik," p. 68.

127. See Ferdinand Wernet, "Instrumentalmusik in den Vereinen," *Volkskunst* 13 (1925): 247.

128. See "99 Jahre 'Musica Sacra,'" p. 29; Walter Berten, "Die Schallplatte in der Musikpflege," *Volkstum und Volksbildung* 4 (1932): 73–79; "Schallplatten-Ecke: Musica Sacra," *Allgemeine Rundschau* 28 (February 21, 1931): 127–28; "Vorträge für die Cäcilien-versammlung der deutschen Gemeinden der Diözese Kattowitz . . . 1931," p. 123; and Horst Feldt, "Schallplatte und Lautsprecher im katholischen Gottesdienst," *Cäcilienvereinsorgan* 61 (1931): 13–16.

129. Willi Schmid (1893–1934).

130. Schmid, "Neue Musik," p. 89.

8. THEATER, CINEMA, AND RADIO

1. Arnold was actually paraphrasing Sarah Bernhardt in an essay that was a trib-ute to the good organization of French drama. See "The French Play in London," in Mat-thew Arnold, *The Complete Prose Works of Matthew Arnold*, ed. R. H. Super, vol. 9, *English Literature and Irish Politics* (Ann Arbor, Mich.: University of Michigan Press, 1973), p. 85.

2. Jakob Overmans, S.J. (1874–1945), associated with *Stimmen der Zeit* from 1910 to 1928; wrote on drama; student chaplain at the Universities of Kiel and Göttingen from 1923 to 1928.

3. Jakob Overmans, "Das Theater als Bildungsstätte," in Meinertz and Sacher, *Deutschland und der Katholizismus*, p. 392; "Der Erzbischof von München gegen die Aus-schreitungen der modernen Bühnenliteratur," *Allgemeine Rundschau* 15 (1918): 396. See also Overmans, *Roman, Theater und Kino im neuen Deutschland*, p. 3; and Wolff, "Spielet Cal-derons geistliche Festspiele!" p. 328.

4. Georg Büchner (1813–1837), German playwright; his best-known play is *Woyzeck*.

5. *Dictionary of Literary Biography*, ed. Wolfgang D. Elfe and James Hardin, vol. 118, *Twentieth-Century Dramatists, 1889–1918* (Detroit: Gale Research, 1992), s.v. "Ger-man Drama from Naturalism to Fascism, 1889–1933," by Roy Cowen, pp. 185–94.

6. W. Thamerus, "Die kulturfördernde Verpflichtung der deutschen Bühne," *All-gemeine Rundschau* 14 (1917): 405; Arthur von Klein-Ehrenwalten, "Die Entwicklung der deutschen Bühne in ihrer Stellung zur katholischen Kirche," *Wissen und Glauben* 24 (1927): 298; Gustav Stezenbach, "Ein Apostolat des Theaters," *Allgemeine Rundschau* 20 (1923): 313; and R. L., "Moderne Bühnenkunst," *Hochland* 24 (October 1926): 126.

7. See *Dictionary of Literary Biography,* vol. 118, s.v. "German Drama from Naturalism to Fascism, 1889–1933," pp. 286, 288, passim; Geuke, "Katholiken und Theaterkultur," *Historisch-politische Blätter für das katholische Deutschland* 159 (1917): 765; and Jakob Overmans, "Unser Kampf um die Bühne," *Stimmen aus Maria-Laach* 85 (1913): 268.

8. Frank Wedekind (1864–1918), German dramatist. Carl Sternheim (1878–1942), German dramatist.

9. Karl Schönherr (1867–1943), Austrian dramatist.

10. Arthur Schnitzler (1862–1931), Austrian short-story writer, novelist, and physician.

11. Oscar Wilde (1854–1900), Irish writer; notorious for his trial as a homosexual.

12. See Ferdinand Klein, "Klerus und Theaterbesuch," *Allgemeine Rundschau* 1 (September 17, 1904): 329–31; "Tapfere Worte gegen die Auswüchse des modernen Theaters," *Allgemeine Rundschau* 10 (1913): 35; W. Thamerus, "Schaubühne und sittliche Erneuerung," *Allgemeine Rundschau* 13 (1916): 613–14; *McGraw-Hill Encyclopedia of World Drama,* ed. Stanley Hochmann (New York: McGraw-Hill, 1972), s.v. "German Drama"; and *Dictionary of Literary Biography,* vol. 118, s.v. "Frank Wedekind," by Steve Dowden, s.v. "Karl Schönherr," by Pamela S. Saur, and s.v. "Carl Sternheim," by Edson M. Chick.

13. Hugo von Hofmannsthal (1874–1929), Austrian poet and dramatist.

14. See Geuke, "Katholiken und Theaterkultur," p. 768.

15. Michael Patterson, *The Revolution in German Theatre, 1900–1933* (Boston: Routledge and Kegan Paul, 1981), p. 22.

16. Klein, "Klerus und Theaterbesuch," pp. 329–31. See also Manes Radow, "Verteidigung des Provinz-Theaters," *Germania,* July 14, 1928, Morgenausgabe; "Clerici theatra ne frequentant," *Kirchlicher Anzeiger für die Erzdiözese Köln* 54 (January 1, 1914): 12; and Volksverein für das katholische Deutschland, 1891–1916, clipping from the *Kölnische Zeitung,* January 8, 1914, Senat der Freien und Hansestadt Hamburg, Stadtarchiv, Hamburg (hereafter HSA), 331–3, Politische Polizei, V 358.

17. Johannes Albani, "Katholische Dramatiker," *Allgemeine Rundschau* 19 (1922): 500. See also W. Thamerus, "Zensurloses Theater," *Allgemeine Rundschau* 16 (1919): 467.

18. See Stezenbach, "Ein Apostolat des Theaters," p. 323; Hans Grundei, "Theaterprobleme und Schauspielerfragen," *Allgemeine Rundschau* 19 (1922): 101; and Patterson, *The Revolution in German Theatre, 1900–1933,* p. 25.

19. Heinrich Heimanns, S.J. (1875–?), writer on belles letters and religion at the Sittard Missionary House in Aachen; editor of several journals, including *Missionswarte.*

20. Heinrich Heimanns, "Der Verband zur Förderung der Theaterkultur und die katholischen Bedenken," *Allgemeine Rundschau* 14 (1917): 892. Gertrud Kaetzel, "Die Gefährdung der Moral des Familienlebens durch die Bühne," *Wissen und Glauben* 26 (1931): 55. See also Thamerus, "Schaubühne und sittliche Erneuerung," pp. 613–14; "Tapfere Worte gegen die Auswüchse des modernen Theaters," p. 35; Overmans, *Roman, Theater und Kino im neuen Deutschland,* p. 5; and Ludwig Ernst, "Die Theaterfrage—eine Frauenfrage," *Allgemeine Rundschau* 13 (1916): 209–10; 229–30.

21. Expeditus Schmidt, "Theaterkultur," *Hochland* 14 (November 1916): 229. See also F. H. Schwank, "Staatstheater und Volkskunst," *Volkskunst* 16 (December 1928): 354; Geuke, "Katholiken und Theaterkultur," p. 769; Stezenbach, "Ein Apostolat des Theaters," p. 313; and W. Thamerus, "Mißbrauchte Theaterfreiheit," *Allgemeine Rundschau* 16 (1919): 557.

22. Friedrich Schiller, "The Stage as a Moral Institution," in Friedrich Schiller, *Essays Aesthetical and Philosophical* (London: George Bell and Sons, 1879), pp. 333–39.

23. See Overmans, "Das Theater als Bildungsstätte," p. 393; Friedrich Mucker-mann, "Kulturfragen der Gegenwart: Auf dem Wege zum nationale Kultspiel," *Germania,* June 5, 1926, Morgenausgabe, Das neue Ufer; H. Jung, "Demokratisierung des Theater," *Germania,* October 23, 1926, Morgenausgabe, Das neue Ufer; Thamerus, "Die kultur-fördernde Verpflichtung der deutschen Bühne," p. 405; Eugen Gürster, "Krisis des The-aters," *Hochland* (1926): 125; and Georg Raederscheidt, "Grundsätzliches zur Begegnung von Theater und Katholizismus," *Das Nationaltheater* 5 (January 1933): 67.

24. Overmans, *Roman, Theater und Kino im neuen Deutschland,* pp. 4–5; Gürster, "Krisis des Theaters," p. 124.

25. Lorenz Kjerbüll-Petersen, "Theater und Drama," *Der Gral* 25 (1930/1931): 60; Jakob Overmans, "Bilanz der Sprechbühne," *Stimmen der Zeit* 117 (1929): 357.

26. Georg Raederscheidt (1883–1974), educator and city councillor of Neuß from 1919 to 1929.

27. H. A. Fischen, "Die katholische Weltanschauung und das moderne deutsche Theater," *Das neue Jahrhundert* 4 (July 21, 1912): 339, paraphrasing Richard von Kralik. Overmans, "Unser Kampf um die Bühne," pp. 269–70; Overmans, "Das Theater als Bil-dungsstätte," p. 393. See also Leo Weismantel, "Die Bühne der Stunde," *Die Tat* 14 (1922): 491; and Raederscheidt, "Grundsätzliches zur Begegnung von Theater und Katholizis-mus," p. 68.

28. Reinhard Johannes Sorge (1892–1916), German dramatist and promoter of the Catholic literary movement.

29. *Dictionary of Literary Biography,* vol. 118, s.v. "Reinhold Johannes Sorge." Bern-hard Stein's collection of Catholic plays *Katholische Dramatiker der Gegenwart* (Ravens-burg: Verlag von Friedrich Alber, 1909) illustrates the debt to Schiller beyond question. See also Raederscheidt, "Grundsätzliches zur Begegnung von Theater und Katholizismus," p. 69; Albani, "Katholische Dramatiker," p. 499; Overmans, "Unser Kampf um die Bühne," p. 269; and Overmans, *Roman, Theater und Kino im neuen Deutschland,* p. 33.

30. Leo Weismantel (1888–1964), Bavarian writer, dramatist, and educator; mem-ber of the Bavarian Landtag from 1924 to 1928.

31. Balduin of Luxemburg (1285–1354), archbishop of Trier.

32. Gustave Stezenbach (1876–1925), editor of *Badischen Gastwirts;* secretary of the Badischer Gastwirtsverband (Innkeepers' Association of Baden).

33. Stezenbach, "Ein Apostolat des Theaters," p. 313. See also *Kürschners Deutscher Literatur-Kalender auf das Jahr 1928,* 24th ed. (Berlin: Walter de Gruyter, 1928), s.v. "Weis-mantel, Leo"; Arno Klönne, "Leo Weismantel—Ein fränkischer Poet und Pädagoge," *Main-fränkisches Jahrbuch für Geschichte und Kunst* 37 (1985): 162–73; Leo Weismantel, "Briefe über katholische Literatur: Die Katholiken und die Bühne," *Das literarische Echo* 25 (1923): 888; Otto Steinbrinck, "Leo Weismantel—ein Wegbereiter des neuen Dramas," *Bücherwelt* 22 (February 1925): 65–71; Wilhelm Spael, "Aus der Bühnenwelt: Zwei rheinische Festspiele," *Bücherwelt* 22 (November 1925): 523–28; and Weismantel, *Mein Leben,* p. 30.

34. Max Mell (1882–1971), Austrian writer and dramatist.

35. See Stezenbach, "Ein Apostolat des Theaters," p. 313; A. Glitz-Holzhausen, "Die Krisis der Provinz-Theater," *Germania,* April 16, 1926, Abendausgabe; Gertrud Kaetzel, "Katholizismus und Bühne im In- und Ausland," *Wissen und Glauben* 26 (1931): 120; and "Wo bleiben die katholischen Theaterbesucher?" *Kölnische Volkszeitung,* June 27, 1928.

36. See R. E. Sackett, "Antimodernism in the Popular Entertainment of Modern Munich: Attitude, Institution, Language," *New German Critique* 57 (Fall 1992): 139.

37. See Franz Eckardt, "Wir Katholiken und das Theater," *Allgemeine Rundschau* 10 (February 15, 1913): 122; Fischen, "Die katholische Weltanschauung und das moderne deutsche Theater," p. 340; and Overmans, *Roman, Theater und Kino im neuen Deutschland,* p. 13.

38. Maximilian Pfeiffer (1875–1926), librarian, historian, and politician.

39. Maximilian Pfeiffer, "Theaterkultur," *Allgemeine Rundschau* 13 (1916): 632.

40. See Heimanns, "Der Verband zur Förderung der Theaterkultur und die katholischen Bedenken," pp. 892–93.

41. See Wilhelm Karl Gerst, "Wie die Katholiken für das Theater aktiviert wurden," *Der Gral* 27 (1933): 359–60.

42. See "Denkschrift über den Bühnenvolksbund," undated, CHAE, Gen. 23.49; Gerst, "Wie die Katholiken für das Theater aktiviert wurden," p. 363; and Emil Ritter, "Der neue Bühnenvolksbund," *Volkskunst* 7 (May/June 1919): 401–5.

43. See *Aus der Arbeit des Bühnenvolksbund: Theaterpflege im christlich-deutschen Volksgeist: Bericht über die Grundversammlung am 8. und 9. April 1919 in Frankfurt am Main,* ed. Ausschuß des Bühnenvolksbund (n.p., n.d.).

44. Adolf Dyroff (1862–1943), professor at the University of Bonn; privy councillor; wrote extensively on philosophy and also on psychology; long-time chair of Borromäus Verein managing committee. Ilse von Stach (1879–1941), German dramatist and writer; convert to Catholicism (1908).

45. See *Aus der Arbeit des Bühnenvolksbund: Theaterpflege im christlich-deutschen Volksgeist;* "Denkschrift über den Bühnenvolksbund," undated, CHAE, Gen. 23.49; Emil Ritter, "Bühnenvolksbund und katholische Vereine," *Volkskunst* 16 (January, 1928): 1–6; Bühnen-Volksbund, *Volksbühne oder Bühnenvolksbund?* (N.p., n.d.), printed leaflet, RBZ, G 1.1 C 16.5g; and Consul Heinrich Maus to the managing committee of the Bühnenvolksbund, November 23, 1927, CHAE, Gen. 23.49.

46. See "Ausbreitung der Bühnen-Volksbundarbeit," *Mitteilungen des Bühnen-Volksbundes* 2 (April/May 1921), in *Volkskunst* 9 (April/May 1921): 187–92; and "An die Freunde deutschen Kulturlebens," [1925], printed, CHAE, Gen. 23.49.

47. See Alexander Drenker, "Wille und Werk des Bühnenvolksbundes," *Volkskunst* 16 (October 1928): 296–98; and Leo Schwering, "Antwort an die Reichsgesellschaft des Bühnenvolksbundes," June/July 1927, mimeographed, RBZ, G 1.1 C 16.5g.

48. Wilhelm Gerst (1887–1968), founded Caritashilfe (Organization for Charity) in 1910; founder and director of Bühnenvolksbund until 1928; candidate in Fulda for the Communist Party in 1949; later Bonn correspondent for the news service of the German Democratic Republic.

49. Otto Brües, *Jupp Brand* (Berlin: Bühnenvolksbund, 1927).

50. See Wilhelm Gerst, director of the Bühnenvolksbund, to minister for science, art, and adult education, June 25, [192]3, Wilhelm Gerst to Cardinal Archbishop Karl Joseph Schulte, June 16, 1926, as well as letters from Dyroff, Grosche, and Stegerwald, CHAE, Gen. 23.49. See also two articles by M. Wilhelm Senn, "'Jupp Brand' oder Katholiken und Bühnenvolksbund," *Schönere Zukunft* (1927) 1054–57, 1076–79, and "Notwendige Neuorientierung in der Literaturfrage," *Schönere Zukunft* 2 (1927): 1098–100; "Zur Krise im Bühnenvolksbund," *Germania,* June 2, 1926, Abendausgabe; Stezenbach, "Ein Apostolat des Theaters," p. 313; and Father Breitung, Weimar, to episcopal vicariate, Fulda, October 20, 1932, FBG, 210–07.

51. See Stezenbach, "Ein Apostolat des Theaters," p. 313; Ritter, "Bühnenvolksbund und katholische Vereine"; "Katholische Vereinsbildungsarbeit im Bühnenvolksbund," undated, RBZ, OA 2105; "Entschliessung Nr. 1, Richtlinien für die Bühnenaufführungen der Vereine des Verbandes . . . ," 1924, CHAE, Gen. 23.54.1; and Bühnenvolksbund to episcopal ordinary, Fulda, April 15, 1930, mimeographed letter, FBG, 210–07.

52. Joseph Damian Schmitt (1858–1939), bishop of Fulda from 1906.

53. See Eckardt, "Wir Katholiken und das Theater," p. 537; "Hirtenwort über die Vergnügenssucht," *Kirchliches Amtsblatt für die Diözese Fulda* 42 (January 13, 1926): 2, FBG, 210–07; and "Kaiser-Feier," *Volkskunst* 3 (March 1915): 177. For a detailed study of amateur theater in Catholic organizations for apprentices and workers, see Gabriele Clemens, *Erziehung zu anständiger Unterhaltung: Das Theaterspiel in den katholischen Gesellen- und Arbeitervereinen im deutschen Kaiserreich*, Veröffentlichungen der Kommission für Zeitgeschichte, ed. Ulrich von Hehl, Reihe A: Quellen, vol. 46 (Paderborn: Schöningh, 2000).

54. See Alois Pichler, "Der Sprung auf die Bühne," *Allgemeine Rundschau* 1 (1905): 286; "Tapfere Worte gegen die Auswüchse des modernen Theaters," p. 35; Stezenbach, "Ein Apostolat des Theaters," pp. 313, 323; Wolff, "Spielet Calderons geistliche Festspiele!" p. 327; and Emil Ritter, "Alte und neue Laienbühne," *Volkskunst* 11 (July/September 1923): 67–71.

55. See Fritz Budde, "Moderne Theaterkunst," *Hochland* (May 1914): 201–14; H. Behm, "Staatstheater: Hauptmanns 'Weber,'" *Germania,* February 6, 1928, Morgenausgabe; Kjerbüll-Petersen, "Theater und Drama," p. 60; and "Theater als Zeitgeist: Ein Rückblick und ein Ausblick," *Germania,* January 1, 1929, Morgenausgabe.

56. See Alois Funk, "Film und Seelsorge," *Pastor Bonus* 41 (September 1930): 338; and Muckermann, *Im Kampf zwischen zwei Epochen,* p. 283.

57. A good, brief summary of German film history can be found in Bruce A. Murray, "An Introduction to the Commercial Film Industry in Germany from 1895 to 1933," in *Film and Politics in the Weimar Republic,* ed. Thomas G. Plummer et al. (University of Minnesota, department of German, distributed by New York: Holmes and Meier, 1982), pp. 23–34.

58. Fritz Wächter, "Zur Kinematographenfrage," *Volkswart* 2 (April 1909): 52.

59. Heiner Schmitt, *Kirche und Film: Kirchliche Filmarbeit in Deutschland von ihren Anfängen bis 1945,* Schriften des Bundesarchivs 26 (Boppard am Rhein, 1979) gives a detailed, chronological account of Catholic film work and this summary draws heavily upon it. Other useful publications include Otto Steinbrinck, "Gesetze der Filmkunst," in *Lichtträger im Chaos 3: Film und Volk* (Essener Volkszeitung, 1925), p. 89; David A. Welch, "Cinema and Society in Imperial Germany, 1905–1918," *German History* 8 (1990): 28–45; D. J. Wenden, *The Birth of the Movies* (New York: E. P. Dutton, 1974), passim; and Frederick W. Ott, *The Great German Films* (Secaucus, N.J.: Citadel, 1986), pp. 9–17.

60. See Schmitt, *Kirche und Film,* pp. 23–29; Richard Muckermann, "Der Film: Sein Werden, Wachsen und Wollen," in *Lichtträger in Chaos 3,* p. 52; and Walther Conradt, *Kirche und Kinematograph* (Berlin: Herrmann Walther Verlagsbuchhandlung, 1910).

61. Karl Walterbach (1870–1952), priest; head of the Süddeutsche katholische Arbeitervereine from 1903 to 1933.

62. See Schmitt, *Kirche und Film,* passim; and Bernhard Marschall, "Wintertagung," *Volkskunst* 14 (1926): 110.

63. See "Kirchl[iches] Amtsblatt für die Diözese Fulda," November 25, 1913, Das Kinematographenwesen, FBG, 210–07; and "Katholische Leitsätze und Weisungen zu

verschiedenen modernen Sittlichkeitsfrage," *Kirchlicher Anzeiger für die Erzdiözese Köln* 65 (January 20, 1925): 17.

64. Their concern was not without foundation. Research published in 1934 confirmed that attitudes could indeed be influenced by films. Solomon P. Rosenthal, *Change of Socio-economic Attitudes under Radical Motion Picture Propaganda,* Archives of Psychology, ed. E. S. Woodsworth, no. 166 (New York, 1934).

65. Richard Muckermann (1891–1981), film expert and journalist; brother of Friedrich Muckermann, S.J.

66. A trick film can be either a film that uses photographic techniques to create a misleading effect, such as superimposing one image on another, or an animated film.

67. Alois Funk (1896–1978), priest; named subdirector of the episcopal seminary in Trier in 1929; received his doctorate from the University of Munich in 1934; later secretary of Catholic Action and editor of the diocesan newsletter.

68. Richard Muckermann, "Film," in *71. Generalversammlung der deutschen Katholiken zu Essen an der Ruhr . . . 1932,* p. 247. See also R. Muckermann, "Der Film: Sein Werden, Wachsen und Wollen," pp. 22–23; and Funk, "Film und Seelsorge," p. 340.

69. See Kr., "Kirche und Film," *Germania,* November 15, 1928, Morgenausgabe, Das neue Ufer; Schmitt, *Kirche und Film* p. 21; Welch, "Cinema and Society in Imperial Germany," p. 28; Eugen Kalkschmidt, "Die Macht des Films," *Hochland* 26 (1929): 637; R. Muckermann, "Film," p. 247; and F. Muckermann, *Im Kampf zwischen zwei Epochen,* p. 283.

70. Friedrich Wolf, "Film im Westen," in *Aufsätze,* vol. 1 (Berlin: Aufbau, 1967–1968), p. 529; Josef Ettl, "Das Pfarr-Kino," *Der Seelsorger* 7 (1930): 18. See also Steinbrinck, "Gesetze der Filmkunst," p. 89; Welch, "Cinema and Society in Imperial Germany, 1905–1918," pp. 28–45; Wenden, *The Birth of the Movies,* passim; Ott, *The Great German Films,* pp. 9–17; A. F. Stenzel, "Katholische Filmforderungen," *Allgemeine Rundschau* 25 (1928): 700; and Kalkschmidt, "Die Macht des Films," p. 633.

71. See Emilie Altenloh, *Zur Soziologie des Kino* (Jena: Eugen Diederichs, 1914), p. 34, quoted in *Film und Gesellschaft in Deutschland: Dokumente und Materialien,* ed. Wilfried von Bredow and Rolf Zurek (Hamburg: Hoffmann und Campe, 1975), p. 18; "Als Kino-Nummer," *Augustinus-Blatt* 26 (May/June 1922): 17; [Joseph Mausbach], "Der Kampf gegen die moderne Sittenlosigkeit," *Volkswart* 5 (September 1912): 135; Willy Rath, *Kino und Bühne,* Lichtbühnen-Bibliothek, no. 4 (Mönchengladbach: Volksverein Verlag, 1913), p. 22; and Richard Muckermann, "Der Film, ein Feind des Theaters," *Volkswart* 24 (1931): 25.

72. See Altenloh, "Zur Soziologie des Kino," pp. 34–53; and J. Chomse, "Rundschau: Psychologie des Kinos," *Bild und Film* 2 (1912/1913): 140.

73. See Victor Schamoni, "Filmkrisis," *Hochland* 26 (June 1929): 329; Murray, "An Introduction to the Commercial Film Industry in Germany from 1895 to 1933," p. 23; Otto Behrens, "Verlogenheiten der weißen Wand," *Germania,* September 30, 1928, Morgenausgabe, Film-Rundschau; and Overmans, *Roman, Theater und Kino im neuen Deutschland,* p. 7.

74. "Als Kino-Nummer," p. 17; Funk, "Film und Seelsorge," p. 338.

75. Luitpold Nusser, "Verwendung des Films zur Verbreitung von Ideen," in *Film und Rundfunk: Zweiter Internationaler Katholischer Filmkongreß, Erster Internationaler Katholischer Rundfunkkongreß,* ed. Georg Ernst and Bernhard Marschall (Munich, 1929), p. 114.

76. Victor Schamoni, "Kino," *Hochland* 21 (September 1924): 620; Karl Schaezler, "Erben des Buches?" *Hochland* 29 (October 1931): 93. See also Malwine Rennert, "Die Kunst des Lichtspieltheaters," *Bild und Film* 3 (1913/14): 128–30; and Willi Warstatt, "Das

künstlerische Problem in der Photographie und in der Kinematographie," *Bild und Film* 3 (1913/14): 7–10;

77. See Mr. Kl., "Die Gefahr der Lichtspielhäuser," *Volkswart* 6 (October 1913): 152–53; and Raimund Eberhard, "Sittliche und unsittliche Kunst," *Volkswart* 17 (December 1924): 177.

78. H. O. Seidel, "Auf zum Kino-Kampf!" *Wissen und Glauben* 27 (1932): 473. See also A. Kneer, "Katholik und Kino," *Allgemeine Rundschau* 22 (1925): 145; Wächter, "Zur Kinematographenfrage," p. 50; "Aus unseren Vereinen," *Volkswart* 5 (May 1912): 74; and "Einfluß des Kinos auf die Sittlichkeit," *Pastor Bonus* 44 (November 1933): 418.

79. Overmans, *Roman, Theater und Kino im neuen Deutschland*, p. 31; Siegfried Kracauer, "The Little Shopgirls Go to the Movies," in Siegfried Kracauer, *The Mass Ornament: Weimar Essays*, trans. and ed. Thomas Y. Levin (Cambridge: Harvard University Press, 1995), p. 292; Behrens, "Verlogenheiten der weißen Wand."

80. Friedrich Muckermann, "Die Katholiken und der Film," in Ernst and Marschall *Film und Rundfunk*, pp. 24–26 (reprinted as "Katholizismus und moderner Film" *Schönere Zukunft* 4 [June 30, 1929]: 823–24).

81. Cardinal Adolf Bertram, April 20, 1923, to the minister of the interior, printed, WAA, I A 25 g 49. See also Seidel, "Auf zum Kino-Kampf!" p. 473; and W. Thamerus, "Die Moral des Kino," *Allgemeine Rundschau* 15 (May 4, 1918): 269.

82. Hütterman, "Schundfilmmoral," *Allgemeine Rundschau* 10 (May 3, 1913): 350. See also Ott, *The Great German Films*, pp. 25–26; Otto Behrens, "Niedergang des Spielfilms," *Germania*, August 12, 1928, Morgenausgabe, Film-Rundschau; and Cardinal Adolf Bertram, April 20, 1923, to the minister of the interior, printed, WAA, I A 25 g 49.

83. "Einfluß des Kinos auf die Sittlichkeit," pp. 418–21. See also H. v. W., "Rundschau," *Bild und Film* 4 (1914/15): 255; and "Das Ergebnis der Kinobesuche . . ." *Volkswart* 15 (March 1922): 34.

84. B[ernhard] M[arschall], "Filmarbeitsgemeinschaft," *Volkstum und Volksbildung* 3 (1931): 185. See also Nusser, "Verwendung des Films zur Verbreitung von Ideen," p. 98; Karl Norbisrath, "Weiterhin Kampf oder Resignation in der Kinofrage? Ein Beitrag zur christlichen Lichtbildkultur," *Allgemeine Rundschau* 19 (1922): 56; and Karl Brunner, *Der Kinematograph von heute—eine Volksgefahr* (Berlin: Verlag des vaterländischen Schriftenverbandes, 1913), pp. 18–19.

85. Brunner, *Der Kinematograph von heute*, p. 11. See also Arthur von Klein-Ehrenwalten, "Wege des Films," *Wissen und Glauben* 24 (1927): 556; "Das Ergebnis der Kinobesuche . . ." p. 33; and Hans Steckner, "Kunst und Kino," *Volkskunst* 13 (1925): 99.

86. Behrens, "Niedergang des Spielfilms."

87. See Joseph Reymond, "Von Haag nach München: Das Intern[ationale] kath[olische] Filmbüro," in Ernst and Marschall, *Film und Rundfunk*, p. 36; Kalkschmidt, "Die Macht des Films," pp. 638–40; Heinrich Lentz, "Film, Kunst und Zivilisation," *Hochland* 22 (August 1925): 598; F. Muckermann, "Die Katholiken und der Film," p. 28; Richard Muckermann, "Kultur-Zivilisation," typescript, ca. 1925, and Richard Muckermann, "Kino und katholische Empfinden," *Festblatt zum 66. Katholikentag in Dortmund, 3. September 1927*, Bundesarchiv, Coblenz (hereafter CBA), NL 154/2; and Klein-Ehrenwalten, "Wege des Films," p. 558.

88. See H. H. Bormann, " 'Panzerkreuzer Potemkin': Ein Meisterwerk russischer Filmkunst," *Germania*, April 30, 1926, Abendausgabe; Erich Pommer, "Der internationale Film," *Germania*, September 23, 1928, Morgenausgabe, Film-Rundschau;

Heinrich Bachmann, "Ein neuer Chaplinfilm: 'Zirkus,'" *Germania*, February 9, 1928, Abendausgabe; and Iwan Grimm, "Filmportrait: Charlie Chaplin," *Germania*, October 21, 1928, Morgenausgabe.

89. Steckner, "Kunst und Kino," pp. 97–100; Marschall, "Wintertagung," pp. 110–19.

90. Otto Steinbrinck (1901–?), newspaper correspondent; wrote on literature and culture.

91. Steinbrinck, "Gesetze der Filmkunst," pp. 93–94.

92. See Funk, "Film und Seelsorge," pp. 345–53.

93. See Albert F. Stenzel, "Filme als Kulturdokumente," *Allgemeine Rundschau* 24 (1927): 149; Schamoni, "Kino," p. 626; and Marforio, "Der Tonfilm zum blauen Engel," *Allgemeine Rundschau* 27 (July 5, 1930): 472–73.

94. See Bormann, "'Panzerkreuzer Potemkin': Ein Meisterwerk russischer Filmkunst."

95. Klein-Ehrenwalten, "Wege des Films," p. 560. See also Funk, "Film und Seelsorge, (Fortsetzung)," p. 410.

96. See F. Muckermann, *Im Kampf zwischen zwei Epochen*, p. 280.

97. See Zentralbildungsausschuß, "Bericht über das Geschäftsjahr 1926/1927," CHAE, Gen 23.54.1; Bernhard Marschall, "Bericht des ZBA," *Volkstum und Volksbildung* 2 (1930): 315; and "Zusammenfassung der Beratungen des Kongresses und Resolutionen," in Ernst and Marshcall, *Film und Rundfunk*, pp. 228–31.

98. See Schmitt, *Kirche und Film*, pp. 38–45, 64–88; and "Auf christlichem Boden stehende Filmunternehmungen," *Augustinus-Blatt* 26 (May/June 1922): 20–24.

99. See Bild- und Film-Zentrale, Cologne, "Filmliste," September 1, 1929, RDA, G 1.1 D 2.4a.

100. See "Gründung einer Film-Aktiengesellschaft" CBA, NL 154/1; Seidel, "Auf zum Kino-Kampf!" p. 476; B[ernhard] M[arschall], "Katholische Filmarbeit," *Volkstum und Volksbildung* 2 (1930): 58; and F. Muckermann, *Im Kampf zwischen zwei Epochen*, p. 289.

101. Ettl, "Das Pfarr-Kino." See also Funk, "Film und Seelsorge, (Fortsetzung)," pp. 410–11.

102. Charlotte Demmig, "Kampf um das Ethos im Film," *Der Gral* 25 (February 1931): 454–55. See also Kneer, "Katholik und Kino," p. 145; Missonne, "Die Zensur für Kinder und erwachsene Jugend," in Ernst and Marschall, *Film und Rundfunk*, p. 216; F. Muckermann, "Die Katholiken und der Film," p. 28; Arthur von Klein-Ehrenwalten, "Zum katholischen Filmkongreß im Haag," *Wissen und Glauben* 25 (1928): 496; and Richard Muckermann, "Der katholische Film," *Lokal-Anzeiger*, June 8, 1930, CBA, NL 154/2.

103. Hans Appelshaeuser, "Rundschau: Der Kinematograph und seine Aufgaben," *Bild und Film* 1 (1912): 47; Lentz, "Film, Kunst und Zivilisation," p. 602; Richard Muckermann, "Film," p. 246; F. Muckermann, "Katholizismus und moderner Film," p. 823; Johannes Hönig, "Die Stellung der Katholiken zum Theater," *Historisch-politische Blätter für das katholische Deutschland* 160 (1917): 543.

104. Demmig, "Kampf um das Ethos im Film," p. 455.

105. See Schmitt, *Kirche und Film*, pp. 73–74; and Funk, "Film und Seelsorge, (Fortsetzung)," p. 412. A 1933 letter from the director of Leohaus to the Bishop of Rottenburg claimed that Leohaus was the only group to have produced Catholic films. See Ernst and Walterbach, Leohaus, to Bishop Johannes Baptista Sproll, February 14, 1933, RDA, G 1.1, D 2.4a/34.

106. See Schmitt, *Kirche und Film*, pp. 88–105.

107. See Richard Muckermann, "Film," p. 248; and Funk, "Film und Seelsorge, (Fortsetzung)," p. 412.

108. See Bernhard Marschall to Kurt Heydecker, May 6, 1931, mimeographed, FBG, 210–07; and F. Muckermann, *Im Kampf zwischen zwei Epochen*," p. 290.

109. Funk, "Film und Seelsorge," p. 338. See also Malwine Rennert, "Im Reich der Mütter," *Bild und Film* 3 (1913/1914): 267–69.

110. Hans von Bredow, quoted in Heinz Pohle, *Der Rundfunk als Instrument der Politik* (Hamburg: Verlag Hans-Bredow-Institut, 1955), pp. 41–44. See also *Brockhaus Enzyklopädie* (Mannheim: F. A. Brockhaus, 1992), s.v. "Rundfunk"; Günther Bauer, *Kirchliche Rundfunkarbeit 1924–1939*, Beiträge zur Geschichte des deutschen Rundfunks, vol. 2 (Frankfurt am Main: Josef Knecht, 1966), p. 25; Alois Funk, "Rundfunk und Katholizismus," p. 115; and Hans Juncker, *Kirchliche Rundfunkarbeit im Bistum Trier von den Anfängen bis 1945* (Trier: Bistum Trier Medien, 2000), pp. 4–7.

111. Heinz Stephan, "Die Volksbildung und der Rundfunk," *Volkskunst* 14 (1926): 97. See also Bauer, *Kirchliche Rundfunkarbeit 1924–1939*, pp. 9, 43; and Bernhard Marschall, "Frühjahrstagung," *Volkskunst* 14 (1926): 324.

112. See K. Th. Haanen, "Rundfunk und Religion," in "Strandgut," *Germania*, April 3, 1926, Abendausgabe, Das neue Ufer; Heinz Monzel, "Der Rundfunk und die Katholiken," *Stimmen der Zeit* 120 (November 1930): 129; Josef Vögele, *Der Rundfunk und wir Katholiken!* (Stuttgart: Schwabenverlag, 1929), p. 5; Alex Drenker, "Rundfunk und Volksbildung," *Volkskunst* 16 (June 1928): 181; and Leo Schwering, "Um den Rundfunk," *Germania*, November 17, 1928, Abendausgabe.

113. See Bernhard Marschall, "Frühjahrstagung," pp. 319–24; and K. J. M. Nielen, "Zum Bildungswert des Rundfunks," *Volkstum und Volksbildung* 4 (1932): 113. Bauer, *Kirchliche Rundfunkarbeit 1924–1939*, disagrees strongly with this view, arguing that Catholics rejected radio as a means of adult education (pp. 28–30).

114. See Bernhard Marschall, "Die Weltbedeutung des Rundfunks," in Ernst and Marschall, *Film und Rundfunk*, p. 288; Heinz Monzel, "Referat," in Ernst and Marschall, *Film und Rundfunk*, pp. 348–50; J. H., "Wie stehen wir Katholiken zum Rundfunk?" *Bücherwelt* 28 (1931): 367; and Marschall, "Frühjahrstagung," p. 322.

115. Berten, "Die Schallplatte in der Musikpflege," p. 78. See also Bernhard Marschall, "Katholische Rundfunkarbeit," *Volkstum und Volksbildung* 2 (1930): 172; B[ernhard] M[arschall], "Rundfunkarbeit," *Volkstum und Volksbildung* 3 (1931): 187; P. J. Kreuzberg, "Rundfunk und ländliche Volksbildung," *Volkstum und Volksbildung* 4 (1932): 90; and Vögele, *Der Rundfunk und wir Katholiken!* p. 24.

116. See Bauer, *Kirchliche Rundfunkarbeit 1924–1939*, pp. 9, 60; and "Protokoll der Fuldaer Bischofskonferenz vom 10. bis 12. August 1926," WAA, I A 25b 35.

117. Erich Przywara, S.J. (1889–1972), theologian and philosopher; associated for many years with *Stimmen der Zeit*.

118. Anton Ernst, Graf Neipperg (1883–1947).

119. See Bauer, *Kirchliche Rundfunkarbeit 1924–1939*, pp. 14, 59, 77; "Katholische Morgenfeiern im Westdeutschen Rundfunk, 1928," *Mitteilungen des Zentralbildungsausschusses*, in *Volkskunst* 16 (March 1928): 95; and Rundfunkarbeitsgemeinschaft der deutschen Katholiken, Sendebezirk Frankfurt am Main, "Bericht des Jahres 1931," FBG, 210–04.

120. See "Anlage 1: Richtlinien für die Mitarbeit der Katholiken am Rundfunk auf Grund der Besprechung vom 3.2.1926 im ZBA" and "Anlage 4: Rundfunk und Kirche," in Bauer, *Kirchliche Rundfunkarbeit 1924–1939*, p. 127.

121. See Bauer, *Kirchliche Rundfunkarbeit 1924–1939,* pp. 33–39; and Marschall, "Katholische Rundfunkarbeit," pp. 170–75.

122. See Rundfunk, Ältere Akten (1927–1933), RDA, G 1.1 D 2.5a.

123. See B[ernhard] M[arschall], "Rundfunk-Hörgemeinden," *Volkstum und Volksbildung* 3 (1931): 245–46; L[udwig] Neundörfer, "Der Rundfunk als Hilfe in den Vereinen," *Volkstum und Volksbildung* 2 (1930): 321–24; and J. H., "Wie stehen wir Katholiken zum Rundfunk," p. 367.

124. See Ernst Hardt, general director of Westdeutscher Rundfunk to Bernhard Marschall, November 28, 1928, MDD, R X/9.

125. Hönig, "Das gute Buch," p. 154.

126. Arnold Ulitz (1888–1971), German novelist.

127. Arnold Ulitz, *Das Testament* (1924), quoted in Schäfer, "Lesertypen," p. 119.

128. Eugène Louis Ernest Julien (1856–1930), bishop of Arras 1917.

129. Julien, quoted in Kr., "Kirche und Film"; F. Muckermann, *Im Kampf zwischen zwei Epochen,* p. 299; episcopal ordinary to Dean Beickert, April 20, 1931, MDD, F XXVI; Lentz, "Film, Kunst, und Zivilisation," p. 598.

9. STRUGGLING WITH THE OBJECTIONABLE: OPPOSITION AND CENSORSHIP

1. Andreas Eberharter, "Die kirchliche Bücherzensur," *Pastor Bonus* 39 (July 1928): 268. At a 1910 meeting of the Bonn branch of a morality group, a school inspector deplored the spread of *Vielschreiberei* (excessive writing), presumably a companion to the *Vielleserei* (excessive reading) of which librarians complained. See "Aus unseren Vereinen: Bonn," *Volkswart* 3 (April 1910): 58.

2. See Mausbach, "Der Kampf gegen die moderne Sittenlosigkeit—eine Kulturaufgabe des deutschen Volkes," p. 295; and "Hirtenschreiben der Bischofskonferenz, 12. August 1908," in Gatz, *Akten der Fuldaer Bischofskonferenz,* p. 121.

3. Hermann Roeren (1844–1920), lawyer, politician, and Center Party member of the Reichstag from 1893.

4. Hermann Roeren, *Die öffentliche Unsittlichkeit und ihre Bekämpfung* (Cologne: J. P. Bachem [1903]), pp. 3–4; also *Ist die Gesundheit unseres Volkes bedroht?* (Volksverein, n.d.). See Gertrude Himmelfarb, *The De-moralization of Society: From Victorian Virtues to Modern Values* (New York: Alfred A. Knopf, 1995) for a discussion of perceptions of morality in England and the United States. The "epidemic" was not a figment of the overheated imagination of the bishops. They may have focused on the incidence of syphilis, but the historian R. J. V. Lenman considers that the social disorder, acute housing shortage, and apparent increase in crime and vice that characterized Germany's large cities "gave genuine cause for alarm." His language is more judicious, but his judgment is the same. "Art, Society, and the Law in Wilhelmine Germany: the Lex Heinze," *Oxford German Studies* 8 (1973/1974): 89. See also "Hirtenschreiben der Bischofskonferenz, 12. August 1908," p. 121; and Eberhard, "Sittliche und unsittliche Kunst," p. 177.

5. Albert, Graf von Oberndorff (1870–1963), German diplomat and member of the old aristocracy of the Upper Palatinate.

6. Oberndorff, "Der sittliche Niedergang des deutschen Volkes und die Aufgabe der Katholiken," pp. 145–50.

7. See Loek Halman, "Is There a Moral Decline? A Cross-National Inquiry into Morality in Contemporary Society," *International Social Science Journal* 47 (1995): 419; Anton Rath, "Wo bleibt die sittliche Erneuerung der deutschen Bühnen?" *Volkswart* 12 (January 1919): 5; Volkswartbund to Bishop Ludwig Maria Hugo, November 7, 1930, MDD, Generalakten, U IV; Schwaer, "Im Dienste der öffentlichen Sittlichkeit," reprint from *Paulus* 8 [1930?]: 3; *Um Sitte und Sittlichkeit: Ein Kommentar zu den katholischen Leitsätzen und Weisungen zu verschiedenen modernen Sittlichkeitsfragen* (Düsseldorf: Verlag der katholischen Schulorganisation, 1926); and "Generalversammlung des Cölner Männer-Vereins z. B. d. ö. Unsittlichkeit am 10. März 1910," *Volkswart* 3 (May 1910): 76. *Um Sitte und Sittlichkeit* included Dr. Magnus Hirschfeld, a Jewish physician who studied human sexuality, in the middle of a list of intolerable trends. The hostility to Hirschfeld can be attributed to his advocacy of a positive attitude to sex, an interest in homosexuality, and his Jewish origins.

8. Thamerus, "Zensurloses Theater," p. 467.

9. See Wolfgang Hütt, ed., *Hintergrund: Mit den Unzüchtigkeits- und Gotteslästerungsparagraphen des Strafgesetzbuches gegen Kunst und Künstler, 1900–1933* (Berlin: Henschelverlag, 1990), p. 10; Kneip, "Katholiken und Literatur," p. 999; "Der Niedergang der deutschen Sittlichkeit," *Allgemeine Rundschau* 5 (1908): 631–33; Bott, dean of Johannesberg to episcopal vicariate, October 26, 1917, FBG, 210–07, Fasz. 1; Borromäus Verein, *Der Borromäusverein und die Not der Zeit* pp. 3–4; Weisweiler, "Gedanken über musikalische Volkserziehung," p. 398; Father Bermoser to episcopal vicariate, January 8, 1926, FBG, 210–07; Dr. Müller, Verein zur Bekämpfung des Schundfilms, to the bishop, February 26, 1920, RDA, G 1.1 D2.4a; and "Das Ergebnis der Kinobesuche . . ." p. 34.

10. Klaus Petersen's definitive study of censorship in the Weimar period, *Zensur in der Weimarer Republik* (Stuttgart, Weimar: Verlag J. B. Metzler, 1995), covers all media and has an excellent bibliography. It has little on art or music, but music was not a popular target of public opposition. The censorship of art is treated in Hütt, *Hintergrund*, and as part of the larger picture in Lenman, *Artists and Society in Germany, 1850–1914*. There is nothing comparable to Petersen for the imperial period, but important contributions include Gary D. Stark, "Pornography, Society, and the Law in Imperial Germany," *Central European History* 14 (September 1981): 200–229; Gary D. Stark, "The Censorship of Literary Naturalism, 1885–1895: Prussia and Saxony," *Central European History* 18 (September/December 1985): 326–43; *Reallexikon der deutschen Literaturgeschichte*, 2nd ed. (Berlin: W. de Gruyter, 1984), vol. 4, ed. Klaus Kanzog and Achim Masser, s.v. "Zensur, literarische," by Klaus Kanzog; Dieter Breuer, *Geschichte der literarischen Zensur in Deutschland* (Heidelberg, 1982); Lenman, "Art, Society, and the Law in Wilhelmine Germany," pp. 86–113; and Gary D. Stark, "Cinema, Society, and the State: Policing the Film Industry in Imperial Germany," in Gary D. Stark and Bede Karl Lackner, eds., *Essays on Culture and Society in Modern Germany* (College Station, Tex.: published for the University of Texas at Arlington by Texas A&M University Press, 1982).

11. See Stark, "Pornography, Society, and the Law in Imperial Germany," pp. 213, 222–26.

12. Theobald von Bethmann-Hollweg (1856–1921), chancellor of the German Reich from 1909 to 1917.

13. See Hütt, *Hintergrund*, pp. 25–32.

14. See Lenman, "Art, Society, and the Law in Wilhelmine Germany," pp. 86–113.

15. The Eichstätt diocesan conference of the Preßverein pronounced: "There are gates into our souls that are broader and more accessible than any other, and through these gates enter death as well as life. In various guises, in captivating colors and forms, as beauty and gleaming gold, death pushes through these gates. But in no form is it so frightful as when it enters in ostentatious words and intoxicating sentences, proceeding via the printed page. It is a whole army, its name is legion. Each of these small black printed pieces is a soldier in its service. But even grace knows that these small black fighters can be put to its service. How often grace speaks in the soul, while the eyes skim, reading the lines! What soul-winning and soul-bewitching, soul-strengthening and soul-destroying strength reading possesses!" ("Die Diözesankonferenz des Preßvereins," *Eichstätter Volks-Zeitung*, June 9, 1914, RBZ, OA 1773). See also *Über die Verbreitung guter Schriften* (Mönchengladbach: Volksvereins-Verlag, 1913), p. 1; and *Bekämpfung der Schundliteratur mit einer Zusammenstellung der bisher getroffenen Massnahmen*, Flugschriften der Zentralstelle für Volkswohlfahrt 5 (Berlin: Carl Heymann, 1911), p. 19.

16. See Calmes, "Schund und Schmutz in ihren vielfachen Erscheinungsweisen," *Volkswart* 21 (August 1928): 113.

17. See Josef Zimmermann, "Das Gesetz gegen Schund- und Schmutzschriften," *Die Bücherwelt* 25 (1928): 31–32; Johannes Braun, "Unsere Stellung zu den modernen Literatur," *Die Bücherwelt* 17 (July 1920): 144; and J. Popp, "Kunst und Moral," *Volkswart* 6 (November 1913): 161.

18. See Margaret F. Stieg, "The 1926 German Law to Protect Youth against Trash and Dirt: Moral Protectionism in a Democracy," *Central European History* 23 (March 1990): 26–33; Detlev Peukert, "Der Schund- und Schmutzkampf als 'Sozialpolitik der Seele,'" in *"Das war ein Vorspiel nur...": Bücherverbrennung Deutschland 1933: Voraussetzungen und Folgen* (Berlin, 1983), p. 52; and Patterson, *The Revolution in German Theatre, 1900–1933*, p. 25.

19. [Albert] Hellwig, "Artikel 118: Meinungsfreiheit, Zensur," in *Die Grundrechte und Grundpflichten der Reichsverfassung*, ed. Hans Carl Nipperdey, vol. 2 (Berlin: Verlag von Reimar Hobbing, 1930), p. 1. See also Petersen, *Zensur in der Weimarer Republik*, pp. 7–8.

20. Martin Schiele (1870–1939), member of the Reichstag from 1914 to 1930; leader of the agrarian wing of the Deutschnationale Volkspartei.

21. See Stieg, "The 1926 German Law to Protect Youth against Trash and Dirt," pp. 33–48.

22. See ibid., p. 49.

23. See Ernst Seeger, "Das Reichslichtspielgesetz in der Rechtsprechung der Filmoberprüfstelle," *Archiv für Urheber-, Film- und Theaterrecht* 1 (1928): 58; J. Halder, Volkswartbund, to episcopal ordinary, March 22, 1929, "Bericht über die Tagung betreffend Schund- und Schmutzkampf am 12. und 13. März 1929 in Berlin," p. 5, RDA G 1.1. F 2.4d; "Bericht über die Zentralarbeitsausschusses der deutschen Katholiken zur Förderung der öffentlichen Sittlichkeit am 13. März 1929 in Berlin," p. 23, BBV; J. Schäfer, "Unsere Ortsgruppen im Kampfe gegen Schund und Schmutz im Rahmen des neuen Gesetzes," *Volkswart* 21 (September 1928): 130; and Calmes, "Schund und Schmutz in ihren vielfachen Erscheinungsweisen," p. 113.

24. "Das Ergebnis der Kinobesuche...," p. 33. See also Franz Kloidt, "Verhindert die Filmzensur den künstlerischen Film?" *Volkswart* 25 (August 1932): 115.

25. See episcopal ordinary to Dean Beickert, April 20, 1931, MDD, Generalakten, F XXVI; and Karl Wolf, "Licht und Schatten des modernen Films," *Volkswart* 25 (July 1932): 99.

26. Klein-Ehrenwalten, "Wege des Films," p. 5. See also Johannes Hambröer, "Vom freien Kino," *Allgemeine Rundschau* 16 (1919): 774.

27. Hambröer, "Vom freien Kino," p. 774.

28. Petersen, *Zensur in der Weimarer Republik,* pp. 7–8.

29. See Germany, *Lichtspielgesetz vom 12. Mai 1920,* ed. Albert Hellwig (Berlin: Stilke, 1921); and R. A. Keller, "Schutz der Jugend vor den Schäden des Kinos," *Germania,* May 27, 1928, Morgenausgabe.

30. Wedding is a section of Berlin, Giesing a suburb of Munich, and Hernals a section of Vienna. The Gedächtniskirche, Frauenkirche, and Stephanskirche are the principal churches and/or cathedrals of the same cities. See Robert Volz, "Uns fehlt das gute Kino!" *Volkswart* 19 (September 1926): 133; Petersen, *Zensur in der Weimarer Republik,* pp. 254–55; "Der Entwurf zur Abänderung des Lichtspielgesetzes," *Volkswart* 18 (November 1925): 162; "Reform des Lichtspielgesetzes," *Volkswart* 18 (March 1925): 39; and "Zur Reform im Lichtspielwesen," *Volkswart* 19 (October 1926): 146.

31. See "Der Entwurf zur Abänderung des Reichslichtspielgesetzes," pp. 33; Redmond A. Burke, *What is the Index?* (Milwaukee, Wisc.: Bruce Publishing, 1952); and Harold C. Gardiner, *Catholic Viewpoint on Censorship* (Garden City, N.Y.: Hanover House, 1958). Although writing after the period, Gardiner and Burke summarize what had emerged as the standard Catholic positions.

32. There is a voluminous literature on the evolution of the family in western Europe. Stark, "Pornography, Society, and the Law in Imperial Germany," p. 202, discusses these issues briefly and gives an excellent bibliography of important writing on the subject in his notes. Nipperdey offers an extensive treatment that is specifically German in *Arbeitswelt und Bürgergeist,* pp. 43–124. See also Seeger, "Das Reichslichtspielgesetz in der Rechtsprechung der Filmoberprüfstelle," pp. 259–60.

33. See Ellen Ammann, "Schutz der Jugend!" *Allgemeine Rundschau* 3 (1906): 528; Calmes, "Aus dem Volkswartbunde," *Volkswart* 21 (March 1928): 40; "Die Kampf gegen die moderne Sittenlosigkeit . . ." *Volkswart* 5 (September 1912): 129–36; Ernst Lennartz, "Der Kölner Katholikentag 1928 und die Sittlichkeitsfrage," *Volkswart* 21 (May 1928): 66; J. Fröhlings, "Zum Geleit," *Volkswart* 25 (January 1932): 3; "Gedanken zur Filmzensur," *Volkswart* 20 (August 1927): 115; and Cato, "Ob Meisterwerke auch unzüchtig wirken," *Volkswart* 12 (May 1919): 65–69.

34. *Um Sitte und Sittlichkeit,* p. 92. See also Renner, "Kunst," p. 547; and Kloidt, "Verhindert die Filmzensur den künstlerischen Film?" p. 115.

35. See Wolf, "Licht und Schatten des modernen Films," pp. 99–101; Zimmermann, "Das Gesetz gegen Schund- und Schmutzschriften," p. 31; "Zynismus," *Volkswart* 18 (November 1925): 171–72; and Joh[annes] Ude, "Der Kaufmannstand als Kulturträger vor dem Richterstuhl des Sittengesetzes," *Volkswart* 9 (January 1916): 7–10.

36. Mausbach, "Der Kampf gegen die moderne Sittenlosigkeit," p. 295. Assistant Bishop Stockums expressed the same view even more emphatically at the rally of the Volkswartbund at the 1932 Katholikentag. Only the Catholic Church represented true Christianity and not an iota, not a dot of the moral laws that came from Christ himself were to be changed. See "Kundgebung des Volkswartbundes auf dem Katholikentage in Essen," *Volkswart* 25 (October 1932): 148.

37. Georg Schreiber (1882–1963), priest, Catholic theologian, professor of church history from 1917 and rector from 1945 to 1950 at the University of Münster; member of the Reichstag (1920–1933); politically prominent for his interest in culture.

38. See Petersen, *Zensur in der Weimarer Republik,* pp. 17–21; Gardiner, *Catholic Viewpoint on Censorship;* H. B.-B., "Die Lektüre der ewig Unmündigen: Ein paar Beispiele von Schund und Schmutz, aber jenseits der Gesetzes," *Bücherwelt* 25 (November/December 1928): 450; and Karl Möhlig, "Aus der Bühnenwelt: Der Streit um den 'Fröhlichen Weinberg,'" *Bücherwelt* 23 (July 1926): 336.

39. See J. F[röhlings], "Was will der Volkswartbund?" *Volkswart* 22 (August 1929): 113; Stark, "Pornography, Society, and the Law in Imperial Germany," pp. 212–13, Petersen, *Zensur in der Weimarer Republik,* p. 277; F. S. B., "A Critic of Catholic Critics," *America,* August 21, 1909, p. 513; and A. A., "Kulturfeindlichkeit," *Historisch-politische Blätter für das katholische Deutschland* 138 (1906): 251.

40. See Ludwig Kemmer, "Fort mit dem Schmutz!" *Allgemeine Rundschau* 1 (1904): 440.

41. Helene Weber (1881–1952), social worker; leader of Catholic women's movement; politician and member of the Reichstag from 1924 to 1933, cofounder of the CDU (1945).

42. The equivalent of "banned in Boston" was as effective a promotional device in Germany as it was in the United States. A refusal to permit Josephine Baker to perform in Munich led to the sale of 360 copies of her autobiography within two days at one Munich bookstore alone. See Consilium a vigilantia, Schreiben Nr. 28, April 18, 1929, "Tagung des Reichsausschusses zur Bekämpfung von Schmutz und Schund," MDD, Abteilung 55.

43. See "Zum Schund- und Schmutzgesetz," *Germania,* November 20, 1926; and "Zitierung des katholischen Dichters Leo Weismantel in der Rede des Abgeordneten Edwin Hoernle (KPD) . . ." in Hütt, *Hintergrund,* p. 173.

44. An article by Raimund Eberhard in *Volkswart,* the journal of the Verband der Männervereine zur Bekämpfung der öffentlichen Unsittlichkeit, an organization dominated by Catholics, does an excellent job of raising questions and does so in a sophisticated way. A prize offered in connection with the trial of Georg Groß for "Ecce Homo" for an essay on what is immoral art stimulated much thinking on the subject at the time. See Eberhard, "Sittliche und unsittliche Kunst," pp. 177–80.

45. See Mumbauer, "Katholische Kirche und moderne Kunst," p. 12.

46. Kneip, "Katholiken und Literatur." See also B.-B., "Die Lektüre der ewig Unmündigen," p. 450.

47. There is interesting discussion of the interdiction of *Il Santo* and about the role of the *Index librorum prohibitorum* in the 1906 and 1907 letters of Johannes Mumbauer and Karl Muth held in the Karl Muth archives at the MBS, Ana 390. II. B. See also "[Lektüre]," *Kirchliche Anzeiger für die Diözese Fulda* 20, May 6, 1897, and "Das Kinematographenwesen," *Kirchliche Anzeiger für die Diözese Fulda* 103, November 25, 1913, FBG 203–01, Fasz. 1, Büchereiwesen: "Borromäus-Verein" 1822–1926; and *Encyclopedia of Library and Information Science,* ed. Allen Kent, Harold Lancour, and Jay E. Daily (New York: Marcel Dekker, 1974), s.v. "Index Librorum Prohibitorum," by Francis J. Witty.

48. See "Anweisung an den Hochwürdigen Klerus über den Kampf gegen Schmutz und Schund," *Kirchlicher Anzeiger für die Erzdiözese Köln* 67 (December 15, 1927): 115–18.

49. Ibid., p. 118.

50. See [Joseph] Froberger, "Gute und schlechte Romane," *Bücherwelt* 12 (March 1915): 118; Otto Hipp, "Schundliteratur und Jugendkriminalität," *Allgemeine Rundschau* 5 (December 12, 1908): 854; Zimmermann, "Das Gesetz gegen Schmutz- und Schundliteratur," p. 35; Schwaer, "Im Dienste der öffentlichen Sittlichkeit," pp. 12–13; Katholischer

Preßverein für Bayern, *Jahres-Bericht pro 1908/09;* Kölner Bezirks-Katholikentag 1928, draft of report, CHAE, Gen 23.30.1.

51. See Rottenburg episcopal ordinary, "Schund- und Schmutzbekämpfung," August 18, 1931, RDA, G.1.1 F 2.4d; "Anweisung an den Hochwürdigen Klerus über den Kampf gegen Schmutz und Schund"; Bernhard Marschall to Cardinal Archbishop Karl Joseph Schulte, July 23, 1927, CHAE, Gen. 23.54.1; Zentralbildungsausschuß to the minister of the interior, January 12, 1927, CHAE, Gen. 23.30.1; minister of the interior to Zentralbildungsausschuß der Katholischen Verbände Deutschlands, January 18, 1927, CHAE, Gen. 23.30.1; and Zentralbildungsausschuß to the minister of the interior, February 1, 1927, CHAE, Gen. 23.30.1.

52. See Father Kohler to episcopal ordinary, May 24, 1921, Schwabenverlag to episcopal ordinary, June 12, 1930, and Nickolaus Ehlen to episcopal ordinary, June 5, 1921, RDA, G 1.1 D 2.4a. *Das Mädchen aus der Ackerstraße* was a film about big-city life.

53. See Michael Meyer, *Theaterzensur in München, 1900–1918: Geschichte und Entwicklung der polizeilichen Zensur und des Theaterzensurenbeirates unter besonderer Berücksichtigung Frank Wedekinds,* Miscellanea Bavarica Monacensia 111 (Munich: Neue Schriftenreihe des Stadtarchivs München, 1982), pp. 39–44; and Mausbach, "Der Kampf gegen die moderne Sittenlosigkeit," p. 286. Morality groups have attracted considerable scholarly interest in recent decades, especially in Britain and the United States. Stark, "Pornography, Society, and the Law in Imperial Germany," p. 204, includes a brief bibliography. Two particularly useful books published since Stark's article appeared are G. I. T. Machin, *Churches and Social Issues in Twentieth-Century Britain* (Oxford: Clarendon Press, 1998), and Alan Hunt, *Governing Morals: A Social History of Moral Regulation* (Cambridge: Cambridge University Press, 1999).

54. Armin Kausen (1855–1913), German editor and publicist.

55. Hans Thoma (1839–1924), German painter and lithographer; known for his landscapes, genre scenes, and religious and allegorical works.

56. Ernst Müller-Meiningen (1866–1944), politician; leader of the Freisinnige Volkspartei (Freethinking People's Party); member of the Reichstag from 1898 to 1918.

57. See Lenman, "Art, Society, and the Law in Wilhelmine Germany," p. 90; Meyer, *Theaterzensur in München, 1900–1918,* pp. 39–44, 309–11, 313–16; and F. Weigl, "Wider den Schmutz," *Allgemeine Rundschau* 5 (1908): 136.

58. Josef Pappers (1877–1911), author and editor.

59. See Ernst Lennartz, "Fünfundzwanzig Jahre Volkswartbund," *Volkswart* 25 (January 1932): 5–6; and "Bericht über die 11. März 1907 in Cöln stattgefundene Versammlung der Vertreter der Männervereine zur Bekämpfung der öffentlichen Unsittlichkeit," CHAE, Bestand Marx, vol. 397.

60. [Ernst] Lennartz, "Warum abonnieren und lesen wir den Volkswart? *Volkswart* 18 (January 1925): 2. See also Fröhlings, "Zum Geleit," pp. 3–5.

61. See "Aus unseren Vereinen," *Volkswart* 2 (January 1909): 7–8.

62. See Verband zur Bekämpfung der öffentlichen Unsittlichkeit to Bishop Georg Heinrich Kirstein, July 28, 1920, MDD, Generalakten, U IV: Unsittlichkeit.

63. See Schaefer, "Kundgebung der vereinigten Sittlichkeitsverbände im Rahmen der 70. Generalversammlung der Katholiken Deutschlands in Nürnberg am 28. August 1931," *Volkswart* 24 (October 1931): 151; newspaper clipping, obituary of Ernst Lenartz, CHAE, Bestand 1010, Fasz. 8, p. 199; Ernst Lennartz to the Fulda Conference of Bishops, August 10, 1922, and Ernst Lennartz to Cardinal Archbishop Karl Joseph Schulte, March 12,

1927, CHAE, Gen. 23.30.; and Pius XI, *Mortalium Animos* (*On Religious Unity*), http://www.vatican.va/holy_father/pius_xi/encyclicals.

64. See "Nr. 66, Moderne Sittlichkeitsfragen," *Kirchlicher Anzeiger für die Erzdiözese Köln* 65 (January 20, 1925): 15–18; and "Kölner Bezirks-Katholikentag 1928," CHAE, Gen. 23.30.1.

65. How much change this brought is debatable. Ernst Lennartz did not feel that the previous interconfessional bylaws needed to be revised. See Lennartz to Cardinal Archbishop Karl Joseph Schulte, March 12, 1927, CHAE, Gen. 23.30.

66. See "Aus den Vereinen: Bericht des Volkswartbundes 1932," *Volkswart* 26 (March 1933): 41; and "Vereinbarung zwischen Volkswartbund (Köln) und Borromäusverein (Bonn) zwecks Bekämpfung von Schund und Schmutz in der Literatur," *Volkswart* (May 1928): 74.

67. Michael Calmes (1894–1958).

68. See "Aus den Vereinen: Der Verband zur Bekämpfung der öffentlichen Unsittlichkeit," p. 180; Calmes, "Zur Geschichte und Arbeit unseres Generalsekretariates!" *Volkswart* 25 (January 1932): 6–7; "Aus den Vereinen: Rechenschaftsbericht des Vorstandes für das Jahr 1929," *Volkswart* 23 (July 1930): 103–4; "Aus der Arbeit des Volkswartbundes," *Volkswart* 24 (February 1931): 17–19; and Volkswartbund, "Rechenschaftsbericht des Verbandsvorstandes für das Geschäftsjahr 1927," CHAE, Gen. 23.30.

69. See Verband zur Bekämpfung der öffentlichen Unsittlichkeit to Bishop Georg Heinrich Kirstein, July 28, 1920, and Volkswartbund to Bishop Ludwig Maria Hugo, November 7, 1930, MDD, Generalakten, U IV: Unsittlichkeit and "Die Arbeiten und Erfolge des Volkswartbundes seit 1927," December 1930, CHAE, Gen. 23.30.2.

70. "10 Gebote für Schundkämpfer," stamped February [9?], 1932, CHAE, Gen. 23.30.2. See also "J. Schaefer, "Unsere Ortsgruppen im Kampf gegen Schund und Schmutz im Rahmen des neuen Gesetzes," CHAE, Gen. 23.30.1.

71. See episcopal ordinary to Father Becker, April 24, 1928, MDD, Abteilung 81/82-20-3; Stanislaus Woywood, *A Practical Commentary on the Code of Canon Law,* rev. Callistus Smith (New York: Joseph F. Wagner; London: Herder, 1962), vol. 2, p. 169; and Consilium a vigilantia der Erzdiözese München und Freising, Rundschreiben Nr. 95, August 12, 1931, and Rundschreiben Nr. 64, November 25, 1930, MDD, Abteilung 55.

72. See "Bericht, Tagung des Zentralarbeitsausschusses der deutschen Katho-Förderung der öffentlichen Sittlichkeit am 13. Mär[z] in Berlin," CHAE, Gen. 23.30.1; Wienke to Cardinal Adolf Bertram, August 18, 1928, WAA, A 25 k 18; and "Konferenz des Zentralarbeitsausschusses der deutschen Katholiken zur Förderung der öffentlichen Sittlichkeit," March 13, 1929, RDA, G 1.1, F 2.4 d.

73. See [Karl] Walterbach, "Katholiken und Film," *Augustinus-Blatt* 26 (May/June 1922): 19; and Karl Leibig, "Die Filmzensur in Deutschland in Gesetzgebung und Praxis," *Allgemeine Rundschau* 26 (1929): 655–56.

74. "Aus den Vereinen: Rechenschaftsbericht des Vorstandes für das Jahr 1929, p. 104; "Rechenschaftsbericht des Vorstandes für die Jahre 1930–1932," *Volkswart* 25 (May 1932): 70; "Aus den Vereinen: Bericht des Volkswartbundes 1932," pp. 41–42; and Lennartz, "Fünfundzwanzig Jahre Volkswartbund," p. 6.

75. See MBS, Ana 390 I. F. 17; and F. S. B., "A Critic of Catholic Critics."

76. See Calmes, "Stand der Schund- und Schmutzbekämpfung in Deutschland und Oesterreich," *Schönere Zukunft* 7 (September 25, 1932); and Volkswartbund to Bishop Lud-

wig Maria Hugo, November 7, 1930, MDD, U IV 9; and Father Becker to episcopal ordinary, April 4, 1929.

77. See Calmes, "Neue Wege der Selbsthilfe im Schundkampf!" *Volkswart* 22 (January 1929): 1–2.

78. Paul Regner, "Der Kampf wider das Gesetz gegen Schund und Schmutz," *Allgemeine Rundschau* 23 (December 4, 1926): 776.

79. Jose[ph] Froberger, *Weltanschauung und Literatur* (Trier: Paulinus-Druckerei), p. 27.

80. A 1926 article that discussed the use of censorship to protect religious sensitivities raised the extremely important question of which religion's sensitivities this meant. The law protected all religious groups in Germany, but not the representatives of religious-philosophical viewpoints. The author specifically mentioned both Islam and Buddhism. See R. V., "Aus der Filmzensur: Welche Filme werden verboten?" *Volkswart* 19 (August 1926): 121.

10. CONCLUSION

1. F. Muckermann, *Im Kampf zwischen zwei Epochen,* p. 286; Johannes Mumbauer, "Die katholische 'Drehkrankheit,'" *Literarischer Handweiser* 25 (1928/1929): 66.

2. Rost, *Katholische Familienkultur,* p. 6.

3. See Muth, *Die literarischen Aufgaben der deutschen Katholiken,* pp. 61–68; Falkenberg, *Wir Katholiken und die deutsche Literatur,* p. 51; and Hürten, *Deutsche Katholiken, 1918–1945,* p. 73.

4. Blackbourn, *The Long Nineteenth Century,* p. 273, explains that historians use the term "urbanization" to mean an increased familiarity with urban material goods, consumption patterns, and behavior in rural areas, as well as to mean the growth of towns in terms of economic history.

5. See Eksteins, *Rites of Spring,* pp. 256–60; and Johannes Mumbauer, "Der wertvollsten Bücher aus der katholischen Literatur der letzten Jahre," *Literarischer Handweiser* 25 (1928/1929): 100.

6. Katholische Vereinsbildungsarbeit im Bühnenvolksbund, quoting Friedrich Muckerman in *Germania,* March 31, 1927, RBZ, OA 2105. See also Schäfer, "Der katholische Dichter in unserer Zeit," p. 83.

7. Schäfer, "Der katholische Dichter in unserer Zeit," p. 83.

8. Pius XII, "The Catholic Church and History," *The Tablet,* September 24, 1955, p. 294.

9. See Lynn Abrams, "From Control to Commercialization: The Triumph of Mass Entertainment in Germany 1900–1925?" *German History* 8 (1990): 278–93.

10. I owe this appreciation to John B. Thompson, *Ideology and Modern Culture: Critical Social Theory in the Era of Mass Communication* (Stanford, Calif.: Stanford University Press, 1990).

11. Quoted in Wenden, *The Birth of the Movies,* p. 80.

12. Heinrich Böll (1917–1985), German novelist, short-story writer, and playwright.

bibliography

ARCHIVES

The following archives and organizations were visited, and usually an assortment of collections relating to the activities of different cultural organizations was used. Because they were so numerous, individual collections are not listed. The most useful were the diocesan archives of Cologne, Fulda, Mainz, Regensburg, Rottenburg, and Wrocław, the Bundesarchiv, and the records of the Borromäus Verein.

Bonn. Borromäus Verein (BBV)
Bonn. Stadtarchiv (BSA)
Coblenz. Bundesarchiv (CBA)
Cologne. Historisches Archiv des Erzbistums (CHAE)
Fulda. Bischöfliches Generalvikariat (FBG)
Hamburg. Senat der Freien und Hansestadt Hamburg, Staatsarchiv (HAS)
Mainz. Dom- und Diözesanarchiv (MDD)
Mönchengladbach. Stadtarchiv (MGS)
Munich. Bayerische Staatsbibliothek (MBS)
Passau. Archiv des Bistums (PAB)
Regensburg. Bischöfliches Zentralarchiv (RBZ)
Rottenburg. Diözesanarchiv (RDA)
Speyer. Bischöfliches Ordinariat, Archiv (SBOA)
Vatican City. Archivio segreto vaticano (VASV)
Wrocław. Archiwum Archidecezjalne (WAA)

PRINTED MATERIAL

A., A. "Kulturfeindlichkeit." *Historisch-politische Blätter für das katholische Deutschland* 138 (1906): 249–62.
Abrams, Lynn. "From Control to Commercialization: The Triumph of Mass Entertainment in Germany 1900–1925?" *German History* 8 (1990): 278–93.
———. *Workers' Culture in Imperial Germany: Leisure and Recreation in the Rhineland and Westphalia.* London: Routledge, 1992.
Achtermann, Bernhard. "1845–1920." *Bücherwelt* 17 (August/September 1920): 165–67.

van Acken, I. *Christozentrische Kirchenkunst: Ein Entwurf zum liturgischen Gesamtkunstwerk.* Gladbeck i. W.: A. Theben, 1923.

Adams, Henry. "The Dynamo and the Virgin." In *The Education of Henry Adams,* 379–90. New York: Modern Library, 1931.

Adorno, Theodor W. *The Culture Industry.* London: Routledge, 1991.

"Die Aesthetik Pius X. im Brief an den Gralbund." *Der Gral* 5 (July 15, 1911): 654–61.

Ahle, J. N. *Ueber Mass und Milde in kirchenmusikalischen Dingen.* Regensburg: Alfred Coppenrath, 1901.

Albani, Johannes. "Katholische Dramatiker." *Allgemeine Rundschau* 19 (1922): 499–500.

Almond, Gabriel, and Sidney Verba. *The Civic Culture: Political Attitudes and Democracy in Five Nations.* Newbury Park, Calif.: Sage Publications, 1989.

"Als Kino-Nummer." *Augustinus-Blatt* 26 (May/June 1922): 17.

Altenloh, Emilie. "Zur Soziologie des Kino." In *Film und Gesellschaft in Deutschland: Dokumente und Materialien,* edited by Wilfried von Bredow and Rolf Zurek, 34–53. Hamburg: Hoffmann und Campe, 1975.

Altermatt, Urs. "Katholische Subgesellschaft: Thesen zum Konzept der 'Katholischen Subgesellschaft' am Beispiel des Schweizer Katholizismus." In Gabriel and Kaufmann, *Zur Soziologie des Katholizismus,* 145–65.

———. "Katholizismus: Antimodernismus mit modernen Mitteln." In *Moderne als Problem des Katholizismus,* edited by Urs Altermatt, Heinz Hürten, and Nikolaus Lobkowicz, 145–60. Eichstätter Beiträge, vol. 28, Abteilung Philosophie und Theologie 6. Regensburg: Verlag Friedrich Pustet, 1995.

Amery, Carl. *Die Kapitulation: oder Deutscher Katholizismus heute.* Reinbek bei Hamburg: Rowohlt, 1963.

Ammann, Ellen. "Schutz der Jugend!" *Allgemeine Rundschau* 3 (1906): 528.

Anderson, Margaret Lavinia. "Afterword: Living Apart and Together in Germany." In Smith, *Protestants, Catholics and Jews in Germany, 1800–1914,* 319–32.

———. "Interdenominationalism, Clericalism, Pluralism: The Zentrumsstreit and the Dilemma of Catholicism in Wilhelmine Germany." *Central European History* 21 (December 1988): 350–78.

———. "The Kulturkampf and the Course of German History." *Central European History* 19 (March 1986): 82–115.

———. "The Limits of Secularization: On the Problem of the Catholic Revival in Germany." *Historical Journal* 38 (1995): 647–70.

———. "Piety and Politics: Recent Work on German Catholicism." *Journal of Modern History* 63 (December 1991): 681–716.

———. *Windthorst: A Political Biography.* Oxford: Clarendon Press, 1981.

Andrea, Alfred J. "Mentalities in History." *The Historian* 53 (Spring 1991): 605–8.

"Antworten und Mitteilungen der Redaktion: In eigener Sache." *Der Gral* 4 (November 15, 1909): 132–35.

"Anweisung an den Hochwürdigen Klerus über den Kampf gegen Schmutz und Schund." *Kirchlicher Anzeiger für die Erzdiözese Köln* 67 (December 15, 1927): 115–18.

Appelshaeuser, Hans. "Rundschau: Der Kinematograph und seine Aufgaben." *Bild und Film* 1 (1912): 47–49.

Arbeitskreis für kirchliche Zeitgeschichte (AKKZG), Münster. "Katholiken zwischen Tradition und Moderne: Das katholische Milieu als Forschungsaufgabe." *Westfälische Forschungen* 43 (1993): 588–654.

Arnason, H. H. *History of Modern Art.* 3rd ed. Revised by Daniel Wheeler. New York: Harry N. Abrams, 1986.

Arnold, Matthew. *The Complete Prose Works of Matthew Arnold.* Edited by R. H. Super. Vol. 9, *English Literature and Irish Politics.* Ann Arbor, Mich.: University of Michigan Press, 1973.

Aron, Raymond. *Progress and Disillusion: The Dialectics of Modern Society.* New York: Praeger, 1968.

Aschoff, Hans-Georg. *Um des Menschen Willen: Die Entwicklung der katholischen Kirche in der Region Hannover.* Hildesheim: Bernward, 1983.

Asselmann, Andrea. "Volksbüchereiarbeit im Spiegel der Zeitschrift 'Borromäusblätter/ Bücherwelt' (1903–1933)." *Bibliothek: Forschung und Praxis* 19 (1995): 322–61.

Aubert, Roger. *The Church in a Secularised Society.* Christian Centuries: A New History of the Catholic Church, vol. 5. New York: Paulist Press, 1978.

———. "Internal Catholic Controversies in Connection with Liberalism." In Aubert et al., *The Church in the Age of Liberalism,* 283–403.

———. "The Modernist Crisis: Reform Catholicism in Germany." In Aubert et al., *The Church in the Industrial Age,* 420–30.

Aubert, Roger, et al., eds. *The Church in the Industrial Age.* Translated by Margit Resch. History of the Church, edited by Hubert Jedin and John Dolan, vol. 9. New York: Crossroad, 1980.

———. *The Church in the Age of Liberalism.* Translated by Peter Becker. History of the Church, edited by Hubert Jedin and John Dolan, vol. 8. New York: Crossroad, 1980.

Auer, Joseph. "Die 16. Generalversammlung des Allgemeinen Cäcilienvereines." *Kirchenmusikalisches Jahrbuch* 16 (1901): 119–28.

"Auf christlichem Boden stehende Filmunternehmungen." *Augustinus-Blatt* 26 (May/June 1922): 21–24.

"Aufgaben und Ziele der kathol[ischen] Literaturbewegung." *Literarische Warte* 2 (1901): 421–24.

"Aufruf!" *Volkswart* 2, Organisationsnummer (March 1909): 1–2.

"Ausbreitung der Bühnen-Volksbundarbeit." *Mitteilungen des Bühnen-Volksbundes* 2 (April/May 1921). In *Volkskunst* 9 (April/May 1921): 187–92.

"Aus den Vereinen: Bericht des Volkswartbundes 1932." *Volkswart* 26 (March 1933): 41–42.

"Aus den Vereinen: Rechenschaftsbericht des Vorstandes für das Jahr 1929." *Volkswart* 23 (July 1930): 103–4

"Aus den Vereinen: Der Verband zur Bekämpfung der öffentlichen Unsittlichkeit." *Volkswart* 19 (December 1926): 180.

Aus der Arbeit des Bühnenvolksbund: Theaterpflege im christlich-deutschen Volksgeist. Bericht über die Grundversammlung am 8. und 9. April 1919 in Frankfurt am Main. Edited by the Ausschuß des Bühnenvolksbund. N.p., n.d.

"Aus der Arbeit des Volkswartbundes." *Volkswart* 24 (February 1931): 17–19.

"Aus unseren Vereinen." *Volkswart* 2 (January 1909): 7–8.

"Aus unseren Vereinen." *Volkswart* 5 (May 1912): 74–76.

"Aus unseren Vereinen: Bonn." *Volkswart* 3 (April 1910): 58–59.

B., F. S. "A Critic of Catholic Critics." *America* (August 21, 1909): 513.

B., H. H. "Drei 'Orplid' Hefte." *Germania,* July 21, 1926, Abendausgabe.

B.-B., H. "Die Lektüre der ewig Unmündigen: Ein paar Beispiele von Schund und Schmutz, aber jenseits der Gesetzes." *Bücherwelt* 25 (November/December 1928): 450–53.

Bachem, Jul[ius]. "Wir müssen aus dem Turm heraus!" *Historisch-politische Blätter für das katholische Deutschland* 137 (1906): 503–13.

Bachmann, Heinrich. "Das Gesicht des katholischen Heimatromans: Zu einigen wichtigen Neuerscheinungen." *Germania* (November 30, 1928) Morgenausgabe, Werk und Wert.

———. "Um den deutschen Roman." *Bücherwelt* 27 (May/June 1930): 167–77.

Baldwin, Burt R. "Formal Volunteer Organization Prevalence among Nations." *Voluntary Action Research* (1973): 75–101.

Bamford, Julian, and Richard R. Day. "Extensive Reading: What Is It? Why Bother?" *Language Teacher Online* 21 (1997). http://languehyper.chubu.ac/jb/jalt/pub/tlt/17/may/extensive.html.

Baresel, Alfred. "Zur Lage der deutschen Unterhaltungsmusik." *Musik im Leben* 4 (April 1928): 53–54.

Barkin, Kenneth D. "The Crisis of Modernity, 1887–1902." In Forster-Hahn, *Imagining Modern German Culture: 1889–1910*, 19–35.

Bauer, Clemens. "Carl Muths und des Hochland Weg aus dem Kaiserreich in die Weimarer Republik." *Hochland* 59 (1967): 234–47.

———. *Deutscher Katholizismus: Entwicklungslinien und Profile.* Frankfurt am Main: Josef Knecht, 1965.

Bauer, Georg Laurenz. *Das Wesen der katholischen Liturgie als Grundlage für die kirchl[ichen] Bestimmungen über die Beteiligung der Frauen am Kirchenchor.* Paderborn: Bonifacius-Druckerei, n.d. Reprinted from *Theologie und Glaube* 4 (1916).

Bauer, Günther. *Kirchliche Rundfunkarbeit 1924–1939.* Beiträge zur Geschichte des deutschen Rundfunks, vol. 2. Frankfurt am Main: Josef Knecht, 1966.

Bauer, Marion. *Twentieth Century Music: How It Developed, How to Listen to It.* New ed. New York: G. P. Putnam's Sons, 1947.

Baumeister, Martin. *Parität und katholische Inferiorität.* Paderborn: Ferdinand Schöningh, 1987.

Baumgartner, Alexander. "Die katholische Belletristik und die Moderne. (Zur Beurteilung der drei Veremundus-Schriften)." *Stimmen aus Maria-Laach* 77 (August 1909): 121–41.

———. "Literarische Gegensätze unter den deutschen Katholiken." *Stimmen aus Maria-Laach* 77 (October 1909): 357–72.

———. *Die Stellung der deutschen Katholiken zur neueren Literatur.* Freiburg im Breisgau: Herder, 1910.

Beals, Ralph L. "Resistance and Adaptation to Technological Change: Some Anthropological Views." *Human Factors* 10 (1968): 579–88.

Bechtiger, Meinrad. "Wir Priester und die kirchliche Kunst von heute." *Theologisch-praktische Quartalschrift* 85 (1932): 106–20.

Becker, Matthias. "Von Werk- und Feierstunden: Der Lesezirkel." *Bücherwelt* 26 (January/February 1929): 28–29.

Becker-Jákli, Barbara. *"Fürchtet Gott, ehret den König": Evangelisches Leben im linksrheinischen Köln, 1850–1918.* Cologne: Rheinland-Verlag, 1988.

Beckmann, Christof. "Katholisches Vereinswesen im Ruhrgebiet: Das Beispiel Essen-Borbeck, 1900–1933." Inaugural diss., Westfälisches Wilhelm-Universität, Münster, 1990.

Beenken, Herman. *Das neunzehnte Jahrhundert in der deutschen Kunst.* Munich: Verlag F. Bruckmann, 1944.

Behm, H. "Staatstheater: Hauptmanns 'Weber.'" *Germania,* February 6, 1928, Morgenausgabe.

Behrens, Otto. "Niedergang des Spielfilms." *Germania,* August 12, 1928, Morgenausgabe, Film-Rundschau.

———. "Verlogenheiten der weißen Wand." *Germania,* September 30, 1928, Morgenausgabe, Film-Rundschau.

———. "Vom unsterblichen Kitsch." *Germania,* June 3, 1928, Morgenausgabe.

Bekämpfung der Schundliteratur mit einer Zusammenstellung der bisher getroffenen Massnahmen. Flugschriften der Zentralstelle für Volkswohlfahrt 5. Berlin: Carl Heymann, 1911.

Belting, Hans. *The Germans and Their Art: A Troublesome Relationship.* Translated by Scott Kleager. New Haven, Conn.: Yale University Press, 1998.

Berger, E. "Über Kirchenchor-Disziplin." *Cäcilienvereinsorgan/Musica Sacra* 59 (1929): 282–87.

Berger, H. A. "Der katholische Zeitungsroman." *Düsseldorfer Tageblatt,* August 24, 1927.

"Bericht über die Jahre 1920 und 1921." *Mitteilungen für die Vereine vom hl. Karl Borromäus* 13/14 (August 1922).

Berman, Russell A. "Literary Criticism from Empire to Dictatorship, 1870–1933." In *A History of German Literary Criticism, 1730–1980,* edited by Peter Uwe Hohendahl, translated by Simon Srebrny, 277–357; 463–69. Lincoln: University of Nebraska Press, 1988.

———. "Writing for the Book Industry: The Writer under Organized Capitalism." *New German Critique* 29 (Spring/Summer 1983): 39–56.

Berten, Walter. "Die Schallplatte in der Musikpflege." *Volkstum und Volksbildung* 4 (1932): 73–79.

———. "Ziele und Möglichkeiten der Volksmusikpflege." *Musik im Leben* 4 (September/October 1928): 134–36.

"Beschlüsse: Vereinswesen, Aeußeres, Formalien." In *Verhandlungen der 43. General-Versammlung der Katholiken Deutschlands . . . 1896,* 454–56.

"Beschlüsse der Vertretertagung des 71. Katholikentages zu Essen über 'Gro[ß]tadt und religiöse Kunst.'" *Die christliche Kunst* 29 (1932): 28.

"Bestrebungen zur Hebung der Kirchenmusik in der katholischen Kirche." *Siona* 27 (1902): 130–32.

Blackbourn, David. *Class, Religion, and Local Politics in Wilhelmine Germany: The Centre Party before 1914.* New Haven, Conn.: Yale University Press, 1980.

———. "The German Bourgeoisie: An Introduction." In *The German Bourgeoisie: Essays on the Social History of the German Middle Class from the Late Eighteenth to the Early Twentieth Century,* edited by David Blackbourn and Richard J. Evans, 1–45. London: Routledge, 1991.

———. *The Long Nineteenth Century: A History of Germany, 1780–1918.* New York: Oxford University Press, 1998.

Blaschke, Olaf. "Die Kolonialisierung der Laienwelt: Priester als Milieumanager und die Kanäle klerikaler Kuratel." In Blaschke and Kuhlemann, *Religion im Kaiserreich,* 93–135.

———. "Das 19. Jahrhundert: Ein zweites konfessionelles Zeitalter?" *Geschichte und Gesellschaft* 26 (2000): 38–75.

Blaschke, Olaf, and Frank-Michael Kuhlemann. "Religion in Geschichte und Gesellschaft: Sozialhistorische Perspektiven für die vergleichende Erforschung religiöser Mentalitäten und Milieus." In Blaschke and Kuhlemann, *Religion im Kaiserreich*, 7–56.

Blaschke, Olaf, and Frank-Michael Kuhlemann, eds. *Religion im Kaiserreich: Milieu— Mentalitäten—Krisen*. Religiöse Kulturen der Moderne, edited by Friedrich Wilhelm Graf and Gangolf Hübinger, vol. 2. Gütersloh: Chr. Kaiser/Gütersloher Verlagshaus, 1996.

Blau, D. "Kulturkrisis der Gegenwart." *Deutsche Blätter in Polen* 6 (April 1929): 173–89.

Blessinger, Karl. "Die Musik als Kulturfaktor." *Musik im Leben* 5 (1930): 172–82.

———. "Musik und Intellekt." *Musik im Leben* 4 (January 1928): 5–8.

Böser, Fidelis. "Christozentrische Kirchenmusik." *Benediktinische Monatschrift zur Pflege religiösen und geistigen Leben* 6 (1924): 1–16.

Bollenbeck, Georg. *Tradition, Avantgarde, Reaktion: Deutsche Kontroverse um die kulturelle Moderne, 1880–1945*. Frankfurt am Main: Fischer, 1999.

"Book Clubs of Central Europe." *Publishers' Weekly* 109 (February 27, 1926): 665–66.

Bormann, Hanns Heinrich. "Franz Herwigs Meisterroman." *Germania*, December 17, 1926, Morgenausgabe, Werk und Wert.

———. "'Panzerkreuzer Potemkin': Ein Meisterwerk russischer Filmkunst." *Germania*, April 30, 1926, Abendausgabe.

———. "Unsere Literaturzeitschriften." *Germania*, June 17, 1926, Abendausgabe, Werk und Wert.

Bornhausen, Karl. "Musik und Religion." *Schlesisches Jahrbuch für deutsche Kulturarbeit im gesamtschlesischen Raum* 1 (1928): 9–13.

Borromäus Verein. *Jahresbericht 1928*. Bonn: J. F. Carthaus, n.d.

———. *Jahresbericht 1929*. Bonn: J. F. Carthaus, n.d.

———. *Jahresbericht 1932*. Bonn: J. F. Carthaus, n.d.

———. *Jahresbericht 1933*. Bonn: J. F. Carthaus, 1933.

Borromäus Verein (Zentralstelle). *Der Borromäusverein und die Not der Zeit*. Bonn: Verlag des Borromäus-Vereins, 1927.

Boving, Remigius. "Aesthetische oder ethische Weltanschauung." *Bücherwelt* 22 (March 1925): 97–107.

Bowman, Sylvia E., ed. *Edward Bellamy Abroad: An American Prophet's Influence*. New York: Twayne, 1962.

Brandt, Hans Jürgen. "Chronik der Pfarrgemeinde St. Josef Schalke." In Brandt, *Schalke 91*, 109–37.

———. "Katholische Kirche und Urbanisation im deutschen Reich." *Blätter für deutsche Landesgeschichte* 128 (1992): 221–39.

———. "Die kirchliche Vereine und Bruderschaften." In Brandt, *Schalke 91*, 353–84.

———. "Kirchliches Vereinswesen und Freizeitgestaltung in einer Arbeitergemeinde 1872–1933: Das Beispiel Schalke." In *Sozialgeschichte der Freizeit: Untersuchungen zum Wandel der Alltagskultur in Deutschland*, edited by Gerhard Huck, 207–22. Wuppertal: Peter Hammer, 1980.

Brandt, Hans Jürgen, ed. *Schalke 91: Eine katholische Arbeitergemeinde im Ruhrgebiet mit Tradition*. Paderborn: Bonifatius Druck Buch Verlag, 1991.

Brasch, Alfred. "Das Volkskonzert." *Musik im Leben* 4 (September/October 1928): 139–40.

Braun, Johannes. "Der Borromäusverein von 1922–1924." *Die Bücherwelt* 22 (January 1925): 25–34.

———. "Die Großstadt als Kulturraum: Das Buch." In *71. Generalversammlung der deutschen Katholiken zu Essen an der Ruhr . . . 1932,* 252–57.

———. "Die Schund- und Schmutzliteratur und ihre Bekämpfung." *Bücherwelt* 7 (April 1910): 124–33.

———. "Unsere Stellung zu der modernen Literatur." *Bücherwelt* 17 (July 1920): 141–46.

———. "Unsre Volksbüchereiarbeit." *Bücherwelt* 17 (August/September 1920): 207–11.

Brechenmacher, Josef Karlmann. "Zeitfragen u[nd] Zeitaufgaben des Jugendbücherwarts." *Bücherwelt* 22 (November 1925): 481–87.

Bredohl, Thomas M. *Class and Religious Identity: The Rhenish Center Party in Wilhelmine Germany.* Marquette Studies in Theology 18. Milwaukee, Wisc.: Marquette University Press, 2000.

Breuer, Dieter. *Geschichte der literarischen Zensur in Deutschland.* Heidelberg, 1982.

Brockhaus Enzyklopädie. 1992 ed. Mannheim: F. A. Brockhaus, 1992.

Broesike, Max. "Die Kino-Frage." *Hochland* 9 (August 1912): 593–601.

Brown, William J., and Arvind Singhal. "Entertainment-Education Media Strategies for Social Change: Promises and Problems." In *Mass Media, Social Control, and Social Change: A Macrosocial Perspective,* edited by David Demers and K. Viswanath, 263–81. Ames, Iowa: Iowa State University Press, 1999.

Bruce, Steve, ed. *Religion and Modernization: Sociologists and Historians Debate the Secularization Thesis.* Oxford: Clarendon Press, 1992.

Brües, Otto. *Jupp Brand.* Berlin: Bühnenvolksbund, 1927.

Brunner, Karl. *Der Kinematograph von heute—eine Volksgefahr.* Berlin: Verlag des Vaterländischen Schriftenverbandes, 1913.

Bry, Carl Christian. "Der Kitsch." *Hochland* 22 (1924/1925): 399–411.

Buchheim, Karl. "Der deutsche Verbandskatholizismus: Eine Skizze seiner Geschichte." In Hanssler, *Die Kirche in der Gesellschaft,* 30–83.

Budde, Fritz. "Moderne Theaterkunst." *Hochland* (May 1914): 201–14.

Bundschuh, E. P. "Katholische Schriftenmission und Kolportage, eine soziale Aufgabe und ein Zeitbedürfnis." *Soziale Revue* 28 (March 1928): 110–16.

Burke, Peter. "Strengths and Weaknesses of the History of Mentalities." *History of European Ideas* 7 (1986): 439–51.

Burke, Redmond A. *What Is the Index?* Milwaukee, Wisc.: Bruce Publishing, 1952.

"Der Caecilianismus—Anfänge—Grundlagen—Wirkungen." *Musica Sacra* 106 (1986): 41–44.

Caecilianus, Fr. "Musica non sacra." *Musica sacra* 24 (1889/1890): 86–88.

Calinescu, Matei. *Five Faces of Modernity.* Durham, N.C.: Duke University Press, 1987.

Calmes, ———. "Aus dem Volkswartbunde." *Volkswart* 21 (March 1928): 40–41.

———. *Der katholische Seelsorger im Kampfe gegen die öffentliche Unsittlichkeit.* Reprinted from *Die Seelsorge* [1930?].

———. "Neue Wege der Selbsthilfe im Schundkampf!" *Volkswart* 22 (January 1929): 1–2.

———. "Schund und Schmutz in ihren vielfachen Erscheinungsweisen." *Volkswart* 21 (August 1928): 113–18.

———. "Stand der Schund- und Schmutzbekämpfung in Deutschland und Österreich." *Schönere Zukunft* 7 (September 9, 1932).

———. "Zur Geschichte und Arbeit unseres Generalsekretariates!" *Volkswart* 25 (January 1932): 6–7

Cardauns, Hermann. "Das literarische Schaffen." In Meinertz and Sacher, *Deutschland und der Katholizismus*, 373–90.

Cathrein, Victor. "Katholische Kirche und Kultur." *Stimmen aus Maria-Laach* 63 (August 1902): 129–46

Cato. "Ob Meisterwerke auch unzüchtig wirken." *Volkswart* 12 (May 1919): 65–69.

Chase, Malcolm, and Christopher Shaw. "The Dimensions of Nostalgia." In *The Imagined Past,* edited by Christopher Shaw and Malcolm Chase. Manchester: Manchester University Press, 1989.

Chefdo, Monique, Ricardo Quinones, and Albert Wachtel, eds. *Modernism: Challenges and Perspectives.* Urbana, Ill.: University of Illinois Press, 1986.

Childs, Peter. *Modernism.* London: Routledge, 2000.

Chomse, J. "Rundschau: Psychologie des Kinos." *Bild und Film* 2 (1912/1913): 140–42.

Clemens, Gabriele. *Erziehung zu anständiger Unterhaltung: Das Theaterspiel in den katholischen Gesellen- und Arbeitervereinen im deutschen Kaiserreich.* Veröffentlichungen der Kommission für Zeitgeschichte, edited by Ulrich von Hehl, series A: Quellen, vol. 46. Paderborn: Schöningh, 2000.

Clement, Paul. "Contemporary German Art." In *Exhibition of Contemporary German Art,* edited by the Metropolitan Museum of Art. New York: Metropolitan Museum of Art, 1909.

"Clerici theatra ne frequentant." *Kirchlicher Anzeiger für die Erzdiözese Köln* 54 (January 1, 1914): 12.

Cohen, C. "Aufgaben des Klerus bezüglich der Kirchenmusik." *Musica Sacra* 33 (1900): 1–6.

Conradt, Walther. *Kirche und Kinematograph.* Berlin: Herrmann Walther Verlagsbuchhandlung, 1910.

Conzemius, Victor. "The Condemnation of Modernism and the Survival of Catholic Theology." In *The Twentieth Century: A Theological Overview,* edited by Gregory Baum. Maryknoll, N.Y.: Orbis Books, 1999.

———. "Kirchen und Nationalismen im Europa des 19. und 20. Jahrhunderts." In *Katholizismus, nationaler Gedanke und Europa seit 1800,* edited by Albrecht Langner, 11–50. Paderborn: Ferdinand Schoningh, 1985.

Cousins, Albert N., and Hans Nagpaul, eds. *Urban Man and Society: A Reader in Urban Sociology.* New York: Alfred A. Knopf, 1970.

Crossick, Geoffrey, and Heinz-Gerhard Haupt. *The Petite Bourgeoisie in Europe 1780–1914.* London: Routledge, 1995.

Dahlhaus, Carl. *Nineteenth-Century Music.* Translated by J. Bradford Robinson. California Studies in Nineteenth-Century Music, edited by Joseph Kerman, 5. Berkeley and Los Angeles: University of California Press, 1989.

———. "Der Streit um die Wahre Kirchenmusik." In *Musik—zur Sprache gebracht: Musikästhetische Texte aus drei Jahrhunderten,* edited by Carl Dahlhaus and Michael Zimmermann, 201–21. Munich: DTV, 1984.

Dalton, Margaret S. "The Borromäus Verein: Catholic Public Librarianship in Germany, 1845–1933." *Libraries and Culture* 31 (Spring 1996): 409–21.

Damberg, Wilhelm. "An der Jahrhundertwende." In Seeber, *Im Aufbruch gelähmt?* 9–24.

Damian, Joseph. "Nr. 2: Hirtenwort über die Vergnügungssucht." *Kirchliches Amtsblatt für die Diözese Fulda* 42 (January 13, 1926): 2.

Dashefsky, Arnold, ed. *Ethnic Identity in Society.* Chicago: Rand McNally, 1976.

Davis, Fred. *Yearning for Yesterday: A Sociology of Nostalgia.* New York: Free Press; London: Collier Macmillan, 1919.

Davis, Natalie Zemon. "The Shapes of Social History." *Storia della Storiografia* 17 (1990): 28–34.

Davison, Peter, Rolf Meyersohn, and Edward Shils, eds. *Culture and Mass Culture.* Literary Taste, Culture and Mass Communication, vol. 1. Cambridge: Chadwyck-Healey; Teaneck, N.J.: Somerset House, 1978.

Demmig, Charlotte. "Kampf um das Ethos im Film." *Der Gral* 25 (February 1931): 454–55.

Dench, Geoff. *Minorities in the Open Society: Prisoners of Ambivalence.* London: Routledge and Kegan Paul, 1986.

Denzer, Heinrich. "Eine katholische Stadt im protestantischen Preußen." In *Geschichte der Stadt Koblenz: Von der französischen Stadt bis zur Gegenwart,* edited by Ingrid Batori, Dieter Kerber, and Hans Josef Schmidt, 253–81. Stuttgart: Theiss, 1993.

"Deutsche Gesellschaft für christliche Kunst." *Volkskunst* 14 (1926): 108.

Dickinson, Edward. *Music in the History of the Western Church.* 1902. New York: Haskell House, 1969.

Dictionary of the History of Ideas: Studies of Selected Pivotal Ideas. Edited by Philip P. Wiener. New York: Charles Scribner's Sons, 1973.

Dictionary of Literary Biography. Vol. 18, *Twentieth-Century German Dramatists, 1889–1918.* Edited by Wolfgang D. Elfe and James Hardin. Detroit: Gale Research, 1992.

"Diskussion der Zeit zu Tanz und Jazz." *Musik im Leben* 2 (October 1926): 147–49.

Dobbelaere, Karel. "Church Involvement and Secularization: Making Sense of the European Case." In *Secularization, Rationalism, and Sectarianism: Essays in Honour of Bryan R. Wilson,* edited by Eileen Barker, James A. Beckford, and Karel Dobbelaere, 19–36. Oxford: Clarendon Press, 1993.

Doering, O. "Die deutschen Katholiken und die Pflege der Kunst." *Allgemeine Rundschau* 6 (1909): 776–78.

———. "Von modernster Kunst." *Allgemeine Rundschau* 13 (1916): 548.

Drenker, Alexander. "Rundfunk und Volksbildung." *Volkskunst* 16 (June 1928): 181–82.

———. "Wille und Werk des Bühnenvolksbundes." *Volkskunst* 16 (October 1928): 296–98.

Drinkwelder, Erhard. "Der geistliche Kirchenvorstand und die Kirchenmusik." *Cäcilienvereinsorgan* 62 (April 1931) and *Musica Sacra* 61 (April 1931): 111–16.

During, Simon. "Editor's Introduction." In *The Cultural Studies Reader,* edited by Simon During, 1–25. London: Routledge, 1993.

Dyroff, Adolf. "Das Buch im Kampf um die Weltanschauung." *Bücherwelt* 17 (August/September 1920): 219–20.

Eberhard, Raimund. "Sittliche und unsittliche Kunst." *Volkswart* 17 (December 1924): 177–80.

Eberharter, Andreas. "Die kirchliche Bücherzensur." *Pastor Bonus* 39 (July 1928): 268–72.

Eberle, Joseph. "Katholiken und Literatur—Eine Auseinandersetzung: Literatur und Pressefragen der Katholiken. (Antwort an Jakob Kneip)." *Schönere Zukunft* 2 (August 21, 1927): 1000–1003.

Ebertz, Michael. "Pluralisierung, Verkirchlichung, alte und neue Kristallisationen." In Seeber, *Im Aufbruch gelähmt?* 25–38. Frankfurt am Main: Verlag Josef Knecht, 2000.

Eckardt, Franz. "Wir Katholiken und das Theater." *Allgemeine Rundschau* 10 (February 15, 1913): 122.

Eckert, Alois. "Grosstadtseelsorge [sic]." In *Das katholische Jahrbuch der Frankfurter Katholiken*, edited by Jakob Herr. Frankfurt am Main: Verlag Carolus-Druckerei, 1928.

Ehrhard, Albert. *Katholisches Christentum und Kultur.* Kultur und Katholizismus 6. Mainz: Kirchheim'sche Verlangsbuchhandlung, 1907.

———. *Der Katholizismus und das zwanzigste Jahrhundert im Lichte der kirchlichen Entwicklung der Neuzeit.* Stuttgart: Jos. Roth, 1902.

Eichert, Franz. "Gralfahrt—Höhenfahrt!" *Der Gral* 1 (October 15, 1906): 1–7.

———. "Das katholische Literaturideal." *Der Gral* 4 (November 15, 1909): 92–100.

———. "Die literarische Inferiorität der Katholiken." *Der Gral* 3 (December 15, 1908): 141–43.

———. "Was ist modern?" *Der Gral* 5 (January 15, 1911): 254–56.

"Einfluß des Kinos auf die Sittlichkeit." *Pastor Bonus* 44 (November 1933): 418–21.

Einheitslieder für die deutsche Diözesan-Gesangbücher. Berlin: Germania, 1916.

150 Jahre Verlag Friedrich Pustet Regensburg, 1826–1976. Regensburg: Friedrich Pustet, 1976.

71. Generalversammlung der deutschen Katholiken zu Essen an der Ruhr . . . 1932. Essen (Ruhr): Fredebeul und Koenen, n.d.

Eitel, Hans. *Alte Eichstätter Grabmale.* Würzburg: Verlag des Verfassers, [1926].

Eksteins, Modris. *Rites of Spring: The Great War and the Birth of the Modern Age.* New York: Doubleday/Anchor Books, 1989.

Elm, Kaspar and Hans-Dietrich Loock, eds. *Seelsorge und Diakonie in Berlin: Beiträge zum Verhältnis von Kirche und Großstadt im 19. und beginnenden 20. Jahrhundert.* Historische Kommission zu Berlin, vol. 74. Berlin: Walter de Gruyter, 1990.

Encyclopedia of Library and Information Science. Edited by Allen Kent, Harold Lancour, and Jay E. Daily. New York, Marcel Dekker, 1974.

Endres, —. "[Katholizismus und Kunst]." In *Verhandlungen der 49. Generalversammlung der Katholiken Deutschlands . . . 1902*, 373–81. Mannheim: Jean Gremm (Neue Mannheimer Volksblätter), 1902.

Englert, —. "Kulturpolitik." *Allgemeine Rundschau* 9 (April 13, 1912): 293–94.

"Der Entwurf zur Abänderung des Lichtspielgesetzes." *Volkswart* 18 (November 1925): 162–63; (December 1925): 177–78; 19 (March 1926): 33–35.

"Das Ergebnis der Kinobesuche . . . ." *Volkswart* 15 (March 1922): 33–35.

Erikson, Erik. *Identity and the Life Cycle: Selected Papers.* New York: International Universities Press, 1959.

"Erlaß der Fuldaer Bischofskonferenz über den sakralen Charakter kirchlicher Kunstwerke." *Die christliche Kunst* 29 (1933): 104–5.

Ernst, Georg, and Bernhard Marschall, eds. *Film und Rundfunk: Zweiter Internationaler Katholischer Filmkongress, Erster Internationaler Katholischer Rundfunkkongress.* Munich, 1929.

Ernst, Ludwig. "Die Theaterfrage—eine Frauenfrage." *Allgemeine Rundschau* 13 (1916): 209–10; 229–30.

"Der Erzbischof von München gegen die Ausschreitungen der modernen Bühnenliteratur." *Allgemeine Rundschau* 15 (1918): 395–96.

Ester, Peter, Loek Halman, and Ruud de Moor. *The Individualizing Society: Value Change in Europe and North America.* Tilburg, Netherlands: Tilburg University Press, 1994.

Estermann, Monika, and Georg Jäger. "Voraussetzungen und Entwicklungstendenzen." In *Geschichte des Deutschen Buchhandels im 19. und 20. Jahrhundert*, edited by Georg Jäger with Dieter Langewiesche and Wolfram Siemann. Vol. 1, *Das Kaiserrreich 1870–1918*, 17–41. Frankfurt am Main: Buchhändler-Vereinigung, 2001.

Ettl, Joh[ann] B. "Das deutsche Volkslied." *Volkskunst* 13 (1925): 514–20.

———. "Theater und Bühne im Wandel der Zeiten." *Volkskunst* 16 (October 1928): 289–96.

Ettl, Josef. "Das Pfarr-Kino." *Der Seelsorger* 7 (1930): 18–23.

Ettlinger, Max, Philipp Funk, and Friedrich Fuchs, eds. *Wiederbegegnung von Kirche und Kultur: Eine Gabe für Karl Muth*. Munich: Kösel und Pustet, 1927.

Evans, Ellen Lovell. *The German Center Party, 1870–1933*. Carbondale and Edwardsville, Ill.: Southern Illinois Press, 1981.

Evans, Richard J. "Religion and Society in Modern Germany." *European Studies Review* 12 (1982): 249–88.

———. *Rethinking German History: Nineteenth-Century Germany and the Origins of the Third Reich*. London: Harper Collins Academic, 1990.

Falkenberg, Heinrich. *Mehr Literaturpflege!* Bonn: Carl Georgi, 1910.

———. *Wir Katholiken und die deutsche Literatur*. Bonn: Carl Georgi, 1909.

Faulhaber, Michael Cardinal von. "Kirche und kirchliche Kunst." *Die christliche Kunst* 26 (February 1930):

Feder, Georg. "Decline and Restoration." Translated by Reinhard G. Pauly. In *Protestant Church Music: A History*, edited by Friedrich Blume. New York: W. W. Norton, 1974.

Felder, Rudolf. "Ueber die sittliche Mission der Musik." *Neue Musik-Zeitung* 42 (1921): 133–35; 149–51.

Feldt, Horst. "Schallplatte und Lautsprecher im katholischen Gottesdienst." *Cäcilienvereins-Organ* 61 (1931): 13–16.

Fellerer, Karl Gustav. "Die Enzyklika 'Annus qui' des Papstes Benedikt XIV." In Fellerer, *Geschichte der katholischen Kirchenmusik*, vol. 2, 149–52.

———. "Grundlagen und Anfänge der kirchenmusikalischen Organisation Franz Xaver Witts." *Kirchenmusikalisches Jahrbuch* 55 (1971): 33–60.

———. "Das Konzil von Trient und die Kirchenmusik." In Fellerer, *Geschichte der katholischen Kirchenmusik*, vol. 2, 7–9.

Fellerer, Karl Gustav, ed. *Geschichte der katholischen Kirchenmusik*. 2 vols. Kassel: Bärenreiter, 1976.

Festschrift und Programm zur Goldenen Jubelfeier des kath[olischen] Kirchenchors Caecilia (St. Paul) Offenbach am Main am 27. Juni 1926. Offenbach am Main: Druck von Albert Kleinsorge, [1926].

Fischen, H. A. "Die katholische Weltanschauung und das moderne deutsche Theater." *Das Neue Jahrhundert* 4 (July 21, 1912): 337–40.

Fischer, E. K. "Die neue Kunst und die Kirche." *Kunstwart und Kulturwart* 35 (1922): 189–94; 286–91; 308–13.

Fischer, W. "Musik, Charakter, Religion." *Der Chorbote* 2 (October 15, 1913): 75–79.

Flemming, Hanns Theodor. "Painting." In *Late Nineteenth Century Art*, edited by Hans Jürgen Hansen. Newton Abbot, England: David and Charles, 1973.

"Förderung des Borromäus-Vereins." *Kirchlicher Anzeiger für die Erzdiözese Köln* 59 (November 1, 1919): 155.

Foerster, Fr[iedrich] W. *Autorität und Freiheit: Betrachtungen zum Kulturproblem der Kirche*. Kempten: Kösel and Pustet, 1922.

"Folgen des Lesens von Schundliteratur." *Die Hochwacht* 1 (October 1910): 7–9.

Forberger, Johannes. *Die wirtschaftliche und kulturelle Rückständigkeit der Katholiken und ihre Ursachen.* Evangelischer Bund, Flugschriften 263/64. Leipzig: Carl Braun, 1908.

Forch, Carl. "Der Kinematograph und das bewegte Bild." *Hochland* (August 1912): 581–92.

Forster-Hahn, Françoise, ed. *Imagining Modern German Culture.* Studies in the History of Art 53. Washington, D.C.: National Gallery of Art, 1996.

Fraser, Theodore P. *The Modern Catholic Novel in Europe.* Twayne's World Author Series, edited by David O'Connell, 841. New York: Twayne Publishers, 1994.

Freudenburg, William R., and Robert Gramling. "Community Impacts of Technological Change: Toward a Longitudinal Perspective." *Social Forces* 70 (June 1992): 937–55.

Froberger, Joseph. "Das 'Ghetto' der deutschen Katholiken." *Schönere Zukunft* 3 (1928): 487–89.

———. "Gute und schlechte Romane." *Bücherwelt* 12 (March 1915): 113–19.

———. "Die Katholiken und die Literatur." *Bücherwelt* 22 (October 1925): 447–51.

———. "Seelische Persönlichkeit und Lektüre." In *Vom Wesen und Wollen katholischer Büchereiarbeit: Vorträge des 14. Kursus für Leiter und Mitarbeiter von Volksbüchereien des Borromäusvereins,* edited by Johannes Braun, 46–54. Bonn: Verlag des Borromäus-Vereins, 1927.

———. "Was will der Volkswartbund?" *Volkswart* 22 (August 1929): 113–15.

———. *Weltanschauung und Literatur.* Trier: Paulinus-Druckerei, 1910.

Fröhlings, J. "Zum Geleit." *Volkswart* 25 (January 1932): 3–5.

Froude, James Anthony. "The Science of History." In *Short Studies on Great Subjects,* vol. 1. New York: Charles Scribner's Sons, 1909.

Fuchs, Friedrich. "Die deutschen Katholiken und die deutsche Kultur im 19. Jahrhundert." In Ettlinger, Funk, and Fuchs, *Wiederbegegnung von Kirche und Kultur in Deutschland: Eine Gabe für Karl Muth,* 9–58.

"Für oder gegen Kirchenkonzerte?" *Kölnische Volkszeitung,* July 30, 1922.

Fullerton, Ronald A. "Creating a Mass Book Market in Germany: The Story of the 'Colporteur Novel,' 1870–1890." *Journal of Social History* 10 (March 1977): 265–83.

Funk, Alois. "Film und Seelsorge." *Pastor Bonus* 41 (September 1930): 338–53; (November 1930): 409–26.

———. "Rundfunk und Katholizismus." *Pastor bonus* 42 (1931): 114–23.

Funk, Philipp. "Der Gang des geistigen Leben im katholischen Deutschland unserer Generation." In Ettlinger, Funk, and Fuchs, *Wiederbegegnung von Kirche und Kultur in Deutschland,* 77–126.

Gabriel, Karl, and Franz-Xaver Kaufmann. *Zur Soziologie des Katholizismus.* Mainz: Matthias Grünewald Verlag, 1980.

Ganghofer, Ludwig. *Lebenslauf eines Optimisten.* New ed. Munich: Drömer-Knaur, 1966.

Gardiner, Harold C. *The Catholic Viewpoint on Censorship.* Garden City, N.Y.: Hanover House, 1958.

Gatz, Erwin. "Katholische Großstadtseelsorge im 19. und 20. Jahrhundert: Grundzüge und Entwicklung." In Elm and Loock, *Seelsorge und Diakonie in Berlin,* 23–38.

Gatz, Erwin, and Lothar Ullrich. "Grundsätzliches zur Minderheitsituation der katholischen Christenheit." In *Katholiken in der Minderheit: Geschichte des kirchlichen Lebens in den deutschsprachigen Ländern seit dem Ende des 18. Jahrhunderts,* edited by Erwin Gatz, vol. 3, 19–36. Freiburg: Herder, 1994.

Gatz, Erwin, ed. *Akten der Fuldaer Bischofskonferenz.* Vol. 3, *1900–1919.* Veröffentlichungen der Kommission für Zeitgeschichte, edited by Konrad Repgen with Dieter Albrecht, Rudolf Lill, and Rudolf Morsey, series A: Quellen, vol. 39. Mainz: Matthias Grünewald Verlag, 1985.

Gay, Peter. *Education of the Senses.* Vol. 1 of *The Bourgeois Experience.* New York: Oxford University Press, 1984.

———. *Weimar Culture: The Outsider as Insider.* New York: Harper and Row, 1970.

"Gedanken zur Filmzensur." *Volkswart* 20 (August 1927): 114–15.

Gehrig, Oscar. "Die Berliner Corinth-Ausstellungen." *Germania,* February 23, 1926; February 24, 1926.

"Generalversammlung des Cölner Männer-Vereins z. B. d. ö. Unsittlichkeit am 10. März 1910." *Volkswart* 3 (May 1910): 75–78.

Gerads, Jos[eph]. "Von Werk- und Feierstunden unserer Volksbildungsarbeit: Volksbücherei St. Jakob in Aachen." *Bücherwelt* 24 (January 1927): 14–16.

Germany. *Lichtspielgesetz vom 12. Mai 1920.* Edited by Albert Hellwig. Berlin, Stilke, 1921.

Gerst, Wilhelm Karl. "Wie die deutschen Katholiken für das Theater aktiviert wurden." *Der Gral* 27 (1933): 359–64.

"Geschäftsbericht für 1913." *Nachrichten für die Vereine vom hl. Karl Borromäus* 12 (September 1914).

Geschichtliche Grundbegriffe: Historisches Lexikon zur politisch-sozialen Sprache in Deutschland. Edited by O. Brunner, W. Conze, and R. Koselleck. Stuttgart: Klett-Cotta, 1972–1984.

"Gesetz zur Bewahrung der Jugend vor Schund- und Schmutzschriften vom 18. Dezember 1926." *Reichsgesetzblatt* pt. 1, 27 (December 24, 1926): 505–6.

Getlein, Frank, and Harold C. Gardiner. *Movies, Morals, and Art.* New York: Sheed and Ward, 1961.

Geueke, ———. "Katholiken und Theaterkultur." *Historisch-politische Blätter für das katholische Deutschland* 159 (1917): 765–75.

Gibson, Ralph. *A Social History of French Catholicism, 1789–1914.* London: Routledge, 1989.

Gietmann, Gerhard. *Allgemeine Ästhetik.* Freiburg im Breisgau: Herder, 1899.

———. "Das Nackte in der Kunst." *Allgemeine Rundschau* 2 (1905): 595–98.

———. "Steht die Kunst in der Kirche nur unter ästhetischen Gesetzen?" *Musica Sacra* 32 (1899): 85–87; 97–99; 109–12; 121–23.

Gleason, Philip. "Identifying Identity: A Semantic History." *Journal of American History* 69 (1983): 910–31.

Glitz-Holzhausen, A. "Die Krisis der Provinz-Theater." *Germania,* April 16, 1926, Abendausgabe.

Götz von Olenhusen, Irmtraud. "Die Feminisierung von Religion und Kirche im 19. und 20. Jahrhundert: Forschungsstand und Forschungsperspektiven." In *Frauen unter dem Patriarchat der Kirchen: Katholikinnen und Protestantinnen im 19. und 20. Jahrhundert,* edited by Irmtraud Götz von Olenhusen. Konfession und Gesellschaft, vol. 7, 9–21. Stuttgart: W. Kohlhammer, 1995.

———. *Klerus und abweichendes Verhalten: Zur Sozialgeschichte katholischer Priester im 19. Jahrhundert: Die Erzdiözese Freiburg.* Kritische Studien zur Geschichtswissenschaft, vol. 106. Göttingen: Vandenhoeck und Ruprecht, 1994.

———. "Klerus und Ultramontanismus in der Erzdiözese Freiburg." In Schieder, *Religion und Gesellschaft im 19. Jahrhundert,* 113–43.

Graff, Harvey J. *The Legacies of Literacy: Continuities and Contradictions in Western Culture and Society.* Bloomington, Ind.: Indiana University Press, 1987.

Grimm, Iwan. "Filmportrait: Charlie Chaplin." *Germania*, October 21, 1928, Morgenausgabe.

Gröber, Conrad. *Das Buch und seine Bedeutung.* Freiburg im Breisgau: Erzbischöfliches Missionsinstitut, n.d.

———. *Kirche und Künstler.* Freiburg im Breisgau: Herder, 1932.

Grosche, Robert. "Über die Möglichkeiten einer Renaissance der christlichen Kunst." In Ettlinger, Funk, and Fuchs, *Wiederbegegnung von Kirche und Kultur in Deutschland*, 241–54.

———. "Volksbildung und Weltanschauung." *Volkstum und Volksbildung* 2 (1930): 193–97.

———. "Was fehlt unserer Volksbildungsarbeit?" *Volkskunst* 13 (January 1925): 4–7.

———. *Der Weg aus dem Ghetto.* Cologne: J. P. Bachem, 1955.

Gross, Michael B. "The Catholic Missionary Crusade and the Protestant Revival in Nineteenth-Century Germany." In Smith, *Protestants, Catholics and Jews in Germany, 1800–1914*, 245–65.

Der Grosse Brockhaus. Leipzig: F. A. Brockhaus, 1929.

"Die Großstadt als Kulturraum." In *71. Generalversammlung der deutschen Katholiken zu Essen an der Ruhr . . . 1932*, 230–70.

"Großstadt und Musik." *Musik im Leben* 1 (June 1925): 81–82.

Die Gründung und Thätigeit des Vereins vom heil. Karl Borromäus: Festschrift zum fünfzigjährigen Jubelfeste des Vereins am 30 May 1895. Bonn: J. P. Bachem, 1895.

Grundei, Hans. "Die Not der katholischen Kulturorganisationen." *Allgemeine Rundschau* 20 (1923): 43–45; 54–55.

———. "Die Rückkehr des Katholizismus aus dem Exil—durch die Wüste." In Hoeber, *Die Rückkehr aus dem Exil*, 57–67.

———. "Sozialistische und katholische Kulturpolitik und Kulturziele in der Nachkriegszeit." *Literarischer Handweiser* 58 (August 1922): 337–46.

———. "Theaterprobleme und Schauspielerfragen." *Allgemeine Rundschau* 19 (1922): 101–2; 113–14.

Gürster, Eugen. "Krisis des Theaters." *Hochland* 24 (1926): 123–26.

Guttsman, W. L. *Art for Workers: Ideology and the Visual Arts in Germany.* Manchester: Manchester University Press, 1997.

———. "Art as a Weapon: Social Critique and Political Orientation in Painting and Print in Weimar Germany." In *The Arts, Literature, and Society,* edited by Arthur Marwick, 181–213. London: Routledge, 1990.

Gystrow, Ernst [Hellpach, Willy]. "Der Katholizismus und die neue Dichtung." *Die Gesellschaft* 1 (1899): 219–28; 421–29; 3 (1899): 88–99; 161–68; 263–67; 4 (1899): 77–86; 185–93; 300–307.

H., Dr. —. "Laien-Gedanken über den Choral." *Cäcilienvereinsorgan* 59 (1929): 224.

H., F. X. "Bildende Kunst und schöne Literatur." *Historisch-politische Blätter für das katholische Deutschland* 156 (1915): 538–44.

H., J. "Wie stehen wir Katholiken zum Rundfunk?" *Bücherwelt* 28 (1931): 365–67.

Haanen, K. Th. "Rundfunk und Religion." In "Strandgut," *Germania*, April 3, 1926, Abendausgabe, Das neue Ufer.

Habersbrunner, Dionys. "Katholizismus und individuelle Kultur." *Der Weg* (1924): 214–20.

Haffner, [Paul Leopold]. "[Lektüre]." In *Verhandlungen der XXXII. Generalversammlung der Katholiken Deutschlands Münster i. W. . . . 1885*, 335–42. Münster: Commissions-Verlag der Actien-Gesellschaft "Westfälischer Merkur," 1885.

Halder, Winfrid. *Katholische Vereine in Baden und Württemberg, 1848–1914.* Veröffentlichungen der Kommission für Zeitgeschichte, edited by Ulrich von Hehl, series B: Forschung, vol. 64. Paderborn: Ferdinand Schöningh, 1995.

Halman, Loek. "Is There a Moral Decline? A Cross-national Inquiry into Morality in Contemporary Society." *International Social Science Journal* 47 (1995): 419–39.

Hambröer, Johannes. "Vom freien Kino." *Allgemeine Rundschau* 16 (1919): 774.

Handbuch für die Geschäftsführer in den Einzelvereinen des Borromäusvereins. Bonn: Verlag des Borromäus-Vereins, 1921.

Hanisch, Ernst. "Der katholische Literaturstreit." In *Der Modernismus: Beiträge zu seiner Erforschung,* edited by Erika Weinzierl, 125–60. Graz: Verlag Styria, 1974.

Hanssler, Bernhard. "Vom katholischen Verein zum Zentralkomitee." In Hanssler, *Die Kirche in der Gesellschaft: Der deutsche Katholizismus und seine Organisationen im 19. und 20. Jahrhundert,* 84–90.

Hanssler, Bernhard, ed. *Die Kirche in der Gesellschaft: Der deutsche Katholizismus und seine Organisationen im 19. und 20. Jahrhundert.* Paderborn: Verlag Bonifacius, 1961.

von Hartmann, Felix, Archbishop. [Report on his speech]. *Nachrichten für die Vereine vom hl. Karl Borromäus* 11 (October 1913).

Hatzfeld, Johannes. "Erneuerung des ländlichen Musiklebens." *Musik im Leben* 1 (March 1925): 34–39.

———. "Ist das Volkslied eine bürgerliche Angelegenheit?" *Musik im Leben* 4 (September/October 1928): 132–33.

———. "Vom Geiste wahrer Kirchenmusik." *Heilige Feuer* 14 (1928): 449–56.

———. "Von katholischer Kirchenmusik." *Die Musik* 8 (1908): 212–24.

Hauptfleisch, Georg. *Praktische Einrichtung von kathol[ischen] Lesezirkeln.* Bonn: Generalsekretariat des Borromäusvereins, 1930.

Hauser, Arnold. *The Sociology of Art.* Translated by Kenneth J. Northcott. London: Routledge, 1982.

Haweis, H. R. *Music and Morals.* New York: Harper and Brothers, 1902.

Hayburn, Robert F. *Papal Legislation on Sacred Music, 95 A.D. to 1977 A.D.* Collegeville, Minn.: Liturgical Press, 1979.

Hebenstreit, Joseph. "Kirchenchor auf dem Lande." *Volkskunst* 14 (1926): 449–56.

v[an] H[eemstede], L[eo]. "Steht die katholische Belletristik auf der Höhe der Zeit?" *Dichterstimmen der Gegenwart: Poetisches Organ für das katholische Deutschland* 13 (1899): 22–27.

Hefele, Herman. "Die Funktion des Katholizismus in der modernen Kultur." *Die Tat* 5 (July 1913): 384–92.

Hegel, Eduard. *Das Erzbistums Köln zwischen der Restauration des 19. Jahrhunderts und der Restauration des 20. Jahrhunderts.* Geschichte des Erzbistums Köln, vol. 5. Cologne: Verlag J. P. Bachem, 1987.

Hehl, Ulrich von, and Konrad Repgen, eds. *Der deutsche Katholizismus in der zeitgeschichtlichen Forschung.* Mainz: Matthias Grünewald Verlag, 1988.

Heidegger, Heinrich. "Die Geschichte der katholischen Pfarrgemeinde nach der Aufhebung des Klosters." In *St. Blasien: Festschrift aus Anlaß des 200jährigen Bestehens der Kloster- und Pfarrkirche,* edited by Heinrich Heidegger and Hugo Ott, 346–65. Zürich: Verlag Schnell & Steiner, 1983.

Heilbronner, Oded. "From Ghetto to Ghetto: The Place of German Catholic Society in Recent Historiography." *Journal of Modern History* 72 (2000): 453–95.

———. "The Impact and Consequences of the First World War in a Catholic Rural Area: The Black Forest as a Case Study." *German History* 11 (1993): 20–35.

———. "In Search of the (Rural) Catholic Bourgeoisie: The Bürgertum of South Germany." *Central European History* 29 (1996): 175–200.

———. "Wohin verschwand das katholische Bürgertum?" *Zeitschrift für Religions- und Geistesgeschichte* 47 (1995): 320–37.

Heimanns, Heinrich. "Der Verband zur Förderung der Theaterkultur und die katholischen Bedenken." *Allgemeine Rundschau* 14 (1917): 892–93.

Heinen, Anton. "Bildungsrummel?" in *Pflug* 3. Abridged in "Im Ringen der Zeit," *Germania,* September 25, 1926, Morgenausgabe, Das neue Ufer.

Heitzer, Horstwalter. "Die soziale und staatsbürgerliche Bildungs- und Schulungsarbeit des Volksvereins für das katholische Deutschland 1890–1933: Zustimmung und Kritik im sozialen und politischen Katholizismus." In Rauscher, *Katholizismus, Bildung und Wissenschaft im 19. und 20. Jahrhundert,* 119–56.

———. *Der Volksverein für das katholische Deutschland im Kaiserreich 1890–1918.* Mainz: Matthias Grünewald Verlag, 1979.

Hellpach, Willy. *Der deutsche Charakter.* Bonn: Athenäum Verlag, 1954.

Hellwig, Albert. "Artikel 118: Meinungsfreiheit, Zensur." In *Die Grundrechte und Grundpflichten der Reichsverfassung,* edited by Hans Carl Nipperdey, vol. 2, 1–74. Berlin: Verlag von Reimar Hobbing, 1930.

———. "Revolution und Lichtspielreform." *Hochland* 17 (September 1919): 635–38.

Hemminghaus, Edgar Hugo. *Mark Twain in Germany.* New York: Columbia University Press, 1939.

Henningsen, Jürgen. *Der Hohenrodter Bund zur Erwachsenbildung in der Weimarer Zeit.* Heidelberg: Quelle und Meyer, 1958.

Henseler, —. "Das Aschenbrodel unter den kath[olischen] Vereinen." *Mitteilungen für die Vereine vom hl. Karl Borromäus* 5 (March 1917): 12–14.

Hepp, Corona. *Avantgarde: Moderne Kunst, Kulturkritik und Reformbewegungen nach der Jahrhundertwende.* Munich: DTV, 1987.

Herf, Jeffrey. *Reactionary Modernism: Technology, Culture and Politics in Weimar and the Third Reich.* Cambridge: Cambridge University Press, 1984.

Hermand, Jost. *Avantgarde und Regression: 200 Jahre deutsche Kunst.* Leipzig: Edition Leipzig, 1995.

Hermand, Jost, and Frank Trommler. *Die Kultur der Weimarer Republik.* Frankfurt am Main: Fischer Taschenbuch, 1989.

Herwegen, Ildefons. "Von dem Wesensgehalt der kirchlichen Kunst." In Herwegen, *Lumen Christi: Gesammelte Aufsätze.* Verband der Vereine katholischer Akademiker zur Pflege der katholischen Weltanschauung, vol. 7, 69–81. Munich: Theatiner Verlag, 1924.

Herwig, Franz. "Rückblick und Ausblick." In Ettlinger, Funk, and Fuchs, *Wiederbegegnung von Kirche und Kultur in Deutschland,* 374–82.

———. *Die Zukunft des katholischen Elementes in der deutschen Literatur.* Freiburg im Breisgau: Herder, 1922.

Herz, Hermann. "Aus dem Vorwort zur dritten Auflage." In *Literarischer Ratgeber der Bücherwelt.*

———. "Die Bücherwelt und ihr literarischer Ratgeber." *Bücherwelt* 17 (August/September 1920): 198–206.

———. "Das freie Volksbildungswesen." In Meinertz and Sacher, *Deutschland und der Katholizismus*, 333–51.

———. "Der Katholizismus in der schönen Literatur Deutschlands im 19. Jahrhundert und in der Gegenwart." *Bücherwelt* 6 (October 1908): 8–12; (November 1908): 29–34.

———. "Unser Weg: Referate des 15. Kursus für Leiter und Mitarbeiter von Volksbüchereien des Borromäusvereins." *Bücherwelt* 25 (September/October 1928): 362–69.

———. "Der Verein vom hl. Karl Borromäus." *Borromäus-Blätter* 2 (October 1904): 10–14.

———. "Das 'wertvolle' Buch der Volksbücherei." *Bücherwelt* 20 (March/April 1923): 49–54.

———. "Zur Beurteilung des Romans." *Bücherwelt* 12 (September 1915): 250–54.

Herzen, Alexander. "Post Scriptum" (1921). In *My Past and Thoughts*, vol. 3. Translated by Constance Garnett. London: Chatto and Windus, 1924.

Hilden, Anna. "Johanna Spyri und ihre Schriften." *Borromäus-Blätter* 1 (October 1903): 12–13; (January 1904): 57.

Himmelfarb, Gertrude. *The De-moralization of Society: From Victorian Virtues to Modern Values.* New York: Alfred A. Knopf, 1995.

Hipp, Otto. "Schundliteratur und Jugendkriminalität." *Allgemeine Rundschau* 5 (December 12, 1908): 854–55.

"Hirtenschreiben der Bischofskonferenz, 12. August 1908." In Gatz, *Akten der Fuldaer Bischofskonferenz, 1900–1919*, 121.

"Hirtenwort über die Vergnügenssucht." *Kirchliches Amtsblatt für die Diözese Fulda* 42 (January 13, 1926): 2.

"Hirtenwort zum Borromäus-Sonntag." *Kirchliches Amtsblatt für die Diözese Fulda* 48 (November 2, 1932): 73.

Hitchcock, James. "Postmortem on a Rebirth: The Catholic Intellectual Renaissance." *American Scholar* 49 (1980): 211–23.

Hoche, P. "Hausfrau und Kunst." *Volkskunst* 7 (March/April 1919): 355–56.

Hoeber, Karl. "Grundsatzlose Literaturkritik." *Kölnische Volkszeitung*, August 18, 1918.

———. *Der Streit um den Zentrumscharakter.* Cologne, 1912.

Hoeber, Karl, ed. *Die Rückkehr aus dem Exil: Dokumente der Beurteilung des deutschen Katholizismus der Gegenwart.* Verband der Vereine Katholischer Akademiker zur Pflege der Katholischen Weltanschauung. Düsseldorf: L. Schwann, 1926.

Höhler, Mathias. "Die kirchliche Geist in der kirchlichen Kunst." *Theologisch-praktische Quartalschrift* 44 (1892): 777–90.

Hönig, Johannes. "Das gute Buch." *Bücherwelt* 23 (October 1926): 451–56.

———. "Das gute Buch." In *Die Reden gehalten in den öffentlichen und geschlossenen Versammlungen der 65. General-Versammlung der Katholiken Deutschlands zu Breslau . . . 1926*, 153–59. Würzburg: Fränkische Gesellschaftsdruckerei, 1926.

———. "Die Stellung der Katholiken zum Theater." *Historisch-politische Blätter für das katholische Deutschland* 160 (1917): 538–48.

———. "Vom Bücherlesen." *Bücherwelt* 24 (February 1927): 49–57.

———. "Von der Tragik der katholischen Volksbildungsarbeit." *Bücherwelt* 26 (May/June 1929): 171–75.

Holl, Karl. "Zur Situation der Musikkritik." *Musik im Leben* 5 (1930): 182–87.

Holtum, Gregor von. "Die Beziehungen der Kirche zur Kultur." *Wissen und Glauben* 24 (1927): 712–21.

Holzmeister, Clemens. "Das Katholische in der modernen Kunst." *Das neue Reich* 9 (1926): 261–65.

Hoven, ——. "Praktische Bekämpfung der Schund- und Schmutzliteratur." *Mitteilungen für die Vereine vom hl. Karl Borromäus* 8 (February 1919): 7–12.

Hübinger, Gangolf. *Kulturprotestantismus und Politik: Zum Verhältnis von Liberalismus und Protestantismus im wilhelminischen Deutschland.* Tübingen: J. C. B. Mohr (Paul Siebeck), 1994.

Hürten, Heinz. *Deutsche Katholiken, 1918–1945.* Paderborn: Ferdinand Schöningh, 1992.

——. *Kurze Geschichte des deutschen Katholizismus, 1800–1960.* Mainz: Matthias Grünewald Verlag, 1986.

Hütt, Wolfgang, ed. *Hintergrund: Mit dem Unzüchtigkeits- und Gotteslästerungsparagraphen des Strafgesetzbuches gegen Kunst und Künstler, 1900–1933.* Berlin: Henschelverlag, 1990.

Hüttermann, ——. "Schundfilmmoral." *Allgemeine Rundschau* 10 (May 3, 1913): 350–51.

Hug, Wolfgang. "Geist und Wirkung des Cäcilianismus in der Erzdiözese Freiburg im 19. Jahrhundert." *Freiburger Diözesan-Archiv* 103 (1983): 245–63.

Hughes, Robert. *The Shock of the New.* New York: Alfred A. Knopf, 1991.

Hughes, H. Stuart. *Consciousness and Society: The Reorientation of European Social Thought, 1890–1930.* New York: Alfred A. Knopf, 1958.

Huneker, James. *Iconoclasts: A Book of Dramatists.* New York: Greenwood, 1969.

Hunt, Alan. *Governing Morals: A Social History of Moral Regulation.* Cambridge: Cambridge University Press, 1999.

Huppert, Philipp. "[Katholische Literatur und Presse]." In *Verhandlungen der 43. General-Versammlung der Katholiken Deutschlands . . . 1896,* 242–51.

——. *Öffentliche Lesehallen: Ihre Aufgabe, Geschichte und Einrichtung.* Cologne: J. P. Bachem, 1899.

Innerhofer, Roland. *Deutsche Science Fiction 1870–1914: Rekonstruktion und Analyse der Anfänge einer Gattung.* Vienna: Böhlau, 1996.

Instruktion für die Beteiligung des Klerus an dem katholischen Vereinsleben der Gegenwart. N.p., n.d.

International Encyclopedia of the Social Sciences. Edited by David L. Sills. New York: Crowell, Collier, and Macmillan, 1972.

Irsch, Nikolaus. "Aus der modernen Kirchenbaukunst in der Dioezese Trier." *Pastor Bonus* 40 (October 1929): 494–500.

Ist die Gesundheit unseres Volkes bedroht? Volksverein, n.d.

J., H. "Tagung für christliche Kunst." *Germania,* October 8, 1926, Abendausgabe.

Jacobs, Romanus. "Gedanken über moderne und religiöse Kunst." *Die christliche Kunst* 20 (1924): 157–62.

Jahrbuch der Hannoverschen Volkszeitung 1912. Hannover-Hildesheim: J. Kornacker, n.d.

"Jahresbericht des Vereins vom hl. Karl Borromäus in der Erzdiözese Cöln für das Jahr 1908." *Kirchlicher Anzeiger für die Erzdiözese Köln* 49 (November 15, 1909): 131.

"Jahresbericht 1903," *Nachrichten für die Vereine vom hl. Karl Borromäus* 2 (September 1903).

Jarausch, Konrad H. *Students, Society, and Politics in Imperial Germany: The Rise of Academic Illusions.* Princeton, N.J.: Princeton University Press, 1982.

Jensen, Jens Christian. "Bemerkungen zu Friedrich Overbeck." In *Johann Friedrich Over-beck, 1789–1869*, edited by Andreas Blühm and Gerhard Gerkens, 12–19. Lübeck: Museum für Kunst und Kulturgeschichte, 1989.

Jerger-Schwennenbach, —. "Religion und Kultur." *Historisch-politische Blätter für das Katholische Deutschland* 137 (1906): 396–400.

Joachmides, Christos M., Norman Rosenthal, and Wieland Schmied, eds. *German Art in the 20th Century; Painting and Sculpture 1905–1985*. London: Royal Academy of Arts: Weidenfeld and Nicolson; Munich: Prestel, 1985.

Johann, Ernst. *German Cultural History from 1860 to the Present Day*. Munich: Nymphen-burger Verlagsbuchhandlung, 1983.

John, Eckhard. *Musikbolschewismus: Die Politisierung der Musik in Deutschland, 1918–1933*. Stuttgart: Verlag J. B. Metzler, 1994.

Johner, Dominikus. "Kirchenmusik und Seelsorge." *Benediktinische Monatsschrift zur Pflege religiösen und geistigen Leben* 11 (1929): 174–92.

Juncker, Hans. *Kirchliche Rundfunkarbeit im Bistum Trier von den Anfängen bis 1945* (Trier: Bistum Trier Medien, 2000).

Jung, H. "Demokratisierung des Theaters." *Germania*, October 23, 1926, Morgenausgabe, Das neue Ufer.

Juschka, —. "Grundsätzliches über Kirchengesang: Richtlinien für Chorsänger." *Gregoriusblatt für katholische Kirchenmusik* 45 (1920): 74–76.

Kaetzel, Gertrud. "Die Gefährdung der Moral des Familienlebens durch die Bühne. (Bühne und Familie)." *Wissen und Glauben* 26 (1931): 55–58.

———. "Katholizismus und Bühne im In- und Ausland." *Wissen und Glauben* 26 (1931): 120–22.

Kaiser, Jochen-Christoph. "Die Formierung des protestantischen Milieus Konfessionelle Vergesellschaftung im 19. Jahrhundert." In Blaschke and Kuhlemann, *Religion im Kaiserreich*, 257–89.

"Kaiser-Feier." *Volkskunst* 3 (March 1915): 177.

Kalk, —, and —Köllen. "Schattenseiten des Vereinslebens." *Pastor Bonus* 13 (1901): 496–503.

Kalkschmidt, Eugen. "Die Macht Films." *Hochland* 26 (1929): 633–47.

"Der Kampf gegen die moderne Sittenlosigkeit . . . ." *Volkswart* 5 (September 1912): 129–36.

"Katholische Leitsätze und Weisungen zu verschiedenen modernen Sittlichkeitsfragen." *Kirchlicher Anzeiger für die Erzdiözese Köln* 65 (January 20, 1925): 15–18.

"Katholische Morgenfeiern im Westdeutschen Rundfunk, 1928." *Mitteilungen des Zentral-bildungsausschusses*. In *Volkskunst* 16 (March 1928): 95.

"Der katholische Roman." *Kölnische Zeitung*, September 25, 1898.

"Katholischer Press- und Literatur-Verein für die Länder deutscher Zunge." *Katholische Revue* 1 (1900): 2–7.

Katholischer Pressverein für Bayern. *Jahres-Bericht pro 1908/09*. Landshut: Jos. Thomann-'sche Buch und Kunstdruckerei, 1909.

———. *Jahresbericht pro 1911*. Munich: G. J. Manz, 1912.

———. *Jahresbericht pro 1913*. Munich: G. J. Manz, 1914.

———. *Jahresbericht 1927*. N.p., 1928

———. *Jahresbericht 1931*. N.p., n.d.

"Katholisches Vereinswesen und katholische Vereinsaufgabe." *Historisch-politische Blätter für das katholische Deutschland* 165 (1920): 709–16.

Kauders, H. "Das Religiöse in der Kunst der Gegenwart." *Das Kunstblatt* 29 (1910): 180–89.

Kaufmann, Doris. *Katholisches Milieu in Münster 1928–1933: Politische Aktionsformen und geschlechtsspezifische Verhaltensräume.* Düsseldorfer Schriften zur Neueren Landesgeschichte und zur Geschichte Nordrhein-Westfalen, edited by Hans-Joachim Behr et al., vol. 14. Düsseldorf: Schwann, 1984.

[Kausen, Armin]. "Unser Programm." *Allgemeine Rundschau* 1 (1904): 1.

Keckeis, Gustav. "Besinnung." *Literarischer Handweiser* 12 (1926/1927): 881–90.

Keiter, Henrich. "Konfessionelle Brunnenvergiftung." *Der Gral* 2 (August 15, 1908): 517–21.

———. *Konfessionelle Brunnenvergiftung: Die wahre Schmach des Jahrhunderts.* Regensburg: Verlag von Heinrich Keiter, 1896.

Keldany-Mohr, Irmgard. *"Unterhaltungsmusik" als soziokulturelles Phänomen des 19. Jahrhunderts: Untersuchung über den Einfluß der musikalischen Öffentlichkeit auf die Herausbildung eines neuen Musiktypes* (Regensburg: Gustav Bosse, 1977).

Keller, R. A. "Schutz der Jugend vor den Schäden des Kinos." *Germania,* May 27, 1928, Morgenausgabe.

Kemmer, Ludwig. "Fort mit dem Schmutz!" *Allgemeine Rundschau* 1 (1904): 440–43.

Kieffer, —. "Die heutigen Tanzbelustigungen vor dem Forum der Moral." *Pastor Bonus* 24 (1912): 458–65; 610–19.

"Das Kinematographenwesen." *Kirchliches Amtsblatt für die Diözese Fulda* 20 (November 25, 1913).

"Kirchenmusikalische Aufführungen." *Kirchliche Amtsblatt für die Diözese Mainz* 66 (December 11, 1924): 39–41.

Kirchlicher Anzeiger für die Erzdiözese Köln 54 (June 1, 1914).

Kirsch, Winfried. "'Nazarener in der Musik' oder 'Der Caecilianismus in der bildende Kunst.'" In *Der Caecilianismus: Anfänge—Grundlagen—Wirkungen: Internationales Symposium zur Kirchenmusik des 19. Jahrhunderts,* edited by Hubert Unverricht, 35–73. Eichstätter Abhandlungen zur Musikwissenschaft, vol. 5. Tutzing: Hans Schneider, 1988.

Kjerbüll-Petersen, Lorenz. "Theater und Drama." *Der Gral* 21 (1926/1927): 713–17.

———. "Theater und Drama." *Der Gral* 25 (1930/1931): 57–64.

Kl., Mr. "Die Gefahr der Lichtspielhäuser." *Volkswart* 6 (September 1913): 152–53.

Kleebeck, K. "Was Arbeiterinnen lesen." *Bücherwelt* 17 (March 1920): 63–64.

Klein, Gotthard. *Der Volksverein für das katholische Deutschland, 1890–1933: Geschichte, Bedeutung, Untergang.* Veröffentlichungen der Kommission für Zeitgeschichte, edited by Ulrich von Hehl, series B: Forschungen, vol. 75. Paderborn: Ferdinand Schöningh, 1996.

Klein, Ferdinand. "Klerus und Theaterbesuch." *Allgemeine Rundschau* 1 (1904): 329–31.

Klein-Ehrenwalten, Arthur von. "Die Entwicklung der deutschen Bühne in ihrer Stellung zur katholischen Kirche." *Wissen und Glauben* 24 (1927): 292–301.

———. "Film und Katholizismus." *Literarischer Handweiser* 67 (1930/31): 237–40.

———. "Wege des Films." *Wissen und Glauben* 24 (1927): 556–61.

———. "Zum katholischen Filmkongreß im Haag." *Wissen und Glauben* 25 (1928): 495–99.

Klimke, Friedrich. "Katholizismus und einheitliche Weltanschuung." *Der Aar* (April 1911): 50–57.

Klinger, M. "Das Problem der modernen Kunst." *Christliches Kunstblatt für Kirche, Schule und Haus* 38 (1897): 38–42.

Klöcker, Michael. *Katholisch—Von der Wiege bis zur Bahre.* Munich: Kösel, 1991.

———. "Das katholische Bildungsdefizit in Deutschland: Eine historische Analyse." *Geschichte in Wissenschaft und Unterricht* 32 (1981): 79–98.

———. "Das katholische Milieu: Grundüberlegungen—in besonderer Hinsicht auf das Deutsche Kaiserreich von 1871." *Zeitschrift für Religions- und Geistesgeschichte* 44 (1992): 241–62.

———. "Katholizismus und Bildungsbürgertum: Hinweise zur Erforschung vernachlässigter Bereiche der deutschen Bildungsgeschichte im 19. Jahrhundert." In *Bildungsbürgertum im 19. Jahrhundert,* edited by Reinhart Koselleck, 117–38, pt. 2, *Bildungsgüter und Bildungswissen.* Industrielle Welt, vol. 41. Stuttgart: Klett-Cotta, 1990.

Klönne, Arno. "Leo Weismantel—Ein fränkischer Poet und Pädagoge." *Mainfränkisches Jahrbuch für Kunst und Geschichte* 37 (1985): 162–73.

Kloidt, Franz. "Filmzensur und künstlerischer Film." *Volkstum und Volksbildung* 4 (1932): 131–37.

———. "Verhindert die Filmzensur den künsterlichen Film?" *Volkswart* 25 (August 1932): 115–18.

Kneer, A. "Katholik und Kino." *Allgemeine Rundschau* 22 (1925): 145.

Kneip, Jakob. "Katholiken und Literatur—Eine Auseinandersetzung: Dichtung und Kirche." *Schönere Zukunft* 2 (August 21, 1927): 999–1000.

———. "Kirche und Dichtung." *Allgemeine Rundschau* 28 (July 11, 1931): 439.

———. "Religion und Dichtung." *Trierischen Landes-zeitung,* supplement, February 7, 1928, n.p.

Knox, Ronald. "Der katholische Roman." *Orplid.* Abridged in "Zeitschriftenschau." *Germania,* September 1, 1928, Morgenausgabe, Das neue Ufer.

Knüppel, A. A. "Christozentrische Kirchenmusik." *Monatshefte für katholische Kirchenmusik* 6 (1924): 2–5.

———. "Werden in Zukunft in unseren Kirchenchören Knaben oder Mädchen singen?" *Cäcilienvereinsorgan* 47 (1912): 71–73.

Koch, Walter. "Der Begriff Modern in der Kunst." *Wissen und Glauben* 17 (1932): 591–95; 646–49.

Kocka, Jürgen. *Bürgertum im 19. Jahrhundert.* Göttingen: Vandenhoeck & Ruprecht, 1995.

———. "Bürgertum und Bürgerlichkeit als Probleme der deutschen Geschichte vom späten 18. zum frühen 20. Jahrhundert." In Kocka, *Bürger und Bürgerlichkeit im 19. Jahrhundert,* 21–63.

———. "The European Pattern and the German Case." In *Bourgeois Society in Nineteenth-century Europe,* edited by Jürgen Kocka and Allen Mitchell, 3–39. Oxford: Berg, 1993.

Kocka, Jürgen, ed. *Bürger und Bürgerlichkeit im 19. Jahrhundert.* Göttingen: Vandenhoeck und Ruprecht, 1987.

Koehler, Oskar. "The Position of Catholicism in the Culture at the Turn of the Century." In Aubert et al., *The Church in the Industrial Age,* 245–56.

Koep, Leo, and Alfons Vodermayer. "Die katholischen Volksbüchereien in Deutschland." In *Handbuch des Büchereiwesens,* edited by Johannes Langfeldt, vol. 2, 387–420. Wiesbaden: Otto Harrassowitz, 1965.

Koep, Leo, ed. *Bücher in Menschenhand: Festschrift zum goldenen Priesterjubiläum des päpstlichen Hausprälaten und Direktors des Borromäusvereins Johannes Braun.* Bonn: Verlag des Borromäus-Vereins, 1955.

Kösters, Christoph. *Katholische Verbände und moderne Gesellschaft: Organisationsgeschichte und Vereinskultur im Bistum Münster, 1918 bis 1945.* Veröffentlichungen der Kommission für Zeitgeschichte, edited by Ulrich von Hehl, series B: Forschungen, vol. 68. Paderborn: Ferdinand Schöningh, 1995.

Kolinsky, Eva, and Wilfried van der Will. "In Search of German Culture: An Introduction." In Kolinsky and van der Will, *The Cambridge Companion to Modern German Culture,* 1–19.

Kolinsky, Eva, and Wilfried van der Will, eds. *The Cambridge Companion to Modern German Culture.* Cambridge: Cambridge University Press, 1998.

Kommt zu uns! Wir sind 400 000 zufriedene Mitglieder der Deutschen Buch-Gemeinschaft. N.p., n.d.

Kossmann. E. H. *The Low Countries, 1780–1940.* Oxford: Clarendon Press, 1978.

Kr. "Kirche und Film." *Germania,* November 15, 1928, Morgenausgabe, Das neue Ufer.

Kracauer, Siegfried. "The Little Shopgirls Go to the Movies." In *The Mass Ornament: Weimar Essays.* Translated and edited by Thomas Y. Levin, 291–304. Cambridge, Mass.: Harvard University Press, 1995.

Kralik, Richard von. *Ein Jahr katholischer Literaturbewegung.* Regensburg: J. Habbel, 1910.

———. *Die katholische Literaturbewegung der Gegenwart.* Regensburg: J. Habbel, 1910.

———. "Katholisches Kultur-'Ghetto', katholische 'Inferiorität'?" *Schönere Zukunft* 3 (1928): 533–35.

———. "Ein katholisches Kulturprogramm." *Historisch-politische Blätter für das Katholische Deutschland* 137 (1906): 1–10.

———. "Kulturideale." *Die Kultur* 3 (1902): 321–29.

———. "Die moderne Kunst- und Literaturbewegung." *Literarische Warte* 3 (April 1902): 385–94.

———. *Tage und Werke: Lebenserinnerungen.* Vienna: Vogelsang-Verlag, 1922.

Kranz, Caspar. "[Johannes Braun:] Persönlichkeit und Werk." In Koep, *Bücher in Menschenhand,* 25–32.

Krauss, Heinrich, and Heinrich Ostermann, eds. *Verbandskatholizismus? Verbände, Organisationen und Gruppen im deutschen Katholizismus.* Kevelaer: Butzon und Bercker, 1968.

Kreiten, W. "Die katholische Kritik und ihr Kritiker Veremundus." *Stimmen aus Maria-Laach* 55 (November 1898): 506–30.

Kreitmaier, Josef. "Der Barometerstand der Kunst." *Stimmen der Zeit* 111 (1926): 453–66.

———. *Dominanten.* Freiburg im Breisgau, 1924.

———. "Expressionistische Kirchenkunst?" *Stimmen der Zeit* 116 (1928): 35–46.

———. "Fünfundzwanzig Jahre Deutsche Gesellschaft für christliche Kunst." *Stimmen der Zeit* 95 (May 1918): 206–8.

———. "Für oder gegen Kirchenkonzerte?" *Stimmen der Zeit* 103 (1922): 231–34.

———. "Konfessionelle Kunst." *Stimmen der Zeit* 104 (1922): 59–69.

———. "Die kranke deutsche Kunst." *Allgemeine Rundschau* 9 (January 6, 1912): 13–15.

———. "Die Krisis der christlichen Kunst." *Stimmen der Zeit* 104 (1923): 377–93.

———. "Musikpessimisten." *Stimmen der Zeit* 107 (1924): 369–81.

———. "Religiöse Kunst der Gegenwart." *Stimmen der Zeit* 124 (1932): 134–36.

———. "Stirbt die Kunst?" *Stimmen der Zeit* 116 (1928): 116–27.

————. "Theologische Grundbegriffe der kirchlichen Kunst." In *Ehrengabe deutscher Wissenschaft: Dargeboten von katholischen Gelehrten,* edited by Franz Fessler. Freiburg im Breisgau: Herder, 1920.

————. "Von der Freiheit der Kunst." *Stimmen der Zeit* 102 (1921): 129–42.

————. *Von Kunst und Künstlern: Gedanken zu alten und neuen künstlerischen Fragen.* Freiburg im Breisgau: Herder, 1926.

————. "Von Piloty zu Picasso." *Stimmen der Zeit* 101 (1921): 323–32.

————. "Zum Problem der religiösen Kunst." *Schweizerische Rundschau* 27 (1926): 237–47.

————. "Zur Kulturaufgabe der christlichen Kunst." *Die christliche Kunst* 23 (June 1927): 284–85.

Kremer, G. "Das Vereinsproblem." *Theologie und Glaube* 14 (1922): 222–25.

Kreuzberg, P. J. "Rundfunk und ländliche Volksbildung." *Volkstum und Volksbildung* 4 (1932): 86–92.

Kroeber, A. L., and Clyde Kluckhohn. *Culture: A Critical Review of Concepts and Definitions.* Peabody Museum of American Archaeology and Ethnology, Harvard University, vol. 47, no. 1. Cambridge, Mass.: The Museum, 1952.

Krose, Hermann A., ed. *Kirchliches Handbuch für das katholische Deutschland.* Vol. 7, *1917–1918.* Freiburg im Breisgau: Herder, 1918.

————. *Kirchliches Handbuch für das katholische Deutschland.* Vol. 11, *1922–1923.* Freiburg im Breisgau: Herder, 1923.

Kürschners Deutscher Literatur-Kalender auf das Jahr 1928. 24th ed. Berlin: Walter de Gruyter, 1928.

Kuhlemann, Frank-Michael. "Protestantisches Milieu in Baden: Konfessionelle Vergesellschaftung und Mentalität im Umbruch zur Moderne." In Blaschke and Kuhlemann, *Religion im Kaiserreich: Milieu-Mentalitäten-Krisen,* 316–49.

Kuhn, Albert. *Die Kirche: Ihr Bau, ihre Ausstattung, ihre Restauration.* Einsiedeln: Benziger, 1917.

————. *Moderne Kunst- und Stilfragen.* Einsiedeln: Benziger, 1909.

"Die kulturelle Inferiorität des Katholizismus." *Das zwanzigste Jahrhundert* 8 (July 19, 1908): 338–40; 8 (August 2, 1908): 365; 8 (August 16, 1908): 393–94.

"Die Kulturkrisis der Gegenwart und ihre Hauptursachen." *Germania,* November 28, 1928, Morgenausgabe.

"Kundgebung des Volkswartbundes auf dem Katholikentage in Essen." *Volkswart* 25 (October 1932): 147–48.

"Die Kunst als Gehilfin der Predigt." *Christliches Kunstblatt für Kirche, Schule und Haus* 32 (1890): 177–86.

"Die Kunst der Kritik." *Germania,* October 20, 1928, Morgenausgabe.

Kurthen, Wilhelm. "Moderne Kirchenmusik." *Gregoriusblatt für katholische Kirchenmusik* 49 (1924): 41–44, 49.

————. "Das Problem des religiösen Ausdrucks in der Musik." *Gregoriusblatt für katholische Kirchenmusik* 45 (1920): 65–68.

L., R. "Moderne Bühnenkunst." *Hochland* 24 (October 1926): 126–28.

Labrie, Arnold. "*Kultur* und *Zivilisation* in Germany during the Nineteenth Century." In *German Reflections,* edited by Joep Leerssen and Menno Spiering, Yearbook of European Studies/Annuaire d'études européenes, vol. 7. Amsterdam: Rodopi, 1994.

[Langbehn, Julius]. *Rembrandt als Erzieher.* Leipzig: Verlag von C. L. Hirschfeld, 1909.

Langen, Gustav. "Christliche Kunst." *Kunstwart* 23 (1910): 158–63; 290–302.

Laqueur, Walter. *Weimar: A Cultural History, 1918–1933.* New York: Perigee, 1980.

Laros, M. "Von christlicher Kunstbetrachtung." *Die christliche Kunst* 23 (May 1927): 252–55.

Latta, ———. "Von Werk- und Feierstunden unserer Volksbildungsarbeit: Ein Jahr Bezirksarbeit im Borromäusverein." *Bücherwelt* 24 (January 1927): 13–14.

Lechthaler, Josef. "Ist die katholische Kirchenmusik inferior?" *Musica Sacra* 57 (1927): 9–16.

———. "Unsere Zeit und die Religiöse Musik." *Musik im Leben* 5 (May 1929): 32–36.

Lees, Andrew. "Critics of Urban Society in Germany, 1854–1914." *Journal of the History of Ideas* 40 (January/March 1979): 61–83.

———. "Debates about the Big City in Germany, 1890–1914." *Societas* 5 (Winter 1975): 31–47.

Leh, Jakob. "Mechanische Kirchenmusik: Schallplatten im Gottesdienst." *Musica Sacra* 61 (1931): 95–96.

Lehnert-Rodiek, Gertrud. *Zeitreisen: Untersuchungen zu einem Motiv der erzählenden Literatur des 19. und 20. Jahrhunderts.* Bonner Untersuchungen zur vergleichenden Literaturwissenschaft, vol. 3. Rheinbach-Merzbach: CMZ Verlag, 1987.

Leibig, Karl. "Die Filmzensur in Deutschland in Gesetzgebung und Praxis." *Allgemeine Rundschau* 26 (1929): 652–56.

"Leitsätze für die Jugendspielscharen des Bühnen-Volksbundes." *Volkskunst* 11 (July/September 1923): 79–80.

Leitsätze der Vorträge des 16. Kursus für Lieter und Mitarbeiter von Volksbücherein. Bonn: Verlag des Borromäus-Vereins, [1928].

["Lektüre"]. *Kirchliche Anzeiger für die Diözese Fulda* 20 (May 6, 1897).

Lemacher, Heinrich. "Die kirchenmusikalische 'Situation' in den Rheinlanden." *Musik im Leben* 3 (October 1927): 139–40.

———. "'Neue Sachlichkeit' in der katholischen Kirchenmusik." *Allgemeine Musikzeitung* 54 (1927): 813–15; 833–34.

Lempp, ———. "Das Kulturprogramm des deutschen Katholizismus." *Evangelische Freiheit* (1914): 185–93.

Lenman, R. J. V. "Art, Society, and the Law in Wilhelmine Germany: The Lex Heinze." *Oxford German Studies* 8 (1973/1974): 86–113.

Lenman, Robin. *Artists and Society in Germany, 1850–1914.* Manchester: Manchester University Press, 1997.

———. "From 'Brown Sauce' to 'Plein Air': Taste and the Art Market in Germany, 1889–1910." In Forster-Hahn, *Imagining Modern German Culture: 1889–1910*, 53–69.

———. "Painters, Patronage and the Art Market in Germany 1850–1914." *Past and Present* 123 (May 1989): 109–40.

Lennartz, Ernst. "Fünfundzwanzig Jahre Volkswartbund." *Volkswart* 25 (January 1932): 5–6.

———. "Der Kölner Katholikentag 1928 und die Sittlichkeitsfrage." *Volkswart* 21 (May 1928): 65–68.

———. "Warum abonnieren und lesen wir den Volkswart? *Volkswart* 18 (January 1925): 2.

Lentz, Heinrich. "Film, Kunst und Zivilisation." *Hochland* 22 (August 1925): 597–604.

Lepovitz, Helena Waddy. *Images of Faith: Expressionism, Catholic Folk Art, and the Industrial Revolution.* Athens, Ga.: University of Georgia Press, 1991.

Lepsius, M. Rainer. "Parteiensystem und Sozialstruktur: zum Problem der Demokratisierung der deutschen Gesellschaft." In *Deutsche Parteien vor 1918*, edited by Gerhard Albert Ritter, 56–80. Cologne: Kiepenheuer und Witsch, 1973.

————. "Zur Soziologie des Bürgertums und der Bürgerlichkeit." In Kocka, *Bürger und Bürgerlichkeit im 19. Jahrhundert,* 79–100.

Levi, Erik. "Music in Modern German Culture." In Kolinsky and van der Will, *The Cambridge Companion to Modern German Culture,* 233–55.

"Leseregeln." *Borromäus-Blätter* 1 (January 1904): 52.

Lichtträger in Chaos 3: Film und Volk. Essener Volkszeitung, 1925.

Lidtke, Vernon L. *The Alternative Culture: Socialist Labor in Imperial Germany.* New York: Oxford University Press, 1985.

Liedhegener, Antonius. *Christentum und Urbanisierung: Katholiken und Protestanten in Münster und Bochum, 1830–1933.* Veröffentlichungen der Kommission für Zeitgeschichte, edited by Ulrich von Hehl, series B: Forschung, vol. 77. Paderborn: Ferdinand Schöningh, 1997.

Lill, Georg. "Christliche Hauskunst." *Die christliche Kunst* 26 (1929): 33–43.

————. "Grenzen und Möglichkeiten: Ein Nachwort zur Essener Ausstellung." *Die christliche Kunst* 29 (1932): 23–27.

————. "Im Streite der Zeit: Rechts oder links in der Kunst? Eine Antikritik." *Die christliche Kunst* (1926): 207–10.

————. "Die kirchliche Kunst der Gegenwart und das katholische Volk: Rede gehalten am 6. September 1927 auf der 66. Katholikenversammlung zu Dortmund." *Die christliche Kunst* 24 (December 1927): 65–78.

————. "Moderne christliche Kunst." Abridged in "Im Ringen der Zeit," *Germania,* May 15, 1926, Morgenausgabe, Das neue Ufer.

————. "Nacktdarstellung und christliche Kunst." *Die christliche Kunst* 23 (1927): 251.

————. "Das Problem der christlichen Kunst." *Die christliche Kunst* 21 (1925): 65–85.

————. "Die religiöse Kunst der Gegenwart und das katholische Volk." In *66. Generalversammlung der Katholiken Deutschlands zu Dortmund . . . 1927.* Dortmund: Gebrüder Lensing, 1927.

Lill, Rudolf. "Der deutsche Katholizismus in der neueren historischen Forschung." In Hehl and Repgen, *Der deutsche Katholizismus in der zeitgeschichtlichen Forschung.*

————. "The Kulturkampf in Prussia and in the German Empire." In Aubert et al., *The Church in the Industrial Age,* 26–45.

Lindemann, Reinhold. "Zur Gegenwartslage der christlichen Kunst." *Bücherwelt* 25 (July/August 1928): 241–44.

Linhardt, Robert. "Kirche und katholische Vereine." *Das neue Reich* 10 (1928): 1085–87.

Literarischer Ratgeber der Bücherwelt: Des Musterkataloges für kath[olische] Volks- und Jugendbüchereien. 4th ed. Bonn: Verlag des Borromäus-Vereins, 1918.

"Das Literaturprogramm des Papstes." *Der Gral* 5 (November 15, 1910): 69–74.

Lloyd, G. E. R. *Demystifying Mentalities.* Cambridge: Cambridge University Press, 1990.

Lönne, Karl-Egon. "Katholizismus-Forschung." *Geschichte und Gesellschaft* 26 (2000): 128–70.

Lohr, Steve. "The Future Came Faster in the Old Days." *New York Times,* October 5, 1997.

Lohrer, Adolf. "Etwas vom Volkstanze." *Volkskunst* 15 (1927): 251–53.

Lorenz, Joseph. "Der Klerus und der moderne Kulturmensch." *Allgemeine Rundschau* 2 (1905): 212–15.

Loth, Wilfried. "Integration und Erosion: Wandlungen des katholischen Milieus in Deutschland." In Loth, *Deutscher Katholizismus im Umbruch zur Moderne,* 266–281.

Loth, Wilfried, ed. *Deutscher Katholizismus im Umbruch zur Moderne.* Konfession und Gesellschaft, Beiträge zur Zeitgeschichte, edited by Anselm Doering-Manteuffel et al., vol. 3. Stuttgart: W. Kohlhammer, 1991.

Lotz, Albert. "Kirche, Kultur und Politik." *Allgemeine Rundschau* 20 (1923): 377–78.

"Der Luther-Film: Oeffentliche Erklärung." *Germania,* March 4, 1928, Morgenausgabe.

Lux, Joseph August. "Gibt es ein deutsches katholisches Literaturleben?!" *Schönere Zukunft* 2 (September 11, 1927): 1071–72.

———. "Kirche und Kunst." *Das neue Reich* 37. Abridged in "Im Ringen der Zeit," *Germania,* June 26, 1926, Morgenausgabe, Das neue Ufer.

———. "Die Not des katholischen Autors." *Schönere Zukunft* 50. Abridged in "Im Ringen der Zeit," *Germania,* September 25, 1926, Morgenausgabe, Das neue Ufer.

———. "Die Tragik des katholischen Dichters: Grundsätzliches zum Literaturstreit." *Allgemeine Rundschau* 24 (1927): 760–61.

Lyon, David. "Rethinking Secularization: Retrospect and Prospect." *Review of Religious Research* 26 (March 1985): 228–43.

McCarthy, John, and Werner von der Ohe, eds. *Zensur und Kultur: Censorship and Culture.* Studien und Texte zur Sozialgeschichte, edited by Wolfgang Frühwald et al., vol. 51. Tübingen: Max Niemeyer, 1995.

McGraw-Hill Encyclopedia of World Drama. Edited by Stanley Hochmann. New York: McGraw-Hill, 1972.

Machin, G. I. T. *Churches and Social Issues in Twentieth-Century Britain.* Oxford: Clarendon Press, 1998.

McLeod, Hugh. "Building the 'Catholic Ghetto': Catholic Organisations 1870–1914." In *Voluntary Religion,* edited by W. J. Sheils and Diana Wood, 411–44. Published for the Ecclesiastical History Society by Basil Blackwell, 1986.

———. *Religion and the People of Western Europe, 1789–1989.* Oxford: Oxford University Press, 1997.

———. "Secular Cities? Berlin, London, and New York in the Later Nineteenth and Early Twentieth Centuries." In Bruce, *Religion and Modernization,* 59–89.

———. "Weibliche Frömmigkeit—männlicher Unglaube?" In *Bürgerinnen und Bürger,* edited by Ute Frevert, 134–56. Kritische Studien zur Geschichtswissenschaft, edited by Helmut Binding, Jürgen Kocka, and Hans-Ulrich Wehler, vol. 77. Göttingen: Vandenhoeck und Ruprecht, 1988.

Macmillan Student Encyclopedia of Sociology. Edited by Michael Mann. London: Macmillan, 1983.

"Der Magdeburger Katholikentag: Der deutsche Katholizismus und die deutsche Kultur." *Germania,* September 9, 1928, Morgenausgabe.

"Der Magdeburger Katholikentag: Die katholischen Vereine und die Kirche." *Germania,* September 9, 1928, Abendausgabe.

"Der Magdeburger Katholikentag: Katholisches Buch, Katholische Presse: Die 2. Öffentliche Versammlung." *Germania,* September 7, 1928, Morgenausgabe.

Magon, Fritz. "Die Freude am Buch in der Großstadt: Einige Beobachtungen und Erfahrungen." *Die Bücherwelt* 25 (March/April 1928): 119–23.

Maier, Hans. "Zur historischen Situation des deutschen Katholizismus heute." In Hehl and Repgen, *Der deutsche Katholizismus in der zeitgeschichtlichen Forschung,* 25–39.

Marforio, —. "Der Tonfilm zum blauen Engel." *Allgemeine Rundschau* 27 (July 5, 1930): 472–73.

Maritain, Jacques. "Christliche Kunst." *Der katholische Gedanke* 4. Abridged from *Art et Scholastique,* translated by Günther Müller, in "Zeitschriftenschau," *Germania,* November 3, 1928, Morgenausgabe, Das neue Ufer.

Marschall, Bernhard. "Aus der Arbeit: Bericht des ZBA." *Volkstum und Volksbildung* 2 (1930): 313–17.

———. "Bericht des ZBA." *Volkstum und Volksbildung* 2 (1930): 313–18.

———. "Einleitungsworte." In *Film und Rundfunk,* 242–44.

———. "Filmarbeitsgemeinschaft." *Volkstum und Volksbildung* 3 (1931): 185–86.

———. "Die Forderungen der Katholiken bezüglich der Handhabung der Zensur." In *Film und Rundfunk,* 286–91.

———. "Frühjahrstagung." *Volkskunst* 14 (1926): 318–24.

———. "Katholische Filmarbeit." *Volkstum und Volksbildung* 2 (1930): 56–60.

———. "Katholische Rundfunkarbeit." *Volkstum und Volksbildung* 2 (1930): 170–75.

———. "Der Rundfunk." In *71. Generalversammlung der deutschen Katholiken zu Essen an der Ruhr . . . 1932,* 240–46.

———. "Rundfunkarbeit." *Volkstum und Volksbildung* 3 (1931): 187–88.

———. "Rundfunk-Hörgemeinden." *Volkstum und Volksbildung* 3 (1931): 245–46.

———. "Die Weltbedeutung des Rundfunks." In Ernst und Marschall, *Film und Rundfunk,* 286–91.

———. "Wintertagung." *Volkskunst* 14 (1926): 110–19.

———. "ZBA-Herbsttagung." *Volkstum und Volksbildung* 5 (1933): 25–27.

———. "Zehn Jahre Zentralbildungsausschuß." *Volkstum und Volksbildung* 1 (1929): 218–22.

———. "Der Zentralbildungsausschuss im Jahre 1930." *Volkstum und Volksbildung* 3 (1931): 47–52.

Marsop, Paul. *Zur "Sozialisierung" der Musik und der Musiker.* Regensburg: Gustav Bosse, 1919.

Marty, Martin E. "The Catholic Ghetto and All the Other Ghettos." *Catholic Historical Review* 68 (April 1982): 185–205.

Marx, [Wilhelm]. "Der Volksverein in alter und neuer Zeit." *Germania,* January 1, 1929, Morgenausgabe.

Matt, Franz. "Die Deutsche Gesellschaft für christliche Kunst." *Allgemeine Rundschau* special issue (July 1911): n.p.

Mauerhof, Emil. "Kunst und Religion." *Allgemeine Rundschau* 3 (March 24, 1906): 163–64.

Mausbach, Joseph. "Der Kampf gegen die moderne Sittenlosigkeit—eine Kulturaufgabe des deutschen Volkes." *Volkswart* 5 (September 1912).

———. *Die Kirche und die moderne Kultur.* Munich: Kösel und Pustet, n.d.

———. "Kultur und Katholizismus." *Theologische Revue* 6 (January 8, 1907): 1–8.

Mayr, Martin. "Der Kampf um die neue Kunst." *Allgemeine Rundschau* 17 (1920): 399.

Mayrhofer, Isidor. "Die katholischen Kirchenmusik auf dem Irrwege?" *Kirchenmusikalisches Jahrbuch* 22 (1909): 124–31.

Meerpohl, Franz. "Zur Kulturphilosophie des Katholizismus." *Literarischer Handweiser* 63 (October 1926): 3–10.

Meinertz, Max, and Hermann Sacher, eds. *Deutschland und der Katholizismus: Gedanken zur Neugestaltung des deutschen Geistes- und Gesellschaftslebens.* Freiburg im Breisgau: Herder, 1918.

Mergel, Thomas. "Grenzgänger: Das katholische Bürgertum im Rheinland zwischen bürgerlichem und katholischem Milieu 1870–1914." In Blaschke and Kuhlemann, *Religion im Kaiserreich*, 166–192.

———. *Zwischen Klasse und Konfession: Katholisches Bürgertum im Rheinland 1794–1914.* Bürgertum: Beiträge zur europäischen Gesellschaftsgeschichte, edited by Wolfgang Mager et al., vol. 9. Göttingen: Vandenhoeck und Ruprecht, 1994.

Meyer, Michael A. *Jewish Identity in the Modern World.* Seattle: University of Washington, 1990.

Meyer, Michael. *Theaterzensur in München, 1900–1918: Geschichte und Entwicklung der polizeilichen Zensur und des Theaterzensurenbeirates unter besonderer Berücksichtigung Frank Wedekinds.* Miscellanea Bavarica Monacensia 111. Munich: Neue Schriftenreihe des Stadtarchivs München, 1982.

Missonne, ———. "Die Zensur für Kinder und erwachsene Jugend." In Ernst and Marschall, *Film und Rundfunk*, 164–206.

Möhler, Anton. *Ästhetik der katholischen Kirchenmusik.* Ravensburg: Verlag von Friedrich Alber, 1910.

Möhlig, Karl. "Aus der Bühnenwelt: Calderons 'Großes Welttheater' auf einer Freilichtbühne in Godesberg am Rhein." *Bücherwelt* 23 (July 1926): 334–36.

———. "Aus der Bühnenwelt: Sechs Personen suchen einen Autor." *Bücherwelt* 22 (August 1925): 382–84.

———. "Aus der Bühnenwelt: Shaws 'Heilige Johanna' und der Katholizismus." *Bücherwelt* 22 (May 1925): 236–39.

———. "Aus der Bühnenwelt: Der Streit um den 'Fröhlichen Weinberg.'" *Bücherwelt* 23 (July 1926): 336.

———. "Die geistigen Strömungen der Gegenwart in der Literatur." *Bücherwelt* 23 (November 1926): 481–87.

Mohr, Josef. *Jubilate Deo! Lieder für den katholischen Gottesdienst . . . .* 12th ed. Regensburg: Friedrich Pustet, 1877.

Mol, Hans. *Identity and the Sacred: A Sketch for a New Social-Scientific Theory of Religion.* Oxford: Basil Blackwell, 1976.

Molitor, F. "Dorfmusik." *Musik im Leben* 1 (March 1925): 39–43.

Mommsen, Wolfgang J. *Bürgerliche Kultur und künstlerische Avantgarde: Kultur und Politik im deutschen Kaiserreich 1870–1918.* Frankfurt am Main: Propyläen Verlag, 1994.

———. *Bürgerliche Kultur und politische Ordnung: Künstler, Schriftsteller und Intellektuelle in der deutschen Geschichte, 1830–1933.* Frankfurt am Main: Fischer Taschenbuch Verlag, 2000.

———. *Imperial Germany, 1867–1918: Politics, Culture, and Society in an Authoritarian State.* Translated by Richard Deveson. London: Arnold, 1995.

———. "Stadt und Kultur im deutschen Kaiserreich." In *Die Welt der Stadt*, edited by Tilo Schabert. Carl Friedrich von Siemens Stiftung, vol. 4. Munich: Piper, 1991.

Monzel, Heinz. "Referat." In Ernst and Marschall, *Film und Rundfunk: Zweiter Internationaler Katholischer Filmkongress, Erster Internationaler Katholischer Rundfunkkongress*, 348–67.

———. "Der Rundfunk und die Katholiken." *Stimmen der Zeit* 120 (November 1930: 123–34.

Mooser, Josef. "Das katholische Milieu in der bürgerlichen Gesellschaft: Zum Vereinswesen des Katholizismus im späten Deutschen Kaiserreich." In Blaschke and Kuhlemann, *Religion im Kaiserreich*, 59–92.

———. "Das katholische Vereinswesen in der Diözese Paderborn um 1900." *Westfälische Zeitschrift* 141 (1991): 447–61.

———. "Volk, Arbeiter und Bürger in der Öffentlichkeit des Kaiserreichs." In *Bürger in der Gesellschaft der Neuzeit*, edited by H. J. Puhle, 259–73. Göttingen: Vandenhoeck und Ruprecht, 1991.

Morsey, Rudolf. "Der Kulturkampf." In *Der soziale und politische Katholizismus: Entwicklungslinien in Deutschland, 1803–1963*, edited by Anton Rauscher, 110–64. Munich: Günter Olzog, 1963.

Mosse, George L. *Fallen Soldiers: Reshaping the Memory of the World Wars*. New York: Oxford University Press, 1991.

Muckermann, Friedrich. *Im Kampf zwischen zwei Epochen*. Veröffentlichungen der Kommission für Zeitgeschichte, edited by Konrad Repgen with Dieter Albrecht, Rudolf Lill, and Rudolf Morsey, series A: Quellen, vol. 15. Mainz: Matthias Grünewald Verlag, 1973.

———. "Der Katholik und das gute Buch." In *Bericht über den Katholikentag zu Magdeburg . . . 1928*. Paderborn: Bonifacius Druckerei, n.d.

———. "Die Katholiken und der Film." In Ernst and Marschall, *Film und Rundfunk*, 24–35.

———. "Katholizismus und moderner Film." *Schönere Zukunft* 4 (June 30, 1929): 823–24.

———. "Kulturfragen der Gegenwart: Auf dem Wege zum nationale Kultspiel." *Germania*, June 5, 1926, Morgenausgabe, Das neue Ufer.

———. "Kulturfragen der Gegenwart: Zur Sondertagung des Verbandes Katholischer Akademiker in Re[c]klinghausen." *Germania*, January 9, 1926, Morgenausgabe, Das neue Ufer.

———. "Die Kulturkrise der Gegenwart und die jüngste Enzykl[i]ka Pius XI." *Germania*, February 11, 1928, Morgenausgabe, Das neue Ufer.

———. "Die Magdeburger Katholikentag: Katholisches Buch, Katholische Presse: Die 2. Öffentliche Versammlug." *Germania*, September 7, 1928, Morgenausgabe.

———. "Mitarbeit der Gebildeten: Aus der Praxis des Lebens." *Germania*, November 17, 1928, Morgenausgabe, Das neue Ufer.

———. "Tanz und Gemeinschaft—Der Laientanz in kultureller und pädagogischer Bedeutung." *Der Gral* 24 (August 1930): 961–67.

Muckermann, Richard. "Film." In *71. Generalversammlung der deutschen Katholiken zu Essen an der Ruhr . . . 1932*, 246–52.

———. "Der Film, ein Feind des Theaters." *Volkswart* 24 (1931): 25–26.

———. "Der Film: Sein Werden, Wachsen und Wollen." In *Lichtträger in Chaos 3*, 89.

———. "Der katholische Film." *Lokal-Anzeiger*, June 8, 1930.

Müller, Dirk H. "Katholische Aktion versus Vereinskatholizismus: Zur kirchlichen Integration und Emanzipation der katholischen Laien." In Elm and Loock, *Seelsorge und Diakonie in Berlin*, 474–97.

Müller, E. Jos. "Die Arbeiter und die Musik." *Musik im Leben* 4 (September/October 1928): 130–32.

———. "Einiges über die Tanzmusik unserer Zeit." *Musik im Leben* 2 (October 1926): 145–47.

———. "Die Frauen und die Musik." *Musik im Leben* 1 (April 1925): 49–51.

———. "Das Kino als—Lehrer." *Volkskunst* 14 (1926): 358–62.

———. "Kirchenmusik." *Musik im Leben* 3 (October 1927): 137–38.

———. "Musik und Erotik." *Musik im Leben* 2 (February 1926): 17–19.

———. "Musikpflege als soziale Pflicht." *Musik im Leben* 1 (1925): 161–63.

———. "Religion und Musik." *Musik im Leben* 1 (1925): 107–8.

———. "Wie können die Frauen an der Hebung des Musiklebens mithelfen?" *Musik im Leben* 1 (1925): 51–52.

———. "Zur Musikpflege in den katholischen Vereinen." *Volkskunst* 12 (July/September 1924): 53–62.

Müller, O. "Die Kulturideale eines kath[olischen] Arbeiters." *Präsides-Korrespondenz* 20 (1907): 230–35.

Müller, Otto. *Die katholischen Arbeitervereine als kirchliche Bildungsvereine*. Mönchengladbach: Volksverein, 1918.

Müller-Freienfels, Richard. "Die psychologische Wirkung der Kunst auf das religiöse Gefühlsleben." *Zeitschrift für Religionspsychologie* 4 (1911): 369–75.

Müller-Gögler, Maria. *Erinnerungen: Bevor die Stürme kamen. Hinter blinden Fenstern. Das arme Fräulein*. Sigmaringen: Jan Thorbecke Verlag, 1980.

Müller-Molitor, ———. "Musikalische Volkserziehung." *Volkskunst* 7 (August 1918): 49–53.

Mumbauer, Johannes. ["Die Beteiligung der deutschen Katholiken am literarische Leben und Schaffen."] In *Bericht über die Verhandlungen der 56. Generalversammlung der Katholiken Deutschlands . . . 1909*, 383–97. Breslau: Goerlich und Coch (Inh. R. Sprick), 1909.

———. "Buch, Buchkrisis und Buchpflege." *Literarischer Handweiser*. Abridged in "Im Ringen der Zeit," *Germania*, August 28, 1926, Morgenausgabe, Das neue Ufer.

———. "Die deutschen Katholiken und die Literatur." *Bücherwelt* 7 (November 1909): 33–41.

———. "Dreißig Jahre katholischer Literaturbewegung und Literaturarbeit." *Literarischer Handweiser* 63 (July 1927): 721–26.

———. "Die katholische 'Drehkrankheit.'" *Literarischer Handweiser* 25 (1928/1929): 65–68.

———. "Katholische Kirche und moderne Kunst." *Der Scheinwerfer* 3 (1930): 10–12.

———. "Ein literarisches Ghetto für die Katholiken?" *Allgemeine Rundschau* 4 (1907): 460–61, 478–79.

———. "Die wertvollsten Bücher aus der katholischen Literatur der letzten Jahre." *Literarischer Handweiser* 25 (1928/1929): 95–100.

Murray, Bruce. "An Introduction to the Commercial Film Industry in Germany from 1895 to 1933." In *Film and Politics in the Weimar Republic*, edited by Thomas G. Plummer et al., 23–34. University of Minnesota, department of German, distributed by New York: Holmes and Meier, 1982.

Die Musik in Geschichte und Gegenwart. Edited by Friedrich Blume. Kassel: Bärenreiter Verlag, 1949–1986.

Die Musik in Geschichte und Gegenwart. Edited by Ludwig Finscher. Kassel: Bärenreiter; Stuttgart: Verlag J. P. Metzler, 1994.

"Musik im Leben. Eine Zeitschrift der Volkserneurung: Einstellung." *Musik im Leben* 1 (January 1925): 1–7.

"Muth gegen Kralik." *Literatur-Beilage* (September 25, 1909): 177–79.

Muth, Karl. "Bilanz: Eine Umschau aus Anlaß des 25. Jahrgangs." *Hochland* 25 (October 1927): 1–23.

————. "Kritik: Vom Gral und den Gralbündlern." *Hochland* 5 (February 1908): 603–610.

————. "Ein Vorwort zu 'Hochland.'" *Hochland* 1 (October 1903): 1–8.

————. *Wem gehört die Zukunft? Ein Literaturbild der Gegenwart.* Frankfurt am Main: A. Foesser Nachfolger, 1893.

————. *Die Wiedergeburt der Dichtung aus dem religiösen Erlebnis: Gedanken zur Psychologie des katholischen Literaturschaffens.* Kempten: Kösel, 1909.

[Karl Muth]. *Die literarischen Aufgaben der deutschen Katholiken.* Mainz: Franz Kirchheim, 1899.

————. *Steht die katholische Belletristik auf der Höhe der Zeit?* Mainz: Franz Kirchheim, 1898.

N., —. "Ende des Cäzilienvereins." *Augsburger Postzeitung,* February 16, 1921.

Narogin, Mudrooroo. *Writings from the Fringe: A Study of Modern Aboriginal Literature.* Melbourne: Hyland House, 1990.

Neundörfer, Ludwig. "Der Rundfunk als Hilfe in den Vereinen." *Volkstum und Volksbildung* 2 (1930): 321–24.

"99 Jahre 'Musica Sacra.'" *Musica Sacra* 100 (1980): 4–42.

New Catholic Encyclopedia. New York: McGraw-Hill, 1967.

The New Dictionary of Music and Musicians. Edited by Stanley Sadie. London: Macmillan, 1980.

The New Oxford Companion to Music. Edited by Denis Arnold. Oxford: Oxford University Press, 1983.

Niebuhr, H. Richard. *Christ and Culture.* New York: Harper and Row, 1975.

"Der Niedergang der deutschen Sittlichkeit." *Allgemeine Rundschau* 5 (1908): 631–33.

Nielen, K. J. M. "Zum Bildungswert des Rundfunks." *Volkstum und Volksbildung* 4 (1932): 113–18.

Niggemann, Wilhelm. *Das Selbstverständnis katholischer Erwachsenenbildung bis 1933.* Beiträge zur Erwachsenenbildung, vol. 15. Osnabrück: A. Fromm, 1967.

Nipperdey, Thomas. *Arbeitswelt und Bürgergeist.* Vol. 1 of *Deutsche Geschichte, 1866–1918.* Munich: C. H. Beck, 1998.

————. *Germany from Napoleon to Bismarck, 1800–1866.* Translated by Daniel Nolan. Princeton, N.J.: Princeton University Press, 1996.

————. *Religion im Umbruch: Deutschland, 1870–1918.* Munich: C. H. Beck, 1988.

————. "Religion und Gesellschaft: Deutschland um 1900." *Historische Zeitschrift* 246 (June 1988): 591–615.

Nissen, Benedikt Momme. "Entwickelung und Entartung christlicher Kunst." *Historisch-politische Blätter für das katholische Deutschland* 171 (1923): 30–43; 65–80.

Noppel, Constantin. "Gärung im katholischen Vereinswesen." *Stimmen der Zeit* 53 (February 1923): 346–57.

Norbisrath, Karl. "Volksbildung und Volkshebung durch Musik- und Gesangespflege." *Wissen und Glauben* 22 (1925): 242–44.

————. "Weiterhin Kampf oder Resignation in der Kinofrage?" *Allgemeine Rundschau* 19 (1922): 56–57.

Norikus, F. *Katholisches Vereinswesen: Ein Beitrag zum fünfzigjährigen Jubiläum der katholischen Vereine.* Munich: Rudof Abt, 1898.

Nusser, Luitpold. "Verwendung des Films zur Verbreitung von Ideen." In Ernst and Marschall, *Film und Rundfunk,* 96–132.

Oberdoerffer, P. "Ein ernstes Wort über unseres katholisches Vereinswesen." *Pastor Bonus* 35 (November/December 1922): 39–44; 77–88.

"Oberhirtliche Empfehlung des christlichen Kunstvereins, des Vereines zur Verbreitung religiöser Bilder, sowie der Zeitschrift für christliche Kunst." *Kirchliche Anzeiger für die Erzdiözese Köln* 44 (January 15, 1904): 6–7.

Oberndorff, Alfred, Graf von. "Der sittliche Niedergang des deutschen Volkes und die Aufgaben der Katholiken." *Volkswart* 24 (October 1931): 145–50.

O'Dea, Thomas. "The Role of the Intellectual in the Catholic Tradition." *Daedalus* 101 (1972): 151–90.

"Öffentliche Bibliotheken und Lesehallen." In *Verhandlungen der 45. General-Versammlung der Katholiken Deutschlands . . . 1898*. Krefeld: J. B. Klein (M. Buscher), 1898.

Oehl, Wilhelm. "Kraliks Kulturprogramm." *Der Gral* 6 (July 1, 1912): 581–96.

O'Meara, Thomas F. *Church and Culture: German Catholic Theology, 1860–1914*. Notre Dame, Ind.: University of Notre Dame Press, 1991.

"The Origins of Mass German Culture: The Case of Imperial Germany (1871–1918)." *New German Critique* 29 (Spring/Summer 1983).

Osinski, Jutta. *Katholizismus und deutsche Literatur im 19. Jahrhundert*. Paderborn: Ferdinand Schöningh, 1993.

Ott, Frederick. *The Great German Films*. Secaucus, N.J.: Citadel Press, 1986.

Overmans, Jakob. "Bilanz der deutschen Sprechbühne." *Stimmen der Zeit* 117 (1929): 353–65.

———. *Roman, Theater und Kino im neuen Deutschland*. Flugschriften der *Stimmen der Zeit* 14. Freiburg im Breisgau: Herder, 1920.

———. "Das Theater als Bildungsstätte." In Meinertz and Sacher, *Deutschland und der Katholizismus*, 391–405.

———. "Unser Kampf um die Bühne." *Stimmen aus Maria-Laach* 85 (1913): 263–75.

"Päpstliche Empfehlung des Borromäusvereins." *Kirchlicher Anzeiger für die Erzdiözese Köln* 71 (February 15, 1931): 50.

Paret, Peter. "Art and the National Image: The Conflict over Germany's Participation in the St. Louis Exposition." *Central European History* 11 (June 1978): 173–83.

———. *German Encounters with Modernism, 1840–1945*. Cambridge: Cambridge University Press, 2001.

Pascal, Roy. *From Naturalism to Expressionism: German Literature and Society, 1880–1918*. London: Weidenfeld and Nicolson, 1973.

Patterson, Michael. *The Revolution in German Theatre, 1900–1933*. Boston: Routledge and Kegan Paul, 1981.

Peabody, Dean. *National Characteristics*. European Monographs in Social Psychology. Cambridge: Cambridge University Press; Paris: Editions de la Maison des Sciences de l'Homme, 1985.

Petersen, Klaus. *Zensur in der Weimarer Republik*. Stuttgart: Verlag J. B. Metzler, 1995.

Peukert, Detlev. "Der Schund- und Schmutzkampf als 'Sozialpolitik der Seele.'" In *"Das war ein Vorspiel nur . . . ": Bücherverbrennung Deutschland 1933: Voraussetzungen und Folgen*. Berlin, 1983.

Pfeiffer, Maximilian. "Theaterkultur." *Allgemeine Rundschau* 13 (1916): 632.

Pfeill, Karl Gabriel. "Neue religiöse Kunst am Rhein." *Die christliche Kunst* 28 (1931/1932): 225–37.

Pflaum, Michael. "Die Kultur-Zivilisations-Antithese im Deutschen." In *Europäische Schlüsselwörter,* edited by Sprachwissenschaftlichen Colloquium (Bonn). Vol. 3, *Kultur und Zivilisation.* Munich: Max Hueber, 1967.

Pichler, Alois. "Der Sprung auf die Bühne." *Allgemeine Rundschau* 2 (1905): 285–86.

Pieper, August. *Zur Frage: Vereinfachung des Vereinswesen.* Reprint from *Führer- Korrespondenz* (1922).

Pius IX. *Syllabus of Errors.* In *Encyclicals and Other Papal Documents of Pius IX. Dated 8th December 1864. Proclaiming the Jubilee of 1865, with the Syllabus of LXXX. Errors,* 19–24, translated by R. Walker. London: George Clark, n.d.

Pius X. "Dilectis Filiis Fancisco Eichert ceterisque sodalibus e Societate litteratorum 'Gralbund.'" *Der Gral* 5 (May 15, 1911): 467–69.

———. *Pascendi Domenici Gregig (Doctrine of the Modernists).* http://www.vatican.va/holy_father/pius_x/encyclicals.

Pius XI. *Mortalium Animos (On Religious Unity).* http://www.vatican.va/holy_father/pius_xi/encyclicals.

Pius XII. "The Catholic Church and History." *The Tablet,* September 24, 1955, 292–94.

Pohle, Heinz. *Der Rundfunk als Instrument der Politik.* Hamburg: Verlag Hans-Bredow-Institut, 1955.

Pommer, Erich. "Der internationale Film." *Germania,* September 23, 1928, Morgenausgabe, Film-Rundschau.

Popp, J. "Kunst und Moral." *Volkswart* 6 (November 1913): 161–66.

Potter, Pamela. *Most German of the Arts: Musicology and Society from the Weimar Republic to the End of Hitler's Reich.* New Haven, Conn.: Yale University Press, 1998.

Pribilla, Max. "Kulturwende und Katholizismus." *Stimmen der Zeit* 107 (July 1924): 259–78.

Prilipp, Beda. "Vom Tanz in unsrer Zeit." *Hochland* 28 (May 1931): 166–72.

"Prof. Thode über Kunst und Sittlichkeit." *Allgemeine Rundschau* 4 (1907): 90–91.

Puhle, H. J., ed. *Bürger in der Gesellschaft der Neuzeit.* Göttingen: Vandenhoeck und Ruprecht, 1991.

Rademacher, Arnold. "Katholizismus und modernes Leben." *Vom inneren Frieden des deutschen Volkes* (1916): 87–104.

———. *Die Kirche als Gemeinschaft und Gesellschaft: Eine Studie zur Soziologie der Kirche.* Kirche und Gesellschaft: Soziologische Veröffentlichungen des Katholischen Akademikerverbandes, vol. 5. Augsburg: Literarisches Institut Haas und Grabherr, 1931.

———. *Religion und Leben: Ein Beitrag zur Lösung des christlichen Kulturproblems.* Freiburg im Breisgau: Herder, 1926.

Radow, Manes. "Verteidigung des Provinz-Theaters." *Germania,* July 14, 1928, Morgenausgabe.

Raederscheidt, Georg. "Grundsätzliches zur Begegnung von Theater und Katholizismus." *Das Nationaltheater* 5 (January 1933): 65–70.

Rarisch, Ilse. *Industrialisierung und Literatur: Buchproduktion, Verlagswesen und Buchhandel in Deutschland im 19. Jahrhundert in ihren statistischen Zusammenhang.* Historische und Pädagogische Studien, edited by Otto Büsch und Gerd Heinrich, vol. 6. Berlin: Colloquium Verlag, 1976.

Rath, Anton. "Wo bleibt die sittliche Erneuerung der deutschen Bühnen?" *Volkswart* 12 (January 1919): 5–10.

Rath, Willy. *Kino und Bühne.* Lichtbühnen-Bibliothek, no. 4. Mönchengladbach: Volksvereins-Verlag, 1913.

Rauscher, Anton, ed. *Katholizismus, Bildung und Wissenschaft im 19. und 20. Jahrhundert.* Beiträge zur Katholizismusforschung. Paderborn: Ferdinand Schöningh, 1987.

———. *Religiös-kulturelle Bewegungen im deutschen Katholizismus seit 1800.* Paderborn: Ferdinand Schöningh, 1986.

Reallexikon der deutschen Literaturgeschichte. 2nd ed. Vol. 4, edited by Klaus Kanzog and Achim Masser. Berlin: DeGruyter, 1984.

van Reeken, Dietmar. *Kirchen im Umbruch zur Moderne: Milieubildungsprozesse im nordwestdeutschen Protestantismus, 1849–1914.* Religiöse Kulturen der Moderne, edited by Friedrich Wilhelm Graf and Gangolf Hübinger, vol. 9. Gütersloh: Chr. Kaiser/ Gütersloher Verlagshaus, 1999.

"Reform des Lichtspielgesetzes." *Volkswart* 18 (March 1925): 39–40.

Regner, Paul. "Der Kampf wider das Gesetz gegen Schund und Schmutz." *Allgemeine Rundschau* 23 (December 4, 1926): 776–77.

Rehmann, Th. B. "Grundsätzliches in der Stellungnahme des Cäcilienvereins zu dem Stilwandel in der Kirchenmusik." *Musica Sacra* (November 1931): 389–96.

Reichenberger, R. "Referat über das Vereinswesen: Leitsätze und Richtlinien." In *Diözesan-Synode für die Diözese Regensburg, abgehalten 1927 am 11. Oktober (Ir. Teil) und 1928 am 2. und 3. Juli (II. Teil): Bericht, Beschlüsse und oberhirtliche Verordnungen,* 63–73. Regensburg: G. J. Manz, 1929.

"Reichsgesetz zur Bewahrung der Jugend vor Schmutz- und Schundschriften." *Kirchlicher Anzeiger für die Erzdiözese Köln* 67 (March 1, 1927): 17–28.

Renner, Gustav. "Kunst: Über die Freiheit der Kunst." *Hochland* 24 (1926/1927): 547–49.

Rennert, Malwine. "Die Kunst des Lichtspieltheaters." *Bild und Film* 3 (1913/1914): 128–130.

———. "Im Reiche der Mütter." *Bild und Film* 3 (1913/1914): 267–69.

Retzbach, Anton. *Das moderne kath[olische] Vereinswesen.* Munich: Buchhandlung Leohaus, 1925.

"Richtlinien für das katholische Vereinswesen." *Kirchliches Amtsblatt für die Diözese Rottenburg* 13 (1931): 262–66.

Rieder, L. "'Grundsätze der Volksbildung.'" *Volkskunst* 2 (1914): 214–18.

"Im Ringen der Zeit: Für das werthaltige Buch." *Germania,* January 3, 1926, Morgenausgabe, Das neue Ufer.

Ritter, Emil. "Alte und neue Laienbühne." *Volkskunst* 11 (July/September 1923): 67–71.

———. "Bühnenvolksbund und katholische Vereine." *Volkskunst* 16 (January 1928): 1–6.

———. "Der Film und die Volksbildung." *Volkskunst* 14 (1926): 49–56.

———. "Gottesdienst und Kunst: Beuroner Erinnerungen." *Volkskunst* 6 (March 1918): 81–85.

———. "Grundsätze der Volksbildung." *Volkskunst* 2 (February 1914): 214–19.

———. "Klassiker auf der Vereinsbühne." *Volkskunst* 1 (July 1913): 345–53.

———. "Kunst und Volksbildung." *Volkskunst* 8 (December 1919): 85–87.

———. "Laienspiel und Bühne." *Volkskunst* 15 (1927): 33–36.

———. "Literatur und Kunstpflege im Verein." *Volkskunst* 7 (January/February 1919): 289–93.

———. "Der neue Bühnenvolksbund." *Volkskunst* 7 (May/June 1919): 401–5.

———. "Eine Rechenschaft." *Volkstum und Volksbildung* 1 (1929): 1–17.

———. "Uber das Verhältnis zwischen Volk und Kunst." *Volkskunst* 2 (February 1914): 181–85.

———. "Unser Programm." *Volkskunst* 1 (October 1912): 1–6.

———. "Vereinsabende und Vereinsfeste." *Volkskunst* 7 (December 1918): 247–53.

———. "Volk und Theater." *Volkskunst* 9 (October/November 1920): 1–6.

———. "Volksbildung und ihre Organisation." *Volkskunst* 13 (1925): 103–8.

———. "Volksbühne und Vereinsbühne." *Volkskunst* 15 (1927): 1–9.

———. "Wo stehen wir?" *Volkskunst* 13 (January 1925): 1–13.

Ritter, Gerhard. "Workers' Culture in Imperial Germany: Problems and Points of Departure for Research." *Journal of Contemporary History* 13 (1978): 165–89.

Rockenbach, Martin. "Jakob Kneip." *Bücherwelt* 18 (October 1921): 201–7.

Roeren, Hermann. *Die öffentliche Unsittlichkeit und ihre Bekämpfung.* Cologne: J. P. Bachem, [1903].

Rohr, G. *Empfehlenswerte Bücher und Schriften für Katholische Töchter.* Godesberg, 1901.

Rohr, Gottfried. "Neue Wege im Borromäusverein: Von der 'literarischen Kommission' 1903–1907." *Die Bücherwelt* 17 (August/September 1920): 193–97.

Rosegger, Peter. "Das Verhältnis des Volkes zur bildenden Kunst." *Das christliche Kunstblatt für Kirche, Schule und Haus* 60 (1918): 259–65.

Rosenthal, Solomon P. *Change of Socio-economic Attitudes under Radical Motion Picture Propaganda.* Archives of Psychology, edited by E. S. Woodworth, no. 166. New York, 1934.

Ross, Ronald J. *The Failure of Bismarck's Kulturkampf: Catholicism and State Power in Imperial Germany, 1871–1887.* Washington, D.C.: Catholic University of America Press, 1998.

Rost, Hans. *Die Katholiken im Kultur- und Wirtschaftsleben der Gegenwart.* Cologne: J. P. Bachem, 1908.

———. *Katholische Familienkultur.* Politik und Kultur 4. Augsburg: Literarisches Institut von Haas und Grabherr, 1926.

———. *Die katholische Kirche die Führerin der Menschheit: Eine Kultursoziologie.* Westheim bei Augsburg: Gangolf Rost Verlag, 1949.

———. *Die Kulturkraft des Katholizismus.* 3rd ed. Paderborn: Bonifacius-Druckerei, 1923.

———. *Die wirtschaftliche und kulturelle Lage der deutschen Katholiken.* Cologne: J. P. Bachem, 1911.

Rumpf, Albert. "Die deutschen Katholiken und der Büchermarkt." *Glaube und Arbeit* 1 (1917): 181–87.

———. ["Die deutschen Katholiken und die Pflege der Kunst"]. In *Bericht über die Verhandlungen der 56. Generalversammlung der Katholiken Deutschlands . . . 1909,* 341–54. Breslau: Goerlich und Coch (Inh. R. Sprick), 1909.

———. "Predigten über gute und schlechte Bücher." *Mitteilungen für die Vereine vom hl. Karl Borromäus* 6 (July 1918): 1–16.

Sachse, Otto. "Des katholischen Dichters Not und Klage." *Allgemeine Rundschau* 24 (August 1927): 488.

Sackett, R. E. "Antimodernism in the Popular Entertainment of Modern Munich: Attitude, Institution, Language." *New German Critique* 57 (Fall 1992): 123–55.

Sambeth, M. "Krisis oder Erneuerung der katholischen Kirchenmusik?" *Theologie und Glaube* 20 (1928): 550–55.

Sauer, Wolfgang. "Weimar Culture: Experiments in Modernism." *Social Research* 39 (Summer 1972): 254–84.

Schäfer, Georg. "Der katholische Dichter in unserer Zeit." *Bücherwelt* 25 (March/April 1928): 81–88.

———. "Lesertypen." *Bücherwelt* 21 (September 1924): 117–28.

Schäfer, J. "Unsere Ortsgruppen im Kampfe gegen Schund und Schmutz im Rahmen des neuen Gesetzes." *Volkswart* 21 (September 1928): 129–33.

Schaezler, Karl. "Erben des Buches?" *Hochland* 29 (October 1931): 92–95.

———. "Jazz." *Hochland* 25 (1928): 439–41.

———. "Das Problem der modernen Kirchenmusik." *Hochland* 30 (1933): 538–46.

"Schallplatten-Ecke: Musica Sacra." *Allgemeine Rundschau* 28 (February 21, 1931): 127–28.

Schamoni, Victor. "Filmkrisis." *Hochland* 26 (June 1929): 326–29.

———. "Katholiken und Film." *Hochland* 26 (September 1929): 669–72.

———. "Kino." *Hochland* 21 (September 1924): 619–36.

Scharnagl, August. "Dr. Franz Xaver Witt und die Erneuerung der katholischen Kirchenmusik im 19. Jahrhundert." *Musica Sacra* 104 (September/October 1984): 362–68.

Scheids, N. "Ist die literarische Kritik eine Kunst?" *Pastor Bonus* 38 (July 1927): 295–99.

Schell, Herman, *Herman Schell: Kleinere Schriften.* Edited by Karl Hennemann. Paderborn: Ferdinand Schöningh, 1908.

———. *Der Katholicismus als Princip des Fortschritts.* Würzburg: Andreas Göbel, 1897.

Schenda, Rudolf. "Alphabetisierung und Literarisierungsprozesse in Westeuropa im 18. und 19. Jahrhundert." In *Sozialer und kultureller Wandel in der ländlichen Welt des 18. Jahrhunderts,* edited by Ernst Hinrichs and Günter Wiegelmann, 1–20. Wolfenbüttel: Herzog August Bibliothek, 1982.

———. *Die Lesestoffe der kleinen Leute: Studien zur populären Literatur im 19. und 20. Jahrhundert.* Munich: C. H. Beck, 1976.

———. *Volk ohne Buch: Studien zur Sozialgeschichte der populären Lesestoffe, 1770–1910.* 1970. Munich: DTV, 1977.

Scherzberg, August Hermann Leugers. "Die Modernisierung des Katholizismus im Kaiserreichs: Überlegungen am Beispiel von Felix Porsch." In Loth, *Deutscher Katholizismus im Umbruch zur Moderne,* 219–35.

Schieder, Wolfgang. "Sozialgeschichte der Religion im 19. Jahrhundert: Bemerkungen zur Forschungslage." In Schieder, *Religion und Gesellschaft im 19. Jahrhundert,* 11–28.

Schieder, Wolfgang, ed. *Religion und Gesellschaft im 19. Jahrhundert.* Industrielle Welt, edited by Reinhart Koselleck and M. Rainer Lepsius, vol. 54. Stuttgart: Klett-Cotta, 1993.

Schiller, Friedrich. "The Stage as a Moral Institution." In Schiller, *Essays Aesthetical and Philosophical Including the Dissertation on the "Connexion between the Animal and Spiritual in Man,"* 333–39. London: George Bell and Sons, 1879.

Schiller, J. "Kunst und Religion." *Allgemeine Rundschau* 17 (1920): 70–71.

Schlenz, J. "Katholische Vereine und kirchliches Hirtenamt." *Theologisch-praktische Quartalschrift* 76 (1924): 12–23.

Schletter, Johann. "Echte und falsche Volksmusik." *Musik im Leben* 1 (February 1925): 23–24.

Schmid, Willi. "Kirchenmusikalische Fragen der Gegenwart." *Katholisches Kirchenmusik-Jahrbuch* 1 (1928): 127–37.

———. "Neue Musik." *Stimmen der Zeit* 118 (1929): 89–96.

Schmidkunz, Hans. "Geschmacklosigkeiten in kirchlicher Kunst." *Der Pionier* 5 (1912): 11–14.

———. "Musik und Ethik." *Allgemeine Musik-Zeitung* 29 (November 21, 1902): 787–89; 805–6.

Schmidt, Expeditus. "Das deutsche Literaturleben und die Katholiken." *Allgemeine Rundschau* 1 (December 11, 1904): 483–85.

———. "Die Stellung der Katholiken im deutschen Literaturleben: Ein Vortrag." In Schmidt, *Anregungen: Gesammelte Studien und Vorträge*. Munich: Verlag Etzold, 1909.

———. "Theaterkultur." *Hochland* 14 (November 1916): 228–37.

Schmidt-Volkmar, Erich. *Der Kulturkampf in Deutschland, 1871–1890*. Göttingen: Musterschmidt, 1962.

Schmitt, Heiner. *Kirche und Film: Kirchliche Filmarbeit in Deutschland von ihren Anfängen bis 1945*. Schriften des Bundesarchivs 26. Boppard am Rhein: Harald Boldt Verlag, 1979.

Schmitz, Eugen. "Der Subjektivismus in der Musik." *Hochland* 10 (1913): 476–81.

———. "Zur Frage der modernen Kirchenmusik." *Hochland* 11 (1913): 92–97.

Schmolke, Michael. "Katholisches Verlags-, Bücherei- und Zeitschriftenwesen." In Rauscher, *Katholizismus, Bildung und Wissenschaft im 19. und 20. Jahrhundert*, 93–117.

Schnettler, Friedrich. "Der Seelsorger und die Gefahren und Auswüchse des modernen Vereinswesens." *Der katholische Seelsorger* (1902): 20–22; 62–65; 115–22.

Schnütgen, Alexander. "Der Verein vom hl. Karl Borromäus geschichtlich gewürdigt." *Zentralblatt für Bibliothekswesen* 41 (1924): 273–91; 327–37.

Schnütgens Schätze: Ein Sammler und sein Museum. Kölner Museums-Bulletin, special issue 1 (1993).

Schulte, Ludgerus. "Kirche und Musik." *Pastor Bonus* 20 (1908): 337–53.

Schulte-Sasse, Jochen. "Toward a 'Culture' for the Masses: The Socio-Psychological Function of Popular Literature in Germany and the U.S., 1880–1920." *New German Critique* 29 (Spring/Summer 1983): 81–105.

Schulte-Umberg, Thomas. *Profession und Charisma: Herkunft und Ausbildung des Klerus im Bistum Münster 1776–1940*. Veröffentlichungen der Kommission für Zeitgeschichte, edited by Ulrich von Hehl, series B: Forschung, vol. 85. Paderborn: Ferdinand Schöningh, 1999.

Schulz, Herbert. "Psychologie des musikalischen Erlebens." *Musik im Leben* 2 (December 1926): 180–82.

Die Schundkampftagung des Borromäusvereins. N.d. [1928].

"Schund- und Schmutzbekämpfung." *Kirchliches Amts-Blatt für die Diözese Rottenburg* 13 (August 10, 1931): 429–30.

Schwaer, —. *Im Dienste der öffentlichen Sittlichkeit*. Reprint from *Paulus* 8 [1930]: n.p.

Schwank, F. H. "Staatstheater und Volkskunst." *Volkskunst* 16 (December 1928): 353–56.

Schwarz, Max. "Kirchliche Kunst und Kleriker." *Die christliche Kunst* 28 (1931/1932): 54–57.

Schwering, Leo. "Um den Rundfunk." *Germania*, November 17, 1928, Abendausgabe.

Schwermer, Johannes. "Der Caecilianismus." In Fellerer, *Geschichte der katholischen Kirchenmusik*, vol. 2, 226–36.

Schwindt, A. M. "Katholische Kunst: Ein offenes Wort an alle, die es angeht." *Allgemeine Rundschau* 16 (1919): 120.

Seeber, David, ed. *Im Aufbruch gelähmt? Die deutschen Katholiken an der Jahrhundertwende*. Frankfurt am Main: Verlag Josef Knecht, 2000.

Seeger, Ernst. "Die Entwicklung des Schundbegriffs durch die Rechtsprechung der Oberprüfstelle für Schund- und Schmutzschriften in Leipzig." *Archiv für Urheber- Film- und Theaterrecht* 1 (1928): 592–97.

———. "Das Reichslichtspielgesetz in der Rechtsprechung der Filmoberprüfstelle." *Archiv für Urheber- Film- und Theaterrecht* 1 (1928): 58–73; 208–23; 255–76.

Seidel, H. O. "Auf zum Kino-Kampf!" *Wissen und Glauben* 27 (1932): 473–77.

Senn, M. Wilhelm. "Notwendige Neuorientierung in der Literaturfrage." *Schönere Zukunft* 2 (September 18, 1927): 1098–1100.

———. "'Jupp Brand' oder Katholiken und Bühnenvolksbund." *Schönere Zukunft* (1927): 1054–57; 1076–79.

Seul, Jeffrey R. "'Ours is the Way of God': Religion, Identity, and Intergroup Conflict." *Journal of Peace Research* 36 (1999): 553–69.

Sharot, Stephen, Hannah Ayalon, and Eliezer Ben-Rafael. "Secularization and the Diminishing Decline of Religion." *Review of Religious Research* 27 (March 1986): 193–207.

Sigl, Max. "Der Cäcilienverein als Organisation." *Korrespondenz- und Offertenblatt für die gesamte katholische Geistlichkeit Deutschlands* 26 (1926): 134–36.

———. "Kirchenmusik und Cäcilienverein." *Musica Sacra* 56 (1926): 38–44.

———. "Organisationsfragen: Musik, Lehrerschaft und Trennungsgedanke." *Musica Sacra* 53 (1920): 45–46; 58–59.

———. "Pfarrer und Kirchenchor." *Korrespondenz- und Offertenblatt für die gesamte katholische Geistlichkeit Deutschlands* 24 (1924): 41–43.

Smend, Julius. "Neue Organisation zur Hebung der katholischen Kirchenmusik." *Monatsschrift für Gottesdienst und kirchliche Kunst* 35 (1930): 115–17.

Smith, Helmut Walser. *German Nationalism and Religious Conflict: Culture, Ideology, Politics, 1970–1914.* Princeton, N.J.: Princeton University Press, 1994.

Smith, Helmut Walser, and Chris Clark. "The Fate of Nathan." In Smith, *Protestants, Catholics and Jews in Germany, 1800–1914,* 3–29.

Smith, Helmut Walser, ed. *Protestants, Catholics and Jews in Germany, 1800–1914.* Oxford: Berg, 2001.

Smith, Robert J. "Comparative Studies in Anthropology of the Interrelations between Social and Technological Change." *Human Organizations* 16 (Spring 1957): 30–36.

Sobania, Michael. "Vereinsleben: Regeln und Formen bürgerlicher Assoziationen im 19. Jahrhundert." In *Bürgerkultur im 19. Jahrhundert: Bildung, Kunst und Lebenswelt,* edited by Dieter Hein and Andreas Schulz, 170–90. Munich: C. H. Beck, 1996.

Söder, Hans-Peter. "Disease and Health as Contexts of Modernity: Max Nordau as a Critic of Fin-de-siècle Modernism." *German Studies Review* 14 (1999): 473–87.

"Sollen wir weiter streiten?" *Fränkisches Volksblatt* 211 (September 15, 1927): n.p.

Sonnenfeld, Albert. *Crossroads: Essays on the Catholic Novelists.* York, S.C.: French Literature Publications Company, 1982.

Spael, Wilhelm. "Aus der Bühnenwelt: Zwei rheinische Festspiele." *Bücherwelt* 22 (November 1925): 523–28.

———. *Das Buch im Geisteskampf: 100 Jahre Borromäusverein.* Bonn: Verlag des Borromäus-Vereins, 1950.

———. "[Johannes Braun] Lebenswerk im Borromäusverein." In Koep, *Bücher in Menschenhand,* 33–40.

———. *Das katholische Deutschland im 20. Jahrhundert: Seine Pionier- und Krisenzeiten, 1890–1945.* Würzburg: Echter-Verlag, 1964.

———. "Religion, Kultur und christliche Kunst." *Kölnische Volkszeitung im Schritt der Zeit,* March 2, 1930: 1–2.

Sperber, Jonathan. *Popular Catholicism in Nineteenth-Century Germany.* Princeton, N.J.: Princeton University Press, 1984.

Stärk, Franz. "Die Erzählung im Sonntagsblatt." *Bücherwelt* 26 (September/October 1929): 344–49.

"Stand wir Katholiken rückständig?" *Der Gral* 3 (January 15, 1909): 181–82.

Stark, Gary D. "The Censorship of Literary Naturalism, 1885–1895: Prussia and Saxony." *Central European History* 18 (September/December 1985): 326–43.

———. "Cinema, Society and the State: Policing the Film Industry in Imperial Germany." In *Essays on Culture and Society in Modern Germany,* edited by Gary D. Stark and Bede Karl Lackner, 122–66. College Station, Tex.: published for the University of Texas at Arlington by Texas A & M University Press, 1982.

———. "Pornography, Society, and the Law in Imperial Germany." *Central European History* 14 (September 1981): 200–229.

———. "Publishers and Cultural Patronage in Germany, 1890–1933." *German Studies Review* 1 (1978): 56–71.

———. "Trials and Tribulations: Authors' Responses to Censorship in Imperial Germany, 1885–1914." *German Studies Review* 12 (1989): 447–68.

Steckner, Hans. "Kunst und Kino." *Volkskunst* 13 (1925): 97–100.

Stehle, A. "Ansprache Sr. Eminenz des H. Kardinals Erzbischof Schulte auf der G.-V. des C.-V. der Erzdiözese Köln in Neuss." *Musica Sacra* 56 (1926): 239–46.

Stehle, G. E. "Ueber die Nothwendigkeit der Popularsierung der cäcilianischen Idee." *Fliegende Blätter für katholische Kirchen-Musik* 10 (February 15, 1875): 9–11.

"Steht die katholische Belletristik auf der Höhe der Zeit?" *Augsburger Postzeitung* (August 30, 1898).

Steiger, Heinhard. "Karl Muth und das Hochland—eine Art 'Kulturkatholizismus'?" In *Kulturprotestantismus: Beiträge zu einer Gestalt des modernen Christentums,* edited by Hans Martin Müller, 261–92. Gütersloh: Verlagshaus Gerd Mohn, 1992.

Stein, Bernhard. *Katholische Dramatiker der Gegenwart.* Ravensburg: Verlag von Friedrich Alber, 1909.

Stein, Henrica. "Vom bayrischen Volksbildungswesen." *Volkskunst* 14 (1926): 311–17.

Steinbrinck, Otto. "Gesetze der Filmkunst." In *Lichtträger in Chaos* 3, 88–95 .

———. "Gibt es eine katholische Literatur?" *Das heilige Feuer* 14 (July 1927): 382–87.

———. "Leo Weismantel—ein Wegbereiter des neuen Dramas." *Bücherwelt* 22 (February 1925): 65–71.

Steinhausen, Georg. *Deutsche Geistes- und Kulturgeschichte von 1870 bis zur Gegenwart.* Halle (Saale): Max Niemeyer, 1931.

Stenta, Norbert. "Der Gesang als Faktor der aktiven Teilnahme des Volkes an der Liturgie." *Bibel und Liturgie* (1928): 6–15.

Stenzel, Albert F. "Filme als Kulturdokumente." *Allgemeine Rundschau* 24 (1927): 149.

———. "Katholische Filmforderungen." *Allgemeine Rundschau* 25 (1928): 700–701.

Stephan, Heinz. "Die Volksbildung und der Rundfunk." *Volkskunst* 14 (1926): 97–101.

Stern, Fritz. *The Politics of Cultural Despair: A Study in the Rise of the Germanic Ideology.* Berkeley and Los Angeles: University of California Press, 1974.

Stezenbach, Gustav. "Ein Apostolat des Theaters." *Allgemeine Rundschau* 20 (1923): 313–14; 320–23.

Stieg, Margaret F. "The Beginnings of Public Library Service in Vienna, 1887–1914." *Journal of Library History* 21 (Summer 1986): 553–73.

———. "The 1926 German Law to Protect Youth against Trash and Dirt: Moral Protectionism in a Democracy." *Central European History* 23 (March 1990): 22–56.

———. *Public Libraries in Nazi Germany.* Tuscaloosa, Ala., London: University of Alabama Press, 1992.

———. "The Richtungstreit: The Philosophy of Public Librarianship in Germany before 1933." *Journal of Library History* 21 (Spring 1986): 261–76.

Stockhausen, —. "Kirchenmusikalische Heranbildung des Klerus." *Caecilienvereinsorgan* 62 (1931): 117–23.

Stockums, [Wilhelm]. "Kundgebung des Volkswartbundes auf dem Katholikentage in Essen." *Volkswart* 25 (October 1932): 147–48.

Stolberg-Stolberg, Christoph, Graf zu. "Kunst und Kultur!" *Allgemeine Rundschau* 10 (June 18, 1913): 485–86.

Storck, Karl. "Gegen die musikalische Schundliteratur." *Der Türmer* (1911): 411–23.

Straßenberger, Georg. "Jazz." *Stimmen der Zeit* 125 (1933): 50–55.

Strieder, Jakob. "Die Deutsche Gesellschaft für christliche Kunst." *Academia* (1927): 33–34.

Strinati, Dominic. *An Introduction to Theories of Popular Culture.* London: Routledge, 1995.

Sun, Raymond Chien. *"Before the Enemy Is within Our Walls": Catholic Workers in Cologne, 1885–1912: A Social, Cultural, and Political History.* Studies in Central European History: Studies in German History. Boston: Humanities Press, 1999.

Tannock, Stuart. "Nostalgia Critique." *Cultural Studies* 9 (1995): 453–64.

"Tapfere Worte gegen die Auswüchse des modernen Theaters." *Allgemeine Rundschau* (January 11, 1913): 34–36.

ten Hompel, Adolph. *Indexbewegung und Kulturgesellschaft: Eine historische Darstellung.* Bonn: Carl Georgi, 1908.

Tenfelde, Klaus. "Die Entfaltung des Vereinswesens während der industriellen Revolution in Deutschland (1850–1873)." In *Vereinswesen und bürgerliche Gesellschaft in Deutschland,* edited by Otto Dann, 55–114. Historische Zeitschrift, supplement 9. Munich: R. Oldenbourg, 1984.

———. "Vereinskultur im Ruhrgebiet: Aspekte klassenspezifischer Sozialismus." *Duisburger Forschungen* 33 (1985): 22–33.

Thamerus, W. "Die kulturfördernde Verpflichtung der deutschen Bühne." *Allgemeine Rundschau* 14 (1917): 405–7.

———. "Mißbrauchte Theaterfreiheit." *Allgemeine Rundschau* 16 (1919): 557–58.

———. "Die Moral des Kino." *Allgemeine Rundschau* 15 (May 4, 1918): 269–70.

———. "Die Pflicht der Bühne." *Allgemeine Rundschau* 12 (1915): 809–10.

———. "Schaubühne und sittliche Erneuerung." *Allgemeine Rundschau* 13 (1916): 613–14.

———. "Zensurloses Theater." *Allgemeine Rundschau* 16 (1919): 466–67.

"Theater als Zeitgeist: Ein Ruckblick und ein Ausblick." *Germania,* January 1, 1929, Morgenausgabe.

Thompson, E. P. "Time, Work-Discipline, and Industrial Capitalism." *Past and Present* 38 (1967): 56–97.

Thompson, John B. *Ideology and Modern Culture: Critical Social Theory in the Era of Mass Communication.* Stanford, Calif.: Stanford University Press, 1990.

Töwe, Carl. "Geschmack und Ungeschmack in der katholischen Kunst." *Theologie und Glaube* [1916?]: 308–11.

Torrund, Jassy [Josefa Mose]. *Hannas Lehrjahr.* Munich: Sonnenland-Bücherei, [1920].

Trommler, Frank. "Working-Class Culture and Modern Mass Culture before World War I." *New German Critique* 29 (Spring/Summer 1983): 64–70.

Ude, Joh[annes] "Der Kaufmannstand als Kulturträger vor dem Richterstuhl des Sittengesetzes." *Volkswart* 9 (January 1916): 7–10.

Über die Verbreitung guter Schriften. Mönchengladbach: Volksvereins-Verlag, 1913.

Ulrich, Karl. *Die katholischen Gemeinden von Nürnberg und Fürth im 19. und 20. Jahrhundert.* Bamberg: St. Otto Verlag, 1989.

"Eine Umfrage und ihr Ergebnis: Die heutige Situation der katholischen Literatur." *Germania*, July 23, 1927, Morgenausgabe, Das neue Ufer.

Um Sitte und Sittlichkeit: Ein Kommentar zu den Katholischen Leitsätzen und Weisungen zu verschiedenen modernen Sittlichkeitsfragen. Düsseldorf: Verlag der Katholischen Schulorganisation, 1926.

Unger, —. "Brauchen wir illustrierte Zeitungsbeilagen?" *Allgemeine Rundschau* 22 (1925): 635–36.

"Unsere 'Literarische Frage'—eine Hononarfrage?: Nebst einigen Besserungsvorschlägen von einem Praktiker." *Literarische Warte* 2 (1901): 242–45.

Ursprung, Otto. *Die katholische Kirchenmusik.* Handbuch der Musikwissenschaft, edited by Ernst Bücken. Potsdam: Akademische Verlagsgesellschaft Athenaion, 1931.

V., R. "Aus der Filmzensur: Welche Filme werden verboten?" *Volkswart* 19 (August 1926): 120–21.

"Vereinbarung zwischen Volkswartbund (Köln) and Borromäusverein (Bonn) zwecks Bekämpfung von Schund und Schmutz in der Literatur." *Volkswart* (May 1928): 74.

Verhandlungen der 43. Gerneral-Versammlung der Katholiken Deutschlands . . . 1896. Dortmund: Gebrüder Lensing, 1896.

Vögele, Josef. *Der Rundfunk und wir Katholiken!* Stuttgart: Schwabenverlag, 1929.

Volksbühne oder Bühnenvolksbund?. N.p., n.d.

Volz, Robert. "Uns fehlt das gute Kino!" *Volkswart* 19 (September 1926): 133–34.

"Von der Hebung des Volksmusiklebens einer Großstadt." *Musik im Leben* 1 (June 1925): 82–85.

"Vorträge für die Cäcilienversammlung der deutschen Gemeinden der Diözese Kattowitz . . . 1931." *Monatshefte für katholische Kirchenmusik* 13 (March/April 1931): 65–78; (May 1931): 113–27.

"Vor vierzig Jahre." *Musica Sacra* 41 (January 1908): 1–6.

W. "Christliche und moderne Kunst." *Hochland* 7 (January 1910): 493–95.

W., H. von. "Rundschau." *Bild und Film* 4 (1914/1915): 255–56.

Wächter, Fritz. "Zur Kinematographenfrage." *Volkswart* 2 (April 1909): 49–54.

Wahl, Alfred. *Cultures et mentalités en Allemagne, 1918–1960.* Paris: Sedes, 1988.

Wallau, René H. "Die kirchliche Rundfunkmorgenfeier: Ihre Gestaltung und Problematik." *Musik und Kirche* 2 (1930): 51–70.

Wallis, Roy, and Steve Bruce. "Secularization, The Orthodox Model." In Bruce, *Religion and Modernization,* 8–30.

Walter, Franz Xaver. *Bildungspflicht und Katholizismus: Das katholische Bildungsideal nach den Grundsätzen der christlichen Ethik.* Schriften des Zentralbildungsausschusses der katholischen Verbände Deutschlands, no. 1. Mönchengladbach: Volksvereins-Verlag, 1922.

Walterbach, Karl. "Katholiken und Film." *Augustinus-Blatt* 26 (May/June 1922): 19–20.

————. *Das katholische Vereinswesen: Leitsätze zur Beratung über dessen Neugestaltung.* N.p., n.d.

Warstatt, Willi. "Das künstlerische Problem in der Photographie und in der Kinematographie." *Bild und Film* 3 (1913/1914): 7–10.

"Was fehlt unserer Volksbildungsarbeit?" *Volkskunst* 13 (January 1925): 4–13.

Weber, Christoph. "Ultramontanismus als katholischer Fundamentalismus." In Loth, *Deutscher Katholizismus im Umbruch zur Moderne,* 20–45.

Weber, Max. "Geschäftsbericht." In *Verhandlungen des ersten deutschen Soziologentages vom 19–22. Oktober 1910 in Frankfurt a. M.* Schriften der Deutschen Gesellschaft für Soziologie, series 1, vol. 1. Tübingen: J. C. B. Mohr (Paul Siebeck), 1911.

Wehler, Hans-Ulrich. *Von der "Deutschen Doppelrevolution" bis zum Beginn des Ersten Weltkrieges, 1849–1914.* Vol. 3 of *Deutsche Gesellschaftsgeschichte.* Munich: Verlag C. H. Beck, 1995.

Weigl, F. "Wider den Schmutz." *Allgemeine Rundschau* 5 (1908): 136.

————. "Wider und—für die Schundlektüre." *Allgemeine Rundschau* 6 (1909): 393–94.

Weiler, Jakob. "Dorfkultur und Dorfbücherei." *Bücherwelt* 22 (September 1925): 393–98.

Weismantel, Leo. "Briefe über katholische Literatur: An den Toren der Kirche." *Das literarische Echo* 25 (December 15, 1922): 327–34.

————. "Briefe über katholische Literatur: Die Katholiken und die Bühne." *Das literarische Echo* 25 (June 1, 1923): 888–901.

————. "Die Bühne der Stunde." *Die Tat* 14 (1922): 485–93.

————. *Mein Leben.* Berlin: Junker und Dünnhaupt, 1936.

Weiss, Eugen. "Abbau des Vereinswesens." *Allgemeine Rundschau* 19 (1922): 246–47.

Weiss, Konrad. "Die christliche Kunst der Gegenwart." *Hochland* 6 (September 1909): 668–84.

————. "Katholische Kulturwille und die neue Kunst: Offener Brief an P. Desiderius Lenz." *Hochland* 12 (May 1914): 191–98.

Weisweiler, J. "Gedanken über musikalische Volkserziehung." *Volkskunst* 2 (March 1914): 397–402.

Weitlauff, Manfred. "'Modernismus litterarius': Der 'Katholische Literaturstreit', die Zeitschrift 'Hochland' und die Enzyklika 'Pascendi dominici gregis' Pius' X. vom 8. September 1907." *Beiträge zur altbayerischen Kirchengeschichte* 37 (1988): 97–155.

Welch, David A. "Cinema and Society in Imperial Germany, 1905–1918." *German History* 8 (1990): 28–45.

Wenden, D. J. *The Birth of the Movies.* New York: E. P. Dutton, 1974.

Wernet, Ferdinand. "Instrumentalmusik in den Vereinen." *Volkskunst* 13 (1925): 246–50.

"Das Wesen der kirchlichen Kunst." *Ecclesiastica* 12 (December 3, 1932): 469–76.

Westerholt, Paul. "Moderne Tanzbewegung und Katholizismus." *Gelbe Hefte* 7 (March 1931): 327–53.

Wetzer und Welte's Kirchenlexikon oder Encyklopädie der katholischen Theologie und ihrer Hülfswissenschaften. 2nd ed. Freiburg im Breisgau: Herder, 1901.

Wick, Karl. "Um die literarische Kritik." *Augsburger Postzeitung,* July 6, 1930.

"Wider den Geist des 'Simplicissimus.'" *Allgemeine Rundschau* 6 (1909): 472.

Wie überwinden wir die Überorganisation und Anarchie des katholischen Vereinswesens? Mönchengladbach: Volksvereinsverlag, 1927.

Wiesebach, Wilhelm. "Zum 'neuen Literaturstreit.'" *Wissen und Glauben* 25 (1928): 162–67.

van der Will, Wilfried. "The Functions of 'Volkskultur,' Mass Culture and Alternative Culture." In Kolinskly and van der Will, *The Cambridge Companion to Modern German Culture*, 153–71.

van der Will, Wilfried, and Rob Burns. *Arbeiterkulturbewegung in der Weimarer Republik.* Frankfurt am Main: Ullstein, 1982.

Williams, Raymond. "The Idea of Culture." In *Culture and Mass Culture,* edited by Peter Davison, Rolf Meyersohn and Edward Shils. Vol. 1 of *Literary Taste, Culture and Mass Communication.* Cambridge: Chadwyck-Healey; Teaneck, N.J.: Somerset House, 1978.

———. *Keywords: A Vocabulary of Culture and Society.* New York: Oxford University Press, 1976.

Wilson, Bryan. *Religion in Sociological Perspective.* Oxford: Oxford University Press, 1982.

"'Wir Katholiken und die deutsche Literatur.'" *Augsburger Postzeitung,* August 11, 1909: 1–2.

Witt, F. X. *Reden an den Cäcilien-Verein. Festgabe für . . . Johannes Overath.* Edited by Christoph Lickleder. Documenta Caeciliana, vol. 1. Regensburg: Allgemeiner Cäcilien-Verband and Feuchtinger und Gleichauf, 1983.

Witt, Franz. "Aufruf." *Probe-Numer: Fliegende Blätter für katholische Kirchen-Musik* 1 (1866): 1–2.

———. "Die erste Generalversammlung des allgemeinen 'deutschen Cäcilien-Vereines.'" *Fliegende Blätter für katholische Kirchen-Musik* 10 (1868): 73–80.

———. "Die Kirchenmusik bei der 18. Generalversammlumg der katholischen Vereine Deutschlands in Innsbruck." *Fliegende Blätter für katholische Kirchen-Musik* 8 (1867): 65–70.

———. "Statuten-Entwurf eines Cäcilien-Vereines für katholische Kirchen-Musik in Deutschland (nebst Oesterreich und der Schweiz)." *Fliegende Blätter für katholische Kirchen-Musik* 10 (1867): 81–83.

———. "Zehn Jahre." *Fliegende Blätter für katholische Kirchen-Musik* 1 (1876): 1–4.

———. *Der Zustand der Katholischen Kirchenmusik zunächst in Altbayern.* Regensburg: Verlag von Alfred Coppenrath (1865).

Witte, Fritz. "Die Erziehung des Klerus zur Kunst." *Zeitschrift für christliche Kunst* 32 (1920): 17–32.

———. "Neue Zeiten—Neue Ziele." *Zeitschrift für christliche Kunst* 32 (1920): 1–15.

———. "Wir und die christliche Kunst." *Christliche Kunst: Korrespondenz für Deutschland, Oesterreich und die Schweiz* 1 (October 1926): n.p.

Wittig, Joseph. "Jesus, soziale Frage und christliche Revolution." *Hochland* 19 (1924): 587–96.

Wittmann, Reinhard. *Geschichte des deutschen Buchhandels: Ein Überblick.* Munich: C. H. Beck, 1991.

"Wo bleiben die katholischen Theaterbesucher?" *Kölnische Volkszeitung,* June 27, 1928.

Wolf, Friedrich. "Film im Westen." In *Aufsätze,* vol. 1. Berlin: Aufbau, 1967–1968, 509–30.

Wolf, Karl. "Licht und Schatten des modernen Films." *Volkswart* 25 (July 1932): 99–101.

Wolff, Hetta. "Buchgemeinde 1927." *Bücherwelt* 24 (March 1927): 116–18.

———. "Das erste Werk der Buchgemeinde." *Bücherwelt* 22 (August 1925): 359–60.

———. "Nochmals: Konzentration oder Zersplitterung? Buchkrise und Buchgemeinschaften." *Germania,* October 9, 1926, Morgenausgabe, Das neue Ufer.

Wolff, Leonhard. "Spielet Calderons geistliche Festspiele!" *Allgemeine Rundschau* 28 (May 23, 1931): 327–28.

"Worin Jakob Kneip recht hat." *Schönere Zukunft,* December 8, 1927: 255–56.

Woywood, Stanislaus. *A Practical Commentary on the Code of Canon Law.* Revised by Callistus Smith. New York: Joseph F. Wagner; London: Herder, 1962.

Wurm, Alois. *Grundsätze der Volksbildung.* Mönchengladbach: Volksverein Verlag, 1913.

Wurzbacher, Gerhard, and Renate Pflaum. *Das Dorf im Spannungsfeld industrieller Entwicklung.* Stuttgart: Ferdinand Enke, 1954.

Wust, Peter. "Die Rückkehr des deutschen Katholizismus aus dem Exil." *Kölnische Volkszeitung,* May 21, 1924; May 22, 1924.

———. "Die Rückkehr des deutschen Katholizismus aus dem Exil." In Hoeber, *Die Rückkehr aus dem Exil,* 16–35.

Yonke, Eric John. "The Emergence of a Roman Catholic Middle Class in Nineteenth Century Germany: Catholic Associations in the Prussian Rhine Province, 1837–1876." Ph.D. diss., University of North Carolina at Chapel Hill, 1990.

———. "The Problem of the Middle Class in German Catholic History: The Nineteenth-Century Rhineland Revisited." *Catholic Historical Review* 83 (April 2002): 263–80.

Zach, Franz. *Modernes oder katholisches Kulturideal?* 3rd ed. Vienna: Herder, 1925.

Zalar, Jeffrey T. "Knowledge and Nationalism in Imperial Germany: A Cultural History of the Association of Saint Charles Borromeo, 1890–1914." Ph.D. diss., Georgetown University, 2002.

———. "The Process of Confessional Inculturation: Catholic Reading in the 'Long Nineteenth Century.'" In Smith, *Protestants, Catholics and Jews in Germany, 1800–1914,* 121–52.

"Die Zersplitterung im ländlichen Chorwesen." *Musica Sacra* 57 (1927): 360–61.

Ziegler, Benno. "Die wirtschaftlichen Grundlagen der katholischen Kirchenmusik." *Neue Musik-Zeitung* 42 (1921): 117–18.

Zimmermann, Josef. "Die Führung des Lesers zum belehrenden Schrifttum." *Bücherwelt* 26 (March/April 1929): 113–15.

———. "Das Gesetz gegen Schund- und Schmutzschriften." *Bücherwelt* 25 (1928): 31–35.

———. "Zur Neuauflage des 'Literarischen Ratgebers des Borromäusvereins.'" *Bücherwelt* 23 (May 1926): 211–12.

Zimmern, ———. "Zum Nackten in der Kunst." *Allgemeine Rundschau* 2 (1905): 637.

"Zitierung des katholischen Dichters Leo Weismantel in der Rede des Abgeordnete Edwin Hoernle (KPD) . . . ." In Hütt, *Hintergrund,* 173.

"Zum Schund- und Schmutzgesetz." *Germania,* November 20, 1926.

"Zur Einführung." *Borromäus-Blätter* 1 (October 1903): 1–2.

"Zur Einführung." *Mitteilungen des Zentralbildungsausschusses der katholischen Verbände Deutschlands* 1 (January 1929): 1–2.

"Zur Krise im Bühnenvolksbund." *Germania,* June 2, 1926, Abendausgabe.

"Zur Reform im Lichtspielwesen." *Volkswart* 19 (October 1926): 145–47; (November 1926): 161–63.

"Zusammenfassung der Beratungen des Kongresses und Resolutionen." In Ernst and Marschall, *Film und Rundfunk,* 228–31.

"Die zweite Generalversammlung des allgemeinen deutschen Cäcilien-Vereines zu Regensburg am 3., 4. und 5. August 1869." *Fliegende Blätter für katholische Kirchen-Musik* 4 (1869): 78–83.

"Zweite Tagung des Zentralbildungsausschusses." *Mitteilungen des Zentralbildungsausschusses* 2 (1924): 5–7. In *Volkskunst* 12 (July/September 1924): 5–7.

"Zynismus." *Volkswart* 18 (November 1925): 171–72.

index

MARGARET STIEG DALTON

is a European historian and professor in the School of Library and
Information Studies at the University of Alabama.